Social Problems

ISSUES, OPINIONS AND SOLUTIONS

Social Problems

ISSUES, OPINIONS AND SOLUTIONS

Brian J. Jones
Villanova University

Bernard J. Gallagher, III
Villanova University

Joseph A. McFalls, Jr.
Villanova University

McGraw-Hill
Book Company
New York / St. Louis / San Francisco / Auckland
Bogotá / Caracas / Colorado Springs / Hamburg
Lisbon / London / Madrid / Mexico / Milan
Montreal / New Delhi / Oklahoma City / Panama
Paris / San Juan / São Paulo / Singapore
Sydney / Tokyo / Toronto

Social Problems
Issues, Opinions and Solutions

34567890   DOCDOC   8932109

ISBN   0-07-022766-7

This book was set in Times Roman by the College Composition Unit in cooperation with Monotype Composition Company, Inc.
The editors were Stephanie K. Happer and David Dunham;
the designer was Jo Jones;
the production supervisor was Diane Renda.
The cover was designed by John Hite.
The photo editor was Elyse Rieder
R. R. Donnelley & Sons Company was printer and binder.

Part- and Chapter-Opening Photo Credits
Part One: Stephen Feldman/Photo Researchers; Chapter 1: Peter Menzel/Stock, Boston; Chapter 2: Charles Gatewood/The Image Works; Chapter 3: Peter Menzel/Stock, Boston; Chapter 4: Linda Benedict-Jones/The Picture Cube; Chapter 5: Mark Antman/The Image Works; Chapter 6: Cathy Cheney/EKM-Nepenthe; Part Two: Arthur Tress/Photo Researchers; Chapter 7: Richard Sobel/Stock, Boston; Chapter 8: Michael Austin/Photo Researchers; Chapter 9: AP/Wide World Photos; Chapter 10: Mike Neveux; Chapter 11: Paul Conklin; Part Three: NASA; Chapter 12: Ira Kirschenbaum/Stock, Boston; Chapter 13: Peter Menzel/Stock, Boston; Chapter 14: Bernard Hoffman, Life Magazine/© Time, Inc.

Library of Congress Cataloging-in-Publication Data
Jones, Brian J.
    Social problems.
    Accompanied by instructor's manual, study guide, and test bank.
    Includes bibliographies and index.
    1. United States—Social conditions—1980–
2. United States—Social conditions—1960–1980.
3. Social problems.   I. Gallagher, Bernard J.
II. McFalls, Joseph A.   III. Title.
HN59.2.J65   1988   306'.0973   87-21523
ISBN   0-07-022766-7

Brian J. Jones, Ph.D., is Associate Professor of Sociology at Villanova University. His graduate work was performed in the Sociology Department and the Fels Center for Public Policy Analysis of the University of Pennsylvania. Social problems is an area of special expertise for Dr. Jones; he has taught the course since 1974 and has written numerous professional and popular articles concerning social issues and public policies. Dr. Jones also regularly consults on applied research projects funded through the Human Organization Science Institute of Villanova University which serve governmental and social service agencies. He is a recipient of the Christian R. Lindback Award for Distinguished Teaching.

Bernard J. Gallagher III, Ph.D., is Professor of Psychiatric Sociology at Villanova University where he has taught various courses on deviant and abnormal behavior since 1971. He holds an M.B.A. from the Wharton School as well as an M.A. and Ph.D. in Sociology from the University of Pennsylvania. His other books include *The Sociology of Mental Illness* and *The Social World of Occupations*. Professor Gallagher's research has centered on the causes of schizophrenia as well as factors affecting authoritarianism, moral development, attitudinal differences between generations, and the psychiatric make-up of criminals. He is a member of the American Sociological Association and the Society for the Study of Social Problems.

Joseph A. McFalls, Jr., a demographer, sociologist, and social biologist, graduated from St. Joseph's University before receiving an M.B.A. from the Harvard Business School and an M.A. and Ph.D. from the University of Pennsylvania. He is currently a member of the Sociology Department at Villanova University and a Research Associate at the University of Pennsylvania's Population Studies Center. His main research interests center on social problems (especially megaproblems), population infertility, and the demography and sociology of the black population in the United States. Professor McFalls is the author of numerous articles, and his other books include: *Psychopathology and Subfecundity* (Academic Press), *Frustrated Fertility: A Population Paradox* (Population Reference Bureau), *Disease* and *Fertility* (Academic Press, with Marguerite McFalls), and *Black Fertility in the United States* (in preparation from Duke University Press, with Stewart Tolnay).

To my family,
creators and solvers
of social problems.

—*Brian J. Jones*

To my mother, Claire,
and to the fine education I received,
at St. Joseph's Preparatory School in Philadelphia.

—*Bernard J. Gallagher III*

To Marquerite, Jeanne Marie, and Joe.

—*Joseph McFalls, Jr.*

CONTENTS

TWO   Macroproblems: Society in the Individual

THREE Megaproblems: American Society in the World

This is *not* just another social problems textbook. First to be explained is *why* it had to be unique (from the perspective of the first author), and then specifically *how* it differs from other texts.

In my tender youth, while daydreaming through another social problems lecture, the concept of "social structure" hit me right between the not-so-intellectual eyes. I suddenly realized that the everyday patterns of society bringing pain and pleasure to individuals were human products, created and maintained by people just like me. I was thunderstruck. This basic principle in the sociology of knowledge has left the lasting impression that the discipline holds a key to social problems, a key to unlocking their mysteries and even their solutions. The more sociology I studied, the more puzzled I became at how people failed to grasp the "true" nature of social problems. In part because I was studying at a university in the middle of a sprawling urban slum, it was baffling that the ghastly human problems all around seemed to receive less public attention than college demonstrators or "free love." Nor was I satisfied by academic treatises suggesting that the public just "didn't know the facts" about social problems. Why didn't they? The conviction started to grow that social progress would require sociological understanding of the processes that forge public opinion about real-world issues. Through the intellectual proddings of colleagues, that conviction has matured into a conceptual apparatus for tracking the roots of social problems both into their public causes and into the public's consciousness.

Now you know the *why* of this book's uniqueness. The *how* of bringing our distinctive approach toward social problems to students is best described through the following special features.

The Subjective Dimension.   How can people ignore the anguish of the homeless while crusading for animal rights? Why is there more public furor about smoking marijuana than smoking cigarettes, when the latter kill hundreds of thousands of people? What explains public opinion becoming inflamed over the pollution issue when the amount of pollution is declining? As suggested in the personal odyssey above, these paradoxes are fascinating to students and professionals alike. They are also puzzles to be solved by sociological concepts. Each chapter presents a full-blown analysis of the specific social forces which control public opinion about social problems.

The Objective Dimension.   Every chapter assesses the human damage wrought by a social problem through an extensive discussion of the various social indicators measuring its harms. In dissecting the theoretical causes of this objective damage, we have attempted to provide an overview of explanations keyed to each specific problem. We have *not* adopted a single theoretical framework as the foundation for the text; nor have we followed an organizational scheme which mechanically scrutinizes each issue under "functionalism," "conflict theory," and "symbolic interactionism" headings. The following pages are rich with theoretical analysis, but *theory has been tailored to the unique outline of each social problem.*

Social Policy.   It is now standard operating procedure for social problems texts to offer some discussion of social policy. One of the features making this book distinctive is, to be blunt, the quality of its policy analysis. Instead of a simple description of current programs, each chapter concludes with an in-depth examination of two opposing contemporary policy positions. After a presentation of the basic arguments on both sides of the issue (in "Strategies for Solution" sections), the opposing policies are scrutinized for real-world obstacles to successful implementation ("Policies into Practice" sections), as well as social scientific data bearing on their relative effectiveness ("Evaluating the Evidence" sections). A quick flip through the back part of any chapter will show that this is clearly *not* just another social problems text in its examination of policy "solutions."

Micro- Macro- Megaproblems.   The logical sequencing of chapters from individual-oriented problems (those most likely to be directly relevant to students at the beginning of the course) up through ever-larger social structures is the arrangement we have found most valuable in our own teaching. For those who lean toward more eclectic combinations, the chapters are effectively self-contained and can be organized in other sequences.

We would like to call special attention to the unique Megaproblems section. In other texts, these three full chapters are often compressed into a single chapter at the end of the book, or even excluded entirely. (Note here a full chapter on nuclear war.) The depth of detail within each of these chapters will no doubt surprise you.

Clarity of Writing.   The first germ of an idea for this project grew from a desire to communicate the breathtaking insights of sociology to students who would remain interested enough to keep breathing. The authors have (blushingly) convinced themselves that they have pulled off the trick of scholarly-yet-interesting writing about social problems for three reasons—

1 Each author has at least ten years' experience teaching about social problems, and about three years' experience mercilessly criticizing (and thus improving) the quality of his coauthors' writing.
2 Each author has been nominated for or received his university's award for outstanding teaching.

3 The reviewers have been most convincing. A modal comment: "The text engages the students without pandering to them or watering down the material."

Supplements.   The textbook is accompanied by a full complement of teaching supplements. In addition to the summaries at the end of each chapter and a comprehensive glossary at the back of the text, there is a test bank, including both objective and essay questions, as well as an unusually extensive *Instructor's Manual* and a student's *Study Guide*. These supplements are literally stuffed with up-to-date boxes and text material directly relevant to in-class issues.

Acknowledgments.   We wish to acknowledge some people who also marked the project with their distinctive stamps. At the top of this impressive list is Lisa Ferraro Parmelee. Among the indispensable functions she performed are: editing, library researching, editing, data analyzing, editing, drawing, editing and psychoanalyzing frenzied authors. We might have been able to do it without her, but not without multiplying our already considerable gray hairs. Steven Kolterman deserves special mention for his word-processing skills and grace under pressure. Similarly, secretary Norma Kehoe was always there in the clutch, usually strapped to her trusty typewriter. Corinne Weaber arrived near the end of the project, and worked happily through her share of headaches. At the bitter end, Barbara Curtin rapidly turned a choppy manuscript into a thing of beauty.

We would also like to acknowledge the intellectual contribution many people made to this book. Arthur Donato, Esq., co-chairman of the Civil Rights Committee of the Delaware County Bar Association of Pennsylvania, helped frame the discussion of the legal aspects of discrimination. Maley Peterson, Esq., furnished a lucid analysis of the state of family law in the United States today. Karen Reardon contributed the dialogue in Box 11.3 based on her professional insights and personal experiences as a volunteer rape counsellor attached to a metropolitan district attorney's office. We also relied heavily on the publications of the Population Reference Bureau and the World Watch Institute in writing Chapter 7 and the megaproblems part of this book, especially the work of Jean van der Tak, Carl Haub, Elaine Murphy, Leon Bouvier, H. Yuan Tien, Lester Brown, and Daniel Deudney. We would also like to thank William Waegel for his invaluable reviews of Chapters 2 and 11.

We would like to express our thanks for the many useful comments and suggestions provided by colleagues who reviewed this text during the course of its development, especially to H. David Allen, University of New Orleans-Lake Front; William D. Amis, Georgia State University; Judith Bootcheck, DePaul University; Phillip W. Davis, Georgia State University; Barbara Gereboff, Bureau of Jewish Education of Greater Phoenix; Eric P. Godfrey, Ripon College; Charles L. Harper, Creighton University; Rudolph C. Harris, Des Moines Area Community College; Arthur L. Johnson, University of Minnesota; James R. McIntosh, Lehigh University; James D. Orcutt, The

Florida State University; Robert Perrucci, Purdue University; Vince Rolletta, Erie Community College; Edward G. Stockwell, Bowling Green State University; Ralph Thomlinson, California State University, Los Angeles; Kendrick S. Thompson, Northern Michigan University; Terry Timmins, Orange Coast College and Nathan Zirl, The University of Texas at El Paso.

In addition, thanks are due to the numerous undergraduate assistants who facilitated the library research process. We also owe a standing ovation to our wives and children for years of tolerating finicky authors, and even their creative arguments as they critiqued each other's work. Finally, we express our gratitude to Villanova University for generous staff assistance and reduced teaching loads without which this project could well have stretched into the 1990s.

Brian J. Jones

Bernard J. Gallagher, III

Joseph A. McFalls, Jr.

SOCIAL PROBLEMS
ISSUES, OPINIONS AND SOLUTIONS

Microproblems:
The Individual in
Society

After the opening chapter's general introduction to
the sociological perspective on social problems,
this part analyzes five substantive issues. What uni-
fies this mixed bag of social problems is their concrete experience at the individual level. Most readers
of this book will know someone who "has" one of
these problems. While they are generally viewed at
the individual level, the chapters reveal the roots of
microproblems in larger social structures.

CHAPTER 1

Social Problems: A Theoretical Overview

Underlying these [utopian] proposals there is always one radical fallacy, namely, that they do not only invent ideal institutions for mankind, but invent an ideal mankind for their institutions.

—*Thomas More*, Utopia

"What do social problems have to do with *me?*"

That is the nagging question that occurs to nearly all students when they first enroll in a social problems course; it is almost certainly on your mind as you read this opening page. In over a decade of professional curiosity about social problems, the authors have had ample time to figure out why we—personally—are so curious. The brief answer offered here is necessarily incomplete, but maybe it can help you to understand why *you* will want to read on.

In the first place, social problems happens to be a fascinating subject. There is something inherently interesting in probing the peculiarities of human behavior, even those involving difficulty or suffering. People may be shocked by teenage suicides or repelled by violent crime, but they hungrily read about both subjects. There is something more here than morbid curiosity. Viewing such phenomena through the lenses of sociology offers a new dimension: explanation. The notion that unfortunate quirks of human behavior may not be quirks after all, that they may be subject to predictable laws of action, is an idea many find irresistibly attractive.

Maybe you do not. Accepting a certain amount of college student cynicism as normal and healthy, this book will offer you a hook on which you can hang your own selfish interests.

At some point each of us is intimately touched by conditions such as unemployment, drug abuse, or mental illness. When facing the personal stress of dealing with them, we may not see our own difficulties as social problems. Why not? Why are we outraged by some suffering that is seen as caused by society while we suffer other socially caused outrages in silence? Moreover, since society is, after all, caused by all of us, how is our own behavior involved in causing our suffering? Stringing all of these question marks together is a blatant attempt to intrigue you. As you read further, we are confident you will be convinced that the answers to

such questions have relevance to an endlessly fascinating subject—you.

SOCIAL PROBLEMS AS SOCIAL BEHAVIOR

The Sociological Perspective

In one sense, society does not exist; in the same sense, the social problems found in societies are not real. These may seem strange statements coming from sociologists. We are, after all, in the business of probing such nonexistent subjects. A word of explanation is clearly in order.

In the first place, who has ever seen a *society?* You probably have walked among thousands of people in an American metropolis; you might even have seen satellite projections displaying the land mass of the entire United States. Neither crowds nor maps, however, offer a direct glimpse at the face of society. Reflect on your own experiences—or lack of them—with the various elements of society. Have you ever bumped into an institution? The school you now attend is frequently referred to as a social institution. Is it really real? One can readily observe the classroom buildings and the individual professors and students who occupy them, but where is this thing called a school? The answer is simple: It is in our heads.

Neither societies nor the social problems besetting them are illusions. Rather, they have a special kind of reality transcending both objects and individuals. Society (with all of its elements) is not only *there,* it is insistently influencing the individuals within it. Your school may forcefully impose its reality upon you by mailing a flunk notice after the social problems exam. And who can doubt the existence of a society which arrests you for income tax evasion? Examples of societal effects may reassure us of the existence of the social world, but they also conjure a disquieting thought: Can these real social things intrude on the lives (and sufferings) of individuals without their knowledge?

The sociological answer is yes. Although no one likes to believe that we dance on unseen strings, consider the following illustration suggesting we all do. The choice of one's friends is among the most personal of decisions. Why did you choose yours? Everyday explanations tend to be individualistic: a friend is a friend because she has a good personality, or because he just relates well to you. There is a wider reality beyond these personal reasons. Although there are always exceptions, you probably have chosen friends of about the same age, religion, and educational level as yourself (how many of your friends are classmates at the same school?). While seemingly exercising free choice, we actually pick friends from within our own social boxes (Jackson, 1977). Perhaps the most intimate choice of all—one's marriage partner—is subject to the same social forces. Mate selection may sometimes occur by the random choice of Cupid's arrow, but the shot is awfully likely to hit two partners of similar social traits (Scanzoni and Scanzoni, 1981). The theme of such examples is this: There is a larger pattern—a "socio-logic" if you will—looming above even our most personal actions.

What do all of these unseen social influences have to do with social problems? Return to the statement that social reality exists in our heads. This is not some philosophical puzzle; it is a plain fact reflecting the subject matter of social problems: people. We the people collectively create the vision of a society or an institution, and so it becomes real.[1] Although it has a different kind of reality than the building that houses it, your school was there before you enrolled, and it will remain after you graduate; the school is something more than the individuals in your classes. Like many other aspects of society, school confronts you as a real, objective thing,

as an undeniable social fact of your life. This is the reason you resist the argument that society is unreal, and it is the key to the reality of social problems. Not only does receiving an F convince you that college exists, it also causes suffering.

Evidence of the social forces acting on friend and mate selection hints at the involvement of such forces in human suffering. We have more than hints. Sociological research strongly suggests that selection of socially similar friends reinforces patterns of discrimination (Berry and Tischler, 1978); furthermore, the social attributes that guide mate selection are also related to divorce and child abuse (Scanzoni and Scanzoni, 1981). Our socially constructed world is real, and it can touch us in mysterious and unmistakably painful ways.

Sociology strives to solve the mystery, and so reduce the pain. The instruments of the discipline are designed to reveal "the patterns of social interaction, the social aggregates, the systems of authority, the social roles, statuses and norms" (Nisbet, 1970:18). These complex phenomena emerge from the socially linked minds of individual people living their everyday lives. The patterns are termed *social structure,* and they are the subject of sociological analysis. Each of us is enmeshed in the web of social structure, and the strands bring us pain as well as pleasure. Why bother to unravel these intricate social-individual effects? In the first place, "when the goal is manipulation of the social environment, knowledge generally enhances the interests of the knower" (Rule, 1978:6). Knowing that certain genetic diseases (such as Tay-Sachs among Jews and sickle-cell anemia among blacks; see Kerson, 1981) are confined within socioethnic boundaries, we can efficiently direct societal resources for diagnosis and prevention; knowing that extensive interpersonal relationships seem to improve one's chances of surviving a heart attack, one can act friendlier to live longer (Caplan, 1981). While there is truth in the truism that "knowledge is

[1] These insights on the nature of man and society received classic expression in the work of French sociologist Emile Durkheim. For an updated presentation, see Peter L. Berger and Thomas Luckmann, *The Social Construction of Reality* (1967).

power,'' the previous paragraphs have been preparing you for an even more profound truth.

Here it is: Social structure is subject to our control. Elements of the social world seem so objective, so real, that it is easily forgotten that we are their creators. The school that does not teach, the court that does not mete out justice, the hospital that does not cure—all these exist only at our whim! The implications for the human control of social problems are staggering. If, indeed, the social play exists only "as an ongoing human production" (Berger and Luckmann, 1967:52), *we* have the ultimate power to rewrite the plot.

Social versus Personal Problems

As you ponder your status as an author of society, you may be reminded of the opening question: "What do social problems have to do with me?" The present section will attempt to clarify your personal relationship to the subject matter of this book.

Obviously, every person in a society has problems. Even the winner of a million-dollar lottery must cope with the stresses of sudden success; there are career decisions to make, investments to choose, and greedy relatives to avoid. Undoubtedly, you would jump at the chance to exchange your problems for those of the instant millionaire, whose frustrations may differ in kind and degree from yours; but getting rich quick can indeed be problematical (Kaplan and Kruytbosch, 1975). If all God's children must suffer, then the question becomes: What suffering is to be attributed to social problems? Which problems flow from the human condition, and which from social conditions?

The issue is complicated by the previously discussed fact that societies are constructed by individuals. It may, therefore, be necessary to search for the cause of a problem within a maze of personal-social links. Consider first the case of fire fatalities. Each year in the United States, approximately 6000 people perish in fires, a death toll about one-third of the annual total of

homicide victims (U.S. Bureau of the Census, 1984). Clearly, each fire death is a tragedy to the individual family suffering the loss. What is less clear is *why* people die in fires. There are some easy answers: smoking in bed, worn-out wiring, lack of a smoke alarm. While one cannot deny the role of personal carelessness and bad luck, such individualistic theories do not account for all the facts. Consider the disturbing results of a cross-cultural comparison of fire fatalities (U.S. Department of Commerce, 1980). According to that study, the fire death rate (i.e., number of victims per 100,000 people) in the United States is five times as high as that in Italy, four times as high as the West German rate, and about twice as high as the rate in the United Kingdom. Note that each comparison is with a country which provided literally millions of immigrants to the United States. Why the substantially greater fire risk in our society? The individualistic theories are inadequate at best. Unless one contends that disproportionate numbers of unlucky firebugs emigrated to the United States, it is hard to see how individuals can take all the blame. As you mentally match the nations compared with us, an objection may occur to you: "But the societies are so different!" Precisely.

Consider a second case: suicide. Few decisions seem more personal (and asocial) than the voluntary destruction of one's self. Again, a widespread tragedy (there were about as many suicide as homicide deaths in the United States last year) can readily be ascribed to the individuals involved in the act. Everyday explanations of suicide often blame mental illness or other personal misfortunes. As in the previous case, it is revealing to compare the quantity of individual tragedies across social categories. In the typical college student's age group—15 to 24—the suicide rate rocketed 40 percent in the 1970s and is now the second leading cause of death (behind accidents). The statistics are chillingly specific concerning casualties within that age range. Among your own classmates, Protestants are more likely to commit suicide than Catholics, and unmarried individuals are more likely to kill themselves than those who are married. Again, the pressing question is *why?*

Any answers should be prefaced by some remarks on the nature of the statistics. The Protestant-Catholic, married-unmarried differences are not based on a count of suicides just last year; the variations by religion and marital status have been reliably observed for over a century. The persistence of this pattern was first explained by the eminent French sociologist Emile Durkheim. Durkheim pointed out that Catholicism is a group-oriented religion whereas Protestantism tends to be individualistic; whatever the quality of their relationships, married couples have built-in company while singles can more easily be socially isolated. In a nutshell, the high-suicide categories contain people with weaker ties to other people (Durkheim, 1897).[2] Of course this is a generalization with numerous exceptions. There are gregarious Protestants, unsociable spouses, and many people whose relationship habits have nothing to do with their suicides. What is unique—and powerful—about Durkheim's approach is its use of statistics to get at the social reality lurking beneath individual cases:

> Such dissociation is indispensable if one wishes to separate *social facts* from their alloys in order to observe them in a state of purity.... Statistics furnish us with the means of isolating them. Since each of these figures contains all the individual cases indiscriminately, the individual circumstances...are neutralized. The average, then, expresses a certain state of the group mind.

> Such are social phenomena, when disentangled from all foreign matter (Durkheim, 1964:8).

[2] A much more recent examination of Durkheim's thesis about social integration and suicide found significant evidence of "egoistic suicide" (associated with weak interpersonal ties) across forty-two contemporary societies (Breault and Barkey, 1982).

Social problems such as homelessness are often viewed as being caused by the individual victims themselves rather than by the workings of institutions and social policies. Consequently, such problems may not be perceived as "social" issues at all. (*Rhoda Galyn*)

The social facts unearthed by the probing of statistical categories can yield startling insights. More important here, though, is the revelation of social forces acting on the individual victims of social problems.

The latter point demands special emphasis in the context of United States society. The American version of rugged individualism is more than a myth; it is a theme running through our everyday social lives. Glorification of personal independence ("Stand on your own two feet!") conditions us to see each individual as wholly responsible for his or her success, or wholly to blame for his or her failure (Arensberg and Niehoff, 1964). This individualism is particularly apparent in the economic realm, but it also subtly shapes our view of social problems. There is a predisposition to regard victims as "nuts, sluts and preverts" (Liazos, 1972), as individuals with personality flaws who have brought problems upon themselves.[3] William Ryan has called this individualistic bias "blaming the victim": drug addicts lack will power, the welfare poor are just lazy bums, and rape victims are promiscuous anyway (Ryan, 1971). In actual fact, well-disciplined physicians have very high rates of drug abuse (see Chapter 3), less than 2 percent of welfare recipients are able-bodied males (Mears, 1977), and rape is primarily an act of nonsexual violence (Chappell, 1977). The factual absurdity of these victim-blaming notions shows that social explanations of problems run against our cultural grain.

It would be folly to assert that individuals—such as yourself—do not contribute to their own problems. Saying that some vaguely defined social environment causes all suffering is saying nothing at all. However, the opposite is also true. Victims cannot be blamed for all victimization. The general approach of sociology is to search for answers between these extreme assumptions. Take the example of academic failure. Clearly, your individual intelligence quotient—or personal preference for soap operas over studying—may contribute to flunking out. Careful educational research has suggested the significance of such individual factors, but it has also determined that the single best predictor of academic performance is family background, a social factor (Jencks, 1972). Rather than accepting on faith that individuals are the cause of any problem, sociological analysis moves

> from the study of individuals already "having" the problem to the study of conditions important in the production of the problem; and from a predominant concern with the individual to a broader concern with the interaction between the individual and the larger social structure (Kohn, 1976:98).

[3] Obviously, victims are not the only people involved in social problems; for every rape victim, there is a rapist. The individualistic explanation tends to shift the attention—and thus the blame—to the former.

It is an approach that has revealed much about people, about societies, and about the suffering that lies in between.

The answers to our recurring question have now fallen into place. You are related to social problems in two distinct ways. Most obviously, such problems may touch you with their *effects*. As a robbery victim, you are directly connected to the crime problem with a bond of pain. Second, there is relationship through *causes*. In the terms of American sociologist C. Wright Mills, there are "personal troubles" for which you are directly responsible, and "social issues" which are widely shared and to which you may contribute through your participation in social structure (1956*b*). Of course, the precise mix of personal and structural causes will depend on the social problem under examination. There is individual evil committed by persons, as well as social evil "caused by the normal, quiet workings of institutions" (Liazos, 1972:112). The methods of sociological research are designed to determine which is which.

Sources of Scientific Insight: Research Methods

To be frank, this is a topic which students (and authors) generally consider deadly dull. Quickly, before you dismiss the subject as boring, consider the presence of sociological techniques in your own life. As it attains maturity, social science is enjoying wider and wider public acceptance; if you doubt it, check the studies summarized in your Sunday newspaper supplement or the "Behavior" section of *Time* magazine. The maturity referred to does not rule out a reality of every science: bad research. A given investigation may "prove" that women are inferior to men, that athletes are really stupid, or that Italians do, in fact, make better lovers. How much (or little) confidence should be associated with these findings, or those in the chapters to follow? The answer will depend on a knowledgeable evaluation of the methods used in the research.

In the present mood of honesty, there is another cliché which must be confronted: The findings of sociological research are nothing more than common sense. The reasoning behind this assertion usually takes two related forms. The first argument is that (*a*) we are human beings, (*b*) we live in the societies constructed by us, and therefore (*c*) we already know all about those societies. While everyday social experience may yield some insights into people and their problems, this argument underestimates the complexity of social facts. Do you know everything about biology because you are an organism? Is an A in physics easily acquired because one's body is composed of atoms? Being part of a complex phenomenon need not bestow a full understanding of it.

Drawing a parallel to the natural sciences raises the second aspect of the commonsense issue. Sociology is often accused of not being a science in the same sense as, say, chemistry because social scientific laws are not rigid enough. While it may be true that theories about people are not as reliable as Boyle's law of expanding gases, there is a certain amount of uncertainty built into every scientific theory. It is an accepted axiom of quantum physics that "if you do know the precise position of an electron, you cannot determine its momentum, and vice-versa" (Heisenberg's uncertainty principle; Mazur, 1968:196). Since they can consciously direct their own actions, human beings are even harder to lock into laws than atomic particles.

Should we abandon scientific aspirations because the subject is a difficult one? A more reasonable claim to scientific status can be made "when the people who know the theories know more about the real world than the people who don't know the theories" (Mazur, 1968: 195). In other words, the science should be nonobvious, yielding research findings that upset the conventional wisdom. Sociological research into social problems can easily pass the nonobvious test. If you have not yet been surprised by the findings reported here, we offer a guarantee of surprises in the pages below. The ambition of sociological science, however, is to be more than startling. The surprises merely confirm that one has adopted a perspective beyond everyday intuition, a scientific perspective that promises to be more effective than common sense in dealing with persistent human problems.

What are the sources of this nonconventional wisdom? Sociologists employ three main strategies in their analyses of social problems. In our brief sketch of these strategies one point will be paramount: The strengths and weaknesses of each research design must be judged in relation to the subject under study.

Participant Observation If one wishes to understand people's problems, a breathtakingly simple strategy is to live among them and observe their behavior. This idea is the basis of *participant observation,* a technique involving much more than just keeping one's eyes open. What distinguishes such a research strategy from journalism is its use of a "generic frame," a set of concepts which provides a wider framework for the social facts that are observed (Lofland, 1974). Rather than merely reporting the exotic events of an unfamiliar lifestyle, the participant-observer interprets daily details in the terms of a more general social theory.

A classic application of this strategy to the poverty problem was performed by Carol B. Stack. After introductions through an ex-community resident who had entered her university, Stack participated in the lives of two black families in The Flats, a fictitious name for a midwestern slum neighborhood. Her three years of observations illuminated a general theoretical issue: How does the kinship system adapt to everyday economic uncertainty? What Stack found was an organization of family life very different from the American middle-class ideal, but admirably suited to the reality of grinding poverty. One of her key findings was an elaborate system of material aid, "a cooperative life style built upon exchange and reciprocity," linking relatives in a network of obligations that most benefited those "down on their luck" (1974:125). The existence of a kinship-based safety net among the impoverished contradicts the public image of the poor as a disorganized rabble; it is also a social reality that should be taken into account in the design of antipoverty policy (Jones, 1982).

Participant observation is a strategy applicable to a wide range of social problems; it will therefore be instructive to use Stack's study to spotlight the general advantages—and disadvantages—of this research design. An impressive advantage is the natural setting of the observed group. Stack's subjects were viewed *in situ,* right in the deprived environment that is the daily background of their behavior. On the negative side of the ledger is, first, the sampling issue. You may recall from above that Stack's research chronicled the activities of *two* families in *one* community. Does that particular community typify the national poverty problem? Are these families even typical of the thousands of others in The Flats? The deeply personal nature of the research (Stack lived among the families for three years) precludes selection of a representative sample of the poor. Consequently, one must be cautious in generalizing beyond the study subjects.

There is a related issue. Keep in mind that the observer is—even with the proper introductions—a stranger entering the lifestyle of a group. Since it is often difficult to disguise the identity of the investigator (Stack was white, her subjects black), the group members under study are liable to *reactivity,* i.e., changing their behavior just because they are being watched (Kidder, 1981). This disadvantage will be particularly pronounced among deviant populations (such as college student drug users) who may feel they have something to hide. Although reactivity of subjects tends to decrease over time (Johnson, 1975), the personal involvement

of the researcher can be expected to increase. The observer's participation, emotional and otherwise, may become very intense. Elijah Anderson, while he was a graduate student doing research among poor street-corner males in Chicago, found himself involved in a near fistfight, the events of which are summarized in Box 1-1. This extreme example raises the general issue of objectivity. An investigator embroiled in face-to-face relations with the people he studies will have personal reactions to them, just as they do to him. It may be no easy matter to untangle one's feelings about the group from one's theoretical observations.

As a research strategy, participant observation offers intimate insights of groups as they actually function in the social world. Such glimpses are bought, however, at the cost of generalizability and possible bias on the part of the researcher and/or research subject. These considerations suggest that, in general, it is a strategy most profitable for exploratory research, for stimulating hypotheses (testable questions drawn from theories), rather than for definitively testing them. Given the present state of development of our theories for many social problems, this is an indispensable service.

Experimental Design   Classifying the sociologist as a scientist associates the individual with laboratories and white coats. The *experimental design* is, however, only one of the tools of sociological study, and it has distinctive strengths and weaknesses in the dissection of social problems. We will evaluate this strategy by again scrutinizing a classic study.

Why are prisons so oppressive? Is the dehumanization caused by the attitudes of the guards, by the behavior of the prisoners, or by the social situation of confinement? Unfortunately, such questions are complicated in real jails by the overlap of all these factors. The problem is a general one. Rather than possessing neatly separable variables like mass and velocity, people have interrelated traits that

---

BOX 1-1

ON THE PERSONAL INVOLVEMENT OF THE PARTICIPANT OBSERVER

One Saturday evening in July, Herman, Terry, and I sat around on the ground in the park near Jelly's. Others, including wineheads, regulars, and hoodlums, sat in other areas nearby. As we talked, Terry began "messing" with me and engaging in what men commonly refer to as "selling wolf tickets." This had been going on for at least two weeks.

Rising to the challenge, I said, "Okay, Terry. Let's go over here on the grass and have this out."

Herman looked surprised and puzzled but said, "A'right now, Terry. You know Eli a pretty strong stud. You know that, don't you? You know that."

"I know that," answered Terry, as he got up and walked toward me.

Since Terry had been "messing" with me for some time in ways that at some point were bound to lead to trouble, I decided to settle his "in for me" then and there. Thus I urged him on. Herman attempted to dissuade us from the match, which Terry and others knew could easily turn into violent fighting. Apparently unmindful of such risks, we found a soft, grassy spot.

"Okay, now. Lie down on your belly, Terry. We gon' arm wrestle," I said.

"Aw, a'right," agreed Terry, assuming a prone position.

We then locked our arms and began to match our strength. The contest drew others. Suddenly Terry and I had an audience, which was really more than we had originally bargained for. Just by their presence the newcomers infused what started out as "play" with a more serious import. Sides could now be taken. The situation was redefined. Slowly I put Terry's arm to the ground.

Herman laughed, "See, I told you to don't be fuckin' wit' Eli!" Terry looked dumbfounded. The others began to laugh and point at Terry.

Then I said, "Okay, Terry. Let's try it with our left arms? A'right?"

"Okay," said Terry, seeing this offer as an opportunity to save face and redeem himself. The others still looked on, expecting, some even hoping, that I would beat Terry again. But this time I let Terry put my arm to the ground.

As we lay on the ground I said, "Damn, Terry. You stronger than I thought you were!"

"You a pretty strong stud, yourself," said Terry, acknowledging his earlier defeat. The others were now silent, as they slowly dispersed and resumed their earlier positions. But a few stayed with the three of us for a while, drinking scotch and water and exchanging stories. After a while Herman and I left.

Elijah Anderson, *A Place on the Corner,* The University of Chicago Press, 1978, pp. 198–199. By permission of the publisher.

---

may be virtually impossible to untangle in the real world. Philip Zimbardo and his colleagues dealt with the overlapping trait problem by creating a mock prison. Volunteers were screened by the experimenters to produce a final set of subjects who were

> mature, emotionally stable, normal, intelligent college students....They appeared to represent the cream of the crop of this generation. Half were arbitrarily designated as prisoners by the flip of a coin, the others as guards. These were the roles they were to play in our simulated prison (Zimbardo, 1972:4).

The strategy was experimental in that it created an artificial situation in order to untangle one factor from the others. Since the college stu-

dents entered the situation with neither the hardened attitudes of prison guards nor the prior criminal records of typical prisoners, the experiment spotlighted the influence of the social situation. What the spotlight revealed was horrifying:

> About a third of the guards became tyrannical in their arbitrary use of power, in enjoying their control over other people. They were corrupted by the power of their roles....We had to release three prisoners in the first four days because they had such acute situational traumatic reactions as hysterical crying, confusion in thinking and severe depression (1972:8).

The experiment dramatically demonstrates that the social *roles* (behaviors expected of people in specific group positions) of guard/prisoner are dehumanizing regardless of the individual personalities who play them. Once one recovers from the emotional punch of the study, however, some questions linger.

Once again, there is the problem of generalizability. The disturbing findings among college students may or may not characterize the reactions of housewives, senior citizens, religious professionals, or the population at large. Even if the twenty-four subjects of this study are assumed to be representative of *all* college students, there is little reason to believe that people such as yourself are mirrors of the whole prison population. This is not a criticism directed specifically at Zimbardo. As a practical matter, most social experimentation has been restricted to samples of college populations (Rubinstein, 1982). Even if the researcher has the money, the often elaborate artificial situation designed to highlight a facet of a social problem (see Milgram, 1973) cannot easily accommodate all the subjects in a nationally scattered sample.

"Artificial situation" is a phrase reflecting the ambivalence of the experimental technique. The contrived circumstances allowing one to tune in on a specific element of human behavior may tune out the real world. Zimbardo's subjects, after all, always knew they could go home; there is no way to ascertain whether the guards were playing at cruelty or being their own cruel selves in the situation. If you are heterosexual and the experimenter assigns you the identity of a homosexual in a campus role-playing experiment, how similar will your actions be to those of a person who *lives* such a sexual identity? Artificial situations may produce artificial behavior. A final problem is reactivity (see above), a real concern for subjects in a predicament obviously arranged so that the investigator can watch.

As with participant observation, our assessment of social experimentation leads to a kind of scientific balance sheet. In the plus column is

the degree of control researchers hold over the situation. This gives the freedom to construct conditions which will spotlight a crucial facet of social problems. Exercise of that freedom is a weakness as well as a strength. The more intense the focus on one social trait, the more unnatural the situation is likely to be. The desire to drain off all of the "bathwater" clouding the view of that trait may result in throwing out part of the "baby": the real context in which the social problem is set. On balance, the utility of social experimentation will be maximized for research issues that are already fairly well understood. If there is a general base of empirical and theoretical knowledge, one should gain the most from a narrowly focused study, and also know enough to control the worst sources of bias due to sampling and artificiality.

Survey Research The final strategy to consider is probably the most familiar. *Survey research* is built upon two techniques which have been widely applied in the real world outside social science. The first of these, random sampling, was deliberately devised to deal with the generalizability issue which haunts observational and experimental research. The problem: to select a sample which accurately represents the various segments of a much larger population. The solution: to give each unit (person or group) in the population an equal chance of being selected. The practical advantages of this seemingly simple concept are enormous. Selection of equally likely units by a random process (bingo balls, computer-generated numbers, etc.) not only tends to yield a true cross section of the population, but also tells us the likelihood of sampling error. The main payoff is generalization. One can say something general about a large population (the United States contains about 240 million people) on the basis of a workably small sample (most Gallup surveys select less than 1500 people). It is important

"Would you say Attila is doing an excellent job, a good job, a fair job, or a poor job?"

(*Drawing by Charles Addams; © 1982 The New Yorker Magazine, Inc.*)

to note that a random sample is not simply many cases gathered in some scattered way. Careful attention to random procedures in a small sample will produce much more representative results than a large sample drawn nonrandomly.

The persons selected into survey samples are generally asked questions through one or more of the following techniques: face-to-face interviews, self-administered questionnaires, or telephone interviews. Each form of questioning has its respective strengths and weaknesses, but all ultimately depend on verbal (oral or written) information. Rather than observing people in their natural groups (participant observation) or watching their behavior under laboratory conditions (experimentation), the survey researcher seeks knowledge about social problems in what the respondents *say*. The strategy thus combines random selection with personal interrogation, but survey research is more than just the use of these two techniques.[4] The choices of both the population to be sampled and the questions to be asked should have their foundation in sociological theory. The guiding concern, after all, is not just getting a cross section of answers to nosy questions; the real goal is settling a general issue bearing on social problems.

A classic application of survey techniques to a theoretical issue is Fernandez and Kulik's recent study of "life satisfaction" (1981). In everyday terms, they explored the determinants of personal happiness—and unhappiness. While this is a matter of individual interest to all of us, the study involves more general issues concerning social problems. Fernandez and Kulik used an advanced form of the statistical

[4] Although sampling experts agree that random selection is usually the ideal procedure, practical considerations (such as time or money) may preclude its use. Not all survey studies, therefore, draw pure random samples.

reasoning explained by Durkheim (see above); specifically, they examined the levels of life satisfaction within the social categories of a nationally representative telephone-interviewed sample of United States adults. These categories were sifted to prospect for social facts underlying individual differences in life satisfaction. Social factors associated with *dis*-satisfaction could plausibly be linked to mental disorders, to drug abuse, to any number of specific problems.

To exemplify the pluses and minuses of survey analysis, we will spotlight several of Fernandez and Kulik's findings. First, they determined that urban dwellers are significantly less happy than those residing in rural areas. You can immediately see a problem with such a statement. Since place of residence is also linked with a host of other factors (income, family size, etc.), how can urban location be isolated as a separate source of unhappiness? To deal with this difficulty, the analysts used the technique known as *statistical control* to hold other factors constant and untangle the specific relationship of interest. After the other variables are controlled, location and—somewhat surprisingly—education are still related to happiness. In the latter case, the link is a negative one; i.e., the higher the number of years of schooling the individuals have completed, the *less* happy (on the average) they are. While you might not find that difficult to believe when cramming for a midterm, it contradicts commonsense American beliefs about the value of education.

Aside from the surprises involved, the results of this application of the survey strategy are impressive for two reasons. First, there is their generality. Conclusions drawn about life (dis)satisfaction can actually be said to characterize the adult population of the United States, rather than one observed group or a few dozen college students. Also, the use of statistical controls permits the spotlighting of particular variables without the artificial conditions of an experiment. Be impressed by survey analysis, but allow yourself some doubts. One reason generalization may be imperfect is that the *population* (total set of individuals or groups about which the researcher wants to generalize) must be defined by some sort of list from which the sample is drawn. Since telephone books and census records—both often used to define populations—are known to undercount certain types of people, a random sample of those lists cannot be perfectly representative.

Another consideration: Do you believe everything you are told? If not, that is further reason to question the infallibility of survey findings. Even if people don't deliberately lie to the interviewer or on the questionnaires, what we say is not necessarily the same as what we really do (consider your most sincere resolutions to study). Researchers have evolved procedures for dealing with both these sources of doubt, but they remain only partially solved problems of the survey strategy.

Which Research Strategy Is Best? Given the inherent weaknesses of *each* research strategy, is the sociological study of social problems to be abandoned as a pointless exercise? No. There are sources of error in the research tools of every science. One must, however, be schooled in the use of such instruments to derive the most knowledge with the least distortion. In the field of social problems, the choice of tools is dictated by the answers to two questions: Who is to be studied? What is it about them you wish to know? Survey research is not better than participant observation in any absolute sense. Rather, the advantages and disadvantages of a strategy must be weighed in relation to a specific subject of study.

In the analysis of deviant populations, just getting close enough to do research is likely to be problematical. The fear of public disclosure and/or official sanctions is a barrier between the researcher and the study of some forms of deviance. Laud Humphreys was able to cross that barrier in his participant observation study of homosexual behavior in a public bathroom known as a "tearoom" (1975). By playing the role of voyeur (an accepted type of homosexual who just watches the action) without identifying himself as a social scientist, Humphreys solved the access problem.[5] Through his observations, Humphreys identified four types of participants in the tearoom trade, each with distinctive characteristics and problems. While one may legitimately wonder how typical this single site is of homosexual behavior, study through participant observation at least offered insights into a virtually unstudied social world. In this case, the generalizability problem was less serious than those which would have been encountered by a survey researcher waving questionnaires, or by an experimenter inviting tearoom regulars into a laboratory.

Once sociological knowledge of a given subject has passed the exploratory stages, interest centers on the wider dimensions of the problem. If the research issue concerns *prevalence* (the total number in a population with a given condition), *incidence* (the number of new cases affected by a condition during a time period), or the *overall relationship between variables* (e.g., is wealth related to the risk of divorce?), then survey research becomes the strategy of choice. An early study of marijuana use probed this (then) relatively rare practice through participant observation among jazz musicians (Becker, 1953). Moving to the next level of scientific generality, recent national surveys have established that the prevalence of pot smoking has generally increased over the past fifteen years, and that the regular use of marijuana is concentrated among young adults (see

Chapter 2). If the scientific priority is to sketch the broad patterns of a problem, the generalizing strength of survey research will outweigh its weaknesses.

The sketch drawn by survey analysis, however, is done in very broad strokes. Data on the distribution of a social condition are typically reported as a *correlation*—a statistical association between variables; Fernandez and Kulik found, for example, that higher happiness and rural residence are correlated. Knowing that two variables tend to vary together creates a seemingly irresistible temptation. The conclusion to which one will be tempted to leap is *causation*, a condition that exists only when a change in one variable directly produces the associated change in the other variable. Which way does the causal arrow run in the relationship between happiness and place of residence? The proper answer is: We can't really tell from Fernandez and Kulik's data. Cities could make people miserable, or unhappy people might move to cities; both causal interpretations fit the general correlation established by the survey analysis. For a more definite answer, we might turn to the experimental strategy, which is "considered to be more powerful than nonexperimental designs in uncovering causal relationships among variables" (Spector, 1981:20). Once correlational analysis has drawn the broad outlines of a social problem, experimental studies are the strategic choice to tease out the causal specifics.

The essence of all this talk about strategies can be distilled into two basic points. First, the sociological study of social problems is based on the application of scientific techniques to theoretical issues. This implies, second, that research findings are not ultimate truths handed down on stone tablets. The quality of the data depends on how skillfully the investigator has wielded the scientific instruments in the dissection of the social problem. Since such skill must be judged in relation to the subject under study,

---

[5] Since Humphreys' covert procedures involved some violation of privacy, they raise the general question of the ethics of social research. Perhaps the issue is best put in this way: Intrusion on the subjects of the research must be balanced against the potential social benefits of the knowledge.

it is necessary to know what the subject matter of social problems *is*.

THE DIMENSIONS OF SOCIAL PROBLEMS

After pages and pages of discussion to set the stage, it is finally time to raise the curtain on a formal definition of a "social problem". Why all the fuss over what might seem so obvious? Explicit statements are necessary precisely because social problems are *not* obvious. Suggestive of their intriguing complexity is the fact that they exist in two dimensions. *The* objective *dimension of a social problem is the concrete, measurable human harm associated with a societal phenomenon; the* subjective *dimension is the general level of concern about that phenomenon registered by the members of a society*. What immediately follows is an introduction to this two-dimensional reality of social problems.

A major point already established is that social problems have a special reality as social facts. Asserting that a problem has social roots is more complex than it first appears. Consider a simple statement that might be found in any local newspaper: "There is growing public concern about drug abuse among college students." Readers might readily accept the argument that social factors—peer pressure, academic anxiety, permissive parents—are involved in such abuse. But what about the first part of the statement? *Who* is so concerned, and *why* is their concern growing? What is the reason for so much public concern about college students and so little concern about drug use in other social segments (see above about physicians)?

The answers to such questions are to be found in the sociological view of self and society. The real social things "out there"—registrar's offices, exam requirements, drug-using friends—are individually perceived "in here" in one's mind. *You* see them, think about them, and emotionally react to them. People collectively create social facts, but they personally experience them as well. It is natural to think of the site of personal experiences—your *self*—as private property, but other people intrude on it all the time. Your personal attitudes about many facets of social life—and not, incidentally, social problems—are shaped by life in society.

Suppose an acquaintance of yours at college has died of a drug overdose. That is an unfortunate fact out there in the real world. Only after you learn of this tragedy from a classmate, however, do you experience an emotional reaction; your personal feelings have been triggered by awareness of the death as well as the death itself. A social event (the conversation with a classmate) has moved the tragedy from the *objective* (out there) to the *subjective* (in here). Almost certainly, your views of college drug abuse will be different than they would have been if you hadn't heard the sad news. The conclusion is clear: Social influences shape not only the objective reality of social problems but also the subjective concern that we feel about them.

This is an unfamiliar idea. The commonsense, nonsociological view is that the depth of public concern reflects the true magnitude of a problem; little suffering in society should logically lead to little public reaction, more suffering to more reaction. The preceding paragraphs seem to reinforce this view by showing both suffering and concern about suffering to be products of similar social forces. It is worth repeating that those forces work in complex ways. Social influences are so intricate, in fact, that the objective (out there) and subjective (in here) aspects of social problems should be seen as separate—and often unequal—dimensions. Here are two cases in point.

Mattoon, Illinois, is a place a novelist would describe as a sleepy little town. In September of 1944, Mattoon's residents experienced a true horror story in the form of dozens of reported attacks by a "mad gasser." His modus operandi was to spray a sweet-smelling gas into the homes of victims who subsequently experienced paralysis and nausea. The Mattoon public became outraged, organizing vigilante patrols, carrying shotguns in their cars (and to bed), and even calling in the FBI. The visits of the mad gasser suddenly stopped, but a number of facts continued to puzzle the authorities. The villain must have been invisible to dogs since they didn't bark to warn the victims; the four victims actually examined by physicians were dismissed as cases of "nervous tension"; finally, the gasser had to have been a mad genius since chemists from the University of Illinois contended that no known substance had the effects claimed by the victims (Johnson, 1945).

This is more than a bizarre episode of mass hysteria. Undoubtedly, the gasser was a social problem to the people of Mattoon; newspaper articles about the attacks took precedence over reports on the concurrent social problem of World War II (Chaplin, 1959). In terms of subjective concern, the mad gasser was the preeminent problem in Mattoon even though, in objective terms, *the person simply did not exist.*

A second demonstration of the independence of objective and subjective dimensions also involves unusual events. The question is: How unusual? Below are five sources of objective damage, i.e., causes of concrete, measurable suffering out there in the social world:

Boats (drownings)
Bicycles (accidents)
Bolts (lightning)
Bugs (venomous insects)
Bites (sharks)

Using deaths as the criterion, which factor causes the most objective damage in the United States in a typical year? Which of the five kills the least? What is the actual number of people who perish from each cause? Such questions might seem unfair and obscure, but that is precisely the point. Even though each factor is killing a relatively stable amount of people out

there year after year, those objective facts probably never reach your subjective awareness in here. After all, you are not hooked up to a sensing device which automatically registers every violent death. If you do know the answers to such questions, it may be because of a recently read magazine article, because you worked as a park ranger, or because a relative nearly died from a bee sting—in short, because of selective social influences. *Such subjective influences are independent of the objective causes of death which operate whether you are aware of them or not.* By the way, the five factors above are ranked in order with approximate annual death tolls as follows: drownings from small-boat accidents, 1300 (U.S. Department of Commerce, 1980); bicycle accidents, 1000 (National Safety Council, 1980); lightning bolts, 100 (U.S. Department of Commerce, 1980); fatal reactions to insect bites, 50 (*American Health,* 1985); and fatal shark attacks, 3.[6] As a final note, observe that shark attack is by far the least significant objective problem. One of the authors submitted a similar list of factors to his students in the summer of 1975, and sharks were selected as the leading cause of death. The reason clearly was not an actual increase in attacks by blood-thirsty sharks; the *objective* death toll that summer was the same as the year before. The reason clearly was a *subjective* social influence—the movie *Jaws* had just been released.

The cases of Mattoon and the death list may not be your idea of social problems. The value of these cases lies not in the momentousness of the topic, but rather in the dramatic contrast they reveal between the outer (objective) and the inner (subjective) dimensions of social problems. This is a general principle which can— and will—be extended to issues such as crime, divorce, even nuclear war. To restate the prin-

---

[6] Data concerning shark attacks were obtained through a personal conversation with John J. McAniff, director of the National Underwater Accident Center.

ciple: *The concrete harm associated with a given problem may vary independently of public awareness and concern.* The objective and subjective dimensions are related (your classmate did actually die before your mind changed about drug abuse), but the relationship is a variable and complex one. To unravel that complexity, it will be necessary to consider separately the social influences bearing on the two major dimensions of social problems.[7]

THE OBJECTIVE DIMENSION: SOURCES OF SUFFERING

> We want to live, but we cannot. We want men to be equal, but they are not. We want suffering to end, but it will not. Honesty permits us to know what is to be accepted and, accepting, to reclaim our humanity and struggle against indignity. It is more than the instrument, it is measurement itself, for it is honesty which allows us to see clearly the ways by which societies must cope. (Calabresi and Bobbitt, 1978)

The present section focuses on human suffering and its origins. In reviewing the tangible evidence on the sources of social problems, honesty is indeed essential. Candor alone, however, will not clarify the complex processes of social (and antisocial) behavior. Honesty must be magnified by science, by a set of theories and techniques designed to be, quite literally, objective. Sociological analysis provides the necessary magnification.

There is still the question of just what to put under the lens. Take a moment to decide which—in your opinion—is the single most

serious social problem in the United States today. Take another moment to decide *why*. Is it the deaths caused by the problem? Is it the physical injury, the mental anguish, or the moral outrage that leads you to your choice of a problem? The point is there are several standards against which suffering may be judged:

> In violence a person is *violated*—there is harm done to his person, his psyche, his body, his dignity....Seen in this way, a person can be violated in many ways; physical force is only one of them (Liazos, 1972:113).

Just as violence cannot be reduced to wounds from street muggings, social problems cannot be seen in terms of only a single type of woe. Proper assessment of cause(s) requires measurement more sophisticated than simple death counts. Social scientists have developed various types of measures—everything from divorce proneness to personal stress scales—to dissect the various types of socially induced harm. Combinations of such measures (sometimes called social indicators) can be used to more fully gauge the objective seriousness of a given problem.

Measurement alone is not enough. A student with a semester test average of 68.5 may have an adequate reading of an inadequate performance, but what is lacking is an *explanation*. In the following pages, we present a number of theoretical perspectives on the causation of social problems. Why is there no single, all-purpose theory? In the first place, consider the wide spectrum of problems—from inflation to infanticide—to be explained. Each problem is unique in many ways, including both the balance of individual versus social forces and the pattern of suffering revealed by social indicators. Even when the focus is on a single problem, though, finding its objective cause is akin to medical research. The complexity of the (physical or social) disease may lead to a profusion of different—and possibly competing—theories, each capturing part of the truth. Set-

---

[7] The relative importance of these two dimensions is currently a matter of scientific dispute. Some analysts contend that the study of social problems should focus entirely on what the public defines as subjectively serious (Mauss, 1975), while others argue for an objectivist definition of social problems to be developed by sociologists (Manis, 1974). Our view is that *both* the objective and subjective dimensions are crucial; what is real and what is real in the public mind are two facets of the same phenomenon—social problems.

tlement of such scientific debates need not concern us here.

The theories below will be presented as *complementary perspectives* providing distinctive insights into the many facets of social problems. While the specific mix of theories to be used in explanation depends on the specific problem under study, there are two stable reference points in our general presentation. First, *all* of these theories are concerned with *causes;* they seek the objective sources of suffering. Second, *all* are to some degree concerned with *social structure,* with tracing the roots of problems into the socially constructed world.[8]

Social Disorganization

While they differ about particulars, the three major theories in this section share a basic assumption about social problems. Their common premise likens society to a blueprint in which social life is arranged according to a specified plan. Like a building designed by an incompetent architect, a society may crush itself. The flaw lies not in the individuals constituting the society—its building materials, if you will—but rather in the plan by which the social structure is built. The social *pattern* is the source of its own problems. This implies that conformity, doing exactly what one is supposed to do, may lead to human misery. Doctors, conforming to the Hippocratic oath and the norms of modern medicine, preserve the lives of thousands of elderly people who have no one to support them. Police, dutifully following the letter of their regulations, enforce unjust laws. College students, overzealously performing the requirements of the syllabus, contribute to unhealthy academic competition and their own ulcers. Since all of these problems are the result of individuals scrupulously conforming to the

---

[8] This is by no means to be an exhaustive list of all theories dealing with all social problems. Our selective presentation focuses here on the major sociological perspectives; later chapters will develop them more fully in combination with additional concepts.

demands of the system, something must be amiss with the system itself.

Functional Theory Of the three major theories to be considered here, *functionalism* has the most formal view of society as a system. Each element of social life is analyzed in terms of the purposes—or functions—it serves in the larger social pattern. Why, for instance, is the ideal family in America a nuclear unit? According to functionalists, an industrial economy demands a mobile labor force, and small easily moved families help that economy to function smoothly. Why are you expected (by law and/or parents) to attend sixteen years of schooling before entering adult life? Because United States society needs highly trained personnel to fill its many white-collar occupations. The theory does not require everything to fit together quite so neatly. In the act of playing their assigned roles, individuals may be caught between conflicting functional expectations. Working women, for example, may hold full-time jobs while also having primary responsibility for child rearing and husband pampering. Caught in a financial aid crunch, college students may be torn between spending hours studying and putting in work hours to earn tuition. These are cases of role conflict (contradictory social expectations) which are problematical for individuals because the social system has not properly organized their functional duties.

Carefully organized social practices can also be a source of problems. Negative effects—known as dysfunctions—often accompany features that positively serve the system. A frontier society instilling violent, macho traits in its adult males may be secure against Indians, but it may also suffer the dysfunction of senseless street killings. A capitalistic society which designs cutthroat competition into its business institutions may gain the advantage of material affluence, but suffer the personal (stress-related illness) and social (pollution) consequences of unrestrained production. Dysfunctions may subside with refinement in the social design or

improved training of individuals, but some social problems must be accepted as the cost of
the beneficial social pattern (Merton, 1976). In
this functionalist sense, societies get the social
problems they deserve.

Conflict Theory If the functionalist view is
that some suffering is part of a higher social
pattern, *conflict theory* sees society as a much
less benign form of social organization.[9] In the
latter view, the blueprint is not a more or less
flawed masterpiece of collective design; rather, it
is the product of conflicting groups trying to
impose their self-serving plans on society. After
all, society is not a colony of identical individuals.
The person in the next desk in class is probably
different from you in a number of ways, such as
sex, ethnicity, and religion. According to the
conflict approach, these diverse social categories
mark off not only different kinds of people but
also different social demands. Particularly in het-
erogeneous societies such as the United States,
those demands—often called interests—are likely
to clash. In the terms of the theory, higher salaries for working women mean lower salaries for
working men; increasing the age of mandatory
retirement expands opportunity for the elderly,
but contracts the job market for new college
graduates. Society's design is a patchwork of
negotiated settlements in which the winning
groups get social rewards and the losers get social
problems.

The most elegant formulation of the conflict
approach focuses on the broad economic divisions of modern societies. In the scramble of
contending groups, the main antagonists are the
higher and lower classes or, more pointedly, the

haves and have-nots.[10] Members of the disprivileged class suffer not due to personal failings
or some technical flaw in society's design, but
because the privileged class controls social institutions for its own benefit:

> Major causes of much actual and potential misery
> in advanced industrial societies, in principle sus-
> ceptible to enlightened change, are the vast ineq-
> uities in wealth and power in these societies
> (Rule, 1978:198).

The proposals of conflict theory for the solution
of social problems hinge on the contradictory
interests of the major classes. The ills of poverty can be cured simply by taking from the rich
and giving to the poor. If the little guy is
exploited by the price fixing and shoddy products pushed by major corporations, impose
stiffer sentences for such white-collar crimes;
the loss in the power of privileged executives
means a gain in justice for the disprivileged.

If this version of conflict theory is correct
and society is a simple us versus them proposition, why don't we (who are poor) clearly see
them (the rich) as the cause of our social
problems? The further argument is that the
reality of class exploitation is deliberately
clouded by ideologies, that is, by beliefs justifying the interests of the ruling class. The idea
that the rich are deserving because they worked
their way up the ladder of success, or that
governmental control of free enterprise violates
our value of personal liberty—these are smoke
screens behind which the rich profit from the
suffering of others. The naked truth is that
social problems are caused by class conflict
which one side has lost. Phrasing the issue in
this way reveals the close kinship of the conflict
view to the theories of Karl Marx. As would be
expected of the intellectual heritage of Marx,
this theory is radical in its societal implications.

---

[9] Some analysts of social problems—notably, those
using a subjectivist or constructionist approach—would not
include conflict theory as a heading under social disorganization (see Rubington and Weinberg, 1981). We emphasize
that only a subset of the many value-conflict concepts is
considered here (those also called radical theory), and that
we have defined social disorganization in unusually broad
terms.

[10] In complex societies like the United States, of course,
the economic conflict can involve more than just two social
classes.

It does not imply refining a basically sound design, as in functional theory; the very idea that society's problems are technical kinks rather than class interests is seen by conflict theorists as just another ideology of the ruling class. If social problems are indeed rooted in self-serving domination by a social subgroup, society needs to be torn up by its roots.

Social Change Theory Relating social problems to society's design tends to freeze discussion in the present. Whether one sees the American divorce rate, for instance, as a dysfunction of the nuclear family (functionalism) or as a result of geographic movement serving business interests (conflict theory), a current problem is generally viewed in relation to current social organization. But clearly, the American family pattern has been transformed over the last few generations (see Chapter 5). Might not today's family disorganization be a by-product of rapid change from yesterday's family pattern? According to the *social change theory*, the answer is definitely yes. Moreover, this type of question should be asked of other social problems, seeking their common source in alterations of society's design.

As an approach to the causation of social problems, this emphasis on the process of change is not as neatly packaged as functional or conflict theories. It is, quite literally, an approach—a point of view highlighting the dynamics rather than the statics of social life. One of the ways by which change can lead to social disorganization (and thus social problems) is through the phenomenon of cultural lag (Ogburn, 1950). The essence of the idea is that social change may proceed at faster rates in some parts of the social structure; the other parts then lag behind and must strain to catch up. The skyrocketing growth of Sunbelt cities, for example, has overloaded housing, highways, and schools in our southern and western states. The problem lies not in the current design of the houses, highways, and schools, but rather in the sudden adjustments they have had to make to the change in residence patterns.

The most frequently analyzed source of cultural lag is technological change. Particularly in an industrial economy like ours which deliberately stimulates technical innovation (through research and development labs, subsidy of science education, etc.), technological change tends to be rapid and constant. Adjusting to this flood of innovations is more than a matter of replacing one piece of hardware with another. Mass production of the automobile provided the American public with a means of transportation far superior to the horse, but there was a lag of decades before political institutions dealt with the associated problems of traffic congestion and air pollution. To extend the Sunbelt example, a major reason for the relocation of thousands of families—and the municipal problems mentioned above—is the rapid expansion of the computer/calculator industry in that region. A technological breakthrough (the invention of the silicon chip) has left a trail of social strains in its wake. Whether technology or some other societal sector leads the way, uneven change tends to be socially disorganizing.

Even if the transition proceeds evenly, the very rapidity of change presents problems. Each of us has felt the disorienting symptoms of "future shock" (Toffler, 1970) in dealing with new situations, new people, new anything. Too much change too fast can disorient individuals about proper social behavior (norms), thus infecting them with the social disease known as anomie:

> Anomie is precisely this state of disorganization where the hold of norms over individual conduct has broken down. When this controlling normative structure is upset...the individual loses himself in a void of meaningless activities (Parsons, 1968:377).

The relevance of the anomie concept here is twofold. First, anomie has been frequently observed in cases of rapid social change; second, the meaningless activities in which anomic individuals are likely to engage include many forms of destructive behavior. A recent case of the rules of everyday social life disintegrating under the shock of too much change occurred in Barrow, Alaska. Most of Barrow's residents are Inupiat Eskimo, a tribe of traditional whale hunters subjected to instant industrialization by the discovery of oil on the North Slope. The overnight change in lifestyle took its human toll. Between 1965 and 1974, the alcohol death rate of the Inupiat nearly tripled (Kraus and Buffler, 1979); over the same period, there were dramatic increases in suicide, homicide, divorce, child abuse—in virtually every objective index of social problems (Klausner et al., 1979). Sudden social change broke down the norms of Inupiat social life, thus creating anomie; personal breakdown soon followed. Similar interpretations have been applied to recent events in Iran and to the rise of fascism in Germany (Fromm, 1965). These extraordinary cases bear directly on ordinary social problems in the United States. As long as we live in a society that is a pacesetter for social change, the social and personal risks of anomie must be accepted as a price of progress.

Where do social problems come from? Each of the above three theories is an attempt to answer that overriding question. While the specifics of their answers differ, the theories agree that the social system is not properly constructed. Disorganization may be a result of sloppy design, selfish class interest, or haphazard change, but these are all flaws of the societal structure in which individuals live.

Deviant Behavior

It is an occupational hazard among sociologists to use social structure to explain everything. The way to control this temptation is through frequent reminders that people create the social structures wreaking all the havoc. Explanation of social problems must bring the individual back into the theories. In addition to serving an intellectual need, such individual-centered theories appeal to common sense. Since not everybody suffers from a given social problem, why not find the individuals with the problem and see how they differ from those without it? As with theories overemphasizing social structure, there are dangers in this down-to-earth approach. For one thing, once the "nuts, sluts, and preverts" have been singled out, it is all too natural to just blame them, especially if they break the rules.[11] Even theories seemingly sympathizing with the sufferers may only dramatize their personal differences from the rest of humanity (Liazos, 1972). By implication, society is blameless. If they would just be more like us....

The point is that wholly social *or* individual theories tend to present only a partial picture of social problems. The present section fills in some of the gaps in the social disorganization approach by focusing on a sin of which we are all personally guilty—deviant behavior. By definition, individuals are deviant when they violate a social norm; you deviate, for example, when you violate widely shared college student rules against too much or too little studying. Why does anyone break the rules? Whatever the blueprint for social structure, people sometimes step outside the lines assigned to them by the norms. The three theories below are concerned with why they do it, what happens when they do, and what difference it makes for the causation of social problems.

Subculture Theory Why aren't you a drug addict, a bigot, or a rapist? Twisting the usual question about deviance around in this way points to some of the sources of your sterling

[11] Again, the rule breaker is not always the one who suffers. The theories in this section focus on the individual act of rule breaking by explaining which social situations are likely to produce deviant persons. There is not necessarily an attempt to predict that a *particular* individual is destined to deviate.

character: caring parents, quality education, supportive friends. Just as the right kind of environment leads you to be a pillar of the community, the wrong environment may lead others to be conscientiously deviant. The last two words are the essence of *subculture theory,* which posits deviance to be approved conformity to certain sets of social standards. Such standards, obviously, are not those shared by pillars of the community. A central tenet of the subcultural approach is the existence of distinctive cultural environments which (directly or indirectly) promote the violation of society's rules.

"Differential association" (Sutherland, 1939) is a variant of subculture theory claiming there are segments of society that define some forms of deviance as good. This cultural minority—hence, *sub*culture—exerts its influence interpersonally. If most of your social contacts (friends, relatives, peers) see violation of the law as acceptable or even desirable, you will probably be persuaded to share both their deviant opinion and their deviant behavior. The views of your different associates—hence, differential association—concerning social norms may lead you to commit acts that the majority of people define as problematic.

The subculture need not directly approve of norm violation. The idea of "present orientation" (Banfield, 1974) is that some segments of American society reject the mainstream emphasis on planning for the future and instead pursue momentary enjoyment. This socially conditioned attention to today rather than tomorrow does not applaud deviance for its own sake; according to the concept, deviant behavior becomes more likely simply because it offers "kicks" now. A present-oriented student will naturally be less concerned with next week's midterm than with tonight's illegal high. Even though it hypothesizes indirect deviant influence, the idea of present orientation has this in common with differential association: Individuals are predisposed to break society's rules not

because such persons are antisocial, but rather because they strive to live up to (or down to) subcultural social standards.

Labeling Theory What is so bad about deviant behavior? A tacit assumption of subculture theory is that some norm violation is intrinsically harmful, that breaking the rules brings social damage. As we have repeatedly noted, though, rules are socially created. Norms are not laws of nature, deviation from which automatically means destruction. The social forces defining the rules decide who is in violation of them while asserting that deviance brings evil.

As a social process, deviant behavior logically separates into two stages: (*a*) the act of violating the norm and (*b*) societal reaction to the act. *Labeling theory* focuses on the latter stage. According to our second major theory of deviance, a society creates its own rule breaking by forbidding certain acts; without laws, no one behaves like a criminal. After the norms are in place, the social definition—or label—is not applied to every deviant. Similar violations of the law may be dismissed as "boys will be boys" among middle-class youths, while lower-class males are convicted of juvenile delinquency (Chambliss, 1973). Socially inappropriate behavior may be seen as eccentricity if the deviant is rich, but mental disorder if the individual is not (Scheff, 1975). Behavior comes first; society then reacts by deciding what deviance is and on whom to bestow the label of deviant.

While it questions the simple deviance equals damage assumption, labeling theory does identify objective causes of suffering. Regardless of where the rule comes from (or whether you actually broke it), there is personal pain when society pronounces you a burglar, bum, or alcoholic. The suffering of the individual who receives such a label can have further consequences. Persons publicly identified as deviant may increase their subsequent rule breaking (Lemert, 1972); this possible result of accepting society's label as one's true identity is a form of secondary deviance. The primary act of deviant behavior (i.e., violating the norm) may or may not be objectively harmful. Attaching a deviant label to an individual, however, causes deterioration of that person's reputation, self-respect, and self-restraint about society's norms. By the lights of labeling theory, it is not so much the breaking as the making of rules (and their enforcement) that causes objective problems.

Opportunity Theory But who is likely to break the rules in the first place, and why do they do it? In the view of *opportunity theory*, primary deviance has its roots in widely shared social ideals—called cultural goals—aspired to by conformist and deviant alike. What separates the two is not what they want out of life, but their chances of getting it. While cultural goals may be nearly universal, the socially acceptable means of achieving them—called institutionalized means—are not.

The uneven distribution of such approved opportunities means that some societally planted desires must go unfulfilled. Social segments (e.g., the lower class) caught between cultural goals (e.g., material success as "the good life") and restricted means (e.g., little educational or occupational opportunity) will be permeated by anomie, a discrediting of the rules of a society which creates such a personal bind. In an anomic state that fosters rule breaking, some individuals will seek escape from their bind through deviant behavior; a poor boy may thus become a financially successful gangster (Merton, 1976). Bred to value academic success (a cultural goal), the struggling student rankles at a college that grants so few A's (restricted institutionalized means), and finds an uninstitutionalized, deviant solution: cheating. In each case, primary deviance arises because of the equal distribution of desires and the unequal distribution of the means for their satisfaction. According to our third theory of

deviant behavior, the individual likely to cause objective problems is in a socially created corner from which deviance offers a way out.[12]

This side of paradise, *why* do social problems exist? The search for the sources of objective suffering out there in society has led to the six theoretical approaches presented above. No one of these theories is definitive. While all are grounded in scientific investigation, none is a universal explanation for the many forms of human misery. Part of the reason is the diversity of social problems and the diverse harms they bring. It would be truly remarkable if the same theory could fully explain illegitimate tax deductions and illegitimate children. Given the present state of knowledge, the multiplicity of theories enriches explanation.[13] For the complex tangle of individual and social strands that is a social problem, each theory provides a unique angle of vision, a vantage point with fresh insights.

These insights may be cumulative. Grouping theories into the broad perspectives of social disorganization and deviant behavior does not imply unrelated realms of knowledge. Although the blend will differ, every social problem can be (productively) seen as a mix of systemic and individual elements. If the system is breaking down, individuals will be more likely to break its crumbling rules; if individuals engage in wholesale violation of the norms, that will erode the social system. Social disorganization and deviant behavior are thus interrelated perspectives glimpsing different sides of the same problematic coin.

---

[12] The opening of this section noted that all the general theories are, to some degree, concerned with social structure. While Merton's conceptual scheme emphasizes maldistributed opportunities, this structural feature is used to explain a specific aspect of social problems—deviant behavior (Merton also isolates other deviance subtypes based on the relationship of cultural goals and institutionalized means).

[13] As our understanding of social problems progresses, scientific sociology will benefit from more parsimonious (i.e., elegantly simple) theories (see H. W. Smith, 1981).

The specific theories also complement each other in substantive ways (Merton, 1975). Consider labeling theory, which focuses on the process of marking some persons as deviants. Opportunity theory explains who is likely to engage in certain acts of deviance, thus making them (the poor) liable to be labeled; conflict theory fills in a further gap by identifying the labelers (the rich). Sets of theories can (and will, in the following chapters) be combined to develop a more complete picture of problem causation. Even if an inspired blend of theories fully explains the objective sources of suffering *out there*, however, there is still the matter of our feelings about the problems *in here*. Explaining personal and public concern *about* objective suffering brings us to the second major dimension of social problems.

THE SUBJECTIVE DIMENSION: SOURCES OF CONCERN

It may seem a violation of common sense to analyze concern about social problems apart from their objective reality. If you still doubt the separateness of these two dimensions, consider a question based on common sense: Do people always know what is good for them? You may have an uncle who is smugly unconcerned about the cigarettes causing his emphysema. Many college students seem to worry themselves sick over grades while consistently making the Dean's list. Objective reality and subjective perception are related, but they are certainly not mirror images of each other.

If the distinction can be made at the level of individuals, it is even clearer at the societal level since we may be doing the perceiving while other people are doing the suffering. There are myriad examples of public indifference to appalling objective harms. By a conservative estimate, job casualties (accidents and deaths from occupational diseases such as miners' black lung) kill 100,000 Americans annually (U.S. Department of Health and Human Ser-

vices, 1980); yet over the past ten years of opinion polling, death on the job has never been selected by even 1 percent of the public as a "problem of concern" to them (Yankelovich, Skelly, and White, 1982b). Until quite recently, there seemed to be more public outrage over cruelty to animals by owners than over cruelty to children by parents (Freeman et al., 1979). The issue is not just apathy, because concern can also appear to overshoot the objective situation. In 1970, the year of the first Earth Day demonstration, pollution actually surpassed the Vietnamese war in opinion polls about the seriousness of social problems (Erskine, 1972). Although public concern was skyrocketing, the objective evidence indicates that some major forms of air pollution had been declining for a number of years (Barber, 1975). Of course, there was (and is) objective reason for worry about pollution, but the level of concern in the public mind and the actual damage in the public domain appear to have moved *in opposite directions*.

These examples are not just anomalies showing the occasional ignorance of the American public; they are, rather, cases illustrating the independence of the subjective dimension. Objective damage may be a necessary condition for public outrage, but it is not sufficient to explain the *degree* of outrage. Subjective concern about social problems seems to move autonomously, rising and falling largely according to its own laws. There is, however, a logic to those laws, and it is social. The present section will spotlight several significant social factors that act directly on the subjective dimension, factors manipulating what we feel *in here* about the objective side of social problems.

Visibility

It was noted earlier that one does not directly sense the harms wrought by social problems. Only rarely will you be an eyewitness to a mugging, an arson, or a suicide. Your main

source of information about social problems—
or anything else—is the communication network of the social environment. Social information channels operate like a selective filter,
readily passing through some reports while
screening out others.

One of the elements of this social filtering
process is the *intrinsic drama* associated with a
given social problem. Some forms of objective
damage are natural attention getters; and the
more dramatic the damage, the more likely we
are to hear about it and emotionally register it.
Consider airplane crashes. A jet spinning down
in flames and killing hundreds of people on
impact is a spectacularly tragic event. Even
though automobile accidents kill at least
twenty-five times as many people as airplane
crashes (U.S. Bureau of the Census, 1984*b*), the
public seems preoccupied with the latter. Urban slums containing block after block of
squalid housing lead many to view poverty as a
problem of the cities. These dramatic concentrations of human misery attract attention
when, in fact, more of the poor live in nonme-
tropolitan areas than in central cities (U.S.
Bureau of the Census, 1984). Whatever the
actual numbers, the drama inherent in (or absent from) specific objective problems directly
affects our response *in here*.

While word of mouth may still be a significant channel of opinion concerning social problems, *media exposure* renders a given problem
visible to millions of people at a time. The glare
of publicity does not shine uniformly on all
objective harms. Rather than simply holding up
a mirror to society, media professionals screen,
select, and edit events on the basis of their
newsworthiness (Lester, 1980). One eminently
newsworthy problem is bombing incidents,
which kill about 50 Americans in a typical year
(FBI Uniform Crime Reports, 1982). Although
this is much lower than the death toll from
automobile accidents in a single day, a bombing—particularly by terrorists—tends to make a
real media splash. Speaking of terrorism, con-

sider the enormous exposure given to its American victims on foreign soil (with dire consequences for the tourism industry) despite the
objectively tiny risks of actually being kidnapped or hijacked. As such examples suggest,
a major factor in the coverage of events is their
emotional impact. Intrinsically dramatic events
are further dramatized by the mass media spotlight.

There is little doubt that media exposure
shapes subjective judgments about social problems. A classic study of crime news found no
relationship between the amount of newspaper
coverage and the actual amount of crime committed in certain communities; a survey conducted in the same communities, however,
found that there was a relationship between the
amount of newspaper coverage and the public's
subjective perceptions of crime (Davis, 1952).
The rapid rise of pollution to the top of social
problems opinion polls was undoubtedly accelerated by the airing of a dozen television specials on that topic in the spring of 1970 (Murch,
1971). Or consider the phenomenon of "*Sixty
Minutes* syndrome," in which previously ignored problems literally leap into the public
mind overnight. The point is both crucial and
simple: The media-heightened drama of selected social problems may have little to do
with their objective significance, but much to
do with subjective consciousness and concern.

Expectations

If you enroll in a social problems course anticipating a grade of C, receiving a C might seem
perfectly acceptable. If you expect an A, however, and then receive a C, you could be
outraged. The actual grade in each case is
exactly the same. The radical difference lies in
your subjective reaction, in the opposite emotions associated with an identical objective situation.

The difference between satisfaction and dissatisfaction often depends on what is expected.
This truth can be applied to cases that seem to

be paradoxes at the societal level. Take, for example, the timing of revolutions, which are more likely to occur when social conditions are *improving:*

> The most perilous moment for a bad government is when it seeks to mend its ways. Patiently endured so long as it seemed beyond redress, a grievance comes to appear intolerable once the possibility of removing it crosses men's minds. For the mere fact that certain abuses have been remedied draws attention to the others and they now appear more galling (Tocqueville, 1955:177).

As Tocqueville observed over a century ago, an improvement in one's lifestyle makes it clear that positive change is possible, and therefore can be expected of the present regime. With the objective standard of living rising but expectations rising even faster, things can get better but feel worse. The resultant subjective dissatisfaction may build to the point where large numbers of people see society itself as the social problem, and revolution as the solution (Brinton, 1960).

Less sweeping views of social problems are triggered by the same subjective mechanism. A case in point is the spectacular success of American medicine in combating some forms of infectious disease. The virtual elimination of polio, for instance, has saved the lives of thousands while convincing millions of the omnipotence of medical science. Given our apparent capacity to wipe out disease, continuing killers such as cancer seem like an outrage; an objective cure makes uncured illnesses seem, in Tocqueville's phrase, "more galling." Mounting subjective concern is reflected in budgets for medical research, which have grown along with public expectations (Shannon, 1976).

The logic of this improvement-expectation-concern cycle can be readily extended to the case of American social problems in the 1960s. Overall societal conditions preceding this period enjoyed a bounty of improvements, including sustained economic growth with controlled inflation, American hegemony in foreign affairs, and dazzling technological breakthroughs symbolized by space flight. These objective triumphs seemed to lift expectations without lifting the national mood. The sixties became an intensely self-critical period during which subjective concern about societal problems reached a peak; many colleges and universities, in fact, only added social problems to the curriculum in that bountiful decade.

Many problems seemed to appear in the public mind out of nowhere. Poverty suddenly became a matter of widespread public concern, as did the related issue of high school dropouts. The objective truth is that both problems were declining. The proportion of people below the poverty line and the proportion not finishing high school had both been dropping through the 1950s and into the 1960s (U.S. Bureau of the Census, 1984b). The paradox: Subjective concern was growing while the objective extent of the problems was shrinking. The reason: Societal triumphs led to the expectation that control of our collective destiny was feasible, thus making unsolved problems seem more tragic. The general point is that expectations have the power to swing the subjective mood of the public independently of—indeed, even *against*—the objective situation.

Values

Earlier in the chapter, you were assured that a sociological analysis of social problems could yield substantive surprises. In case after case, subsequent sections have revealed the remarkable lack of correspondence between the measured seriousness of social problems and their seriousness in the public mind. The immediate goal is not to startle you with the contrast between the objective and subjective dimensions, but rather to isolate the independent sources of the latter.

A major force operating on general opinion about social problems is values. A value is defined as a "collective conception of that which is desirable'' (Miley, 1981:295); such conceptions vary enormously across societies and groups. Value differences may swing the reaction to an identical objective condition from outrage to apathy depending on the group's values. The power of values over the subjective dimension is based on the truth that "nothing can be defined as 'problematic' without some definition of what the world should be" (Rule, 1978:24).

Because values are general evaluations of the real world out there, they condition public concern about the whole spectrum of potential problems. *Values may magnify the objective harm caused by a given social condition.* Consider the case of narcotics addiction. The subjective seriousness of heroin abuse has been sufficient to support a federally funded Heroin Hotline for reporting pushers. President Nixon even pronounced heroin addiction "public enemy number one." There is objective reality to this problem, one aspect of which is the approximately 600 deaths a year attributable to the drug (National Institute on Drug Abuse, 1981). To put that figure in relative perspective, consider that addiction to another drug—nicotine in cigarettes—kills well over 600 people *every day* (Surgeon General, 1980).

Since death rates reflect only one of the harms associated with heroin, it is desirable to use other social indicators of its objective significance. An alternative method of gauging the drug's human damage is an overall count of the number of addicts. Current estimates indicate that the narcotics addiction rate in America is actually lower than it was in 1900, and is far lower than the rate of addiction to alcohol (Hunt and Chambers, 1976). Why does heroin seem to be a mountainous problem when, in fact, it is a statistical molehill? Clearly, the public image of the junkie is that of a deviant drug fiend who has rejected our cherished lifestyle. The individual has, at best, dropped out of society and, at worst, preyed on society through crime to finance the habit (Califano,

1982). In short, the junkie's behavior is such a shock to our system of values that heroin's harms loom larger than they really are. The point is not that narcotics addiction is so trivial that it should be ignored; the point is that it is not ignored because the lenses of our values magnify heroin's real harms.

This effect also operates in reverse: *Values may minimize the objective harm caused by a given social condition.* Automobile accidents currently kill about 44,000 Americans a year. Since that oft-cited statistic does not seem to register emotionally (which, of course, is the issue), objective comparisons are instructive. The annual death toll for criminal homicides and suicides *combined* barely exceeds that of the automobile; car crashes cause more deaths each year than the American combat death toll in Vietnam over the entire sixteen years of the war (U.S. Bureau of the Census, 1980a).

Even with additional social indicators showing millions of injuries and billions in economic costs (U.S. Department of Transportation, 1976), the carnage of the car ranks low on the scale of public concern. The reason is values. The automobile is more than a device of convenience. One's car symbolizes status, personal independence, even sexual maturity. The automobile is so firmly lodged at the heart of the American value system that most of its harms are ignored or passively accepted.[14] As in the case of heroin addiction, the reaction is not keyed in directly to the objective damage; *first* the social condition itself is ranked in relation to the value system, and *then* the significance of the statistics is weighed. Values can reduce an objective mountain to a subjective molehill.

These two cases are exceptions only in the dramatic way they prove this rule for ranking

[14] An interesting exception that has developed in recent years is drunk driving. The selective public attention devoted to this issue has been due in large part to high media visibility generated by organizations such as MADD (Mothers Against Drunk Drivers; see Chapter 11).

social problems. Why is inflation always among the top national issues in United States public opinion polls (Lauer, 1976)? Its threat to the value of material success inflates our sense of inflation's damage. Another economic issue that consistently leads the social problems polls is unemployment. In one recent survey, in fact, the nation's youth picked unemployment as the most important problem facing the country today. Even more so than with inflation, there is clear objective significance to this problem: approximately 10 million people were out of work at the time of the latter poll, with a doubling of the national unemployment rate among youth and a quadrupling of the national rate among black youth. The high value accorded to work in American culture readily explains our subjective reaction to objective joblessness.

Values also explain the *lack* of reaction to the dangers of *having* a job. Earlier it was observed that work kills at least 100,000 Americans a year; a recent Associated Press article headlined the statistic that work-related injuries and illnesses surged nearly 12 percent in 1984. Both of these facts fail to strike a nerve in public opinion not because of heartlessness or apathy, but rather because we care so deeply about our jobs. Employment is so brightly lit by the value system that unemployment is in the subjective spotlight whereas work's real and present dangers are obscured by the value's rosy glow. The Jekyll-and-Hyde character of work again proves the rule for ranking social problems: values associated with a specific social condition have the power to adjust (up or down) subjective concern about its objective harms.

Like the proverbial tree falling in the woods, social suffering may or may not be heard. The central point is that the objective falling and the subjective hearing are separate processes, and that the crash we hear (or don't hear) can be explained. The three factors—visibility, expectations, and values—offered in explanation of

the subjective dimension are not an exhaustive list, but each is a major socially based force acting directly on the public mind.

Two complications should be noted. First, the factors may interact with one another in producing awareness or apathy. Reporters tend to give media exposure to events bearing on their values (Gans, 1979), and high technological expectations make well-publicized airplane crashes seem all the more shocking. In the second place, how is the public mind to be read? Quite obviously, all the diverse segments of the American public are not unanimous in their reactions to every social problem. Some segments see the use of marijuana as undesirable, while others define the laws against pot as problematical. *In the present usage, the subjective dimension refers to widely shared attitudes reflected in public opinion.* Concern about a problem may begin with the opinion of a small number of significant people (pronouncements by celebrities or politicians, for example), but of primary importance here is the subjective concern of a significant number of people in the American public.[15]

These are just refinements of the central idea that social problems have a dual nature. Because theory and research (and our examples) show the indispensability of objective *and* subjective aspects in assessing the human condition,[16] this book focuses on both. It is necessary to consider the objective dimension of a specific social problem through a rigorous analysis of the available social indicators. Public opinion is anything but infallible, and is an unreliable guide to quantitative scales of suffering. This unreliability is no accident; it is based

---

[15] Obviously, the two are often related. A number of significant people may be influential enough to help convince a significant number of people that a given problem is serious.

[16] An impressive body of cross-cultural research (summarized in Tomasson, 1978) has documented distinct objective and subjective components in the assessment of social welfare.

on the fact that the subjective dimension is guided by its own set of social causes. The independent influence of these subjective factors explains why social problems appear to have a life of their own in the public mind [Armand L. Mauss (1975) has written extensively on the life cycle of social problems movements]. The subjective side must not be ignored if only because of the powerful impact of public opinion on attempts to solve societal problems.

The interplay of the objective and subjective dimensions is a major theme of the chapters to follow. These dimensions blend differently for each social problem, but our theoretical approach will remain constant: The sources of concrete harm and the sources of public opinion must be analyzed separately (see Table 1-1). Subjective concern may be greater than, less than, or even equal to objective damage. To conclude the distinction with a blunt illustration: Whatever the suffering out there caused by a particular problem, your awareness of it in here will be altered by one subjective factor among others—this book.

SOCIAL POLICY: IN SEARCH OF SOLUTIONS

Why is society imperfect? Throughout history, the debate has raged over whether individuals or institutions are to be blamed for the failure to achieve utopia. The sociological perspective reveals this to be a misguided argument. Since institutions are socially constructed by individuals, and since individuals are influenced by the social worlds in which they live, the key to the perfect society is not an either/or proposition. If we are to unlock our social problems and approach the "Heavenly City" dreamt of since America's origins,[17] it will be crucial to recognize the interrelationships of people and social structure.

[17] The phrase is taken from Puritan Cotton Mather's famous essay "Theopolis Americana" (1710).

This is not merely paying lip service to a theme of the chapter. Understanding the social logic linking individuals and institutions is crucial here because "history is strewn with the wrecks of social movements that lacked the knowledge requisite to their success" (Nisbet, 1970:398). Uninformed attempts to solve society's problems through social policy may be useless or worse. Good intentions must be tempered by sociological knowledge for this reason: *The theory of causation of a social problem indicates the appropriate solution.* Faulty theory therefore implies faulty policy. If the problem of poverty is viewed as a result of weak moral fiber, then the "disreputable poor" should not be coddled by giveaway programs; the solution lies in preaching to them to encourage self-improvement. A theory blaming campus protests by college students on permissive child-rearing practices suggests the appropriate answer: stricter parents. Once the cause of the social symptoms has been diagnosed—correctly or incorrectly—it is natural to write a particular type of policy prescription. There is thus a premium on skillful sociological diagnosis of objective causation.

The interrelationship of problem diagnoses and prescriptions brings to mind a specific trend in American social policy. In the place of simplistic victim-blaming theories (like that of the disreputable poor), there is a widespread tendency to view problem people as not responsible for their personal "failings." The therapeutic model absolves deviants of evil by declaring them to be sick (Horowitz, 1968). If alcoholics, rapists, and child abusers are troubled by something that can be called illness, the proper policy is one that gives them personal therapy. The failure of such treatments to cure all social problems suggests the limits of the therapeutic theory.

Consider the contemporary issue of religious cults. It is commonplace to refer to cult members as brainwashed and to attempt to remove that unhealthy condition from the individual

TABLE 1-1   THE DIMENSIONS OF SOCIAL PROBLEMS
(A student guide)

The objective dimension	The subjective dimension
(I) Primary measurement: social indicators of actual conditions	(I) Primary measurement: public opinion polls and evidence of attutudes about social conditions
(II) Sources of suffering: theories concerning the causes of problematic conditions	(II) Sources of concern: factors affecting attitudes toward problematic conditions

(A) Social disorganization: what is wrong with society's design?
    (1) Functional theory
    (2) Conflict theory
    (3) Social change theory
  (B) Deviant behavior: what are the causes and consequences of rule breaking?
    (1) Subculture theory
    (2) Labeling theory
    (3) Opportunity theory
	(A) Visibility
	    (1) Intrinsic drama
	    (2) Media exposure
	  (B) Expectations
	  (C) Values
	    (1) Magnification of harms
	    (2) Minimization of harms

personality through deprogramming (Robbins and Anthony, 1982).[18] The diagnosis and the prescription ignore the fact that cult converts tend to be middle-class college students with unsatisfying interpersonal relationships (Champlin, 1978)—in short, overlooked is the fact that *social* forces are involved. The point is not that all deviant personalities are completely healthy; the point is that diagnosing the problem as only being illness within the individual personality excludes influential social forces from the theory and, consequently, from policy. Abused children may need counseling to deal with stress symptoms, but they more desperately need help changing the family situation which causes the stress.

Given its obvious limitations, why do we find the therapeutic model of social policy so very attractive? The well-known individualism of American culture naturally leads us to see problems as inside individuals, and to see solutions as to be found in one-to-one relationships with a healthy personality (the therapist). As a result,

our values can blind us to socially based solutions. The sociological perspective can be an antidote to this shortsightedness, but it raises a further question. Note the use of the words *we* and *us* in this paragraph, and face a disquieting fact: Sociologists are people, too. Can sociological theories be accepted as scientific when the researchers are members of the very society they research? After all, one of the guiding norms of scientific inquiry is that investigation be free of preconceptions and biases—that it be value-free (Weber, 1949).

As people, sociologists have values. Those who study social problems, moreover, are usually taking an evaluative stand: we oppose the suffering and want to reduce it. This need not disqualify the sociological perspective as science. Consider the parallel to health researchers, who both get sick and oppose illness. Just as the latter seek to understand (and ultimately control) disease through the scientific method, analysts of social problems seek the ideal of objectivity by adherence to the rules of research methods. Since we are flesh-and-blood members of real societies, sociologists cannot help our personal views and even our choice of subjects to study being colored by collective

---

[18] Robbins and Anthony indict the whole medical approach, citing evidence that joining cults may improve mental health and reduce drug abuse; that is, cult membership can sometimes make individuals *healthier*.

values. We can, however, prevent value-induced blindness by putting on the lenses of a scientific approach. Sociology is a disciplined way of seeing the objective and subjective complexities of a social problem, a way of seeing that can guide the hand of social policy.

But how much control is exercised over society's "hand"? One of the founders of modern sociology, Auguste Comte (1854), foresaw the emergence of "sociocracy," a sort of sociological priesthood that would rule society by scientific principles. The failure of Comte's dubious utopia to materialize (none of the authors of this book has yet been nominated for such an elevated position) underscores the policy significance of the objective-subjective distinction. Simply put, subjective concern about a given social problem is a gauge of political support. Whatever sociological analysis suggests about objective causes and cures, public perceptions of a problem importantly influence the resources that will be available for its solution.

The subjective dimension not only represents social support for *some* policy solution but also dictates *which* policies are acceptable. Even if poverty is objectively decreasing, increasing public awareness may independently generate demand that the public sector "do something!" What should be done? The very values shaping subjective concern about the poor—the work ethic, for instance—also shape public opinion about acceptable policy options (Kitsuse and Spector, 1973). No matter how technically efficient a socialist income program would be in dealing with the objective sources of poverty, current American values render it politically infeasible. The subjective dimension of social *policy* is critical for the translation of abstract theories into practical solutions.

So why are social problems unsolved? Even with the limits imposed by the subjective dimension, the case made here for scientific sociology might make you wonder why you live in a society in which social problems textbooks are necessary. We are all part of the reason.

The interrelationship of individuals and institutions is an intricate one, presenting imposing barriers to both understanding and change. One of the services sociology can render is an identification of these roadblocks on the path to utopia.

Value Trade-Offs

With or without sociological knowledge, you can readily think of a solution for any social problem! Crime? Simply give the police unlimited powers of search and seizure while instituting mandatory life sentences for all felons. Urban blight? Just liquidate the assets of the 500 largest American corporations and add the money to municipal treasuries. These solutions seem absurd because of the enormous sacrifices they demand. The value to be gained by solving the crime and urban blight problems must be weighed against the value to be lost in civil rights and economic freedom. Technical ability to reduce one form of objective damage is not the bottom line. Social policies must be assessed by a kind of value accounting, in which benefits are balanced against costs.

Some of these costs can be represented in monetary terms. Consider the fact that there is only so much public concern about social problems, and therefore a limit to the resources to be allocated for social policies. Consequently, a dollar more in one program budget may mean a dollar less to deal with some other form of human suffering.[19] The million dollars spent to save a single balloonist from drowning in the ocean could protect the lives of thousands if it were appropriated for shore patrols; an additional million spent for fire prevention could convert into 100 drug addicts that will go untreated (Calabresi

[19] Of course, the money is generally not shifted in so straightforward a manner; for example, higher police salaries might mean that nothing is left in the budget for the teachers' raise. It should be noted that the *overall* level of public support for domestic social policy can rise (as in the 1960s) or fall (as under the Reagan administration).

The site of this demonstration was deliberately chosen by the participants to call subjective attention to the poverty problem. The demonstrators' message also suggests how a social policy designed to solve one problem (e.g., inflation or national security) may involve severe human costs. (Jean-Louis Atlan/Sygma)

and Bobbitt, 1978). Although they are generally not viewed in such cold-blooded terms, budgetary decisions reflect values being traded-off among competing social policies.

It is important to note that values do vary among subgroups of the society. There will rarely be full consensus, therefore, about the relative worth of social policies. All Americans do not assign the same priority to law and order, and the above proposal for liquidating major corporations would be anathema to mainstream America but a blessing to some political groups.

The final mix of actual policies tends to closely represent the values of the most powerful social segments.[20] The differing values in our complex society, moreover, are subject to change. Controversial Affirmative Action programs giving preference to minority applicants to professional schools (thus practicing reverse discrimination against nonminority college students) have been based on mounting public concern about equality, which now may be on

[20] The ability of special interest groups to influence public policy is well documented (Mauss, 1975; Domhoff, 1967).

the wane. These refinements do not change a basic truth about attempted solutions to social problems: When it comes to the values pursued by various policies, there is no such thing as a free lunch.

The Linkages of Social Problems

To return to a central theme of the chapter, social problems have both individual and social aspects. At each of these levels, problems tend to overlap. Individuals addicted to one drug are likely to be abusing several other substances as well; the alcoholic and the junkie are often the same person. At the social level, neighborhoods with high rates of street crime also tend to have concentrations of poverty and broken homes. The point is that social problems are interrelated, and the implications of this point for policy are crucial.

If social problems are indeed linked, effects exerted on one can reverberate through the others as well. Ironically, this linkage may mean that solving problem A actually worsens problem B. Finding the cure for cancer would remove an enormous source of objective suffering, but would exacerbate the problem of caring for the elderly; finding a practical way to harness solar power could solve our energy problem, thus allowing industry to produce at full capacity and use up more natural resources. The discussion of value trade-offs showed that the *creation* of a given policy implies social sacrifices. Here we face the further paradox that a successful policy may intensify problems linked to the one that is being solved. The latter point can be refined by the realization that the advantages (and disadvantages) of an effective policy are not uniform across all segments of society. An end to poverty might fulfill the material dreams of the lower class, but cause a nightmare of job transfers and adjustments among middle-class employees of the welfare bureaucracy. One group's solution may be another group's problem.

The intricacy of the web of problems is suggested in Table 1-2, which displays the estimated effects of a 1 percent increase in unemployment on suicide, mental disorder, crime, alcohol-related disease, and cardiovascular-renal disease (Brenner, 1978). Such substantial interproblem connections indicate the partial nature of a direct attack on, say, suicide; installing emergency hot lines would be an attempt to prune the branches of suicidal motivation while its roots are apparently somewhat tangled with other social problems. Similarly, school guidance programs to counsel youths against law breaking leave unchanged a potent force precipitating lower-class theft—poverty. One major implication for policy is the importance of a broad-based societal strategy. A coordinated assault on a number of related problems should yield more objective benefits than a problem-by-problem approach. If problem linkages are well understood, such interconnections can be a strength rather than a weakness. The right policy intervening at the right point in a tangle of problems (for example, reducing unemployment in Table 1-2) may set off a positive chain reaction in which progress against problem A reduces problems B and C, thus leading to further progress against A.

Implementation Issues

A general conclusion of the two preceding sections is that social problems should not be viewed in isolation from one another. Similarly, it is unwise to separate a specific policy from the social context in which it is to function. Implementation is the act of putting policies into practice, of transforming ideal solutions into everyday operations. This transformation is attempted *inside* a society filled with other institutions, with individual personalities, and even with opposition to the policy. Thus far our discussion of linked values or problems has assumed the policy does work according to plan. That assumption needs to be examined. Even though theoretical diagnosis of a problem

TABLE 1-2 ESTIMATED EFFECTS OF A SUSTAINED 1 PERCENT INCREASE IN UNEMPLOYMENT ON RELATED SOCIAL PROBLEMS

Social indicator of related problem	Percent increase in social indicator
Suicide mortality	4.1
State mental hospital admissions	3.4
State prison admissions	4.0
Cirrhosis of the liver mortality	1.9
Cardiovascular-renal disease mortality	1.9

Source: Adapted from M. Harvey Brenner, "The Social Costs of Economic Distress," *Consultation on the Social Impact of Economic Distress,* American Jewish Committee, New York, 1978, pp. 3–6. By permission of the publisher. Subsequent research has derived differing estimates of the size of the effects, but has not refuted the basic point about the interrelations of the social problems. Other investigators, in fact, have also linked increases in unemployment to child abuse, physical injuries, and marital problems.

may suggest a policy cure, policy implementation is a more complex process than giving aspirin for a headache.

Unfortunately, there are many instances of counterproductive policies that prove this point. Driver education courses for teenagers have been instituted to promote traffic safety within this high-risk group; research suggests, however, that the courses may *increase* traffic fatalities because more youths get their driving licenses (Robertson and Zador, 1978). Or consider the attempt to control heroin addiction by prohibition of the drug. According to one expert opinion, the profitability of the entire narcotics black market depends on untiring efforts of law enforcement agencies to hold the available supply down (Brecher, 1972). The policy thus causes heroin pushing to be *more* lucrative. These programs appear to be malfunctioning and, in some respects, actually exacerbating the very problems they were designed to solve.

Unproductive or counterproductive policies are not tragic mysteries; they occur for reasons that can be revealed by a sociological analysis of program implementation in the real world. A simplified version of a policy system is shown in Figure 1-1, which represents the complex interplay of forces in and around any social program. One point of breakdown can occur between the policymakers (politicians who

write the laws and authorize the funds) and the policy experts (social scientists who evaluate current policies and invent new ones). A major factor hampering the War on Poverty was, quite simply, that the experts lacked sufficient knowledge to decide what should be done (Moynihan, 1970). Because of pressure from the policymakers who could not wait for the necessary studies to be completed, the social science experts had to make recommendations on the basis of partially researched theories. Uncertainty about the basic strategy for fighting poverty contributed to legislation that was vague and ambiguous. Policy agents (the social workers, administrators, and all those hired to put the programs into practice) thus lacked a clear, workable plan of attack (Friedman, 1977) in this War.

The public in the background of Figure 1-1 is not a passive audience to this play of policy specialists. Just as public concern about the problems of the poor hastened the declaration of the War on Poverty, the subjective dimension can intrude at many points in the implementation process. Consider popular enthusiasm for education in the United States. Schooling has been widely conceived to be a panacea, an all-purpose solution giving individuals the ability to solve their own problems. While upgrading of education has clearly benefited major subgroups of American society, it

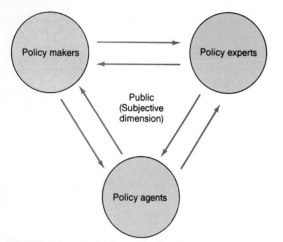

FIGURE 1-1   Social forces involved in policy implementation.

has also contributed to problems of labor shortage and overqualification (Berg, 1970). Or take the related case of manpower training. The provision of job skills to underprivileged persons through schooling and experience is an idea that has received much public acclaim—and money—over the past two decades. As with general education, such wide public support has an effect on policymakers who, after all, want to be reelected. Recent evaluations by policy experts suggest that manpower training programs have, in the main, failed (Rossi et al., 1979). Not only have special interest groups exploited the policy (Larson and Nikkel, 1979), but the basic individualistic strategy is flawed. Unless changes in the occupational structure are also implemented, individuals are left with skills but no job in which to use them.

These case studies show that policy implementation is not magic. Theoretical solutions do not leap off the drawing board into reality. Any program is a complex combination of public attitudes, group interests, and people pursuing careers in the everyday world. Just like the problem it is designed to solve, a policy is a social process which can benefit by sociological scrutiny.

These three dilemmas of social policy stress the need for enlightened action, not the futility of trying. Such barriers have been overcome in a number of successful collaborations of sociologists with policymakers. Even more exciting, though, is the *potential* for success. In its development as a science, sociology is becoming better and better equipped to answer the applied questions posed by social problems.[21] Policymakers, moreover, are increasingly disposed to listen to and implement these answers (see Rein and White, 1977). The convergence of both groups in the solution of social problems is an issue we will examine in some detail.

In each of the chapters to follow, the discussion of a given problem will be concluded by a special section on social policy. After a sketch of the two major Strategies for Solution of the problem, each alternative policy will be analyzed in terms of its ability to reduce human suffering in the real—i.e., social—world. The latter discussion (entitled Policies into Practice) will recall the lessons just learned about the barriers to social problem solving. A final policy segment will engage in Evalvating the Evidence about the past, present, and future effectiveness of the alternative social programs.

Even in this overview chapter, it is easy to get lost in the complexities of concepts and policies. While such intricacies are necessary for the full illumination of social problems, one simple insight should guide you through the maze: Society, with all of its problems, is created by *us*. That sociological reality is the key both to your understanding of social problems and to our aspirations to solve them.

[21] The development of policy analysis and evaluation is one of the major currents in contemporary sociology (Claassen, 1980). The Presidential Address at the 1981 convention of the American Sociological Association further encouraged us to find "Social Inventions for Solving Human Problems" (Whyte, 1982).

SUMMARY

1 Society is our collective creation. We the people create the social structures in which social problems—and potential solutions—are set.

2 Sociological analysis of social problems is based on a scientific perspective. The quality of the insights to be gained from the major research strategies (participant observation, experimental design, and survey research) depends on the social problem subject under study.

3 Social problems have a dual nature. The objective dimension is one side of that nature, and it concerns the concrete harm associated with a given problem "out there" in society. The subjective dimension is public awareness and concern about that same problem, which often does not correspond to the objective level of suffering.

4 There are numerous theories concerning the sources of objective suffering in society. One set of theories can be grouped within the social disorganization perspective, which emphasizes defects in the design of social structure. Deviant behavior theories focus on individual rule breaking, a form of behavior many members of the society find problematic.

5 The fact that subjective concern often does not match objective damage demands sociological explanation. Several socially rooted factors (visibility, expectations, values) have been shown to influence public opinion about problems independently of those problems' objective significance.

6 Despite our collective efforts to solve them, social problems are a continuing reality of United States society. The barriers to simple solutions (value trade-offs, problem linkages, and implementation issues) have been revealed by sociological analysis. That revelation may improve the design of social policies by minimizing their collision with such barriers.

Drug Abuse: Altered Consciousness and Social Reality

Cut it any way you want to—drug use is here. It's not "in," "out," "cool," or anything else—drug use is. Drug use has lost the frenzy it had in the psychedelic sixties and the anxiety it aroused in the seventies. Drug use is housebroken—it's tolerated by many, condemned by some, profitable to a few, but illicit drug use has found a niche in our culture. That fact must astound and amaze anyone over 40, baffle and infuriate those over 50, and confirm the fact for those over 60 that the world is, indeed, on the fast track to the nether world. If you talk to the very young—the early teens—drugs are an everyday part of their life, in and out of

health classes: No big deal! High school and college students may have some appreciation of the transition period they have lived through, but for many, drugs are like sex: something that agitates their parents, upsets their teachers, but is to be enjoyed mostly in a low-keyed way.

Oakley Ray, Drugs, Society, and Human Behavior, *1983:3*

While it is true that drugs have become an increasingly common part of our everyday lives, it is also true that drug abuse has become a major public policy issue. Increasing concern over the dangers of drugs has led to growing support for mandatory urine testing among personnel managers since the military began using it in 1982. And, in 1986, President Reagan declared a "war on drugs," calling for mandatory drug testing of hundreds of thousands of federal workers, the death penalty in some drug-related murder cases, and a 3.1 billion dollar drug abuse program. In 1987, Reagan partially reversed himself by calling for a 915 million dollar cutback in funding for 1988.

In the past, alcohol and tobacco were the common avenues to pleasure, but today a whole spectrum of different chemicals is used (and abused) by millions of Americans. Alcohol is still a common drug, reaching the bloodstreams of some 100 million people each year.

Reasons for drug use vary enormously from person to person. So do the effects of drugs, partly because drug experiences are social psychological and partly because people take drugs in different ways. Some inject directly into a vein, feeling a rapid maximum response. Others smoke, experiencing less of a jolt since some of the drug escapes into the air. Oral ingestion generally diminishes but prolongs the effect of drugs, although the result depends on the individual's physical system. It is important to remember that drugs are not simply chemicals; they are a complex phenomenon with social, psychological, and physical effects.

This chapter is not simply about the physical effects of drugs, but about drugs as a major social problem in contemporary America. Things that used to be considered a normal part of life, such as anxiety and dissatisfaction, are now often dealt with by altering consciousness through chemicals. This is a reflection of relaxed attitudes of physicians toward prescribing drugs, the competition of American life, and a

host of other factors. While the end result is staggering economic, social, and health costs, costs which objectively qualify drug use as a major social problem, some see drugs as a problem because they are part of a lifestyle that flaunts conventional middle-class values and threatens the American way of life. However, we will show in this chapter that drugs are part of the American way of life, and explain how this has come about.

DRUGS: AN OVERVIEW

Common Terms

The sociolegal term *drug* refers to any habit-forming chemical substance that affects perception, mood, or consciousness. There are four classes of legal psychoactive drugs: prescription drugs, over-the-counter (OTC) drugs, social drugs (such as alcohol, caffeine, and nicotine), and drugs sold for nondrug purposes that can affect mood and awareness, such as airplane glue and nutmeg. There are also illegal psychoactive drugs such as heroin, cocaine, and marijuana, and legal psychoactive drugs used illegally, such as stimulants and depressants sold on the street.

The term *narcotic* is used in a variety of ways. Pharmacologically, it refers to opium and opiate derivatives such as heroin, morphine, and codeine, as well as other drugs which kill pain and/or produce sleep. Subjectively, the term narcotic has come to mean almost any drug assumed to be habit-forming. See Table 2-1 (pages 42-45) for a detailed breakdown of types and facts about controlled drugs.

The National Commission on Marijuana and Drug Abuse (1973) outlined five forms of drug use. These include *experimental use,* which is of a short-term trial nature. In this instance, a person may use a drug only once or twice to experience its effects. *Social recreational use* is occasional indulgence among friends to share an experience or enhance interaction. *Circumstantial-situational use* is restricted to specific pressing circumstances, such as taking a drug to stay alert for an exam. *Intensified use* is long-term, habitual, and regular use of a drug. *Compulsive use* is frequent use of a drug to the point where a person cannot face life without it and becomes physiologically and/or psychologically dependent.

What is a *drug problem?* The term means different things to different people. To some, the use of drugs is itself a serious problem, but to others the *effects* of the drug use may constitute the problem. Those holding the latter view feel that as long as drug use does not harm society, the government should not interfere with individual choices (Strategy Council on Drug Abuse, 1976). The most common view of a drug problem involves the social definition of some drugs as unacceptable regardless of effects. This highly subjective view typically reflects the values of mainstream culture and does not always reflect the objective harm of different drugs. Heroin, for instance, is used largely by minority groups and has traditionally been repressed by society. Yet it causes fewer health problems than alcohol and cigarettes, which are socially acceptable. Marijuana is another case in point. At one time it was highly unacceptable, but when its use shifted in the 1960s to middle-class college youth, attitudes toward it were liberalized.

There are important distinctions between *drug use, drug abuse,* and *drug addiction.* The simple use of drugs is not necessarily problematic, but drug abuse is. Abuse is the improper use of drugs to the point where the individual and/or social group suffers, as when drugs are taken for nonmedical purposes (to feel good, to get high, and so on), are used excessively, or are damaging to health. The American Psychiatric Association considers drug abuse a form of mental disorder, classified as substance use disorder, and defines it as

regular use of substances that affect the central

nervous system....Examples...include impairment in social or occupational functioning as a consequence of substance abuse, inability to control use of or to stop taking the substance, and the development of serious withdrawal symptoms after cessation of or reduction in substance abuse (American Psychiatric Association, 1980:163).

Addiction, a severe form of abuse, is considered by some to be behavior which leads to *dependence,* a recurrent psychological and/or physical craving for a drug. Others use the term *addiction* loosely to include any regular use of a drug with or without dependence on it. Here the term addiction is restricted to conditions where dependence occurs from withdrawal of the drug. The evidence is clear that addiction in this sense can occur with a number of drugs, most notably alcohol, cigarettes, the barbiturates, and the opiates. One special form of addiction is *medical addiction,* addiction to a drug prescribed by a physician. A common form of this is the overprescription of Valium and Librium to housewives, a problem that was the subject of 1979 Senate investigative hearings.

Overprescription is one factor which can lead to another form of drug behavior, *cross addiction,* the simultaneous dependence on more than one drug. Traditionally, the most common form of cross addiction has been mixing prescription drugs (such as tranquilizers) and alcohol, a practice which led some 50,000 people to treatment in 1986. Recently, with the rise in the popularity of cocaine, many users have developed a dependency on sleeping pills to get some rest. The effects of cross addiction are difficult to estimate. Social or recreational use is usually harmless, but intensified or compulsive use can prove fatal. This was true in the case of Elvis Presley, the king of rock and roll. Although Presley's official death report stated he died from heart disease, cross addiction was probably the real cause. Presley's body contained high levels of Quaalude, codeine, and ten other drugs. During the thirty-one months be-

TABLE 2-1   TYPES AND CHARACTERISTICS OF DRUGS

Drugs	Often prescribed brand name	Slang name	Medical uses	Dependence physical	Potential: psychological	Tolerance	Duration of effects (in hr)	Usual methods of administration	Possible effects	Effects of overdose	Withdrawal symptoms
Narcotics											
Opium	Dover's Powder, Paregoric		Analgesic, antidiarrheal	High	High	Yes	3–6	Oral, smoked	Euphoria, drowsiness, respiratory depression, constricted pupils, nausea	Slow and shallow breathing, clammy skin, convulsions, coma, possible death	Watery eyes, runny nose, yawning, loss of appetite, irritability, tremors, panic, chills and sweating, cramps, nausea
Morphine	Morphine	White stuff, M	Analgesic	High	High	Yes	3–6	Injected, smoked			
Codeine	Codeine		Analgesic, antitussive	Moderate	Moderate	Yes	3–6	Oral, injected			
Heroin	None	H, horse, junk, scag, smack, dope	None	High	High	Yes	3–6	Injected, sniffed			
Meperidine (pethidine)	Demerol, Pethadol		Analgesic	High	High	Yes	3–6	Oral, injected			
Methadone	Dolophine, Methadone, Methadose	Dolly	Analgesic, heroin substitute	High	High	Yes	12–24	Oral, injected			
Other narcotics	Dilaudid, Leritine, Numorphan, Percodan		Analgesic, antidiarrheal, antitussive	High	High	Yes	3–6	Oral, injected			

Depressants

Drugs	Often prescribed brand name	Slang name	Medical uses	Dependence physical	Potential: psychological	Tolerance	Duration of effects (in hr)	Usual methods of administration	Possible effects	Effects of overdose	Withdrawal symptoms
Chloral hydrate	Noctec, Somnos	Poppers, locker room, rush	Hypnotic	Moderate	Moderate	Probable	5–8	Oral	Slurred speech, disorientation, drunken behavior without odor of alcohol	Shallow respiration, cold and clammy skin, dilated pupils, weak and rapid pulse, coma, possible death	Anxiety, insomnia, tremors, delirium, convulsions, possible death
Barbiturates	Amytal, Butisol, Nembutal, Seconal, Phenobarbital, Tuinal	Downs, downers, barbs, reds, yellow jackets, tooies	Anesthetic, anticonvulsant, sedation, sleep	High	High	Yes	1–16	Oral, injected			
Glutethimide	Doriden		Sedation, sleep	High	High	Yes	4–8	Oral			
Methaqualone	Optimi, Parest, Sopor, Quaalude, Somnafac	Ludes	Sedation, sleep	High	High	Yes	4–8	Oral			
Tranquilizers	Equanil, Librium, Miltown, Serax, Valium, Tranxene		Antianxiety, muscle relaxant, sedation	Moderate	Moderate	Yes	4–8	Oral			
Other depressants	Clonopin, Dalmane, Dormate, Noludar, Placydil, Valmid		Antianxiety, sedation, sleep	Possible	Possible	Yes	4–8	Oral			

Drugs	Often prescribed brand name	Slang name	Medical uses	Dependence physical	Potential: psychological	Tolerance	Duration of effects (in hr)	Usual methods of administration	Possible effects	Effects of overdose	Withdrawal symptoms
Stimulants											
Cocaine	Cocaine	Coke, snow, toot, blow	Local anesthetic	Possible	High	Yes	2	Injected, sniffed	Increased alertness, excitation, euphoria, dilated pupils, increased pulse rate and blood pressure, insomnia, loss of appetite	Agitation, increase in body temperature, convulsion, possible death	Apathy, long periods of sleep, irritability, depression, disorientation
Amphetamines	Benzedrine, Biphetamine, Desoxyn, Dexedrine	Speed, ups, bennies, dexies, pep pills, black beauties	Hyperkinesis, narcolepsy, weight control	Possible	High	Yes	2–4	Oral, injected			
Phenmetrazine	Preludin		Weight control	Possible	High	Yes	2–4	Oral			
Methylphenidate	Ritalin		Hyperkinesis	Possible	High	Yes	2–4	Oral			
Other stimulants	Bacarate, Cylert, Didrex, Pre-Sate, Plegine, Ionamin, Sanorex, Voranil, Pondimin		Weight control	Possible	Possible	Yes	2–4	Oral			

Drugs	Often prescribed brand name	Slang name	Medical uses	Dependence physical	Potential: psychological	Tolerance	Duration of effects (in hr)	Usual methods of administration	Possible effects	Effects of overdose	Withdrawal symptoms
Hallucinogens											
LSD	None	Acid, sugar, trips, blotter	None	None	Degree unknown	Yes	Variable	Oral	Illusions and hallucinations (with exception of MDA), poor perception of time and distance	Longer, more intense trip episodes, psychosis, possible death	Withdrawal syndrome not reported
Mescaline	None	Mesc	None	None	Degree unknown	Yes	Variable	Oral, injected			
Psilocybin, psilocyn	None	Magic mushroom	None	None	Degree unknown	Yes	Variable	Oral			
MDA	None		None	None	Degree unknown	Yes	Variable	Oral, injected, sniffed			
PCP	Sernylan	Angel dust, superjoint	Veterinary anesthetic	None	Degree unknown	Yes	Variable	Oral, injected, smoked			
Other hallucinogens	None		None	None	Degree unknown	Yes	Variable	Oral, injected, sniffed			
Cannabis											
Marijuana, hashish, hashish oil	None	Pot, dope, hash, grass, joints, smoke, reefer	None	Degree unknown	Moderate	Yes	2–4	Oral, smoked	Euphoria, relaxed inhibitions, increased appetite, disorientated behavior	Fatigue, paranoia, possible psychosis	Insomnia, hyperactivity, and decreased appetite reported in a limited number of individuals

Source: Adapted from U.S. Department of Justice, Drug Enforcement Administration, Drugs of Abuse, Washington, D.C., Government Printing Press.

fore his death, Presley's physician had prescribed 19,000 depressants, stimulants, and painkillers! Actually, it is remarkable that Presley lived as long as he did.

Some drug addicts graduate from one drug to another. Wepner and Agar (1971) studied over 1000 heroin addicts and found that 60 percent had first been abusing a different drug. Thirty-five percent named marijuana, nearly 18 percent named alcohol, and the rest listed various drugs, including cough syrup. Multiple use (and cross addiction) may stem from a curiosity about experimenting with new drugs rather than being caused by use of the previous drug. It may also result from *tolerance,* the ability of the body to adapt to progressively larger doses of the drug, making ever larger amounts necessary to achieve the desired effects. This is particularly apparent with alcohol and heroin. At some point another drug may be added (or substituted), and a new cycle proceeds toward tolerance. With certain drugs, such as LSD, tolerance develops rapidly. If LSD is taken once a day for a week, the effect on the fifth or sixth day is only a fraction of the effect of the first day's dose.[1] Multiple drug use exemplifies the linkage among different forms of a social problem.

Household Drugs

As stated earlier, a significant amount of the drug problem involves the abuse of prescription drugs and OTC drugs. This is not surprising in light of the fact that the average American family has about thirty different drugs in its medicine chest. These come from 60,000 retail locations where some 150,000 pharmacists fill 750 million new and 650 million refill prescriptions written yearly by one of the 500,000 physicians in the United States. The OTC drugs are self-prescribed and self-administered for self-diagnosed reasons. Such drugs are potentially dangerous, yet Americans eagerly purchase some 6 billion dollars

worth annually. There are about 300,000 different OTC products grouped into twenty-six classes, ranging from sleep aids to analgesics to stimulants. The most widely abused is aspirin. Almost 30 million pounds of aspirin are consumed each year in the United States, an unsettling fact responsible for many ulcers and other gastrointestinal disorders.

About 70 percent of all prescriptions are for psychoactive drugs; 6.2 prescriptions per person were dispensed in 1986. It is well documented that women are more likely than men to use these drugs, a probable result of differences in family role responsibilities between the sexes (Cafferata, Lee, Kasper, and Bernstein, 1983). One of the most popular and frequently abused of these drugs is Valium.[2] Although it is a tranquilizer designed to relax muscles and reduce anxiety, it is often used as a psychological crutch. Until 1978, Valium was *the* number one legal drug with annual sales of 2 billion dollars. Valium—like Librium, Miltown, and other so-called minor tranquilizers—is commonly abused by housewives and elderly widows who have little difficulty getting physicians to prescribe for them indefinitely. It is also frequently abused by those who find it difficult to get through a day's work without a drug to alleviate job-induced stress. But the price of this chemically induced sense of peace can be stiff in terms of long-term problems, such as family disharmony. Fortunately, current rates of tranquilizer abuse are declining as physicians have become more aware of the possibility of abuse and psychological dependency. In the mid-1970s, more than 60 million prescriptions for Valium were sold annually, but by 1982, only 24 million crossed pharmacy counters.

There has also been a dramatic decrease in the use of other psychoactive drugs, such as sleeping pills and sedatives. Physicians now prescribe one-third fewer of these drugs than they prescribed in the mid-1970s. Despite these

---

[1] When tolerance develops quickly, it also diminishes quickly. If a person with a tolerance for LSD refrains for a week, the full effects will return.

[2] Valium literally means "to be strong and well."

reductions, there is still much abuse of legal drugs, but the fact that they are legal means people who use them are respectable addicts (housewives, businesspeople, or students) who are dependent on pills to make life a little easier to face. Their "hidden addiction" (Moffitt and Chambers, 1970) is an unrecognized facet of the overall drug problem.

A number of factors contribute to hidden addiction and overmedication in general. One is the practice of drug companies to market products in questionable ways. For example, many ads in medical journals glorify the wonders of a drug but relegate a lengthy list of serious side effects to fine print. Another cause of overmedication is physicians (a minority of about 1 percent) who write prescriptions without much concern for—or knowledge of—the misery and addiction that can result. About 5000 physicians annually prescribe or dispense some 200 million doses of controlled drugs—an amount greater than the total prescribed by the other 495,000 physicians! The elderly are especially likely to be overmedicated. People over age 65 make up only 11 percent of the population but consume 30 percent of the drugs prescribed each year. Do not get the impression that this simply reflects the ill health of the elderly. They are twice as likely to be hospitalized for drug-induced problems as people under 60, which suggests that drugs are doing more than curing their sicknesses. What is especially sad is that some of the elderly were given drugs to help people around them, not themselves. This happens with old people living with relatives who keep them medicated so they will not be a nuisance. See the chapter on health for a discussion of the failure of physicians to communicate effectively with elderly patients.

THE OBJECTIVE DIMENSION OF DRUGS

Economic Costs of Drugs

A number of estimates have been made on how much drugs cost society economically. In 1983, a former secretary of Health, Education, and Welfare reported that Americans' addiction to alcohol and other drugs drains from the economy more than 100 billion dollars a year in reduced productivity, days away from work, and medical bills. A more conservative estimate, offered in 1982 by the Alcohol, Drug Abuse, and Mental Health Administration, reported that American society loses about 50 billion dollars each year because of alcohol abuse and around 17 billion dollars because of abuse of other drugs. This report equated economic costs with loss in worker productivity. In 1986, the National Institute on Drug Abuse estimated that on-the-job drug and alcohol abuse by workers cost United States automakers $175 per vehicle in lost productivity and increased injury claims. There are many other indirect costs paid to support drug-dependent persons which should be added to the total bill; these include treatment and control of drug abuse, welfare funds to support the unemployable drug abuser, and the costs of processing drug users through the criminal justice system. Although it is difficult to measure accurately the total economic costs of drug use, it clearly exacts a huge financial toll on society. The 1984 annual report of the International Narcotics Control Board stated that drug trafficking and the abuse of illegal narcotics have become so pervasive worldwide that national economies are being disrupted and the very security of some countries threatened.

Drugs also constitute big business in the United States. Legal sales of the 1.5 billion prescriptions filled each year tally 11 billion dollars. In 1986, there were about 30,000 "head shops" which sold close to 2 billion dollars in drug accessories such as water pipes, rolling papers, "roach clips," vials, and scales. If money spent illegally on such drugs as marijuana and cocaine were added to the sales figures, the total would show that the drug business may be the largest American industry. It may also be the most dangerous in light of the fact that illegal drugs are often sold on the street as something different from their actual chemical makeup (see Table 2-2).

Drugs and Other Social Problems

A number of linkages connect drugs to many other contemporary social problems. The link to crime is evidenced by the large number of federal and state prison inmates who are drug offenders. Each year there are close to a million arrests for drug law violations. The most common drug-related crimes (aside from possession or distribution) are burglaries and muggings to support drug habits. Heroin especially is related to stealing, since a heroin addict may need over $100 a day to get high. Of all the drugs, alcohol is most highly correlated with violence. In 1985 the Bureau of Justice Statistics reported that more than half of jail inmates convicted of violent crimes had been drinking before committing the offenses. Wife abuse, child abuse, fighting in bars, rape, and a long list of other forms of violence are frequently associated with alcohol abuse.

Drug abuse affects people who have a variety of other social problems such as poverty, unemployment, alienation, or discrimination. Heroin addicts are likely to experience *all* of these difficulties. Drug abuse is also profoundly involved with family life because it is inextricably bound up with the causes and consequences of marital problems and instability. The skyrocketing divorce rate in our country may be due in part to the rise in drug use. Since 1958 the divorce rate has been steadily increasing, as has drug use, although it is difficult to tell whether drug use is a cause or a result of failing marriages.

Drugs are also involved in accidents which injure and kill not only the drug user but innocent victims as well. Alcohol use, for instance, is blamed for half of the yearly total of automobile fatalities, not to mention the 1 billion dollars wasted annually on property damage and medical expenses caused by alcohol-related car

accidents. The effect of other drugs on highway accidents is not fully known, but it is safe to assume that large doses of psychoactive drugs impair driving ability.

A number of mental and physical health problems are also associated with drugs. The fact that large numbers of people turn to drugs in order to feel comfortable may indicate a deep dissatisfaction with the quality of their lives. Or perhaps they are psychologically disturbed people who use drugs to escape their troubled psyches. Physical health problems of drug abusers are more tangible than psychological complications. In general, drug abusers are more likely to suffer from a number of physical consequences including malnutrition, retarded sexual maturation, anemia, infections, hepatitis, poor dental health, and high death rates. Some health problems occur even before birth, such as congenital disorders (*fetal alcohol syndrome*) caused by mothers drinking alcohol during pregnancy. The most telling fact regarding the effect of drug abuse on physical health lies in a 1984 report from the National Institute of Drug Abuse. That study found that the addictive use of many psychoactive substances—such as alcohol, tobacco, heroin, cocaine, amphetamines, barbiturates, and hallucinogens—has made *drug abuse the leading cause of death in the United States*. This striking fact has been neglected because of the failure of "physician sentinels" to certify things like smoking as the underlying cause of death. In 1984, the World Health Organization said cigarette smoking alone was responsible for a million premature deaths worldwide each year.

Are there any positive aspects of drug use? Functionalists believe drug use can have beneficial effects, such as acting as a social lubricant by allowing people to relax and be sociable as well as helping some unwind after work. Sometimes this idea can be deadly. Butyl nitrite ("poppers"), a drug used to enhance sex, reportedly weakens the body's ability to resist infections such as AIDS. Some drug users feel that our social problems

TABLE 2-2 DRUGS ON THE STREET
Do It Now Foundation National Street Drug Analysis Summary, 1979–1984

% actual ingredients

Alleged ingredients	Amphetamine	Methamphetamine	Caffeine, phenylpropanolamine, ephedrine	Cocaine	Cocaine and lidocaine	Cocaine and mannitol	Cocaine plus 2 or more additives	Barbiturate	Methaqualone	Methaqualone plus 2 or more additives	Valium	Heroin	Heroin & adulterants	LSD	Opium & opiates	Phencyclidine (PCP)	MDA/MDM	Marijuana	Mescaline	Psilocybin	Other substitutes	Unidentified	Contains no drugs	% of deceit
Amphetamine (speed)	8	9	74	0.8				0.4			0.2			0.09							3.8	1	2.9	92%
Methamphetamine	6	74	11	0.3					0.3												3.6	2.7	1.2	26%
Cocaine	0.1	0.3	0.4	45	7.7	11	29		0.06		0.08										8.1	1.3	0.7	55%
Quaalude		0.2	0.3					3/3	18	36	30				0.2						17	1	0.3	82%
Heroin		2							1.2			11	60								12	7	6	89%
LSD		0.3	1											88						0.3		1	9	12%
Marijuana															0.6	1		88			2.3	1	7.4	12%
MDA/MDM														0.5		0.5	90				1.6	2.7	4.4	10%
Mescaline														70		2			13		4.3	2	8.7	87%
Psilocybin														31						18		8	43	82%
PCP/angel dust										1		2		6		49		6		1	19	3	13	51%
Opium and synthetic opiates (including Methodone, Morphine, Demerol, Dilaudid, Darvon, etc.)								1.5			0.7				75						4.5	4.5	6	25%

Source: © 1984 Do It Now Foundation. Data for this summary is based on a five-year analysis of 12,283 samples.

could be reduced if drugs were used more widely—a common attitude among pot smokers who believe the mellowing effect of marijuana reduces aggression. Drugs are also beneficial for those who make a living growing, processing, and selling them, as well as for physicians and the patients they serve. Another example of the utility of drugs is their use with mental patients. Before the introduction of psychopharmacological drugs in the 1950s, mental patients had little hope of ever escaping their agonizing symptoms. Now medication can help control many forms of mental disorder and allow the disturbed to return to the community. The discovery of Ritalin, for instance, has been an invaluable aid to hyperactive children. But when drug *use* turns to drug *abuse,* it is very difficult to find *any* positive results.

Drug Abuse and the Changing Age Structure

The National Institute on Drug Abuse (NIDA) has made some interesting predictions about the extent of the drug problem in 1995. Since the highest percentage of drug abusers is in the young adult (18 to 25 years old) population, and since there will be a decline in the size of that age group between now and 1995, it is reasonable to assume that the number of drug abusers will decline. The institute predicts this decline in the use of all drugs. Consistently, 47 percent of high school seniors reported using an illicit drug sometime in 1982, down 6 percent from the peak of 53 percent in 1979. Therefore, the projected decline in drug use among youth may not simply be the result of fewer young people in the population but an actual decline in the *rate* of use.

THE SUBJECTIVE DIMENSION OF DRUGS

Although drug abuse is not usually one of the most important problems in current public opinion polls, many surveys report that the drug problem is perceived by a majority of Americans as a threat to society. Drugs were considered a major social problem until 1974 when the Nixon administration announced to the American people that it had won a great victory over drugs. In fact, this was a cover-up which occurred at a time when drug abuse was actually reaching the highest levels in our history (Richardson and Frank, 1977), another case of the objective and subjective dimensions moving in opposite directions. Currently, there is far from a smooth matchup between the subjective and objective dimensions of specific drugs. Some of the most harmful drugs are widely accepted, while some of the most innocuous drugs are heavily stigmatized. Why? Because, like many social problems, drugs are evaluated on the basis of values and emotional responses rather than factual information.

The effect of *values* on the acceptance or rejection of different drugs can be clearly seen with all drugs, including nicotine and caffeine. A century or two ago the use of tobacco and coffee was considered to be morally abhorrent. In England, people who smoked cigarettes were sometimes punished by having their noses cut off or split. Today, labeling the users of some drugs as deviant and the users of others as normal is largely a political process whereby, as conflict theory suggests, politically powerful groups approve the use of some drugs (such as alcohol and tobacco) and punish those who use others (such as marijuana).

The major social reaction to drugs is not determined simply by the actual dangers of each drug, but by the values of members of mainstream culture. Often these values are inconsistent with reality, as in the case of marijuana. In 1974, a Senate Judiciary Committee issued a report saying that the use of pot threatens the national security of the United States because it changes young people into "amotivational zombies" who are incapable of defending against a foreign invader! In reality, marijuana does not even compare to alcohol and cigarettes in terms of documented objective damage experienced by users.

Subjective views toward drugs are also determined by the type of people who use them. If the users are "respectable," the drugs are likely to be accepted, but if the drugs are used primarily by the poor, criminals, or minority groups, they are more likely to be viewed as undesirable. Public opinion about a particular drug also varies by such factors as the social class of the user. A middle-class alcoholic, for instance, is seen as a person with a medical problem, but a lower-class alcoholic is seen as a derelict or bum (Pittman, 1967).

The subjective association of a drug with use or abuse is partly the result of the media's powerful influence over people's attitudes toward drugs. The public has little knowledge of the actual properties of drugs and has little tolerance for drugs the media portray as disreputable. Nowhere is this more *visible* than the media-sponsored view of drug users as dope fiends and violent criminals. The 1936 film, *Marijuana: Assassin of Youth,* later retitled *Reefer Madness,* portrayed high school students smoking pot and swiftly turning to murder, rape, prostitution, and mental disorder. A 1986 *Parade Magazine* study reported that at least sixty major motion pictures made in the previous five years had glamorized the use of illegal drugs. These include *Poltergeist, Private Benjamin,* and *Mask,* in which Cher, the mother of a deformed child, smokes pot and snorts cocaine. The ideas many people have about the connection between drugs and sex are especially likely to be far off the mark. (See Box 2-1 for a discussion of the effect of drugs on the sex drive.) Many older people still think of marijuana as the road to vice, even though smoking it is not actually associated with aggressive behavior of any kind, except for that among dealers. In fact, the idea that drug users turn to crime is not universally true; in one study, more than 70 percent of drug abusers with criminal records were crim-

inals before they turned to drugs (Zinberg, 1967).[3]

The attitudes many Americans have toward drugs are a reflection of popular myths and the dramatic treatment of certain drugs in the media. There is no real connection between the objective dangers of drugs and the social reaction to them. In terms of health damage, deaths, and the pains of withdrawal, alcohol is much worse than heroin, yet drinking and smoking are accepted because they are done by mainstream people. Ries (1977) found that alcoholics are more stigmatized than "normal" people. Alcoholics generally are attributed unfavorable characteristics, and a majority of people reject them in close relationships. However, alcoholics are much less stigmatized than users of other drugs, such as heroin. The real drug problem is the abuse of legal and "harmless" drugs such as tranquilizers, cigarettes, pep pills, and alcohol. This is not to say that illegal drugs cause no harm. They certainly do. However, a 1982 General Accounting Office (GAO) study reported that *more Americans die or suffer medical emergencies from using prescription drugs improperly than from all illegal drugs combined!*

Are there any indications that public opinion toward drugs is changing? Most social scientists believe that public tolerance of illegal drugs is rising on all levels of American society. Concerns about marijuana and cocaine have become less salient in recent years as their use has moved into mainstream society. This is largely the result of an increasing number of young people using substances which were unavailable to previous genera-

---

[3] There are numerous examples of how misinformation about drugs is transmitted by the media. One form of distortion is all the attention paid to heroin when alcohol causes more objective damage, such as drunk-driving deaths. Yet the high visibility and intrinsic drama of heroin make it a highly feared drug. All over the country there are heroin hot lines, even though 75 percent of all heroin addicts are in three cities: New York, Chicago, and Los Angeles.

BOX 2-1

DO DRUGS ENHANCE SEX?

Most of the lurid stories of drug and sex orgies are complete myths. Not only are drugs not true aphrodisiacs—substances that increase the physical aspects of sexual arousal—but they actually depress sexual sensations and functions and even diminish sexual dreaming (Jones and Jones, 1977). In fact, some addicts become motivated to stop drug use after they fully understand that drugs are the cause of their loss of libido. It is true, however, that some drugs taken for pleasure may give the user a temporary sense of self-confidence and euphoria and, in that sense, aid sexual pleasure.

The popular belief that alcohol increases sexual desire and performance is simply not true. Small doses may help by releasing inhibitions, but larger amounts actually inhibit sexual response. This is especially true for males, who are known to have a diminished ability to achieve and maintain erection the more they drink (Lemere and Smith, 1973). An experiment designed to measure the effect of alcohol on sexual arousal of college females also demonstrated that increased alcoholic intake results in decreased *physiological* arousal along with self-reports of increased sexual arousal (Wilson and Lawson, 1976).

Quaalude, the so-called love drug, can offer only psychological assistance to people who are sexually repressed by releasing inhibitions. It has no true abilities to cause physiological arousal. Stimulants, such as cocaine and amphetamines, are slightly different. Like alcohol, Quaaludes, and a number of other drugs, they are not really aphrodisiacs, although they can prolong the sense of excitement during intercourse by postponing (or eliminating) climax. Sometimes a person on amphetamines, particularly a male, cannot climax until the effects of the drug have subsided.

What about pot? Some people who smoke it claim it makes sex more erotic and exciting, and even makes finding a sex partner easier. Once again, these are probably people who are inhibited to begin with. The sexual effects of marijuana vary from person to person, but there is evidence that it actually interferes with the physical aspects of sexual performance and therefore is not a true aphrodisiac. Like pot, any reported sexual enhancement of LSD is simply illusory (Gay and Sheppard, 1973).

If drugs actually interfere with the physical aspects of sexual pleasure, why does the term *aphrodisiac* even exist? Because it is an interesting topic with a high level of intrinsic drama. This has led the public down the road to gross misunderstanding. There are only a few exotic drugs that may qualify as true aphrodisiacs. One is the nitrites (amyl, butyl, and isobutyl), commonly referred to as poppers and sold in head shops and adult bookstores by such vividly euphemistic names as Rush, Climax, and Locker Room. When inhaled, the nitrites cause a dizzying, heart-pounding rush of intense exhilaration and a marked drop in blood pressure. This results in a relaxation of every soft muscle in the body for about ninety seconds. It is popular among gay men because it eases discomfort from anal sex. The drug itself is medically dangerous and may cause cancer. Now the use of nitrites is spreading to the heterosexual community. Another drug which may qualify as a true aphrodisiac is Contharidin (Spanish Fly). It is an extract containing dried and powdered blister beetles which irritates the urethra and causes severe itching. This, in turn, lends to an increased need for physical contact.

---

tions. These changes should not be seen as progress; acceptance of illegal drugs does not necessarily help anyone. A truly beneficial change in subjective views toward drugs would be an increased awareness of the dangers of the ''acceptable'' ones.

As this book is being written, tolerance for drugs appears to be declining. Much of this apparent change has resulted from the appearance of a menacing drug on the American scene: crack. These dangerous little pellets of cocaine have destroyed many lives and completely taken others. Regular media reports of the dangers of crack have accompanied the well-publicized cocaine deaths of American idols, such as University of Maryland basketball star Len Bias. These incidents, along with Reagan's war on drugs, appear to be turning public attitudes from growing tolerance into bitter resentment.

THEORIES OF DRUG ABUSE

Psychologists have traditionally believed that drug abusers are people cut from inferior material. Today, that view appears erroneous since psychologists have been searching for the so-called addictive personality for decades but have yet to find it. Alcoholics have been described as anxious, repressed, fixated, immature, and frustrated, among other things. There may be individual factors involved in using drugs, such as seeking pleasure or avoiding pain. However, it would be a mistake to look at drug abuse simply as a psychological problem since predisposing social factors are frequently involved (Galizio and Maisto, 1985). Certainly some may turn to drugs after the loss of a loved one or as an expression of self-destructive urges. But the major social theories of drug abuse (summarized below) are indispensable explanations of general patterns of abuse as well.

Role Strain

The difficulty some people experience in meeting their role obligations is known as *role strain*. There are numerous examples in our society, including the harried executive, the college student with a demanding set of courses, and the overworked laborer. Role strain may develop when people are taking on new roles, such as when students graduate from college and enter the workforce. Strain may also occur when role obligations are ambiguous, or when a role makes contradictory demands. The result is a "social squeeze," a lack of fit between the individual's needs and the demands of the role. Some turn to drugs to avoid or alleviate the stress. This theory appears to be an appropriate explanation for the high use of psychoactive drugs by young and future physicians (McAuliffe, 1984).

Culture of Industrialism

Why do some societies, like the United States, have high rates of drug abuse while other places, such as rural Africa, have little difficulty with the problem? Since most of the societies with significant drug problems are highly industrialized (Lynn, 1971), it stands to reason that the cultural values associated with industrialism may be a cause. One of these values is an emphasis on individual achievement: occupational, financial, and educational. This orientation increases role strain and tightens the social squeeze since the need for achievement makes people feel they have to perform their roles better, and better, and better.

Rise of Anomie

Drug abuse can also be triggered by social change, particularly *rapid* social change which, according to social disorganization theory (see Chapter 1), can cause an imbalance in the social system. Such change can cause *anomie,* a confusion of norms in society. The result is a lack of social solidarity; individuals do not have adequate ties to the conventional social order. Because people are less integrated into families, schools, organizations, and communities, two factors occur which encourage drug use. One is the sense of isolation individuals experience. With it comes reduced external control over their behavior, since few social restraints are present to keep them from deviating. Second, individuals who are anomic are miserable. They are driven to drink or to seek refuge in other drug experiences. In industrialized societies, there is a built-in layer of anomie because of continual change and technological discoveries. But in traditional societies which are modernizing, accelerated change can lead to many forms of destructive behavior, particularly alcohol abuse. A case in point is the Inupiat Eskimos discussed in Chapter 1. Their overnight change in lifestyle nearly tripled the alcohol death rate.

Social Learning

Drug abuse can also occur when a person is a member of a subculture whose values conflict with those of mainstream society. If drug use is acceptable among a particular group of people, then, from their point of view, it is normal. Drug use may be part of a *social learning process* by which people become deviant through conforming to a set of standards rejected by the larger society. Heroin use may occur mainly in the ghetto because it is part of everyday life there. On a more microsocial level, children can turn into drinkers by modeling drinking parents. Additionally, marijuana use is now filtering down to children under 8 years old who are smoking under the influence and supervision of their parents. The Adlers have labeled this phenomenon *tinydoping* (1978). Thus, drug use may be a form of social behavior acquired through direct conditioning and through imitation, or modeling, of others' behavior (Akers, Krohn, Lonza-Koduce, and Radosevich, 1979).

There are also many people with drug problems who are not members of oppressed minority groups but are simply following the lead of a *reference group*—a social network an individual uses to guide his or her own behavior (Kaplan, Martin, and Robbins, 1984). The fact that most users are hooked on drugs prescribed by a physician demonstrates they are simply conforming to the suggestions of the medical world. At cocktail parties, guests are expected to drink alcohol as part of the social ritual. College students who use drugs are typically the ones whose friends (*reference individuals*) do. In fact, there is no better predictor of whether a student smokes pot than whether the student's friends do (Ginsberg and Greenley, 1978). And people who use tranquilizers are more likely to have friends and family members who also use them (Radelet, 1981). Perhaps social ties are as much a cause of the abuse of prescription drugs as the physicians who overprescribe them.

Social Conflict Theory

Conflict theorists consider heroin abuse in the ghetto as a tool for social control which serves the interests of the powerful. Those with the power oppress those without it and create a host of problems for the lower social classes. To ease the sting of oppression, some poor people turn to drugs which tranquilize them and prevent them from rebelling against the oppressor.

Aside from the five social theories of drug abuse presented above, there are also a number of psychological theories. In addition, there are biological explanations of some drug problems. This is particularly true of alcoholism, which has been linked with a metabolic disturbance, endocrine deficiencies, glandular dysfunctions, and inherited traits. The problem with most of the biological theories is that it is impossible to tell whether alcoholism stemmed from a biological abnormality or was the cause of it. One exception is genetic theory, where innate factors precede any behavioral problems. Clearly, there are many different theories of drug abuse. Their value depends on the drug under question, since some theories fit better with certain drugs than with others.

ALCOHOL

Alcohol, a natural substance formed by the reaction of fermenting sugar with yeast spores, has many forms. The kind in alcoholic beverages is ethyl alcohol—a colorless, inflammable liquid with an intoxicating effect. Because of its ability to alleviate pain and relieve tension, alcohol has been highly valued in many societies. It is a drug which can produce feelings of well-being, sedation, intoxication, or unconsciousness, depending on the amount and manner in which it is consumed. Alcoholism, an addiction to the drug, has been defined by some as a disease and by others as a mental disorder. Clearly, alcoholism involves drinking which exceeds societal norms and which affects the drinker economically, socially, and/or physically. One useful definition of alcoholism classifies it as

(1) loss of control—the victim finds himself drinking when he intends not to drink, or drinking more

than he planned; (2) presence of functional or structural damage—physiological, psychological, domestic, economic, or social; (3) use of alcohol as a kind of universal therapy, as a psychopharmacological substance through which the person tries to keep his life from coming apart (National Institute on Alcohol Abuse and Alcoholism, 1975:15).

In 1973, the National Commission on Marijuana and Drug Abuse identified alcoholism as "without question, the most serious drug problem" in the United States. Approximately 80 million Americans drink, each consuming on the average 3 gallons of pure alcohol a year. Although the estimates on the number of alcoholics vary widely, the government believes there are at least 10 million—almost 5 percent of the total population! Unfortunately, the problem seems to be spreading, particularly among adolescents, over half of whom drink at least once a month (National Institute of Alcohol Abuse and Alcoholism, 1982).

Patterns of Use

Traditionally, alcoholism has been found mainly among males. It still is, but the gap between the sexes has significantly diminished since the 1950s, when only 1 in 6 alcoholics was female; today the rate is nearly 1 in 5. If women continue to achieve greater equality in the United States, their drinking patterns will come closer to those of men. One consequence of equality is the opportunity of women to share the undesirable problems of men, such as drinking as a response to occupational pressures (see Chapter 10). Wilsnack (1973) found that alcoholic women were substantially more "masculine" in their sex role identity than nonalcoholic women. In the past, other kinds of problems typically led women to drink.

Other demographic factors related to heavy drinking are ethnicity and religion. For example, Italian-Americans and Jews have very low rates of alcoholism, while Irish-Americans have high rates. This is a reflection of the alcoholic-use norms of the different groups. It is part of Italian culture to use wine at meals. Even the young do so. In the traditional Jewish community, alcohol is used as part of the religious ritual. The Irish typically grow up in families where alcohol has been forbidden, so drinking takes place apart from meals and away from home, and male drunkenness is tacitly admired. When rates of alcoholism are compared among Catholics, Protestants, and Jews, Catholics consistently have a greater percentage of alcoholic members. This is partially because of the specific contribution of the Irish, who are disproportionately Catholic.[4] In 1975 the National Institute on Alcohol Abuse and Alcoholism (NIAAA) found that, consistent with the known differences in drinking patterns between the Irish and the American ethnic groups, low rates of alcoholism are correlated with several group-related factors: the use of low alcoholic beverages such as wine; children using alcohol as part of family or religious tradition; alcohol consumed at mealtime; and drinking viewed as a custom, not a moral question. All three of these factors account for low rates of alcoholism among Italian-Americans and Jews. Additionally, church attendance is inversely related to the use of alcohol and any drug (Nelson and Rooney, 1982).

Although there are no clear differences in drinking patterns among the races, social class does affect the probability of being an alcoholic. In general, problem drinking is most common among younger males from the middle class. However, because middle-class people are more likely to drink at home, their problems are less visible than those of lower-class alcoholics who are more likely to drink on the street. As a result, the public has the subjective misperception that most alcoholics are skid row bums.

[4] One of the earliest studies to examine for differences in the rates of alcoholism among religions was conducted by Roberts and Myers in 1954. In that study, Catholics constituted almost 70 percent of the alcoholic population.

The truth is that a significant number of alcoholics are business and professional people—the so-called pillars of their communities. There are many "normal" people who become alcoholics, and even "smart" people develop a problem without realizing it. Only about 5 percent of all alcoholics are the skid row type.

Americans who do drink are drinking more and more per capita. In fact, from 1960 to 1979, there was a 42 percent increase in beer consumption, a 44 percent increase in whiskey consumption, and a doubling in wine consumption (*Statistical Abstract,* 1980). Economic factors, such as taxes and recessions, can sober alcohol sales, but a certain segment of the population will continue to drink regardless of the price. The heaviest-drinking 5 percent of the population consumes roughly 50 percent of the total alcohol consumed (Moore and Gerstein, 1981). There is a positive side to all this: One third of the adult population is abstinent, and another third drinks very little over the course of a year. According to a 1984 *Psychology Today* report, alcohol consumption may have been worse in earlier times; Revolutionary-era Americans drank twice as much alcohol per person as their contemporary counterparts. Compared to other Western industrial nations, the United States has a remarkably high proportion of adult abstainers.[5] The Americans who do drink are not randomly distributed throughout the country but are concentrated in particular states, such as Nevada.

Objective Damages of Alcoholism

Although much of the public does not perceive alcohol as a dangerous drug, the Alcohol, Drug Abuse, and Mental Health Administration esti-

mated in 1982 that American society loses about 50 billion dollars each year because of alcohol abuse. This includes the costs of lost production (absenteeism, wasted time, accidents, extra sick leave, and the like), health and medical expenses, automobile accidents, violent crime, and fire losses. Then there are the immeasurable social costs associated with alcohol. A 1982 Gallup poll found that alcohol-related problems occur in 1 of every 3 homes, problems such as divorce, desertion, sexual nonfulfillment, and emotional problems for the drinker and his or her family. Alcohol is also frequently associated with crime. A third of *all* arrests are related to abuse of the drug. Some of these are for minor offenses like public drunkenness, but alcohol is also frequently involved with violent crime. About 10,000 murders occur each year in situations involving alcohol. A majority of aggravated assaults and one-half of all forcible rapes are alcohol-related.

The health costs of alcohol abuse are staggering.[6] Although many consider alcohol a stimulant, it is actually a protoplasmic poison with a depressant effect. About 65,000 deaths are attributed to alcohol each year. In terms of the number of people injured and diseased, alcoholism is responsible for much more damage than heroin, which causes only hundreds of deaths each year. Alcoholics can expect to live ten to twelve years less than nonalcoholics, partly because of a poor diet resulting in vitamin deficiencies, which in turn lead to a lowered resistance to infectious diseases. Alcohol also destroys liver cells, leading to cirrhosis of the liver, the sixth most common cause of death in the United States. Additionally, alcohol is a factor in about one-third of all suicides annually and about half of all deaths from car accidents. It is the third major cause of birth defects and

[5] In some countries around the world, alcoholism is reaching epidemic proportions. Consumption is skyrocketing in Japan. No people in the world drink more hard liquor than the Poles. In Barrow, Alaska, 72 percent of the population (mainly Inupiat Eskimos) is alcoholic; and in Greenland, where 42 percent of the population is alcoholic, the government is distributing alcohol coupons to control consumption.

[6] For reasons not completely known, moderate consumption of alcohol (three drinks or less a day) reportedly improves health by reducing the risk of heart attack, lessening symptoms of exhaustion, and encouraging desirable social interaction (Darby, 1978).

can impair all the major organs of the body with prolonged use. Alcoholics also run the risk of permanent brain damage, causing memory loss and occasional psychotic behavior.[7] The combined effect of drinking and smoking enormously increases the risk of cancer of the mouth and throat; the cancer rate is fifteen times greater than for those who neither drink nor smoke.

Few suffer more than the family of the alcoholic. The suffering takes many forms. Marital breakup, sexual dissatisfaction, and damage to children's personalities have already been mentioned. It is not unusual for an entire family to be stigmatized because of an alcoholic member. Physical abuse is also common in the households of alcoholics. Some experts attribute 65 percent of child abuse to a drinking parent, and 80 percent of wife battering to a drinking spouse. Moreover, batterers who abuse alcohol are more violent than batterers who do not drink (Eberle, 1982). It is difficult to enumerate all of the different types of problems that alcoholism can cause (see Figure 2-1 for some of the more common drinking problems and how they differ by social class). This is one of the features that makes alcoholism such an objectively weighty social problem—the fact that it is linked with so many other problems including unemployment, poor mental and physical health, family instability, mortality, alcohol-related poverty, crime, suicide, and abuse of other drugs.[8] Because these problems are intimately linked with alcoholism, any policy designed to ameliorate the alcoholic prob-

lem should employ a social strategy broad-based and sophisticated enough to untangle this complex web of interrelated problems.

Types of Drinkers

Since not all heavy drinkers share the same drinking habits or dependency levels, a distinction is usually made between problem drinkers and alcoholics. Problem drinkers are nonaddicted alcoholics who chronically drink to the point of inebriation. The roots of their drinking are typically social or psychological, unlike alcoholics, who are physically dependent on heavy drinking. Deprived of alcohol, alcohol addicts will develop painful withdrawal symptoms including sweating, nausea, shaking, and elevated heartbeat. The development of physical dependence requires the consumption of large amounts of alcohol for a period of three to fifteen years. Some researchers have identified distinct phases of this process.

Alcoholics vary in their drinking habits. A binge alcoholic may stay sober for a while and then rush to oblivion when the need strikes. A skid row alcoholic, on the other hand, drinks continually and lives in squalor. Other alcoholics may lead outwardly successful lives while consuming enough alcohol to kill the average person. Although the motivations of alcoholics may vary,[9] it is common for them to deny their drinking problem and reject any attempt to define their use of alcohol in negative ways.

How can you tell if someone is an alcoholic? Not by their outward appearance, but by their behavior. Some tip-offs include pouring a drink when faced with a problem; missing work; driving while drunk; getting into trouble with authorities for no logical reason; intolerable home life; and being involved in inexplicable accidents.

[7] *Korsakoff's psychosis* results from brain damage associated with alcoholism. It is characterized by amnesia and disturbance of attention. *Delirium tremens* is caused by the withdrawal from prolonged use of alcohol. It is characterized by hallucinations, tremors, delusions, and occasional convulsions, and may lead to death. See the chapter on mental disorder for definitions of psychosis, hallucinations, and delusions.

[8] Alcoholics who use barbiturates walk an especially thin line since alcohol increases the intensity of the barbiturate and increases the risk of overdose.

[9] Unlike other drug addicts who seem primarily motivated to avoid the fright of withdrawal, many alcoholics report that their drinking is a search for euphoria. This is an interesting twist since withdrawal from alcohol is much more painful than withdrawal from most drugs.

		Blue-collar worker	Harvard group
	Employer complaints	38%	31%
	Multiple job losses	28	8
	Family or friends' complaints	87	100
	Marital problems	66	88
	Alcohol-related arrest	73	19
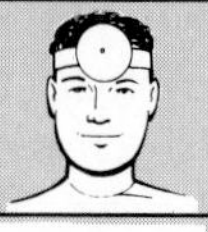	One hospital, clinic, or A.A. visit	46	31
	Gone on the wagon	70	58
	Tardiness on job or taking sick leave	43	12
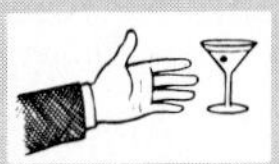	Admitted problem of controlling drinking	72	92

FIGURE 2-1   The sorrows of drink. Percentage of alcoholics in each study group who experienced specific drinking problems. (*Time, April 25, 1983. By permission of the publisher.*)

Effects of Alcohol Levels

Earlier we detailed a lengthy list of health costs associated with alcohol abuse. There are other physiological aspects to drinking which even moderate drinkers encounter. One of the more important of these is the established relationship between alcohol levels in the body and psychological/physical changes in the drinker.

Drinking certainly has a psychological side; the American Psychological Association has found evidence that people can get high (and aggressive) simply by believing they are drinking alcohol—even if all they are drinking is soda. But an important chemical basis also affects a person's response to alcohol, as Table 2-3 indicates. Table 2-3 includes alcohol concentration

TABLE 2-3   PSYCHOLOGICAL AND PHYSICAL EFFECTS OF VARIOUS BLOOD ALCOHOL
CONCENTRATION LEVELS*

Number of drinks†	Blood alcohol concentration	Psychological and physical effects
1	0.02–0.03%	No overt effects, slight feeling of muscle relaxation, slight mood elevation
2	0.05–0.06%	No intoxication, but feeling of relaxation, warmth. Slight increase in reaction time, slight decrease in fine muscle coordination
3	0.08–0.09%	Balance, speech, vision, and hearing slightly impaired. Feelings of euphoria. Increased loss of motor coordination
4	0.11–0.12%	Coordination and balance becoming difficult. Distinct impairment of mental facilities, judgment, etc.
5	0.14–0.15%	Major impairment of mental and physical control. Slurred speech, blurred vision, lack of motor skill. Legal intoxication in all states (0.15%)
7	0.20%	Loss of motor control—must have assistance in moving about. Mental confusion
10	0.30%	Severe intoxication. Minimum conscious control of mind and body
14	0.40%	Unconscious, threshold of coma
17	0.50%	Deep coma
20	0.60%	Death from respiratory failure

*For each one-hour time lapse, 0.015% blood alcohol concentration, or approximately one drink.
†The typical drink—three-fourths ounce of alcohol—is provided by:
● A shot of spirits (1½ ounces of 50 percent alcohol—100-proof whiskey or vodka)
● A glass of fortified wine (3½ ounces of 20 percent alcohol)
● A larger glass of table wine (5 ounces of 14 percent alcohol)
● A pint of beer (16 ounces of 4½ percent alcohol).
Source: Dorothy E. Dusek and Daniel A. Giordano, *Drugs: A Factual Account,* New York, Random House, 1987:64.

in the blood up to 0.60 percent. At the 0.30 percent level, an individual cannot respond to the environment and may go into a stupor; at the 0.40 or higher percent level, a person will lapse into a coma and may die. Of course, there is some variation in the effect of alcohol on different people, depending on body weight and development of a certain degree of tolerance over time.[10] Some drinkers are susceptible to alcohol-induced blackouts—periods of time during drinking when the person appears nor-

[10] There is much controversy as to whether alcoholics can stop drinking if "they really want to change," a belief some refer to as the "myth of alcoholism." Some research suggests that certain alcoholics can become normal drinkers after they are cured of alcoholism. Recently, it has been reported that "controlled drinking" is appropriate only for certain groups of alcoholics (Heather and Robertson, 1981).

mal but which are completely forgotten later. Needless to say, blackouts not only indicate alcohol abuse but also are dangerous experiences which can cause a number of additional problems.

Excessive alcohol intake always leads to another unpleasant result of drunkenness—the hangover—a combination of gastritis, nausea, anxiety, headache, and extreme fatigue. There are many supposed cures for a hangover, but none of them work. Vitamins, coffee, raw eggs, tranquilizers, oxygen, oysters, exercise, chili peppers, steak sauce, or the "hair of the dog that bit you" (more alcohol) have all been touted as hangover cures. The only things that can help are aspirin, rest, solid food, and patience. But they only help. The real way to avoid a hangover is to avoid drunkenness. It is as simple as that.

Drinking and the Law

Because alcohol affects perception and motor responses, it seriously impedes an individual's ability to perform physical tasks. This is especially apparent in automobile driving, in which a blood alcohol level (BAL) of 0.10 percent increases the likelihood of an accident sevenfold. The legal BAL in most states is 0.10 percent. For most people, two whiskeys consumed over a period of hours will produce the illegal level. Because of the widespread acceptability of alcohol, the laws regarding intoxication are often ignored, a major reason over 1.5 million Americans are arrested each year for drunk driving, and over 25,000 are killed annually on the nation's highways because of it.[11] In 1985, the College of American Pathologists estimated that alcohol may be involved in 90 percent of all car accidents. Consistently, the Crime Control Institute reported in 1986 that national statistics on drunken driving are inaccurate because police let most drivers leave the scene without being tested for alcohol abuse.

Drunk driving may elicit some social reaction, but traditionally little has been done to control it. Typically the legal penalty is no penalty at all, a direct reflection of public acceptance of drinking. Jurors often have been reluctant to punish drunk drivers because they sympathize with them. Recently, however, many are becoming angry at the carnage of drunk driving and are calling for such punitive measures as sending more people to jail, a

[11] Apart from traffic deaths, alcohol causes many injuries. Public Health officials in Washington State found that 10 percent of people injured in falls had alcohol in their blood. Moreover, 60 percent of the people who died and 22 percent of all people who were injured at home had alcohol in their systems. New York City officials report alcohol is involved in 47 percent of the fire victims there. Baltimore health officials find alcohol involved in 47 percent of adult drownings, and almost 50 percent of pedestrians killed in Pennsylvania had been drinking.

punishment some feel is justified for acts amounting to negligent manslaughter. America's patience seems to have run out, and outraged parents of drunk driver victims have formed groups to push for stiffer penalties. Mothers against Drunk Drivers (MADD) has already prompted several states to enact tougher laws. Pennsylvania is a case in point; in 1983, the state senate approved rigid drunken driving legislation that requires a person convicted of a first offense to enter an alcoholism treatment program or spend a minimum of forty-eight hours in jail and pay a $300 fine. Mandatory minimum sentences for repeat offenders are thirty days in jail for a second conviction, ninety days for a third, and one year for any subsequent convictions. In its first year, the law had a sobering effect. Regardless of the effect of this kind of law, it is timid compared to some of the laws in countries where drunk driving is subjectively perceived as a more serious act. In the Soviet Union, drunk drivers lose their license for life. In Turkey, they are driven 20 miles away from home and forced to walk back with a police escort. And in Bulgaria, repeat drunk drivers face the ultimate punishment: execution!

This response to drunk driving exemplifies the life cycle of social problems discussed in Chapter 1 (Peyrot, 1984). The incipiency phase involved mounting subjective awareness about the dangers of driving and drinking but little organization to do anything about it. During the coalescence phase, groups like MADD raised society's consciousness to the point where their efforts paid off politically with laws bringing about the institutionalization segment of the life cycle. Will the drunk driving problem be controlled by these stricter laws, or will concern about the issue recede and the laws fade away? That is difficult to tell, although some moral and practical questions have already been raised about the laws. Some people are concerned with the toll the laws will take on already crowded jails and with the toll harsh prison life

Drinking and rowdiness have become increasingly common among college-age women in the 1980s. (*Alan Carey/The Image Works*)

will take on America's newest convicts: the middle-class drinkers. Others believe the laws will not work because the police and judges will be less likely to apply laws which are so punitive. There clearly is a value conflict between limiting the damage incurred by drunks and individual freedoms. Whatever the outcome, one thing is certain: Subjective awareness of drunk driving is now increasing. One idea recently proposed is to equip cars with devices that can detect a drunken driver and prevent the car from working. One possibility is a breath alcohol analyzer built into the car; another is a skill tester requiring the driver to punch random numbers into a tiny computer. If the person were to fail either type of test, the car simply would not start (unless the equipment had been altered).

One of the most prominent violators is the teenage drunk driver. Some observers actually anticipated that recent drops in the legal drinking age would reduce drinking problems, reasoning that there would be less drinking for rebellion. In fact, since the swing to lowered drinking age occurred in the 1970s, the rate of auto accidents among young people has risen.

Teenagers from 16 to 19 make up just 7 percent of licensed drivers but are involved in nearly 15 percent of fatal crashes in which alcohol is a factor. Since 1976, twenty states have increased the drinking age by one to three years. The results have been dramatic: In at least eight states, the higher drinking age was followed by a 28 percent reduction in nighttime fatal accidents involving 18- to 21-year-olds. What may be needed now is a uniform drinking age among all states so that teenagers cannot drive to a neighboring state with a lower drinking age. In essence, state-by-state differences force people to drive if they want to drink.

Drinking among Youth

It is no secret that many high school students are getting drunk on a regular basis. This is especially visible in the suburbs where drunken teenagers knock down vulnerable letter boxes that stand temptingly by the road (mailboxing) and tear up lawns with cars (turfing). The NIAAA estimates that over 3 million teenagers have gotten into trouble because of their drinking. Of these, about 1.3 million have a *serious* drinking problem. Not only are teenagers drink-

TABLE 2-4   ALCOHOL ON COLLEGE CAMPUSES: PATTERNS AND PROBLEMS

Characteristics of students, 1982 survey	Drinkers*	Heavy drinkers†
All students	82.1%	20.6%
Males	86.4%	32.3%
Females	79.4%	12.7%
Whites	85.4%	22.7%
Blacks	58.3%	3.8%
Freshmen	80.6%	23.1%
Sophomores	83.0%	22.0%
Juniors	81.8%	19.1%
Seniors	84.0%	17.3%
Roman Catholics	90.2%	24.5%
Protestants		
Denominations that allow drinking	87.3%	23.6%
Denominations that do not allow drinking	56.7%	10.7%
Jews	90.5%	12.3%
Other religion or none	82.9%	20.1%
Religion very important	78.3%	17.4%
Religion not very important	92.5%	29.2%
Grade-point average		
4.0	68.9%	10.7%
3.5	78.0%	11.4%
3.0	83.6%	20.7%
2.5	84.6%	23.8%
2.0	80.8%	27.3%
Less than 2.0	84.8%	38.0%

*Students who said they drank alcoholic beverages at least once in the past year.
†Students who have six or more drinks at any one sitting, more than once a week.
Source: Ruth C. Engs and David L. Hanson, "Drinking Patterns and Drinking Problems of College Students: 1983," *The Chronicle of Higher Education,* Jan. 19, 1983: 9. By permission of publisher.

ing more these days, but they are starting at an earlier age; typically children now take their first drink before age 13. Teenage drinking is complicated further by their lack of experience in coping with alcohol's effects. This is why intoxicated adolescents are more likely to get involved in other difficulties and become highly visible drinkers. One national survey found that 88 percent of all high school seniors had used alcohol at least once and 72 percent drank at least once a month (Hindelang, Gottfredson, and Flanagan, 1981). This is not a problem peculiar to big cities and urban states; the Nebraska Prevention Center for Alcohol and Drug Abuse found that almost 70 percent of the

students in grades seven through twelve had used alcohol at least once a month and that more than 40 percent had been drunk during that period!

Drinking among college students reached epidemic proportions in the 1970s. Now, of the approximately 82 percent of college students who drink, 21 percent identify themselves as heavy drinkers, consuming six or more drinks at a sitting at least once a week (Engs and Hanson, 1983). Heavy drinking is especially common among college students with low grade-point averages and is frequently a factor in vandalism and other forms of campus violence. Some of the specific facts about alcohol on college campuses are presented in Table 2-4.

MARIJUANA

Marijuana (from the hemp plant, Cannabis sativa) is one of the most popular psychoactive drugs in the United States and many parts of the world. The active chemical ingredient is delta-9-tetrahydrocannabinol (THC). It is concentrated in the sticky resin exuded by the tops of the plants and is usually consumed in user-rolled cigarettes known as joints or reefers. Hashish, commonly referred to as hash, is made by packing the sticky resin into bricks. The effects of hash are about seven times as potent as those caused by smoking the other parts of the plant. Marijuana acts on the central nervous system and typically produces feelings of well-being, distortion of time and distance, hunger, talkativeness, and eventual drowsiness. After they have been regular smokers, users may feel anxious or depressed, the probable results of tolerance to the drug. Anxiety is even more likely among inexperienced users.

Marijuana was legal until the earlier part of this century, when it became subjectively associated with wild behavior among blacks and Chicanos. In 1937, the federal government outlawed its use, but consumption of the drug quietly continued. In the 1960s, it became a national issue when middle-class youths began smoking it as part of a subcultural movement away from their parents' values and lifestyles. Suddenly it was perceived to be a social problem. Today pot has become more acceptable as many of the 1960s youth continue to use it and others have followed their lead. A 1982 Gallup poll showed that 13 percent of the American population would welcome more acceptance of marijuana usage. Nationally, the number of people older than 12 who have tried marijuana has more than doubled since the early 1970s—from 24 million in 1972 to 56 million in 1982. In the 1960s, some social scientists believed that marijuana was replacing alcohol as a drug of choice of the new generation. Now it is clear that it was adopted in addition to alcohol and not as a substitute. Alcohol is still the most widely used drug of all.

Patterns of Use

About 20 million people use marijuana daily. They spend 25 billion dollars a year and collectively consume about 130,000 pounds a day. There is some concern about the fact that THC potency in marijuana products has increased significantly over the past decade; in 1982, the National Institute on Drug Abuse reported that the potency of street samples increased fivefold since 1978. This is reflected in elevated prices, which range from $50 to $200 an ounce, quite a jump from the $15 ounces of the sixties.[12] The Colombian Connection—a network of farmers, smugglers, and dealers that extends more than 5000 miles from Bogota to the great markets of New York, Chicago, and Los Angeles—provides roughly two-thirds of all pot smoked in the United States. Most of it is smuggled through Florida, where a recent crackdown by drug agents has had only a small effect on the distribution network. About 10 to 20 percent of what is smoked is domestic, a fact which has made pot a major cash crop in several states since the late 1970s. In California, marijuana is the biggest and best-selling crop in the entire state. In places like Mendocino County in northern California, the emphasis is on high-quality *sinsemilla* (without seeds), the stuff that sells for up to $250 an ounce.[13]

The use of pot cuts across all sociodemographic lines, but certain patterns are clearly visible. Use peaks among 18- to 21-year-olds and falls off in the mid-thirties. Americans are using more potent marijuana at increasingly early ages and may be damaging their lungs as much

---

[12] Part of the increase, of course, is simply due to inflation, and part to enforcement efforts driving up the price.

[13] *Sinsemilla* is a high-potency marijuana produced by weeding out the male cannabis plants before they can pollinate the female plants, resulting in the production of more resin in the flowering buds.

as with heavy cigarette smoking. As with alcohol, more men smoke marijuana than women, although patterns of use vary according to many factors, including family relationships such as marriage and being a parent (Yamaguchi and Kandel, 1985). One of the most consistent findings of marijuana research is the relationship between use of the drug and drug-related attitudes of peers: people whose friends smoke marijuana are especially likely to become involved with the drug themselves. This is a major reason for the high prevalence of pot use among students; its very acceptance promotes further use. Will consumption increase in the future? The federal government does not think so. In fact, the National Institute on Drug Abuse (1981) projects that use will decline over the next ten years simply because the United States will have an older population (see Chapter 7).

The Effects of Marijuana

One interesting thing about marijuana is that its effects are conditioned. In an early study, Becker (1953) reported that marijuana use is pleasurable when an individual learns how to smoke pot correctly and how to recognize and enjoy the effects it produces. He describes the experience as socially acquired—similar to acquiring a taste for oysters or dry martinis. At first the user is not sure whether the effects (dizziness, thirst, misjudgment of time and distance) are pleasurable. Through interaction with other smokers, the user starts to view the effects as enjoyable. Initially, the effects can be frightening. Some simply experiment with the drug a few times and stop. Others use the drug occasionally, and a third group uses it to the point where it dominates their lives through psychological dependence. All three groups tend to be lumped together by the public.

What happens to people who smoke pot regularly? This is one of the most controversial questions in drug research today. Some researchers are convinced that pot smokers undergo a number of negative mental and physical health effects. These include lowered motivation and productivity, lung disease, chromosome damage, reduced reproductive function, brain dysfunction, impaired driving ability, short-term memory loss, heart damage, interference with the immunological mechanisms of the body, basic alterations in cell metabolism, and toxic psychosis from high doses. Many of these findings were uncovered by government-supported research,[14] but for every study reporting harmful consequences of pot smoking, there is another that refutes it. A National Institute of Mental Health study of heavy users in Jamaica (1975) noted "no significant physical abnormality" in any of the smokers. These were people who smoked over ten joints a day. The only harmful consequence was impaired lung function due to smoke (marijuana or tobacco) inhalation. A number of other studies confirmed what people suspected from observing pot smokers for ten years or more: There is now no convincing evidence that marijuana causes brain dysfunction (National Academy of Sciences, 1982). A 1983 UCLA study of members of a religious sect who smoked up to 4 ounces of marijuana (each!) per day for over seven years found no effect on cognitive functioning or IQ[15] Marijuana use is also reported to have no negative influence on students' grades (Picou, Wells, and Miranne, 1980) or achievement orientations (Miranne, 1979).

It is agreed that marijuana is not physically addictive and does not cause withdrawal symptoms in users who are deprived of it, although long-term users may develop a tolerance. Only a few long-term effects of marijuana use have

[14] For a comprehensive review of research on the negative consequences of prolonged marijuana use, see Robert Margolis and Nancy Popkin, "Marijuana: A Review of Medical Research with Implications for Adolescents," *Personnel and Guidance Journal*, September 1980:7–14.
[15] Despite evidence to the contrary, the American Medical Association presently holds that marijuana does impair brain functions, although it changes its opinion periodically.

Among members of the Rastafarian religious sect, marijuana smoking is often a constant ritual. (© *Alon Reininger/Contact 1982*)

been firmly established. One is a harmful influence on the lungs, and another is the "permanent congestion of the transverse ciliary vessels of the eye and an accompanying yellow discoloration" (Geiss, 1972:156). The idea that marijuana is a stepping-stone drug that leads to harder drugs has no supporting evidence. Peer pressure is the primary cause of multiple drug use, not the effect of one specific chemical. This is not to say that marijuana has no long-run physical hazards. The important point is that aside from indicating a negative effect on the lungs, yellow eyes, and increased risk for people with damaged hearts, the data on marijuana are inconsistent. Despite the lack of evidence that marijuana causes all the ill health effects with which it has been charged, the debates still continue.

Marijuana is a widely misunderstood drug largely because of the media, which selectively report the negatives and often overlook the positives. A marijuana high is certainly more manageable than alcohol intoxication. In addition, pot has an assortment of medical uses. Earlier in the century, marijuana could be pur-

chased without a prescription to treat a variety of ailments including muscular tension, migraine headaches, insomnia, excessive menstrual bleeding, ulcers, spasms, pain, and tooth decay. Recent preliminary studies indicate marijuana and its derivatives are useful in treating glaucoma, severe nausea, vomiting caused by cancer chemotherapy, asthma, and certain types of epileptic seizures (Maugh, 1982). Because of the benefits of marijuana, in 1982 the National Association of Attorneys General supported legislation to legalize the use of marijuana for medical purposes. The complete legalization of pot is a pressing question which is treated separately in the social policy section of this chapter.

Changing Views toward Pot

Over the past fifty years, marijuana has been charged with causing a variety of undesirable behaviors. In the 1930s it was accused of provoking crime and violence; in the 1950s, it was believed to lead to heroin addiction; and in the 1960s, new charges of lowering motivation and productivity were levied against it. Despite the current lack of objective evidence supporting such changes, a majority of the public is still opposed to the legalization of marijuana, on the grounds that it is physically addictive and leads to the use of hard drugs.

There are few topics on which public opinion and the views of many experts are as sharply divided as they are on the subject of pot and its effects. Marijuana is a social problem because it is perceived by the public as such; it is a social problem because of moral values, not because of any hard objective evidence that it is dangerous to the mind or body. Some of the "scientific" studies which concluded that marijuana is dangerous to health were based on observations of monkeys forced to smoke hash three times a day for six months—a situation far removed from the smoking pattern of the average user. Clearly, pot, like cigarettes, can damage the heart and lungs. But does this justify the social cost of arresting over 450,000 people annually for possession of small amounts, and the 600 million dollars in law enforcement annually spent on marijuana arrests and prosecution? We will deal more fully with this question later in the chapter.

At this point, we do not want to give the impression that smoking pot is completely harmless. On the contrary, it may interfere with the normal development of adolescents, who have enough trouble coping with new emotions and the intellectual demands of school without being in a haze as well. Unfortunately, marijuana use is starting at an earlier age today, although its overall use among teenagers has declined since the peak year of 1978. A 1982 Gallup Youth Survey found that teenagers' attitudes toward pot have become increasingly negative. Does this mean the youth of America is becoming increasingly drug-free and opposed to the liberalization of drug laws? No, in fact the real news is bad news: Pot use among teens has declined, but there has been an accompanying increase in more dangerous drugs, particularly alcohol.

THE OPIATES

The opiates are powerful depressants that severely affect the respiratory and central nervous systems. They are derived from the poppy flower and are the source of heroin, morphine, codeine, and paregoric. In 1969 it became illegal to import this flower, and growing it in the United States was outlawed in 1942. Heroin is the most widely abused opiate. It is a derivative of morphine and was originally considered to be a harmless drug with numerous medical uses. At the turn of the century, a 2-ounce vial could be purchased for 45 cents through the Sears catalog. Although there were more heroin addicts at that time than there are today, heroin use was not a social problem because it was not subjectively perceived as one. Shortly afterward, heroin became recognized for what it is: a dangerous drug which is physically addictive. The country was reminded of the problem of this drug during the Vietnamese war, when scores of American soldiers turned to heroin to ease the stress of combat and returned home addicted. Most heroin reaches the United States from three countries in Southeast Asia known collectively as the Golden Triangle: Laos, Burma, and Thailand.

Heroin is also known as smack, scag, horse, junk, or H, and it can be taken in a variety of ways. These include sniffing (snorting), injection into the skin (skinpopping), and injection into the bloodstream (mainlining). Mainlining is used most frequently by addicts because it takes less heroin and less time to get the desired effects. The latter include elevated self-esteem, peacefulness, euphoria, and an eventual stuporous feeling. The appetite and sex drive are dulled, although most users describe the initial "rush" as similar to sexual orgasm. An excessive dose may lead to coma or death by respiratory failure. This is more likely to happen to occasional users, who, contrary to public opinion, are more numerous than hard-core addicts who develop a tolerance for large amounts of purer doses. Addiction develops after regular use—perhaps after only a few weeks—depending on the frequency of use and the purity of the drug. Tolerance soon occurs, and the user requires larger or purer doses to attain the desired effects. Addicts deprived of heroin experience very unpleasant withdrawal symptoms including nausea, chills, cramps, diarrhea, excessive sweating, and rapid weight loss. Dangers associated with heroin use include the threat of harmful impurities (see Table 2-2), risk of infection from injecting into the veins, hepatitis, and AIDS. The high cost of the drug leads many addicts to steal to support their habit. Thus, some of the problems of heroin stem from the fact that it is illegal. Subjectively, heroin has long been the most widely feared drug in the United States. Despite the objective harms of heroin noted here, alcohol kills more people and leads to more severe withdrawal symptoms.

Glutethimide, a potent hypnotic prescription drug, has recently become popular in some circles because it provides an inexpensive high which mimics heroin. Known as the workingman's heroin, it is swallowed along with potent pain relievers (such as codeine) to produce a heroin high without the risks of infection or the necessity to steal to pay for it. A "load"—typically two glutethimide tablets and four pain relievers—costs about $10 to $15 in the street, compared to a street price of $25 for an average heroin dose. In 1986, federal drug agents arrested a research chemist in Delaware for production of a new synthetic heroin substitute: 3-methylfentanyl. The heroin substitute is about 1000 times more powerful than heroin. One ounce of the substitute equals about 3000 pounds of street-level heroin. Other so-called designer drugs pose a larger threat than the Delaware chemist's substitute because their exact molecular structure is not covered by existing drug laws.

When heroin is scarce on the streets, some users turn to an alternative drug combination known as T's and Blues. T's are peach-colored tablets called Talivin, the trade name for the prescription painkiller pertazocine. Blues are an over-the-counter antihistamine traded under the name Pyrilenzomine (scientific name: tripelenn-amine). Ground up together, dissolved in hot water, and injected, the two make a heroin-like drug soup which often proves fatal. In the short run, the combination can cause seizures and suppression of breathing; overdoses can bring about psychotic behavior as well as death.

Patterns of Use

Despite the widespread fear of heroin as a killer in our country, fewer people use it than almost any other drug mentioned in this chapter. About a half million people regularly inject heroin—a handful compared to the number of people who abuse alcohol. Some of these injectors are simply recreational users. The hardcore addicts are typically poor, uneducated, young males who live in the slum, unlike alcoholics who are frequently respected members of the community. Because heroin addicts are often from the lower class, attitudes toward heroin have consistently been negative compared to drugs like cocaine, which are popular among middle-class people. However, this may change, since in the 1980s there has been a significant increase in recreational use of heroin by the middle class. In 1986, the President's Commission on Organized Crime reported an increase in middle-class heroin users, including addicts and nonaddicts who began to use the drug because of their dependency on cocaine. In fact, about 6 percent of college students have used heroin at least once (McFalls, 1979). An alarming usage among the young occurs in Pakistan, where a 1983 survey of 500 engineering and medical students at the University of Karachi revealed that 12 percent are addicts.

Most addicts are on a schedule of three to four injections a day—a habit that is very difficult to break. For some reason, they often spontaneously give up heroin when they are in their mid-thirties. Some switch to marijuana or methadone, a heroin substitute which allows them to function in society. Until recently, most authorities expected heroin use to decline, but the alarming increase in recreational use by middle-class people makes that prediction highly unlikely. In the high school class of 1979, for instance, 1.1 percent reported having used the drug (Fishburn, Abelson, and Cisin, 1979).

Objective Damages of Heroin

Contrary to the subjective impressions of the public, heroin and other opiates do not regularly produce any organic diseases, such as those found with alcoholism and cigarette smoking. Heroin is actually one of the safest psychoactive drugs, although it can cause some minor physical problems, such as constipation, sweating, menstrual irregularities, and diminished sexual potency. Taken in moderation, it cannot kill like other drugs. Some users, called "chippers," can use heroin regularly, experience no serious side effects, and lead productive and otherwise crime-free lives. Morphine has a real medical value in reducing the emotional response to pain, and the recent government authorization to test the effects of heroin in reducing the pain of terminal cancer patients may result in a change in the public's attitude toward the drug.

Of course, it would be very irresponsible to portray heroin use as a bed of roses. Like all drugs used to excess, it can kill. In 1982 alone, over 700 people died from heroin overdoses.[16] Some people die because they use more heroin than their systems can handle; long-term users can tolerate higher levels than recreational users. Others die because heroin is not regulated and consequently may be cut with impure substances that kill. One example is Hong Kong rock heroin, which causes blood vessels to expand and burst, often resulting in fatal hem-

orrhages. Some of these substances do not dissolve and become lodged in small capillaries in the lungs. The long-term result is lung abscesses which stress the heart and can lead to severe swelling. Like alcoholics, female heroin addicts can undergo *fetal narcotic syndrome,* which causes a host of physical problems to their newborns including an inborn addiction to the drug, sneezing, nausea, and difficulty in gaining weight. Heroin-addicted women undergo spontaneous abortion in 30 percent of their pregnancies and have stillbirth rates four times greater than those of the general population (McFalls, 1979).

Aside from the disrupting effect heroin abuse has on individual lives, there are also significant social costs. Heroin exacts a large economic toll. It costs addicts $7000 to $50,000 a year. Much of this is supported through criminal activities, particularly stealing, to the tune of some 3 billion dollars a year. This exemplifies the linkage of social problems, in this case between drug addiction and crime. But keep in mind that there are many wealthy addicts who support opiate habits without turning to crime—like addicted physicians. Also, many addicts were criminals before turning to heroin. Although heroin clearly imposes some heavy damage on both user and society at large, its objective toll is a small fraction of that of alcohol.

As mentioned earlier, misconceptions about heroin are widespread and will likely decline in the future as the public becomes more educated about the drug. Some misconceptions, however, are worth special mention here. First, mainlining heroin does not always induce an intense pleasure unequaled by any other experience; some initial users experience only nausea and discomfort. Second, withdrawal from heroin is not always an excruciatingly painful experience. This generally occurs only among heavy users who withdraw without medication. Third, it is not true that you are hooked for life after one shot of heroin. No drug can do that.

---

[16] While this is a significant number of deaths, it is not as high as in the peak years of heroin-related deaths: 1974 through 1976.

COCAINE

$C_{17}H_{21}NO_4$. A derivative of Erythroxylon coca. Otherwise known as cocaine, coke, C, snow, blow, toot, leaf, flake, freeze, happy dust, nose candy, Peruvian, lady, white girl. A vegetable alkaloid derived from leaves of the coca plant. Origin: eastern slopes of the Andes mountains. Availability: anywhere, U.S.A. Cost: $2,200 per oz., five times the price of gold. Whatever the price, by whatever name, cocaine is becoming the all-American drug. No longer is it a sinful secret of the moneyed elite, nor merely an elusive glitter of decadence in raffish society circles, as it seemed in decades past. No longer is it primarily an exotic and ballyhooed indulgence of high-gloss entrepreneurs, Hollywood types and high rollers, as it was only three or four years ago—the most conspicuous of consumptions, to be sniffed from the most chic of coffee tables through crisp, rolled up $100 bills. Today, in part precisely because it is such an emblem of wealth and status, coke is the drug of choice for perhaps millions of solid, conventional and often upwardly mobile citizens—lawyers, businessmen, students, government bureaucrats, politicians, policemen, secretaries, bankers, mechanics, real estate brokers, waitresses. Largely unchecked by law enforcement, a veritable blizzard of the white powder is blowing through the American middle class, and it is causing significant social and economic shifts no less than a disturbing drug problem (*Time*, July 6, 1981:56).

By most accounts, cocaine is quickly becoming the most popular drug of the 1980s. The sense of alertness, power, and euphoria yielded by cocaine has literally hooked millions of new users overwhelmed by its charms. Although the "high" produced by cocaine is similar to that produced by amphetamines (speed), the effects do not last long—about forty minutes for two average "lines."

The drug was virtually ignored until 1906 when it appeared in a drink promoted for its medicinal uses: Coca-Cola. Sigmund Freud, the founder of psychoanalysis, advocated its use as an antidepressant which increased energy and creative output. Even the fictional detective Sherlock Holmes regularly injected a 7 percent solution for sheer pleasure. Today, cocaine is not usually injected but is snorted into the nasal passages, where it is readily absorbed. Some melt the impurities, leaving pure cocaine (free-base) which can readily be smoked for an intense high. Some people seek further kicks by mixing cocaine and heroin, a technique known as "speedballing." As in the case of actor John Belushi, speedballing can be a deadly high.

Crack

In 1986, a new form of cocaine reared its head. Known popularly as crack, it is a pea-sized, crystallized form of cocaine that users smoke. Some refer to it as a fast-food version of cocaine, since it gives users an intense five-minute high. Crack dominated media attention during the 1986–87 surge in drug coverage. At this writing, crack is still a mysterious drug which has whipped the American public into a worried frenzy. Much of the perceived fear of crack stemmed from the media, which may have overdosed on print and television coverage of crack horror stories. The Federal Drug Enforcement Administration, for instance, claims that the media have collectively hyped the nation's crack problem by exaggerating the extent of its use. Hopefully, the objective dimension of crack will be uncovered in the near future.

Patterns of Use

Approximately 4 to 5 million Americans use cocaine regularly. Perhaps 1 million of those are deeply dependent on it. From 1981 to 1983, the number of Americans who have used the drug climbed from 15 million to 20 million, and every day an estimated 5000 neophytes snort their first line of coke (*Time*, Apr. 11, 1983:23). Most users are in their late twenties and thirties, although use is spreading among younger people as well. Among high school seniors in the United States, the percent who report ever

Cocaine, the chic drug of a few years ago, has recently caused new public alarm through the deaths of famous people. (*Tannenbaum/Sygma*)

having tried cocaine increased from 9 percent in 1975 to 17 percent in 1981 (Ray, 1983:301). Since that time, a number of national surveys have reported an important turnaround in young people's attitudes about drugs and the use of them. But progress in reducing drug use among high school students stalled in the mid-1980s. In 1985, an annual survey of 16,000 seniors conducted by the Institute for Social Research at the University of Michigan reported that cocaine use is at an all-time high. Cocaine use among college students is also increasing at an astonishing rate.

Like most drugs, the amount of cocaine use determines the long-term effect on the user. Recreational users ("weekend warriors") reportedly do not run the risk of serious psycho-logical or physical impairment. The same cannot be said for daily users, who can become so enslaved by the drug that their entire life structure is altered by sleeplessness, loss of appetite, hallucinations, and paranoia. Increasing heavy use is indicated by a 60 percent jump in cocaine-related admissions to emergency rooms from 1979 to 1981 (Ray, 1983:301). The number of deaths associated with cocaine increased more than four times between 1975 and 1980. Most deaths result from a combination of cocaine and alcohol.

Although some report wider cocaine use among males than females, this may simply reflect the greater visibility of use among males who snort for the high. Females, by contrast, seem more likely to use coke to accomplish tasks, or achieve better orgasms. There is no question that cocaine use is spreading at epidemic rates among both sexes. It also seems clear that some areas of the United States have justified a reputation for heavy use. The flow of cocaine into southern California, for example, has risen dramatically in the past few years, and Aspen, Colorado, is so pervaded by coke it is known as Toot City.[17]

Cocaine is currently a very fashionable drug, partly because its high cost makes it chic and also because it is widely used by the upper middle class. Of course, the large number of success junkies (people deeply dependent on the need for achievement and recognition) on coke could be a spurious correlation, because only the wealthy can afford it. If the price of cocaine declines (as is predicted), use will undoubtedly spread further to all sectors of society. It is simply that alluring. That is a scary proposition, since the end result will be more and more Americans balancing their lives on a thin white line.

Cocaine Is Big Business

The best guesstimate of the volume of cocaine smuggled into the United States is 45 tons a year, selling for an estimated 25 billion dollars. If all the dealers who supply the drug to the United States were to form a single corporation, that company would rank around seventh on the Fortune 500 list—right up there with Ford Motor Company and Gulf Oil Corporation. In other countries, cocaine occupies an even more prominent position in the economy. In Bolivia, for instance, cocaine exports surpass the value of the country's largest legal industry: tin. In Colombia, cocaine exports are rivaling the value of the coffee crops.

No discussion of the economics of cocaine would be complete without mention of Miami,

the center for the illegal entry and distribution of cocaine in the United States. Miami is truly the Wall Street of the South American drug trade as evidenced by the fact that Miami banks are the most economically stable in the country. In 1983, a customs inspector in Miami poked a screwdriver into a cardboard carton unloaded from a Colombian cargo jet and found what became the nation's biggest cocaine seizure: 3748 pounds of Colombian coke with a street value of almost 1 billion dollars.

The financial power of drug traders is simply too much for the governments of the United States and South American countries to counteract. In short, they are losing the war against cocaine production and smuggling. Part of the power of the traders stems from the huge profits generated by cutting the coke with a number of substances each time it changes hands. A kilo (2.2 pounds) of uncut, nearly pure cocaine from South America sells for about 60,000 dollars in New York City. Changing hands several times and adulterated with a cheap stimulant such as speed, a simple carbohydrate such as mannitol or lactose, or a local anesthetic such as procaine or lidocaine, a gram of coke ends up retailing (at 12 percent purity) for about $120 on a New York street corner.

Objective Damages of Cocaine

There is not much evidence available about the dangers of cocaine since the primary user group is young and, consequently, little is known about long-term effects. It does appear that moderate users are not usually affected negatively[18], but excessive use is another story. Some heavy users feel so much anguish after a high that they are compelled to use more to

---

[17] In Aspen, people sometimes tip or pay their bills with coke, and professionals may offer coke to their clients instead of martinis.

[18] The kinds and magnitude of adverse reactions can vary from one individual to another. Some people can consume several grams a day without any noticeable negative impact, while others may become ill by taking just a few lines. Len Bias perished on a relatively small amount.

combat the distress. Others experience hallucinations of touch, taste, and smell. One strange result of cocaine abuse is cocaine psychosis (*formication*)—the paranoid belief that bugs or snakes are crawling under the skin. In fact, one Hollywood actress required plastic surgery after she clawed her face open to kill "cocaine bugs."

Technically, cocaine does not produce true physical dependence with definite withdrawal symptoms. However, continual use can create a strong psychological dependence, particularly in those who freebase or administer cocaine intravenously. Some get so "strung out" on coke they turn themselves in for help from support groups such as Cokenders, a parallel to AA. Others are hospitalized. Some even try to trick themselves into stopping through self-blackmail.

Although the jury is still out on the physical dangers of cocaine, it would be unwise to view it as safe, especially in light of the fact that it appears to increase the risk of spontaneous abortions and causes unresponsive, erratic behavior in newborn infants. Additionally, there has been a 91 percent rise in cocaine-related deaths in the United States from just 1980 through 1983.

AMPHETAMINES

The amphetamines are a family of stimulant drugs including Methedrine, Benzedrine, and Dexedrine. They often go by such names as speed, fast, pep pills, dexies, drivers, bennies, footballs, robins' eggs, smith, and black beauties. Amphetamines are uppers, originally designed to keep people alert and awake. Dieters use them to decrease appetites. They have also proved effective in reducing activity in hyperactive children and in controlling the sleep attacks of narcoleptic patients. During World War II, there were many reports that Germany was using amphetamines to motivate its soldiers.

Speed differs from cocaine in two respects. First, the high produced by amphetamines lasts a long time compared to cocaine. Second, the effects of cocaine are much more subtle than speed, which packs a larger wallop. A lot of illegal speed is manufactured in eastern Pennsylvania, southern New Jersey, and Delaware. A pound of methamphetamine (crank) usually costs about 2500 dollars to manufacture, although it wholesales for about 10,000 dollars. After it is cut with a variety of cheap, often dangerous, substances, it is sold on the street for about 1000 dollars an ounce. Recently, look-alike pills (boots) sold over the counter and loaded with caffeine have become one of the nation's latest drug dangers leading to an undetermined number of deaths due to caffeine overdose.

Patterns of Use

An estimated 13 million Americans have used various forms of amphetamines without medical supervision. The prevalence rate has reportedly increased in the 1980s, but the increase may be exaggerated due to a rise in the use of look-alike pills. Statistics show the typical user is white, male, and between the ages of 20 and 29, although there are reports that speed is becoming increasingly popular among teenagers, particularly females who are lured by the drug's ability to instill confidence and induce weight loss. Speed is also popular among college students, who may use it in times of stress, such as when they are preparing for exams. Athletes also commonly use amphetamines (and cocaine) to get psyched up for games.

Objective Damages of Amphetamines

Moderate doses of speed may produce desirable results, but they are usually followed by irritability, tension, insomnia, and occasional loss of reflective judgment. Frequent large doses may produce a host of undesirable side effects, including speech disturbances, brain damage, paranoia, grinding and decay of teeth, long-term personality disorders, depression, liver damage, and a depletion of vitamins and protein. Some users take barbiturates (downers) to calm down and get to sleep. This can lead to a repeated cycle of uppers and downers with devastating results. Persons who inject amphetamines (speedfreaks) are potentially violent when they are coming down from the effects of the drug, and hence are more likely to commit crime.

BARBITURATES

Barbiturates, originally developed in Germany by Dr. A. Bayer of aspirin fame, essentially act to depress the central nervous system. Thus they are useful with a wide variety of medical conditions including insomnia, anxiety, epilepsy, and high blood pressure. They are also commonly prescribed before and during surgery. Because of our culture's preoccupation with eight hours of sleep, some develop a phobic fear of insomnia and overuse barbiturates to close the curtains of their minds.

When they are abused, barbiturates produce effects similar to alcoholic intoxication, including loss of inhibition and slurred speech. The most widely known barbiturates are pentobarbital (Nembutal), phenobarbital (Luminne), secobarbital (Seconal), and amobarbital (Amytal). These prescription drugs are often abused because they are so readily available. Drug companies are partly responsible for this; they manufacture dozens of unnecessary different barbiturates simply to increase sales.

Some heroin addicts use barbiturates as a heroin substitute, but more often barbiturates are used to enhance the effects of other drugs, such as alcohol. Sometimes they are used to offset the stimulating effect of drugs like cocaine and speed. In the 1970s, there was a shift toward nonmedical use of a new drug chemically different from barbiturates but with similar effects: methaqualone. Commonly known as Quaalude, it has dangerously increased in popularity among the young. Loss of motor coordination is greater with Quaalude than with the other barbiturates. This is why some refer to the drug as "wallbanger." Mixed with alcohol, the effects of Quaalude often prove fatal. Respiratory failure and car accidents are two of the more common pathways to death. In 1981, the Drug Abuse Warning Network named Quaalude in 4782 overdoses and 165 deaths nationwide. As a result of these dangers, the manufacturer of the drug halted production in 1984.

Patterns of Use

Over 400 tons of barbiturates are produced in the United States each year. That translates into almost 4 billion doses! In 1980 about 4 tons of Quaalude was made and legally distributed throughout the country. Possibly another 100 million tons was smuggled in during that year.

Barbiturates are one of the few drug types that bridge the generation gap. People are more likely to abuse them as they grow older because of an increased frequency of insomnia, while the younger abusers are generally looking for a high. According to the National Center for Health Statistics, the use of barbiturates as sleeping pills is more common among blacks, the poor, and people with little education (Bonham, 1979). Women are more likely to abuse these drugs than men. This is especially true of the so-called minor tranquilizers, such as Valium and Librium, which are overprescribed by physicians. They are widely used to tranquilize women who exhibit anxiety or discontentment with their roles.

Objective Damages of Barbiturates

Prolonged use of barbiturates can cause physical dependence with symptoms similar to those produced by opiate addiction. Some feel barbiturate addiction is even more dangerous and difficult to treat than heroin addiction. Withdrawal typically involves body tremors, fever, excessive sweating, anxiety, and hallucinations. Sometimes fatal convulsions occur.

Although barbiturates can be fatal by themselves, some users also die because of cross effects with other drugs. Alcohol and barbiturates constitute one such deadly combination, since alcohol increases the potency of barbiturates and therefore the likelihood that the user will take an overdose. Uppers (amphetamines) and downers (barbiturates) used together also can cause profound psychological and physical deterioration. Some barbiturate users die because as tolerance develops, they take progressively stronger doses which eventually become lethal. Others die because of the interaction of barbiturates and other drugs. Every year, about 27,000 Americans die from accidental (or suicidal) overdoses of barbiturates alone (Altroche, 1980:535).

THE HALLUCINOGENS

In Basel, Switzerland, in 1938, Dr. Albert Hofmann synthesized d-lysergic acid diethylamide (LSD). In 1943, he tasted it and went on the world's first "trip." Drugs like LSD and other hallucinogens later became known as *psychedelic* because of their profound effects upon the nature of the conscious experience. Simply stated, hallucinogens cause hallucinations—visual and other types of imagery that ordinarily would not be perceived. Some of these drugs produce only minor alterations in consciousness and, surprisingly enough, are found in most households. Such minor psychedelics include nutmeg and banana skins. Mescaline, psilocybin, and LSD are major psychedelics. As such, they cause gross disturbances in thought and perception. Mescaline and psilocybin are available in natural form—mescaline from the buttons of the peyote cactus and psilocybin from a type of mushroom. In the 1960s, synthetic mescaline and psilocybin were manufactured to meet the growing demand for

"safe" hallucinogens—safe relative to LSD, which is so potent that 1 ounce is equivalent to 300,000 human adult doses.

The LSD trip sometimes begins with nausea, headache, sweating, and chills and proceeds to scramble the nerve impulses so that colors become kaleidoscopic, music can become confused with smell, and objects appear to expand and contract. The exact nature of the trips varies according to the personality of the user, the purity of the drug, and the social situation in which it is taken. It is almost always severely mind-altering—a radical and dramatic way to avoid the stress of "social squeeze" by changing the perception of everyday reality.

The latest and most dangerous hallucinogen is phencyclidine (PCP), also known as angel dust. Used mainly by naive teenagers, it produces psychotic symptoms which may spark assaultive behavior and even murder. Larger quantities can induce seizures, coma, and death. "Getting dusted" can be a permanent experience. In 1985, the hallucinogen MDMA reared its head in certain circles, most notably among college students and young professionals. Known popularly as Ecstasy, it had been used in psychotherapy to make people trust one another and to break down barriers between lovers, parents and children, therapists and patients. It became illegal on July 1, 1985, after research showed that a single dose could cause permanent brain damage.

Patterns of Use

There is some controversy regarding the prevalence of LSD use. It clearly was most popular in the 1960s, when countercultural youth used it to "expand their minds." In 1977, about 20 percent of young adults surveyed by the National Institute on Drug Abuse admitted to having used hallucinogens at some time in the past. The institute expects that figure to drop dramatically in the 1980s and 1990s, but recent newspaper accounts suggest that LSD use may, in fact, be on the rise.

Authorities believe the prevalence of angel dust use (and associated deaths) far exceeds the number reported. Some 8 million Americans have reportedly tried the drug, and use appears to be spreading rapidly (Nicholi, 1983).

Consequences of Hallucinogens
A microscopic amount of LSD can temporarily affect a person's entire relationship to the world and turn upside down the learning and habits of a lifetime. This is particularly true in the case of a "bad trip," a panic state most likely to occur in a person who is disturbed or anxious at the time of taking the drug. LSD can also produce a flashback effect weeks or months after being taken. Flashbacks are spontaneous recurrences of previous trips. Sometimes they are brought on by smoking marijuana.

Like some other drugs, LSD has useful medical applications. It has been used as an aid to psychotherapy, as a painkiller for terminal cancer patients, and as treatment for alcoholism. It is also reported that LSD therapy can be helpful with suicidal patients (Masters and Houston, 1971), quite a contrast to the widespread subjective belief that LSD regularly induces some people to kill themselves. Other misconceptions about LSD include the idea that the drug's chemical properties cause chromosomal breakdown.

CIGARETTE SMOKING
Some of you may be surprised to see cigarettes included in this discussion, since many do not consider them to be drugs at all. The truth is that tobacco is an addictive drug which can cause a wide array of objective damage. As such, compulsive smoking is listed as a mental disorder by the American Psychiatric Association. Because smokers usually consume large quantities of cigarettes, the health hazards are much greater than those associated with the average drinker or marijuana user. The addictive component in tobacco is nicotine, although other ingredients, such as tar, can cause enormous health problems. Smoking is also a significant economic problem, since some 25 billion dollars a year is wasted on various tobacco products.

Patterns of Use
Despite the dangers of smoking, some 35 percent of adult Americans continue to puff their lives away. Use increases with age, peaking in middle adulthood. Traditionally, men have smoked more than women, although this is changing, particularly among young smokers. Unprecedented numbers of teenage girls and young women now smoke. As a result, women who smoke like men will also start to die like men. In fact, women under age 50 who smoke heavily are seven times more likely to have a heart attack than nonsmokers.

Level of education seems to influence the probability of smoking, since lower-class people have the highest consumption rates. Blacks, who are overrepresented in the lower class, smoke more than whites and have correspondingly higher death rates. It has also been noted that occupationally imposed stress causes people to smoke more (Conway, Ward, Vickers, and Rahe, 1981).

The only positive side to smoking is that fewer people are doing it, particularly among high school youth, who increasingly disapprove of this dangerous habit. Apparently, the widely publicized warnings of the dangers of smoking have had an effect. Some people may have quit or cut back in recent years because of a number of governmental actions, but smoking will never be seriously curtailed without strong federal laws outlawing it. This cannot happen while people continue to see it as an accepted pastime rather than as a dangerous path to addiction and early death. In addition, the media and lobbyists of the American Tobacco Institute exert a strong influence to keep cigarettes legal. Institutions like these make huge profits from cigarette sales, even though people die in the process.

Consequences of Cigarette Smoking

Because of the long list of health hazards engendered by smoking, we can mention only a few in the space available here. Cigarette smoke, like alcohol or heroin, is habit-forming. Smokers who stop display withdrawal effects, including drowsiness, headaches, diarrhea, constipation, increased appetite, and anxiety. The effects on the human body of many of the substances found in cigarette smoke are devastating. Of particular importance are heart disease, lung disease, and cerebrovascular disease. It has been estimated that were it not for cigarettes, there would be 11 million fewer cases of chronic illness each year in the United States (Mays, 1973). The Surgeon General reports that cigarette smoking is the chief preventable cause of death in this country. A 32-year-old male smoking thirty cigarettes a day increases his likelihood of death 340 percent over that of a nonsmoker, and, on the average, he decreases his life expectancy by 7.3 years (Crowell and Hirst, 1979). The American Cancer Society estimates the annual direct medical cost of treating smoking-generated diseases at 15 billion dollars. The director of the National Institute on Drug Abuse recently named tobacco the deadliest drug, accounting for 350,000 deaths annually—seven times the fatality rate of car accidents and more than the total number of Americans killed in World War I, World War II, and the Vietnamese war combined. Additionally, the wages lost by workers and production lost by society because of illness and premature death attributable to smoking have been valued at 12 to 18 billion dollars annually.

SOCIAL POLICY: MARIJUANA

Strategies for Solution

Although their names appear as section headings, this chapter is not about drugs. Its proper subject, rather, is people and how the patterns of their behavior convert drugs into a social problem. A central point is that these many and varied chemicals can be understood in terms of common sociological denominators. Despite pharmacological differences, drugs have been consistently characterized by the social influences, the social groups, and the social policies relating to their use and abuse. Such general *social* patterns are viewed as more important than whether the chemical is an upper or a downer. This sociological theme is highlighted because of the crazy quilt of laws, agencies, and programs designed to deal with drugs in the United States. While a comprehensive overview of America's maze of drug policies cannot be presented here, we will offer an in-depth analysis of alternative strategies for the marijuana problem. The common sociological factors underlying our multifaceted drug problem suggest that many of the issues to be discussed below also apply to social policies for cocaine, alcohol, heroin—in fact, to each of the drugs discussed in this chapter.

To those who would overhaul present policies pertaining to pot in the United States, the very phrase "marijuana problem" is misleading because the drug itself is not problematic. In our sociological perspective, serious subjective concern about a drug in the public mind does qualify it as a social problem. The pro-marijuana forces are attempting to change minds by presenting objective evidence. There has been an enormous amount of scientific investigation searching for the health effects of pot smoking. Such studies have found some negative effects (see above), but the evidence for significant physical damage is inconclusive. The latest in the series of blue-ribbon panels (this one convened by the National Academy of Sciences) to assess the mountain of health studies draws this conclusion: "At this time, our judgment as to behavioral and health-related hazards (of marijuana) is that the research has not established a danger both large and grave enough to override all other factors affecting a policy decision"

(Lasagna and Lindzey, 1983:69). Nor would such evidence necessarily override the efforts of those lobbying for a new marijuana policy. They properly point out that alcohol and tobacco are documented to be killing hundreds of thousands of people a year, yet both drugs remain legal. Whatever medical ill effects are ultimately revealed by research, marijuana reformers contend that laws are harming people right now.

Since pot is illegal, it is sold in a black market with no controls on purity, and thus may contain really dangerous drugs or even toxic substances (see Table 2-2). Aside from these health hazards, the prohibition of pot means enormous costs to our criminal justice system and to the people processed through it. Over 600 million dollars of law enforcement resources are annually allocated to handle marijuana offenders, who are twice as numerous as the total arrested for rape, robbery, and murder combined (Federal Bureau of Investigation, 1982). Not only could these resources be devoted to the reduction of these objectively more serious crimes, but there is a price in personal suffering paid by the marijuana offender. The typical offender is young, has had no previous brush with the police, and is arrested for possessing less than 1 ounce of the drug. For running afoul of our current pot laws, this individual may do hard time in prison, and will carry the stigma of a narcotics record to all future job interviews.

These exorbitant costs are often cited by interest groups such as NORML (National Organization for the Reform of Marijuana Laws) in support of marijuana *legalization,* in which the government would permit controlled production and distribution (as with alcohol). This alternative strategy is vehemently opposed by defenders of the present system of marijuana *prohibition,* outlawing both sales and possession.[19] They read the health evidence

differently, citing the same blue-ribbon panel quoted on the other side of the issue. The National Academy of Sciences reported accepted studies showing that marijuana impairs driving skills (auto accidents are *the* major killer of people your age), and further stated that the "likelihood of developmental damage to some young users make(s) marijuana use a cause for extreme concern" (Lasagna and Lindzey, 1983:77). As for the inequity of legal alcohol and illegal pot, the pro-prohibition side argues against compounding the drug/health problem. Just because we have opened the national bloodstream to some harmful substances is no reason to accept every potentially dangerous drug that comes along. Since legalization can quite plausibly be expected to increase the prevalence of marijuana use, its critics contend that the criminal justice costs may be a bargain compared to the long-term price tag in physical suffering.

Policies into Practice

This is not just an academic debate to decide whether marijuana should or should not magically disappear from our society. A down-to-earth sociological issue for both sides in the debate is the concrete impact of the alternative policies when implemented in the real world.

Can marijuana be made to disappear under a restrictive legal policy? It was noted above that 56 million people have tried the drug despite its present illegality. Nearly 90 percent of high school seniors in national surveys say that marijuana is "fairly easy" or "very easy" for them to get, and it is certainly no more difficult for college students. Proponents of prohibition respond to such figures by arguing for more vigorous enforcement efforts, and their arguments apparently have been heard. The federal government recently launched a so-called war on drugs, for which the Drug Enforcement

---

[19] The major federal law prohibiting marijuana is the Comprehensive Drug Abuse Prevention and Control Act of

1970. Penalties for the violation of state laws vary widely, with maximum sentences ranging from two years to life imprisonment.

Agency is being remodeled in the image of the FBI, and the Navy and Air Force have even been enlisted in a stepped-up attack against drug smugglers. Such active policing obviously involves value trade-offs in terms of invasion of innocent citizens' privacy and diversion of citizens' money that could be spent on other social problems,[20] but prohibitionists can point to *billions* of dollars worth of drug seizures. Much of this contraband, moreover, includes other drugs that are considered dangerous by those promoting marijuana legalization.

The latter group assesses these enforcement efforts by reminding us of another case of prohibition: alcohol. Despite thousands of arrests and millions of gallons seized, alcohol consumption actually increased during the short-lived Eighteenth Amendment. As in that case, prohibition of pot creates an incredibly lucrative criminal industry. With sales in the billions of dollars, law enforcement losses can be written off as a business expense, and, in fact, they drive up the price and profitability of the drug. The purposes to which these profits are put by organized criminals again show the linkages among social problems. Clearly, pot provides a funding base for other illegal activities, including development of a marketing system for dangerous drugs such as PCP, amphetamines, and barbiturates. There is even speculation that individuals socially labeled as criminals because of their involvement with marijuana may "become socialized into other illegal activities" (Lasagna and Lindzey, 1983:70). According to advocates of legalization, this secondary deviance as well as the normal violence of doing illegal business is the direct result of the prohibition policy. Their view is that the *law* is the real social problem.

[20] A concerted effort to seal off drug traffic across the Mexican border known as Operation Intercept caused public outrage because of its cost and inconvenience, and was quickly halted (Gooberman, 1974).

Proponents of marijuana legalization are not only against prohibition but also in favor of a concrete policy which must also be evaluated in terms of implementation issues. Their general goal is the creation of a regulated, revenue-producing (and tax-producing) industry similar to that for alcohol. Because of the widespread concern about the effects of marijuana on the long-term health and development of adolescents, reformers generally propose plans attempting to limit access for young users. As you might know from your experience as an alcohol "minor," these legal limits are pretty easy to beat. Consequently, legalization could very well increase the number of young users. Such practical problems of this alternative strategy are part of the reason the majority of the American public now opposes legalization. Acceptance of the idea does seem to be spreading, however, particularly among young adults (ages 18 to 24), 49 percent of whom favor while 51 percent oppose legalization (Gallup, 1982). Such an even subjective split shows that this is very much a live issue for the future of your age group.

Evaluating the Evidence

Besides prohibition and legalization, there is a third major option for drug policy. It is known as *decriminalization,* in this case the abolition of criminal penalties for marijuana possession (without government controlled production and distribution). We have no need to present the armchair arguments of its supporters because hard evidence is available from the real world. Eleven states (with one-third of the United States' population) have adopted some form of marijuana decriminalization. Preliminary indications from this massive policy experiment are that law enforcement costs have dropped markedly and, surprisingly, that marijuana use has increased more slowly in the decriminalized states than in states where pot is still outlawed (Lasagna and Lindzey, 1983). Neither prohibition nor legalization advocates are satisfied with such results. The former respond that aggressive enforcement of prohibition could *reduce* use and, therefore, long-term health harms. Pro-legalization elements note that prosecution of pot *pushers* still costs tax dollars, and still buys limousines for organized criminals.

Charting the future for marijuana policy is hazardous because of the swirling of interest groups around the issue. Besides single-issue organizations such as NORML, those supporting reforms of our current marijuana laws include the American Medical Association, the American Bar Association, and the National Council of Churches. Powerful forces are also pressing for continued prohibition, among them the weight of present public opinion and, by some accounts, lobbyists for organized crime. The degree of public controversy about marijuana—and other legal and illegal drugs—suggests two sociological predictions. First, policy change is likely in the decade ahead. Second, the shape of that change will not follow a rational policy blueprint. As the conflict theorists remind us, policy is not created on an academic drawing board, but rather in the clashing interests of groups in the real social world.

SUMMARY

1 There are a wide variety of drugs available to Americans. Because many use drugs for pleasure rather than for health problems, drug abuse constitutes one of our major social problems. Subjective concern about drugs approximates the objective damage of the problem, but people often fear the less harmful drugs and overlook the widespread damage of socially acceptable drugs, such as alcohol and cigarettes.

2 There are a number of theories of drug abuse. These include the idea that people turn to drugs because of role strain, the competition in industrial society, anomie, social learning, or social conflict.

3 Alcoholism, one of the worst drug problems of all, appears to be on the rise. Although the public does not perceive alcohol as a dangerous drug, the economic, health, and social costs of alcohol abuse are staggering.

4 Some of the other drugs abused by Americans include marijuana, heroin, cocaine, amphetamines, barbiturates, and hallucinogens.

5 The alternative policies examined for dealing with the marijuana problem are prohibition—the present system outlawing sale and possession—and legalization—the government overseeing production and distribution. Major issues bearing on both policies are health hazards, the effect of statutes on patterns of use, and linkages to the crime problem.

CHAPTER 3

Health and Illness: Social Sources of Disease

The organization of medicine is not a thing apart which can be subjected to study in isolation. It is an aspect of culture whose arrangements are inseparable from the general organization of society.

—*Walter H. Hamilton,* Medical Care of the American People

Nobody escapes the problem of physical illness. The clinical term *symptoms* encompasses everything from the gentle indignities of the all-too-common cold to the sudden havoc of a heart attack. Everyman—and everywoman—suffers from such conditions in the privacy of the physical self. But if illness is indeed a matter of the individual body, how does it qualify as a social problem?

From a sociological perspective, your symptoms are not yours alone. The roads leading both to and away from personal illness follow the contours of the social landscape. The simplest way to demonstrate this truth is to compare groups at the national level. In a cross-national comparison of life expectancy—one rough barometer of a population's health—the United States fares surprisingly poorly. At birth, Americans can look forward to fewer years of life than people in seven other societies. The relatively greater hazards begin at a tender age, with the United States registering only the seventeenth lowest rate of infant mortality. Given high levels of material, technological, and intellectual resources, why does our society lose lives that are saved elsewhere? An answer to such questions will require the full chapter that follows, but simply posing the issue in this way spotlights the present point: Health differences do reflect societal differences.

That point can be further focused if we examine social patterns *within* the massive group that is American society. Consider, for example, the members of the Church of Jesus Christ of Latter-Day Saints, popularly known as the Mormons. By any measure, individuals with that religious affiliation enjoy extraordinarily good health. The Mormons have a life expectancy far above the United States norm, and their rates of cancer and suicide are unusually low. Why? The reasons that have been proposed—abstinence from alcohol and tobacco, traditional family values, encouragement of education and exercise—have a common denominator. All of these health-promoting fac-

tors originate in a single social fact: The individuals are linked by their membership in the group that is the Mormon church.

The social roots of life and death can be revealed in a more general way through large-scale changes in mortality rates (i.e., deaths per year per 1000 people). There is good news and bad news. Overall, the death rate of the American population has declined significantly over the last generation. The bad news specifically applies to you in the college-age group.[1] Not only has the 15 to 24 age category not shared in the death decline of *every* other age group, but the risk for young adults is actually higher now than it was twenty years ago! The statistical reason is an upsurge in violent deaths, such that 3 out of every 4 fatalities in the 15 to 24 age group are the result of homicides, suicides, or accidents (U.S. Department of Health and Human Services, 1980). The explanations proposed typically involve family breakdown, drug use, academic and career competition—in short, social factors. As in the Mormon case, one's biological fate is sensitive to sociological forces. Also note that each major cause of young adult fatalities is a social problem in its own right. The impact of homicides, suicides, and accidents upon your health risk again shows the linkages between human problems. Glowing health, draining disease, premature death—the most intimate facts of one's physical existence cannot be separated from other social problems or, ultimately, from the social worlds we inhabit.

SOCIAL DEFINITIONS OF HEALTH PROBLEMS

You wake up feeling terrible. In the rush to get to school, the pain in your stomach is dismissed as a by-product of a greasy late night snack.

---

[1] Here and at several other points in the chapter the term *college age* refers to its traditional meaning of ages 18 through 21. We recognize that a sizable (and increasing) portion of the college students reading this book are beyond this tender age.

Despite your attempt to put the problem out of your mind, the cramps will not go away. Midway through the first class of the day, it strikes you that this is not just indigestion. The discomfort has been distracting long enough for you to decide, "I am sick." On the advice of friends, you go to the campus infirmary, and the physician diagnoses an intestinal virus.

This commonplace experience introduces two key points. Consider that the virus was in your body doing its evil work long before you decided that the condition must be illness. On a simple level, this suggests the essential distinction between the objective and subjective dimensions of problems. While the germs have actually been there all along (i.e., objectively present), you have avoided seeing the symptoms as serious enough to be sickness (i.e., a subjective definition) until they interfered with your social duties. Point one, therefore, is that the objective and subjective features of your case are related, but not in any direct way. You probably know people who, with the same objective symptoms, would have subjectively defined the illness immediately and cut class; other equally sick people would finish the day's classes and never go to the doctor.

These varying reactions to the same germ suggest the second major point: Illness is a sociological as well as a biological process. Each plot twist in the above story bears the mark of the social world. You ignore the symptoms to fulfill the *social* expectations of a student, and stop ignoring them when you cannot perform that *social* role; your *social* contacts then prod you to visit the physician, who gives you the official *social* title of "patient." Where did you get the virus in the first place? Perhaps *socializing* with a sick relative. The point warrants repetition. Illness is not merely something between you and your body; it is a pattern of behavior that is socially sensitive at every stage from infection to recovery.

Social Aspects of Sickness

This sociological view contradicts common sense about illness, and it might contradict the view of your campus physician. Nevertheless, social influences have been documented at the most basic physiological levels. Even individual reactions to pain vary by social context. It has been reliably observed that football players and combat soldiers can block out enormous amounts of pain while performing their respective roles. In one ingenious (if sadistic) study, volunteers were tested for pain tolerance using a blood pressure cuff fitted with hard rubber teeth that pressed into the subjects' arms (Lambert et al., 1960). Before a second administration of the test, the same subjects were told that the researchers would check whether this experimental group could stand more pain than another group. The change in the social meaning of the ordeal led the subjects to tolerate significantly more discomfort during the second trial.

A separate study of ethnic differences in reactions to pain in a New York City hospital indicated that Jewish and Italian patients respond to pain in an emotional way, that WASPS tend to be more stoic, and that the Irish more frequently deny the discomfort (Zborowski, 1952). Clearly, these group differences overshadow individual guts or character in withstanding pain. The experience of discomfort is not a simple response to excited nerve endings. Social roles, social situations, social groups—all shape what we feel *about* what we feel.

Such evidence of sociological intrusion into the seemingly simple sensation of pain can be readily extended to the other stimuli which we may choose to call illness. The point again will be that there are a variety of social definitions that may apply to the same physical state. Anthropologists researching American Indian groups report the latter ignoring physical states other Americans would define as serious illness, while reacting with alarm to symptoms which non-Indians would ignore (Foster and Anderson, 1978).

There are also wide variations across socio-economic groups in the United States in the symptoms considered to be matters of medical concern. But beyond these cultural and class differences in the recognition of disease, there is the question of which symptoms will be recognized as sickness *within* specific groups. The issue is a puzzling one since, at any given time, most people could qualify as sick! Studies of supposedly healthy populations have revealed that over 90 percent of all individuals have physical disorders, many of which are clinically serious. Out of a bottomless pit of symptoms, the ones most likely to be defined as sickness are those that cause social interference. Take the example of thyrotoxicosis, whose victims generally complain of quite ordinary symptoms, such as nervousness and trembling. These commonplace complaints are converted into a quite out-of-the-ordinary disease by the socially embarrassing staring eyeballs (see photo) characteristic of the condition. Similarly, acne is defined not so much by the

physical as by the social suffering it inflicts. Large-scale investigations indicate that individual decisions to take medical action depend heavily on the degree to which symptoms disrupt everyday activities (Mechanic, 1978). As in the fictional case of your in-school stomachache, illness may be defined less by physical *feelings* than by socially visible *failings*.

What about physicians? The medical profession wields the authority to *officially* label illness, presumably by scientific classification of symptoms. Despite an imposing arsenal of biological knowledge and technological expertise, there is more to a diagnosis than blood tests. For one thing, physicians perform a role that is indisputably social, and therefore subject to social demands. Combat doctors are less likely to grant a soldier with a given set of symptoms the dispensation of sickness when the needs of the army unit outweigh the needs of the individual. Company doctors must adapt their diagnoses to the dual social pressures of the individual's desire to be released from work and management's desire to keep the individual working (Walters, 1982).

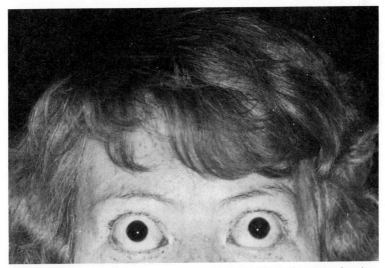

A case of thyrotoxicosis, an illness defined less by its physical ravages than by the social impact of its starting eyeballs. (*Armed Forces Institute of Pathology*)

The general point about social influences on the (formal or informal) definition of illness is nicely illustrated by a common form of physician self-diagnosis. Approximately 70 percent of would-be doctors fall victim to medical student's disease, a condition in which common symptoms are attributed to some fearsome illness, such as gas pain which they diagnose as a heart defect (Mechanic, 1978). The syndrome appears to arise from the educational stress of the medical student role combined with the subject matter learned in that role. Interestingly, the "disease"—if not the symptoms—generally disappears after a consultation with a physician faculty member, who understands the social sources of the imagined illness, and who therefore refuses to apply a clinical label. As in the previous studies, the general point concerns the social process of defining illness. The belief that one's body is sick is more than a matter of instinctive sensation or scientific diagnosis. Even the objective state of death is medically ambiguous (e.g., how long must a coma last?), and is therefore socially defined by the so-called death statutes which have been passed in some states.

What happens to you *after* the social label of sickness has been applied? According to medical sociologists, the person defined as ill faces a revised set of social expectations (Parsons, 1951). This *sick role* grants the right to be excused from one's usual social responsibilities. The intestinal virus is viewed as beyond your immediate control, thus exempting you from duties such as the sociology midterm or cleaning your room; the role also entitles you to a certain amount of pampering and sympathy. In return, you have the new responsibilities of (a) acknowledging the undesirability of your incapacitated state and (b) doing everything possible to speed recovery so you may resume your social duties.

Aside from recalling your own experiences of playing (or faking) the sick role, the best way to show the significance of the concept is to explore its boundaries. One peripheral case is childbirth. If pregnant women are considered sick, they are subject to the rights—and restrictions—of that role. The natural childbirth movement rejects the sick label, which drastically changes the social treatment of the mother (Fox, 1977). She is less pampered during pregnancy; during the birth, she receives more support from her husband and less treatment from the physician; since the mother is not under the pall of the sick label, she is also more likely to enjoy the birth process (Doering, Entwisle, and Quinlan, 1980).

Another borderline case is obesity. Is it sickness or personal weakness? If it is the former (due to some diagnosed condition, such as a glandular disorder), the individual may be excused from the cultural norms of appearance and self-control. Lacking this official label, an overweight person is likely to be blamed for the condition. Experimental studies of adolescents suggest that obese people not medically admitted to the sick role will be stigmatized and unpopular (DeJong, 1980). The marginal cases of childbirth and obesity prove the general rule: The social definition of illness has crucial consequences for the attitudes toward and the behavior of the ill individual.

The sick role concept is useful in spotlighting the societal as well as the individual consequences of illness.[2] According to functional theorist Talcott Parsons (1951), the sick person is a deviant from the standpoint of society. Not only does defined illness suspend the norms that would otherwise apply—a kind of permissible deviance like an exam exemption—but some sick roles themselves carry a deviant stigma. Venereal disease and alcoholism, for instance, may taint the individual character because they are construed as one's own fault. There are functional advantages to making all

---

[2] While the reality of the sick role is still widely accepted, researchers now emphasize the variations in the definition of the role across sociocultural groups (Segall, 1976).

sickness a somewhat undesirable role, "so that people resist the temptation to assume a pose of illness to escape the stress of their role obligations" (Salloway and Baruch, 1973:72).

The well-known individualism of American society tends to reinforce the general unsavoriness of being sick by blaming the victim for *any* illness. This presumption of personal responsibility is apparent in such everyday phrases as "He cut himself" and "She picked up the flu." In Mexican usage, one is "struck by" a cold; across the border in the United States, one actually "catches" a cold, presumably because the person pursues it by not getting enough rest (Foster and Anderson, 1978). The functional advantages for the society of stigmatizing the sick role remind us again that illness is not just an individual problem. The sociological dimension is revealed in both the social influences on the definition of sickness and the social consequences of being defined as sick.

Subjective Aspects of Health Problems

How do Americans *view* the problem of ill health? The emphasis in the question reflects the key distinction between the objective and subjective dimensions of this—or any—social problem. Assessing subjective concern about health leads us away from real morbidity and mortality statistics to their image in the public mind. There is little doubt that we are growing more aware of health problems. According to one national sample, a full 70 percent of adults interviewed believe that Americans are more concerned about their health than they were a few years ago (Yankelovich, Skelly, and White, 1979). An intriguing aspect of this surge in illness concern is that it does not appear to be fueled by increasing illness. According to the overall medical statistics, Americans are certainly no less healthy than a decade ago, and yet we are more concerned about the health of the nation. Why?

Again we are presented with a puzzling imbalance between the objective and subjective dimensions of a problem, and again sociological analysis presents us with an explanation. The social problem of ill health offers—if you'll excuse the expression—a textbook case of the subjective factors at work. Consider, first of all, the *visibility* of various health events. Recent studies of college students asked people like you to estimate fatality frequencies for each item on a list of numerous causes of death. The research found that "overestimated items were sensational, whereas underestimated items tended to be unspectacular events, which claim one victim at a time" (Slovic et al., 1980: 183–184); dramatic diseases like brain tumors and botulism are overly feared, while objectively common conditions such as diabetes and asthma are underrated killers. The investigators also noted a close connection between the subjective seriousness of lethal events and the amount of newspaper coverage they had received.

On the broader issue of the rise in overall health concern, just think of the impact of mass media on the visibility of medical matters. Publicity about real or potential breakthroughs not only heightens our awareness of health issues but also creates an image of imminent cure. The media spotlight trained on interferon and other futuristic therapies may explain the optimism shared by over three-quarters of the American public that a cure for cancer will be found "any day now" (Yankelovich, Skelly, and White, 1979:133).[3]

Clearly, public awareness of the startling advances of medical technology has created high *expectations* for an end to illness. Such unbounded optimism ignores the objective barriers to stopping cancer or the common cold and anticipates a dazzling panacea like the polio vaccine. High expectations create high dissat-

[3] Interferon is a substance which was widely hailed as a potential cancer cure-all several years ago. Despite making the cover of *Time* and still offering considerable promise, interferon has not yet lived up to therapeutic expectations in this country.

isfaction when the "magic bullet" is not quickly shot. While freedom from disease has always been prized, there is some evidence that health *values* have been on the rise (Fox, 1977). The mounting militant attitude toward the medical establishment (reflected in rapidly rising rates for malpractice insurance) suggests that proper health care is increasingly viewed as a patient's personal right rather than a physician-controlled privilege. As the social value placed on health climbs, so does people's frustration when physical perfection does not appear. The joint operation of these three social factors (visibility, expectations, and values) on the public mind clarifies both the surge in subjective seriousness of the health problem and the stiffer demands for a policy system that will objectively reduce disease.

THE PRODUCTION OF ILLNESS: SOCIAL CONTEXTS

Despite the undeniable impact of subjective aspects, the foregoing should not suggest that illness is an illusion. Rather than being a national case of hypochondria, the social problem of health exacts a staggering toll in real human misery. Whether it is assessed quantitatively at the societal level or qualitatively in terms of individual anguish, the objective significance of sickness is beyond question.

Many social indicators can be used to probe the problem. Consider first the loss of the most precious resource of all, namely life. The U.S. Department of Health and Human Services has estimated the cost of four major disease categories in years of life lost, based on current life expectancies at age of death (1980). A category with special relevance to your age group—accidents, poisonings, and violence—will annually steal approximately 5,565,100 years of life from the United States population, and that category is *less* significant than two diseases on the list! While the value of lost life to the individuals suffering premature death—and to

their loved ones—is incalculable, the costs of disease to our society have been estimated in dollar terms. The bill now totals to over 425 billion dollars annually, an amount greater than either the defense budget of the United States or the gross national product of Canada (International Monetary Fund, 1985)!

Such societywide figures indicate the enormity of health problems, but they are too general to tell the entire objective story. To add depth to this sketch, it is instructive to look more closely at the human reality of illness as it touches individual lives (see Box 3-1). You have experienced a share of the objective dimension of disease. Recent health surveys report that an average American adult will spend about five days in a sickbed and be forced by illness to limit usual activities for fifteen days in a typical year (American Public Health Association, 1982); of course, these averages underestimate the suffering of the millions of your peers with more persistent forms of disease, such as hemophilia and diabetes. Particularly in such chronic cases, individual sickness may develop social symptoms. The everyday burden of disease can strain—and even sever—the social relationships of patients with their spouses, family members, and friends (DiMatteo and Hays, 1982). A final reading on the human toll of illness is its association with personal unhappiness. One recent national study identified health status as the single best predictor of Americans' life satisfaction (Fernandez and Kulik, 1981).

Where does all of this objective affliction come from? Now that we no longer view pestilence and early death as inevitable scourges of the human condition, and particularly now that medical science offers hope to improve that condition, a major goal is finding the real cause(s) of ill health. The pursuit of that goal has again revealed the interrelatedness of individual and social factors in our societal problems.

Take the complex case of high blood pressure (the severe form is called hypertension), a

BOX 3-1

THE SILENT EPIDEMIC

My mother said, "She won't let me see the little doggy, sweet little doggy here." She pointed to the ashtray of the car and then began to trace with her finger along the pattern in her dress.

"But it tugs, not tugs really but, but..." She made a fist and hammered the dashboard with a raging frustration I'd never seen in her.

"It's gone," she said, shaking her head, the anger breaking into sorrow and fear. "It's gone."

What had seemed individually to be merely instances of the forgetfulness of aging had become, in total, frightening. It was like watching someone in a room in which first the chairs broke when he sat on them, then the windows were stuck shut, and the telephone cord was found to be cut, and the doorknob came off in his hand, and there was no way out, and confusion turned to fear.

For my mother, it had started (I *think* it started this way; in the beginning it sneaks up like a thief) with an inability to write checks, to make change, to deal at all with simple math. It had spread to her ability to do things in a logical progression, to make sentences (soon she would be putting nonsense words in the blanks), to care for herself. When a neighbor of hers called to say my mother had locked herself out of her house and didn't seem to know how to use her key to get back in, I decided to bring her to Chicago and renew the search for whatever was stealing her mind.

We were on the way that sunny day to Billings Hospital where a neurologist—the second I'd taken her to that year, in addition to two psychiatrists, a psychological testing clinic, a geriatric specialist, and an internist—finally would put a name to her suffering.

That was the last cloudless day.

Alzheimer's disease sounded exotic and rare at the time. I know now that it's neither, that 1 ½ million Americans—5 to 6 percent of the 65-and-over population—are victims, that the devastation it visits on families multiplies the number of those affected by a factor of 3 or 4, that it accounts for nearly half the admissions to nursing homes, that 12.5 billion dollars this year—an average of some 17,000 dollars a patient, an expense virtually uncovered by insurance or government until the family finances are depleted to public aid level—will be spent on nursing home care for Alzheimer's sufferers, and that those annual costs are expected to rocket to 20 billion dollars within the next few years.

If you are a taxpayer, Alzheimer's will savage your wallet; if you get the disease, it will destroy your mind and cut your life expectancy in half; if someone you love gets it, someone like the 68-year-old woman sitting next to me on the trip down to Billings Hospital, it will break your heart.

Lewis Thomas, chancellor of Memorial Sloan-Kettering Cancer Center in New York, has called dementia (of which Alzheimer's is the most common form)

a disease of the century...the worst of all diseases, not just for what it does to the victim but for its devastating effects on family and friends. It begins with the loss of learned skills, arithmetic and typing, for instance, and progresses inexorably to a total shutting down of the mind. It is, unmercifully, not lethal; patients go on and on living, essentially brainless but otherwise healthy, into advanced age, unless lucky enough to be saved by pneumonia.

One thing certainly can be said about what Alzheimer's is. Jerome Stone, president of the Alzheimer's Disease and Related Disorders Association, looked at Alzheimer's accounting, directly or indirectly, for up to 120,000 deaths a year. He looked at the vast number of Americans suffering from the disease (roughly the population of Detroit) and the tremendous costs involved. He considered what little publicity Alzheimer's has received (only in the last few months has the description of the disease in the popular press changed from "rare form of dementia" to "most common form of dementia"), and he realized what Alzheimer's disease is. "It is," Stone says, "a silent epidemic."

(*Authors' note:* Updated estimates place the annual objective costs of the disease in excess of 30 billion dollars. Quite recently, the subjective silence about Alzheimer's disease has been shattered by high media visibility, including a *Newsweek* cover and a television movie.)

Adapted from Charles Leroux, "The Alzheimer's Disease and Related Disorders Association Reprint" from the *Chicago Tribune*, copyright 1981.

condition which affects some 60 million people and which is a major risk factor in both heart disease and stroke, two of the leading life stealers in our society. Since nearly everyone knows a hypertensive person, you are undoubtedly aware that personal habits such as smoking and high salt intake contribute to the disease. Less obvious— but no less real—are the social forces pushing up the needle of the blood pressure gauge. Like many other illnesses (see Social Stress below), hypertension is correlated with unemployment, residential migration, work pressure, and various other stressors that are parts of our everyday social lives. Hypertension has been pronounced a disease of modern society because of its comparatively high rates in industrial nations such as the United States, and because of the rapid rise in average blood pressure among people suddenly exposed to modern lifestyles (Eyer, 1975). The present point is that hypertensive Uncle Harry's high risk of heart attack or stroke is not caused entirely by his personal habits. The general point—to be considered in the following sections—is that individual lifestyle and health risk must be viewed in the larger social contexts within which individual lives—and deaths—are set.

Social Background

A major theme of this chapter has been the transpersonal nature of illness—the idea that your physical ailments have social roots. Simple but compelling evidence for this not-so-obvious point appears when individuals are grouped with other individuals of similar background. Everyday social categories (such as sex, age, income, and race, which will be considered here) are intricately related to a spectrum of health indicators. Since general death rate variations are extensively discussed in Chapter 7, the analysis here will highlight special issues in *morbidity* (sickness) and *mortality* (death).

Someone of college age can now expect to live fifty-five more years (Hacker, 1983). Like

most statistics, this projected average contains a lot of individual variation. A look at your fellow students will reveal general social traits that change the fifty-five-year projection, and also the likelihood of being sick this week. Consider a simple social category such as sex. As noted in Chapter 7, the typical female will outlive the typical male by about eight years. Given the mortality differential, it is somewhat surprising to find morbidity differences in the opposite direction. Females are comparatively *more* likely to report symptoms from commonplace illnesses (such as colds, flu, and headache), and are also more likely to visit a doctor than males of the same age.

Research has not yet unraveled the reasons for this intriguing difference between the sexes, but there are a few very intriguing hypotheses. Some investigators posit that women are no sicker; they are simply more willing to admit their aches and pains because the cultural role of a female permits expression of feelings, whereas males are supposed to be strong, silent, and vigorously healthy. Other researchers hypothesize that the female sex role directly produces illness because nurturing means more strain and more germs (Mom gets up at night to wipe noses). Still others assert that females' reproductive function is physically responsible for many of their maladies (Verbrugge, 1985). Whatever the actual pattern of biological and sociological causes, the nature of the sex correlation can be succinctly stated: Women get sick, but men die.

Morbidity and mortality also vary strikingly by age category, and not only through the obvious process of physical decline. Many of the health problems of old age (such as heart disease and senility) have their roots in personal habits established by the time you reach college, and some current health problems are statistically dominated by the college-age group. Adolescents and young adults account for 75 percent of the 12 million new cases of sexually transmitted disease (STD) contracted annually. Pelvic inflammatory disease alone will result in over a quarter of a million hospitalizations, 50,000 surgical procedures, and 50,000 cases of sterility each year (U.S. Department of Health and Human Services, 1980). Genital herpes is an objective epidemic, affecting as many as 20 million Americans and up to 20 percent of young people. This incurable disease is also an instance of a health problem made suddenly *visible* by the media. Subjective awareness of herpes and other STDs is so great, in fact, that nearly a quarter of all young, unmarried adults are reportedly changing their sexual behavior.

Easily the most terrifying of the STDs, with special relevance to young, sexually active adults, is acquired immune deficiency syndrome (AIDS). This disease has been likened to a biblical plague; it is incurable and apparently always fatal. Victims often die of so-called opportunistic infections, attacks by germs that noninfected people can easily ward off (e.g., pneumonia). As of 1985, an estimated 1 million Americans are believed to have been infected with the AIDS virus, and the total is thought to be climbing by as many as 2000 people a day (Boffey, 1985*b*).

It is unknown in 1985 what proportion of infected persons will remain symptomless carriers of the virus, possibly capable of infecting others, and what proportion will become ill. Studies have shown, however, that 5 to 19 percent of exposed persons develop AIDS within the first five years of infection, and another 20 to 30 percent experience a less severe condition called AIDS-related complex

A part of the subjective storm surrounding the AIDS epidemic. (*Tannenbaum/Sygma*)

(ARC). It seems likely that the proportion infected who become gravely ill will continue to rise with time. William Haseltine, a leading AIDS researcher at the Harvard Medical School, believes the worst-case projections will probably come true, noting: "We must be prepared to anticipate that the vast majority of those now infected will ultimately...develop life-threatening illness" (Boffey, 1985*a*:C3). The Surgeon General of the United States projects 179,000 AIDS deaths by the end of the decade and a health services cost between 8 and 16 billion dollars in 1991 (1986).

In 1985 in the United States, AIDS is largely a disease of male homosexuals. But in some other countries the disease has primarily afflicted heterosexuals, and there is evidence that the virus is moving increasingly into the heterosexual population of the United States via bisexuals and prostitutes. Prostitutes have become a reservoir for AIDS in much the same way as they have for gonorrhea, herpes, and other STDs. It is estimated that heterosexuals in New York who visit prostitutes have a 20 percent chance of contracting the virus (Boffey, 1985*a*). These "johns" (and bisexuals) can then infect their lovers and wives and, ultimately, their children. In the future it is possible that more heterosexuals than homosexuals will be infected, because the former outnumber the latter, and because of the generally high rates of premarital and extramarital sex. A chilling thought: Haseltine expects that the AIDS virus will eventually infect up to 30 percent of college students! Enough college administrators have been chilled by the thought so that courses on AIDS and AIDS-victim residence policies have already been adopted at some institutions.

With the notable exception of AIDS, sexually transmitted diseases are rarely fatal in modern societies. Such is unfortunately not the case with another special problem for the college age group which we have discussed at several points: namely violence. Objective analysis of this health issue reveals a major

reason young men are more likely to die than young women. Males predominate in the fatality statistics not only for homicides and suicides but also for deaths from burns, drownings, drugs, and even medical complications (Hacker, 1983).

A more significant revelation concerns the behavioral basis for this carnage. The largest single killer of young adults is motor vehicle accidents, for which there are well-known risk factors: drinking, driving fast, and not wearing a seat belt. All three of these factors are clearly subject to social influence (e.g., males are culturally pressured to be risk takers). The conclusion is twofold. First, violence, like sexual disease, is primarily a product of individual and interpersonal behavior rather than biological breakdown. Second, the social roots of both special problems for the college-age category suggest that they are highly preventable.

It probably will not surprise you to learn that socioeconomic traits (especially income) are correlated with health status. Common sense leads us to expect people with less money to spend on health care to be sicker. They are, but not simply because of being shut out of the medical system. While all physician visits are obviously not of equal quality, poor people actually average *more* visits in a year than the nonpoor (American Public Health Association, 1982). This surprising fact suggests the need for a look beyond the doctor's office to general social conditions.

Such a look uncovers mounting evidence of ill health as one looks down the income ladder. Only about half as many people earning less than 7000 dollars a year report their present health to be excellent, compared to those making over 25,000 dollars (American Public Health Association, 1982). Low income inflates an individual's risk of arthritis, diabetes, anemia, measles, tuberculosis—in short, of just about every major and minor disease. The conventional wisdom has it that upper-class job pressures (deadlines, decision making, etc.) will produce heart attacks, while the poor joke through their miseries. The sociological wisdom is the opposite, since cardiovascular disease rates increase at the lower rungs of the income ladder. The available data clearly support this basic contention: The objective significance of health problems rises as income drops.

As Chapters 7 and 9 indicate, death rates vary substantially across the races in the United States. The excess mortality of nonwhites is paralleled in the morbidity statistics, which clearly show that blacks are sicker than whites. To cite only a few of the more serious diseases, blacks have comparatively higher rates of hypertension, diabetes, and tuberculosis. It is distressing to note a greater chance of getting cancer among blacks; it is downright terrifying for black individuals with cancer to have to face the fact that they also have a worse chance of surviving the disease (U.S. Bureau of the Census, 1980b; American Cancer Society, 1983). Some of the race differential in sickness, of course, is explained by racial differences in income. However, even if income category is controlled, blacks have more restricted activity days per person per year than whites for every age group, starting in young adulthood (American Public Health Association, 1982).

This last clarification suggests a major point to be made about the neat summaries in this section on Social Background: The categories are abstractions. Every black or white person has an income level, an age, and a sex. Flesh-and-blood people have all of these traits, thus creating complex patterns of objective risk. A typical example of interwoven social categories is presented in Box 3-2, which brings abstract national statistics down to the human scale of a single neighborhood. The individuals living in Philadelphia Census Tract 152 are haunted by an infant mortality (and morbidity) rate much higher than that of nearby districts in the city, and comparable to the rate in medically unsophisticated South Korea. The discussion of this shocking situation in the excerpted article re-

veals the following profile of the mothers in Tract 152: they are poor, young, and black. Such overlapping of personal traits of course does not mean that social categories do not matter for health risk, but rather that they really do matter in complex ways. Attention to the intricate forces of social background exposes the general contexts in which individuals get sick or stay healthy.

Social Stress

"Calm down! You'll make yourself sick!" This statement expresses the commonsense view that stress may lead to illness, but it also reflects a more profound sociological truth about the way we perceive ourselves. In the wording, it is apparent that the *you* refers to the mind and the *self* to the body. The separation of personal identity into a physical and a psychic self is an idea with deep cultural roots (dating back at least to Plato), which seems to be validated every time the body betrays you by getting sick. It is important to recognize, however, that *all* of you suffers from the illness.

Even more important is the growing recognition by researchers of the mind-body connection. Of course you are aware that unpleasant thoughts can make you sweat and pleasant thoughts can make you blush, but there are less obvious consequences of the link between body and mind:

> Imagine a caveman who suddenly sensed a lurking sabre-toothed tiger. Adrenaline poured into his blood, giving him instant, much-needed energy through the use of sugar and other stored energy supplies. His blood pressure rose sharply with his increased respiration and quickened pulse rate. At the same time, other functions stopped instantaneously to allow his system to make an undivided demand on his vital "adaption energy" so that he could meet this crucial moment of survival (Selye, 1978:66).

Although the social problem of saber-toothed tigers has subsided, it has been replaced by

BOX 3-2

FIVE BLOCKS THAT OFFER SLIMMEST HOPE TO A BABY

In all of Philadelphia, there is not a worse place to be a baby than Census Tract 152.

In that little chunk of North-Central Philadelphia, amid the boarded-up homes and the housing projects and the trash-strewn streets, more babies have died before their first birthdays in the last few years than in any other area of comparable size in the city.

It is an area just five blocks square, but more than twenty-seven babies have died there since 1978.

That means, for instance, that in 1980, Census Tract 152 had an infant mortality rate of 34.7 per 1000. That was more than double the rate for Pennsylvania (13.2) or the nation (12.5). And it is just short of double the 18.1 rate in Philadelphia, which itself appears to have a feeble record for keeping babies alive and in good health.

Because the social service cuts proposed by President Reagan could make matters even worse in places such as Census Tract 152, a nun named Sister Teresita Hinnegan and a group of health advocates called the Maternal Care Coalition have studied in detail just what makes it so hard for mothers to take good care of their babies in North-Central Philadelphia.

As Sister Hinnegan and her allies knew, the simple answer was poverty. But she does not consider poverty an excuse for poor public health care; rather, it is a mandate for better planning. By pulling together statistics on everything from infant health to housing, unemployment, welfare, and the location and nature of all available health care, Sister Hinnegan found what City Health Commissioner Stuart H. Shapiro and other health officials have acknowledged as one of their major problems: neglect that results from poor coordination of health care. In Census Tract 152 in 1980, she learned, more than 1 mother in 10 received no prenatal care or none until the last trimester of pregnancy.

INFANT MORTALITY RATE 1980
(PER 1000 LIVE BIRTHS)

	Census Tract 152	USA
Infant deaths (up to age 1)	34.7	12.5
Neonatal deaths (in first twenty-seven days)	20.8	8.4

"There is no citywide tracking system to explore why (women) received inadequate prenatal care or the condition of their babies in the first year of life," Sister Hinnegan wrote. "The communities in Philadelphia have no interaction with hospitals or health centers about maternity-care program content or pregnancy outcome problems."

She also learned that a baby in Census Tract 152 was twice as likely to be born underweight than other babies in the state. In 1980, the rate of babies born at 5 pounds 8 ounces or less in Pennsylvania was 6.5 per 1000 live births; in Census Tract 152 it was 13.5.

Few of the mothers were married, indicating that at least some of them had no one to help with child care. Statewide, 17.6 percent of new mothers were single in 1980; in Census Tract 152 that year, 87.8 percent of new mothers were unmarried.

And 1 out of 5 new mothers who lived in the tract that year was under the age of 18.

Adapted from an article by Mary Bishop, published in the *Philadelphia Inquirer*, Apr. 5, 1982.

various ferocious concerns of contemporary living. The bodily responses to the modern mind's worries are very much the same as those described above.

The mind-body state of stress has been associated with a veritable encyclopedia of medical conditions. Chronic stress is associated with known risk factors of heart disease, such as hypertension and hardening of the arteries, but also is increasingly recognized to be a risk factor in its own right. Some cardiologists are actually prescribing stress-management techniques (meditation, physical activity, etc.) for their high-risk patients. Cancer, another major killer, has also been linked to mental pressure. Recent research has even identified bodily compounds secreted under certain kinds of stress which may promote the growth of malignant tumors (Lewis, 1983). Stress has also been related to less life-threatening forms of objective suffering. According to most authorities, psychic stress is responsible for the majority of sexual dysfunctions, such as impotence. There is a well-known association of stress with headaches, ulcers, colitis—with so many symptoms, in fact, that some medical authorities view from one-half to three-fourths of all physical disorders as at least partially caused by emotional disturbances (McFalls, 1979*b*). This view is not confined to health experts. Nearly one-third of the families polled in a recent national survey saw stress as "the main reason (they) were not as healthy as (they) could be" (Yankelovich, Skelly, and White, 1979:65).

All of this evidence of the stress-sickness relationship may seem surprising because of the cultural power of the mind versus body idea. Still another false dichotomy is the idea that the individual mind is separated from the *social* body. One conclusion that might be drawn from this section is that individuals should just *calm down*. Such a recommendation is simplistic for a major reason: much stress is socially created. Studies have suggested the social nature of major stresses by showing just how objectively common they are. Four out of ten individuals in a recent national sample lived through at least one traumatic event (death of a relative, divorce, unemployment, or hospitalization) in the previous year (NORC, 1985). Being an individual cell in a stressful social body can be very hard on the cell. Experiencing an excessive number of such pressure-producing events is associated with health risks as diverse as suicide and heart attack (Dean and Lin, 1977).

One intriguing study of children from birth to age 4 indicates that the physical ravages of stress reverberate through the social unit of the household. Children whose families had experienced at least twelve stressful events were six times as likely to have been hospitalized for sickness or accident as were children from families with three or fewer events (Christ Church Hospital Research Group, 1983). The point is that stress is not simply a personal experience. As members of group bodies—families or societies—individuals are naturally exposed to the strains within the structure of the social organism.

To further spotlight this social-individual illness connection, consider that the United States is a world leader in heart disease. There is evidence that this dubious distinction is based in part on our cultural ideal for personality. The Type A personality is ambitious, impatient, aggressive—in short, the very kind of person you will try to convince a prospective employer you are. While they may impress job interviewers, the bad news is that Type A's are likely candidates for heart attacks. Even if other major cardiovascular risk factors are controlled, this personality type has *double* the coronary risk of the non-Type A (Friedman, 1974).[4]

Why do people become Type A? Competitive, hard-driving traits are highly valued as the qualities of a successful American executive or professional; in fact, the original Type A data came from a study of medical students. Recent research suggests that socialization plants the seeds of the Type A by age 6, and that up to half of American adults have acquired this personality style. If you are hurrying to finish reading this so you can get to other assignments and raise your grades in the classroom competition, you may be a case in point. The social pattern produces a stressful individual behavior pattern, which in turn produces risk of disease.

---

[4] The research on the Type A personality is very suggestive, but not yet definitive. Some recent reports indicate that it may be the anger and hostility often associated with a hard-driving personality which actually affect disease risk.

Social Relationships

Relatives and friends are a mixed blessing. Our interpersonal relations can provide help when we need it and fun when we want it, but they also mean nagging, arguments, and distractions when trying to study. There is even a saying that the other person in a bad relationship is "making me sick." Recent sociomedical research suggests that our intimate relations really are intimately linked to our physical health.

The literature supporting the healthful effects of social relationships has emerged from a variety of sources. Experimental studies of monkeys fed a low-fat diet found that those in unstable social settings developed more and worse hardening of the arteries than monkeys in groups with stable members (Kaplan, Cassell, and Gore, 1979). While generalization from the artificial setting of animal experiments to the social setting of people must be done cautiously, the evidence for the benefits of human contact is similarly impressive.

One research project examining 7000 individuals in Alameda County, California, discovered a two- to threefold higher death rate among those who were relatively isolated compared to those with more extensive social ties (Berkman and Syme, 1979). Evidence of morbidity differences also abounds. Persons integrated into cohesive networks of relatives and friends are less likely to suffer from pregnancy complications, heart attacks, arthritic joint swelling, accident proneness, postsurgical pain, and many other conditions (Caplan, 1981). As one authority sums it up, "Social support...has beneficial effects on a wide variety of health variables throughout the life course from conception to just before death, and on the bereaved who are left behind after death" (Cobb, Dematteo, and Hays, 1979:113).

That last remark sounds supernatural in its reference to postmortem effects, but there is sound evidence that the loss of a loved one can actually break your heart—and a variety of other bodily organs. It is well established, for instance, that widowed (and divorced) people are sicker than those with a spouse in terms of the rates of many diseases (Lynch, 1977). A study conducted by the Johns Hopkins University School of Hygiene and Public Health controlled a variety of key variables (including race, sex, and education) and still found a much higher mortality rate for individuals who had lost a spouse than for the still married (Helsing et al., 1981). Interestingly, spouse loss significantly elevates death risks for every age category—including yours—and the death risk is significantly lowered by remarriage. While the latter finding suggests a social antidote to the effects of grief, the broader point concerns the relationship between social relationships and social stress.

Please note that many of the traumatic events mentioned above (and several of the stressful life events listed in Table 4-1) involve shocks to or through members of one's social network. This fact supports the findings of the network literature that *not* all social relations are pro-health (Wellman, 1981); as the opening paragraph of this section suggests, some network relations may indeed help make you sick. One theory which would account for the generally beneficial effects of personal relationships on the many health conditions cited above views relatives and friends as de-stressors, that is, as supporters who may soften the impact of life's shocks on the mind and body of the individual.[5] Relationships may cushion stress, relationship problems may cause stress, but relationships are certainly involved with stress and its physical manifestations.

A final illustration of the overlapping effects of stress and relationships can be found in the

---

[5] This is the so-called buffer theory of social relationships and stress, the research on which is reviewed by Peggy Thoits (1983).

fascinating case of the World War II bombing of London (Titmuss, 1950). Living day to day amid such destructive explosions is obviously quite stressful. Studies of children who grew up during the blitz show, amazingly though, that the stress of living through war with one's family appears to have been less harmful than the stress of being separated from the family to escape the bombings!

What does all of this research have to do with you? Since you have undoubtedly felt the physical sensations of stress, it may be easy to accept data which show that a sympathetic friend can reduce long-term wear and tear on your body. But since the symptoms of stress-linked diseases like ulcers and hypertension generally do not arrive until later in adulthood, you may find it difficult to relate to this knowledge beyond making vague resolutions to relax with friends or visit Grandma. How about the minor—but objectively common—ailments that actually keep college students from, among other things, attending classes? In still another demonstration of the nonobvious nature of sociological knowledge, more social contact has been shown to be associated with less minor illness. Whereas common sense would put you in quarantine to avoid colds, isolated individuals actually face an increased chance of getting respiratory diseases (Kaplan, Cassell, and Gore, 1979).

In their own study of college students, the authors of this text presented respondents like you with a list of everyday illness symptoms such as cough, abdominal pain, and headache. Students were asked to indicate how frequently they had experienced each symptom in the previous two months; respondents also provided information about the nature of their relationships within their social networks. Our results confirm the relevance of relationships to your physical health. Kin appear to be the key network members in this regard, since the degree of interaction with relatives is significantly related to the number of symptoms reported by

students.[6] Interestingly, the healthful effects of kin seem to be more protective of males than females. This finding is relevant both to your present health problems and to our larger point about the intricate involvement of social context with individual illness.

SOCIAL CONTROL OF ILLNESS

Health is a state of complete physical, mental and social well-being and not merely the absence of disease or infirmity.

—*The World Health Organization*

Disease Trends

Although we do not approach the WHO's ambitious definition of a truly healthy society, the United States has made startling strides toward the absence of disease in some of its forms. A major reason that an American baby can now expect to live twenty-six years longer than one born at the turn of the century is our social control of infectious diseases such as tuberculosis, diarrhea, diphtheria, and polio. To gauge the objective gains in health, consider this: If the 1900 death rates for those four diseases had remained constant, they would kill an additional 840,000 Americans *every year* (U.S. Department of Health and Human Services, 1980).

One breakthrough in the control of communicable diseases was the so-called antibiotic revolution in medical science. Before the widespread use of these drugs in the United States, some 30,000 young adults died annually from tuberculosis alone; currently, the casualties in your age group number in the hundreds (Lawrence, 1976). Clearly, we have gained considerable social control over many of the age-old plagues of the human condition.

---

[6] Our college respondents were asked: "How many relatives living outside your current residence do you see or have a conversation with at least several times a month?" (Jones, Gallagher, and McFalls, forthcoming).

An ominous undercurrent to this tide of progress against *acute* (short-term) disease is our relative helplessness against the rise of *chronic* (long-term) conditions. Heart disease and cancer combined for 12 percent of mortality in 1900, but account for over half of all deaths today (Council on Environmental Quality, 1975). To some degree, the disease shift simply reflects medical success. If you die of tuberculosis at age 20, you cannot be around for a heart attack in your sixties. While it may be interesting to note this example of the solution to one social problem leading to another problem, a crucial question remains: Are we gaining control over the new diseases that are replacing the old ones?

In many cases, the answer is no. Despite the recent decline in deaths from heart disease, it is still our No. 1 killer. Cancer is expected to eventually strike about 1 out of every 4 readers of this book. Not only are overall rates of lung cancer still rising, but the likelihood of surviving this deadly disease has remained virtually unchanged since 1960 (U.S. Department of Health and Human Services, 1980). Again, it is important to remember the morbidity of the living. Whether they survive or not, people generally are saddled with chronic conditions for years or even decades. Such diseases as arthritis and multiple sclerosis may not kill immediately, but they do sentence millions to long-term suffering. Over 30 million Americans must live with chronic, sometimes incapacitating, pain that does not respond to surgery and/or drugs (Kotarba, 1983). Despite medicine's selective success against some conditions, many chronic diseases stubbornly resist the miracles of modern science:

> Indeed the medical triumphs...of the past few decades have been so impressive and so widely acclaimed that the general public now seems to believe that any ailment can be cured by the ministrations of health professionals. But there is overwhelming evidence that, although many of the most common ailments may be relieved symp

The dazzling success of modern medicine against acute diseases such as tuberculosis has not been matched for chronic, degenerative conditions which afflict many Americans with daily suffering. (© *Alon Reininger/Contact 1984*)

tomatically, their courses cannot be significantly altered by entering the health-care delivery system (Rushmer, 1975:15–16).

Much treatment is "carative" rather than curative, merely attempting to reduce discomfort as chronic symptoms progress.

This stalemate in the war against chronic disease has prompted a reevaluation of the simple strategy of treating the individual's illness. Historical studies indicate that major reasons for the victories over acute disease are social rather than medical. General societal conditions—such as industrial development and the levels of income and education—seem to produce substantial health gains independently of medical advances (Fuchs, 1974).

There is a need to look beyond individual symptoms and treatment to the general forces bearing on health. Figure 3-1 is a schematic diagram showing three relevant factors other than "Medical Care." To apply the diagram to the case of cancer, the health risk of a malignant tumor is affected by heredity (whether a parent had cancer, "Genetics" circle A), the breathing of carcinogenic material from the air ("Environment" circle B), and the "Lifestyle" habit of smoking cigarettes (circle D), in addition to the detection and treatment of the tumor (circle C). Moreover, the circles interact in complex ways to multiply disease risks. An individual whose parent had coronary disease and who overeats while living in a stressful environment has many times the average likelihood of a heart attack. The conceptual apparatus in Figure 3-1 is applicable to a wide spectrum of health issues, and it should attune you to the health significance of what goes on outside the doctor's office.

Aside from the rise of chronic conditions, there is another noteworthy trend relating to society's management of disease. It has been tabbed *medicalization*, and it concerns the increasing tendency to call behavior "illness." The earlier discussion noted that persons labeled ill have a kind of official excuse for deviance since the disease is assumed to be beyond their control. More and more ex-"sins" are being seen as sickness, including gambling, drug addiction, and crime. Consider the tamer issue of hyperactive children. The fidgety, impulsive behavior pattern that used to be called mischief was formally defined as a disease after some cases were successfully managed with drugs (Conrad, 1981). Despite the current controversy about the very existence of hyperactivity as a physical state (Satterfield, 1983), those defined as hyperactive are now the province of physicians rather than the police.

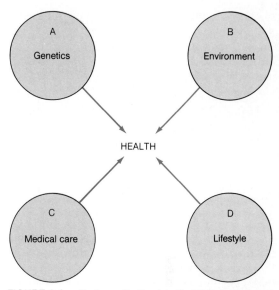

FIGURE 3-1   Factors affecting health. (*U.S. Department of Health and Human Services, Health United States 1980, p. 268.*)

Another medicalization question concerns your relatives and, eventually, yourself: Is old age a disease? If the answer is no, getting old simply means adjusting to a somewhat limited but still independent lifestyle. If the answer is yes, the decline in physical capacities symptomatic of advancing age suggests institutionalization in a nursing home.

The momentum of the medicalization trend flows from forces deep within American culture. One mainspring in the public mind is the success of medical science. The dazzling defeats of acute disease that have fed the subjective expectation of a cancer cure also promise a scientific solution to some of our stickier deviance problems. Even as we see the cultural causes of the medicalization trend, its consequences must be carefully examined. It is tempting to view alcoholism as a simple physical ailment which can be medically treated with antabuse (a drug inducing vomiting if any alcohol is consumed); but addiction appears to be only a symptom of deeper, nonphysical difficulties untouched by the drug. The consequences of trying to cure deviants with pills are exemplified by the case of hyperactivity:

> By focusing on the symptoms and defining them as hyperkinesis we ignore the possibility that behavior is not an illness but an adaptation to a social situation. It diverts our attention from the family or school and from seriously entertaining the idea that the problem could be in the structure of the social system (Conrad, 1981:596).

A recent writer on the medicalization of old age similarly states: "It is widely suggested that this phenomenon represents a medical solution to what are essentially social problems" (Morgan, 1982:40). The point is not that a medical approach is valueless, but rather that its value must be weighed in relation to the wider contexts of the "disease." The multidimensional model in Figure 3-1 has special relevance to the control of deviance which, after all, is a peculiarly social sickness. Saying "They're sick and need treatment!" (i.e., in circle C) may seem to be an enlightened way to handle rule breakers, but medicalization benefits neither the deviant nor society by forgetting the sociological sources of the "sick" person's behavior.

Access to Quality Health Care

> Accordingly, if I carry out the provisions of this solemn oath, and if I do not violate any of them, may it be my reward to enjoy life and the practice of my profession, honored always by all men; but if I transgress any provision or falsely swear to this oath, may I suffer the opposite fate.
>
> —The Hippocratic Oath

For most Americans, the control of personal illness means one straightforward step: get to a doctor. The high achievements of medical science in stamping out various diseases are reflected in the high social standing of physicians. According to a recent national poll, over 80 percent of the population perceives medical doctors as making relatively large contributions to the general good of society; nearly 7 out of every 10 persons of college age rate the occu-

pational prestige of physicians to be very high (Gallup, 1981:19 and 43). These subjective attitudes are matched by the social rewards showered on medical doctors. The median income of physicians is roughly 100,000 dollars, which pays them at least twice as much as the average professional working in the United States!

The get-to-the-doctor approach has clearly benefited medical practitioners, but many sick people still find the getting difficult. The United States has one of the highest physician-to-population ratios in the world, and that ratio is projected to increase through 1990. Nevertheless, hundreds of communities are actually doctorless, and literally millions of people continue to suffer limited access to professional care because of where they live. To spotlight two badly underserved groups, blacks in the rural South and Hispanics in the Southwest are significantly more likely than the general population not to see a doctor, and to spend more travel and waiting time if they do make an office visit (American Public Health Association, 1982).

Where are the doctors who are so sorely needed in such places? Quite simply, they are where the money is. It would be a mistake to suggest that physicians' offices are packed into affluent areas purely due to greed, but there clearly is a surplus in the suburbs and a shortage in both the inner city and outer rural areas. Aside from monetary considerations, physicians set up practice where they do because of better hospital facilities, more stimulating medical problems, and better working conditions (Rushmer, 1975). In short, physicians are people who pick places to live and work for pretty much the same reasons as anybody else. Unlike most people's locational decisions, however, physicians' choices directly affect the access of the sick and the dying to professional health care.

The maldistribution of medical doctors is not the only hurdle between the individual and proper care. A second access issue is the *type* of physician, regardless of location. Over the past fifty years, there has been a virtual stampede of medical school graduates into the specialties. In 1930, there were five general practitioners for every medical specialist; now, that ratio is reversed. Again, one reason for the choice appears to be monetary. Specialists may charge up to twice as much as general practitioners—$32 versus $16—for a fifteen-minute office visit (U.S. Bureau of the Census, 1980*a*). But part of the motivation is the understandable desire to apply the scientific advances within the specialized fields of modern medicine.

While many people recognize the advantages of going to a specialist, there are also disadvantages in too much specialization of care. What is your usual reason for visiting a doctor? According to a national study of doctor visits, you are most likely to seek access for everyday illness such as cough, muscle ache, and abdominal discomfort (National Center for Health Statistics, 1983). Who in the maze of specialists should deal with these general symptoms? It is apparent that the reward system of modern medicine does not pay off for the treatment of such common ailments. There is too much glamour (and money) in exotic operations like organ transplants, and too little training to deal with the symptoms from which most people actually suffer.

But suffer they do, and in the search for relief frequent use is made of two undesirable alternatives. Lacking a general family doctor, millions of people take their nonemergency complaints to a hospital emergency room, which is nobody's idea of personalized medical care. The other available option is to follow a string of specialists until a remedy is found. Even if this scattered search is successful, it is expensive and depersonalizing. How can the continuing relationship necessary to treat the *whole* person be cultivated when the physician is an expert only on the patient's liver? An unfortunate side effect of medical specialization

is the lack of ready access to the appropriate form of care.

The title of this section contains a word that has not yet been directly considered: quality. Given the (essentially true) conventional wisdom about the intellectual qualifications and scientific training of American physicians, it is natural to assume that if one manages to get over the two hurdles of local availability and overspecialization, healing will occur. However, a third barrier between you and health looms even in the office of the "right" doctor. The objective statistics to follow may surprise and even shock you, and they could be subjectively ignored only in a society which holds medical professionals in such high esteem. Despite its impressive potential for healing, the present system of health care kills thousands and harms millions of people who come seeking help. This double-edged property of modern medicine is reflected in the term *iatrogenic disease,* meaning health problems caused by the physician. The size of the problem is controversial, but there is no controversy about the fact that many people die each year because of doctors' decisions (Lanza-Kaduce, 1980).

It is more than a matter of human error in the face of a life-threatening situation. According to a congressional report, 15,000 people die in the United States every year in unnecessary operations (U.S. House of Representatives, 1976)! The routine medical practice of bladder catheterization (inserting a tube for urination) causes about half a million infections a year, and those getting infected have triple the death risk of the average patient (Platt et al., 1982). In a typical year, over 3 million physician visits will result in the prescription of drugs (National Center for Health Statistics, 1982). Undeniably, a multitude of people are helped by the medication, but it cannot be denied that many are harmed, since up to a million and a half each year are hospitalized and 30,000 die as a result of adverse drug reactions (Makofsky, 1977). Given all of these dangers, it is understandable that about one-third of the nurses responding to a recent professional poll would refuse to be treated at their own hospitals!

Whatever your personal reaction to these deadly "cures" administered by the medical profession, it is striking how little societal reaction is generated by so much human damage. Despite some evidence of public dissatisfaction with physicians (such as the surge in the number of malpractice suits), the level of subjective concern is so low that most people dismiss these outcomes as the tragic result of necessary medical risks. The objective statistics above highlight how questionable this assumption is, and they call for a search for deeper causes. One cause is unfit physicians. Although medical training in the United States may be the most advanced in the world, the Federation of State Medical Boards recently concluded that about 5 percent of the nation's physicians are definitely incompetent. Of course this means that the vast majority are competent, but how comfortable would your flight be if you knew that 1 out of every 20 air traffic controllers had inadequate skill?

Overlapping with the competency issue is doctor deviance. Not only does physician fraud in government health programs cost taxpayers billions each year, but such criminal actions "likely deprive some persons of the satisfactory treatment that they otherwise would receive" (Pontell, Jesilaw, and Geis, 1982:125). In spite of their high achievements, physicians are people, and we ignore that fact at our own peril. It is conservatively estimated that 1 out of every 100 physicians develops drug dependency, and 6 out of every 100 become alcohol abusers (Morrow, 1982).

The whole story, though, is not the human weakness of some physicians. Doctor deviance occurs within a professional arena woefully lacking in social controls. One obvious shortcoming is the end of professional certification shortly after graduation from medical school. Rather than the brushup courses and relicens-

ing exams required by some other critical occupations (like air traffic controllers), the only routine "control" on practicing doctors is encouragement from the American Medical Association to keep up with the scientific literature. In lieu of a formal societal process for weeding out unfit physicians, the profession depends on peer review according to a code of medical ethics.

How much self-enforcement by physicians actually occurs? The answer is not much. Despite the frightening number of unnecessary deaths and iatrogenic diseases, fewer than seventy physicians a year even have their licenses suspended. Over a five-year period, seven entire states "reported no disciplinary actions of any kind, not even a reprimand" (Klavv, 1975:97). A flagrant example of lax self-policing is the case of Irving W. Potter, an obstetrician widely known to have practiced a dangerous method of childbirth for nearly fifty years (Bullough and Groeger, 1982:109).[7] Even if physicians were predisposed to blow the whistle on their professional colleagues—and they clearly are not—what goes on between doctor and patient in the scattered offices of our medical system generally remains confidential.

It is worth repeating the point that physicians' shortcomings are a symptom of the social organization of modern medicine in the United States. Not only does society exercise no systematic control over MDs, but the current organization of medical education fails to provide physicians with key skills. Technical training is necessary, but it is not sufficient for the practice of medicine on human beings. Evidence has accumulated in recent studies of doctor-patient interaction that people need more than a body mechanic. The physician's skill in communication has been shown to affect everything from the success of treatment to the likelihood of a

---

[7] Potter employed the pedialic internal version technique (feet-first delivery), which was considered hazardous even in his day.

malpractice suit (Bush, 1983). Nevertheless, most doctors receive no serious training in this crucial facet of their bedside manner and, in fact, tend to become more distant and authoritarian as they progress through medical school. No wonder 1 out of every 8 drug prescriptions in hospitals is in error, often because of simple misunderstandings (Davis and Cohen, 1981).

The question is why doctors continue to make lethal mistakes, which leads to the larger question of the organization—or lack of it—of health care. Physicians' choices of location, of speciality, even the choice of words to a patient—all affect your access to real healing. These choices must be seen in the context of the wider social structure within which physicians practice.

The Social System of Health Care Delivery

Even with no improvement whatsoever in the competency of physicians, the morbidity and mortality of the contemporary United States could be dramatically improved. General application of already well-known techniques could eliminate 400,000 cases of hospital infection and save up to 20,000 lives a year. The dangerous acute diseases against which modern medicine has already been so successful (e.g., tuberculosis and pneumonia) can be further reduced at least 25 percent simply by applying current knowledge (U.S. Department of Health and Human Services, 1980). Physicians and other health care providers have the technology, resources, and skills to save us from so much suffering and death, yet these real health benefits remain beyond our grasp. Why? The answer leads us past individual practitioners directly to the social structure of American medicine.

Drawing a thumbnail sketch of our health care institutions is difficult because of their enormous complexity. Consider the scale of the system. It contains some 7,000 hospitals and employs about 4 million people, and it is growing rapidly. Coordination of this mountain of workers and material is a herculean task. Many

health resources are underutilized, many are overutilized, and many are providing the same service to the public. Perhaps the best way to see why all of the impressive pieces do not fit together is to spotlight the process of health care *delivery*. Recognizing that getting the newspaper to your door is a practical problem separate from the quality of the printed product, we have many fine healing skills and services being delivered in a haphazard way. Beyond the level of the hospital room or the doctor's office, the institution of medicine is not a "system" for serving public health needs.

The proper instruments for diagnosing the symptoms of this system are sociological. Specifically, the social disorganization of American medical delivery will be spotlighted from the theoretical perspectives introduced in Chapter 1. As one surveys the social landscape of health care in the United States, the most prominent institutional setting is the hospital. It is worth noting that hospitals were originally places where deviants could live and where the poor went to die.

Today hospitals are the organizational center of modern medicine, taking in over 1.3 billion dollars a year and collectively housing about 1 million individuals every day. While certain centers command so many qualified people and resources that they have been called medical empires, there is precious little coordination of services across hospitals. It is not uncommon for two hospitals in the same community to acquire the exotic and expensive equipment needed for open heart surgery, when one facility would be more than enough for the entire region. Wasteful duplication of services helps to explain why 1 out of every 4 costly hospital beds is unfilled (U.S. Department of Health and Human Services, 1980).

Lack of interhospital cooperation costs lives as well as money. Research approved by the American College of Obstetrics and Gynecology suggests that consolidation of several hospital maternity units into one larger, well-equipped childbirth center can reduce maternal mortality by two-thirds (Rushmer, 1975). The reason many such life-saving opportunities are missed is simple: Hospitals are not parts of an overall system cooperating to serve public needs. As a rule, hospitals are independent units actively competing against one another for patients' dollars and medical status.

The lack of coordination among hospitals is paralleled by confused social structures within the hospital door. Despite impressive evidence indicating that the organizational chart does influence patients' care and satisfaction (Mechanic, 1978), hospitals have notoriously haphazard management practices. To a *functionalist*, the lack of both external and internal hospital organization is symptomatic of a faulty functional system. This theory would recommend viewing each part of the health care system—a hospital ward, for example—in terms of its overall contribution to the general goal of healing. If the hospital ward serves the positive function of helping 100 people but diverts 1000 people from more helpful forms of therapy, its net health effect is negative, or dysfunctional. Functional analysis would attempt to integrate all of the hospital parts together into a true medical system, rather than a loose collection of people dispensing various sorts of healing.

To a *conflict* theorist, the symptoms of hospitals—and the entire health care sector—are well diagnosed. The reason the system is not a streamlined structure delivering health is simple: Various groups are pursuing the more immediate value of profit (Ehrenreich and Ehrenreich, 1971). The conflict perspective bases its analysis on the fact that medical care in the United States is delivered in largely the same way as cars or mink coats, that is, by being bought and sold in the open market. Consequently the profit motive is seen as eclipsing the healing motive. Private, for-profit hospitals compete with one another not just because no authority has arranged them into a better func-

tional system, but rather because they are each scrambling for a bigger cut of the billions in hospital revenues. Such coordination as does occur is most apparent in capitalistic medical management groups such as the Hospital Corporation of America, which has been called The McDonald's of the Health Business. Hospitals that are losing in this cutthroat competition for profits—many in already underserved inner-city areas—will shut their doors in spite of crying public need.

The conflict of profit versus public values argument has also been leveled at the behavior of physicians. MDs mostly move into suburban, specialized practices because that is where the money is, even though it means moving away from public needs. The death-dealing decisions of doctors cited above can be viewed as mistakes occasioned by haste to get to the next patient paying $30 for fifteen minutes. Since time literally is money for physicians, conflict theorists contend that surgery and drugs are preferred treatments despite their documented dangers. They further note that the American Medical Association has steadfastly opposed any public policy that might bear on the economic interests of physicians. The AMA fought vigorously against government health clinics in the 1920s, and even against Medicare and Medicaid (to be discussed below) in the 1960s. Most recently, the Association lobbied against a 1977 medical cost-control bill by making campaign contributions to nearly all the members of the two congressional subcommittees screening the legislation (Common Cause, 1978); as the theory would predict, the bill was killed. Such considerations argue for an end to the professional dominance of physicians and other economically powerful interest groups (Friedson, 1970). Conflict theorists call for a restructuring of the system so that the health care needs of consumers will gain priority over the profit-seeking motives of producers.

One factor complicating this sketch of the social system of medical delivery is that the subject will not hold still. The ever-changing face of American health care is reflected in the recent trend toward natural childbirth. If you check with your parents, they will probably relate that you entered the world with your mother under general anesthesia, as in any surgical operation. In less than a full generation, medical opinion has moved to accept the idea that birth should not be treated as a disease; consequently, more and more fathers are present to share the birth process with their fully conscious spouses (Nelson, 1982).

Speaking of your parents, the last generation has also witnessed a sudden shift in the living patterns of aging Americans. Between 1963 and 1979, the number of nursing home residents in the United States nearly tripled (U.S. Bureau of the Census, 1980a). This trend in the treatment of aging family members reflects still other health-related changes. Increasing national life expectancy is rapidly increasing the fraction of the populace older than 65. New policies inside the medical sector—notably changes in Medicare and Medicaid legislation—have also contributed to the instant industry of nursing homes by bankrolling them. Patient abuse within nursing homes and the ambivalent attitudes many people have about sending their parents away are both evidence of culture lag, the delay required for the rest of the social structure to adjust to rapid changes in its parts.

This concept is a facet of *social change* theory which has special relevance here. If you consider the deluge of medical innovations in your lifetime—organ transplants, artificial hearts, even cures for acne—it is not surprising that the system is unsettled. It takes time for the government to approve the techniques, time for patients to accept them (Do I want my life artificially prolonged?), and time for hospitals to implement them. In the meantime, the social structure of health care is a disorderly blend of the old and the new. Whatever the potential for good in a medical breakthrough, the change that it requires means a potentially disorganizing

shock to health care's social system. Together with the other sociological theories, this paradox of social change is a key to understanding a medical delivery system that seems to be less than the sum of its very impressive parts.

Financing Medical Services

Perhaps the most shocking changes in the whole medical arena concern costs. Even without looking at the numbers, the steeply rising lines in Figure 3-2 trace a fantastic record of price escalation. A hospital room now costs over eight times as much as it did around the time many of you were born! Totaling up the bill on a national basis, health care costs nearly twice as great a percentage of the gross national product as in 1960. Totaling up the bill in individual terms, every man, woman, and child in America spends an average of over 1300 dollars a year on medical services. Moreover, this heavier and heavier cost burden is not borne equally. Families struck by so-called catastrophic illness (such as cancer or kidney disease) may be financially crushed by huge treatment bills over a period of years. About 1 family in every 20 spends over 5000 dollars a year for needed care! From any angle, the objective picture shows a price tag for healing that is growing more and more exorbitant.

Skyrocketing medical costs have not escaped the attention of the public paying the bills. A recent national survey studying major problems facing families today found more worry about the costs of medical care than about illness (Yankelovich, Skelly, and White, 1979:64). Subjective concern over the price of healing is reflected in behavior as well as public opinion. There is evidence that high costs are leading to a practice known as doctor shopping, in which people search for bargain care that may be no bargain for their health (Kasteler et al., 1976). In either its objective or subjective dimension, the cost of health care is a classic case of a "solution" becoming a social problem. The financial system we have built to pay

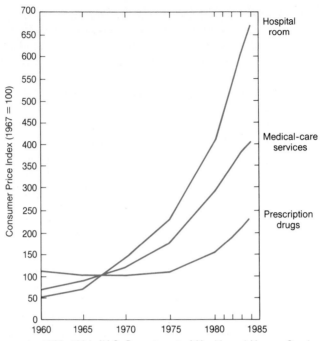

FIGURE 3-2   Medical care costs, 1960–1984. (*U.S. Department of Health and Human Services, Health United States 1985, p. 126.*)

for the control of illness has itself become problematic.

A keystone of this financial structure—and a key to exploding costs—is third party payments, otherwise known as medical insurance. In general, the private and public insurance systems have woven quite an impressive safety net for covering runaway health prices. About 85 percent of the population of the United States is covered by some form of medical insurance, and roughly 70 cents on the dollar of medical bills is funded by the government or private insurers (U.S. Department of Health and Human Services, 1985). Such aid may be indispensable for a stroke victim paying up to $600 a day for an intensive care room, but the scale of the costs must also be considered when viewing the holes in the insurance net. Over 30 million people have no coverage at all, and 30 cents of each of the billions of dollars paid must come out of pocket. The insurance net is full of

holes below the poverty line. Despite the previously discussed fact that the poor are less healthy than the nonpoor, approximately 1 out of 5 persons below the federal poverty line is unprotected by any form of medical insurance (American Public Health Association, 1982).

This last point may surprise you because of the widely publicized governmental programs providing medical care for the needy which have, in some respects, delivered significant health benefits (Davis and Schoen, 1978). Medicaid is a medical plan designed specifically for the poor; in dollar terms, it is the largest single welfare program in the United States. Medicaid payments help with the health bills of approximately 10 percent of the population, but states differ widely in their eligibility requirements for people and services. Consequently, millions of the poor are not covered despite the billions of dollars spent. Medicare is a part of the Social Security system which automatically includes the vast majority of Americans over the age of 65, but the program is not by any means free. The (often poor) senior citizen must pay some portion of hospital bills, and only about half of the nation's physicians accept the Medicare allowance as an adequate fee. Given these coverage gaps and galloping medical costs, the elderly are now spending the same percentage of their income (about 20 percent) on health care as they did before Medicare began!

Such payment gaps do not apply only to the public programs. Private insurance plans have similar limits on office visits, hospital days, and diagnostic tests, thus leaving up to half the population open to financial ruin through catastrophic illness (Dye, 1981). In sum: Over 30 million people appear to be in an insurance no man's land, with too much income to qualify for public care and too little to afford private insurance; for those who are covered by the insurance net, many major expenses still drop through as personal burdens.

A powerful stimulus for the development of our current insurance structure has been careening costs. It would be a mistake, however, to view third party (insurance) payments as only a response to medical inflation. The guarantees of the insurer mean that the first two parties—the physician and patient—have very little incentive to cut costs. Since their bills will be paid, patients naturally seek the best (and often most expensive) care available. Physicians can actually triple their incomes by adding on quite defensible procedures and tests that are not necessary for a given patient (Moloney and Rogers, 1979). Doctors have further financial motives to practice costly defense medicine because of their own insurance premiums for medical malpractice, which top 1.5 billion dollars a year (Williams, 1983).

Even with this evidence that insurance has been a cause as well as an effect of runaway health charges, there are many other potent inflationary forces, such as increased public demand for health care, an aging (thus more

chronically ill) population, and new high-priced technology. Fueled by these many forces, medical costs are literally out of control.

But are they *beyond* our control? Admittedly, attempts at medical cost containment have been laughably inadequate. The impotence of recent control programs stems partly from the fragmented nature of the health care system. The organizational complexity discussed earlier makes it exceedingly difficult to design fair and workable financial limits. Moreover, the system has too many loosely connected parts to apply only one financial bandage at a time. Even if hospital costs are effectively controlled, physicians are free to charge higher fees in their unregulated offices; putting the lid on Medicaid and Medicare charges may mean only higher costs for nonpoor patients (Williams, 1983). Consequently, the lines in Figure 3-2 continue to go through the roof.

In the eyes of many expert analysts, cost-control legislation is ineffectual because it treats symptoms rather than the underlying disease.[8] Their diagnosis of the financial condition is simple: a case of contagious profit. Drug companies, physicians, and hospital stockholders are not deliberately trying to create the social problem of medical costs; they are merely pursuing profit in a free enterprise system. With care providers commanding whatever prices they want in the medical marketplace, it is hardly surprising that health costs are rising feverishly. The malady of medical finance in the United States may be brought under control, but it would require radical surgery on the entrepre-

[8] Most cost and quality control programs that have been implemented (such as Professional Standards Review Organizations overseeing Medicare and Medicaid) have been dominated by physicians, thus leaving control in the hands of health care providers. The new prospective payment plan written into federal law in 1983 will assign hospitalized patients into one of 467 diagnosis-related groups, and then limit Medicare payment to a flat fee. Evaluating cost and health effects of this new program will have to postdate its full implementation in 1986.

neurial structure of the present system (Waitzkin, 1983).

Treating Illness versus Preserving Wellness

Even with the billions of dollars pouring into the health care market, the buck has to stop somewhere. Financial limits force resource decisions which mean some people will live while others die. Unfortunately, these decisions often lead to questionable—even tragic—choices. Consider the fact that the government spends about 30,000 dollars annually to keep a kidney patient alive at a dialysis center rather than the 1765 dollars a year it would cost to save a heart patient's life with a mobile cardiac unit (Rhoads, 1978). Or consider that the development of an artificial heart costs much more than the most expensive prevention program which might stop many heart attacks each year. Part of the problem is the social disorganization of a medical system with no general authority making life-and-death decisions according to public needs. Instead, resources are allocated depending on ability to pay, or even the degree of subjective support drummed up for a given disease by celebrities in the mass media (Kerson, 1981).

A deeper source of such questionable decisions is the preoccupation of American medicine with illness. Of course doctors should treat the sick, but prevention of sickness is unquestionably more efficient. There are now excellent cure rates for some forms of cancer, but lives, money, and anguish could be spared if individuals never got the disease in the first place. Melanoma, the most serious form of skin cancer killing some 5000 Americans annually, almost always has an early innocent stage during which the disease can be prevented by simply removing the malignant mole.

It is not as though prevention is an unproven strategy within the medical system. There have been spectacular savings in lives through immunization programs for polio and whooping cough, both treatable diseases (Kaplan, Cassell, and Gore, 1979). Infant mortality has dropped dramatically over the last generation, in part because of preventive measures in pre-natal care (U.S. Department of Health and Human Services, 1982). Despite the enormous potential for keeping people well rather than treating them when they are ill, *less than 4 percent of the nation's expenditures for health are devoted to any form of preventive activity.*

Why? There are several reasons for the pro-treatment bias of the American health system, all with deep sociological roots. An intellectual basis for this approach is germ theory, which has been called "the most powerful single idea in the history of medicine" (Twaddle and Hessler, 1977:11). Essentially, the discovery of microorganisms producing acute disease has focused the attention of the medical profession on killing germs once they are already in people. The focus on treating those sick from infection has generated some miraculous cures, but it has also sidetracked measures which could eliminate the need for miracles. Organization of physicians' training around this medical model means the neglect of potentially potent—but nonbiological—sources of disease.

A second factor promoting treatment over prevention is the structure of social rewards. Most physicians in the United States practice on a fee-for-service basis, which pays off on the amount of treatment given rather than the amount of treatment avoided. Prestige (and grant money) in medical research seems to be showered on those espousing exotic treatment techniques, such as laser surgery and organ transplants. The incentives are less concrete for those preaching and practicing prevention.

A closely related third factor is the American love affair with technology. Aside from the rewards they may bring medical practitioners, innovations in treatment hardware appeal to us as a kind of technological fix, a quick, painless solution through the magic of science. Our cultural admiration for high technology is behind the rapid diffusion of electronic fetal monitors, laser surgical equipment, and CAT scan devices throughout the medical arena. Hospitals continue to spend millions of dollars on such advanced equipment, while proven (but unglamorous) prevention programs receive pennies. Together, these three factors indicate why the overwhelming response to the social problem of ill health is more and better cures for people who are already ill.

Please return now to Figure 3-1. The previous paragraphs explain that most of the eggs of our medical resources are in the one basket of circle C; other sources of disease—and its possible prevention through circles A, B, and D— are deemphasized by the medical establishment. The number of lives lost because of behaviors outside circle C borders on the incredible. Consider the case of cigarette smoking, which has nothing to do with germs but induces profound changes inside the body:

> Within seconds after a smoker inhales cigarette smoke, his blood pressure starts rising by 10 to 20 points, his heart rate increases by 25 beats per minute, his skin temperature drops 5 or 6 degrees—and even his eyesight is adversely affected. And when he exhales, up to 90 percent of that true tobacco taste stays in his tissues as submicroscopic particles of about 1,200 chemicals, most of which are in chimney smoke or automobile exhausts (Byrd, 1976).

Dr. Byrd's repeated use of "his" is ironic in that a rapidly rising proportion of young females are experiencing these physiological effects, a fact that has been tied to new social pressures on women (Silverstein, Feld, and Kozlowski, 1980). For both sexes, smoking is a facet of "Lifestyle" (circle D) which causes astronomical objective damage. Over 85,000 people will die this year from cigarette-induced lung cancer alone (American Cancer Society, 1983). Dr. David Sachs of the Case Western Reserve University School of Medicine (1983) reports that smoking-linked diseases killed more Americans in 1982 than all the battles in World War II! It is estimated that those of you

with the habit lose about as much life span as is spent smoking—about 5½ minutes per cigarette (Eckholm, 1978a). Moreover, the "Lifestyle" effects of smoking interact with "Environment" (circle B) and other facets of circle D in deadly ways:

> Risks of cancers of the respiratory system are more than tripled when heavy smokers are exposed to certain toxic agents or dusts in the work environment. Risks of stroke among women using oral contraceptives are more than doubled among the subset who smoke (U.S. Department of Health and Human Services, 1980:269).

While the medical system scrambles to find cures for smoking-related diseases, cases pour in because of unchecked behavior in circles A, B, and D. Treatment continues to receive the higher priority, even though *no single measure would lengthen the life or improve the health of Americans more than preventing cigarette smoking* (Richmond, 1980).

Oddly, the neglect of prevention by the health care system is running against the tide of public opinion. The highly visible fitness boom appears to be a full-blown social movement based on a subjective vision of preserving health. More than 9 out of 10 respondents in a national poll agreed with this statement: "If Americans ate more nutritious food, smoked less, maintained our proper weight, and exercised regularly, it would do more to improve our health than anything doctors and medicine could do for us" (Harris, 1978). It is uncertain whether this popular attitude reflects lowered expectations about the magic of medicine or heightened value placed on personal wellness. It has, however, produced real changes within the "Lifestyle" circle. Evidence of new patterns of preventive health behavior is displayed in Figure 3-3, which shows marked reductions in the percentage of cigarette smokers—with the notable exception of teenage females. Additional facets of this lifestyle shift involve

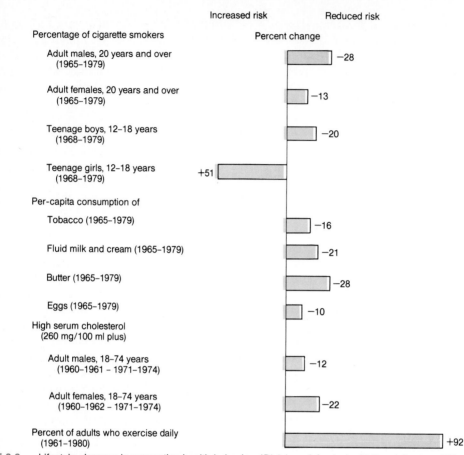

FIGURE 3-3   Lifestyle changes in preventive health behavior. (*Division of Analysis, National Center of Health Statistics.*)

nutrition and exercise, which will be considered in turn.

In terms of health effects, diet is an area for which an ounce of prevention really does seem to equal a pound of cure. Nutrition research is not yet definitive on the causal role of dietary factors, but there is little question of their involvement in the production and prevention of our most serious diseases. Diabetes is a condition affecting about 11 million and contributing to the deaths of over 100,000 people a year in the United States (American Diabetes Association, 1983). Although diet is generally accepted as a factor in the development of the disease, much of the medical research is geared to the development of new technology to manage insulin levels rather than to dietary prevention. Research has advanced to the point of isolating dietary risk factors for the four major killers in America: heart disease—foods elevating serum cholesterol; cancer—fat intake and specific substances such as saccharin; stroke—salt intake related to hypertension; accidents—alcohol, particularly for the college age group (U.S. Department of Health and Human Services, 1980).

But perhaps the most well-established diet-health link concerns the quantity rather than quality of nutrients. Obesity is so objectively common and a risk factor in so many diseases that its prevention would add more years to the average life expectancy than the elimination of cancer! As the national obsession with dieting suggests, Americans are indeed concerned about this lifestyle issue; 96 percent of the public considers being overweight a "serious health threat" (Yankelovich, Skelly, and White, 1978:94). High subjective concern with diet is reflected in eating behavior. Three out of every four consumers polled claim to be "more interested in nutrition than they were a few years ago" (Yankelovich, Skelly, and White, 1978:32), and Figure 3-3 suggests that they have acted on that interest by reducing fat intake. Whatever the priorities within medical institutions, many Americans are moving to prevent ill health by changing what they put—or do not put—in their mouths.

Another facet of the social movement toward preserving wellness involves exercise habits. Since research priorities have focused on fixing up sickness rather than shaping up those not yet sick, this is another area in which firm conclusions are just starting to be drawn. But again, the promise of disease prevention appears to be gigantic. Consider a killer in which the United States is among the world leaders: heart disease. Despite the conspicuous absence of exercise emphasis in hospitals and physicians' offices, several medically supervised programs for strenuous physical activity have successfully reduced the symptoms of coronary disease victims, presumably reducing the chance of a future heart attack. Lack of regular exercise is both a reflection of our societal habits (Do you walk or drive to campus?) and an official risk factor for cardiovascular disease. A report in the *Journal of the American Medical Association* actually quantified exercise's preventive potential: individuals who engage in vigorous exercise (aerobic activity at least three times a week for twenty minutes or more) have half the likelihood of heart attack of sedentary persons (Peters et al., 1983).

As in the case of nutrition, people's perceptions and personal lifestyles are being altered in advance of the medical establishment. Eight out of ten individuals feel they are not getting enough exercise (Yankelovich, Skelly, and White, 1979), and there are strong indications that Americans are starting to work up a sweat (see the bottom of Figure 3-3). Just over half of the adult population now exercises regularly, and participation in endurance sports—jogging, biking, and other activities affecting the cardiovascular system—is up sharply (Gallup, 1983). The health-through-fitness movement is running at its fastest pace through certain social segments. Particularly striking is the relationship of exercise and nutrition consciousness to socioeconomic status. Both facets of shaping up increase with educational and occupational level, a fact that foretells a further widening of the health gap between the poor and the nonpoor (Gallup, 1983; Yankelovich, Skelly, and White, 1979).

This last point brings us back to the role of the health care system. The unequal spread of the fitness movement—and the number of misinformed, get-rich-quick operators riding on the boom—shows that the neglect of prevention should not be left to the public to heal by itself. Changes in individual behavior are required to cut off the flow of disease from circles A, B, and D (Figure 3-1), but changed priorities within the "Medical Care" circle could multiply the health benefits. More active immunization, screening, and outreach efforts by medical institutions would mean an almost immediate drop in morbidity and mortality (U.S. Department of Health and Human Services, 1980). There is objective evidence that medically supervised programs can influence the smoking, diet, and exercise habits of the public, and subjective evidence of the public's interest in health education (American Hospital Association, 1978). Clearly, social action can strengthen individual action in the preservation of wellness. The general principle about the individual-social aspects of social problems is made personally relevant to your body in Table 3-1.

SOCIAL POLICY: NATIONAL INSURANCE

Strategies for Solution

Just as individual illness has roots in wider social patterns, the system of medical care is a social institution rooted in a particular society. As such, it is created by human behavior and can thus be creatively changed. But the sociological view of medical care, which reminds us that social systems are subject to our control, has deeper implications as well. Policy treatments for the ills of the medical system must be tested for social side effects, for their compatibility with the living patterns of the society.

People's reservations about policy cure-alls for the social problem of illness are reflected in the history of national health insurance. As early as 1912, Theodore Roosevelt proposed a comprehensive program to protect every American from the financial and physical ravages of disease. Throughout the twentieth century the idea of a federally organized health system has remained a public issue (Feder, Holahan, and Marmor, 1980), and many of the arguments for this alternative policy have recently been considered in major legislation before Congress. Proponents of medical reform view our care delivery system cross-culturally, noting that the United States is the *only* advanced industrial society without some universal health care program for its population. They see irony in the fact that education is valued as a basic right (actually, a compulsory right) of every citizen, financed and planned by the government, whereas medical care is a service bought and sold in the marketplace.

Although there have been many proposals for increased governmental involvement in the health arena, most serious discussion centers on national health insurance, in which the government would *guarantee* payment of the medical costs of all its citizens. Some strengths of such a financing scheme are apparent from the objective statistics in this chapter. Universal coverage would patch the gaps in the present private-public insurance system, instantly creating a financial safety net for the 30 million Americans now unprotected; some of these millions would thus escape the ruinous effects of catastrophic illness striking a family member.

Another oft-cited advantage of a national insurance system is that it *is* a national system. The governmental body created to administer universal insurance would be a natural center from which to coordinate the widely scattered and overlapping hodgepodge of health agencies. Supporters of federal insurance contend that the board could plan health care decisions on the basis of public need rather than private profit, thus reducing much of the wasteful—and lethal—disorganization discussed in The Social System of Health Care Delivery section. With its power over the purse strings, the agency might similarly oversee access to the health work force in terms of the demands of communities rather than the desires of physicians. The latter administrative functions proposed in some plans are much more controversial than the insurance function because they involve government in changing the structure of health care delivery rather than just underwriting costs.

This is not to say that national health insurance itself has been free of controversy. Even though proposals originated around the turn of the century, not one has yet been enacted in the United States. Backers of the present system—which here will be called free enterprise medicine—argue that governmental centralization of medical care would endanger both the fiscal and physical health of the nation.

Perhaps the most common attack against national health insurance concerns cost. Our previous discussion of the inflationary impact of third party payments raises the prospect of

TABLE 3-1   YOUR PERSONAL HEALTH INVENTORY

Directions:

If uncertain, leave blank.

Place scores (given in parentheses) on lines provided in the plus (+) or minus (−) columns.

Total the (+) and (−) columns and subtract the lower number from the higher to find the total (+ or −) for each section.

Follow the instructions for calculating your medical age at the end of the appraisal.

1. Lifestyle inventory

	+	−
Disposition. Exceptionally good natured, easy going (−3); average (0); extremely tense and nervous most of time (+6).		
Exercise. Physically active employment or sedentary job with well-planned exercise program (−12); sedentary with moderate regular exercise (0); sedentary work, no exercise program (+12).		
Home environment. Unusually pleasant, better than average family life (−6); average (0); unusual tension, family strife common (+9).		
Job satisfaction. Above average (−3); average (0); discontented (+6).		
Exposure to air pollution. Substantial (+9).		
Smoking habits. Nonsmoker (−6); occasional (0); moderate, regular smoking 20 cigarettes, 5 cigars, or 5 pipefuls (+12); heavy smoking 40 or more cigarettes daily (+24); marijuana frequent (+24).		
Alcohol habits. None or seldom (−6); moderate with less than 2 beers or 2 oz. whiskey or hard liquor daily (+6); heavy, with more than above (+24).		
Eating habits. Drink skim or low-fat milk only (−3); eat much bulky food (−3); heavy meat (3 times a day) eater (+6); over 2 pats of butter daily (+6); over 4 cups of coffee, tea, or cola daily (+6); usually add salt at table (+6).		
Auto driving. Regularly less than 20,000 miles annually and always wear seat belt (−3); regularly less than 20,000 but belt not always worn (0); more than 20,000 (+12).		
Drug habits. Use of street drugs (+36).		
Part 1 total		

2. Physical inventory

	+	−
Weight. "Ideal" weight at 20 was ___ pounds. If current weight is more than 20 pounds over that, score (+6) for each 20 pounds. If same as age 20 or less gain than 10 pounds (−3).		
Blood pressure. Under 40 years, if above 130/80 (+12); over 40 years, if above 140/90 (+12).		
Cholesterol. Under 40 years, if above 220 (+6); over 40, if above 250 (+6).		
Heart murmur. Not an "innocent" type (+24).		
Heart murmur. With history of rheumatic fever (+48).		
Pneumonia. If bacterial pneumonia more than three times in life (+6).		
Asthma (+6).		
Rectal polyps (+6).		
Diabetes. Adult onset type (+18).		
Depressions. Severe, frequent (+12).		
Regular* medical checkup. Complete (−12); partial (−6).		
Regular* dental checkup (−3).		
Part 2 total		

*"Regular" refers to well people who have thorough medical exams at a minimum according to this age/frequency: 60 and up, every year; 50–60, every 2 years; 40–50, every 3 years; 30–40, every 5 years; 25–30, as required for jobs, insurance, military, college, etc. More frequent medical checkups are recommended by other authorities. Dental exams: twice yearly.

TABLE 3-1   YOUR PERSONAL HEALTH INVENTORY *CONTINUED*

3. Family and social inventory

	+	−
Father. If alive and over 68 yrs., for each 5 yrs. above 73 (−3); if alive and under 68 or dead after age 68 (0); if dead of medical causes (not accident) before 68 (+3).	___	___
Mother. If alive and over 73 yrs., for each 5 yrs. above 73 (−3); if alive under 68 or dead after age 68 (0); if dead of medical causes (not accident) before 73 (+3).	___	___
Marital status. If married (0); unmarried and over 40 (+6).	___	___
Home location. Large city (+6); suburb (0); farm or small town (−3).	___	___
Part 3 total	___	___

4. For women only

	+	−
Family history of breast cancer. In mother or sisters (+6).	___	___
Examines breasts monthly (−6).	___	___
Yearly breast exam by physician (−6).	___	___
Part 4 total	___	___

Calculations

	+	−
Enter total from Part 1 (placed in appropriate column)	___	___
Total from Part 2	___	___
Total from Part 3	___	___
Total from Part 4	___	___
Enter the totals of each column	___	___
Compute the chart total (+ or −)	___	___
Enter current age	___	___
Divide chart total by 12, and enter that (+ or −) **figure**	___	___
Add or subtract above figure to/from your current age to determine your medical age	___	___

Source: Based on adaptation by Center for Health Education, Blue Cross and Blue Shield of Greater New York, from "How to Be Your Own Doctor...Sometimes" by Keith W. Sohnert, M.D., with Howard Eisonberg. Grosset & Dunlap.

a dizzying cost spiral if the federal treasury would indeed write a blank check for health. There is little question that the Medicare and Medicaid programs funded by the government since the 1960s have steepened the spending increases shown in Figure 3-2 (Feder, Holahan, and Marmor, 1980). Defenders of the free enterprise model also maintain that national insurance would buy us less health for more money. The present system of solo practice physicians who are paid on a fee-for-service basis contains, they contend, powerful incentives for high-quality care. If the alternative program compromised the profit motive, not only might patients suffer but there would be less motivation to discover and adopt life-saving medical innovations (Helms, 1978).

There is also concern about governmental red tape. The bureaucracy required to administer such a vast system could mean endless regulations choking the provision of care, especially if the agency attempted to reorganize service delivery. Defenders of the free enterprise model claim that more is at stake than standing in lines to receive impersonal medical care. There is the wider issue raised in this section's opening paragraph. A national medical system would trespass against one of our most cherished cultural values, substituting governmental control for the freedom of patients to choose their care and the freedom of physicians to practice their profession (Fuchs, 1974).

These are serious charges, which undoubtedly feed the public's misgivings about national health insurance. But advocates of the alternative policy have a rebuttal for each charge. On the fear of more depersonalized health care, reformers respond that care is already depersonalized due to overspecialization (see above), and that a national insurance board could increase incentives for family practice physicians to be distributed where they are needed most. They further argue that the profit motive does not necessarily promote health. The present fee-for-service system ties payments to the amount of testing and therapy, not to curing.[9] More important, a national agency could launch a broad-based program of education and training for disease prevention, which offers little in the way of short-term profits but enormous long-term health dividends.

Cost is a real concern of national health insurance supporters, but they see more reason for concern about the *present* system's price tag. Hospitalization is the most expensive form of care, and it is strongly encouraged by private insurance, which often will not pay if you seek outpatient (nonovernight) services. National insurance could cut costs through funding alternative forms of care, and also through coordinating hospital services so that they serve local needs rather than rival hospital stockholders. Many experts agree that real cost control is impossible without comprehensive authority over the medical sector (Williams, 1983), a feature built into national health insurance. Proponents concede that costs would be high because of increased care delivered to underserved segments of our population, but perhaps not so high as they are now climbing under free enterprise medicine.

National insurance reformers even deny that the present system is indeed the free enterprise valued by American culture. Physicians, after all, have a virtual monopoly over medical care, and the AMA has actually called competition unethical. Moreover, its backers claim the encroachment of national health insurance on personal freedom has been greatly exaggerated. The federal government is already deeply involved in the regulation of medical technology (Rettig, 1980). Any of you who has recently tried to pay a medical bill (or get into a hospital) knows that private insurance can create quite a snarl of red tape, and the paperwork of public programs such as Medicare and Medicaid has kept many people from even applying (Feigelman, 1980). Under the alternative system, eligibility would be automatic for everyone, thus cutting administrative complexity and costs (Cohen, 1976). The advocates of national health insurance appeal to traditional American culture as well, arguing that small losses in individual liberty are overbalanced by large gains in the honored values of equality, efficiency, and health.

Policies into Practice

These arguments for national health insurance are not new, nor are the arguments of the free enterprise advocates. While the reasoning of the latter group clearly has struck a chord in public opinion (particularly since many in the group are physicians), popular hesitancy about the alternative health system is, at least partly, fear of the unknown. When the known—the present system of modern medicine—is highly esteemed, there will naturally be reservations about changing so vital and familiar a feature of our daily lives, even if some elements of the present system are to be maintained. Nevertheless, there are signs that the public mind is starting to change. Political speeches now regularly refer to a health care crisis. An intensive study in Iowa showed a majority of the 30,000 people polled favor ten major changes in med-

---

[9] The fee-for-service approach is considered particularly inappropriate for the rising volume of chronic conditions discussed under Disease Trends (Sidel and Sidel, 1977).

ical delivery, including fixed hospital fees and preventive health and education (Yankelovich, 1982a). Subjective support is indispensable to the success of a public policy, and the present policy appears to be losing it. General willingness to change, however, is not necessarily support for a specific program of national health insurance.

Whatever the exact ingredients in a reform proposal, it is vital to remember that more is involved than giving the nation a better pill for its health. Like the old policy, national health insurance is a social system which must function in a living, breathing society.

Recognition of societal realities leads to the implementation question, the matter of putting an abstract idea into everyday practice. One issue is obvious: Supporters of free enterprise medicine will actively oppose national health insurance. The AMA has a history of nearly hysterical opposition to government programs. Some members actually called Medicare "fascist control" before it was enacted (Langor, 1975:336). The subsequent acceptance of this health reform shows the unlikelihood of medical professionals sabotaging a national health program, but its opponents claim that enactment would sabotage *other* vital programs. Unless national health insurance is implemented with careful utilization controls, people could overuse the system, swamp its budget, and force the diversion of funds from the solution of other social problems (Feder, Holahan, and Marmor, 1980).

Reformers observe that this danger also exists in the present system's feverish cost increases, a fever that can be brought under control by (a) taking fee setting for medical services out of the hands of care providers (i.e., physicians) and (b) billing individuals for some portion of the cost according to their ability to pay (Seidman, 1977). Such steps toward a practical reform program appear to be persuading some medical professionals. The American Public Health Association and certain groups of

physicians agree that some national health plan should be implemented (Waitzkin, 1983; Pontell, Jesilaw, and Geis, 1982).

Evaluating the Evidence

Although experience teaches that evaluating health care reforms before they are implemented is a risky business, there is a body of evidence on field-tested national health programs in other nations. The best known case is the United Kingdom, in which the National Health Service is financed entirely out of general tax revenues, care is free to all citizens, and physicians are paid primarily by salary and capitation (i.e., a lump sum for each patient) rather than by fee for service. By most objective measures, the British are healthier than we are: they have a longer life expectancy, a lower infant mortality rate, and much less hospitalization and surgery—all at a cheaper cost per capita (Anderson, 1972). Subjectively, the National Health program is the most popular government service in Britain.

Canada may be a better policy reference point because of its broad similarities to the United States. In the Canadian system of comprehensive national health insurance (which has been operating since 1971) the government pays physicians on the fee-for-service basis experts think might remain a facet of care delivery in an American version. Taking a broader view, international studies comparing the United States to several other societies with national health programs suggest that implementing such a policy here would indeed be a more efficient treatment for the social problem of ill health than our present system (Sidel, 1977; U.S. Bureau of the Census, 1980b). The trouble with such studies is simple: however close the parallel, these other societies are not the United States.

Another source of data on the pros and cons of national insurance is a health innovation emerging within the present medical system.

Health maintenance organizations (HMOs) are prepaid insurance plans in which a fixed premium is charged no matter how many medical services you consume. The rationale behind this payment scheme involves economizing through prevention. Because physicians on the HMO staff cannot increase their incomes by ordering extra procedures, they are encouraged to practice preventive medicine that will render expensive and risky treatment unnecessary. The idea seems to work in the real world of *this* society. Since a 1973 federal law which stimulated employer participation in prepaid plans, the HMO model has expanded to cover over 8 million Americans. There are concrete reasons for such rapid growth. HMO subscription costs are substantially lower than those in private insurance plans, mainly because of less hospitalization (Luft et al., 1980). Significantly, such savings are not bought at the price of inferior care. In twenty-seven separate studies evaluating HMO performance, nineteen found the quality of care to be superior to that in other settings; in no case was HMO care found to be inferior (Consumers' Union, 1980). Although HMOs are not without their troubles and complaints, most members appear to be subjectively satisfied with this innovative form of care delivery.

What do HMOs have to do with the free enterprise medicine versus national health insurance debate? The evidence of their effectiveness is a sword (or scalpel) which cuts both ways. On the one hand, it shows the private sector to be capable of ingenious solutions to the social problems associated with medical care. On the other, the solution's genius appears to lie in its cutting out the fee-for-service heart of the free enterprise model. Whichever side deserves the credit, the present private insurance market seems to be slowing HMO development, thus indefinitely delaying access for millions. National health insurance could quickly extend the HMO approach to a rising number of chronically ill Americans for whom fee-for-service medicine seems inappropriate (Sidel and Sidel, 1977).

This is by no means a textbook debate. Much of the evidence here is being cited in speeches supporting or opposing the health-related legislation now before Congress. In the charged atmosphere of subjective concern about health reform, some speak of the implementation of a national health insurance plan in the next few years as "inevitable." Now alerted to the sociological dimensions of health problems and policies, you may exercise your powers as an informed social creator (and voter) to improve the inevitable.

SUMMARY

1 Social factors have documented effects on illness behavior in terms of personal reactions to symptoms, the social role played while sick, and official medical definitions of sickness.

2 Subjective concern about ill health as a social problem has been increasing in spite of a stable (or even improving) national health prognosis. This development is traced to specific health-related features of visibility, expectations, and values.

3 Social background categories such as sex, age, income, and race are demonstrably related to the likelihood of morbidity and mortality. Disease and death are likewise related to social stress and social relationships.

4 The social system of health care in the United States is theoretically viewed as functionally disorganized, rapidly changing, and dominated by profit considerations rather than social needs.

5 The present system of free enterprise medicine is contrasted with the alternative strategy of national health insurance, which implies governmental intrusion into the health care arena, but offers the advantages of universal coverage and coordination according to social needs.

CHAPTER 4

Mental Disorders: Social Bases of Mental Health

To give you some idea of how the mentally ill are being treated in the United States today, I will mention a dirty little secret among some mental health professionals. In some cities, the mentally ill are being "treated" with a bus ticket to another city. Thus one area's problems are reduced by shipping the mentally ill off somewhere else, an unethical practice known as "Greyhound Therapy."

—*Bernard J. Gallagher*, The Sociology of Mental Illness, *1987:370.*

The mass media frequently devote a lot of attention to detailed descriptions of bizarre behavior. Who, for instance, will ever forget the gruesome slayings at the home of actress Sharon Tate by Charlie Manson and members of his "family"? Another mind-boggling case was that of John George Haigh. A man of outward charm, he was actually the notorious English murderer of the late 1940s known as the Acid-Bath Blood Drinker. Haigh's fetishistic thirst for blood was relieved only by shooting a victim through the nape of the neck, making an incision in an artery, and drinking a few inches of blood in a glass. He later disposed of the body by dissolving it in acid. In 1981, a California teenager murdered his 14-year-old girlfriend, hid her body in the woods, and brought dozens of friends to ogle it as if they were at a carnival sideshow. Incredible as it may seem, not a single one of the murderer's friends reported the crime to the police.

Around the same time, a jury was deciding the fate of one of the nation's most vicious sex killers, the now-famous Hillside Strangler. Decades before, another strangler terrified Boston for years by sneaking into women's apartments, murdering them, raping them, cutting out their sexual organs, and hanging pieces of their flesh on picture nails on the walls. More recently, David Berkowitz, popularly known as the Son of Sam, went on a rampage of blasting young couples with a 44-magnum pistol in New York City. When he was arrested, he claimed that his mind was controlled by a neighbor's dog. He now states that he was the hit man for a killer cult.

THE SUBJECTIVE DIMENSION OF MENTAL DISORDER

Clearly these people were all deranged in some manner. But are they representative of the ways mentally disordered people *typically* think

and act? They certainly are not. What they represent is what makes a good news story—one that is interesting and unusual. In 1981, the *New England Journal of Medicine* reported that prime-time television programs are especially likely to portray mentally ill characters as violent. Unfortunately, this gives the public the highly *subjective* impression that "crazy" people rant, rave, murder, and rape. In reality, (or objectively speaking), mentally disordered people are rarely dangerous or assaultive. They typically lead miserable lives (often in secret), have uncontrollable feelings of worthlessness or anxiety, often cannot handle a job, and are faced with personal and social difficulties that seriously affect them, their family, and friends. The anguish of mental illness is vividly illustrated by the woman in the photograph at the beginning of this chapter.

THE OBJECTIVE DIMENSION OF MENTAL DISORDER

Mental disorder is not only an agonizing personal experience but also a major social problem, as evidenced by a large number of studies reporting that an alarmingly high percentage of the American population is mentally disordered. Although there is a wide array of estimates, the National Institute of Mental Health reported that in 1984 approximately 20 percent of Americans had some type of mental disorder. Additionally, perhaps 80 percent of the population have mild psychiatric symptoms at some point in their lives.

What is particularly distressing is that the prevalence of mental disorder (the total number of cases at a particular time) appears to have grown since World War II. It was during the war itself that the problem first became evident. Psychiatrists evaluating men for the service rejected an estimated 1.8 million among the 15 million examined because of alleged psychiatric disabilities. This high psychiatric rejection rate stirred the government and the public to action, and in 1946, mental health care became a serious concern. The National Mental Health Act was passed that year, and three years later the National Institute of Mental Health was established. Records of the number of episodes of mental disorder were compiled with greater care, and over the years they showed an estimated sevenfold increase in the prevalence of mental disorder between the end of World War II and 1975 (Dohrenwend, 1975). Although some of this increase is probably due to better reporting methods and a broader definition of mental disorder, much of it may simply result from the increased stress of modern living in the United States.

There were 1.7 million cases of treated mental disorder in 1955. By 1975, that figure rose to 6.4 million cases. Today the number is well over 10 million. These figures do not include the 6 million people defined as mentally retarded or the 1 in 8 Americans that suffer from serious depression at some point in their lives. They also do not include patients under the care of psychiatrists in private practice, clinical psychologists, various types of counselors, or psychiatric social workers. Certainly many more people are being treated today than a few decades ago. However, there has been an actual decline in the mental hospital population because of a widespread movement toward outpatient care. This is largely the result of tranquilizing drugs which were discovered in the 1950s.

Estimates of the rate of mental disorder are drawn from studies using known treated cases as the criterion for the prevalence of mental disorder. Certainly many other people have real mental health problems and never receive help. How many of these people are there? Some researchers have tried to answer this question by studying large groups of people who are not being treated to see what the real rate (*true prevalence*) of mental disorder is. They report that between 20 and 30 million Americans actually need some kind of mental health care, although only a fraction receives it. The rest go unrecognized.

Perhaps no other issue better exemplifies the dramatic difference between the objective and subjective aspects of social problems than mental disorder. Because so many victims go untreated, the objective dimension of the problem is broader than any official statistics indicate. Yet even the official statistics would shock most people because mental disorder has traditionally been denied, ignored, or explained away as something else. Only recently have magazine articles, television programs, and books on mental health helped to improve public awareness. Still, the gap between the actual extent of the problem and the average person's subjective awareness is enormous. In fact, mental disorder never even appears in Gallup surveys of Americans' opinions concerning the issues that are important social problems. This tremendous gap between the objective and subjective dimensions of mental disorder as a social problem is partly due to the low *visibility* of mental disorder in the popular press, as well as the fact that many Americans have *values* about mental disorder which minimize the objective harm associated with it.

The public is also unaware of the total costs of mental disorder to American society. Although the costs cannot be precisely determined, a very conservative estimate is offered by the Alcohol, Drug Abuse, and Mental Health Administration, which, in 1982, figured the direct costs to be 40.3 billion dollars annually. This figure includes private fees and taxpayer dollars. The average annual cost of caring for each patient in a state mental hospital alone is over 15,000 dollars. There are other indirect costs that should be added to the direct costs of patient care, such as a 25 percent loss of productivity to the workforce due to employee illness and inefficiency. More difficult to estimate are the increases in divorce, crime, drug addiction, and child abuse that stem from mental disorder. Objectively, mental health problems may be the most extensive and expensive health problems of all, yet the public knows very little about them.

CONCEPTS OF MENTAL DISORDER

Another question not fully understood is just what constitutes mental disorder. There are some useful everyday definitions, such as behavior which exceeds the tolerance of others. It is, for instance, all right to talk to God, but woe to the person who hears God talking back. Others view mental disorder as behavior which is inappropriate to the circumstances, such as laughing when a tragedy occurs. Still others feel the seriousness of the behavior separates the mentally disordered from people who are simply eccentric. Thus the person who babbles incoherently and walks naked in the street is seen in a light different than the old lady who lives as a recluse. Of course, many people employ no definitions at all and indiscriminately label deviants as "weirdos," "nuts," "kooks," and "lunatics."[1] These slang terms are widely used in our so-called enlightened era.

Although the public shows some very primitive attitudes toward mental disorder, there was a time when beliefs were even more backward. Some preliterate people believed mental disorder was the work of Satan. The course of treatment was to exorcise the devil from the person through prayers, loud noises, or foul odors. If these did not work, the person would be whipped and starved. One particularly deadly and barbaric practice was *trephination*, which involved chipping holes in the person's skull so the devil could escape.

Ancient Greeks and Romans assumed mental disorder was a disturbance within the body itself. Hippocrates, for instance, believed the causes stemmed from an imbalance among the four "humors" of the body (yellow bile, black bile, blood, and phlegm). However, in ancient Palestine there was a resurgence of the idea that insanity was connected with the supernatural, and magical practices were designed to cast out the demons of madness as preliterate people had done centuries before.

The mentally disordered were never more abused than during the Middle Ages. In London (circa 1400), one of the first mental institutions was built—the Bethlehem Hospital, commonly referred to as Bedlam. The conditions were appalling. In fact, the hospital even sold tickets to the public so they could gawk at the more violent patients ranting in their cells! At this time, treatment was partly in the hands of priests who believed they were dealing with the devil's work. Consequently, they would sprinkle the disordered person with holy water and shout obscene words at Satan to hurt his pride. By the end of the fifteenth century, many unfortunates were labeled as witches and accused of causing pestilence and floods. The medieval Catholic[2] and Protestant churches furthered the fear of witches and prompted a multitude of arrests, hangings, and other grotesque executions of suspected witches, many of whom were actually suffering from mental disorder.

During the eighteenth century in Europe, the mentally disordered were no longer killed or tortured. Instead they were chained and confined in jail with criminals. In the United States, public insane asylums kept them isolated from the rest of society. The first such asylum—the Lunatic Hospital at Williamsburg, Virginia—was opened in 1769.

Humane treatment was begun in France through the efforts of Phillipe Pinel (1745-

---

[1] The term *lunatic* was originally based on the idea that abnormal behavior was caused by lunar or astrological forces.

[2] In 1484 Pope Innocent V11 issued a papal doctrine urging the clergy to search exhaustively for witches. This was largely responsible for a violent and tragic period. In western Europe alone, about half a million people were executed for being witches.

1826), a founder of modern psychiatry. At the Bicêtre Hospital, he removed the patients' chains, allowed them access to hospital grounds, and instructed the staff to employ kindness. Many patients who were considered incurable recovered. This policy of non-restraint, promulgated by Pinel and other reformers of the time, such as Tuke, was tested in the United States by Benjamin Rush (1745–1813), the founder of American psychiatry. He introduced social reforms based on humane treatment at the Pennsylvania Hospital. However, some of his treatment methods were far from progressive. He not only employed blood-letting but also invented the gyrator (a rotating board to which patients were strapped) and the tranquilizer (a chair to which patients were strapped with their heads in a fixed position).

In 1841, Dorothea Lynde Dix (1802–1887), a Massachusetts school teacher, began a lengthy campaign to eliminate the deplorable and brutal conditions prevalent in asylums. She is responsible for the system of state-supported hospitals that still exists today. Even though Dix was an important force in dramatically increasing the portion of the mentally disordered population that received help, she was disappointed that mental patients were still not being cured after her hospitals were built. Again the hospital conditions deteriorated. In the early 1900s, Clifford Beers, a former patient, played a vital role in attempting to reform institutional practices. Things improved slightly, but public mental hospitals still had the reputation of being "snake pits."

During the nineteenth and twentieth centuries, a considerable number of shifts occurred in psychiatrists' concepts of the causes of mental disorder. In the 1800s, most psychiatrists rigidly adhered to the belief that pathological bodily conditions and brain tissue dysfunctions were solely responsible for abnormal behavior. This perspective became known as the *somatogenic* view, since it looked in the body (soma)

for the origin of mental disorder.[3] In the late nineteenth century, a great struggle occurred between somatogenic theorists and a new school of thought which held that mental disorders could be caused solely by a disturbance in a person's psychological state. This approach, known as the *psychogenic* view, was first established within modern psychiatry through the study of hysteria, a condition which appeared to be purely somatic. Hysterical patients suffered from such symptoms as loss of sight, mutism, deafness, or anesthesia of a body part. In France, Charcot and Janet hypnotized normal persons and demonstrated that they could produce hysterical symptoms simply through suggestion. They also discovered that if hysterical patients are hypnotized, they no longer manifest symptoms. Clearly the disorder was the result of abnormal psychological processes.

A major breakthrough in psychiatric research occurred in the late 1800s through the classic studies of Sigmund Freud and Joseph Breuer. They found that the psychological problems that led to hysteria occurred during childhood and were deeply hidden in an unconscious part of the personality. Freud developed a number of techniques to analyze the unconscious, such as the interpretation of dreams. His discoveries and theories of mental disorder provided the cornerstone of *psychoanalysis,* a lengthy and intense "talking out" approach between a patient and therapist.

Until recently, psychoanalysis was the dominant perspective in psychiatric research and treatment. Currently there is a *medicalization* of mental disorder. This means abnormal behavior is defined as a medical problem which should be treated by physicians only. This is partly a reflection of the inordinate political power the medical profession has to define its

---

[3] One important piece of research that supported the somatogenic view involved the study of *dementia paralytica,* a condition in which persons suffer from paralysis and the loss of their mental powers. Fournier and Krafft-Ebing discovered that this disorder resulted from untreated syphilis.

own area of concern. Alternative professions, such as clinical psychology and psychiatric social work, are not taken as seriously as other possible approaches. Another reason for the medicalization of mental health problems is the limited success of social approaches to mental health care, such as the community-based mental health clinics. As we will see later in this chapter, the medical approach has provided some important discoveries about the causes and treatment of mental disorder. However, because it is a one-sided approach, it hinders an awareness of how social and psychological forces influence mental health. At a time when psychiatric research is still in the dark regarding the real nature of mental disorder, any such unilateral view can seriously impede progress.

DIFFICULTIES IN DIAGNOSING MENTAL DISORDER

Mental disorder cannot be diagnosed in the same way as an illness of the body because the mind is an abstract concept, not simply a physical entity. As the eminent British psychiatrist Sir Aubrey Lewis points out, attempts to diagnose mental disorder use a host of terms undefinable in themselves, such as lack of joy of life, no will to live, discontentment, and inability to adjust.

A further diagnostic problem is that indexes of mental disorder are relative because the *social context* in which a particular behavior occurs affects whether it is adjudged normal or abnormal. There are numerous examples of this. The seventeenth century religious leaders who had witches and heretics burned at the stake were considered respected members of the community, but today they would be committed to an institution. A sexually promiscuous woman is called a whore or a nymphomaniac, but the sexually active male is lauded for his talent with females and considered to be a real stud. To many people, those who speak unintelligibly are definitely abnormal unless

they act that way in a church where speaking in tongues is common. In the United States, political dissent is often praised, but in the Soviet Union, many dissenters are sent to insane asylums. This includes poets, writers, and intellectuals who would be highly revered in the West. In 1986, a battle raged over the severe distress and anxiety some women suffer in association with menstrual cycles. The American Psychiatric Association wanted to include it in the basic manual of mental illnesses, but the Association of Women Psychiatrists argued that such maladies are physical and that lumping them with mental illness will contribute to discrimination against women.

Certainly the social context of behavior affects whether it is diagnosed as abnormal or acceptable. However, this is not the only diagnostic problem, since there are certain forms of behavior found only among certain people of the world. One such culturally specific disorder is *pibloktoq*, sometimes called *Arctic hysteria*, which occurs among the Polar Eskimos of the Thule District of northern Greenland. At first, the victims are irritable and socially withdrawn. Then they suddenly become wildly excited and may tear off their clothing, break furniture, attempt to walk on ceilings, shout obscenely, throw objects, eat feces, dive into snowdrifts, or jump off icebergs. Eventually they undergo convulsive seizures, collapse, and coma. When the victims recover, they behave perfectly normal and have no recollection of what occurred.

Another exotic disorder is the *whitiko psychosis* which occurs among male Ojibwa Indians in Canada. The victim becomes obsessed with the idea that he is possessed by the spirit of the whitiko monster and perceives those around him as fat, appetizing animals which he wishes to eat. At this stage he is usually killed, since the Ojibwa believe the craving for human flesh will never leave once it has been fulfilled. Finally, males in mainland China suffer from a problem unknown elsewhere. It is called *shook yang* and involves the overwhelming fear that the penis will dissolve from masturbation and nocturnal emission.

Clearly, it is next to impossible to diagnose mental disorder in a completely objective and cross-culturally meaningful way, but how good are American psychiatrists at diagnosing members of their own culture? Practical experience has shown that certain sets of symptoms tend to occur together in what is known as a *syndrome*. However, psychiatric diagnoses are still much more difficult to render than strict medical diagnoses. In fact, much of the diagnosis depends on the theoretical orientation and depth of knowledge of the psychiatrist. In addition, psychiatrists are susceptible to suggestions in their diagnoses. In one study (Temerlin, 1968), therapists were asked to diagnose interviewees who were normal. One group was given no prior information. A second group of therapists was told the people were quite normal. A third group was told the interview was part of a job selection process for an industrial research scientist. A fourth group was told it was part of a sanity hearing, and the fifth group was told that the interviewees were mentally ill. Although the interviews were the same for all five groups, only the fifth group diagnosed the people as disordered.

Aside from suggestion, another reason diagnoses are often unreliable is that they are made on the basis of only brief personal contact. This is risky because symptoms can change over time, at least the symptoms seen at the first interview. Although diagnoses conducted under ideal circumstances (including a number of interviews) are usually more valid, the experiments to assess the validity of diagnosis rarely employ favorable conditions. They will, instead, parade normal people and disordered people before a panel of psychiatrists, give them a few minutes to ask questions, and then expect a very specific diagnosis. Consequently, it is not unusual that the psychiatrists in the experiments agree with one another less than 50 percent of the time (Ash, 1949; Chodoff, 1960;

Stoller and Giertsma, 1963). There is, however, another side to the question of diagnostic reliability. When the psychiatrists use broad diagnostic categories, such as healthy and abnormal, instead of very specific diagnoses, they are much more consistent in their opinions. In one such study (Rosenzweig, 1961), a team of therapists agreed 96 percent of the time.

The problems of diagnosis received national attention in 1973 when David Rosenhan, a psychiatrist, studied admissions procedures at mental hospitals around the country. Specifically, Rosenhan wanted to see what would happen if perfectly normal people applied for admission, so he arranged for some of his associates to present themselves at twelve different hospitals. They were instructed to complain of hearing a voice saying a word such as "hollow," "empty," or "thud." All of the pseudopatients were diagnosed as severely disordered and admitted. However, the most alarming outcome occurred when they acted normal after they were admitted and no longer claimed to hear voices. Not a single staff member of any hospital realized they did not belong there! The only people who caught on to the experiment were the real patients. The pseudopatients were held for an average of nineteen days. During that time, all their behavior was interpreted on the basis of their respective diagnoses. One woman, for instance, became so frustrated with the situation that she began taking handwritten notes about her experiences. She was further diagnosed as having compulsive handwriting!

After publishing his exposé, Rosenhan warned another mental hospital that he would be sending a pseudopatient there between January and March. Of the 193 patients admitted during that period, 43 were designated as pseudopatients by the staff. Actually, Rosenhan had not sent any fake patients! Such imprecision in the diagnosis of mental disorder is a major obstacle to gaining accurate knowledge on how to effectively handle this major social problem. As Rosenhan notes:

We seem unable to acknowledge that we simply don't know. The needs for diagnosis and remediation of behavioral and emotional problems are enormous. But rather than acknowledge that we are just embarking on understanding, we continue to label patients...as if in those words we had captured the essence of understanding. The facts of the matter are that we have known for a long time that diagnoses are not useful or reliable...(Rosenhan, 1973).

Psychiatrists are also frequently unable to predict how patients will behave once they are released from a mental hospital (Greenley, 1979). This is especially evident in their inability to predict whether a person will be violent sometime in the future (Steadman and Ribner, 1981). Of course, it is understandable that predictions of dangerousness are inaccurate. After all, they are made in an institutional setting, far removed from the time and situation in the open community where the dangerous behavior occurs. To compensate for this problem, psychiatrists tend to overpredict dangerousness (Levinson and Ramsay, 1979). This serves to protect them from censure by the community when a released patient causes harm.

The problems of psychiatric diagnosis are further compounded when they occur in a court of law. In many states if a person is not responsible for a crime, then the person is not guilty by reason of *insanity.* Insanity is a legal concept which has no technical status in psychiatry. It is used most often to refer to persons who suffer from *psychosis,* a severe mental disorder involving loss of contact with reality.

One law designed to separate insane people who commit criminal acts from mentally competent people who do so is the widely used M'Naghten rule. It provides that defendants may establish a defense of insanity if they did not know they were doing something wrong in the eyes of society. However, there are many people who suffer from mental disorder and realize that they are doing something wrong. Their problem is they do not care because they lack a conscience. Because of the primitive decision-making process underlying the M'Naghten rule, they are sent to prison rather than a psychiatric facility where they might be helped. Of course, this was not true in the case of presidential assailant John Hinckley, who successfully pleaded insanity and was sent to a mental hospital. Because the case was widely publicized, the public received the subjective impression that criminals frequently avoid jail through an insanity defense. The objective truth is that the insanity defense is rarely employed, and when it is, it usually does not work.

VARIETIES OF MENTAL DISORDER

Clearly, what constitutes a mental disorder depends, in part, upon social definitions and what professionals say it is (masturbation and homosexuality, for instance, used to be considered illnesses). Today the official position is that a condition qualifies as a disorder if it causes distress or disability to the person. Ideally, a classification system should be based on cause, but since the causes of mental disorder are so elusive, classification is actually carried out on the basis of manifest symptoms. Fortunately, there is a growing consensus on the subtypes of psychiatric disorders, largely due to the efforts of the World Health Organization (WHO).

In 1980, the American Psychiatric Association (APA) published the third edition of the *Diagnostic and Statistical Manual of Mental Disorders (DSM-III).* It represented a great expansion of the definition of mental disorder. While this may prove to be a real help in making more accurate diagnoses, some feel that the APA included too many behaviors and created a psychiatric imperialism. This complaint is voiced especially loudly among health insurance companies, which, for obvious reasons, would prefer fewer categories. Before *DSM-III,* there were essentially four major categories of disorder. They are briefly described below:

Neurosis

The central symptom of all neuroses is *anxiety,* a felt fear from within. Neurosis takes different forms depending on how the personality attempts to manage the anxiety. Some neurotics have fears (*phobias*) of specific situations or things. Others (*obsessive-compulsives*) engage in repetitive rituals such as hand washing or checking and rechecking the door lock or the jets on the stove. Still others (*hypochondriacs*) believe they suffer from physical ailments which, in fact, do not exist. Neurosis is one of the milder forms of disorder and, although it may cause anguish, neurotic people are usually able to function on an everyday basis.

Closely related is *anorexia nervosa,* the intense fear of becoming obese. Anorexic persons, almost always teenage females, refuse to eat and consequently experience significant weight loss. Another eating disorder, often found among female college students, is *bulimia.* Bulimics go on eating binges (typically consuming about 40,000 calories) followed by self-induced vomiting or heavy use of laxatives. There is a case in the literature of a girl who, for dessert one night, ate a candy bar, two bags of cookies, an éclair, three sandwiches, crackers and dip, a jar of peanut butter and half a jar of jelly, raisins and berries, two slices of bread with cheese and mayonnaise, a large pizza, and four bowls of cereal. Then she made herself throw up. A 1986 Stanford University study found that 1 in 8 high school sophomores tries to lose weight by vomiting or using laxatives or other drugs.

Psychosis

Psychotics are severely disturbed people who have actually lost contact with reality. The symptoms of the psychoses (often referred to as the *functional* psychoses because of their assumed psychological origins) are very bizarre. The most common form is *schizophrenia* in which a schizophrenic's thought processes become so disordered that the person may regu-

larly fantasize, have delusions, and/or hallucinate. The other common psychosis is the manic-depressive illness in which the person undergoes extreme mood swings involving excitement and/or depression. Additionally, there are *paranoid disorders* in which a person suffers from persecutory or grandiose delusions.

Organic Psychosis

People with this condition are also severely disordered, but their problems stem from a biological cause such as cerebral arteriosclerosis, which can cause senility. Other types include cranial infection, brain trauma, mental retardation, epilepsy, and alcoholic psychosis.

Personality Disorders

People with personality disorders are free of neurotic and psychotic symptoms, but they behave pathologically. Many of the personality disorders are simply conditions which typically precede a full-blown psychosis or neurosis. One that does not lead to another condition is the *antisocial personality disorder,* a widely researched condition that is often used interchangeable with the term personality disorder. Antisocial people regularly violate social mores, and can rape, murder, or steal with no remorse because they lack a conscience. Traditionally, the sexual deviations have been listed as personality disorders as well.

It is hoped that the greater specificity of disorders in *DSM-III* will aid in future diagnoses. However, because it will take some time for the new nomenclature to be widely adopted, the research reported here will employ the traditional fourfold breakdown: neurosis, functional psychosis (schizophrenia and manic-depression), organic psychosis, and personality disorder.

THE CAUSES OF MENTAL DISORDER

There are a number of theories regarding the *etiology* (causes) of mental disorder. Although today there is an emphasis on medical explanations, research since the time of Freud has shown quite convincingly that social and psychological forces often play an important role. While this is particularly true for the neuroses and personality disorders, even schizophrenia may be psychosocial in origin, as evidenced by a large amount of research showing that family socialization has an effect in precipitating the psychosis. Schizophrenics frequently come from families that are importantly different from "normal" families. Sometimes they are simply impervious to the children's needs. Sometimes the children are raised by parents who constantly subject them to contradictory messages. They may, for instance, communicate feelings of warmth and feelings of rejection at the same time, putting the child in a position of *double bind*. They are damned if they do and damned if they don't.

Another pathological family pattern conducive to schizophrenia is the *schismatic* family. Here the family is divided into two warring camps, each headed by a parent who forces the child to choose a side. Where the family is *skewed,* one parent dominates the group, usually through excessive dependency on the other parent. In the process, the child's needs are ignored.

Macrosocial forces also contribute to the problem of mental disorder. This is especially apparent during recessions and economic downturns when the unemployment rate is high (Marshall and Funch, 1979). Brenner (1973), examining admissions data of New York state mental hospitals from 1842 to 1967, found that admissions increase significantly when unemployment climbs, a pattern recently reconfirmed by Dooley and Catalano (1984). A more dramatic example of the effect of unemployment on mental health is reported by Srole (1978), who found the psychological status of people raised during the Great Depression significantly worse than that of those raised later.

The psychiatric costs of recessions and depressions have been explained in a number of ways. It may be that economic change causes *new* disorder by imposing stress. It is also possible that economic downturns affect the tolerance and ability of family and friends to care for people who are *already* disordered. It is interesting to note that unemployment is especially likely to cause depression among men, particularly those without supportive marital relations or ties to the extended family or peer groups (Gore, 1978). A 1985 national sample of married couples found that economic hardship is increased by being young and having young children. Economic hardship, in turn, increases both spouses' depression levels (Ross and Huber, 1985).

Certainly no list of social causes of mental disorder would be complete without mention of the devastating effects of war. These are particularly evident in long-term war zones such as Northern Ireland, Israel, Lebanon, and Cambodia. The personality effects of extended chaos are immeasurable. The risks are especially great for the children of war, the ones raised in environments where fear, torture, mutilation, bombings, and hatred are part of their "normal" lives. It would not be surprising that many of these children grow into bigoted, antisocial adults, since they were raised in a world that was emotionally disturbed.

While many factors contribute to psychiatric problems, the major theories can be classified into four groups: the medical (genetic and biochemical), psychoanalytic, behaviorist, and labeling theories. They are briefly summarized below:

Genetic Theory

There is persuasive evidence that some mental disorders, particularly schizophrenia and manic-depression, are partially caused by genetic factors. The children of schizophrenics have an unusually high probability of becoming schizophrenic themselves. Approximately 10 percent of children with one schizophrenic parent and 50 percent of those with two schizophrenic parents also develop the disorder. Of course, it is possible that this is the result of being *raised* by schizophrenics rather than heredity per se. A more direct test of the etiological role of genes in schizophrenia is to measure how often (*concordance rate*)[4] both members of a pair of identical twins exhibit schizophrenic symptoms. Identical twins can be alarmingly similar. For example, England's Chaplin twins, although not necessarily schizophrenic, seem like halves of a single personality. They are 37-year-old identical twins who dress alike, walk in step, take two-hour baths together, and frequently talk—and sometimes swear—in unison. If separated, even for a moment, they wail, scream, and wet their pants simultaneously.

F. J. Kallman (1953), the most widely cited of the genetic researchers, reports an 86.7 percent concordance rate among monozygotic (identical) twins where one twin is a diagnosed schizophrenic. This is an *average* of identical twins who had not lived together for some years as well as those who were raised together since birth. In the nonseparated group, the concordance rate is 91.5 percent, but in the separated group, it drops to 77.6 percent. In other words, concordance decreases when the social environment is changed.

Research by Gottesman and Shields (1973) has helped define the role of heredity in schizophrenia. They took fifty-seven identical twin sets in which one twin was a diagnosed schizophrenic and divided the sets into four groups separated by severity of symptoms. They found that concordance increased as severity of symptoms increased. This suggests that severe cases of schizophrenia may result from a genetic defect, while milder cases may not be related to genes at all.

[4] This frequency, known as a *concordance rate*, is expressed as a percentage.

Some research has been conducted to counter the criticism that twin studies do not adequately separate nature (genes) from nurture (environment). Heston (1966) traced the psychiatric history of people born to schizophrenic mothers in state hospitals. The infants were separated from their mothers at birth and raised in foster homes. Over 16 percent of the children became schizophrenic, well above the average for the population at large. Other studies of the adopted-away offspring of schizophrenics support the idea that there is a *vulnerability* to schizophrenia which is transmitted genetically (Kety et al., 1971; Garmezy, 1978).

The evidence that manic-depression may result from heredity is rather impressive. Rosenthal (1970) measured concordance among manic-depressives and their immediate families and found that the family members are ten times more likely to be manic-depressive than people in the general population. The rates of manic-depression among monozygotic and dizygotic (fraternal) twins whose co-twins are diagnosed manic-depressive are revealing. It is well documented that the concordance rate among fraternal twins is approximately 13 percent, while the rate among identical twins is over 60 percent (Gershan, Targum, and Kessler, 1977). The fact that the pathology is more common among relatives of manic-depressives than in the general population, and that it increases as genetic similarity increases, lends strong support to genetic theory. Research by Weitkamp and Stancer (1981) has helped pinpoint the specific gene(s) that cause susceptibility to depression. They report it is one gene, or possibly more, at a specific point on the sixth chromosome. It is found near a cluster of genes that control a part of the body's immune system.

There is also some evidence that the antisocial personality disorder may have a genetic foundation. Antisocials, almost always males, suffer from a defect in their consciences. As a result, they can commit immoral acts such as rape and murder and feel no remorse. The disorder may be the result of an extra male (Y) chromosome. This chromosomal abnormality (XYY) could cause an excessive amount of aggressive behavior which can lead to antisocial acts. However, the XYY pattern, considered to produce "supermales," may account for only 1.5 percent of antisocial behavior (Rosenthal, 1970).

The strength of genetic theory depends upon the disorder under consideration. With certain conditions, such as some of the organic disorders, genes play an obvious role. With other disorders, such as neurosis, genetic factors are inconsequential. Schizophrenia and manic-depression seem to be somewhere in between. That is, genes appear to be frequently but not universally involved since concordance among monozygotics is not 100 percent. At this writing, the best guess is that what is transmitted genetically is a *vulnerability*—a predisposing factor but not a sufficient cause. The vulnerability must be combined with certain environmental stresses (such as double-bind parenting) to produce the full-blown psychosis.

Biochemical Theory

The other school of medical thought is biochemical. It is based on the proposition that mental disorder is caused by an imbalance in body chemistry. Actually, the genetic and biochemical perspectives are compatible since genetic factors may well lead to a biochemical imbalance. Consistently, biochemical research appears to be relevant to the same groups of disorders which have been linked with heredity. Of course, there is much evidence to support biochemical correlates of many of the organic disorders, but disturbed biochemistry is also reported among schizophrenics and manic-depressives.

A number of specific chemicals, when present in abnormal amounts, are believed to cause schizophrenia. Some researchers postulate schizophrenia stems from a metabolic failure causing a deficiency in *serotonin*, a cerebral hormone. Researchers found a protein substance, *taraxein*, in the blood serum of schizophrenics and claimed it was responsible for their mental condition (Heath and Krupp, 1967). They hypothesized that taraxein interacts with other bodily chemicals to produce a toxic substance resembling a copper-containing globulin. Autopsies on schizophrenics uncovered amounts of taraxein which correlated strongly with the severity of the psychosis preceding death; the more taraxein present, the more serious the psychotic symptoms had been. A third biochemical theory holds that schizophrenia results from excessive amounts of *dopamine*, producing the exact opposite condition of people with Parkinson's disease. In the 1980s there has been much speculation that schizophrenia is linked to opiatelike chemicals manufactured in the brain.

There is growing acceptance of the theory that biochemical factors play a role in the origin of manic-depression, particularly because the disorder responds so favorably to antidepressant pharmaceuticals, such as lithium carbonate. One biochemical hypothesis involves electrolyte metabolism. Two of the electrolytes, sodium and potassium chloride, play an important role in the functioning of the nervous system. Alterations in the distribution of sodium and potassium affect the excitability of the nerve cell. Manic-depressives are reported to have elevated intracellular sodium levels. Another biochemical hypothesis postulates that mania and depression stem from fluctuations in the metabolic system. Metabolic dysfunction is suggested by a number of symptoms found among manic-depressives, such as loss of appetite, insomnia, cessation of menstruation, heart rate alterations, skin difficulties, and gastrointestinal disorders. These symptoms may appear because the autonomic nervous system is operating in a deranged manner, resulting in the production of abnormal amounts of epinephrine. Depression may be caused by a deficiency of epinephrine, and mania by an excess of the same substance.

Biochemical researchers have made some discoveries about antisocial personalities as well. They report that antisocials may be less sensitive to social mores because of a defect in the autonomic nervous system that in turn reduces arousal levels. Simply stated, antisocials may act immoral and break the law because normal modes of pleasure do not excite them. If this is true, then they should act like normal people if their arousal levels are increased. Schachter and Latone (1964) tested this hypothesis by injecting a group of antisocials with adrenaline, a chemical which stimulates the autonomic nervous system. Under the influence of the chemical, they did act more like normal people with consciences.

All the biochemical theories are subject to one very important criticism: Simply because mental disorders and abnormal biochemistry are found together does not necessarily mean biochemistry is causing the disorder. It is quite possible that disturbed biochemistry is the result of the disorder rather than the cause. This criticism is particularly relevant in light of common knowledge of how emotions can cause physiological changes, such as when fear induces increased heart rate and sweating.

Psychoanalytic Theory

Psychiatric researchers are in general agreement that psychosocial factors play an important role in the etiology of certain disorders, such as the neuroses, sexual disorders, and some of the personality disorders. Most psychiatrists (not psychologists) hold to the psychoanalytic theory, or at least some variant of it. Essentially, the theory rests upon the idea that unconscious motivations stem from life experiences, especially childhood experiences.

Initiated by the work of Sigmund Freud, psychoanalytic theory holds that the personality is composed of three interdependent parts. One, the *id*, consists of biological drives, such

as sex and aggression. The *ego*, acquired in early childhood, acts as a mediator between the pleasure-seeking id and social reality as well as between the id and the moral component of the personality, known as the *superego* (commonly referred to as the conscience). These three personality components must be in harmony for mental health to be enjoyed. If any particular part dominates the personality, the groundwork is laid for a psychiatric problem.

What causes a component of the personality to be unusually demanding or weak? Psychoanalysts believe the answer lies in the infant and childhood years—the time when the personality is being formed. This period is crucial because the social experiences that occur then can have lasting effects on the individual's makeup. These years are divided into what psychoanalysts call *psychosexual* stages, specific periods of maturation during which needs connected with certain body parts strive for satisfaction: first the oral zone, then the anal zone, and then the genital zone. If everything proceeds normally, the developing personality continues to move through the remaining stages of development (adolescence and young adulthood) toward full and healthy maturation.

Unfortunately, not everyone experiences a conflict-free childhood. Some undergo severe traumas that cause mental disorder. Freud reported that traumas often arise from a disturbance in the parent-child relationship, as in the case of the mother who provided little love to her infant or the child who was severely punished for failing to live up to parental toilet training demands. Contemporary psychoanalysts feel that any number of threatening interpersonal childhood experiences can inflict severe damage, including achievement failure in school or social rejection by one's peers. These conflicts cause an arrest of personality development at a particular psychosexual stage. This phenomenon is known as *fixation,* and psychoanalysts contend that fixations at specific stages lead to particular types of disorder. The unloved infant, for example, fixated at the oral stage, is likely to turn into a socially withdrawn adult, and may eventually become schizophrenic.

Psychoanalysts believe personality defects are deeply hidden in the unconscious recesses of the mind. Therefore, the only way to effect cure is to analyze a person's unconscious motivations and memories. That is why psychoanalysts who treat disturbed people use a variety of techniques to gain access to the unconscious, such as dream interpretation and hypnosis.

The psychoanalytic theory of mental disorder has been criticized on a number of grounds. However, it is important to separate the valid criticisms from those based on ignorance. Many psychologists, for instance, dismiss Freudian views without completely studying them. Some activist groups, such as radical feminists, often voice anti-Freudian slogans simply because of a few concepts such as penis envy. One *substantive* criticism of the theory is that it is too deterministic in assuming one's personality is chained to the past and therefore unable to grow and change. The theory has also been validly criticized for emphasizing the parent-child relationship to the point where it seems as if other forces in the psychosocial environment play no active role. Psychoanalysts have also been criticized from a sociological perspective for being biased toward Western culture and not accounting for socialization practices of other societies, particularly preliterate ones.

Behaviorist Theory

Behaviorists hold that mental disorder results from *learning*, a change of behavior that takes place through practice or experience. While behaviorism has been applied mainly to neurosis (particularly phobias), there is some evidence that it may be relevant to the etiology of other disorders, such as the functional psychoses. There are different learning processes by which abnormal behavior is developed. In *conditioning*, the behavior results from a pairing of a particular object or experience with intense anxiety, as when a person develops a phobia toward automobiles after having been in a bad accident.

Another behaviorist mode of learning is the process of *modeling*. This occurs when significant others encourage abnormal behavior. Often the significant others are parents who are disordered themselves. Thus, the children become like the parents because of the natural tendency of children to imitate their elders. For example, overprotective parents who constantly warn their kids about physical health may be raising hypochondriacs. Sometimes modeling may be at work in unusual phenomena such as group hysteria. In 1987, for example, sixty-three employees and shoppers at a New Jersey department store became lightheaded and nauseous in chain reaction form. Hospital tests showed nothing physically wrong with any of them.

Behaviorists have been criticized for not separating the symptoms and causes of mental disorder. As a result, they may be examining only surface behavior and therefore ignoring underlying etiology. Unlike psychoanalysts, behaviorists do not recognize the existence of an unconscious or believe that the social experiences which lead to disorders necessarily occur only during childhood. While psychoanalysis and behaviorism share the idea that mental disorder stems from psychosocial experiences, all parallels end there. For the most part, these two perspectives are at serious odds with each other.

Labeling Theory

Labeling theory is a reaction to the failure of medicine to fully explain the origin of mental disorder, and also to the arbitrary ways in which psychiatric diagnoses are reportedly made. Some labeling theorists, such as Thomas Szasz, are themselves psychiatrists, but most are sociologists.

Labeling theorists believe that psychiatrists do more to create mental disorder than to cure it. This idea is prominent in many of Szasz's books (1970, 1974, 1978), in which he insists that mental disorder does not exist but is simply a label applied to a socially powerless person who has committed a deviant act. The act was much like one committed by all people at some time in their lives. Some, however, were caught by an authority figure and labeled as crazy. Although they may not have had anything more than problems in living, their behavior *becomes* what is labeled as the disorder. This occurs through a process by which the individual moves from *primary deviance* to *secondary deviance*. Primary deviance is the original deviant act, which may have had a wide variety of causes. Secondary deviance results from being caught and *labeled* a deviant. At this point, the person may unconsciously adopt a prescribed set of role-related behaviors that are consistent with the label, such as being a "good mental patient." Labeling theorists believe some people prefer this situation over the intolerable conditions of their lives in outside society. It is a *strategy* adopted as a means of escaping the reality of an unlivable world. Recently, the labeling approach to mental illness based on the reactions of *others* has been developed to include the notion of *self*-labeling as well (Thoits, 1985).

Closely related to the labeling theory view is the *symbolic interactionist* view (Rosenberg, 1984). Although both theories focus on the societal reaction to mental illness, symbolic interactionism rests on the idea that mental health and mental illness are the result of role-taking success or failure.

Some tenets of labeling theorists appear to be quite valid among certain groups of people. One such group is women who become severely depressed at menopause. These women are a blatant example of the secondary and harmful influence of labels on mental health. Interestingly, the women who succumb to menopausal depression are the very ones who believe the social stereotypes of what supposedly happens to women at this stage of life. The stereotypes describe hot flashes and impending madness, the very symptoms these women report. What they are reporting, however, is a self-fulfilling prophecy; they experience what they expect. There is much evidence for this. First, menopausal depression cannot be the result of hormonal changes since replacement hormone therapy has no effect at all. Second, the women who are susceptible to the disorder are not those busy with a career but housewives whose self-definitions center on having children and raising them. When both functions are gone, they feel worthless and become depressed.

Others who fit the labeling theorists' predictions are people committed to mental hospitals, as was evident in the Rosenhan study of pseudopatients. A solid body of research clearly indicates that the inappropriate attitudes and expectations placed on these people often make them worse. In fact, the evidence is so great that it has been divided into three phases (before, during, and after hospitalization: Gallagher, 1981). The findings are summarized later in this chapter.

Labeling theorists have been widely criticized for contending that mental disorder does not objectively exist. Obviously, some conditions are genetic and/or biochemical and therefore not simply the acting out of a role. Mechanic (1969) argues that a severe condition like schizophrenia cannot be explained by labels, especially when there are such vast differences in recovery from one patient to another. Another criticism is that labeling theory assumes the person reacts passively and has no autonomy to make choices. It also assumes that the labeling caused the deviant behavior, but it does not explain deviance that existed long before the label was applied. Typically, disordered people have months or even years of difficulties before they are labeled and treated. Additionally, Weinstein (1983) found that labeling theory underestimates the degree to which patients and ex-patients think favorably about mental disorder and past hospital experiences.

At this point, it should be clear that the causes of mental disorder are still mysterious. All that exist are theories, each with its own pile of supporting evidence. However, no theory can explain all cases of any type of disorder. In the face of such uncertainty, the only safe view is an *eclectic* perspective, one that combines all the approaches into a broader sociomedical view. For example, there probably are many people who are genetically and/or biochemically vulnerable to schizophrenia, but psychosocial factors determine which ones will actually be affected and how they will react.

STRESS AND MENTAL DISORDER

One of the factors related to the onset of mental disorder is stress. Most people who seek treatment have experienced an unusual number of stressful events in the weeks or months prior to their breakdowns. In some instances, stress may be a direct cause of mental disorder and not simply a precipitant. Holmes and Rahe (1967) have measured the amount of stress produced by various types of events. Although some of the events in their list are intrinsically pleasant, all the events are stressful because they require people to readjust their lives. Table 4-1 presents the rank ordering of these events according to the amount of stress each event generates. Holmes and Rahe report that people with a high life crisis score during a particular period of time are especially likely to become disordered. Others find that high scores on life-events scales are related to suicide attempts and heart disease as well as psychiatric symptoms (Dean and Lin, 1977).

Life events are stressful because they disrupt a person's usual activities. That is why events that appear to be positive are actually experienced as stressful. This was apparent in a study of poor people being helped by an income maintenance program. Even though their material well-being was improved, they underwent significant stress simply because of the change in their lives (Thoits and Hannan, 1979).

Of course, not all people are affected equally by changes. While some appear to have an emotional insulation against stress, others are quite vulnerable. The vulnerable people (the genetically predisposed, the biochemically imbalanced, or those who were improperly socialized) may react dramatically to seemingly trivial events. This may be because the events uncover old, recurring problems and give them new meaning, as in the case of the rejected woman whose sister gets married.

It is likely that stressful life events cause strain, which in turn erodes self-esteem, leaving the person especially vulnerable to depression. It is also possible that mentally disordered people *cause* stressful events to occur in their lives, although most researchers believe this is less common than the reverse.[5] Additionally, there is evidence of a problem linkage between physical health and mental health. Physical illness, for example, is a known precursor of depression (Aneshensel, Frericks, and Huba, 1984). Among children, there is little question about the direction of the causal relationship since the ones who become mentally disordered usually come from families that stressed them. Berkman (1979) found that the family experiences most likely to create stress in young children are broken homes, quarreling parents, and parents in poor physical health.

There is no doubt that stressful life events can deteriorate mental health over time. It is also evident that particular social roles, such as the stressfulness of womens' family roles, can affect psychological well-being (Kandel, Da-

---

[5] A major determinant of violent behavior among discharged patients is the patients' life experiences after release (Levinson and Ramsay, 1979). This is one reason it is so difficult for psychiatrists to predict dangerousness. Patients who are not predicted to be dangerous often are because of stress-inducing events which occur after they leave the hospital.

TABLE 4-1 SOCIAL READJUSTMENT RATING SCALE

Rank	Life event	Mean value
1	Death of spouse	100
2	Divorce	73
3	Marital separation	65
4	Jail term	63
5	Death of close family member	63
6	Personal injury or illness	53
7	Marriage	50
8	Fired at work	47
9	Marital reconciliation	45
10	Retirement	45
11	Change in health of family member	44
12	Pregnancy	40
13	Sex difficulties	39
14	Gain of new family member	39
15	Business readjustment	39
16	Change in financial state	38
17	Death of close friend	37
18	Change to different line of work	36
19	Change of number of arguments with spouse	35
20	New mortgage	31
21	Foreclosure of mortgage or loan	30
22	Change of responsibilities at work	29
23	Son or daughter leaving home	29
24	Trouble with in-laws	29
25	Outstanding personal achievement	28

Source: Adapted from T. Holmes and R. H. Rahe, "The Social Readjustment Scale," *Journal of Psychosomatic Research,* 11, 1967: 213–218. By permission of publisher.

vies, and Raveis, 1985). Is it also possible that specific people are vulnerable to stress while others are hardly affected? A number of studies report that the reaction to stress depends on whether the person has adequate social supports, such as friends and relatives (Pearlin et al., 1981; Turner, 1981; Williams, Ware, and Donald, 1981). Some believe that supportive people can act as a buffer against stressful events by providing sympathy and advice. Inadequate social supports may be why certain groups (such as the lower class and single people) have high rates of mental disorder; life events have a greater impact on them because supportive others are not available to mediate the effects of the stress.

The reaction to stress is an important determinant of mental health. In fact, it is so important that it can even affect the development of the unborn. Nuckolls, Cassel, and Kaplan (1972) found that the pregnancy complication rate is much higher among women who experienced many life events during pregnancy but had few social supports (such as a good marriage) than for those who also experienced many life events but had supportive others.

There are other possible mediators between life events and mental disorder besides social support systems. Some report that personality characteristics are also involved (Kobasa, Maddi, and Courington, 1981). They propose that *hardy people* are more resistant to stressful life events because they thrive on personal development through change. Hardy individuals have a lot of curiosity and find life events interesting and meaningful. They expect change to be the norm, and they believe they can be influential through what they imagine, say, and do. This is an interesting finding which has been tested on university campuses. College students who feel in control of their lives are less likely to feel stressed by life events than those who feel they are controlled by others (Johnson and Sareson, 1978). Another reported correlate of stress is place of residence. For example, those who live in the Middle Atlantic states (New York, New Jersey, and Pennsylvania) report more stress (and less happiness with life) than those who live in other parts of the country.

One group in American society especially likely to experience a number of life events is teenagers. Perhaps this is why there is an epidemic of adolescent suicides. One team of researchers (1981) reports that teenagers experience about nine life events annually, (Newcomb, Huba, and Bentler, 1981). Some common events among teenagers include falling in love, deciding whether to go to college, and starting work. The process of applying to college can be especially stressful. This is evident in a number of ways, including a notable increase in blood pressure (Hansell, 1982). There are certain groups of students which are especially stressed by preparing for college, such as class leaders, high achievers, and those under inordinate pressure by their parents. College life is no cup of tea either. Pressures to do well in school, to pay off loans, and to have a career orientation are expressed by such things as increased vandalism, graffiti, wild drinking binges, and acting out physically.

The events which affect teenage males are different from the ones which affect teenage females (Newcomb, Huba, and Bentler, 1981). Males more often get in trouble with the law, steal valuable objects, get in trouble at school, and get or give venereal disease. The females are more often affected by parental divorce, falling in love, thinking about suicide, having their family move, and gaining a lot of weight.

THE EPIDEMIOLOGY OF MENTAL DISORDER

The fact that mental disorder appears more frequently in certain social groups than others is an important clue to underlying causes. The many studies social scientists have undertaken of the distribution of mental disorder among social groups are part of a research field known as *epidemiology*. These studies are based on the assumption that if there is a difference in the prevalence of mental disorder among different groups of people, then the social factors that differentiate the groups may be related to etiology. If, for example, rates differ between males and females, sex roles may be a causal factor. Lower rates among married people as compared to single people may indicate that married life is more conducive to mental health.

Below is a brief review of the major findings of epidemiological research, including the relationships between rates of mental disorder and sex, marital status, religion, ethnicity, migration, place of residence, social class, and race. Gallagher (1987) provides a complete review of all the research on epidemiology. For instance, there is a clear difference in the patterns of mental disorder between males and females, with women having higher reported rates than men, although a 1984 NIMH study found that there may no longer be significant differences in rates of mental disorder between the sexes. See Chapter 10 for a discussion of mental health differences between the sexes.

Marital Status

Single persons have a higher prevalence of mental disorder than married persons (Gove, 1972). There is also a relationship between prognosis, length of stay in a mental hospital, and marital status; single persons have a poorer prognosis and longer stays than those who are married. Because of these associations, some consider marital status to be one of the best single demographic predictors of the chances of becoming mentally disordered and recovering from it (Hafner, 1986).

One theory holds that the high rate of mental disorder among single people is the result of a social selection process which prevents the mentally ill from marrying because they are not perceived as good mates. Another theory is that marriage is a mental health haven which offers interpersonal security (social support) not available to single people, who suffer more economic hardships and social isolation. Thus, single people may be stressed more by those life events not mediated by supportive others (Eaton, 1978). However, today there appears to be a new and different breed of singles who chose singlehood and find each other's support through their own clubs and organizations. Some preliminary evidence indicates that the mental health of these people is not grossly different from that of their married counterparts.

Married women have higher rates of disorder than their husbands. Gove (1972) believes this is because women find marriage more difficult than men. The traditional housewife role is not very gratifying. Keeping house is frustrating, requires little skill, offers little prestige, but must be constantly performed. Because the housewife role is vaguely defined, the woman becomes responsible for everything that must be done in the house. Children cause even more stress, and when they grow up and move out of the home, the lives of housewives become more meaningless, a phenomenon known as the empty nest syndrome. However, depression among married women is much less in those relationships where marital power is shared by husband and wife (Mirowsky, 1985).

Those married women who work are in better mental health than those who do not (see Chapter 10), although they are still somewhat more impaired than employed husbands

Depression among people locked into the housewife role is not an unusual problem. (© *Joel Gordon 1985*)

(Aneshensel, Frericks, and Clark, 1981). In the nontraditional marriages in which both husband and wife are employed, mental health differences between the sexes decrease. This is probably because working wives feel a greater sense of purpose than housewives, something which is also true for divorced and separated women (Krause and Markides, 1985).

In direct contradiction to the popular stereotypes of the carefree bachelor and the rejected spinster, single men are more frequently disordered than single women. Why is this so? Perhaps impaired males are more noticeable during courtship than impaired females since males are expected to play a more active role. Therefore, disordered males may be less likely to marry in the first place. It is also possible that single women have fewer symptoms than bachelors because they are better able to form attachments with others and avoid the anguish of social isolation.

The once married (separated, divorced, and widowed) have the highest rate of mental disorder of any marital grouping. They also have an extremely high suicide rate. Because depression is so common among the once married, they experience a number of health and work-related problems. The greatest amount of psychiatric impairment occurs among those who recently experienced a marital break up, particularly separated men.

Religion and Ethnicity

An early study by Roberts and Myers (1954) examined the religious denominations of mentally disturbed people in New Haven, Connecticut. They found that Protestants were slightly underrepresented in the psychiatric population compared to their number in the general population (31 to 33 percent). Catholics appeared in the psychiatric population in proportion to their numbers in the general population (approximately 57 percent). What is noteworthy about Catholics is an inordinately high rate of alcoholism. In the Roberts and Myers study, almost 70 percent of all alcoholics were Catholic. Further analysis revealed that this is due largely to the specific contribution of the Irish strain of Catholics, not Catholics in general.

Jews were overrepresented in the psychiatric population (12 to 9.5 percent). Most of the Jewish patients were neurotic, and none of them suffered from alcohol or drug addiction. In a later study of psychiatric patients in private therapy in New York, Chicago, and Los Angeles, Jews were again far overrepresented as patients (Marx and Spray, 1972). On the one hand, since they typically seek help for neurotic problems, Jews are unimpaired relative to members of other religions who have more serious disorders. At the same time, Jews seek psychiatric help more frequently than others. *Why is it that the least impaired group receives the greatest amount of psychiatric treatment?* One possible reason is that Jewish people are concentrated in the higher social classes and therefore are better able to pay for treatment. They are also highly educated, a trait which

makes them sensitive to the nuances of human psychology and knowledgeable about where to go for help. Jews who feel distressed are simply cautious and educated enough to take their problems to a therapist. In the process, they become registered patients even though their symptoms are mild or transient. Another likely factor in the high treatment rate among Jews is the great number of therapists who are Jewish. This allows the Jewish person to easily find help from a similar other.

It is sometimes difficult to isolate the singular effects of ethnicity on mental health because ethnicity is often intimately associated with religion, as is the case of Puerto Ricans, who are largely Catholic. However, unlike Catholics in general, Puerto Ricans in the United States have a relatively high rate of disorder. Mexican-Americans (Chicanos) have low reported rates, but this may be because they are not likely to be treated by professionals, since they try to solve their own problems or take them to witch doctors. Both Japanese-Americans and Chinese-Americans have exceptionally low rates of disorder and, in fact, appear to be free of antisocial tendencies. This may be the result of the tightly knit family structure that is common among both groups. Polish immigrants have above-average rates. German immigrants have average rates. The lowest rates are found among those who migrated from England, Italy, and Russia.

Migration

One experience believed to produce stress is migration, of which there are two types. One is *international* migration, whereby a person moves from one country to another, and the other is *internal* migration, whereby a person moves within the same country. It is a well-documented fact that international migrants have a much higher rate of disorder than those who remain in their native countries. This may be the result of stress (culture shock) generated in adapting to a new environment, particularly when the two countries are culturally different, as when a person moves from New Guinea to New York. Another factor determining whether international migration is stressful is the reason for leaving the old environment. A refugee who is forced to leave has no rationale for choosing a new home and thus is stressed more than a voluntary migrant. The attitude of the new country toward immigrants is also important. For instance, Israel's positive attitude toward immigrants is reflected in low rates of mental disorder.

The psychological effects of internal migration vary according to the type of move. People who move within a city have higher rates of disorder than those who migrate from one city to another. This is probably because the reason for moving typically varies between intercity migrants, who are often moving because of a job promotion, and intracity migrants, who are often rootless individuals moving to avoid bill collectors and landlords.

Place of Residence
A number of studies find the rate of mental disorder slightly higher among urban dwellers compared to rural dwellers (Dohrenwend and Dohrenwend, 1974). Popular opinion has it that this results from the strains of urban living, but there are other factors at work as well. Since treatment facilities (including office-based psychiatrists) are more available in and around cities, more urban people seek help and become registered cases. In addition, cramped living conditions make disordered people more visible in urban areas. Consequently, urban dwellers are more likely to be brought to treatment centers.

Within urban areas there is a notable concentration of mental disorder, especially schizophrenia, in the ghetto areas of the inner city, and a regular decrease to the periphery of the city. Faris and Dunham first discovered this phenomenon in Chicago in 1939 and offered their "social isolation hypothesis" to explain the high rates of schizophrenia in the inner city. Their theory holds that the anonymity of life in inner-city areas creates an extreme sense of isolation which triggers a schizophrenic breakdown.

Most cases of schizophrenia in inner-city areas are lower-class, single, separated, or divorced men living alone (Levy and Rowitz, 1973). Cases of manic-depression are distributed randomly throughout the city, with a slight concentration among suburbanites. These ecological patterns of mental disorder have been reported in a number of American cities. The causes, however, have raised a good deal of speculation. Besides the theory that the inner city actually produces mental disorder, there is another view which holds that unstable people move into the socially disorganized inner city because it suits their disturbed makeup.

Social Class
The high rate of mental disorder in inner-city, skid row districts may not be caused simply by the low quality of life in those areas but may instead be the result of lower social class. Perhaps no other demographic variable has been studied more thoroughly than social class. Almost all the studies to date have found the greatest prevalence of disorder among the lower class, the same group which populates inner-city areas. In 1950, Hollingshead and Redlich undertook a landmark study analyzing the relationship between social class and mental disorder in New Haven, Connecticut. Their data included hospitalized patients, as well as clinic and private patients. The social class breakdown of a random sample of the New Haven community was compared to the class breakdown of the psychiatric population.

In short, they found that the proportion of mentally disordered persons to normal persons was importantly different in each of the five major social classes. For example, in New Haven, the upper class contains 3.1 percent of the community's population but only 1.0 percent of all known psychiatric cases. Upper middle, lower middle, and working class people are also underrepresented in the patient population. On the other hand, *the percentage of lower-class people in the patient population is more than twice as great as their number in the general population.* This is especially true for lower-class males, who have the highest rate of hospitalization. In addition, lower-class people are hospitalized longer than patients from higher classes.

A later study of a random cross section of the entire population of midtown Manhattan involved interviews with 1660 people to see if they had ever sought psychiatric help, had a "nervous breakdown," or shown neurotic symptoms (Srole, Langner, Michael, Kirkpatrick, Opler, and Rennie, 1975). Psychiatrists rated the degree of psychiatric impairment of each person in the sample. The degree of mental disorder strongly correlated with social class. The psychiatrists rated nearly 1 person in every 2 in the lower class as impaired, but the rate declined to 1 in 8 in the upper class. In addition, lower-class people were the least likely to seek help. Therefore, the lower social class was the one most in need of help but the one receiving the least of it. By 1987, more than fifty studies of the relationship between the rate of mental disorder and social class have found that the highest rate occurs in the lowest class.

Why is there such a high concentration of reported mental disorder among the poor? Labeling theorists believe part of this is due to the fact that psychiatrists, who are overwhelmingly middle class themselves, are unfamiliar with the values, language, and behavior of lower-class people. Consequently, they are prone to confuse social class differences with pathological symptoms.

A more popular explanation of the class-disorder relationship is the *social stress hypothesis.* It holds that the miserable conditions of lower-class life generate stress, which in turn fosters psychiatric impairment. Stress in the lower class takes many forms, including childhood deprivation, broken homes, social isolation, discriminatory treatment, and, especially, unemployment.

Another theory of the preponderance of disorder in the lower class is the *drift hypothesis,* which holds that social class is not a cause but a consequence of mental disorder. According to this view, mentally disordered people are likely to be members of the lower class because their illness did not allow them to function at a higher class level. Consequently, they become downwardly mobile and drift into the lower class. A number of studies have been undertaken to evaluate the stress and drift theories. Some find that the poor are exposed to more stress (Kessler, 1979*a*), while others report that mentally disordered poor people often come from higher classes (Antunes, 1974). This is not surprising because the two theories are not mutually exclusive; class can determine disorder in one case and disorder can determine class in another.

In addition to their findings on the prevalence of mental disorder among the different social classes, the New Haven researchers also discovered a relationship between type of mental disorder and social class. They found a concentration of the neuroses at the higher class levels and the functional psychoses at the lower levels of the class structure (see Figure 4-1).

A number of other studies also report an inverse relationship between psychosis and class and a direct relationship between neurosis and class. Some of these studies have looked at types of psychosis and found some interesting patterns. Schizophrenia, for instance, is especially common in the lower class, while manic-depression appears more frequently in higher-class groups. Neurotic type also varies: obsessive compulsive neurosis is most common among the higher class, while phobic neurosis occurs more frequently among the lower class, as does antisocial behavior.

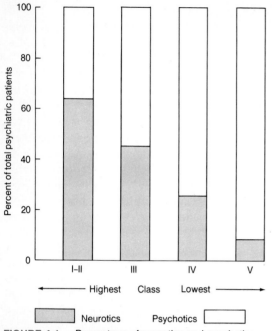

FIGURE 4-1   Percentage of neurotics and psychotics among total psychiatric patients, by class. *(Reprinted from August B. Hollingshead and Frederick C. Redlich, Social Class and Mental Illness: A Community Study (1958), John Wiley and Sons. By permission of the authors and publisher.)*

Does type of psychiatric treatment vary by social class, along with rate and type of mental disorder? The New Haven researchers found distinct differences in the type of care administered to patients of different classes. In that study, treatment was grouped into three categories: psychotherapy, organic therapy, and custodial care. Psychotherapy involves verbal interaction between a patient and a therapist. This ranges from the highly individualistic and lengthy psychoanalytic approach to the cheaper group therapy technique often employed in state hospitals. Organic therapy includes chemotherapy (the use of drugs) and electroshock therapy. Custodial care, a polite term for no treatment at all, is based on the assumption that the person cannot be rehabilitated and must be segregated from society for security reasons.

The New Haven study found an inverse relationship between social class and quality of care. The highly regarded psychotherapies were used almost universally with higher-class patients but with only 59 percent of the lower class. The less desirable organic and custodial treatments were used most frequently with lower-class patients. In addition, the lower-class patients who did receive psychotherapy were typically administered group therapy and treated for a shorter period.

Some argue that the poor receive inferior treatment because they are usually psychotic and not amenable to psychotherapy. There is more to it than that, since patients of different classes with the same diagnoses are not treated in the same way. In one study, only 17 percent of depressed lower-class patients were referred for psychotherapy in contrast to 100 percent of the depressed in the upper class (Karno, 1966).

What are the causes of the discriminatory treatment of lower-class patients? Psychotherapists claim poor people do not respond to psychotherapy because they do not understand it, are uninterested in it, and lack verbal skills. However, it is well known that psychotherapists, who are almost always from the middle class themselves, have an elitist bias toward higher-class patients (Kandel, 1966). Even psychotherapists from the lower class prefer higher-class patients (Rowden, 1970). These biases are found in state mental hospitals as well as among psychotherapists in private practice (Marx and Spray, 1972). Schofield (1964) calls the type of patients most preferred by psychotherapists YAVIS— young, attractive, verbal, intelligent, and successful. The end result is that psychotherapy is given to the privileged, the ones who need it least. Even community mental health centers, which were established to give everyone equal access to treatment, are victimized by the middle-class bias which defines a ''good patient'' on the basis of social worth.

Race

There is a greater prevalence of mental disorder among blacks than among whites. A likely reason for this is that in a racist society, blacks are relegated to the lowest social class. In other words, blacks have high rates for the same reasons lower-class people do. Consistently, blacks are also susceptible to the same types of disorders as the poor, particularly schizophrenia. Some cases of schizophrenia among blacks may be caused prenatally by the inadequate diets of poor pregnant women. This is a problem especially common during the winter and may account for the unusual number of winter-borns who became schizophrenic (Gallagher, McFalls, and Jones, 1983). Organic disorders also appear more frequently among blacks. For example, organic brain syndromes caused by chronic alcoholism are reportedly nine times more common among blacks than whites (Pasamanick, 1962). Blacks also have higher rates of mental retardation, a disorder associated with premature birth and pregnancy complications, both of which are more common in the lower class. Antisocial personality disorders also appear more frequently among blacks, as they do among poor people in general.

Surprisingly, blacks living in northern states have higher rates of disorder than those residing in the South. This may be because unstable blacks migrate to the North, or because most northern blacks are urban dwellers and most southern blacks live in rural areas. However, it is also possible that northern blacks are more frustrated than southern blacks because they have greater aspirations but no more opportunity to achieve them than they would have in the South. Thus, northern blacks are more stressed by the larger discrepancy between their expectations and their actual accomplishments. Regardless of place of residence, blacks are especially vulnerable to mental disorder relative to whites, although this vulnerability is somewhat controlled by social support systems such as a tightly knit extended family (Dressler, 1985).

Ironically, there has been a tremendous increase in the black mental hospital admission rate since the civil rights movement. This is most apparent in the high rate of impairment among young blacks (under 30). This group was raised during and after the civil rights movement and is especially likely to demand and expect equal treatment. However, their real opportunities are limited compared to their aspirations, and the resulting stress seems to have taken its toll on their mental health.

PSYCHIATRIC TREATMENT

Today there are a wide variety of treatment modalities. They can be broadly grouped into two classes: organic therapies (brain surgery, electroconvulsive therapy, and chemotherapy) for psychotics and psychotherapy (psychoanalysis, behavior modification, client-centered therapy, and milieu therapy) for less disturbed patients.

Organic Therapy

The most extreme (and controversial) organic therapy is brain surgery, commonly referred to as frontal lobotomy, an operation in which the frontal nerves of the brain are severed in order to calm a violent patient. In the 1950s, some 50,000 lobotomies were performed in the United States. Although lobotomies eradicated a patient's violent tendencies, they often transformed the person into a mindless zombie as well. For that reason, they have been severely restricted since that time to extreme cases. Today lobotomy procedures have been refined through the use of microelectrodes, which deactivate very specific parts of the brain.

In electroconvulsive therapy (ECT), electrodes are placed on the patient's head and an electric shock (between 80 and 100 volts) is sent into the brain. The shock produces a convulsion and brief loss of consciousness. When this method was first used in the 1930s, there were many undesirable side effects, including broken bones and spines from the convulsive writhings. Today anesthetics and muscle relaxants are used to reduce the risk of injury, although amnesia may still result. ECT is especially useful with patients who are severely depressed. There are many people opposed to ECT because they claim it is a cruel, barbaric treatment which is often used to punish uncontrollable patients and which can cause permanent brain damage. Despite these fears, the use of ECT has increased in the 1980s, even though no one knows how it works.

Chemotherapy makes use of a wide variety of drugs from mild tranquilizers, such as Valium, to antidepressant medication, such as lithium carbonate. Psychotropic drugs were introduced in the 1950s as a way of controlling symptoms so that patients could respond better to their therapists and others around them. Drugs do not cure mental disorder. They only alleviate symptoms, the way insulin does for a diabetic. However, in some understaffed state mental hospitals, drugs are the dominant form of treatment, a type of medicinal straitjacket that keeps patients under control. On the other hand, it is important to recognize that drugs have been a big help in eliminating suffering. One drug, lithium carbonate, has been a godsend for depressed people, many of whom are simply troubled by a biochemical disturbance.

Psychotherapy

Psychotherapy is a form of treatment that attempts to change personalities, not bodies. All forms of psychotherapy use a talking-out technique whereby patients are helped to understand the nature of their problem. The process hinges on some type of interaction between the patient and the therapist to reach this understanding and work out a solution.

There are many variations of psychotherapy. The oldest is the psychoanalytic technique developed by Freud. Psychoanalysts treat people by uncovering unconscious conflicts, memories, fears, and wishes that may have led to the problem. They use a variety of techniques to explore the unconscious, such as dream interpretation, the famous inkblot test, and free association. A fundamental principle of psychoanalytic treatment is *transference,* the process by which patients transfer to the analyst their feelings toward parents and other significant people from childhood. This allows the patient to rework the experiences that led to the problem. Needless to say, psychoanalysis can take a long time (possibly years) and be quite expensive.

Behavior modification is a newer form of psychotherapy. It is based on the assumption that behavior is learned and therefore can be unlearned. Accordingly, undesirable behavior is punished and appropriate behavior is rewarded. This approach is used on a wide variety of patients. For example, schizophrenics in mental hospitals are often taught basic social skills through a token economy program. If patients properly perform such tasks as grooming or dressing, they are rewarded with a token that can be redeemed for a reward, such as a small item at the hospital store. Behaviorists might treat outpatients, such as phobics, by *desensitizing* them. This typically consists of teaching the person to relax while presenting the phobic object in increasing doses. For example, a behaviorist may treat a college student with an overwhelming fear of talking in class by arranging the fear on an anxiety hierarchy, from the least threatening fear to the most threatening. The behaviorist would then help the student to relax, first with the simple thought of speaking in class and finally with actually giving a speech. Behaviorist treatment is cheaper and less time-consuming than psychoanalytic treatment. However, it may work only with people whose problems result from learning. More complex problems may require a more in-depth approach.

Client-centered therapy was developed by Carl Rogers. Like behaviorism, it emphasizes current issues rather than unconscious motives from the past. This type of therapy centers on patients interpreting their own needs and shortcomings to help them become more self-aware and improve their relationships with other people.

In group therapy, people share their problems with one another in order to gain insight through interaction with similar others. It is useful, for example, with groups of alcoholics or sex offenders. One subtype of group therapy is family therapy, in which members of a family work with an outside therapist to resolve their problems.

Many other varieties of psychotherapy have come in and out of vogue over the years, such as transcendental meditation, total awareness, transactional analysis, primal therapy, and encounter groups. Self-help books, designed to demonstrate ways of avoiding a nervous breakdown or living with a neurotic, are also popular in some circles. However, most of these awareness approaches are very simplistic and simply not suitable for people with serious problems.

Life in the Mental Hospital

People with serious mental disorders often end up in mental hospitals. This can be either a helpful experience or a devastating one. The outcome depends partly on the design of the hospital. Today there are two major types of psychiatric hospitals: the traditional custodial hospital and the emerging therapeutic hospital. The custodial hospital is primarily concerned with segregating the patient from the rest of society. In this setting, the patient is expected to conform to the authoritarian routines of the hospital and passively accept impersonal organic treatment including ECT and drugs. The therapeutic hospital is concerned with rehabilitating patients rather than simply controlling

them. In this setting, the patients' problems are treated individually, and patients play an active role in rehabilitation, especially through psychotherapy.

Generally, large state hospitals are custodial and small private hospitals are therapeutic. There are a number of reasons for this. The ratio of staff to patients in state hospitals is so low it is impossible to tailor treatment to individual patients. Additionally, private hospital patients usually come from a higher class and suffer from disorders, such as neurosis, which can be treated through psychotherapy. State hospital patients are often poor people suffering from schizophrenia, a condition which presently can be controlled only through drugs.

In the United States today there are approximately 475 mental hospitals, 293 of which are run by state governments. The state hospitals have the reputation of being snake pits for a number of reasons. First of all, the design of the buildings is so depressing that the patients may actually be emotionally harmed. The architecture is usually antiquated and bleak: huge wards of half-walls lined with rows of identical beds, long gloomy corridors, high ceilings, no privacy, drab colors, factory-type lighting, and, of course, the infamous glass observation cubicle in the dayroom, where patients sit for hours on uncomfortable furniture, watch television, and smoke cigarettes to the butt. The closed wards for chronic patients are even worse because they are locked and offer little opportunity for change.

Another problem with state hospitals is their small and undertrained staff. State hospitals typically house several thousand patients who are supervised largely by psychiatric aides. For the most part, aides are undereducated and employed basically to keep things quiet. The hospital staff is too small and of poor quality because the hospital budgets are so low. As a result, professionally trained personnel are attracted to private practice, where the salaries are much higher. Most patients have regular contact only with aides. They rarely have as much as a five-minute conversation a week with the nurses. The psychiatrists have even less patient contact and spend most of their time on the ward writing medical orders and handling administrative duties.

It is not surprising that the condition of state hospital patients often gets worse because, in a sense, they are ignored. In some instances, they are actually forgotten. In 1971, five patients were released from an Ohio institution. Although they had been sent there merely for observation, they had been kept for periods ranging from twenty-one to forty-one years because the staff had forgotten about them! In Chicago alone, more than 300 patients died from neglect between 1977 and 1981. Some who wandered away were found floating in rivers or dismembered on railroad tracks. Others died from exposure to the elements while still on hospital grounds. Some committed suicide while aides were busy with other patients. Recently, ex-patients, such as Kenneth Donaldson, have politicized and demanded improvement of hospital conditions. Donaldson was involuntarily committed to the Florida State Mental Hospital by his parents. For fifteen years he was forced to live in crowded conditions and work to the point of exhaustion. He spoke with psychiatrists for a total of only five hours in all that time. After his repeated attempts to gain release, a federal court ruled that the hospital knew Donaldson did not belong there, yet continued to force a prisonlike existence on him. He was released and awarded 38,500 dollars in damages.

Subjective versus Objective Attitudes of Life in the Mental Hospital

There is an interesting sidelight to the experiences of patients in mental hospitals: Most of the horrors are *subjectively* reported by outsiders, such as social scientists, the media, and people masquerading as patients. There is little mention of the researchers who have conducted *objective* studies of how the patients react to the hospitals. The fact is there is an enormous difference between the subjective reports of outsiders and the objective attitudes of real patients. Most studies of patients' attitudes show that a large majority have favorable attitudes toward hospitalization (Weinstein, 1981). Perhaps the outsiders' reports are biased by the preconceived idea that all mental hospitals are hell holes. Or perhaps mental patients do not mind hospital life because it compares favorably with their previous miserable lives in the outside world.

Institutionalization

Regardless of how patients view mental hospitals, there is little doubt that they can be damaged by a long stay in a custodial type of hospital. In these places, their lives are so highly regulated that they fall victim to a syndrome which is not part of their original mental disorder. The syndrome, usually referred to as *institutionalization,* frequently develops in patients who have been hospitalized for two or more years. The symptoms of institutionalization usually consist of apathy, lack of concern for one's future, deterioration in personal habits, oversubmissiveness, and an excessive dependency on the hospital and staff. This may be the result of the authoritarian, impersonal routines in the mental hospital, which force people to succumb to institutional demands and minimize their individual needs. Goffman (1961) argues that long-term patients adjust to being hospitalized through what he calls *conversion,* the process by which patients accept the hospital's judgment of them as sick and belonging in an institution. The patients' self-concepts are so damaged that they come to view themselves as simply sick patients rather than individuals. The submissiveness and dependency decrease a patient's chances for recovery even further because the proper sick role of a psychiatric patient (unlike that of a medical patient) requires an active, independent participation in one's own rehabilitation.

To eliminate the adverse effects of a stay in a mental hospital, some cities have Short Procedure Units to evaluate and treat psychiatric emergencies and help the practicing psychiatrist and other physicians deal with problems that ordinarily cannot be handled in the physician's office. These procedures include electroshock, laboratory workups of depressed patients, and the like. The utility of a Short Procedure Unit is that it can be a bridge that enables patients to continue to be treated by their own physician without the cost of hospitalization or the traumatic experience of going to an emergency room.

LIFE AS AN EX-MENTAL PATIENT

Today, because of tranquilizing drugs and the widely recognized dangers of lengthy hospitalization, the average stay is about forty-one days (Horowitz, 1982). However, there are still many patients who have been hospitalized for most of their lives simply because they were committed before the movement to short-run treatment.

Criteria for Discharge

Unlike medical hospitals, which discharge patients on the basis of symptoms, mental hospitals do not have objective standards for evaluating patients for release. The behavior of a mental patient is not a useful discharge criterion because the patient may appear quite well in the hospital but fall apart in the outside world. Unfortunately, psychiatrists are generally unable to predict how a patient will do after release (Greenley, 1979).

As a result, hospitals often discharge patients for reasons completely unrelated to a patient's condition (and welfare). One reason is *statistical pressure,* a polite term for hospital overcrowding, which can result in the premature release of patients who still need help. Another factor is that psychiatrists, unable to

accurately predict ability to function in the outside community, are often influenced by a patient's life circumstances. For example, whatever their disorder, patients have a better chance of release if they have a job and a place to live (Rock, Jacobsen, and Janopaul, 1968). Perhaps the best example of how life circumstances (rather than symptoms) affect release is the important role played by the patient's family. The attitudes of the family are more likely to affect length of hospitalization than the degree of the patient's impairment (Greenley, 1972). If the family favors release, the patient is likely to be discharged. This is especially true among patients from higher-class families which have the finances for outpatient follow-up treatment. Conversely, release is unlikely if the family does not favor it or if the patient has no family. What determines the attitudes of the family toward release? Typically they are based on factors having nothing to do with the patient's condition, such as the need for help with child care, loneliness, guilt, or even the timing of a vacation.

Problems of Mass Discharge

Although the average length of stay in mental hospitals has declined over the last few decades, there are just as many (and reportedly more) admissions. The result is a mass discharge of disordered people into the community. Community mental health clinics are supposed to be treating these people, but they have largely failed to do so. Many of the patients released from state hospitals have moved into inner-city areas or neighborhoods near the hospital, creating psychiatric ghettos. They live in boarding homes that house only schizophrenics, manic-depressives, the retarded, alcoholics, drug addicts, and the marginally menacing. The boarders mostly wander aimlessly around mildly sedated, or lie on their beds sorting out bewildered thoughts. They have been simply dumped into the community, still hearing voices, still hallucinating, still paranoid, and still with the unmistakable look of the deranged. Others are not fortunate enough to even have a roof over their heads. They constitute part of the growing number of destitute people commonly referred to as street people (See Box 4-1.) This is a classic case of a social policy causing a new social problem.

In 1976, the United States Senate Subcommittee on Long-Term Care documented the horrible conditions of the boarding homes in these ghettolike areas. Not only is there a blatant lack of therapeutic and rehabilitative care, but most of the boarding homes' revenue comes from federal funds! The government is actually contributing to a very profitable industry which many see as illegitimate. Although the authors of this book feel that there is a high percentage of mentally ill people among the homeless, a 1986 assessment of the plight of the homeless in Texas reports that this is a myth (Snow, Baker, Anderson, and Martin, 1986).

Readjustment into the Community

Because discharged patients have such unpleasant experiences, it is no small wonder they have difficulty readjusting to outside life; in fact, almost half are readmitted within a year after release. Part of this may be the crippling result of institutionalization, but some of the blame must be placed on what ex-patients face in the form of discrimination, stigma, and lack of effective follow-up care.

The patients who successfully reenter society are usually the ones returned to certain types of interpersonal situations. (Grusky, Tierney, Manderscheid, and Grusky, 1985). For instance, there is a high rate of rehospitalization among discharged patients who live alone, but those who are returned to families have much higher performance levels. This is particularly true if the patient returns to a spouse rather than a parent. Spouses are more beneficial because they have higher expectations of the way in which the ex-patient should function. Unfortunately, many ex-

The mass release of mental patients into the community has added to the numbers of homeless street people. (© *Alon Reininger/Contact 1984*)

BOX 4-1

THE FORSAKEN: AMERICA'S STREET PEOPLE

Dawn was just beginning to brighten the eastern sky. It was a sunrise that went unnoticed by the man asleep on the steam grate opposite Rittenhouse Square, folded up between a concrete trash receptacle and a newspaper vending machine. The sleeping man was wearing baggy corduroy pants, a wool hat, a shirt and a dirty blanket worn over his shoulders like a shawl. His eyes still closed, he reached into his open shirt to scratch at the lice, as he had been doing all night. It took a long time, maybe 15 or 20 minutes, for him to wake up fully, but by 6:15 his eyes were open wide, staring down the elegant street that had been his home for three years. At first he did nothing but sit, stare, and scratch. Another day was beginning for Jim Logue Crawford, 69, a former mental hospital patient.

Despite appearances, Jim Crawford is neither an alcoholic nor a Skid Row bum too lazy to work. He is instead a victim—a victim of a 20-year-old, $2.5 billion government program that didn't work right. A program called "deinstitutionalization." Since it began, that program has released between 700,000 and 1.5 million mental patients from the state mental hospitals into the cities and towns of America. Most are better off now than they ever were in the back wards of mental hospitals where they were warehoused and ignored. But thousands of others were released into a world unprepared, or unwilling, to care for them. They are now living, and occasionally dying, in alleys, parks and vacant lots of America, with little more than garbage for food, rags for clothes and no shelter or medical care at all.

Crawford stood up and took off all the clothes above his waist, exposing an emaciated chest and a bloated belly. It was midwinter and a heavy snowstorm had been predicted. The digital display in the bank window now gave the temperature: it was 28, but Crawford did not seem to mind the cold. Standing half-naked on the street corner, as though under a shower, he started rubbing at his skin and picking off lice, invisibly tiny annoyances that he threw away with the contempt of a Charlie Chaplin character. He spent many minutes trying to get the lice off his body. He reached over his left shoulder and scratched and then twisted his body in an awkward way so he could reach the small of his back and scratch. He scratched his armpits and scratched the back of his neck and scratched his bloated belly and his pale chest. Closing his eyes again, Crawford scratched away at his body again and again with long yellow fingernails that protruded two or three inches beyond his fingertips. Crawford brought a small comb from his pants pocket and started combing the stubble on his face. Without a mirror, he had to feel his way across the contours of his face. He carefully pulled his comb through his crew cut, being sure to comb his entire head. Completing this part of his morning preparations, he replaced the comb in his pocket, bent down and picked up the coat and blanket that lay at his feet, shaking them vigorously as though to get rid of something. He was probably trying to shake the lice loose.

It was almost 7 now, and men and women dressed in business clothes were starting to appear on the street. A man with an attaché case, who had just come from a nearby indoor parking lot, walked over to Crawford, handed him a dollar without speaking or smiling, and left. Crawford stuffed the money into his pants pocket and finished pinning the blanket shut around his head and chest. Once again dressed, Crawford walked over to the curb. Although it was a one-way street, he looked in both directions for cars. Seeing none, he walked over to the park and crouched behind a stone entranceway, where he urinated.

Source: Donald C. Drake, "The Forsaken," *The Philadelphia Inquirer*, July 18, 1982. By permission of publisher.

---

patients cannot return to spouses since so many marriages deteriorate to the point of separation or divorce before commitment and release. The relationship between mental disorder and marital dissolution, by the way, illustrates again the linkage of social problems to one another.

Another factor related to posthospital adjustment is social class. Higher-class ex-patients function better in the community because, as with spouses, their relatives place more expectations on them. Another factor is stigma, the albatross of mental patients, which is more profound among lower-class people because they tend to be uneducated. This, in turn, forces the lower-class ex-patients into social isolation rather than suffer the ridicule of friends and neighbors.

Stigma

A major reason millions of troubled Americans avoid help is the stigma attached to being a mental patient. Ex-patients experience many forms of rejection in the community because the public considers them a separate class of undesirable beings. This is a widespread problem which is not confined to the uneducated: even general medical practitioners have negative attitudes toward the mentally disordered. So does the law, which permits psychiatric treatment to be used as grounds for divorce, invalidating a contract, revoking a driver's license, and losing voting rights.

Stigmatization of mental patients is a prime example of the vast difference between the subjective and objective dimensions of a social problem. The public is convinced mental patients are dangerous, stupid weaklings who sponge off others. Nothing could be further from the objective facts, yet patients returned to the community are treated as if they are dangerous, stupid, and weak. The degree of stigma varies from patient to patient: schizophrenics are stigmatized more than neurotics, and patients released from state mental hospitals suffer more stigma than those who have been in private hospitals.

Where do these inappropriate and damaging views come from? Much of the blame must be placed on the mass media, which do not report on ex-patients who are good citizens. For example, although only a small percentage of ex-patients commit violent crimes, the public knows only about them because of media exposure. The subjective effect of distorted news stories about former mental patients is largely responsible for stigmatization (Steadman, 1981). This was apparent in the case of Senator Thomas Eagleton, a vice presidential candidate in 1972. Because his past treatment for depression was widely publicized, he was forced to withdraw from the Democratic ticket. On the other hand, Abraham Lincoln, a manic-

depressive who was not treated, was widely respected.

The only way to alter the public's harmful attitudes toward the mentally disordered is to attack the myths about the alleged dangerousness, stupidity, and unpredictability of mental patients. Simply stated, most Americans are ignorant about mental disorder and need to be reeducated. Of course, this is easier said than done. The most effective approach is through direct contact with patients, an experience which can have a tremendous impact on a person's attitudes. Students who visit the closed wards of a state mental hospital as part of course work typically go (with shaky knees and sweating palms) expecting to encounter stark-staring, mad people screaming in padded cells. Instead, they find friendly people who have been quietly tucked away in a corner of the world. The students go to the hospital with fear. They leave sad, depressed, but enlightened about the objective situation.

SOCIAL POLICY: DEINSTITUTIONALIZATION

Strategies for Solution

Today the major issue in mental health care is whether the mentally disordered should be hospitalized or treated in the community (*deinstitutionalization*). This issue is generally discussed in terms of state hospitals because they represent a major component of our social policy. At this point, it should be clear that there are many risks associated with hospitalization, including the institutionalization syndrome and stigma. On the other hand, some definite benefits are enjoyed by psychiatric inpatients, such as being separated from the demands and stresses of everyday living. Additionally, hospital treatment is quite helpful in controlling the symptoms of people with organic problems requiring constant monitoring.

However, some new policies for running mental hospitals are needed to make them more efficient. One such policy is the *therapeutic community,* an attempt to treat inpatients without their developing a dependency on the hospital. This is accomplished with a large, well-trained staff (including nurses, aides, psychiatrists, and social workers) that has regular contact with every patient. The concept of the therapeutic community involves the patients playing an active role in their own rehabilitation. The treatment is personalized, patient autonomy is encouraged, and patients share decisions with the staff in regard to many aspects of hospital life. Of course, none of these policies can be undertaken without a large staff which is properly trained and well motivated. This may be possible in many of the well-funded private hospitals, but state hospitals simply do not have the money to be structured on a truly therapeutic basis. As a result, there has been a widespread movement to treat the mentally disordered in community-based facilities.

The community movement began in the early 1960s after the mental hospital population swelled to over half a million people. Some states have tried to phase out all their mental hospitals and treat disordered people in their own communities, where they are not threatened by institutionalization. However, most states have kept their hospitals open for chronic patients with severe disorders. The community treatment movement is based on a public health approach, a policy designed for the *primary prevention* of mental disorder. The community is regarded as a therapeutic tool. Interested citizens and institutions such as schools, hospitals, and law enforcement agencies are encouraged to participate in programs that will prevent mental disorders. Many of the programs are designed to help high-risk groups, such as children and the poor.

Community treatment was clearly enunciated as a public policy with the passage of the Community Mental Health Centers Act in 1963. Conceived by the Kennedy administration, the law provided poor people with outpatient treatment. The establishment of federally funded community mental health centers was a reaction to the abuses and dehumanization that often occurred in state mental hospitals. It was also an outgrowth of Kennedy's observation that the mental health care of the poor was being widely ignored. President Carter developed primary prevention programs designed to understand the causes of mental disorders and control such stresses as crowding, social isolation, noise, and economic fluctuations. Most of the progressive community-based programs have been developed and expanded during Democratic administrations and seriously curtailed in Republican administrations, particularly President Reagan's.

Community-based care programs include day hospitalization, immediate crisis intervention (such as suicide hot lines), brief stays in a foster home, and, most recently, the multipurpose community mental health clinic. A primary function of these clinics is to promote positive mental health attitudes in the community as a whole. A second function is to shorten the length of illness through early evaluation and treatment. A third function is to assist patients returning from the mental hospital to the community. In 1987 there were over 1000 community mental health clinics whose most significant public role is assisting ex-patients to rejoin society. To accomplish this end, temporary living arrangements, known as halfway houses, have been established in communities all around the country.

Policies into Practice

The policy of the hospital therapeutic community is a good idea insofar as it directs help to the specific problems of individual patients and encourages them to play an active role in their own rehabilitation. However, from a practical perspective, it is somewhat limited. The major problem with the hospital therapeutic community is that it requires a large, well-trained, and highly motivated staff. This is something which can be found in private hospitals where there is adequate funding from high patient fees. It is fine for the rich but no help to the average person who simply cannot afford private treatment. The state hospitals are certainly affordable, but this is largely due to a limited payroll which can support only a modest staff. The end result is that therapeutic communities are only available in hospitals beyond the financial reach of the average person.

The hospital therapeutic community is also challenged by the ideology of psychiatric training, which predisposes psychiatrists toward biogenic forms of treatment. The idea of treating patients by encouraging patient autonomy is directly opposed to drug therapy, which is known to produce a number of side effects that seriously limit a patient's ability to think and act independently.

The policy of community treatment does avoid some of the risks involved with hospitalization, but there are a number of trade-offs as well. On the positive side, deinstitutionalization preserves people's freedoms by not forcing them into an inpatient facility. On the negative side, a large number of essentially incompetent people, who are deeply troubled and in need of help, are left with no place to go. Such is the case with the so-called bag ladies, ventmen, and duck ladies who roam the streets because the state has turned over to the community what was once a commonwealth problem. Local businesses are especially prone to complain that the presence of street people in their doorways scares off customers. Disordered people who live at home and receive treatment at community clinics also pose problems since their very presence in the house may seriously disturb the emotional well-being of other family members. The family members' economic well-being may also be jeopardized if they are required to stay home from work to care for the disordered person.

Another practical problem with the community approach is that the clinics are not properly equipped to handle certain types of mental patients, particularly psychotics. Those patients require supervision which cannot easily be provided within a community treatment setting; and the treatments they require—lithium and other medication, for example—are much more appropriately administered in a hospital.

A third practical problem of the typical community clinic is staffing. In many instances, the clinics have even fewer professionals than the state hospitals. In fact, psychiatrists represent less than 5 percent of the total personnel of community clinics. These clinics are simply unappealing to many mental health workers, particularly psychiatrists who often lack the training in the social sciences which the community approach requires. Psychiatrists also find private practice more attractive because it is so much more lucrative than community psychiatry.

Another difficulty with community mental health clinics is the uncertainty of funding from the federal government. Citizens and their local governments have had to raise more than 50 percent of the funds for these centers. The federal funds were seriously curtailed after the Kennedy administration. The Nixon administration was publicly unsupportive of community clinics and attempted to phase out the funds already appropriated to run them. The change in social priorities during the Reagan administration resulted in a significant decline in social spending. This was very obvious in the reduced number of jobs available for psychiatric social workers.

Aside from the practical problems of handling psychotics, staffing, and funding, the community approach to mental health care is also challenged by a number of attitudinal difficulties. Psychiatrists are generally not tuned in to the community mental health approach. They are trained to change individuals, not society. It is much more convenient for them to set up their own private practices and treat less disturbed patients who can afford their fees. This is a major reason the clinics and the halfway houses are run by such poorly trained people.

The attitudes of the public toward community-based programs are especially negative. Many people simply fear a mass invasion of mental patients into their neighborhoods. Consequently, they often fight the establishment of community-based programs, particularly halfway houses for ex-patients. They use city ordinances, zoning codes, fire regulations, police arrests, and various informal approaches to exclude ex-patients from the community. As a result, ex-patients may be neglected in the community more than in state hospitals (National Institute of Mental Health, 1976). Public resistance would be even greater if the halfway houses were established in well-maintained neighborhoods rather than neighborhoods which are already deteriorated.

Evaluating the Evidence

The real measure of the effectiveness of the community approach treatment is whether it has significantly reduced the prevalence of mental disorder. Unfortunately, it is not now possible to answer this question objectively. There is no shortage of researchers who have tried, however; and, consequently, there are a number of conflicting reports regarding the supposed merits and disadvantages of the community approach.

On the positive side is the commonly cited fact that since the creation of community clinics, hundreds of thousands of people have received care who would never have been reached before. This is consistent with experimental studies which report that as many as three-fourths of patients scheduled for hospital admission could be maintained in the community with medication. Some of the community programs are reportedly quite effective, particularly in the area of emergency services. There

are also such programs as New York City's Fountain House, which serves about 2000 patients and provides them with jobs, apartments, meals, and day and night therapy programs. The program, founded in 1948 by former mental patients, has been quite successful. However, the staff is highly motivated and works with an annual budget of over 1 million dollars.

On the other hand, critics of the community programs charge that they are no more effective than the state hospitals. The community programs are not part of an organized system, they say, and as a result, patients get lost. Questions have also been raised regarding the efficacy of short-term and day hospitalization, both of which require immediate prescriptions of high drug dosages for psychotics and allow little time for careful observation of symptoms. Short-term hospitalization has certainly increased the number of discharges to the point where they outnumber new admissions. However, readmissions have also increased dramatically since the initiation of short-term hospitalization and community follow-up. The label *revolving door phenomenon* aptly describes the combined effect of shortened periods of hospitalization with a high probability of readmission. Although the community programs have never evolved as planned, many state hospitals are discharging patients as if these services exist.

What changes are needed to make community programs function better? Certainly we need an organized, well-funded system that can properly diagnose the mentally ill and then refer them to the most appropriate help source. This type of operation exists in many European countries. If it were developed in the United States, the quality of the staff should improve since salaries would be higher. It would also be very helpful if therapists were drawn from all class backgrounds, reducing the class and cultural differences between them and their patients. Then psychotherapy could be more evenly provided to people of all classes. The problem of public acceptance of community programs could be minimized through social programs by which patients and outsiders can mix and mingle. This would help to further close the gap between objective reality and subjective perceptions. In fact, there is real evidence that this can lead to greater public acceptance of community programs (Roman and Floyd, 1981).

Aftercare programs could be vastly improved if they were tailored to the particular needs of ex-patients. This could be accomplished by gradually reintegrating people into the community by giving them increased doses of responsibility. Each new dose should go beyond the current level of performance. This can lead to higher self-expectations, a condition vital for improvement. Suddenly dumping patients into the community without adequate preparation is a sure path to rehospitalization. Aftercare programs should be integrated with inpatient care so that patients will view a posthospital, community-based program as a natural next step. In addition, research on the chemistry of the brain should continue to develop drugs that can *cure* mental disorder and not simply alleviate symptoms.

We also need programs that really effect primary prevention, rather than dealing with mental disorder after it begins. Specifically, we need ways of protecting individuals at risk (such as the poor and the divorced) from mental health hazards. Environmental and social design projects are needed to change the situations that debilitate people, such as removing a child from abusive parents or providing social support to people undergoing stressful life events. Until these changes come, and until the general public becomes more sensitive to psychological problems, mental disorder will continue to take what could be a normal life and twist it into a hellish nightmare.

SUMMARY

1 Objectively, mental disorder is a major social problem; it affects millions of Americans, costs over 40 billion dollars annually, and reduces the productivity of the workforce by an estimated 25 percent. Subjectively, mental disorder is a hidden social problem which is widely denied, ignored, and misunderstood by the public.

2 Over time, concepts of mental disorder have changed dramatically. Originally mental disorder was considered to be the devil's work. Today it is considered to be the result of some mysterious combination of biological and psychosocial factors.

3 There are many well-defined categories of mental disorder. These included neurosis, schizophrenia, manic-depression, organic psychosis, and personality disorder. However, diagnosing mental disorder is not an easy task since there is great cross-cultural variation in what is seen as abnormal as well as much variation in the individual diagnostic techniques of psychiatrists.

4 Although the causes of mental disorder are not entirely known, recent research indicates that genetic and biochemical factors are frequently involved in schizophrenia and manic-depression. Neurosis and personality disorder appear to result from factors in the social environment such as childhood traumas or conditioning. Many cases of mental disorder seem to be precipitated by stressful life events.

5 Epidemiological studies have shown that certain groups in American society have high reported rates of mental disorder. These include married women, single men, Jews, international migrants, inner-city dwellers, lower-class people, and blacks.

6 Psychiatric treatment can be grouped into two broad classes: organic therapies (brain surgery, shock therapy, and chemotherapy) for psychotics and psychotherapy (psychoanalysis, behavior modification, client-centered therapy, and milieu therapy) for less disturbed patients.

7 Mental hospitals can help or hinder a patient's recovery, depending on whether they are designed to be therapeutic or custodial. Therapeutic hospitals (often small, well-funded, and private) pay particular attention to the problems of individual patients. Custodial hospitals (often large, poorly funded state institutions) are often structured to warehouse patients rather than truly rehabilitate them.

8 Mental patients face enormous problems when they are released into the community. These include lack of effective follow-up programs, having nowhere to live, and widespread stigmatization which makes it difficult to find a decent job or be accepted as a member of the community.

9 There has been a movement away from the social policy of treating people in hospitals toward treatment in community-based programs (deinstitutionalization). Community programs were created to avoid some of the undesirable side effects of hospitalization, such as institutionalization. However, community clinics currently have a number of practical problems including an inability to handle psychotics, poor staffing, uncertain funding, and negative subjective attitudes of the public.

CHAPTER 5

The Family: Society's Nucleus Under Strain

FAMILY PROBLEMS: AN OVERVIEW

The conflicting aims and assumptions of those involved in planning the [White House Conference on the Family] surfaced as soon as the [Carter] Administration tried to devise a definition for "family." The Census Bureau's definition, "a group of two persons or more related by birth, marriage, or adoption and residing together," was too restrictive to encompass the new family forms, while the alternative offered by the Family Service Association of America, "a person-to-person mutual aid system" providing "emotional support...and the assurance of economic and physical survival of the total constellation" would, one traditionalist noted, include "a pair of winos sharing a boxcar and a bottle."

—*Lawrence Grossman (1985)*

In 1976 presidential candidate Jimmy Carter made family problems one of his major campaign themes. He argued that the American family was in serious trouble, and promised to aid the institution if elected. As President, Carter did propose a White House Conference on the Family to be held in 1979. But that conference never really got off the ground. One reason for this failure, as the passage by Grossman above indicates, was that those involved in planning the conference could not even agree on what the *family* was. The Conference's planners ultimately decided to sidestep this definitional dispute by naming the project a White House Conference *on Families* rather than *on the Family*.

We have begun this chapter with this story to emphasize two things at the outset. First, there is wide disagreement about what constitutes a family; consequently, there is similar disagreement about the nature of family problems and about possible solutions. Indeed, the solutions offered by some are viewed as problems by others. Second, this dispute over the definition of the family was not just a silly argument over words. It was an impassioned confrontation over basic values. The same value conflicts that made the definition problematic surfaced throughout the rest of the planning activities of the conference and ultimately caused it to be severely scaled down and virtually abandoned. These value conflicts are a major subtheme of this chapter.

Family problems are not one of those problem areas where the objective dimension towers over the subjective dimension. Just about everyone agrees that the family faces serious problems and that many of these problems seem to have intensified since the 1950s. Indeed, because the family is the central institution in American life, it cannot help but be linked as cause and/or effect to virtually every problem in American society. You will see its imprint clearly in almost every chapter of this book, and its role with respect to the problems of teenagers and young adults (e.g., drug abuse, crime, sex, and suicide) is particularly vivid. Before discussing specific family problems, we will focus on the big picture. We will address the questions: What is happening to the American family, and why does it have problems?

The Traditional American Family

There has never been a society in which the family was perfectly designed and problem-free. Historical accounts of the family in many cultures invariably include lists of deficiencies and troubles. And this has also been true of the American family, stretching back to its colonial beginnings. For example, the proportion of children, especially black children, living in households without a father present is currently very high: 53 percent in 1984 (U.S. Bureau of the Census, 1985b). But it was also high just before World War I in the then predominantly Irish Middle West Side of New York, where about half the families were fatherless (Banfield, 1970). Similarly, some of the present trends considered by some to be problematic—like the declining proportion of people who marry (see Box 5-1) or of mothers who are full-time housewives—are really just a return to past patterns. There is not space in this book to trace the entire history of American family problems. Instead, we will pick up the thread in the 1950s and proceed from there.

The typical family in the 1950s consisted of a breadwinning husband, a stay-at-home wife, and their dependent children. This organization—which we will call the *traditional family*—was society's ideal, and about two-thirds of the nation's families conformed to it. Any deviation from this social norm was considered a problem per se. Divorce was a problem because it shattered an ideal marriage and led to a broken home for children. Voluntary and involuntary childlessness were problems because they resulted in incomplete families. And a working mother could not be a "good" mother (Bassis, Gelles, and Levine, 1982).

BOX 5-1

THE DECLINING POPULARITY OF MARRIAGE

One way to weaken the family institution is to decrease the proportion of the population who participate in it. This is what is happening in the United States. The proportion of people who never married was only about 4 percent in the 1950s. Today experts estimate that about 10 to 15 percent of women presently in their early twenties will never marry. Conservatives are particularly concerned that this proportion will continue to rise in the future. They point to Sweden as an ominous bellwether. The actual number of marriages declined by 30 percent there between 1966 and 1975 (Westoff, 1978b), and by the mid-1980s about 20 percent of Swedes never married (Brodin, 1983).

One reason why the proportion never marrying in the United States will likely continue to rise is that American men and women are increasingly delaying marriage. The result of this practice is usually that large numbers will ultimately never marry. In 1984, the median age of first marriage for women was 23 years—the highest since 1890. The median age for men was 25.4 years, approaching the 1890 pinnacle of 26.1 years. By comparison, the median ages in 1956 were 20.1 for women and 22.5 for men. Moreover, the rate of increase in the median age has increased particularly sharply since 1976 (U.S. Bureau of the Census, 1985a). What is even more striking are the large increases that have occurred in the proportion of women and men under 35 years old who have yet to marry. For example, between 1970 and 1984, the percentage of men aged 30 to 34 who never married increased from 9 to 21 percent, and for women of the same age the proportion rose from 6 to 13 percent (U.S. Bureau of the Census, 1985a).

However, even though it was considered ideal by the public, the traditional family had problems. Many husbands, wives, and children simply refused to abide by the social norms regulating desirable family and marital behavior. Consequently, such problems as divorce, premarital sex, extramarital sex, and family violence troubled many families. Because these problems were either less common and/or less reported than they are today, sociologists commonly viewed them through the prism of deviant behavior theory. Particular attention was focused on the society's reaction to deviant individuals and on the ensuing suffering and social dislocations that reaction brought about. The unmarried, the divorced, the out-of-wedlock mothers, the childless, and other deviants were all stigmatized, and were cut off in many ways from full participation in American life. In addition, subculture theory was used to explain why entire social groups, invariably lower-class or ethnic ones, failed to conform to the norms of the traditional American family.

Other problems of the traditional family were thought to be best understood through functionalism, the theory that each element of social life—like the family—can be analyzed in terms of the purposes—or functions—it serves in the larger social pattern. According to functionalists, the traditional family is a nuclear unit because an industrial economy demands a mobile labor force, and small, easily moved families help that economy to function smoothly. But functionalism does not presume that society's blueprint is perfect, that everything fits together neatly, and that there are no conflicting functional expectations. Indeed, due to the change brought about by industrialization and urbanization, the traditional family was unable to adequately perform some of the customary family functions which the extended family took in stride.

The extended family includes three or more generations. One feature of the extended family is that it contained a large pool of potential care givers for its dependent members: small children, the handicapped, the old, and the sick. It could, for instance, easily provide support for the wife and dependent children of a husband-father who was incapacitated, missing, or dead. By contrast, the traditional family could be devastated by such an occurrence. Similarly, the extended family provided a secure place and a respected role for the elderly, whereas the traditional family frequently supplied neither.

There were also critics of the family who saw the problems not as deviations from desirable norms or as imperfections in an otherwise sound and functional institutional design. They saw the problems as being intrinsic to the institution itself. The principal source of their criticism came from the feminist movement, which erupted from whiffs of smoke in the 1950s to a raging fire in the 1960s. The feminist movement had both a radical and a moderate wing. The radical wing believed that women were the most oppressed of all people and that the family was an institution designed by men to subjugate women. As Berger and Berger (1984) note, the family was viewed as an age-old evil, heterosexuality was rape, motherhood was slavery, and all relations between men and women were a struggle for power. Thus, the family was looked upon as a major obstacle to the radicals' value-bound goal of the total liberation of women. This radical critique hearkens back to the ideas of Frederick Engels (1942), who also believed that the family was an oppressive institution which should be radically changed.

The more influential moderate wing of feminism did not indict the family per se, just the traditional family. The flash point of the feminist movement occurred in 1963 with the publication of Betty Friedan's *The Feminine Mystique*. This book criticized the domestic role of women in the traditional family. It provided a springboard for the more moderate feminist view, largely championed by the National Organization for Women, that the self-abnegating role that the wife played in the traditional family was problematic not only

for herself but for her husband and children as well. Women were encouraged to develop a larger, more varied identity, principally by leaving the household and entering the labor force. In short, feminism considered the traditional family to be a remnant of patriarchy and, as such, problematic in itself.

Sociologists used value conflict theory to understand the struggle of such opposing groups to impose their self-serving plans (in this case, plans concerning the nature of the ideal family) on society. They also used this theory to interpret conflict over specific value-bound issues related to the family, such as abortion, premarital sexuality, and alternative lifestyles.

The Family in Transition: 1950–1980

In modern industrial societies, social change is inevitable and unceasing, and it was particularly rapid in the United States between the 1950s and the early 1980s. No institution remained unscathed, but the traditional family was one of the hardest hit. Much of this change was caused by the continued rise and evolution of the modern industrial state—the continuation of trends toward industrialization, urbanization, economic growth, individualism, social mobility, and personal freedom. Technological change, as usual, played an important role. For example, med-tech advances led to longer life expectancy which, among other things, increased the potential duration of marriage, the time spouses play nonparental roles (i.e., the empty nest period), and the probability of divorce (Stub, 1982). The traditional family was also affected by government policies such as those which contributed to the rise of the post-New Deal American welfare state. One critic (Murray, 1984), for example, contends that many social programs of Lyndon Johnson's Great Society contributed to the breakup of families (in addition to rising crime and falling educational standards). Similarly, judicial decisions such as the Supreme Court's legalization of abortion had a profound impact on the family.

Moreover, virtually all the major social and cultural movements of that period were antagonistic to the traditional family. One of these, of course, was the feminist movement, probably the most influential of the bunch. Others were the sexual liberation movements, such as the gay and lesbian movements, and elements of the singles subculture, which were all, by definition, opposed to the hegemony of the traditional family. There were also the iconoclastic nonconformist groups and the "beat" generation of the 1950s and early 1960s, which rejected middle-class values and institutions. Similarly, the black culture movement dismissed traditional family norms as white impositions. The New Left and the counterculture groups (e.g., the hippies) of the mid-1960s to early 1970s found serious fault with all elements of traditional American society, including the family. And the growth psychologies of the 1960s and 1970s (like the encounter movement) and the "me" generation of the 1970s emphasized self-realization and the primacy of the individual over any type of family (Berger and Berger, 1984).

Although not nearly as organized and visible as the feminist movement, there was also a battle going on between 1950 and 1980 for the hearts of men. Men, too, were encouraged to rebel against their sex roles, particularly the bread-winner role they played in the traditional family. Indeed, Ehrenreich (1983) contends that contrary to popular belief, it was men, not women, who *first* rebelled against their sex roles and undermined the traditional American family.

Between 1950 and 1980 these forces, movements, and a myriad of other phenomena (e.g., major events like the Vietnamese war) changed the face of the American family almost beyond recognition. One change was that the family got significantly smaller. The size of the average American household declined about 20 percent between 1950 and 1980, from 3.4 persons to 2.7. The popularity of marriage was down too. The

proportion of people in a typical generation who never married by age 45 was just 4 percent in the 1950s. But by 1980 it appeared that about 10 percent (Thornton and Rodgers, 1983), and possibly as high as 15 percent (Family Service America, 1984), of American women born after 1960 would never marry. Divorce went through the roof in this period. The annual rate increased sharply from about 1 percent of existing marriages in 1950 to 2.3 percent in 1980. And the proportion of children born after marriage who experienced a parental marital dissolution by age 16 rose from about 25 percent in 1950 to about 36 percent in 1980 (Thornton and Freedman, 1983).

The percent of currently married adults also declined markedly during the period. For instance, about 66 percent of women aged 20 to 24 were currently married and living with their husband in the 1950s, compared to less than 40 percent of women that age in the early 1980s. On the other hand, the proportion of unmarried adults sharing living quarters with an unrelated person of the opposite sex escalated dramatically. By the early 1980s they constituted about 4 percent of all couples maintaining a separate household, up from a mere fraction of 1 percent in 1950 (U.S. Bureau of the Census, 1960; 1983b).

There was also less childbearing going on in America. The average number of children per woman dropped from about 3.5 in the 1950s baby boom era to about 1.8 in the early 1980s. Similarly, the percentage of women remaining childless is expected to increase from the 1950s' 10 percent range to as high as 30 percent for women in the midst of their prime reproductive period during the early 1980s (Bloom, 1982). Moreover, more of the childbearing that did take place occurred outside the traditional family. Indeed, the percentage of all American births that occurred out of wedlock catapulted from a mere 4 percent in 1950 to an alarming 18 percent in 1980. The increasing availability and utilization of abortion was one reason for the overall decline in childbearing. By 1980 there were more than 1.5 million abortions being performed annually in the United States (Henshaw, Forrest, Sullivan, and Tietze, 1982), many times the number carried out in 1950.

Premarital sexual activity increased enormously, too, between 1950 and the early 1980s, particularly among teenagers. Judging from the famous Kinsey study data, less than 10 percent of never-married women aged 15 to 19 had premarital sexual intercourse in 1950. By 1980 this figure had risen to nearly 50 percent (Zelnick and Kantner, 1980). Not surprisingly, premarital pregnancy among teenagers followed suit. The proportion of all women aged 15 to 19 who had been premaritally pregnant swelled from just a few percentage points in 1950 to about 16 percent in 1980 (Zelnick and Kantner, 1980). And the actual birth rate for unmarried women aged 15 to 19 rose by more than 200 percent over the same period (National Center for Health Statistics, 1978, 1982b).

Finally, a veritable revolution occurred in women's work patterns between 1950 and 1980. In 1950, only 25 percent of all married women were working for pay or looking for a job outside the home. By 1980, 51 percent were in the labor force. Even more dramatic is the fact that most of this change was due to the movement of married women with preschool children into the world of work. Fully 49 percent of these women were in the labor force in 1980 compared to a mere 12 percent in 1950. Married women with school-age children also entered the workforce in droves. In 1950, just 31 percent were in the labor force; by 1980, the figure was up to 64 percent (U.S. Bureau of Labor Statistics, 1982; Thornton and Freedman, 1983). As a result of these labor force trends, the proportion of preschool and school-age children who had a full-time mother present in the home plummeted between 1950 and 1980.

In short, people were marrying less, divorcing more, remarrying less, and having fewer children. More wives and mothers were in the labor force, more children were growing up without full-time mothers, and more sex and childbearing was taking place outside of the family.

The Conservative Reaction

By 1980 the American public could be divided into three groups. About 17 percent of Americans were deeply committed to a philosophy of personal self-fulfillment—a value system in which ego needs, sensation, and excitement take priority over the needs of others, including spouse and children. We will call this group the *liberals* in the sense that they want to liberate the individual from traditional family and other norms. Another 63 percent of Americans subscribed to this self-centered philosophy in varying degrees, which means that they also continued to embrace some traditional values. Etzioni (1982) labels this group "the ambivalent majority." We will simply call them *moderates*. Only 20 percent of the American public still clung to a broad range of traditional values, including those that underpin the traditional family (Yankelovich, 1981). We will call this latter group *conservatives* in the sense that they want to conserve the traditional family and the traditional roles within the family (between the sexes, between spouses, between the generations). They are also in favor of traditional concepts of moral responsibility, not only with respect to the family and sexuality but over a broad range of social behavior (Berger and Berger, 1984). In the ideological struggle between the conservatives and the liberals, the moderates split, depending upon the issue. For example, some moderates are pro-abortion while others are antiabortion.

The conservatives were keenly dismayed not only about the changes that the family was undergoing after 1950 but also about where these trends were leading. In recent decades two Scandinavian countries, Sweden and Denmark, have been in the avant-garde of social change in the developed world. The family changes that occurred there tended to be mimicked by countries like the United States a decade or so later (Westoff, 1978b). Conservatives believed that they could see the American family's future unfolding in places like Sweden, and they were horrified by what they saw. For instance, Sweden has had an extraordinarily low birth rate (1.5 children per woman, far below that·required for replacement of the population), and has experienced exceptionally high rates of marital disruption, nonmarriage, illegitimacy, and abortion (half of all pregnancies are aborted). Moreover, Sweden has adopted many radical family policies such as compulsory child day care (even for children of mothers who are not in the labor force), prosecution of parents who administer corporal punishment to their children, and government subsidies to employers for hiring individuals in jobs traditionally held by the opposite sex (Brodin, 1983).

But even though conservatives were upset about ongoing and anticipated family changes, there was little organized opposition to these changes until well into the 1970s. It was then that a backlash phenomenon emerged. In retrospect, it is surprising that it took so long for conservatives to mobilize, given the central role the family played in people's lives and the shocking quality of much of the change. Nevertheless the pro-traditional family movement was not really ignited until the Supreme Court barred the states from outlawing abortion in 1973. This decision galvanized the opponents of abortion, and a well-organized antiabortion movement quickly materialized. The antiabortion movement then served as a seed crystal for the whole pro-traditional family movement. It was soon allied with such entities as the Moral Majority and Fundamentalist Protestantism, as well as with independent conservatives. The pro-traditional family movement ultimately included people with many different concerns, especially opposition to feminism, the sexual revolution (particularly homosexual aspects),

pornography, secular humanism (especially the prohibition of prayer in public schools), and abortion. While these groups and individuals could not always be aligned, the pro-traditional family movement did achieve enough consensus to become an influential cultural and political force by 1980.

The American Family in the 1980s

During the 1980s the mood of the American people veered toward conservatism, and the erosion of traditional family values slowed down and even rebounded in some areas. Eight percent more Americans rated their family life highly satisfying in 1982 than in 1974. And 92 percent of Americans in 1982 believed that there should be more emphasis on traditional family ties (Gallup, 1984). The divorce rate stopped increasing in 1981, and actually declined 8 percent by 1984 (National Center for Health Statistics, annually). And Americans were more critical of divorce than in the 1970s. Fifty-four percent of the public in 1982 thought divorce should be more difficult to obtain; in 1977, only 44 percent thought that (*Public Opinion,* 1983). The abortion rate also declined slightly after reaching its peak in 1981. And the sexual revolution lost many of its followers. After nearly quadrupling between 1970 and 1982, the number of unmarried-couple households leveled off in 1983 and 1984 (National Center for Health Statistics, 1985c). And by 1982 only 1 person in 4 wanted to see "more acceptance of sexual freedom" (Gallup, 1984). However, one conspicuous exception to this trend toward more traditional family values was the continuing movement of wives and mothers into the workforce.

Despite the shift toward conservatism, the traditional family was still fading fast in the mid-1980s. Remember, in 1950, nearly two-thirds of the nation's families conformed to the traditional family model. By 1984, only 18 percent continued to do so (U.S. Bureau of the Census, 1985b). But even these startling figures

By the 1980s single-parent families were common in the United States, and many like this one lived in poverty. (*David E. Kennedy/Texastock*)

underestimate the real decline of the traditional family as the basic institution of American life, because there were proportionately far fewer families *of any type* in 1984 than in 1950 (meaning there were proportionately more nonfamily households like a male householder living alone). Another statistic gives us a better view of the true immensity of this trend. In 1950 the traditional family constituted about 70 percent of all households. But by March 1984 this figure had dropped to a mere 10 percent (U.S. Bureau of the Census, 1985*b*). And experts believe the proportion will continue to shrink in the future. So in a very real sense, the traditional family is dying.

But this does not mean that the family institution itself is doomed, as conservatives (and radicals) often predict. The family has repeatedly proved itself to be a very resilient institution by adapting to the changing worlds of the past, and it is likely to continue to do so. The

United States has now become a more variegated society with different kinds of families, no one of which predominates. Yet most Americans still consider their actual or planned family, regardless of type, to be central to their happiness and well-being. This is clear from in-depth community studies [e.g., the Middletown study (Caplow, Bahr, Chadwick, Hill, and Williamson, 1982)] and from public opinion polls (e.g., Gallup, 1984). Indeed, the Family Life Survey found that strong ties still exist between grown children and their parents, brothers, and sisters, as evidenced by the extraordinary amount of socializing they do. For example, grown children visit one or both of their parents about fifty-five times a year.

Family Problems in the 1980s

But just as the family will likely survive in one form or another, so will family problems. Indeed, recent changes in the family have brought with them a raft of psychological, social, and economic problems, like the feminization and "childization" of poverty.

Liberals contend that many of these problems are just temporary, that they will be ironed out in the future once the necessary policies (e.g., passage of an Equal Rights Amendment for women and a Bill of Rights for children) are adopted and implemented. But conservatives disagree. They maintain that many of the traditional values have survived several thousand years because they work. As Marshner (1985) notes: "Human nature is so constructed that certain things tend to make people happy and certain things do not. Traditional values are really an enumeration of what makes people happy, and the 'thou shalt nots' are really enumerations of what causes human unhappiness." Because of this, conservatives argue that high rates of divorce, premarital and extramarital sex, abortion, illegitimacy, and the like will always create serious problems for American society. Conservatives also insist that traditional values provide the only framework for society in which capitalism can survive. They contend, for example, that as the family unit weakens, the only thing that can happen is for the welfare state mentality to become more entrenched and for the entitlement programs to become more bloated (Marshner, 1985). But it is important to note that some liberals are not committed to capitalism per se and that many others would rejoice at the prospect of greatly expanded entitlement programs. So once again, what is a problem for the conservatives is often a solution for the liberals and vice versa.

Sociologists view family problems today using the same prisms they used in 1950, although the mix is different. The deviance approach is used less today because deviance from traditional norms (e.g., those against premarital sex and divorce) is so prevalent that the behavior can no longer be considered deviant. Indeed, as Rossi notes, "What we defined a decade ago as 'deviant' is today labeled 'variant', in order to

suggest that there is a healthy, experimental quality to current social explorations into the future 'beyond monogamy', or 'beyond the nuclear family' " (Rossi, Kagan, and Hareven, 1978:1). Moreover, since few new widely accepted norms have taken the place of the traditional ones, the absolute number of norms to deviate from has declined. The deviance approach is still used, however, to understand deviance from the few remaining widely accepted norms (e.g., those relating to family violence).

On the other hand, social change theory is utilized somewhat more than it was in the 1950s. After all, the traditional family went from being the dominant mode to being just a small minority of households in the space of a single generation. According to social change theory, the fantastic speed of this collapse alone is responsible for much of today's family disorganization.

Functionalism remains a useful approach as the family continues to give up or improperly perform traditional functions, and other institutions fail to adequately adopt them. For example, the family continues to seek adequate government assistance for child care and social services for the elderly. But the government has been unwilling to fully provide this support, and the private sector is not equipped to take up the slack. As a result we have, among other problems, "latch key" children and suicides among the elderly.

Finally, value conflict theory continues to be useful in understanding the struggle between opposing groups, like the conservatives and the liberals, and in interpreting conflict over specific family-related issues, like abortion and alternative lifestyles.

THE SUBJECTIVE DIMENSION OF FAMILY PROBLEMS

Earlier in this chapter we made the point that Americans are committed to the institution of the family. Upwards of 80 percent tell poll-sters that their family is one of the most important facets of their lives and that they are highly satisfied with their own marriage and family. Nevertheless, the average American believes the family institution itself is in serious trouble—that it is deteriorating, decaying, even dying. This information again comes largely from public opinion polls. For instance, the Gallup Organization reported in 1980 that Americans see the family threatened on all sides; and family-related problems made the Gallup Organization's list of the ten most important problems throughout the first half of the 1980s (*Gallup Report,* various years). The Middletown study provided a microcosm of this paradox. When Middletown people compared their own families to what they thought was the typical family, nearly all of them related that their own families were much more affectionate, secure, and peaceful. In other words, they were saying, "I'm fortunate, my family is okay. It is other people's families that are falling apart" (Caplow et al., 1982).

Conservatives in particular are anxious about the demise of the family and, subsequently, of society itself, since the family is often viewed as the building block or cornerstone of society. They see themselves involved in a historic battle with liberals over the fate of the family and society. And they think they are losing that battle. As one conservative expresses it: "There is a war going on for the preservation of society and the pagans are already within the walls" (Berger and Berger, 1984:31).

The idea that the family is dying or succumbing to moral decay is not new. It has haunted many societies, including the Roman Empire in its latter stages and the United States during the Great Depression. But whatever its problems, the family always seems to muddle through. Apparently there is a timeless tendency for the subjective dimension of family problems to exceed their objective dimension, no matter how great the latter might be. So it should not surprise us that this situation exists in the United States today. Why does this tendency exist? The answer revolves around three social factors: visibility, expectations, and values.

Family problems are highly *visible*. There is intrinsic drama in such phenomena as free love, incest, open marriage, illegitimacy, palimony, child abuse, divorce, childlessness, abortion, child poverty, stepfamilies, and involuntary singleness (see Box 5-2). Always looking for a good story, the media are quick to capitalize on this real-life drama. There is a constant stream of highly emotional films (e.g., *Kramer vs. Kramer*), gripping television documentaries, and in-depth coverage in the print media on virtually every family problem.

The second social factor causing the subjective dimension of family problems to be too high is *expectations*. The basic principle here is this: The more controllable a problem seems to us to be, the more we tend to view its objective dimension as outrageous ("Why isn't somebody *doing* something about this?!?"). Since families are the most personal and intimate environments in which we live, they *seem* eminently tractable ("If parents would just discipline their children, there would be much less crime"). Problems like child abuse, spouse abuse, and parent abuse are so upsetting to us because they are the last things we *expect* from parents, spouses, and children.

The family is also the focus of many of our most cherished *values*, ones sanctified by religion and overlaid by tradition. Since the basic principle here is that objective damage done to things associated with the value system gets magnified (a drug addict *seems* worse than an alcoholic because the former is seen as rejecting conventional society), family problems loom larger than life. The reverence for family as an institution—and the

---

BOX 5-2

PROBLEMS WITH THE MARRIAGE MARKET

One social problem in the United States is the fact that there are more women ready to marry than there are men. Goldman, Westoff, and Hammerslough (1984) examined the relative availability of unmarried men and women in 1980, making the judgment of suitability principally on the basis of race, age, and education. They found that white women under 25 were the only female group that was in a good position to find a mate. There were 121 suitable men for every 100 suitable women. After age 25, however, the marriage prospects of single white women plummeted. By ages 30 to 34, for instance, there were two college educated women available for every suitable man. And by ages 60 to 64, available college educated women outnumbered the men by 7 to 1. The situation for black women was similar, just somewhat worse; and there was no age at which there were enough black men to go around.

This imbalance in the numbers of eligible men and women is due primarily to different sizes of birth cohorts (Chapter 7), educational differences between men and women, and the tendency for men to marry women younger than themselves. Sexual preference also works against women, for there are several times more men than women who are homosexual.

Being unable to marry is not just a personal tragedy for the individuals involved. Research has shown that the sex ratio of available marriage partners has profound social, psychological, and economic effects on the basic structure of society. The availability of too few marriage partners affects the comparative status and power of men and women, norms of sexual behavior, marriage rates, family stability, and childbearing practices. In the United States, the growing surplus of women not only increases the percentage who remain single but also is related to many other family-related trends of the past two decades. These include the rising age at marriage, falling marital fertility, increasing rates of divorce, growing rates of out-of-wedlock childbearing, rising female employment, and increasing female earnings.

---

related notion that it is the cornerstone of society—means that each statistical addition to divorce, illegitimacy, and the like *seems* more ominous than objective slippage in other areas. This is one reason why the issues most fiercely contested in the United States (e.g., abortion and sex education) focus directly on central aspects of the family.

Strong values also boost the subjective dimension of family problems by making people hyperaware of problem linkages. For example, since people hold that the family is the building block of society, they believe that when the family goes wrong, so does everything else. Unfortunately, people have a tendency to go overboard. They give family problems too much credit for society's other woes. Family problems are often blamed for everything from crime waves to declining college board scores. This is in sharp contrast to many other social problems like prejudice and poverty, which frequently are given too little credit for their problem linkages.

SEXUAL ACTIVITY AND CHILDBEARING AMONG THE UNMARRIED

Prevalence and Trends

Increased sexual activity and childbearing among the unmarried are growing social concerns in the United States. There are no solid statistics on the extent of sexual activity among all unmarried women, but data on premarital sexuality and the rising rates of contraception, cohabitation, and childbearing among the unmarried indicate that it is substantial and growing. One recent national study (Bachrach and Horn, 1985) on premarital sexuality, for instance, found that 80 percent of women who married in the years 1975–1979 did not wait until marriage to begin sexual activity. This was a sharp increase from the 1960–1964 period, when only 52 percent had had sexual intercourse before marriage.

Childbearing among all unmarried women grew steadily from 1940 to 1983 (National Center for Health Statistics, 1985c). In 1983, more than 3 percent of unmarried women gave birth, the highest rate ever observed in the United States. The rise in the proportion of women who are unmarried, the increase in their childbearing rate, and the declining childbearing rate of married women have, since 1960, combined to boost the proportion of all American births that are illegitimate. Only about 4 percent of all births occurred to unmarried women in 1960, but by 1983, more than 20 percent were illegitimate. In 1983, 13 percent of white births and 58 percent of black births were out of wedlock (National Center for Health Statistics, 1985c).

Sexual activity and childbearing among unmarried *teenagers* have also increased steadily and are now widespread. The proportion of never-married women aged 15 to 19 who have had premarital intercourse increased from less than 10 percent in 1950 to 46 percent in 1979 (42 percent of white women and 65 percent of black women). Moreover, 69 percent of never-married 19-year-old women and 78 percent of 19-year-old men were no longer virgins in 1979. As a result of (1) this increased sexual activity, (2) the low proportion of sexually active teenagers who always use contraception (only 34 percent), and (3) the careless or inefficient practice of contraception by many who do use it, premarital pregnancy among teenagers has skyrocketed. By 1979, 16 percent of all women aged 15 to 19 had been premaritally pregnant (14 percent of white women and 30 percent of black women) (Zelnick and Kantner, 1980).

Unmarried teenage women deal with premarital pregnancy three ways: (1) by legitimating them through marriage prior to delivering the baby, (2) by having an abortion, or (3) by having an out-of-wedlock birth. The first response—marriage—has lost popularity in recent years. Only 16 percent chose this solution in 1979, compared to about twice that many in 1971. One reason for this decline was the increased availability of abortion. The proportion who took this alternative increased 60 percent over that interval, from 23 to 37 percent.

Out-of-wedlock childbearing among teenagers also rose over this period, as it has been doing uninterruptedly since 1940. In 1983, 3 percent of unmarried women aged 15 to 19 gave birth, a figure four times higher than it was in 1940 (National Center for Health Statistics, 1985c; 1978b). The 1983 rates for white and black 15- to 19-year-olds were 2 percent and 9 percent, respectively. Out-of-wedlock childbearing accounted for more than half of all births to women in this age category in 1983. The increase in illegitimate births among teenage women was due not only to the increase in premarital pregnancy but also to a growing reluctance to legitimate such births via traditional shotgun marriages.

Consequences of Unmarried Sexuality

Unmarried sexual activity has been a social problem in America from colonial days. It has been a traditional theme in American culture, as exemplified by Hawthorne's *The Scarlet Letter* (1850). And it was a major topic in the social problems texts of the mid-twentieth century. Unmarried sexuality was viewed as a threat to the traditional family and as a symptom of moral decay. It was also considered problematic because of its links to other problems like illegitimacy, abortion, and sexually transmitted diseases (STDs).

Abortion   The unmarried are disproportionately represented among those who terminate pregnancy by abortion (Henshaw, Binkin, Blaine, and Smith, 1985). Eighty-one percent of all abortions in 1981 were obtained by unmarried women, even though they constituted only about 43 percent of all women aged 15 to 44. And unmarried women are increasingly using abortion. In 1974, the year after abortion was legalized, 3 percent of unmarried women had one. This figure rose to 5 percent in 1981. In contrast, the percentage of married women who had abortions, only 0.9 percent in 1974 and 1 percent in 1981, was much lower and changed little over the period.

Unmarried teenage women (and teenage women in general) were also increasingly utilizing abortion, and using it out of proportion to their numbers. In 1974, 2.7 percent of women aged 15 to 19 had an abortion; in 1981, this figure had risen to 4.3 percent (4.4 percent for just unmarried teenagers). Women aged 18 to 19 had the highest rate of abortion of any age group, with more than 6 percent having an abortion in 1981. Though they represented only 18 percent of all women aged 15 to 44, women aged 15 to 19 obtained 28 percent of all abortions in 1981. This is one reason why the antiabortion forces are vehemently opposed to teenage sexuality.

Sexually Transmitted Disease The incidence of sexually transmitted diseases (STDs) has skyrocketed over the past several decades. This increase is generally linked to many of the social changes discussed in this chapter, particularly the growing number of young, sexually active people who are its principal victims. Indeed, more people are infected with STDs than ever before because an increasing number of individuals are beginning interpersonal sexual activity at an earlier age, are having multiple sex partners, and are staying unmarried for a longer time.

AIDS, which is increasingly moving into the heterosexual population of the United States, is just one star in a burgeoning constellation of sexually transmitted diseases (Chapter 3). There are twenty-four other sex-related afflictions that affect tens of millions of Americans. One of these is genital warts, a condition linked to cancer which plagues up to 4 million Americans. Another is genital herpes, a disease with 20 million victims that causes genital sores and can lead to blindness and mental illness in offspring. Chlamydia troubles 3 million Americans, including 20 to 30 percent of college

women. Like gonorrhea (1 million victims in 1984), chlamydia can cause lifetime sterility and miscarriages even after the disease has been cured (McFalls and McFalls, 1984).

STDs are major causes of sickness and death, and are also responsible for an immense amount of emotional distress. Consider for a moment the anguish of a sterile couple unsuccessfully trying to have a baby, or the suffering of a herpes victim who is treated like a sexual outcast. In addition, STDs annually cost the United States billions of dollars.

As noted above, conservatives argue that traditional values have endured because they work and that STDs provide a case in point. Allegiance to norms against sex outside of marriage would greatly reduce the prevalence of STDs and their accompanying problems. However, the cost would be a severe reduction in personal sexual freedom, so this is a good example of value trade-offs.

Attitudes toward Premarital Sex and Out-of-Wedlock Childbearing

Despite the serious and growing problems linked to premarital sexuality (and more generally to unmarried sexuality), its subjective dimension has plummeted in recent decades. In 1969, 76 percent of Americans considered premarital sex to be unacceptable; by 1985, only 42 percent thought that (*Gallup Report,* 1985). But as the 42 percent figure suggests, there are still sizable groups—most notably conservatives and/or religious individuals—with values opposed to sex outside marriage. For example, in 1985, 60 percent of those who claimed that religion was very important in their lives thought premarital sex was wrong.

Out-of-wedlock childbearing is almost universally considered a problem. Conservatives oppose illegitimacy per se. They see it as a symptom of moral decay and as a threat to the traditional family. They argue that the stigma society applies to unwed mothers and their illegitimate children is necessary (or functional) because it helps ensure that most births take place within the nuclear family, the ideal structure for child rearing. Liberals see out-of-wedlock childbearing as a problem because they recognize that illegitimate children and their mothers often suffer from negative economic and social consequences, not the least of which are the problems children confront in a fatherless home. Another consequence is the aforementioned stigma, which liberals have opposed and have helped to reduce in recent decades. Liberals and conservatives alike are alarmed over the sheer number of illegitimate children being born and their rising proportion of all births; and over the huge cost of programs to reduce illegitimacy and to mitigate the negative consequences faced by out-of-wedlock children and their mothers.

All groups are also particularly concerned over the trend in out-of-wedlock childbearing among teenagers, because the unfavorable social and economic circumstances associated with teenage childbearing in general are especially problematic for unmarried teenagers (Thornton and Freedman, 1983). Adolescent mothers get less schooling than other teenagers, and this, together with child care problems, retards their quest for and commitment to an occupation. As a result, many turn to the welfare system for support (Baldwin, 1980). In addition, women who begin childbearing early tend to have relatively more children than those who do not. So the problems of the teenage mother are often quickly multiplied. Finally, women whose first child had been conceived or born out of wedlock have relatively high rates of marital disruption (O'Connell and Rodgers, 1984).

While liberals and conservatives agree that out-of-wedlock childbearing is a problem, they disagree strongly on what social policies should be adopted to solve it. Liberals want to lower the costs of averting illegitimate births by making contraceptives and abortion cheaper and easier to obtain. They also argue persuasively

for more and better sex education in the schools (see Jones et al., 1985). Conservatives would rather increase the disincentives for having an illegitimate baby by reducing Aid for Dependent Children payments, food stamp programs, and other subsidies, and by creating work requirements for unwed mothers. They also favor strenuous measures to force fathers to support their illegitimate offspring. Again, the conservatives' solutions are viewed by the liberals as merely trading existing problems for new ones, and vice versa.

FAMILY VIOLENCE

Overview

Family violence can be defined as an attack on a family member with intent to hurt. It can be a physical attack ranging from a hard slap to a murder. Or it can be verbal or nonverbal threats of bodily injury as well as psychological or emotional abuse. While there are no complete statistics on the occurrence of any kind of family violence, it is beyond dispute that extraordinary numbers of children, wives, parents, grandparents, and even husbands are being brutalized by other family members. In fact, family violence may be the most common type of violence in the United States.

Violence toward family members dates back at least to the dawn of written history and undoubtedly beyond (Davidson, 1977). It is found in most contemporary societies (Gelles and Cornell, 1983), and has always been common in the United States. But despite its towering objective dimension, family violence has traditionally had a low subjective dimension and still does in much of the world. Family violence was not considered to be a serious social problem in the United States until the mid-1970s, when three developments came together to raise our social consciousness (Bassis et al., 1982).

One of these developments was an increasing national sensitivity to violence of any kind, a reaction to the highly dramatic and visible public violence of that era—the Vietnamese war, political assassinations, urban riots, and the escalating homicide rate. Another development was the emergence of the women's movement, which publicly challenged the traditional values that caused and concealed family violence, especially wife battering and marital rape. Finally, due in part to the first two developments, social science trained its sights on family violence systematically for the first time in the 1970s, discovering that it was prevalent, that it cut across all socioeconomic groups, and that it was not simply confined to the mentally disturbed.

This line of research repeatedly stunned the public when it was reported in the press, and these shocks were amplified in the late 1970s and early 1980s by gripping films (e.g., *The Burning Bed*) about wife abuse and documentaries which vividly portrayed the horror of family violence. One consequence of this heightened subjective dimension was that the number of reported cases of family violence in the United States rose sharply after the mid-1970s.

Many experts believe family violence occurs because it is built into the social structure of the family itself. Straus, Gelles, and Steinmetz (1980) have identified four such structural causes of family violence. The first cause is *intimacy*, the fact that family members know each other very well, and know best how to torment each other. Cruel attacks, especially from a trusted loved one, have the potential to create intense anger and subsequent violence. The second structural cause is the value of *privacy*, the fact that in American society what happens within the home has traditionally been considered a private family matter, both by family members and by outsiders such as neighbors, friends, physicians, teachers, and legal authorities. Cultural *norms* that either tolerate, support, encourage, or mandate violence against family members are the third structural cause of family violence. For instance, Straus

et al. (1980) found that most parents believe children benefit from such parental violence as spanking. Finally, the process of *socialization* within the home perpetuates family violence because children learn through experience that violence is an acceptable way to control the behavior of other family members. Hence, children of battered women are prone to become battering husbands and battered wives; and they also grow up predisposed to batter their own children and their parents.

Family violence has many negative consequences for society besides the deaths, injuries, blasted psyches, and ruined lives of those immediately involved. It uses up valuable police, judicial, and social services that could be applied to other problems. For instance, it consumes one-third of the time of the nation's police (O'Reilly, 1983), and in the process, it accounts for more police fatalities than any other type of crime (Gelles, 1979). In addition, family violence is a cause of other family problems such as marital disruption, one-parent households, teenage runaways, drug addiction, alcoholism, mental illness, and suicide (Andersen, 1983). It has also been linked to violent criminal behavior outside the home. Studies of prison populations indicate that more than 90 percent of all inmates claim that they had been abused as children (Magnuson, 1983).

Types of Family Violence

Child Battering Annual estimates of the prevalence of child battering range from 920,000 cases (American Humane Association, 1984) to 1.9 million cases, the differences depending largely on the definitions and methodologies employed. The latter estimate is based on a classic study by Straus and his associates (1980) in which they asked members of a cross section of American families how each dealt with family conflicts. Nearly 8 percent of the parents admitted to kicking, biting, or punching a child during the preceding year; 4 percent reported beating up a child; and 3 percent confessed to threatening a child with a gun or a knife. Parents who admitted beating their children did it about six times a year. The authors also concluded that about 2000 children are slain by their parents annually.

Despite evidence of child battering throughout the ages, its "discovery" as a social problem is a recent phenomenon (Pfohl, 1984). Indeed, child battering did not even warrant an entry in the *Readers' Guide to Periodical Literature* until 1968. Since then, however, the problem has changed from a small, private-sector charity concern to a multi-million-dollar public social welfare issue (Nelson, 1984). One reason for this transformation is the quantum leap taken by its subjective dimension since the mid-1970s. In 1976, for instance, surveys indicated that only about 10 percent of Americans considered child battering a serious national

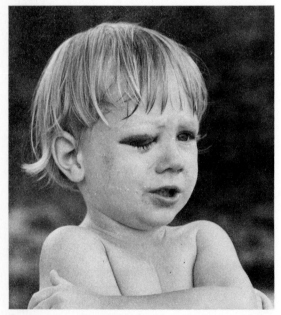

Family violence is probably the most common type of violence in the United States. Even little children, like the girl shown here, are often brutalized by another family member, usually a parent. (*James R. Holland/Stock, Boston*)

problem. But by 1983, the figure had risen to 90 percent (Magnuson, 1983).

Child Sexual Abuse   Kempe (1978) defined child sexual abuse as "the involvement of dependent and developmentally immature children and adolescents in sexual activities that they do not fully comprehend, to which they are unable to give informed consent, or that violate social taboos of family roles." Child sexual abuse can cause both physical and psychological trauma, and one study found that child molestation involved violence in half of the cases surveyed (Hobbs, 1982). It can be considered a form of family violence because about 75 percent of abusers are parents, stepparents, other relatives, and family friends (Vrazo, 1984).

Reports of child sexual abuse have soared since the mid-1970s. The American Humane Association found that between 1976 and 1982 the number of reported victims in the United States grew from about 7,500 to 57,000. By 1984, the National Committee for the Prevention of Child Abuse put the figure at 123,000. But most experts are quick to note that such reported cases represent just the tip of the iceberg. The FBI, for instance, believes that only about 20 percent of all sexual assaults on children are reported. And all the surveys on child sexual abuse concur. For example, Kinsey and Gebhard (1953) found that 9 percent of their sample of women had been sexually victimized as children; Finkelhor (1979), 20 percent; and Russell (1984), 28 percent. The proportions for men were much lower, yet still substantial (15 percent of reported child sexual abuse victims are males, and boys are the target of both heterosexual and homosexual abuse in the home). If these survey figures are anywhere near accurate, then child sexual abuse is epidemic in the United States. Indeed, Finkelhor (1984) has calculated that even if just 10 percent of all girls and 2 percent of all boys are sexually abused, there would be 210,000 new cases of sexual abuse every year.

The world has a long history of sexual exploitation of children (Schultz, 1980). Over the last several decades, a few scholars, physicians, and child protection advocates have tried to alert the public to the objective dimension of child sexual abuse, but their efforts for the most part fell on deaf ears. The subjective dimension of child sexual abuse began to rise in the late 1970s in conjunction with the growing awareness of child abuse in general. Then in the early 1980s a series of jolting incidents of sexual abuse occurred in child care centers across the nation. Due mainly to the media publicity surrounding these dramatic cases, the sexual abuse of children went from being a minor public concern to a major social problem. Intense public interest and fear led to new child sexual abuse laws, books on child protection, educational television shows and newspaper series, and childhood safety programs.

Much of the increase in reported cases of sexual abuse is attributed to this rising subjective dimension, but part of the increase could be real. Trends that may be related to increasing rates of sexual abuse include the recent touting of the very young as sex objects in the media (particularly in commercials and rock and roll songs), the growing use of strangers to care for children outside the home, and the increases in divorce and single parent households which leave children, especially girls, vulnerable to advances from stepfathers and their mothers' boyfriends.

Child sexual abuse is linked to the usual secondary problems associated with family violence in general (e.g., drinking problems, drug abuse, mental disorders) and child abuse in particular (e.g., children running away from their homes). The federal government estimates that 2 million children run away from their homes each year, half because of physical or sexual abuse. Many of these children turn to prostitution, child pornography, and crime in order to survive. Parents also push children into prostitution and pornography (Masters, John-

son, and Kolodny, 1985). Not surprisingly, sexually transmitted disease has become a common sickness of children. Most tragic of all, 20,000 to 50,000 children in the United States who are reported missing each year are never heard from again by their parents. Many are either abducted or preyed upon by sex killers. Several thousands of these children are found murdered each year.

Wife Battering   The statistics on wife battering are grim. Somewhere between 1.8 million (Straus et al., 1980) and 6 million (Andersen, 1983) wives are beaten in their homes every year. Wife abuse occurs at some time in about two-thirds of all marriages (Roy, 1982), and is chronic in about one-third (Grossman, 1983a). One survey in Texas reported that 25 percent of battered women were abused at least once a week. Researchers have found that wife battering is responsible for 20 percent of the visits of women to emergency medical services, 25 percent of suicide attempts by women, and 25 percent of female murder victims (Cultural Information Service, 1984). Each year some 2000 to 4000 women are beaten to death by their husbands (O'Reilly, 1983).

Wife abuse cuts across all socioeconomic strata. In 1985, for example, a top federal government executive resigned his position after public disclosures that he had beaten his wife periodically during their eighteen-year marriage. His physical and emotional abuse included beating her on the abdomen while she was pregnant and yanking her by the hair over a banister. Among other injuries, she suffered a broken eardrum, wrenched neck, and several black eyes. However, wife abuse, like other forms of family violence, is most common among lower socioeconomic groups (Bassis et al., 1982).

Women have been subjected to battering from their husbands throughout history. And for most of that time it was not considered to be a problem. Feminists in Britain and the United

States tried to curb wife abuse several times since 1850, but the public failed to respond with support or even sympathy (Dobash and Dobash, 1981). During the 1950s and 1960s wife abuse remained an unacknowledged problem. Indeed, most Americans laughed rather than cringed when Ralph Kramden, Jackie Gleason's character in the television series *The Honeymooners,* threatened to punch out his ever-loving wife. "I'm gonna send you to the moon," he roared, gesturing with his clenched fist. "To the *moon*, Alice" (Andersen, 1983). It was not until the 1970s that wife battering began to be taken seriously as a social problem, largely through the efforts of feminists and academics (Ferraro and Johnson, 1984).

By the 1980s wife battering was no longer considered a private matter by the majority of Americans, and the issue was placed higher on the social agenda. Throughout the country, wife battering was gradually being redefined as a breach of the woman's civil rights, and was increasingly being treated by the legal authorities as a criminal act of assault. This mounting subjective dimension and the resulting social change were part of the reformation in the United States of social values concerning the rights and roles of women (O'Reilly, 1983).

Marital Rape   Historically, marital rape was not viewed as a social problem in the United States. In fact, it was considered an impossibility, a contradiction in terms. American law on this matter was based on English common law, which held that wives were the property of their husbands and that husbands had sexual rights to their wives' bodies. These principles guided legal thinking until well into the 1970s. In short, marital rape was a legal form of wife abuse (Finkelhor and Yllo, 1985).

Since the early 1970s, however, feminists have worked hard to raise the consciousness of Americans about marital rape. They argued against the notion that wives are the property of their husbands, to be treated as the latter see fit.

They insisted that wives are independent people who do not cede sexual rights over their bodies to their husbands as part of the marriage contract. Moreover, if a husband does force his wife to have sex, they contended that he should be charged with the crime of rape and that marital rape should not be distinguished from other rapes.

The feminists and a growing number of allies were influential in changing the way marital rape was treated legally in many places. By 1978, four states had dropped the marital exemption from their rape laws or had decided to prosecute marital rape under laws that were blind to marital status. It was in that year that the first husband, John Rideout, was tried on charges of raping his wife while they were still living together. Although he was acquitted, the fact that the case even made it to trial was viewed as a major victory by advocates of marital rape statutes. This highly publicized trial also enormously boosted the visibility of this heretofore unacknowledged problem. By early 1985, twenty-three states allowed spouses living together to be prosecuted for rape.

The rising subjective dimension of marital rape is due in part to changing values concerning women's sex roles and the nature of marriage. Nevertheless, much of American society still does not agree with the idea of having a law permitting marital rape charges. There are two principal objections. One is the fear that vindictive wives will threaten to or actually claim rape to gain leverage in divorce proceedings. But experts contend that this is not a problem because frivolous and fraudulent charges are screened out by the legal system, and that only obvious and particularly brutal cases ever go to trial. This perspective is supported by the evidence. As of December 1984, only twenty-three cases had been tried (indicating that the legal system is highly selective), and there were nineteen convictions (indicating that the selected cases were well supported by evidence).

The second objection is that marital rape is not really rape, and should be distinguished from other rapes because it is less traumatic to the victim. However, domestic violence counselors have found that marital rape is as bad or worse than other rapes. This is difficult for many individuals to accept. But ask yourself this question: Which is worse, a child being sexually molested by a stranger or by a father? This analogy to child sexual abuse is an apt one. The crime is often worse for the victim if it is being perpetrated by a loved one, not only because of the violation of trust and intimacy involved but because the victim must frequently live with the abuser afterward, often enduring repeated attacks. There is also evidence that marital rape victims suffer the same kinds of psychic trauma experienced by other rape victims. For example, many have difficulty afterward establishing relations with any man (Yllo, 1985).

The number of marital rapes is not negligible. One study of 930 randomly selected women found that 14 percent of ever-married women had been raped by their present or former husbands (Russell, 1982). Criminalization of marital rape will exert downward pressure on its prevalence, but there is at least one counterforce: the sexual revolution. Apparently, sexual freedom among the young has been accompanied by a greater incidence of rape in dating (Beneke, 1982). One reason for this is that increasing numbers of young men expect sex to occur as part of a date, and are angered if it is withheld. The concern is that these men will also be more apt to force sex upon their wives.

Husband Battering A 41-year-old Pennsylvania man died of asphyxiation due to chest compression in 1984 when his much heavier wife sat on him for ten minutes during a domestic quarrel. This case was not an isolated incident. A 1979 FBI report stated that 10 percent of men killed were murdered by their wives (O'Reilly, 1983). And for the last half century,

about the same number of husbands have been slain each year by their wives as vice versa. Moreover, about the same number of husbands are battered by their spouses each year as the other way around. Straus et al. (1980) estimate that about 2 million husbands are physically attacked and nearly 300,000 are severely thrashed by their mates (Steinmetz, 1977).

Although the prevalence estimates are similar, it is not fair to conclude that husband battering is on a par with wife battering as a social problem. Wives are more likely to be seriously hurt in domestic battles (Straus et al., 1980). Also, in many cases of husband battering, perhaps even in the majority, wives are simply striking out in self-defense (Gelles, 1979).

But there are many innocent men who are battered by their wives, some too sick or old to fend off the attack. Others are able-bodied, even he-men types, like Blenda Gay, a hulking lineman for the NFL's Philadelphia Eagles, whose mentally ill wife slit his throat in his sleep. Another kind of victim is the passive, dependent man who seeks out a strong woman to protect him from life's problems—only to find, ironically, that his wife beats him up.

Parent and Elder Abuse The problem of elder abuse involves far more than just a few frail elderly and their mentally ill offspring. Indeed, estimates of elder abuse, or "granny bashing" as it is sometimes called, range as high as 3 million or 12 percent of the nation's old people (cf. U.S. House of Representatives Select Committee on Aging, 1985). But offspring do not confine their violence to the elderly. Straus et al. (1980) found that each year up to 1 million teenagers victimized their parents. One in five children abused a parent, and 1 in 10 severely attacked a parent, sometimes using deadly weapons. Abuse of the elderly and parents takes many forms such as violence and neglect, and children slay about 2000 parents annually in the United States (Bassis et al., 1982).

This problem may increase in the future for several reasons. One is the unprecedented growth in the over-65, and especially the over-75, population that is occurring as the population ages. Another is the low birth rate which results ultimately in fewer adult care givers, thus concentrating the burden of caring for an elderly parent on fewer and often just one child. Finally, the typical care giver, usually a middle-aged daughter or daughter-in-law, is increasingly working outside the home and/or caring for dependent children because of postponed childbearing. The stress of added duties to an already grueling schedule can contribute to elder abuse.

While the problem of elder abuse has always been well known among social workers, it was hidden from the public until the late 1970s. Fortunately, its subjective dimension is now rising, and it has attracted the increasing concern of social scientists, social workers, health care professionals, and legislators. As of 1985, legislation requiring mandatory reporting of elder abuse had been adopted in thirty-seven states.

Prognosis

Society has responded in many ways to family violence. There are telephone hot lines for child abusers, crisis centers for battered children, peer support groups for chronic and potential child abusers, shelters for battered wives, rape treatment clinics for sexually abused children, and improved legal procedures to prosecute all forms of family batterers. But so far, society's response has been grossly insufficient. For example, while nearly 2 million United States women are battered each year, there were only about 700 shelters in the mid-1980s offering battered women and their children a safe environment free from violence (Cultural Information Service, 1984). That works out to about 3000 women per shelter. Moreover, federal budget cutbacks and inflation have forced drastic cuts in funds at the state and local level for family violence services. These federal cuts were due in part to the influence of conservatives who were dismayed by what they called encroaching federal intervention in the family domain.

Ridding society of family violence would take more than the above responses, even if they were properly funded. It would necessitate major changes in the family, such as the eradication of norms that support the use of violence on family members and elimination of the socialization process that teaches children to associate violence with the family. It would also require major changes elsewhere in the society, changes that would minimize and eliminate the circumstances that foster family violence. These include values that legitimize violence for certain purposes such as corporal punishment in the schools and capital punishment in the criminal justice system, business and government policies that isolate families through forced relocation, poverty and unemployment that make living difficult and set family members on edge, and sex role stereotypes that force the sexes and the generations apart (Straus et al., 1980; Bassis et al., 1982).

DIVORCE

Prevalence and Trends

The best way to understand the prevalence of divorce is to ascertain what proportion of first marriages of women marrying in a certain year—a so-called *marriage cohort*—eventually end in divorce. The trend in this proportion has been upward in the United States for most of the past century. Only about 5 percent of marriages that took place in 1860 ended eventually in divorce. Present marriage cohorts in the United States have already greatly exceeded that figure, even though they have many years yet to add to their totals. And the proportions divorcing have risen sharply among the most recent marriage cohorts. For example, nearly

30 percent of the 1952 marriage cohort were divorced by their twenty-fifth wedding anniversary. The same 30 percent figure was attained by the 1957 cohort in twenty years; by the 1962 cohort in fifteen years; and by the 1967 cohort in just ten years (Thornton and Freedman, 1983). If the present age-specific divorce rates persist indefinitely, some 52 percent of the marriages that take place after 1975 will end in divorce (Preston, 1983).

Marriages can also be dissolved by separation and by the death of a spouse. In fact, about 14 percent of the first marriages of women aged 15 to 44 in 1982 had terminated due to these causes (Bachrach and Horn, 1985). This means that considerably more than 52 percent of United States marriages in the last quarter of the twentieth century probably will not escape marital dissolution of some sort. Moreover, the proportion of all marriages that are disrupted would be much higher yet if we counted disrupted consensual unions (couples living together indefinitely), some of which have children (Davis, 1983).

Many of those who divorce eventually remarry. In fact, nearly 60 percent of the women aged 15 to 44 in 1982 whose first marriages had ended by divorce or death of a spouse had remarried by that year. Forty-eight percent had done so within five years. But the likelihood of remarriage declined between the 1960s and the late 1970s (Bachrach and Horn 1985; National Center for Health Statistics, annually). And the divorce rates among remarried couples are even higher than those for once-married couples.

Reasons for the High Divorce Rate

Why is it that we have reached this extraordinary level of family instability when collectively we have better health, more teeth, better odor, more orgasms, and more happiness with our mates of the moment? Preston (1984) argues that there are two main explanations for this paradox. The first is that the trend in divorce has been due to increased incentives to termi-nate a marriage. The husband's disposable income greatly increases after divorce. The higher potential earnings of women have made it relatively less attractive for them to maintain a household and raise children, even on a part-time basis. The economic benefits of joint living are made easier to forgo by the higher incomes of husbands and wives, and both are able to purchase more freedom from the expectations and needs of the other by setting up separate residences. Expanded public programs, especially Aid to Families with Dependent Children, increase the incentive for poor couples to divorce because these programs financially penalize them for staying together. Finally, industrial changes have concentrated more people in metropolitan areas, led to less sex segregation at the workplace, and increased the proportion of jobs that deal with people rather than raw materials and machines. These changes widened the exposure of spouses to alternative partners. In short, more people than ever before have had the resources and opportunity to act on their preference to terminate a marriage.

But there must be more to it than these structural explanations. Other societies have roughly similar circumstances but have much lower divorce rates. For instance, United States divorce rates are about twice those of the most prosperous European nations. And here in the United States, the Mormons are one of the most economically and educationally advanced groups, yet they have remarkably strong marriages, high birth rates, and exceedingly low divorce rates.

This is where Preston's second and, in his view, more important explanation comes in. He contends that divorce has mushroomed because of "the increased prevalence of a world view that legitimizes calculations based upon individual self-interest" (1984:445). He alludes to the work of the eminent family historian Lawrence Stone, who found that there has been a growth over the past several centuries of *affective individualism,* the recognition of the self as a unique being with the right to pursue selfish goals (Stone, 1982).

The connection between these individualistic values and divorce is strong and transparent. Individuals who hold such values are less constrained by the welfare of a spouse or children to stay in what they view as a suboptimal marriage. This is one reason why opinion polls find that an increasing proportion of women (51 percent in 1962 versus 82 percent in 1980) and men believe that divorce is an acceptable solution to the problems of not getting along with a spouse, even when there are children in the family (Thornton and Freedman, 1983).

There are many other possible reasons for the upsurge in divorce. It may be that people have increasingly expected more from marriage, and have been unwilling to settle for less. One possible indication of these higher expectations is that the proportion of people reporting problems in their marriages rose from 46 percent in 1957 to 61 percent in 1976 (Veroff, Douvan, and Kukla, 1981). Another possible reason was the diminished prevalence of negative attitudes toward divorce, although this could have been as much a consequence as a cause of the divorce trend. Then there was the postponement of childbearing and the decline in family size which facilitated divorce, especially for women. And changes in divorce laws, particularly the adoption of no-fault divorce in every state except South Dakota, have helped grease the skids for many troubled marriages (Thornton and Freedman, 1983).

Consequences of Divorce

There is a growing recognition that some couples are better off ending a conflict-ridden marriage than trying to preserve it. This is often particularly true for families that are plagued by serious problems such as family violence. In such cases, divorce can be in the best interests of both the parents and the children. Neverthe-

less, divorce presents serious problems for society and for many individuals. It is linked to many of the other problems discussed in this book, such as poverty, physical and mental health problems, and drug abuse.

Divorce (and illegitimacy) is a principal cause of the growing poverty among women and children in the United States. Between 1959 and 1983, female-headed families in the United States increased from 4.3 million (9.8 percent of all families) to 10.4 million (14.3 percent of all families). Female-headed families are more than four times as likely to be below the poverty line than male-headed ones. In 1960, female-headed households contained 18 percent of the poor; by 1983, they accounted for 35 percent of the 35 million poor in the United States (O'Hare, 1985).

In the 1980s more than 1 million children a year were involved in divorces (National Center for Health Statistics, 1985*a*), and it is estimated that two-thirds of children born in wedlock in 1980 will experience the disruption of their parents' marriage by the time they reach age 17 (Hofferth, 1983). A large percentage of these children will spend many years in female-headed families where they will be impoverished. There were 13.8 million children under age 18 in below-poverty-level households in 1983, and 6.8 million (49 percent) of them lived in households that were headed by women. Fifty-five percent of children in female-headed families were poor, compared to only 13 percent of those in other types of families (O'Hare, 1985).

Divorce has led to the impoverishment of large numbers of women and children in spite of the trend toward more equitable property settlements. This is due in part to the fact that the dividable assets of couples are often meager. Because husbands typically have better educations and work skills, they end up much better off than their former spouses after a divorce (Hoffman, 1977). And women confront job markets that are still biased toward them (Chapter 10).

Child support is grossly inadequate in the United States. It is often a small sum and frequently temporary. Moreover, only 69 percent of white women and 34 percent of black women with minor children from an absent father were entitled to child support in 1982, and even smaller fractions actually received it. Indeed, only 75 percent of divorced and separated women due child support got any payments in 1981 (U.S. Bureau of the Census, 1981). A well-publicized case of this occurred in 1984 when a 5.6 million dollar lottery winner was hauled into court for failing to pay 125 dollars a month in child support for his 11-year-old daughter. Even when child support is received, it is paid in full only about half the time (Thornton and Freedman, 1983).

As a result of all these factors, one study (Weitzman, 1985) found that wives and minor children experienced a 73 percent decline in their standard of living in the first year after a divorce, while husbands experienced a 42 percent increase in the same period.

The negative health consequences of divorce can also be substantial. It can exact a greater, and in many cases longer-lasting, emotional and physical toll than virtually any other life stress, including the death of a spouse. Numerous studies have found that divorced adults have higher rates of emotional disturbance, accidental death, and death from heart disease, cancer, pneumonia, high blood pressure, and cirrhosis of the liver than the married, never married, and widowed. National mortality data show that the divorced are worse off than those in other marital statuses in 8 of 10 categories related to psychological functioning. For example, the suicide rate for women who were separated or divorced was about four times higher than that of married women, and about twice as high as that of single or widowed women (Jacobson, 1984).

Divorce has also been negatively linked to the well-being and behavior of children in both the short run and the long run (Preston, 1984).

These children have higher rates of suicide (Furstenberg and Allison, 1984); of stress and emotional trauma (Zill and Petersen, 1982); of drug use (Nicholi, 1983); of low school achievement (Hetherington, Camara, and Featherman, 1983); and of deviance such as running away, truancy, arrests, and smoking (Rankin, 1983).

These effects on children are due not only to the emotional trauma of the divorce itself but also to factors in its aftermath. One of these factors is the abandonment of children by their father, not only financially but personally as well. One study (Furstenberg and Nord, 1982) found that 52 percent of children with a nonresidential father saw him less than once a year, and another 16 percent saw him less than once a month. Other deleterious factors include the problems children have dealing with their now separated biological parents, and the problems of adjusting to the complex of old and new relationships present in stepfamilies (Thornton and Freedman, 1983). Noncustodial parental kidnappings also expose children to mental and physical abuse. Estimates vary, but as many as 500,000 children each year may be victims of these kidnappings.

Spouses and children are not the only ones who suffer from divorce. For instance, grandparents are sometimes devastated when grandchildren vanish as a result of their child's divorce (or death). And society is negatively affected in many ways. For example, family law cases clog the civil courts.

Attitudes toward Divorce

Divorce has been recognized as a serious social concern in the United States as far back as the late eighteenth century. It has traditionally been thought of as an act of failure, irresponsibility, and immorality, and divorced individuals were treated as social outcasts. Over the last several decades, however, negative attitudes have declined enormously as Americans became more disposed to see divorce as a solution for bad and even marginal marriages. Divorce is no longer widely regarded as disreputable, and divorced persons are now included in the normal patterns of social life.

Nevertheless, divorce remains a value conflict area between liberals and conservatives. Liberals see it in positive terms as a vehicle for personal change, development, self-fulfillment, opportunity, and freedom. Feminists in particular see it as a major weapon in their historical struggle with men. Moreover, liberals do not believe that the high rate of divorce constitutes a threat to the family. They argue against that thesis by noting that most spouses state they are happy with their present marriages and that most divorced people remarry. Often these arguments are backed up by this quote from

Mary Jo Bane's classic book, *Here to Stay: American Families in the Twentieth Century:*

> The majority of marriages do not end in divorce. The vast majority of divorced people remarry. Only a tiny proportion of people marry more than twice. We are thus a long way from a society in which marriage is rejected or replaced by a series of short-term liaisons (1976:31).

Conservatives on the other hand are extremely concerned about the impact of high divorce rates on the family. They are highly suspicious of the happiness statistics quoted by the liberals, noting that there has to be something misleading about them when more than half of these "happy" marriages are projected to end

Some of our most cherished values—and the groups that espouse them—collide with the abortion struggle. For instance, the personal freedom to control one's body championed by many feminists like the ones in this photograph conflicts with the widespread value on the sanctity of human life emphasized by the antiabortion demonstrators in the adjoining photograph. (*Gatewood/The Image Works, Inc.*)

The intrinsic drama in the emotional family issue of abortion is highlighted in a steady stream of documentaries, dramas, and demonstrations. Interest groups on both sides, like the antiabortion demonstrators above, have succeeded in keeping the issue in the news and in the minds of the American public. (*Anna Clopet/U.S. News & World Report*)

in divorce or separation. Besides, they argue that it is not what people say that is important, but what they do. And spouses are fleeing their at least once-happy marriages in droves. Conservatives also contend that the Bane quote above is no longer true, noting that the majority of recent marriages are now projected to fail. They also emphasize that while the majority of divorced people do still remarry, the rate of remarriage is declining, and the divorce rate is extraordinarily high among the remarried too. They also take no solace in the fact that a tiny proportion of people marry more than twice. The fact that huge numbers marry more than once is, in their view, sufficiently worrisome.

Conservatives also warn that society has yet to witness all the long-term effects of widespread divorce. Most of the unprecedentedly large number of people who divorced after 1960 have yet to run their entire life course, and so have their children. What problems might these generations pose for society in coming years? Will the children of divorce, particularly the 37 percent or so who are most traumatized by the disruption (Wallerstein and Kelly, 1980), make good parents or workers? Will those who are low achievers or discipline problems in school bring those problems to the workplace? Conservatives are also concerned that today's children of divorce will have even less regard for marital stability than their divorce-prone parents, who were themselves the offspring of relatively low divorce generations. The fear is that each time the wheel goes around, the family will become weaker, and the social order will become a little less stable (cf. Marshner, 1985).

SOCIAL POLICY: LEGALIZED ABORTION

Strategies for Solution

As strong as the controversy over divorce is, it is dwarfed by the fire storm that swirls around abortion. Abortion is the most fundamental and searing of human dilemmas, a problem that has been compared to slavery in its ability to divide the nation.

Abortion has always been an issue in the United States, and for most of our history there were strict antiabortion laws in force. Sentiment favoring the liberalization of these laws escalated after 1960, however, and in 1973 the Supreme Court struck them down in its *Roe v. Wade* decision. This decision allowed women the option to have an abortion for any reason in the first two trimesters of pregnancy, and in the third trimester if their physical or mental health was jeopardized by the pregnancy. This decision virtually mandated abortion on demand, since most women could find physicians who would certify that their pregnancy was a threat to their mental health. By 1987, more than 18 million legal abortions had been performed in the United States, and they were proceeding at the rate of more than 1.5 million a year. For some Americans this legalized abortion is an acceptable solution to the problems unwanted pregnancies pose for individuals and society; for others, it is the greatest holocaust in the history of the world. This controversy once again demonstrates the principle that one group's solution to a social problem (i.e., unwanted pregnancies) can become another group's social problem (i.e., abortion).

We use the term *antiabortion* for those against legalized abortion rather than *pro-life*, because the latter is an attempt to elicit support for the antiabortion cause by associating it with the general value Americans place on human life. This association is misleading, however, because many antiabortion people favor such antilife things as capital punishment and aggressive military policies, and because it implies that pro-abortion people are against life as such. Similarly, we use the term *pro-abortion* for those favoring legalized abortion rather than *pro-choice,* because the latter is an attempt to elicit support for the pro-abortion cause by associating it with the general value Americans place on freedom of choice, thus diverting attention from the more complex and controversial issue of abortion itself. The term pro-choice also implies that opponents are against political democracy. There are some individuals who are personally opposed to abortion, but who believe that women should have the right to choose. Nevertheless, such individuals still support legalized abortion and are, therefore, pro-abortion from a policy standpoint. In any event, the terms pro-life and pro-choice are political rather than analytical.

Arguments for Legalized Abortion   The first argument for abortion is one advanced by radical feminists. They hold that a woman has the right to control her own body, including reproductive processes. This right supersedes all other consideration, including any rights of the *conceptus* (the medical term for the product of conception from fertilization to birth). A woman has a right to obtain an abortion at any time without having to seek permission from the father or anyone else in the society. If this were not the case, the argument runs, women would still be dependent on and subordinate to the male-dominated society.

The second argument for abortion is that women should have the option to utilize this form of birth control to reduce the incidence of unplanned and unwanted children, and to help them confidently plan the timing and number of their children. It permits women to rationally integrate their childbearing decisions with education, career, and other plans. In particular, women are able to participate more fully and effectively in the labor market if they have access to abortion.

The third argument for abortion is that pregnancy sometimes endangers the mother's physical or mental health. Pregnancy can be dangerous in women with, for example, chronic diseases of the heart or kidneys; and it can also affect their emotional well-being, especially when pregnancy is the result of such things as incest and rape. Young girls who become pregnant also face emotional risks. Similarly, abortion can be used to prevent the birth of children with known birth defects. Tietze (1984) estimates that legal abortions averted the birth of thousands of defective infants between 1973 and 1983. While therapeutic abortions to protect the mother and to avoid children with birth defects occurred prior to the legalization of abortion, they were restricted by society (especially by the medical profession) and difficult to get.

Another argument for legalized abortion is that society can regulate the operations and make them safer. Illegal abortion used to be a major cause of death related to pregnancy and childbirth, especially among the poor, who were less able to travel to countries that permitted abortion or to pay the fees demanded by physicians who would risk performing an illegal abortion. Abortion advocates buttress this argument by recounting cases such as that of a 14-year-old girl who died from an illegal abortion after she had been gang raped by six men (Goodman, 1985). Once abortion became legal, deaths attributed to it plummeted. Tietze (1984) estimates that legal abortions saved 1500 women from pregnancy-related deaths between 1973 and 1983. Illegal abortion also caused far more subsequent infertility than legalized abortion now does (McFalls and McFalls, 1984).

Other arguments for legalized abortion are that it prevents women from becoming crimi-

nals and from having to deal with the criminal subculture (Henslin and Light, 1983), it might save unwanted children from physical abuse and emotional deprivation, and it reduces welfare expenditures enormously (each welfare child costs the taxpayer about 20,000 dollars) because the poor and minorities disproportionately use abortion (Henshaw et al., 1985).

Often an advocate of abortion will advance many of these arguments simultaneously. For instance, in a 1985 speech Geraldine Ferraro stated:

> [Abortion] has tremendous economic implications for all women....[It] is inseparable from our struggle for economic independence....For the poor woman, it means the choice of not being driven further into poverty by the costs of caring for a child she cannot afford. For the young woman, it means a choice of not having to leave her high school or job training program. For the woman with other children, it means the financial freedom so she and her children can have the educational opportunities and health care they deserve. For our society, too, it means avoiding an unequal and unfair system where the rich can get safe medical abortions and poor women cannot. For all these women it means not letting someone else—in this case male dominated conservative religious interests—make our decisions for us (1985).

As noted above, some of those who favor legalized abortion do not believe it is morally right. They see it as the lesser of two evils—abortion as a preferable option to mistreated or defective children, dead or sterile women, or having to endure an incest-caused pregnancy. For many proponents, all the above arguments are rife with value trade-offs and problem linkages.

Arguments against Legalized Abortion   The principal argument against abortion is that the conceptus is a human being and, as such, has the right to life. Most opponents of abortion believe that this right is bestowed at the moment of conception.

Abortion foes often argue for the right to life of the conceptus by pointing out how early in gestation it acquires its human anatomy and body functions. For instance, they note that its heart begins beating on the eighteenth day after conception; that it already has the beginnings of eyes, spinal cord, nervous system, thyroid glands, lungs, stomach, liver, kidneys, and intestines within four weeks, before most women are even aware they are pregnant; and that its forebrain appears around five weeks. At about ten weeks the conceptus begins sucking, and the face becomes expressive. It can squint, frown, or look surprised. All the major organ systems are laid down by the thirteenth week, the end of the first trimester (Curtis, 1977). Abortion foes conclude such descriptions by noting that many second trimester abortions are carried out on beings that look like a baby, suck their thumbs, cry, and have the senses of hearing, sight, and touch.

To fully appreciate the viewpoint of abortion opponents, you must understand that they consider the conceptus to be a *baby*. (The words *baby, son,* and *daughter* are italicized in this discussion to emphasize that these words are used by abortion foes and that others do not consider them to be valid.) This baby/conceptus identity is the abortion foes' fundamental premise, and all their other arguments are based upon it. In general, they contend that all other considerations are subordinate to the *baby*'s right to life, with one exception: if the abortion is an incidental by-product of a necessary effort to save the mother's life (e.g., removing a cancerous uterus).

Abortion foes respond to the pro-abortion arguments like this: First, a woman does have the right to control her own body. But all rights are limited, especially when they conflict with the rights of others. The right to free speech, for example, is limited by the right of others not to be libeled. In this case, the *baby* has the *same*

right to life as the woman. The woman does not have the right to kill another human being to make life easier or better for herself.

Similarly, abortion opponents maintain that it is wrong to kill a *baby* in order to finish school or advance a career. They believe that pregnancies resulting from rape or incest are tragic, but argue that you should not compound that tragedy by killing a *son* or *daughter*. In like manner, they argue that while it is lamentable when a child (or young teenager) becomes pregnant, you cannot solve that child's problem by killing another *child*. They also insist that a *baby* with birth defects has the same right to life as any other baby, even though it may cause the parents great trouble and ineffable anguish. They reject the idea of killing such *babies* for their own sake. C. Everett Kopp, a renowned pediatric surgeon and Surgeon General of the United States in the 1980s, addressed this point like this: "It has been my constant experience that disability and unhappiness do not necessarily go together. Some of the most unhappy children whom I have known have all of their physical and mental faculties, and on the other hand some of the happiest youngsters have borne burdens which I myself would find very difficult to bear" (Nathanson, 1979:235). Abortion opponents buttress their position by relating stories like the one about Baby Jane Doe, the severely handicapped child who was the center of a bitter legal battle in 1984. Her parents wanted to withhold surgical procedures that would have prolonged her life. Later an operation was performed, and on the occasion of her first birthday her parents said that the red-haired, blue-eyed youngster was "comfortable and happy, and had become so special to us" even though she was unable to do anything on her own (Milton, 1984).

By the same token, abortion foes argue that you do not kill a *baby* to save it from physical abuse or emotional deprivation. They also point out that most children with blighted childhoods survive to lead relatively normal lives (Goleman, 1984).

Opponents of abortion do not dispute the claim that abortion has always taken place and will continue if it is recriminalized. But they argue that there will be far fewer *babies* terminated if abortion is made illegal. They also contend that you cannot legitimize the killing of 1.5 million *babies* a year to save the lives of the 150 women who die as a result of killing their own *babies*. Minimizing welfare is also viewed as an unacceptable reason for killing *babies*, and the *babies* of the poor and minorities are seen as just as worthy of life as those of other groups. Indeed, some black leaders both in and out of the antiabortion movement hold the view that abortion "is a class war against the poor and genocide against blacks" (Williams, 1984; Leo, 1986), because such groups are principal targets of the family planning establishment and have a disproportionately high share of all abortions.

Value trade-offs are also recognized by abortion foes. They are not insensitive to the plight of incest victims or to the monumental problems children with birth defects create for their parents. But the value gained by solving these kinds of problems with abortion is weighed against the value against killing innocent *babies*, and the former is found wanting.

Attitudes toward Legalized Abortion American public opinion regarding legalized abortion has changed enormously since the 1950s, when only a small minority approved of it for most reasons. Approval rose steadily until 1972, when large majorities of Americans approved of abortion if the mother's health would be seriously endangered by the pregnancy, if there were a strong chance for a serious defect in the baby, or if the pregnancy were the result of rape. Large minorities approved of abortion if the family had a very low income and could not afford more children, if the woman were unmarried and did not want to marry the man, or if the woman were married and did not want more

children. The proportions approving of legalized abortion for various reasons remained roughly constant from 1972 to 1982. But approval dropped about 7 percent between 1982 and 1985 (*FPP*, 1985), a decline seemingly consistent with the overall trend toward conservatism in the United States, and with the slight decline in the number of abortions that were taking place. In any event, a Gallup poll in 1985 found that 21 percent of Americans believed that abortions should be legal under all circumstances; 55 percent, only under certain circumstances; and 21 percent, under no circumstances (Gallup Organization, 1985). Thus, the number of ardent pro-abortion and antiabortion individuals is roughly the same.

However, while most Americans (76 percent) approve of abortion for at least one reason, most Americans oppose most abortions. This is because the vast majority of abortions are performed for reasons of low income, birth control, and singleness, and the majority of Americans are opposed to abortion for these reasons. Abortions for reasons of rape, birth defect, or serious health problems probably constitute less than 5 percent of all abortions. Thus, when asked if they favor or oppose a ban on all abortions except in the case of rape, incest, or when the mother's life is endangered, 58 percent of Americans said they were in favor of such a ban, while only 36 percent said they were opposed (Gallup Organization, 1985). This means that in 1985 the majority of Americans were opposed to the so-called convenience abortions, a fact that should be kept in mind when evaluating the practical problems facing the present abortion on demand policy.

Policies into Practice

In this part of the social policy section, pro-abortion and antiabortion policies are scrutinized in terms of practical implementation (i.e., Can the policy be successful in the real world?).

Implementation Problems for Pro-Abortion Policy The present policy of virtually unrestricted legalized abortion faces serious opposition from the antiabortion movement.

After the Supreme Court's *Roe v. Wade* decision that led to de facto abortion on demand, the antiabortion opposition, most vocally represented by Catholics and Fundamentalist Protestants but by no means limited to these groups, began to mobilize. Their primary goal was to outlaw abortion; their secondary goal was to minimize the number of abortions that occurred in the meantime.

Abortion foes can achieve their primary goal three ways. One way is to have the United States Congress pass a strong antiabortion law that would define human life as beginning at conception and that would entitle the conceptus to the right to life. Another way would be through the passage of a constitutional amendment that would give Congress and states joint authority to limit or stop abortion. The final way would be to get the Supreme Court to overturn its own decision.

Abortion foes have pursued all three of these strategies using two main tactics. First, they have tried to elect antiabortion politicians and to defeat pro-abortion ones. So far they have had considerable success at this, especially at the state level. Their greatest triumph was in helping Ronald Reagan become elected. Reagan was an antiabortion candidate, and abortion foes hoped that once elected he would have the opportunity to appoint similarly minded judges to the Supreme Court. Second, abortion foes have worked to change the values of those who favor legalized abortion. Obviously, if this occurred, politicians would be even more responsive to the pressure of abortion foes.

Abortion foes have tried to swing public opinion onto their side by debating the issue wherever possible, and by demonstrations such as their annual mass march on Washington, D.C. They have also attempted to raise concern by publicizing what they consider to be the worst aspects of abortion. They have explained in graphic detail what happens to the conceptus when it is killed—that in saline abortions, for example, the fetus is burned by the injected solution over its entire body; and that in dilation and evacuation (D&E) abortions, the living fetus is crushed and/or torn apart and evacuated in pieces. Abortion foes have displayed pictures of burned, mangled, and dismembered fetuses at every opportunity. And in 1985 they began showing a sonogram videotape of an abortion called *The Silent Scream,* which graphically depicts a D&E abortion from inside the womb.

Other potentially troubling aspects of abortion publicized by abortion foes include the deaths of live-born babies resulting from abortion, fetal research such as an experiment in which the heads of live-born fetuses were severed and kept "alive" by supplying blood through the carotid artery (Henslin and Light, 1983), the improper disposal of aborted fetuses such as the case of the 16,433 fetuses found in a steel bin outside Los Angeles in 1982, the fact that abortion is being used by many individuals as the primary form of birth control (60 percent of women who have abortions had not tried contraceptives first) (Grossman, 1985), the use of late abortion for sex selection of children, and the anguish of women who now feel their abortions were wrong and that they killed their own babies.

Abortion foes have tried many ways to achieve their secondary goal of minimizing the number of abortions that took place until the law could be changed. These included boycotting hospitals until they stopped doing abortions; picketing abortion clinics; trying to persuade clinic clients not to go through with the abortion; harassing present and prospective clients and clinic personnel; holding sit-ins in the clinics themselves; posing as patients, then splashing paint in waiting rooms, chaining themselves to examining tables, dropping stink bombs, and otherwise disrupting the work of the clinics; and operating phony abortion clinics where abortion clients are presented with antiabortion information. In addition, radical abortion foes began bombing abortion clinics in the 1980s, a tactic that was denounced by most antiabortion activists.

Another interim tactic of abortion foes was to limit the scope of the Supreme Court decision. Their major success in this area was the Hyde Amendment, which was passed in 1977 and upheld by the Supreme Court in 1980. It prevented the use of Medicaid funds for convenience abortions, thus stopping some poor women from obtaining them. Abortion foes also pushed through at the state level restrictive abortion laws that were clearly unconstitutional but which often took the courts years to strike down. These stopgap measures cut down the number of abortions while they were in effect, and could be replaced with new laws once they were overturned (Henshaw et al., 1982).

But abortion foes do not pose the only implementation problems for legalized abortion. As noted earlier, many pro-abortion people are not strong supporters of abortion per se (seeing it as a lesser of two evils), and are unwilling to support or implement abortion policy. Clinics have a difficult time finding medical directors because many physicians do not want to be publicly identified as abortionists. Some physicians who personally condone abortion will not do them because of personal reasons. In fact, in 1980 only 1 in 10 obstetrician-gynecologists in private practice performed abortions in their offices. Others restricted them to before a certain gestational age. In 1980, 30 percent of abortion providers would do them only before eleven weeks gestation; an additional 49 percent drew the line at fifteen weeks. Hospitals, too, including many secular ones, refused to do abortions or restricted them to early gestational ages. Others limited them by erecting bureaucratic and financial barriers (Henshaw et al., 1982). The result of all this was that abortion services were not readily available to all United States women, especially teenagers (Henshaw

et al., 1985). Indeed, as late as 1980, 78 percent of United States counties had no abortion provider, and 59 of the nation's 305 major metropolitan areas had no facility providing abortions (Henshaw et al., 1982).

Implementation Problems for Antiabortion Policy One alternative to the present pro-abortion policy is a return to the policy which existed prior to 1973. An abortion was then illegal except for serious health reasons. That policy certainly had implementation problems, which is one reason why it failed. And if it is reinstituted, there would be serious social consequences again. These would include dangerous illegal operations, although perhaps not as many as in the past because of the availability of better technology and a reservoir of personnel with abortion experience. For the antiabortion policy to be effective, there probably would have to be a tremendous ground swell of public opinion against the practice. Otherwise, an underground abortion industry would perform a sizable fraction of the abortions that are being done under present policy.

The antiabortion policy would also bring with it an increase in unwanted, poor, and illegitimate children unless it was accompanied by effective family planning and sex education programs (Jones et al., 1985). But the antiabortion movement contains segments that are opposed to contraception and sex education as well, and these groups may be able to short-circuit these programs too. The presence of growing numbers of these children as well as those with birth defects would require increased public spending, but again there are groups in the society that would oppose increased government expenditures for welfare programs. In short, making abortion illegal would exacerbate some of the other social problems that led to the legalization of abortion in the first place. This would be a serious problem for antiabortion policy, because although the majority of those who supported a ban on abortion for most reasons in 1985 were reconciled to the fact that there would be social consequences (Beck, 1985), once they became a reality, many people might reconsider.

Another serious problem for antiabortion policy would be the activity of women's rights organizations. To them abortion rights are indispensable, so much so that they do not support liberal women candidates for political office who disagree with them on just this one issue (e.g., United States Representative Mary Rose Oaker of Ohio). The adoption of an antiabortion policy would energize the women's movement and cause it to go back on the offensive. Indeed, there were already signs in the mid-1980s that this was happening in response to the growing success of the antiabortion forces. The National Organization for Women elected a president in 1985 who promised to give the organization a more aggressive attitude on abortion; and the National Abortion Rights Action League began a national campaign to reacquaint the public with another set of facts: the difficult problems some women face with an unwanted pregnancy and no recourse to legal abortion (Goodman, 1985).

An antiabortion policy would also add extra incentive for the women's movement to press for the passage of the Equal Rights Amendment. If the ERA becomes part of the United States Constitution, it could lead to unrestricted tax-funded abortions. In states such as Pennsylvania, Hawaii, and Massachusetts that have made the ERA part of their state constitution, pro-abortion groups have already used it to push their abortion goals. For example, in Massachusetts abortion activists went to court claiming the state discriminated against women in violation of that state's ERA, when it refused to grant tax funds for abortions. The court agreed, and the state was forced to pay for abortions with tax funds.

Abortionists would also seek to overturn an antiabortion policy. Abortion is much more profitable for physicians than seeing a woman through a nine-month pregnancy. Abortionists in clinics can make more than 1000 dollars on an eight-hour shift, and some work two shifts a day. They would fight hard to regain their billion-dollar annual business.

Evaluating the Evidence

Because the pro- and antiabortion policies have actually been tried in the United States, there is ample evidence concerning their success and failure in solving their respective social problem (i.e., unwanted pregnancies and abortion). This evidence has already been presented in the two previous sections. Here we will simply discuss what the future might hold for abortion policy.

Many compromises have been suggested for the abortion problem. One is that the beginning of life should be judged by the same standard we use to determine the end of life: the presence or absence of brain function. Since the conceptus has brain function at the end of eight weeks, abortion would be permitted only before that. Another compromise would permit abortions before twenty to twenty-two weeks but would outlaw them after that, except for threats to the mother's health or serious genetic defects. But neither of these compromises would be accepted by abortion foes because both still permit the majority of abortions to be performed.

Another compromise has been proposed by the American Law Institute. It would permit a physician to terminate a pregnancy if there were a substantial risk that continuance would seriously impair the physical or mental health of the mother, or that the child would be born with a serious physical or mental defect, or that the pregnancy resulted from incest or rape. Two physicians would have to certify in writing why the abortion was justified (at least one of which would have to be a member of an organization set up to *impartially* review such cases). And all abortions would be performed in hospitals. This compromise would have a chance of being accepted by both sides. It would appeal to all but the most hard-core pro-abortion people because it permits abortion for the most compelling reasons. It would appeal to all but the most hard-core abortion foes because it would eliminate more than 95 percent of the 1.5 million legal abortions performed each year. Indeed, Jerry Falwell, an influential antiabortion leader, announced in 1985 that he would support a similar compromise. And we have already noted that 58 percent of Americans would too (Gallup Organization, 1985). So such a compromise may well be the future of abortion policy in the United States. Even if President Reagan succeeds in stacking the Supreme Court with antiabortion judges, it would not be surprising if the justices, too, arrived at the same compromise.

An abortion pill that could be used to terminate early-stage pregnancies—and, hence, would be an alternative for most abortions—is also on the horizon. It will have profound social implications by, for example, increasing privacy and decreasing physical and emotional trauma. Antiabortion groups will oppose the pill and may even succeed in making it illegal. But judging from experience with other illicit drugs, the abortion pill will be available if the demand exists. Thus, the abortion pill will greatly reduce the role of the political institution in the abortion controversy and increase the power of individual women. This means that the clash between abortion advocates and foes will be, more than ever before, a struggle for the hearts and minds of American women.

SUMMARY

1 There is wide disagreement about the nature of family problems and possible solutions, which arises from differences in basic values. The traditional family is disappearing fast, easing some family problems and intensifying others.

2 The common tendency for the subjective dimension of family problems to exceed their objective dimension revolves around the social factors of visibility, expectations, and values.

3 Sexual activity is increasing among the unmarried, leading to social, health, and economic problems for unmarried mothers and their children.

4 Extraordinary numbers of children, wives, parents, grandparents, and even husbands are brutalized by other family members in the United States.

5 Epidemic divorce is caused primarily by increased incentives to terminate marriage and the increased prevalence of a world view that legitimizes calculations based upon individual self-interest. Divorce poses serious problems for individuals and society.

6 Abortion is the most divisive social problem in America today. For some Americans, legalized abortion is an acceptable solution to the problems posed by unwanted pregnancies; for others, it is the mass slaughter of innocent babies.

CHAPTER 6

Sexual Variance:
Lifestyles and Disorders

A number of witnesses have testified about the effects on their own sexual relations, usually with their spouses, of the depiction on the screen and in magazines of sexual practices in which they had not previously engaged. A number of these witnesses, all women, have testified that men in their lives have used such material to strongly encourage, or coerce, them into engaging in sexual practices in which they do not choose to engage. To the extent that such implicit or explicit coercion takes place as a result of these materials, we all agree that it is a harm.

Attorney General's Commission on Pornography,

Final Report, 1986

It may surprise some of you to realize that the statement above is one of many conclusions reached by the now famous Meese Report without the benefit of scientific evidence. However, by the time you finish this chapter, you may be surprised by a lot of things. One point will become increasingly clear as you read about sexual variance: *The topic is loaded with personal opinion and subjective values.* The following discussion of Inis Beag and Mangaia underscores this point rather dramatically.

SEXUAL VARIANCE: AN OVERVIEW

In Inis Beag, a small island off the coast of Ireland, sex is rarely discussed or practiced (Goode, 1978). Premarital or adulterous sex is unknown, and only marital, man-on-top intercourse is allowed. Affection and foreplay between spouses are rare. So also is intercourse, which takes place in long undergarments which unbutton at the appropriate places. In this sexually repressed society nudity is abhorred. Female sexual pleasure is not valued either, and female orgasm is unknown. So are many other sexual practices such as french kissing and oral sex. Thousands of miles away in the South Pacific is the small island community of Mangaia. There sex is a central concern; premarital and extramarital intercourse occur regularly and are considered normal (Goode, 1978). Men are rated on their ability to sustain vigorous intercourse for long periods of time without ejaculating. The average person has intercourse three times a night, seven nights a week.

No two groups of people could be more dissimilar in their attitudes toward sex than those who live in Inis Beag and Mangaia. However, they are not the only ones who are sexually exotic by American standards. The Etoro people of New Guinea, for example, are a predominantly homosexual group which prohibits heterosexual intercourse for most of the year. As a consequence, they have trouble maintaining the size of their population. And in Russia today, where violence and alcohol often rule the male-female relationship, many women are so physically scarred that they lose interest in sex. To Soviet men, orgasm is a masculine privilege, partly because of the belief that holding back an ejaculation to satisfy the woman is an immoral act.

It was not that long ago when our own culture was dominated by sexual attitudes which appear odd today. One example is Victorian morality, in which almost all forms of sex were considered a sickness, and which even demanded prudery within husband-wife relationships. In the famous novel *1984,* George Orwell predicted that attitudes toward sex would return to a Victorian orientation during the 1980s.

Sex presents an excellent example of how subjective views define what is allowed in a society. In the United States today, sex, religion, and politics, as the old adage goes, are three topics which do not make for good conversation at the dinner table. Of the three, sex is probably the one most emotionally charged. It is also associated with a number of social problems discussed in other chapters, including venereal disease, illegitimacy, marital problems, and crime. Apparently, it has an alarming connection with health care as well, as evidenced by the growing number of reports of physicians who use their patients for sex. Because the subjective features of sexual behavior are both so personal and so cultural, studying sex scientifically is a challenging task, as the Meese Commission demonstrates.

The Sexual Continuum

What is the proper subject of this chapter? Just as everyone consumes food but only certain eating behaviors are problematic (e.g., obesity and anorexia), not all forms of sexual behavior are matters of societal concern. To extend the analogy, food is the subject of radical differences of opinion across social groups. Some people view high-protein diets as healthful muscle builders, while vegetarians see those same foods as destructive—"One man's meat is another man's poison." The point is twofold. First, the problem of sexual variance is preeminently a matter of social definition. Second, not all segments of United States society agree on the basic terms of that definition. These complications suggest that the proper subject of this chapter must be specified using both the objective and subjective dimensions of sexual behavior.

Consider Figure 6-1. The horizontal line represents a continuum of sexual practices, varying from the normative (i.e., defined by the norms) extreme of widely accepted behaviors on the left, to the deviant extreme of the least accepted sexual orientations on the right. Rising from left to right is the line indicating the level of subjective concern. The essential idea is this: The greater the departure from the sexual norm, the greater the degree of societal concern. Within the nearly infinite variety of acts which constitute the sexual practices line, we have inserted into the figure two major classes of behavior for the present discussion. Sexual lifestyles involve actions which are recognized to vary from ideal norms of sexual conduct, but which have come to be tolerated as "their business" if not flaunted in mainstream society. Further to the right—and therefore with a higher level of subjective concern looming above them—are the sexual disorders. Contained within this class are several practices which are the polar opposite of cultural norms, and which occasion severe stigma for their practitioners. Although it is invaluable in casting the complex issue of human sexuality into the concepts of a social problem, Figure 6-1 should be considered a very general model. We are about to see that this positioning of behaviors along the sexual practices line is only the average of various widely varying segments of public opinion.

The topic of sex may finally be out of the closet, but the closet door did not open on well-oiled hinges. One remaining problem is determining which forms of sexual variance are lifestyles and which are disorders. Although this is an extremely difficult task to carry out objectively, there are some deeply ingrained positions. Part of the sexual conservative position is that any act which is nonheterosexual or a violation of a law is a disorder. This notion upholds a strict adherence to rigid sexual mores. The problem with the conservative view is that it begs the question: If strict sexual mores

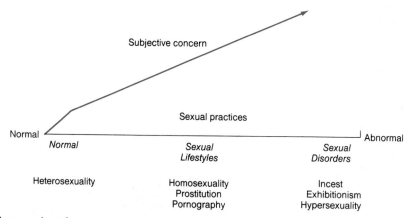

FIGURE 6-1   The sexual continuum.

are necessary, why are so many of them regularly violated? The permissive position is that all sex acts are normal as long as they occur between consenting adults and no one is harmed. The permissive position also holds that all sex is natural and private and hence should not be regulated in any way. This also begs the question: If all sex is normal, why have humans always had rules about sexual conduct? The prevailing sociological view is that certain acts are variant if they are preferred to heterosexual activities. According to this position, some forms of variance are parts of acceptable lifestyles—such as prostitution and pornography—and other variances—such as incest, exhibitionism, and hypersexuality—indicate a definite disorder. The central point to keep in mind is that sexual orientations are viewed on a continuum of social acceptability.

Simply taking a sociological position on human sexuality does not allow us to safely categorize every sexual orientation as either a normal act, a variant lifestyle, or a disorder. The behavior that may be a lifestyle for one person, such as a well-adjusted homosexual, may be a disorder for another, such as a homosexual who is very troubled about being gay. In other words, an orientation such as homosexuality can be either a lifestyle or a disorder, or some combination of the two, depending on how the person deals with being gay and how society deals with that person. There are other examples of this individualized idea. Take the case of voyeurism. A person may enjoy sexual watching on occasion, but if he or she is not obsessed with it, there is no disorder. Thus there is an important difference between a person who uses field glasses to look in the window of a women's dorm as a pastime and the Peeping Tom who can achieve sexual excitement *only* when climbing fire escapes. Human sexuality is a complex topic which is difficult to categorize. The way different sex acts are classified along the sexual continuum may reflect the opinion of many people, but it is not carved in stone.

When you read this chapter, keep in mind that it is as much about opinion as it is about sex.

THE OBJECTIVE DIMENSION OF SEXUAL VARIANCE

Surveys of Sexual Behavior

A number of researchers have tried to assess objectively human sexuality and people's opinions toward it. Freud conducted the first study in European society toward the end of the Victorian period. He frequently found sexual material in the recollections of his patients, and he postulated that the sex drive was a critical part of personality formation. Later, Alfred C. Kinsey systematically studied sexual behavior using the techniques of survey research. Kinsey's *Sexual Behavior in the Human Male* (1947) reported a wide discrepancy between the actual sexual behavior of some 5300 white males he interviewed and the stated sexual mores of society at that time. Many people found that their secret sexual desires and acts were shared by others. One-third of those studied had had a homosexual experience since puberty, 92 percent had masturbated, over 80 percent had had premarital intercourse, and half of those married had had extramarital sex. The real shocker came in 1952 when Kinsey published *Sexual Behavior in the Human Female,* in which he reported that premarital intercourse, homosexuality, masturbation, and adultery were much more common among women than most people believed.

The Kinsey findings caused quite a national stir by documenting the wide gap between sexual practices and sexual values. In terms of Figure 6-1, much of people's behavior was further to the right than was commonly believed. Later surveys comparable to Kinsey's indicated a significant increase in the acceptance or practice of different sexual behaviors. In 1973, more than half of the women and three-fourths of the men approved of premarital intercourse (Hunt, 1974). The same survey reported a tremendous increase in the acceptance of oral sex, anal sex, and masturbation, behaviors rarely discussed in earlier years and frequently condemned as sinful even if they were commonly practiced. However, both the Hunt and Kinsey surveys have been widely criticized for methodological reasons, particularly sampling bias.

Since the 1970s, there has been a proliferation of so-called sex surveys oriented toward peeping at, assaying, analyzing, and tabulating the sex lives of Americans. More formally, they purport to tap the objective type and frequency of actual sexual behavior. Four popular magazines (*Cosmopolitan, Playboy, Ladies' Home Journal*, and *Redbook*) have asked a total of 396 highly intimate questions of 389,000 willing people. The results have sold a lot of magazines, but have done so by duping the public into believing that the surveys are scientific and accurate. In fact, they are highly biased toward people who read those magazines and want to talk about themselves. For example, the *Ladies' Home Journal* asked for responses from *happily married* women, and then not surprisingly concluded that American wives are more happily married than is commonly believed! Since these polls depend on a self-selected group of respondents—rather than random samples drawn by professional survey samplers—they make it difficult to assess the objective dimension of human sexuality.

The dubiousness of the data is suggested by the amazing diversity of their findings. Over 100,000 readers of *Cosmopolitan* magazine provided accounts of multiple lovers, slapping during sex, anal intercourse, and simultaneous partners. According to the *Cosmo* survey, 54 percent of the wives had been sexually unfaithful. Consider the contrasts with the findings of the *Ladies' Home Journal* mass poll (83,000 respondents), which paints a picture of traditional connubial bliss. About 85 percent of the *LHJ* readers claim to be basically satisfied with their married sex lives (18 percent said they

occasionally have sex with hubby in the car), with only 21 percent admitting infidelity. The enormous differences in "objective" behavior appearing in these two typical studies point to a common flaw: unscientific sampling. Magazine sex surveys *should* be biased along obvious lines: they poll only their own readers (are *Cosmo* readers a cross section of American females?) and, like any survey research on such a sensitive topic, will be much more likely to get responses from people with more interest in and fewer inhibitions about the topic.

An honest, scientific assessment of the available data on actual sexual behavior leads to a simple conclusion: We know precious little about it. Random—and thus representative—samples of the American population are practically nonexistent on this topic. Consequently, the boundaries of "normal" sexual practices remain undefined. This forces us into the peculiar position of reporting objective statistics on problematic aspects of sexuality without having an objective baseline against which to measure them.

THE SUBJECTIVE DIMENSION OF SEXUAL VARIANCE

As mentioned earlier, it is difficult to assess the nature of sexual variance and be scientifically objective because there is so much disagreement over what constitutes normality and the various degrees of abnormality.[1] Many of the behaviors commonly included in the list of disorders are nothing more than exaggerations of popular sexual activity. Since we live in an age of moral differences and changes, many groups in society have their own set of sexual standards. Conservatives, for instance, endorse the idea that what is sexually acceptable is only what is legal.

[1] For a detailed discussion of this topic, see Clifton D. Bryant, *Sexual Deviance and Social Proscription: The Social Context of Carnal Behavior*, New York, Human Sciences, 1982.

If existing laws were taken as a true definition of acceptable activity, an enormous amount of the everyday sexual life of Americans would be adjudged abnormal. The only form of sex that is legal in every state is heterosexual intercourse between a husband and wife, at night, in bed, in an upper room, with the light out, and in the missionary style position (man on top of woman). In Texas, Rhode Island, and Arizona, two unmarried adults who have intercourse can be fined or imprisoned. A majority of states still prohibit homosexual acts between consenting adults as well as heterosexual oral-genital contact. Clearly, these state laws are inconsistent with the sexual behavior of many Americans. Religious institutions such as the Catholic church have a hand in this. In 1983, Pope John Paul II urged United States bishops to push harder for Americans to accept the conservative church teachings on sexuality, including opposition to divorce, premarital sex, and lust for one's spouse. Other influential groups, such as the Moral Majority, also have conservative sexual values.

Perhaps no group in our society is more maligned and misunderstood than homosexuals. We will use homosexuality here as a case example of Americans' subjective views toward various forms of sexuality. The myths about gay persons are problems themselves because they reinforce negative attitudes. One such myth is that homosexuals have specific physical attributes. Some psychiatrists helped foster this belief in the past. One, for instance, describing a "typical" homosexual stated, "He is thin and has slender limbs; his cheeks are flushed, his face soft, and his appearance and manners pleasant. Hair on the chest, axilla, and pubes is scarce. He behaves like a girl, walks like a girl, and smiles like a girl. He may like to cook and sew" (Abrahamsen, 1967:169). This stereotype is unfounded and has not been supported by empirical studies, and most psychiatrists today are aware of this. The homosexual athlete attests to it. So also did such aggressively masculine figures as Julius Caesar and Alexander the Great, as well as militant groups such as the Spartan warriors.

Gays are seen as effeminate because effeminacy is scorned since it is closely linked to the general devaluation of women in our society. An objective study of gay males found that most are indistinguishable from other people (Westwood, 1962). Yet these subjective misconceptions are propagated, even by some supposed experts on the topic, and they are often accepted as objective fact by the public. Lesbians do not escape this attitudinal harassment. They are typically viewed as masculine people in the wrong bodies. In reality, a clear majority of lesbians have an appropriately feminine appearance (Saghir and Robins, 1973).

Other subjective views about gays include the unfounded ideas that their relations with members of their own sex are sexually loaded and that they are eager to seduce children. Opinion polls indicate that approximately two-thirds of the American people feel that homosexuals are "harmful" to society and regard gays with "disgust, discomfort, or fear" (Clinard, 1974:547). A 1983 Gallup poll did not uncover any significant softening in subjective views toward gays. Most people think gays would rather be straight. This is simply not true. Contrary to the popular belief that gay parents are incompetents who promote homosexuality in their children, a number of studies have found that gay parents are very ordinary people with very ordinary children. Clearly, many Americans have subjective misconceptions about homosexuals. In some people these distorted attitudes foster an intense fear of homosexuals, a condition known as *homophobia*.

Many Americans regard the sexual preference of homosexuals as the overriding factor in understanding the entire personality of the gay person (Gagnon and Simon, 1973). In reality, most gays think no more about sex than heterosexuals. The subjective impression that gays share a distinct and consistent personality type persists, despite much scientific evidence to the contrary. One result of this myth is the assump-

Gay males, such as Julius Caesar, make it clear that the notion of effeminate gays is simply a myth. (*The Bettmann Archive, Inc.*)

tion that gays are suited only for certain jobs. For instance, a gay interior designer is assumed to have chosen that occupation because it intrinsically attracts homosexuals. A Harris poll in the 1960s reported that a majority of people felt gays should be allowed to work as artists, beauticians, florists, and musicians, but were unfit to engage in occupations of influence and authority. Attitudes have changed significantly since those days. A 1983 Gallup poll found that a majority of people believe homosexuals should have the same job opportunities as heterosexuals, with the notable exceptions of elementary school teaching and clergy work. In sharp contrast to an enlightened view about the acceptability of gay people, a 1984 American Civil Liberties Union (ACLU) report uncovered thirty years of infiltration of gay organizations to collect prejudicial information on activists' personal lives. In 1985, the ACLU filed suit against Big Brothers of Los Angeles, alleging that the organization discriminates against homosexual men who want to participate.

In the 1960s, the issue of gay rights reached the public consciousness through the actions of various groups commonly referred to as the gay liberation movement. This clearly raised the visibility of homosexuality as a social problem. Mental health professionals were persuaded to reconsider whether homosexuality is a sexual disorder or simply a variant lifestyle. In view of the lack of evidence that gays are more emotionally disturbed than heterosexuals, the Trustees of the American Psychiatric Association unanimously voted in 1973 that it is not objectively valid to consider homosexuality as a disorder since, in and of itself, it implies no impairment.[2] However, those homosexuals who are troubled by or in conflict about their sexual orientation are now classified as having a *sexual orientation disturbance,* officially known as *dyshomophobia.*

At the same time, the American Psychiatric Association cried out against discriminatory practices in employment, housing, and licensing and also urged the repeal of all laws against homosexual acts performed by consenting adults in private. The penalties for such acts are severe; in many states the punishment is five years' imprisonment. In other states the penalty ranges from ten years to life imprisonment. Currently, there is a movement to eliminate such legislation, but changes have been slow because of the widespread belief that homosexuality is immoral. Public attitudes toward homosexuality are presently in a state of considerable flux, and it will apparently be some time, if ever, before subjective impressions of gays are consistent with the findings of empirical research about them.

Myths and misconceptions about sexual variance are not limited to homosexuality. Many of the topics in this chapter involve deeply ingrained subjective beliefs which often ignite hostile feelings. To many people, for instance, pornography is a shameless, disgusting, and degrading phenomenon capable of triggering sex crimes. Others have different feelings; they may feel pornography is distasteful but also a useful substitute for criminal acts. Probably no forms of sexual vari-

ance are more heavily stigmatized than those involving children. Many people recoil in horror at the thought of child pornography or child molestation.

Surveys of public perceptions of various forms of sexual variance have uncovered some interesting findings in how people view a wide array of sexual behavior. Rist, Haggerty, and Gibbons (1973), for example, found a good deal of tolerance toward specific sexual variations commonly identified as lifestyles (homosexuality, prostitution, and pornography) but little patterning of viewpoints across the different lifestyles. A person who tolerates prostitution, for instance, may not tolerate homosexuality.

The case of homosexuality is, of course, only one key aspect of the multifaceted phenomenon addressed in this chapter. Actually, a wider lens on the phenomenon permits a focus on the subjective dimension of the general social problem. This wider view is necessary to counterbalance the extremely individualistic approach most people take to the topic. Usually, sexual variance is viewed as a deviant act for which the *individual* committing it is personally responsible; similarly, the reaction to the behavior is typically viewed in terms of *individuals'* attitudes toward the "deviant," which may range from approval to outrage. By analyzing the social patterns joining these individual attitudes together in public opinion, we can develop a sociological perspective on the subjective dimension of this complex social problem.

A major complication here is the many facets of the problem, remarked on above. As Figure 6-1 suggests, the collective reaction to deviations from the sexual norm is not uniform; behaviors that differ drastically from "normal" sex (those at the right-hand extreme of the continuum) will be considered much more problematic than those nearer the norm (close to the left extreme). Picture the sociological factors working on public opinion as forces that may alter the subjective curve. The *visibility* factor, for example, may increase public concern about

---

[2] The issue of whether or not homosexuality is a mental disorder has not been completely settled. A 1978 poll of members of the American Psychiatric Association found that 69 percent believed homosexuality is usually a pathological condition (*Time,* 1978:102).

a given sexual variation when a particularly dramatic case comes to light.[3] A homosexual senator being found in the closet with a teenage congressional page could raise the height of the subjective curve above homosexuality. On the other hand, the aggregate effect of many such revelations in the mass media may be one of declining shock and increased permissiveness. If general tolerance does result from the heightened visibility of the sexual smorgasbord, the whole subjective curve in Figure 6-1 will tend to drop. Since most church doctrines proscribe sexual permissiveness, individuals with strong religiously based *values* tend to define such acts as problematic throughout the continuum in Figure 6-1. Among people whose value systems emphasize civil liberties, on the other hand, the height of the subjective curve should be lower across the board.

The major purpose of this chapter is to delineate the known forms of sexual variance, examine the empirical research, and note discrepancies between the real nature of these acts and public opinion about them.

HOMOSEXUALITY

Cross-Cultural Views

Throughout history, some societies have maintained very positive attitudes toward homosexuality. It was practiced extensively by ancient Babylonians, Egyptians, and Greeks. A number of important historical figures openly engaged in homosexuality, including Plato, Sappho, Alexander the Great, Socrates, Virgil, and Julius Caesar. In ancient Greece, male homosexuality was widely practiced. Two notable contemporary examples are novelist Truman Capote and playwright Tennessee Williams.

In non-Western societies, homosexuality is often considered a normal part of life. Ford and Beach (1951) investigated seventy-six such societies and discovered that homosexuality is socially acceptable in forty-nine (64 percent) of them. They found two broad patterns of accepted homosexuality: the institutionalized homosexual role, and relations between men and boys who are otherwise heterosexual. Among the Siwans of North Africa, males of all ages are expected to perform homosexual acts. In fact, the Siwans consider it abnormal for a man not to have homosexual experience! In New Guinea, Keraki bachelors universally engage in anal intercourse, a homosexual ritual which is viewed as a necessary part of growing up. After a year of playing the passive (recipient) role, the Keraki male spends the remainder of his bachelorhood actively administering anal intercourse to the newly initiated. Some of the other societies in which homosexuality is accepted are the Mojave Indians of California and Arizona, the Aranda of central Australia, and many Moslem societies.

Although the general attitudes of Western societies toward homosexuality are not as liberal as those of non-Western cultures, there is a great divergence among the legal positions held toward homosexual acts.[4] In most western European societies, homosexual acts carried out in private between consenting adults are not considered crimes. In the United States, on the other hand, homosexual acts are often met with harsh legal reprisals. What is behind these unusually severe sanctions? Certainly the Judeo-Christian heritage, which condemns homosexual acts as unnatural, plays a part.[5] Some feel that homosexuality is incompatible with the

[3] For an examination of how public opinion and media coverage affect the development of homosexual rights, see Steven F. Cohn and James E. Gallagher, "Gay Movements and Legal Change: Some Aspects of the Dynamics of a Social Problem," *Social Problems*, 32, 1984:72–86.

[4] For a comprehensive overview of the scientific, religious, and social dimensions of homosexuality, see Ruth Tiffany Barnhouse, *Homosexuality: A Symbolic Confusion*, New York, Seabury, 1977.
[5] There are groups in the United States which attempt to change gay people into heterosexuals through what is called the principles of Christian Healing.

long-term preservation of the family, while others fear that if gays were accepted by society, they would actively attempt to seduce the young.[6] Negative attitudes toward gays are not unique to American heterosexuals. Our society has been so saturated with these views that one-quarter of the gays themselves believe that they are abnormal (Bell and Weinberg, 1978).

Prevalence of Homosexuality

Given their stigmatized status in the laws and culture, it is difficult to know the true prevalence of homosexuality in the United States. Nevertheless, a number of researchers have attempted to derive objective estimates. Kinsey's study of male sexuality reported that, at some time following the onset of puberty, 37 percent of males have at least one homosexual experience resulting in ejaculation. However, this is *homosexual behavior,* which does not necessarily indicate *homosexuality.* Kinsey's data indicated that most males having these experiences go on to lead heterosexual lives, and only 4 percent are exclusively homosexual throughout life. Kinsey's data have been criticized on a number of grounds. First, some of his respondents were recruited from gay groups and gay bars. Second, homosexual behavior was liberally defined to include 12-year-old boys dropping their pants on a dare as well as college boys "mooning." Both of these problems may have increased the estimate of the size of the gay population. Despite these problems, the Kinsey figures are still widely cited today.

A later study by Hunt (1975) reported that 10 percent of males have had some type of homosexual experience after the age of 15, but only 1 percent was exclusively gay. In 1975, *Time* magazine, without the benefit of carefully collected data, conservatively estimated that 5 million Americans are exclusively homosexual.

Gay Pride Day in San Francisco. (*Paul Conklin*)

Gay activists use numbers which greatly magnify these estimates. They claim that 20 million people are gay when closet homosexuals are included. Thus, in the homosexual community, there is frequent use of the estimate 1 in 10 Americans.

Despite the controversy over the actual size of the gay population, most researchers agree there are more gay males than lesbians. We are told that lesbians are only one-third to one-half as numerous as male homosexuals. Some interpret this guesstimate as an indication that male sexual development has special characteristics and problems. A more accurate interpretation may be that it is even harder to estimate the real frequency of female homosexuality because it is less overt. As a result, most lesbians are undiscovered. Because male homosexuals are more open than lesbians and because effeminate

---

[6] In 1985, the Pennsylvania Superior Court ruled that a parent's homosexuality can be considered in determining who gets custody of children after a divorce.

196

THE INDIVIDUAL AND SOCIETY

males are more often erroneously associated with homosexuality, it may simply be a popular misconception that female homosexuality is less common. In the future, the frequency of lesbianism will be better known as a result of women achieving greater equality to men in sexual expression.

Causes of Homosexuality

Although no one definitively knows what causes people to be gay, there is no dearth of theories and research on the topic. Presently, there is no known cause of homosexuality, just as there is no known cause of heterosexuality. But since heterosexuality is considered "normal," few have bothered to question its origin. This is not true of homosexuality. In the 1800s, Ulrichs, a homosexual himself, theorized that homosexuality is the product of abnormal embryonic development which causes a person to have the genital organs of one sex and the brain of the other! Recent theories are less primitive than Ulrichs' but not necessarily more valid. One biased thread running through most of today's theories is a failure to consider differences between gay males and lesbians; they either ignore the origin of lesbianism or simply assume that what is true for male homosexuals can be easily converted to fit female homosexuals. This is simply sexism reflected in research.

The environmental theories of male homosexuality really run the gamut. On the one hand, Freudians have always pushed the idea that gays have an unresolved Oedipal crisis stemming from an overbearing mother and a disinterested father. The result is an overidentification with women, resulting in an attraction to men as lovers. This is just one of the many versions of the psychoanalytic theory. Others include an unconscious fear of women as well as an overattachment to the father, resulting in a lust for men. Behaviorists have their own favorite pile of guesses. Some behaviorists contend gays were born to parents who wanted a

child of the opposite sex. Others believe homosexuality results from being punished for erotic curiosity about girls. Still others contend that gays were led into homosexuality during childhood by being seduced by older homosexuals. In a nutshell, none of the environmental theories seem compelling, since many of the experiences that purportedly cause homosexuality also happen to people who end up as heterosexuals.

Biological theories have also been contradicted as much as they have been supported. Genetic studies of patterns of homosexuality among identical twins have failed to uncover anything significant. Those that have were either tainted by biased sampling[7] or not sophisticated enough to separate out environmental factors. Other biological ideas have been tossed around, including the notion that gay males have testosterone deficiencies, respond differently to injections of female hermones than heterosexual men or women, or were stressed while in the womb. Although the research on prenatal stress has been conducted largely on rats, some feel comfortable making the great leap of faith to the world of humans. Obviously, it is risky to assume that what is true about rats is also true about humans.

There is a glimmer of hope in all the confusion about the etiology of homosexuality. A major study of homosexual men and women by the Kinsey Institute for Sex Research recently found little or no support for most of the traditional theories. However, the researchers concluded that a homosexual orientation usually seems to emerge from a deep-seated predisposition, possibly biological, that first appears as a failure to conform to society's stereotype of what it means to be a boy or a girl.[8]

[7] Kallman, for instance, reports 100 percent concordance for homosexuality among identical twins. Most of his data were based on hearsay rather than actual investigation.
[8] Interestingly enough, a large proportion of gays have long thought homosexuality is biological (Hooker, 1966).

Psychological Profiles

Closely related to the issue of causality is the question of whether there are differences in the psychological makeup of homosexuals and heterosexuals other than sexual preference. The popular belief is that gays are more disturbed, since many people consider healthy psychological adjustment and homosexuality to be mutually exclusive. Some mental health experts believe this, but only a handful of studies support them. Cattell and Morony (1962), after examining only sixteen male homosexuals, reported that their psychological profiles were similar to those of neurotics. Kenyon (1968) reported the same results for lesbians. Saghir and others (1970) concluded that gay males are more disturbed than male heterosexuals, but their measures of psychopathology were questionable. They used drug abuse, attempted suicide, and use of a psychotherapist as measures of disturbance. Clearly these behaviors may simply reflect homosexuals' despair over a world that rejects them rather than homosexuality itself. Other reports of high rates of attempted suicide among lesbians (Bell and Weinberg, 1978; Martin and Lyon, 1972) should be interpreted with the same caution.

The more sophisticated analyses of the psychological status of gay people show that homosexuality per se is typically not a pathological syndrome. This was established as far back as 1959 by Hooker's report that a team of psychologists who examined the performance of thirty male homosexuals and thirty male heterosexuals on standardized psychological tests agreed that two-thirds of the gays were average to superior in adjustment. Hedblom (1972) conducted in-depth interviews with sixty-five lesbians and found no indication of psychopathology. The 1978 Kinsey Institute study of homosexuals (published as the book *Homosexualities*) reported that a minority of gays are indeed disturbed, but the majority function as well psychologically as heterosexuals. A number of studies of lesbi-

ans report them to be *better* adjusted than female heterosexuals in terms of autonomy, spontaneity, and sensitivity to their own needs and feelings (Friedman, 1975), and to have more relatively stable work histories (Gagnon and Simon, 1968).

Apparently the American Psychiatric Association made an appropriate decision in designating homosexuality as a disorder only if the gay person is unable to accept his or her homosexuality. A majority of the studies indicate that gays lead ordinary lives and have the same everyday concerns that others have. Their relationships with other people are influenced more by their sex—the fact of being a man or a woman—than by their sexual orientation (Peplau, 1981). Despite these objective facts, stigmatization of gays is still subjectively rooted in negative attitudes.[9]

Gay Lifestyles

Societal rejection encourages homosexuals to form their own distinctive subculture, often with a special language and a well-known territory in some cities. Two of the largest gay neighborhoods are the Castro District of San Francisco and Greenwich Village in New York City. In these places, there are many gay institutions which provide services and function as social centers, such as public baths, gyms, bars, and gay businesses, including barber shops, bookstores, and travel agencies. In some cities there are also gay churches, and in 1985 a school for homosexual teenagers unable to cope with straight city high schools opened in a Greenwich Village church annex.

Some transitional gay neighborhoods are characterized by hostility between the homosexuals who move in and earlier residents of the

[9] The same people who stigmatize gays support the repeal of equal rights laws for homosexuals, proclaiming the danger of gays mixing with children. The fact is that children *raised* by homosexual parents are not dramatically affected and are typically heterosexually oriented (Green, 1978).

area. Many of the gays are affluent whites who can afford to restore buildings in dilapidated areas. As a result, they are displacing poor blacks and Hispanics. This is another example of the linkages of social problems: gays form neighborhoods in response to sexual discrimination, and impoverished minority members are forced out because of economic discrimination. Despite their common maltreatment, resentment of gays among the displaced runs high and sometimes takes the form of violent attacks against "faggots" by macho members of minority youth gangs.

Some male homosexuals never declare themselves and lead secret, painful lives in straight society, often married to women. A minority of these people seek sexual release in public places. This phenomenon was studied by Humphreys (1970), who conducted participant-observation research on gay males meeting for impersonal sex in public rest rooms, called "tearooms" (see Box 6-1 on gay bathhouses). By posing as a "watch queen," an accepted tearoom role of one who warns when strangers are nearing, Humphreys observed the gestures homosexuals used to initiate sex at a urinal before moving to a toilet stall for quick, anonymous oral sex. This usually took place without a single word being spoken. Humphreys found that almost 40 percent of the tearoom participants were married men with predominantly heterosexual orientations who simply made quick stops for sex with little risk of getting caught. How did he know they were married? By taking down their license numbers, tracing their home addresses, and later visiting in disguise as a researcher, an ethically questionable tactic for which he has been sharply criticized.

Promiscuity also occurs among gays who have decided to come out of the closet. In 1986, much of the promiscuous behavior in gay bathhouses and sex clubs came to an abrupt halt. In San Francisco, for instance, city officials ordered the closing of these places, saying they were a principal cause of AIDS. Gay bars, gay

parties, and parks are also some of their favorite gathering places. But this is only true for a certain segment of the gay male population and is relatively rare among lesbians. Why? It has nothing to do with homosexuality per se but with differences in personalities of the sexes, as noted in Chapter 10. If males are socialized toward sex, we would expect them to interact more on that level with one another. Lesbians, on the other hand, are more likely to seek long-term relationships based on romance.

Several formal voluntary organizations can help gay people learn about the homosexual community. These include the Gay Activists Alliance, the Society for Individual Rights, and the Mattachine Society. They organize various activities and furnish a number of services to homosexuals, including counseling. If present trends continue, we can expect the development of homosexual organizations to represent gays in all walks of life. Perhaps someday even the Teamsters will have a gay chapter.

Types of Gays

Given all the studies confirming that homosexuals are not that psychologically different from heterosexuals, does it make any sense to categorize them?[10] This is a controversial question, but since some feel that homosexuals are split into very different subgroups, a short review is in order. Among gays, there is a clear difference between those who flaunt a defiant lifestyle and the closeted, who may grant that overt gays have called attention to homosexuals' plight but who would never dream of emulating them. Many of the closeted are in heterosexual marriages (as alibis) and are simply traumatized at the thought of coming out for fear of destroying their careers or social standing.

---

[10] One factor that makes it difficult to accurately categorize homosexuals is that some heterosexuals behave homosexually in certain settings. This is known as situational homosexuality. It occurs most frequently among people segregated from the opposite sex for extended periods of time, as in the army or in prison.

BOX 6-1

GAY BATHHOUSES

New York City has many different types of places where homosexual men can find sex, but nowhere is the hunting better than at the baths. Every major city has gay bathhouses, and some, like New York, have several. One of the most famous is the St. Marks Bath, housed in a four-story historically designated building at 8th Street and Third Avenue in the East Village.

It was a quiet weekday night a few months ago when Rodger McFarlane, the representative of a gay group, went there with a reporter, who wanted to see these places that were so popular with homosexuals who got AIDS. The clerk stood silently and looked at the two customers who had just walked into the lobby. Behind him, the spools of a big tape recorder turned slowly, playing Pachelbel.

Money was given to him. It cost $6.75 a person, including a $2 deposit for each locker key. Neither smiling nor talking, the clerk returned the change, gave each man a towel and key, and buzzed open the door. Rows of lockers, thin and brightly colored, were to the left and up a short flight of steps. A small bar was to the right. No one spoke. The only sounds were the music and the noise of the metal locker doors clanking open as the two newcomers hung up their street clothes. The lighting was subdued, and fanned out in such a way that only the bottoms of people were lit, while their heads remained in shadow. The reporter and Rodger, now dressed only in towels, went down to the basement, which housed the pool and steam room, which was empty. Two men, one wearing a towel and the other nude, sat on ledges around the pool and stared at Rodger as he walked by, headed for the rooms upstairs.

Walking up narrow stairs painted black, Rodger went to the second floor, which, like the third and fourth floors, was a labyrinth of narrow hallways and little rooms. All told there were 150 cubicles on the three floors, each little room opening onto a hallway, lit only by the warehouse lights.

Rodger headed down one of the hallways. In one of the cubicles, a man was lying on a cot in such a way that his naked backside was seductively displayed to all who passed. In the shadows of another cubicle, a man sat masturbating. Down the hall could be heard moaning. It came from behind any one of a dozen closed doors.

Rodger climbed another flight of stairs to the third floor, silently passing two more men who were coming down the stairs. The two men looked with interest at Rodger, but he neither spoke nor looked at them. Rodger said people didn't talk much in the baths. It wasn't necessary because the sex rituals were known to all. If you see someone who interests you, he said, you touch him. If he's not interested, he brushes your hand away and you go elsewhere. If he is interested, Rodger said, he acquiesces and you go further or he touches you back.

Soon you are in one of the cubicles and you are having sex—oral, anal, probably both. Another person may join you. You change positions. And then maybe it is on to another cubicle or the steam room for group sex or perhaps the bar for a drink and rest before finding another person and another cubicle. People stay for hours, Rodger said, frequently all night. He adds that men come with gym bags loaded down with belts and chains and lubricants for sexual variety.

Rodger made his way back down to the locker room, which was getting busier. Three more men had just come in and were standing naked, looking back and forth at each other without saying anything. One of them touched Rodger, but he pushed the man's hand away. Then he and the reporter got dressed and walked out.

Mozart was playing on the tape machine now, and five men were standing at the desk, waiting for the man in the tight-fitting T-shirt to take their money. Two of them wore leather jackets, the type World War II bomber pilots used, two had polo shirts, and the fifth wore a conservative three-piece business suit and carried an attaché case.

Source: Adapted from *The Philadelphia Inquirer Magazine,* May 22, 1983. By permission of the publisher.

Today, more and more gays are coming out and leading more rewarding lives. Some are completely candid about it, work in fields where homosexuality is not stigmatized, and have social lives revolving almost completely around their homosexuality. Others come out for idealistic reasons, such as changing public opinion or challenging discriminatory laws. But most gays lead rather conventional lives that are simply homosexual counterparts to heterosexual marriages, with less role playing.

Bell and Weinberg (1978) paint a more

negative picture of homosexual types. They report that only 10 percent of the males and 28 percent of the females are "close coupled," with long-standing relationships analogous to straight marriage. About 17 percent of both males and females are "open coupled," living together but "cruising" public places in search of new partners. Bell and Weinberg classify 15 percent of the males and 10 percent of the females as "functionals" who have a great number of sexual partners and little interest in permanent relationships. About 13 percent of the males and 5 percent of the females are labeled "dysfunctionals," troubled people who regret being homosexual and are especially inclined to cruise. "Loners" constitute 16 percent of the males and 11 percent of the females in Bell and Weinberg's schema. These are people with low sexual activity, much unhappiness, and the highest incidence of suicidal thoughts.

Even if these pessimistic scenarios are true of some gay people, it is important to remember that they are more likely to result from society's reaction to gays than from homosexuality itself. The stress of the social stigma attached to being gay is one reason for the high rates of alcoholism and drug abuse among homosexuals. This fits with the subcultural theory of drug abuse discussed in Chapter 2: Some turn to drugs to ease the burden of belonging to a subculture whose values/lifestyles conflict with those of mainstream society. Curiously, the public is subjectively aware of the fact that homosexuals are more likely to have problems with alcohol and other drugs than nonhomosexuals. In a 1982 Gallup poll, almost 50 percent of a national sample felt that homosexuals have rates of drug abuse well above the average for other groups.

Differences between Gay Males and Lesbians

Female homosexuality[11] has remained more of a secret than male homosexuality. This may be because lesbianism is less objectively common, but part of the mystery surrounding lesbians is due to the fact that lesbianism is less visible. American social customs permit kissing, dancing, and holding hands in public among women. These same behaviors among men, however, are met with shock and snap judgments of homosexuality.

Studies on lesbians and gay males have uncovered differences that are typical of men and women in general rather than gay people only. These differing characteristics, particularly those involving sexuality, are reviewed in Chapter 10 on sex roles. It is important to remember that male and female homosexuals are as individually different as male and female heterosexuals, although there are some general differences between lesbians and gay males. For instance, lesbians are more likely to seek long-lasting relationships based on romance and mutual fidelity (Wolf, 1979). Gay males, like men in general, are more likely to promiscuously seek sexual satisfaction. In fact, Bell and Weinberg (1978) report that almost half of the gay males in their study have had at least 500 sexual partners.[12] Lesbians are much less likely to have one-night stands, and therefore they spend less time cruising in gay bars, which are central to the lives of many gay males.

For lesbians, like women in general, the discovery of love relations precedes the discovery of sexuality, the reverse of many males (Simon and Gagnon, 1967). Because they tend to explore their homosexuality later, lesbians typically "come out" two or three years later on the average than their male counterparts. This is a reflection of differences in sexual socialization for men and women. Men learn

---

Lesbos. There she wrote sensuous poems about the love of woman for woman.

[12] There are conflicting reports on the degree of promiscuity among gay males. Saghir and Robins (1973) found that 61 percent had a deep emotional relationship with at least one other male for a relatively long time.

---

[11] The term *lesbian* originated with Sappho, the first literary advocate of female homosexuality in the Western world. She lived in the sixth century B.C. on the island of

earlier to articulate their sexual needs without having to legitimize them through romantic love. About five years elapse for both groups between first expressing sexual feelings for people of the same sex and considering themselves homosexual (Cronin, 1974).

There are some differences between lesbians and gay males regarding heterosexual experiences. Schafer (1977) found that over half of the lesbians have had heterosexual intercourse at least once, but only one-fifth of gay males have. In addition, most lesbians reported that their first sexual experience was with a man, yet all of the gay males in the study had had sex with another man before experimenting with women.

There are, of course, numerous perceived differences between male and female homosexuals that are simply the result of stereotypical thinking by the public at large. Many believe that gay people play roles that mimic heterosexual relationships. One stereotype of the gay male is the effeminate, passive person who walks with a swish and limply hangs his wrists. A common characterization of the lesbian is the masculine butch or dyke who seeks out a passive partner (known as a femme) to rule and dominate. While these behaviors may be characteristic of a tiny minority of gays, the public feels they typify the whole group. This often happens to the stigmatized: the public generalizes from a small yet visible minority to the entire group. Perhaps 1 gay male in 100 holds his wrists limp, but all are assumed to do so.

Another popular but unfounded view of gay people involves lesbian mothers. The stereotype of the man-hating amazon has caused more than one judge to award custody to the father. The objective evidence clearly indicates lesbian mothers cling firmly to highly traditional notions of child rearing and experience the same delights, disappointments, strains, and stresses as any other group of single mothers. There is also no evidence that lesbianism in the mother has a specific effect on the child in terms of gender-related problems, sex-role confusion, or general development.

The Gay Rights Movement

Since the 1960s, gay people have become politically organized to fight discrimination and repeal antihomosexual laws. Presently, under Army regulations, homosexual acts are considered crimes punishable by court-martial proceedings or dishonorable discharge. In Miami, male homosexual prisoners are locked up with female inmates. These practices, as well as formal laws such as the homosexuality exclusion clause of the 1952 Immigration and Nationality Act, again exemplify the linkages of social problems, since they are grounded in prejudice as well as sexism. Lesbians are rarely the target of such practices and infrequently run into trouble with the law because of their lower visibility and greater acceptability than gay males.

Today restrictive laws are attacked as attempts to legislate private morality and violate constitutional rights. Those in favor of the laws argue that decriminalizing homosexual behavior will result in more gays and more seductions of young boys (see the section on pedophilia later in this chapter for a discussion of this issue). Opponents argue that there are enormous economic and psychological costs inflicted by denying persons access to certain careers and other important parts of life simply because of sexual preference.

The gay rights movement symbolically originated on June 28, 1969, at the Stonewall Inn, a gay bar in Greenwich Village. On that day, the police burst into the bar and were met with outrage rather than passivity. Men gathered in front of the bar shouting and cursing and hurling a barrage of missiles. The demonstration went on for three days, a period now known as the Raid Heard Round the World. Soon gays were pouring out of closets, and bewildered straight Americans realized that they had a homosexual second society in their midst. Since then, the struggle has been fought on many levels, but the movement's victories are now barely balancing its defeats. A move to amend the 1964 Civil Rights Act by adding ''affectional or sexual preference'' to the list of other ill-treated groups does not appear to have much chance of passing Congress in the near future. And, in 1976, the Supreme Court upheld the constitutionality of state antihomosexual laws. There will certainly be a continuation of the battle between militant gays and those who oppose granting them full civil liberties. However, until national legislation is passed, gays will probably continue to make inroads in some areas and lose political contests elsewhere.

Some states have liberalized laws concerning homosexuality by eliminating penalties against private sexual relationships, both homosexual and heterosexual, between consenting adults. Generally, there has been a marked growth of tolerance toward gays. Some police units that once were notorious for harassing homosexuals can now be found playing goodwill softball games with them.

It is ironic that the well-publicized antihomosexual crusade of singer Anita Bryant in 1977 actually provoked gays and prodded them to join gay rights organizations by the tens of thousands. Now gay politicians are no longer certain losers. In 1984, about 100 elected officials nationally were openly gay. During the same year Democratic presidential candidates affirmed gay rights and actively sought gay support. All of this was unheard of a decade ago. Since then, the gay liberation movement has had a tremendous personal and political impact on many gays. Now their self-images are changing from shame to pride, they *demand* adequate research funds for AIDS, and, most important, the general political climate for gay reform looks promising for the near future. Widespread stereotypes still exist, but there is evidence of progress.

PROSTITUTION

Prostitution, the World's Oldest Profession, is almost always found, or at least reported, among women only. It is another sexual variance which, while at odds with societal values, is not necessarily indicative of a sexual disorder. This applies to both prostitutes and their customers (johns). Attitudes toward prostitution have varied enormously throughout history and within societies. In ancient Greece, a prestigious group of prostitutes called the *hetairae* was made up of distinguished people who served leading citizens. The well-educated hetairae provided intellectual companionship as well as sexual gratification to their clients. Their portraits and statues were placed in public buildings next to those of important statesmen and famous generals.

Prostitution has also been revered when linked with religion. In ancient times, inhabitants of the Mediterranean area associated prostitution with worship of the gods. In some instances, a woman was required to perform an act of prostitution in a temple before she was married. One respected class of prostitute in modern Japan is the *geisha,* or dancing girl. Trained in singing, dancing, and other forms of entertainment, many of these women selectively provide sexual services for certain customers.

In the United States today, attitudes toward prostitution vary widely. Some people view prostitutes as helpless, exploited victims, some as dangerous criminals, and others simply as unorthodox working girls. Generally speaking, prostitution is tolerated, but certain forms are less stigmatized than others, as when the prostitute is selective of her customers, combines other roles with sexual pleasure, or uses her earnings for a socially acceptable goal.

Functions of Prostitution

There are a number of reasons prostitution is not widely condemned. To functionalists, it benefits society and provides certain individual advantages over sex within marriage. Prostitution is impersonal, impartial, and, according to Kinsey, more economical than attracting and seducing a nonprostitute. The traveling salesman away from home or the sailor in a port finds it much easier to visit a prostitute than go through the difficult task of finding a stable relationship on the road.

Quick, anonymous sex also appeals to some men who are not separated from their wives or girlfriends but have a strong need for sexual variety or certain sexual practices (such as oral sex) which are taboo with their mates. Many of these men are clearly satisfied with the sexual aspect of their marriages. Others crave more unconventional forms of sexual activity, such as sadomasochistic practices, desires which they are ashamed to reveal. Still others turn to prostitutes because they have physical handicaps which they might feel compel them to buy sex. In addition, separated or divorced men frequent prostitutes since their stable sexual relationships have been dissolved.

To all of these men, a prostitute is appealing because she is readily available, not interested in emotional commitment, knowledgeable about different sexual acts, and willing to forget the encounter after she has been paid. By meeting the needs of these various groups, prostitution functions as a form of social control over sexual needs. Prostitutes themselves report that they serve important social functions because of individuals' extensive and varied sexual needs (Bryan, 1966b). This serves to protect individuals and social institutions from destructive ruptures. Prostitutes believe that their availability leads to a decrease in the number of rapes and murders. They also believe that marriages are more enduring because prostitutes hold them together as marriage counselors do. This sentiment was voiced long ago by St. Augustine (A.D. 354–430), who argued that prostitution stabilizes the family and protects "good" women.

Of course, what some may see as socially

functional others may see as simple degradation. Using a *conflict* perspective, feminists argue that prostitution epitomizes men's domination of women. This, they say, stems from the attitude that women are the sole sexual property of men; and, consequently, they must choose between becoming domestic slaves within marriage (see Chapter 10 on sex roles) or prostitutes who are directly paid for sex. To feminists, prostitution is simply a blatant symptom of a sexist society.

Whatever its sociological interpretation, many Americans subjectively define prostitution as a definite social problem. Some see it as essentially immoral, others as part of a larger social problem: social injustice toward women. To others, it is a social problem because it destroys "good" neighborhoods. A fourth view is that prostitution is a social problem because it violates the law (except in certain regions of Nevada). Whatever its status as a social problem, one thing about prostitution is quite clear: It has always existed and will likely exist in the future. The only circumstance which could reduce prostitution would be a totally permissive society in which anything goes sexually. This is not likely to happen, and even if it did, the less attractive might still end up paying the more desirable for their bodies.

Prevalence of Prostitution

Although no separate data are available on the number of male prostitutes, there is a general consensus that there are between 250,000 and 500,000 male and female *hookers* (a term originating from the female Civil War camp followers of General Joseph Hooker) in the United States today. This is a sharp decline from the estimated 1.2 million prostitutes in 1945. Why the large decrease since World War II?[13] Loos-

[13] There is still some debate over whether the number of prostitutes has actually declined. However, recent reports of United States women being lured to Japan for prostitution suggest that the need for prostitutes here at home has been satisfied.

ening of attitudes and behavior toward sex probably plays some role. Premarital and extramarital sex are not as widely tabooed today. As one disgruntled old hooker put it: "Why should a john pay a professional for it, when other girls are giving it away for free?" One striking aspect about the prevalence of prostitution is its apparent increase among the young. Experts estimate that 1.6 million children run away from their homes in this country each year and that 25 to 50 percent of them end up in prostitution.

Is there a typical client (or john or "trick") who patronizes prostitutes? The majority are reportedly middle-aged married men (Wells, 1970). In the late 1940s, Kinsey reported that 69 percent of the white male population had or will have had some contact with prostitutes. More recent studies indicate that the use of prostitutes is all but dying out among young college educated males. This is probably a direct result of sexual freedom among the young, something that today's older males missed in their younger days. The men who do visit prostitutes today are finding the times a bit tough, especially in places like New York City and Minneapolis, where the names of people caught with prostitutes have been publicized.

Forms of Prostitution

Essentially, prostitution is dispensing sexual favors on a mercenary basis with no emotional attachment. It can take many forms, depending on how and where the services are rendered. Prostitutes differ from one another in terms of the trappings surrounding the method and place of the sexual contact. On the basis of these factors, there is actually a social hierarchy of prostitution, ranging from the expensive call girl to the lowly streetwalker. The different forms of prostitution are listed below, from the most prestigious to the least prestigious types.

1 *Call girls,* the crème de la crème of prostitutes, dress tastefully, live in fashionable apartments, and have a wide choice in selecting

their clients. They generally service their customers on a regular basis. Their name derives from the fact that their meetings are prearranged by direct telephone contact, answering service, or message machine. Their sophisticated approach to prostitution commands as much as 100 to 200 dollars a visit. Some call girls are aspiring entertainers with some reputation in the world of show business. As such, these women, sometimes referred to as *pony girls,* can charge even more.

2 *Hotel prostitutes* work their own particular hotels, where they split their fees with hotel employees. Sometimes they pose as salespeople or secretaries at conventions, roaming the lobbies and cocktail parties for potential johns. Some convention organizers may prearrange services with this type of prostitute.

3 *Stag party girls* are a cut below the hotel hookers. They entertain men by serving as topless waitresses, doing strip shows, and al-

Mayflower Madam, Sidney Biddle Barrows, who allegedly ran a high-class call girl ring in the 1980s. (*UPI/Bettmann Photos*)

lowing the men to fondle them. Intercourse and other sexual acts are usually arranged with individual men after the party.

4 *House prostitutes* are hookers who operate out of a building commonly referred to as a whorehouse, brothel, or "cat house." Here the john has a choice of a variety of girls who split their fees with the madam or pimp who manages the house. Houses of prostitution, such as the famous Kit Kat Ranch, are legal only in certain regions of Nevada. In earlier times, brothels were readily identified by a red light in the front of the house. Today, houses in "red light districts" have been replaced by more secretive settings, where women work long hours for a fraction of call girls' pay. Sometimes, groups of these women will move from one house to another (between or within cities) to avoid detection and provide more variety for customers. This phenomenon is known as a "traveling circus."

5 *Bar girls* are near the bottom of the prostitution hierarchy. Also known as "B-girls," they spend their time hustling drinks in bars, where potential johns pay exorbitant amounts for the "lady's drink." Their trick is to lure clients to a nearby hotel or rooming house, where the sex comes quick and cheap or not at all. Usually these houses have financial arrangements with bar and hotel employees, splitting their fees for drinks hustled and rooms provided. Some suspected prostitutes working in bars peddle their wares in exhibitionistic ways on a stage.

6 *Streetwalkers* are bottom-of-the-line hookers who approach strangers directly on the street. They are quite visible, not only because they dress like stereotypical whores but also because they wave at passing motorists and sometimes knock on doors of cars stopped at lights. Sexual negotiations are quickly carried out, and arrangements are finalized in a nearby cheap hotel or in the john's car. These women turn a lot of tricks a night and they show it. Streetwalkers are especially likely to come

from impoverished backgrounds and to be hooked on drugs. More prestigious hookers, such as call girls, may skid to the streetwalker level as they age and their appearance deteriorates. Today, young runaways, only 14 or 15 years old, are more frequently turning to streetwalking to support themselves. Regardless of their backgrounds, most streetwalkers lead sad and desperate lives.

Today, prostitution is not limited to the six forms described above. A number of changes and innovations have occurred which are mainly designed to make prostitutes more available and more discreet. One such innovation is the massage parlor, a national phenomenon which has customers pay for sexual services under the guise of getting a legitimate rubdown from a masseuse. Usually the customer pays a set amount ($25 is common) for a massage and then negotiates for extra sexual services when he is alone with the woman. Although many forms of sex are available, these places specialize in masturbation, commonly referred to as a "local" exercised by a "hand whore."

Other innovations in American forms of prostitution include escort services, which are really a cover for something more than a dinner date, and corporate prostitutes, who are supposedly hired as secretaries and office workers, but are actually on the payroll for the sexual pleasure of a firm's clients. Now streetwalkers have also developed innovations to avoid arrest. Some are letting their fingers do the walking by calling public telephones, engaging in erotic conversation with men who answer, and arranging meetings with any interested parties.

Male Prostitution

Although most prostitutes are women who cater to men, both sexes sell sex. Males usually have a male clientele. Reportedly, there are some men, known as gigolos, who are paid to have sex with women, but gigolos may be more myth than reality. Because of the traditional differences in attitudes toward sex between men and women, it is extremely unusual for a woman to have to pay a man to have sex with her. There may be a few women who *are* that desperate. They are the ones likely to contact a male escort service. These men are rarely arrested because most solicitation laws refer only to female heterosexual prostitution. There are exceptions, however. In 1981, a 21-year-old man was arrested as a "call guy" in Des Moines after offering to have sex with an undercover female police officer for $20.

So much for the exceptions. Male prostitutes almost always service gay males. Like female prostitutes, they also come in different forms. There are macho-dressed hustlers who walk the streets, call boys, and child prostitutes known as "chickens." Their numbers seem to be increasing. Boy prostitutes have become a particularly alarming objective social problem. Most are runaways between the ages of 13 and 16 who are often escaping from poverty and family upheaval (Lloyd, 1976). There may be as many as 100,000 of these boys selling their bodies, generally to middle-aged married men known as "chicken hawks." This is one of the undesirable by-products of keeping homosexuality in the closet and an example of the linkages between two subproblems of sexual variance.

Solicitation by older males may be initiated in a public place like a park or bar. Sometimes it occurs in a male house of prostitution, where clients make their selections from a book of nude photographs, a practice also found in female houses of prostitution. The male houses commonly bill themselves as modeling agencies.

Men who patronize male prostitutes may find them through ads in underground newspapers. Some of the ads are placed by drifters, and others provide direct access to call boys— the elite of the world of male prostitution. It is especially interesting to note that many male hookers, while providing homosexual services, are straight themselves. Perhaps this is linked with a greater sense of desperation and emo-

tional upheaval among male prostitutes who, contrasted to female prostitutes, are acting against their heterosexual tendencies.

Causes of Prostitution

The reasons that women become prostitutes are widely varied, although there is some information about their backgrounds. Next to nothing is known about the causes of male prostitution. One common finding of research on the background of female prostitutes is the broken home experience (Katchadourian and Lunde, 1975). Many prostitutes come from families where the parents fought constantly (if they were even still together), and there was an absence of warmth between daughter and parents, particularly the father. Prostitutes report that emotional deprivation was an everyday life experience during childhood. More important, many report they were sexually abused, usually by a father or stepfather (Goldman, 1985).

Given all of these stresses, it is not surprising that children who later become prostitutes often had difficulty in school and were regarded by teachers and neighbors as "oddballs" or troublemakers. In general, the psychological analyses of prostitutes typically find that they were victimized in many ways as children.[14] They come to see sex as something they can barter for needed affection. This is not to say that all who enter prostitution are emotional basket cases: some may sell themselves simply because they can make a lot of money in a relatively short time.[15] This may be especially true for teenagers who drift into prostitution because they lack the skills for other kinds of work.

As noted earlier, there are different forms of prostitution, ranging from the lowly streetwalker to the high-priced call girl. Do all types

---

[14]The studies of male prostitutes also find a high percentage of broken homes and frequent self-reports of being unwanted or misunderstood (Ginzburg, 1977).

[15] It is reported that in the economically booming Silicon Valley of California, prostitutes earned an average of 74,000 dollars in 1985.

of prostitutes have similar background characteristics? Most studies to date have focused on streetwalkers who were arrested. What about the more discreet call girls? Greenwald (1958) interviewed twenty call girls and found that, unlike streetwalkers, call girls come from the upper echelons of society. However, Greenwald found an amazing similarity among the family atmospheres into which these women were born. Not one of the women reported growing up in a happy home. Most of the homes were broken before the women reached adolescence. As in the case of streetwalkers, the attitude of the parents toward the children was one of general rejection. It was in this context of neglect and rejection that many of the women had a special kind of experience: they reported engaging in some form of sexual activity for which they were rewarded in their exploitive environments. A sad footnote to the Greenwald study is the fact that 75 percent of the call girls interviewed reported having attempted suicide.

Stages of Prostitution

Nanette Davis (1978) interviewed thirty streetwalkers and found a recurring three-stage pattern through which these women had become prostitutes. The first stage in the process was a gradual *drift* from simple promiscuity to the first act of prostitution. This usually took several years; Davis' subjects typically had had intercourse by age 13 and had begun prostitution around age 17. The second stage is called *transitional deviance.* This lasts about six months. At this time, the girl is learning the skills of prostitution on a part-time basis. She does not yet consider herself a prostitute and is ambivalent about the role. She rationalizes her behavior by normalizing it, viewing the selling of sex as she would the selling of anything else, and placing the blame on men who approach her rather than on herself. Eventually she stops kidding herself about what she is doing and enters the final stage of prostitution, which Davis calls *professionalization.* Now she thinks

of herself as a prostitute, makes sex her vocation, and centers her life on it. She may also defend her deviant identity by claiming that all people prostitute themselves in one way or another. A few of Davis' subjects were able to lead a dual life by maintaining homes with children, although it was a difficult act to juggle—an illustrative case of role conflict.

Barbara Heyl (1975) investigated the process involved in becoming a house prostitute. Here the socialization process is different from that of a streetwalker in that there is a formal training program conducted by a madam, the manager of the house. The woman is taught specific sexual skills and ways of persuading customers to spend more money.

Although most prostitutes probably go through the three stages of drift, transition, and professionalization, there are additional experiences that some types of hookers have. Call girls, for instance, are recruited in specific ways. Bryan (1966a) found that these higher-status prostitutes start with a personal contact with another call girl or a pimp. The next stage is an *apprenticeship,* a period of training usually lasting two or three months. Like a student teacher, the woman is supervised in an apartment which serves as the classroom. The instructor may be an experienced call girl or a pimp.

Bryan reports that certain attitudes are also transmitted at this time. These include the belief that men are corrupt and dishonest, so it is acceptable to exploit them. This view is supported by rationalizing that men cheat on their wives, members of the clergy break oaths, and johns sometimes "stiff" (cheat) the prostitute. Call girls are taught rules about cleanliness, the techniques of "french culture," and methods of dispensing with the john as soon as possible. A major purpose of the apprenticeship is to develop a clientele so that the woman can eventually set up business in her own place. At the streetwalker level, training is nonexistent or haphazard at best; streetwalkers literally walk onto the job, fumble for an organized approach, and hope that they can make a living without regular arrest or physical harm, two of the many threats associated with being a prostitute.

PORNOGRAPHY

Historically, pornography was loosely related to prostitution, since writings by and about prostitutes were originally referred to as pornography. Today pornography and prostitution are by no means one and the same, although they may be found together, as when hookers hang around adult bookstores in areas known as "combat zones." More important, there may be a linkage between pornography and crime. In 1986, the Attorney General's Commission on Pornography heard testimony that hard-core pornography was used by a majority of child molesters, rapists, and incest offenders. Of course, a correlation between crime and pornography does not mean one is the cause of the other.

What is pornography? This is a difficult question to answer since different people may see the same sexual material in radically different ways (Malamuth and Billings, 1984). Generally speaking, pornography may be defined as a depiction of sexual behavior which is designed to sexually excite the viewer. Although it has existed for centuries in the United States, it is more prevalent and varied today than ever before.

In 1957, the Supreme Court ruled that materials are pornographic if they appeal to essentially "prurient interests," oppose "contemporary community standards," and are "utterly without redeeming social value." Clearly, the intention of the Supreme Court was to set objective standards of obscenity, but the standards have not worked because they have widely different meanings to different people. Consequently, sexual material is labeled pornographic if members of the Supreme Court say it is, and this label may be the simple result of whatever affects them rather than some objective quality of the material.

Attitudes toward Pornography

Many Americans—a full 91 percent of the population, according to one survey (Hindelang, Gottfredson, and Flanagan, 1981)—are opposed to pornography, feeling that it should be either restricted or totally banned. This is particularly true of women. In fact, a 1986 nationwide *Washington Post*-ABC news poll found that men are fairly evenly divided on whether the laws dealing with pornography are strict enough. The views of women were much different. By about 3 to 1, women said pornography is harmful and should be banned. One form of pornography which is especially stigmatized is "kiddie porn," although many either are unaware of it or deny its existence.

People oppose pornography for different reasons. Some feel it is morally wrong and inherently disgusting. Others believe it stimulates disordered needs and dehumanizes women. Another perspective is that pornography is acceptable because it increases sexual freedom, is more desirable than censorship in terms of value trade-offs, and acts as a safety valve for those who are already oriented toward sexually disordered acts. The question of whether pornography increases or decreases sex crimes will be analyzed in the Social Policy section of this chapter.

Some feminists have been especially vocal about pornography in recent years. They contend that pornography teaches people to view women as sex objects to be used for men's pleasure. They are especially enraged by pornography which includes violence against females—a depiction which they believe contributes to the general victimization of women in society. One feminist group, Women against Pornography, has declared an all-out war on pornography. Its activities (such as group demonstrations) are fueled by the supposition that pornography is a significant factor in the nation's disturbing rate of violence against women and children.

Critics worry about groups such as Women against Pornography because they believe their methods could undermine free speech, encourage the suppression of ideas, and possibly even lead to book burnings. Whether the feminists are right or wrong, their actions have helped to push pornography through many phases of the life cycle of a social problems movement (see Chapter 1). Presently pornography seems to be at the institutionalization stage of the life cycle. It is now a highly visible problem. However, if present trends continue in sales of videocassette recorders and the wide availability of porno tapes in all types of retail outlets, fragmentation and eventual demise of the movement may be just around the corner. Objective behavior may very well outrun subjective concern.

Patterns of Consumption

Subjective concern about pornography was widespread in 1968 when President Johnson appointed a National Commission on Obscenity and Pornography. The commission found that exposure to porno was commonplace; 84 percent of the men and 69 percent of the women had seen some type of sexually explicit material. Exposure was especially widespread among younger adults and people with some college education. The commission concluded that around 20 to 25 percent of the male population in the United States *regularly* encountered sexually explicit materials, including depictions of intercourse, oral sex, or sadomasochistic activities. The study also found that porno appeals more to the religiously inactive than to the religiously active, and more to the sexually experienced than to the sexually inexperienced. One notable finding was that women are as aroused by watching porno as men. This runs counter to the traditional role expectations about sexual behavior.

While it is true that the typical customer of a "dirty" bookstore today is a white, middle-class, married male, aged 26 to 55, many forms of porno are branching out to other sectors of society, including college campuses. The commission found that people have been exposed to porno at increasingly early ages; a significant majority of men and women had encountered explicit sexual materials before age 21, and 30 percent of the men and 17 percent of the women before age 15. Now there is a growing emphasis on marketing porno for women, as evidenced by magazines such as *Playgirl,* which contains nude male centerfolds, and by the increased production of porno flicks with a romantic theme.

When polled, people may *say* they are opposed to pornography, but the actions of much of the American public suggest otherwise. Pornography is a well-organized business which grossed an estimated 7 billion dollars in 1984. It seems safe to assume that pornography will become even more popular in the future as home video recorders become commonplace. Today there is a proliferation of videocassette rental centers, some in exclusive shopping malls or in corners of food markets. Porno is moving from peep houses to sleekly packaged video stores, from the trench coat crowd to chic social gatherings. The future of porn will include an interesting collision between women who no longer watch porno movies through nearly closed fingers and feminists who call for its abolition. Right now, the fingers are opened, and feminist rage does not seem to be having much effect on actual practice. We may, however, see a significant change in the content of porno, especially away from female degradation and violent behavior. It appears especially likely that control of so-called kiddie porn will be increased. Child pornography was once an anonymous shame, but it has recently emerged as a key feature in heightened subjective concern about the victimization and sexual molestation of children. Federal and state laws have established tougher standards and penalties for child pornographers. Even the Netherlands, the world's child pornography center, has responded to public concern by enacting laws making child pornography a crime. The magazine *Family Weekly* reported that at least 300,000 children under the age of 16 were involved in child pornography in the United States during 1985.

THE SEXUAL DISORDERS

The most severely stigmatized sexual variances (see Figure 6-1) are known as sexual disorders. They are called disorders not only because they are socially unacceptable but also because they usually indicate a psychological abnormality. This is true in the case of a person who can be stimulated only at the sight of a certain object, such as a shoe. Others may have a preference for children as sex partners. Some prefer to make love to a cadaver, while others are stimulated only if they spy on a stranger getting undressed. The list of sexual disorders is quite lengthy. One helpful way to classify the different behaviors is according to whether the behavior involves an abnormal *type* of sexual object, an abnormal *mode* of gratification, a gender *identity* or role disorder, or an abnormality in the *intensity* of the sex drive.

Abnormalities in type of object include *pedophilia* (child partner), *incest* (family member), *fetishism* (inanimate object), the *excretory perversions* (feces or urine), *necrophilia* (corpse), *bestiality* (animal), and *pyromania* (fire).

Abnormalities in mode of gratification include *exhibitionism* (displaying one's genitals), *voyeurism* (watching others), *sadism* (inflicting pain), *masochism* (receiving pain), and *frotteurism* (rubbing the penis against a stranger).

Gender identity disorders include *transvestism* (dressing in the clothes of the opposite sex) and *transsexualism* (persistent wish to be a member of the opposite sex).

Abnormalities in intensity of desire include *nymphomania* (excessive desire for coitus in a female) and *satyriasis* (excessive desire for coitus in a male).

You may wonder how some of these acts could be considered social problems since they seem so private. On the surface they may appear to be personal, but *as a collectivity,* all of the individual sexual disorders affect an objectively substantial number of people. Some of the sexual disorders are still pretty mysterious and have hardly been researched. The better-known ones are described separately below, while the more mysterious are briefly discussed under the heading Miscellaneous.

Pedophilia

Pedophiles are attracted to prepubescent children of the same or opposite sex. Most offenders are males. Because of the great potential for psychological and physical harm to the child, this disorder has more serious consequences than most forms of abnormal sexual behavior.

About 100,000 children are sexually molested each year in the United States. Most victims are 10 to 12 years old. An equal number of boys and girls are abducted and molested, but boys report it less often. Over 40 percent of the victims are molested between 3 and 6 p.m. in March and April. Asking for help or directions is the most common lure used by child molesters. In the late 1980s, chilling stories of child sexual abuse have regularly been making the headlines. These include reports of conspiracies of pedophiles who run nursery schools and reportedly have abused hundreds of children.

Cavanagh (1966) classifies pedophiles into two groups: the *tender type* and the *aggressive type*. The tender type is usually homosexually directed toward young boys, whereas the aggressive type is more frequently oriented toward young girls. Like most sexual disorders, pedophilia reportedly is committed overwhelmingly by males. The aggressive type may physically harm the child, and may even panic and kill. Ironically, both types of pedophiles tend to be rigidly religious and moralistic (Davison and Neale, 1974).

Although little research has been done on homosexual pedophiles, the mental status of heterosexuals has been evaluated. One team of investigators found that heterosexual pedophiles cluster into three age groups: adolescence, mid to late thirties, and mid to late fifties (Mohr, Turner, and Jerry, 1964). In general, the adolescent pedophiles lack sexual experience with people of their own age, and they do not desire it. Many pedophiles in their thirties are severely socially maladjusted and intoxicated during the sex act. The pedophiles in their fifties tend to suffer from social isolation and prefer young children to relieve their loneliness.

Pedophilia is one topic which has recently come out of the closet and gained the public's attention. Consequently, many people have become outraged at this sexual disorder because it can inflict permanent damage on children. Some feel offenders should be dealt with harshly, including the use of so-called medical castration. This involves drugs such as Depo-Provera, a female hormone which reduces the sex drive.

The increase in subjective awareness of pedophilia has also contributed to a rather appalling development on the sexual front: groups devoted to child molester's lib. Spokesmen for the North American Man-Boy Love Association (NAMBLA) are now arguing in newspapers and on television for the right to have sex with underaged youngsters. The pedophilic Réne Guyon Society of Los Angeles is especially strident: its crude motto is "Sex by eight or else it's too late." The British Pedophile Information Exchange (PIE) wants the age of consent dropped as low as 4! To make matters worse, some respected sex researchers are fanning the flames by declaring that very young children should be allowed, and perhaps encouraged, to conduct a full sex life without interference from parents and the law. In many ways, pedophilia is a sexual variance problem which appears to be headed toward a highly volatile future. It is also closely linked to other social problems, such as child pornography, alcoholism, and incest.

Incest

Incest refers to sexual relations among members of the same family, such as between a parent and child or a brother and sister. When it occurs between a parent and underaged child, it is a form of intrafamilial pedophilia. Although the legal definition of incest varies from state to state,[16] incestuous feelings appear to be commonplace. There are strong cultural and psychological defenses against incest, usually referred to as the *incest taboo.* With the possible exception of murder, no other act has been so widely condemned cross-culturally. Some reported exceptions throughout history have been the pharaohs of ancient Egypt, the royalty in Hawaii centuries ago, and an isolated Malaysian tribe which is presently repopulating itself through incest.

Because incest is so subjectively stigmatized, prevalence data are extremely difficult to collect due to unreported cases. In the 1950s, the Kinsey researchers found about five cases of incest reported for every 1000 members of the population. In the 1960s, the reports swelled to almost 4 percent of the population (Gebhard, 1965). Today's estimated figures are even higher. These increases are probably not the result of a true rise in incest, but rather because people are reporting it more. Why? Because, like many other tabooed sexual topics, incest is finally being exposed as a real psychological and social problem. For instance, a 1984 tele-movie about father-daughter incest, *Something about Amelia,* had an enormous impact on reporting incest. Apparently, the true prevalence figures are just beginning to be uncovered.

[16] In some states incest is defined to include sexual relations between cousins. In Ohio, incest laws also include people who are related only by marriage.

Certain patterns of incest are reflected in the cases which *do* come to light. The most common form appears to be that between a father and daughter, although some studies have concluded that brother-sister incest is more common. We cannot be sure which is true, although it is certain that brother-sister sexual relationships are not viewed by society with the same repugnance as father-daughter or mother-son incest. This is because brothers and sisters are generally close in age, and sex between them can be rationalized as "harmless" kids' play. Mother-son incest is reportedly rare, although a 1984 case in Tennessee, where a mother and son married each other, may have altered subjective awareness about its existence. There are now data indicating that father-son incest is more widespread than previously supposed (Dixon, Arnold, and Calestro, 1978). One common misconception about incest is that it occurs more frequently in lower-class families. Incest may be reported more often in lower-class families since it is more likely to be discovered by police, but in reality, incestuous acts are more common among higher socioeconomic families (Hunt, 1974).

Incest, especially the parent-child type, is usually initiated through emotional intimidation rather than physical force. In father-daughter incest, for instance, the father typically goes through a whole series of steps to entice and engage the child and to play upon his position and power as an adult. This does not mean that the long-term consequences to the victim are minimized. The fact is that many children grow into seriously disturbed adults because of the experience, although the effects vary from child to child. The only positive aspect of incest in the United States today is that victims are finally beginning to seek help in growing numbers. Some incest victims have even filed suit to collect money from the offender for the damage inflicted. Unfortunately, the cries for help may not be getting the sympathetic responses they deserve because some so-called sexologists are

now claiming that incest can sometimes be a beneficial learning experience and that the taboo against it is a mindless prejudice.

Sadism and Masochism

A sadist is sexually aroused by inflicting pain on, restricting, or humiliating another person, usually a masochist. Sadism is a term derived from the Marquis de Sade, a novelist who was afflicted with the disorder himself. He cataloged some 600 different ways of inflicting pain. One channel for sadists is beating prostitutes who offer such services at extra cost. The most extreme form of sadism is practiced by the sex killer (*necrosadist*), who derives erotic pleasure from killing his victims.

It is not known how many Americans have sadistic impulses, but it is important to note that porno films portraying lust murder ("snuff films") command a sizable audience in this country. The least extreme form of sadism is *moral sadism*. Moral sadists have a need to discharge their aggressions against society, and they express these aggressions through verbal humiliation of others rather than through physical attack. Closely related to sadism is rape. The number of men who would force themselves on a woman in this way may be shockingly large. For instance, at the 1986 New York Academy of Sciences conference, results of a national survey of more than 1000 men revealed that more than 50 percent said they were likely to force a woman into having sex with them if they could get away with it.

Masochism, a term derived from the Austrian novelist Leopold von Sacher-Masoch, refers to people who obtain orgastic gratification by receiving pain. Some masochists like to be whipped or beaten. Others like to wear uncomfortable garments. *Bondage* is a variant of masochism. In this practice, a willing victim is constrained by ropes, chains, or handcuffs and then placed in vulnerable positions. Often he or she is beaten as well. Masochists requiring anal stimulation insert various objects into their rec tums and derive erotic pleasure from the result-ant pain. In its extreme forms, masochism may lead to serious injury and even death. There are reports, for instance, of young men who hang themselves to achieve erection and orgasm (Resnick, 1972) and of females who increase their sexual pleasure by partially suffocating themselves (Wiesman, 1967). Interestingly enough, many activities which appear sadoma-sochistic to others, such as those common to the male homosexual leather scene, are not conceptualized by participants in that way at all (Weinberg, Williams, and Moser, 1984).

Sadomasochism is a disorder in which the same individual can derive pleasure by either receiving or inflicting pain. In its pure form, sadism is held to be more common among men, while masochism usually occurs among wom-en. This difference may be the result of a misinterpretation of American sex roles by which men are expected to be domineering and aggressive and women passive and submissive. Sadism and masochism can be viewed as patho-logical extensions of these sex role expecta-tions.

The true extent of sadism and masochism is not known. It cannot be inconsequential, how-ever, as evidenced by the increasing number of sex shops catering to the needs of these people (see Box 6-2 for a description of a house for sadists and masochists). Kinsey estimated that 3 percent of the women and 10 percent of the men are sexually responsive to sadomasochistic stimuli. Now there is rising concern about the use by teenage boys and others of an extremely dangerous sexual practice in which self-induced erotic pleasure is enhanced by near asphyxia-tion, usually accomplished by a noose around the neck. Some accidentally die from *autoerotic asphyxiation*, although their deaths are often reported as suicides. In 1984, some experts on the topic estimated that 500 to 1000 deaths caused by autoerotic asphyxiation occur annu-ally in the United States. There are also shock-ing reports of practices involving sex and vio-lence on college campuses, where as many as 60 percent of the students may have encoun-tered some kind of violence while dating. This may not always be fostered by sadomasochistic needs, but it is still alarming that so many students report being punched, slapped, or shoved by their dates or lovers.

Intensity of Desire

Although it is impossible to say what an "ideal" amount of sexual interest is, clearly some peo-ple with extreme desires are not normal. For instance, there are people who have inhibited sexual desire (ISD), the current jargon for asex-uality. They come in a wide range of types: lonely outsiders, happily married individuals, chronic complainers, and high achievers. Some of the married ones have never consummated their marriage and are not sure why. Some experts guesstimate that 20 percent of all adult Americans have desire problems, a form of sexual anorexia nervosa. Of course, this figure may also include temporary impotence, which frequently occurs among men who have been traumatized by, as one example, loss of a job.

At the opposite end of the libido scale is *hypersexuality*—excessive sexual desire that cannot be satisfied. Again, it is impossible to say how many Americans are hypersexual be-cause most cases go unreported. It is also difficult to ascertain the prevalence of hypersex-uality by sex because of biased stereotypes of the "normal" sexual conduct of men and wom-en. The man who beds every woman he ap-proaches may well be afflicted with some dis-order, yet his friends envy his great "talent." On the other hand, the woman who is not sexually monogamous may be branded promis-cuous, although this stereotype is fading.

Hypersexuality among females is widely known as *nymphomania*. Typically, the nym-phomaniac dislikes foreplay and wishes only for intercourse, but often the act does not produce orgasm. If orgasm is achieved, the desire for further intercourse usually returns within min-

BOX 6-2

STOMPING AND WHOMPING GALORE: SADOMASOCHISM COMES OUT OF THE CLOSET—
WHIPS, CHAINS, AND ALL

The client, a Los Angeles judge, is so eager that he has arrived an hour early. "Have some coffee and relax," says the chubby receptionist. "I will," the judge mutters. "Hard day, lots of cases." He is there to be whipped and abused for 40 minutes or more at a minimum cost of $40, payable by Visa or MasterCard. Refreshed by his regularly scheduled flogging, he may well rush home into the arms of his wife or mistress and startle her with his renewed ardor.

The scene is the Chateau, a two-story modern house in West Hollywood with a nondescript exterior and an exotic interior: four dungeons full of racks, pillories, cages, whipping posts, shackles and wooden crosses for spread-eagling clients. The house does not offer sexual intercourse, only sexual theater and enough pain to set any masochist aglow. A staff of 13 women—six dominants, three submissives and four switch-hitters—provides personalized sadomasochistic services for 1,000 or more well-heeled customers, many of them staid professional men such as judges, doctors and executives, who want to be bound, gagged, stretched, beaten and understood.

Like many who sell sexual services nowadays, the "mistresses" at the Chateau consider themselves therapists of a kind. Says one of them, Juliet Williams: "We provide customers mental relief from pressures, the fantasies and desires that have built up in them." Doctors and dentists too, she points out brightly, sometimes have to hurt people to help them.

Freud considered sadism and masochism among the darkest eruptions of the primitive in human nature. He did not live to see them transformed into well-lit, credit-card banality, dispensed by women piously mouthing the jargon of social work. Nor, mercifully, did he survive to witness all the trendy commercial appropriations of sadomasochistic themes in U.S. popular culture. Some rock groups have

pushed S-M messages for years. Fashion photographers, notably Helmut Newton, made the theme high chic in the late '70's, and it is routine today. In a recent display in the lingerie department of one of Joske's department stores in Dallas, a female mannequin wearing a black garter belt hovered over a male mannequin, brandishing handcuffs.

S-M hardware, always the big ticket item in sleazy porn shops, now sells briskly in sparkling clean "sex boutiques" for the respectable middle class. Patty Wheat, owner of six sex shops in the Miami area, says her clientele is largely "Suburbia, U.S.A." Blindfolds and ankle and wrist restraints are in demand at Patty's Place. At the Pink Pussy Cat Boutique in trendy Coconut Grove, Fla., police handcuffs and whips are big sellers, and a $70 male body harness is moving well. S-M trade has picked up so sharply in the past six months that the Pink Pussy Cat plans to open a wholesale mail-order department. "People are getting less and less inhibited," says Wheat. "S-M is something new to try, like redecorating your bedroom."

Though no one knows whether hard-core S-M activity is actually increasing—many therapists think not—it is clearly becoming more open and inching closer to public acceptance. One reason, say the therapists, is that in the advanced age of sexual liberation, the bored are looking for new taboos to break, new jolts and new ways to shock the sexually square. Sex manuals, starting with Alex Comfort's *The Joy of Sex,* which approves of "bondage games," now treat "loving" S-M as just another sexual variation. S-Mers often use the same arguments that homosexual liberation groups used a decade ago: if it is consensual activity that pleases both partners, where is the harm? Such galloping tolerance makes it seem somehow unsporting to point out the obvious: that bashing and thrashing have little to do with affection.

Source: *Time,* May 4, 1981, p. 73. By permission of the publisher.

utes. *Satyriasis* (old goat) is the term for the insatiable male who feels compelled to have intercourse with every attractive female he sees. This is the *Don Juan,* also known as the *compulsive womanizer.* As soon as he conquers a woman, his thoughts turn to the next potential partner. Hypersexuality in men and women can trigger a number of social problems, including

venereal disease, unwanted pregnancies, and divorce.

By some signs, hypersexuality appears to be growing in prevalence and acceptance. "Swinging" among married couples is practiced by a substantial number of Americans, most of them middle-class suburbanites who are reportedly conservative in their political attitudes (Bartell,

1970). Once in the closet, swinging is now an industry. There are international conventions for swingers in well-known hotels, where up to 1000 people may attend seminars on the swinging lifestyle. Some seminars may be devoted to management of a swing club, such as the famous Plato's Retreat in New York City. With such things as orgy rooms filled to capacity with virtual strangers, there is nothing platonic about these places.

Exhibitionism

The exhibitionist, commonly known as a "flasher," usually displays his sex organs to strangers of the opposite sex. The typical exhibitionist does not want actual sexual contact with the "victim." Instead, he achieves gratification simply through drawing attention to his exposed genitals. It is questionable whether this is only a disorder of the sex drive, since not all exhibitionists have an erection during the act of exposure. It is also questionable whether researchers are accurate in reporting that there are no female exhibitionists. This may simply reflect the American view of sex-appropriate behavior. If a man takes off his clothes in public, somebody usually calls the police, yet if a woman does the same thing, she may very well gather an applauding audience. Stereotypical sexist attitudes have led many to believe that a man looking at a nude woman is a voyeur, but a woman looking at a naked man is watching an exhibitionist.

The exhibitionist's behavior is patterned. He often returns to the same place, usually a public place, such as a street, subway, or elevator. An exhibitionist may display his penis from a window of a house. Others drive around in cars with their pants pulled down and lure victims close by asking for directions. The timing of the act is also ritualized in that exhibitionists frequently expose themselves at the same time of day. The number of offenses increases noticeably in summer for obvious reasons. Another stereotyped aspect of the exhibitionist's behavior is his clothing. Many wear a special outfit known as flasher's gear: a long coat underneath which the man is nude from the waist down, his pants secured above the knee by elastic.

The true prevalence of exhibitionism is unknown since many incidents are not reported. However, it is known to be one of the most common sexual disorders leading to arrest, constituting one-third of all officially processed sexual offenses (MacDonald, 1973). An exhibitionist is typically a 15- to 30-year-old male, who is often married.

Closely related to the exhibitionist is the obscene phone caller. Usually, this person randomly selects a female's number from the phone book and masturbates while making an obscene statement or quietly listening. Many obscene phone callers also have histories of exhibitionistic behavior (Nadler, 1968).

Voyeurism

Also closely allied to exhibitionism is voyeurism. The voyeur, or Peeping Tom, derives sexual pleasure by looking at a member of the opposite sex in some state of undress, in a sexual act, or in the act of excretion. This behavior is considered a sexual disorder when it is the person's preferred sexual activity or when it is undertaken at serious risk, such as climbing the fire escape of a guarded woman's dorm. The voyeur is usually a timid person who is sexually inhibited and often impotent. He is nearly always a heterosexual and habitual masturbator. In 95 percent of reported incidents, he observes strangers in situations in which his risk of being caught is great (Katchadourian and Lunde, 1975).

There is mixed opinion about the dangers voyeurs pose to others. Most researchers describe them as withdrawn persons who do not graduate to a more threatening pathology. However, there is evidence that some voyeurs can become tomorrow's rapists (Oliven, 1974).

Like exhibitionism, voyeurism is said to be exclusive to men, but it is questionable whether this simply reflects behavior allowed males through sex roles or whether there actually are other differences between the sexes in regard to sexual pleasure derived through watching. Certainly men act as if they are more aroused through sexual watching than women, but as mentioned in the section on pornography, this may be changing.

One recent development is *phone sex.* Erotic phone systems consist of recorded or live messages that titillate dialers with aural sex, specifically the breathless sounds of a sexual liaison in which the imaginative caller can pretend that he or she is a participant. These calls are often long-distance calls made by employees, who are discreetly racking up expensive phone bills for their companies. Some phone sex is live, caters to the caller's individual needs, and is paid for with a standard charge card. Thirty dollars for three minutes of dirty talk is not unusual. This may contribute to a new trend known as auditory voyeurism.

Miscellaneous Disorders

Fetishism   Fetish, a term derived from the Portuguese word *feitico,* for "charms," is frequently used to refer to a special object viewed as magical by preliterate people who employ it in their religious rituals. As a sexual disorder, it refers to the use of a body part or inanimate object to achieve orgasm. Fetishism, like many sexual disorders, is reportedly peculiar to men, and it usually appears in adolescence.

Men with fetishes are involuntarily and irresistibly stimulated by articles of clothing, inanimate objects, or parts of the body not generally viewed as erotic, such as feet. Some men with fetishes can have sexual intercourse without the fetish object, but they must force themselves to do so, and usually fantasize about the fetish during intercourse. The fetish may dominate much of the person's life, as in the case of a man who is so enthralled by women's feet that he becomes a shoe salesman.

There are different forms of fetishism (Randell, 1976). One form is *adherent fetishism.* Here the fetish object is worn and, in some instances, makes contact with the genitals. *Olfactory fetishism* involves the smell of rubber, leather, or other substances, such as car upholstery. *Beast fetishism* refers to the use of fur or animal skins. In *pygmalionism* there is an attraction to statues or life-sized rubber-doll versions of women, as are commonly advertised in porno magazines today.

Subjective attitudes toward men with fetishes range from humor to disgust. However, few people recognize that some fetishistic preoccupations can proceed to the point where members of society can become victims. One 17-year-old student, for example, committed three brutal murders only because he was caught in the act of burglarizing women's apartments to steal their underwear (Kennedy, Hoffman, and Haines, 1947). And who knows how much misery Boston would have been spared if the Boston Strangler had not been fetishistically motivated to cut out his victim's sexual organs and hang pieces of their flesh on picture nails on the walls? Fortunately, most men with fetishes are not driven to such macabre actions. Most alleviate their urges in secretive ways without bothering others. The origin of this disorder, like most forms of sexual behavior, remains a mystery.

Transvestism   A transvestite achieves sexual gratification by wearing clothing associated with members of the opposite sex. Less often, transvestism involves a wish to be viewed as a person of the opposite sex. Female impersonation is sometimes called *drag,* which stands for *dr*essed *a*s a *g*irl. Transvestism is often mistakenly confused with other sexual orientations, such as fetishism and homosexuality.

Available evidence indicates that transvestism and homosexuality are not usually found in the same person. In fact, the typical transvestite is a married male with children, who is

Female impersonators have become increasingly visible in recent years. (*John Veltri/Photo Researchers, Inc.*)

exclusively heterosexual (Weinberg and Bullough, 1986). Many cross-dress before they have sexual relations with their wives.

One unanswered question about this disorder is whether it is as rare among women as it is reported to be. It is possible that transvestism is as common among women as it is among men, but is simply less noticeable since it is socially acceptable for women to wear men's clothes in our society. As a result, a woman dressed in jeans and boots raises no suspicions, but a man in a prom gown will certainly raise eyebrows.

Although cross-dressing often begins in early childhood, it may not become manifest until young adulthood. Many wives of transvestites do not discover the truth about their husbands until well after the wedding. Their reactions vary. Some leave their husbands immediately. Others stay as long as they do not have to see the act. Others actually become supportive of their husbands' habits and aid them with useful tips on feminine dress, walk, and makeup! Some couples may even live together as two

females and call each other by female names. What is especially surprising about transvestite fathers is that if the children find out, they prefer him in female attire because he reportedly treats them better when he is cross-dressed (Randell, 1976).

Transsexualism This gender identity disorder occurs among those who have a total aversion to their biological sex, although they are physically normal. From early childhood onward, they have a strong desire to change sex. Some eventually undergo sex change surgery, and others assume the identity of the opposite sex without surgery. A transsexual should not be confused with a *hermaphrodite,* who is a person born with the physical attributes of both sexes. Transsexuals *wish* they had the physical features of members of the opposite sex, but they do not. When they request surgery, most transsexuals come cross-dressed. The males may have had their facial hairs removed through electrolysis, and may be taking female hormones. The females often bind their breasts flat. Sex change surgery is difficult to obtain in the United States. Some psychiatrists fear the operation will transform a delusion into a reality; surgeons fear malpractice suits; hospital board members often oppose such operations on moral grounds. In addition, many transsexuals forgo surgery when they find out they will have to undergo psychiatric evaluation to confirm their suitability for the sex change.

The male-to-female surgery involves removing the scrotum and penis (*penectomy*). A vagina is created from a loop of intestine or a plastic pouch (vaginoplasty). The Adam's apple is shaved down. Female hormones are administered to stimulate breast development and to reduce hair growth. Silicon injections are used to enlarge breasts, buttocks, and hips.

The female-to-male surgery is much more complex. It requires a number of operations over a period of six months to a year. The breasts and internal sex organs are removed. Labial tissue is used to make a scrotum. A penis is devised by grafting skin onto a tube that encloses an artificial urethra. Then the clitoris is embedded in the artificial penis to retain orgasmic capacity. The person is also administered androgen, which produces facial hair and causes a weight increase. Until transsexuals undergo the operation by which their bodies complement their minds, they are completely miserable.

Necrophilia is sexual gratification obtained by having sex with a corpse. This disorder has traditionally been viewed as found exclusively among males. Like all disorders, necrophilia is as old as humankind. Some necrophiliacs choose occupations that give them easy access to dead bodies, such as graveyard attendant, undertaker, or hospital worker. Others become sexually aroused after funerals, masturbate in graveyards, or enhance sexual intercourse by the presence of a coffin. Necrophilia is fantasized as well. For instance, some prostitutes provide specific services for necrophiliacs by cooling their skin, lying still in coffins, and making themselves up like cadavers with a pallid appearance. Some researchers have suggested that those who have sex with actual dead people are committing a peculiar form of rape.

Some persons obtain sexual gratification through intercourse with living animals, a practice known as *bestiality* or *zoophilia*. It is most common among adolescent boys who live in rural areas. In fact, Kinsey found that one-third of the males in rural areas have had intercourse with animals. Goats, sheep, and dogs are usually involved, but there are also case reports of sexual acts with horses, ducks, and even crocodiles. Some think this disorder results from a scarcity of human beings in underpopulated rural areas (like prisoners committing homosexual acts), but the official definition of the American Psychiatric Association holds that an animal must be preferred no matter what other forms of sexual outlet are available.

Another miscellaneous and mysterious disorder is *pyromania*. The pyromaniac derives sexual pleasure from starting and watching fires. Often he obtains particular stimulation—to the point of ejaculation—from seeing the fire extinguished. For this reason, there are probably an inordinate number of these people who are fire fighters. Pyromania differs from *arson;* both the pyromaniac and the arsonist deliberately set fires, but only the pyromaniac does so for sexual reasons. Needless to say, pyromania is a dangerous sexual disorder which is responsible for an unknown number of lives lost. Like the other miscellaneous disorders, it is a bizarre practice of unknown origin.

SOCIAL POLICY: PORNOGRAPHY

Strategies for Solution

Since there are many forms of sexual variance, we have chosen one—*pornography*—for social policy evaluation. Presently there is a lot of controversy over whether pornography should be *outlawed* in the interest of public morality or *decriminalized* as an expression of individual liberty. These two positions are represented by conservatives and civil libertarians, respectively.[17]

Conservatives believe pornography cheapens and demeans human sexuality. They are especially concerned that pornography encourages sex crimes, a common fear fed by officials such as the late J. Edgar Hoover. Antipornography crusaders, such as Citizens for Decency through Law, Inc., are fearful that pornography is conceived by the "most insanely perverse minds" and will become a dangerous but accepted part of American life. It is curious that conservatives have been joined in their fight against pornography by feminists. Although there is no natural political alliance between conservatives and feminists, the women's movement has been especially opposed to porno because of its perceived exploitation of women and the fear that porno creates hostility toward women which, in turn, increases sex crimes committed against them.

Feminists and conservatives are not alone in their concern about pornography. In 1970, a national opinion poll found that about 50 percent of the people thought erotic materials led to a breakdown of morals and also led people to commit rape. More recent polls in the 1980s indicate that the subjective fear of porno leading to sex crimes has increased.

On the other side of the debate over pornography are the civil libertarians, who believe that government has no business regulating morality since the First Amendment guarantees freedom of expression. They argue that this right does not hinge on judgments of artistic merit or even redeeming value. They argue further that a number of useful functions are served by sex-oriented material. First, they say that pornography provides an opportunity to explore and indirectly experience sex situations which are otherwise inaccessible. A person may see a certain act and thereby facilitate an expression of his or her fantasy while not risking it in everyday life. Second, pornography may offer an important avenue of expression for persons who, for whatever reasons, have no sex partners. It may not only give a fantasy release but also provide detailed information that is otherwise unavailable. Couples may also find that their ability to communicate about sexual matters may be enhanced by looking at pornographic materials together. Additionally, exposure to pornographic materials could be a useful preparation for adult sexual functioning. A third argument of the civil libertarians is that pornography may be a useful adjunct to psychotherapy for people with sexual problems. It can help them cut through defenses or feelings of guilt or anxiety.

There are many policy positions between ultraconservatives, who want to prohibit any display of nudity, and ultralibertarians, who feel that even the most lewd and prurient display must be tolerated. Most people are for or against pornography based on their own subjective feelings about its morality. But such morality matters cannot be settled simply by sociological analysis, particularly if the analysis attempts to be value-free. Consequently, we are going to concern ourselves here with one specific question which can be objectively analyzed: Does pornography lead to sex crimes? Conservatives believe it does and therefore should be outlawed. Civil libertarians believe that it acts as a safety valve and actually decreases sex crimes.

Policies into Practice

Which policy on pornography makes the most sense in terms of working in the real world of the contemporary United States? Is the conser-

---

[17] For a comprehensive review of the determinants of antipornography attitudes, see Michael Wood and Michael Hughes, "The Moral Basis of Moral Reform: Status Discontent vs. Culture and Socialization as Explanations of Anti-pornography Social Movement Adherence," *American Sociological Review*, 49, 1984:86–99.

vative approach better able to reduce human suffering—sex crimes in this instance—than the libertarian approach? The real answer to this question lies in the next section of this chapter, for it is only by examining scientific studies of the hookup between pornography and sex crimes that any meaningful answer to this question can be found. However, there are some serious practical limitations to implementing pornography policies which should be considered first in terms of the outlawing approach of the conservatives. If widespread legal action is taken against porno, it is highly unlikely that any real reduction in its use will occur. The great volume of pornography available today meets a public demand which will not go away simply because new laws are passed.

The Supreme Court has ruled that local rather than national standards should be used in determining whether material is pornographic and whether it should be banned. The practical result of this decision is an increase in the number of court cases aimed at overturning locally imposed bans. These cases are starting to end up back in the Supreme Court's lap for their reevaluation. In 1986, for instance, the Supreme Court struck down a novel Indianapolis ordinance that sought to crack down on pornography by characterizing it as a form of discrimination against women. Current attempts to legally restrict porn could very well add up to one large legal mess. In a nutshell, the major implementation issue with the conservative policy is that it may be as impossible to stop the massive flow of pornography as it was to stop the flow of alcohol during Prohibition. Certainly it would be cumbersome.

From a practical perspective, toleration of pornography could be accomplished through decriminalization. Porno businesses could be licensed and taxed. This would eliminate a major source of police corruption and produce a major source of tax revenue. Restrictions over zoning, age participation, and the like would ensure that porno reaches only those who want it. This all begs the big unanswered question: Does porno lead to sex crimes? If it does, then the impracticality of banning porno and the practical aspects of legalizing it are secondary issues.

Evaluating the Evidence

The trigger theory of pornography, supported by conservatives, holds that porno stimulates deviant drives and thus increases sex crimes. The safety valve theory, supported by libertarians, holds that porno allows the private release of sexual fantasies and thus protects people by decreasing the occurrence of sexual offenses. The two theories have been evaluated both in experimental settings and in the real world (Malamuth and Donnerstein, 1984).

In general, the evidence to date favors the idea that pornography acts as a safety valve, although some studies support the trigger theory. For example, in Britain, the Longford Committee Investigating Pornography reported in 1972 that exposure to pornography leads to sexual assault. Unfortunately, much of the antipornography evidence was based on hearsay and selected cases. A more scientific analysis of the question involved an experiment on college students (Zilman and Bryant, 1982). The results indicated that exposure to large amounts of pornography tends to trivialize attitudes about rape (they see rape as less serious) among both men and women and harms them by creating calloused attitudes about sex. Additionally, the 1986 Attorney General's Commission on Pornography conducted interviews with sex crime victims and concluded that pornography is linked with such crimes. The Meese Report, referred to in the beginning of this chapter, concluded that there is strong evidence that sexually oriented materials bear a causal relationship to sex crimes. The same commission also uncovered an important social problems linkage: the association of organized crime with the distribution of pornography. The commission's conclusion on pornography and violence has been sharply criticized by social scientists and the American Civil Liberties Union. The report based its findings on a few social science experiments and often reached conclusions on the unquestioned testimony of a single witness. Further, if the recommendations of the commission were enacted, theater owners could be prosecuted for showing movies such as *Pretty Baby,* starring a 13-year-old Brooke Shields, and *Taxi Driver,* starring 14-year-old Jodie Foster.

On the other hand, numerous studies support the safety valve theory. Although there is evidence that the more sexually active individual is more likely to be exposed to pornography, sexual activity is not the same as sexual crime. In fact, most major studies of the pornography-crime correlation find that sex offenders had less experience with pornography in their youth than control normals (Wilson, 1971). Gray (1982) reports there is little evidence that exposure to hard-core pornography affects men's attitudes toward women or produces aggressive behavior in men. However, levels of aggression *in already angered men* may be increased by exposure to hard-core materials, particularly ones with violence.

Another factor in support of the safety valve theory is the use of pornography in psychotherapy. People who harbor feelings of guilt or anxiety about sex often feel less guilty or anxious after seeing sexually explicit material (Kadis and Winick, 1973). Pornographic films have also been used to successfully treat sex offenders, many of whom come from families where the discussion of sex is taboo. Of course, much of the therapeutic value of pornography may depend on the type of film viewed. For example, an aggressive-erotic film may well be counterproductive compared to a film which is simply erotic.

The most compelling evidence in support of the safety valve theory comes from the so-called Danish experiment in which virtually all legal controls on pornography were abandoned in the mid-1960s. Shortly afterward there was a significant reduction in sex crimes: a 48 percent decline in rape, a 61 percent decline in exhibitionism, a 77 percent decline in voyeurism, and a 78 percent decline in homosexual crimes (Kutchinsky, 1970).[18] As a result of the Danish experiment and other pro-pornography findings, in 1970 the National Commission on Obscenity and Pornography recommended the repeal of laws prohibiting the sale, exhibition, or distribution of sexual materials to consenting adults. This was in line with a good deal of evidence suggesting that exposure to such material is part of growing up in many normal individuals.

The commission also recommended prohibiting sales to young persons and unsolicited advertisements, which would offend many people. These sensible recommendations could be accomplished through zoning laws aimed at concentrating porno shops within small areas of cities or dispersing these shops throughout the commercial areas of cities while restricting their number. Both strategies would avoid exposing citizens to pornography against their wills. Future legislation should also place careful restrictions on so-called kiddie porn. There is no evidence that involving children in producing pornography does anything but traumatize developing personalities and inflict serious psychological damage.

SUMMARY

1 Human sexuality is an issue which is highly charged with subjective feelings. Consequently, it is impossible to evaluate all forms of sexual behavior objectively. This chapter is based on the idea that sex can be viewed as a continuum from normal behavior to variant lifestyle to sexual disorder.

---

[18] Today there is some controversy over whether porno increases rape. However, the reported rise in rapes in countries where porno has been liberalized may be the result of a greater willingness of victims to report rape rather than any influence of pornography.

2 Homosexuality is typically viewed as a variant lifestyle. Although little is known about its origins, it is a fact that many homosexuals are troubled people because of the rejection they experience from others.

3 Prostitution, another variant lifestyle, has always existed throughout history and is widespread in the United States today. There are some positive functions of prostitution which reduce the objective aspects of this social problem.

4 Sexual disorders are abnormalities involving type of object, mode of gratification, gender identity, intensity of desire, as well as a group simply classified as miscellaneous. By and large the disorders are mysterious behaviors which are largely ascribed to males.

5 The alternative policies for dealing with pornography are to either outlaw it or decriminalize it. Since available evidence indicates that porno may actually reduce sex crimes, decriminalization appears to be the rational choice.

Macroproblems: Society in the Individual

These issues are *not* distinguished from the micro-problems by operating beyond the level of personal suffering. Clearly, poverty and discrimination bring everyday anguish to individuals. The essence of the macroproblems is the well-documented fashion through which looming social structures bring anguish to whole categories of people. As the subtitle above says, these social problems are the working of society in the individual.

CHAPTER 7

Population Problems in the United States

There is simply nothing so important to a people and its government as how many of them there are, whether their number is growing or declining, how they are distributed as between different ages, sexes, and different social classes and racial and ethnic groups, and again, which way these numbers are moving....

—*Daniel Moynihan (1977)*

As this statement by Senator (and sociologist) Moynihan indicates, people should be interested in the nature of the populations of which they are members. This is because the size, composition, and distribution of a population, as well as the forces which determine these characteristics—fertility, mortality, and migration—are powerful causes of or contributors to many problems (see Box 7-1).

Population problems in the United States include, to name a few, scarcity and waste of social resources caused by baby booms and busts; premature death in the general population and particularly in certain groups; concentration of people in some areas and depopulation elsewhere, with all that implies for the quality of life in both places; social disturbances due to changes in the population's racial and ethnic composition resulting from differences in fertility or immigration; and population growth that undermines the quality of life for present and future generations.

The last problem mentioned, population growth, is especially important because it tends to aggravate other social problems. For example, a growing population leads to more congestion and crowding in metropolitan areas, provides the impetus for the destruction of prime agricultural land due to the expansion of urban areas, and accelerates resource depletion. The Presidential Commission on Population and the American Future (1972) concluded that population growth in the United States since World War II has intensified many of our domestic

---

BOX 7-1

THE ELEMENTS OF DEMOGRAPHY

Demography is the study of human populations, including their size, composition, and distribution, as well as the causes and consequences of changes in these factors. The *composition* of a population is its characteristics. Marital status, socioeconomic status, religion, education, race, age, and sex are key compositional variables. The *distribution* of a population is how the people and their population actions are spatially dispersed. Demographers are particularly interested in distributions by state, by region, by urban and rural area, and by segments of metropolitan areas (e.g., central city, suburb, etc.).

The three immediate causes of demographic change are fertility, mortality, and migration. *Fertility* refers to the number of births that actually occur, and is generally expressed as a yearly birthrate or as the average number of children born to a group of women or couples. *Mortality* refers to the number of deaths that occur in a specific time period, and is usually expressed as a yearly death rate or by life expectancy. *Migration* refers to the movement of people across a specified territorial boundary for the purpose of changing residences. The term *international migration* refers to moves between countries, and the term *internal migration* refers to movement between different areas within a country. Migration is generally expressed as a yearly migration rate.

The size of a population can *change* only through fertility, mortality, or migration. This situation is expressed by the following equation:

$$\text{Population growth} = (B - D) + (I - 0)$$

where for any specified time period, B, D, I, and O are, respectively, the number of births, deaths, people moving in, and people moving out of the population. The expression $(B - D)$ is called *natural increase;* and $(I - O)$, *net migration.* Thus, population growth is the sum of natural increase and net migration. Population growth can be positive, as in a growing population; negative, as in a population that is actually declining in size; or zero, as in a population which is neither gaining nor losing size. This last case is a special one and is called *zero population growth.*

Fertility, mortality, and migration also determine a population's *racial composition* and *age-sex composition.* The latter is the relative number of males and females in each age category of a population. Fertility, mortality, and migration also help determine other compositional characteristics such as marital status, class, religion, and education. Population distribution also reflects local levels of fertility, mortality, and migration.

problems and has made their solution more difficult. And since population growth is not likely to stop in the United States for many decades, these problems will continue for quite some time. For instance, population growth may more than offset any strides the United States may make toward solving our energy problem. The problems caused by continued population growth are considered in detail later in this chapter in the discussion of zero population growth. But because of its links to other social problems, you will also see the imprint of this continued growth in many other chapters of this text.

Like population growth, the age structure of a population is a demographic variable which leaves its mark elsewhere in this book. Social problems rarely have causes or consequences independent of age. The persons involved come disproportionately from certain age groups. For instance, criminals are disproportionately young adults, while the chronically ill are disproportionately elderly. What this means is that the prevalence of a social problem may rise or fall because of changes in the age structure of the population, that is, simply because the age group(s) most involved with the social problem increase or decrease their proportion of the population over time. Thus, changes in the age structure of the population can increase or decrease the damage caused by a social problem even if there is no change in the underlying social causes. The rate of increase in violent crime in the United States has recently tapered off, for instance, in part because there are relatively fewer individuals each year in the violent-crime-prone ages (especially males aged 14 to 24).

Population problems should be of keen interest to you because you are a population actor. Your living, procreating, moving, and dying have a direct effect on many of the problems discussed in this chapter. The number of children you decide to have affects United States population growth and the relative size of dif-

ferent generations. Your habits and lifestyle have a strong bearing on your risk of dying prematurely. If you are between ages 18 and 30, as most of you are, you are now in the most mobile period of your life. Common occasions for movement in this age bracket include entering and leaving college, starting an independent household, seeking better housing, starting a new career, and changing jobs. In any event, your movement may contribute to population problems either in the places you leave or in the places to which you go. And it is you who will have to compete with immigrants for jobs and social resources. Thus, your present and future population acts are collectively either part of our population problems or part of their solution.

THE SUBJECTIVE DIMENSION OF POPULATION PROBLEMS

The objective damage population problems cause is indisputable. For example, hundreds of thousands of Americans—many, like you, in the prime of their lives—die prematurely each year from socially preventable causes. However, subjective concern about population problems usually falls far short of their objective damage. It is true that people do have general opinions regarding such issues as the desirability of population growth, what the ethnic or racial makeup of the population should be, and the appropriate level of immigration. And it is also true that subjective concern about a particular issue occasionally flares up. In the early 1980s, for example, subjective concern escalated over the huge flow of legal and, particularly, illegal immigrants into this country. This was due in part to the weak economy, which heightened fears of increased job competition, and to the media exposure invariably drawn to such emotionally charged situations.

Nevertheless, despite an ongoing low level of concern about population problems and the occasional flare-up of a particular issue, population problems in general are not subjectively viewed by most Americans as being among our most pressing problems. One reason for this is their low visibility. Unlike many other major problem areas, population problems usually lack the dramatic event—the riot, the calamity, the outrageous incident—that galvanizes attention and action. Thus, they tend to be overlooked, even as they insidiously develop from the accumulation of individual births, deaths, and migrations.

BABY BOOMS AND BUSTS

The level of fertility refers to the average number of children born to members of a population. Later in this chapter we will discuss the long-term level of fertility—the average number of children over, say, the next fifty or one hundred years. And we will see that it is extremely important that the average remain relatively low, that is, somewhere around two children per woman. However, regardless of the long-term level of fertility, generational or temporal variations in fertility, in the form of baby booms and busts, are not just possible, but likely. A long-term average of, for example, two children can be achieved by every generation averaging that number, or by different generations having offsetting rates above and below that average. One generation, for instance, might average 1.7 children, although the next might average 2.3 children. While the end result in terms of population growth is practically the same, a society is much better off if it can minimize generational variation in fertility. This is because different sized generations cause a great many problems independent of the overall level of fertility.

The Social Tunnel

Why is this so? To answer this question, we will look first at the effects of baby booms and busts on a hypothetical society that has achieved zero population growth and which is closed to immigration and emigration. In this imaginary population, the number of births and deaths is equal, and each year's crop of babies is about the same size as that of every other year. This hypothetical situation will help us see more clearly the impact of baby booms and busts on a society. While this idealized population has no real counterpart, many advanced societies, especially in Europe, resemble it very closely. And it is likely that the United States will more closely resemble it in the future.

To understand why different sized generations cause many problems, it is also useful to think of this hypothetical society as a railroad tunnel through which railroad cars of a fixed length pass, carrying different generations or age groups (see Figure 7-1). Let us stick with one-year age groups here for simplicity. These groups are composed of all those born in a given calendar year and are known as *birth cohorts*. Let us also assume that no one survives beyond age 114 (in actuality, few, if any, people do). If you had an x-ray view of the tunnel, you would see that inside it were 114 railroad cars, each carrying all the people of a certain age group. The last car into the tunnel carries those under age 1; the car about to emerge empty from the far side carries those who are age 114. Because the length of a car is fixed (at one year in length), its variable dimensions are its height and width. The height and width of each car as it enters the tunnel are determined by the number of people who are born in that year. Since this number is constant, each car or birth cohort entering the tunnel will initially be the same size. The society—or social tunnel—will build itself to fit that size car.

Carrying this analogy one step further, the society will tend to provide the right number of age-related services and products all along the tunnel. For example, where those cars carrying children are, there will be the right number of schools and teachers; in the section surrounding the young adults, there will be the right number of jobs; further on there will be the right

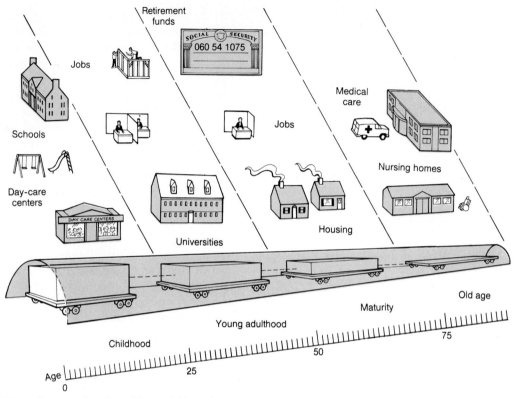

FIGURE 7-1   Cross-section view of the social tunnel.

number of housing units; and toward the end will be the right number of nursing home spaces and geriatric services. Actually, because members of a birth cohort gradually perish throughout the tunnel, it is gradually tapered from the beginning to the end, and the birth cohort cars also get progressively smaller as they move through the tunnel. The society does not have to provide nearly as many wheelchairs or nursing home spaces as tricycles or jobs. In short, each year a car of the same size will enter the social tunnel and begin the lifelong process of efficiently utilizing the age-related goods and services provided at the appropriate places along the way.

Impact of Large and Small Cohorts

But what happens if there is social change that affects fertility? What happens if an unusually small or large cohort is born? In the analogy of the tunnel, an unusually small cohort would require only a small car which would pass through the tunnel *underutilizing* the resources and services at every age. From society's point of view, this would result in waste and inefficiency—too many teachers per student, too many jobs left unperformed, and so forth. Needless to say, for the members of the small cohort, this windfall of goods and services and the relative lack of peer competition would lead to a relatively easy ride through life, all other things being equal. Many of you have parents who are members of such highly advantaged (small) cohorts, those born during the 1930s.

On the other hand, an unusually large cohort entering the tunnel in Figure 7-1 would either burst the social tunnel all along the life cycle, like the fat man trying to get into the thin man's pants, or cause the tunnel to compress the railroad car and the members of that cohort, who would pass through life crowded and uncomfortable. The cohort would face a scarcity of resources and services at every age. From society's point of view, this again would be problematic, because society would have a more difficult time performing its basic tasks such as providing education and employment for the cohort. There would be too many students per teacher and school building, too few housing units and jobs, and so forth. For the members of the large cohort, this scarcity of goods and services and the excess of peer competition would lead to a relatively rough ride through life, all other things being equal.

Many of you are members of large cohorts born during the baby boom years, and no one needs to tell you that you have experienced your share of educational problems (like crowded classrooms) and that you now face an especially difficult job and housing market. What makes this particularly hard for some of you baby boomers is that your parents are members of those aforementioned small cohorts, born in the 1930s, who had it easy (although many are not aware of it). You may find yourself hard-pressed to match either their performance or their expectations for you. On the other hand, the younger readers of this book are members of increasingly smaller cohorts and they will have things easier.

In many sociology textbooks, an analogy is drawn between a large cohort passing through life and a swallowed pig passing through a python. But this analogy is flawed, because society cannot unhinge its jaws to swallow the cohort and its structure is not elastic like the python's. It is relatively inelastic and brittle. Society, unlike the python, is harmed (socially disorganized) if it is forced to accommodate a load larger than the dimensions of its social structure.

Unusually large or small cohorts have many disorganizing effects. If society anticipates that the change toward small or large cohorts will be fairly permanent, then it will go to the trouble and expense of adjusting. It will build a bigger or a smaller tunnel. But if it is perceived that the change is just temporary, society will not make major changes but will stick to stopgap remedies. The problem for planners, therefore, is to try to know in advance whether a set of unusually large or small cohorts is just an aberration preceding a return to the usual size, or whether it is the beginning of a new level of fertility. This is one reason why societies and governments spend tremendous sums on fertility research. The accurate prediction of fertility would save society trillions of dollars, and would make life more pleasant for many individuals.

The Effect on Real Societies

To this point, we have focused mainly on a hypothetical population characterized by zero population growth, same-sized birth cohorts, and no migration. This permitted us to show you more clearly the effect of baby booms and busts on a society. The impact on real industrialized societies is very similar, although the situation is more complicated for two principal reasons. First, although all advanced societies maintain low fertility as a rule, their birth cohorts are not exactly equal in size. However, they do tend to vary fairly closely around the long-term average. This means that the social tunnel must have a little slack built into it to accommodate small variations in cohort size.

Second, some real industrialized societies also must deal with an irregular influx of immigrants. Unusual booms and busts in immigration have the same unsettling impact on society as baby booms and busts. An unexpectedly large group of immigrants strains or fractures the social tunnel; an unexpectedly small group can lead to waste and inefficiency. For instance, immigrants gladly perform some undesirable jobs which natives refuse to accept; and consequently, a shortage of immigrants can result in these jobs going unperformed. Those industrialized societies that receive large numbers of immigrants therefore face disorganizing effects from irregular patterns of both fertility and immigration. The United States is such a society.

Parenthetically, baby booms and busts do not pose problems for high-fertility developing societies. These populations grow very rapidly, and each birth cohort is usually substantially larger than its predecessor. Tragically, a good deal of the resources of these societies are devoted to constantly expanding the social tunnel to accommodate ever-larger cohorts rather than improving the standard of living of their inhabitants.

The Situation in the United States

It is difficult enough for a society to deal with a set of unusually large or small cohorts. But it is far more problematic if the society has to deal with both, alternating from small to large to small, and so on. This is exactly the situation the United States has been in during the last fifty years. Drastic swings in the average number of births have occurred, from the then-historic low of the 1930s, to the baby boom peak of 1957, down to the baby bust low of the 1970s. These swings have severely distorted the age distribution of the United States population, and have led to serious disturbances in the socioeconomic system.

Consider, for example, the educational problems the nation has faced over the last several decades. Much of this stemmed from the baby boom which began in 1945 and resulted in the growth of enrollments, first in elementary schools in the early 1950s, then in secondary schools in the early 1960s, and finally in colleges in the mid-1960s. The educational institution was not designed to handle these student gluts, and consequently there were severe building and teacher shortages, the latter due in part to the small number of births in the 1930s.

Wrongly anticipating that the three-child family was here to stay, United States society adjusted its educational institution upward. It constructed many more buildings, tremendously expanded its schools of education, and trained legions of new teachers. Even while this expansion was taking place, the birthrate was well on its way down, having begun to fall in 1957. But no one had any inkling that a genuine baby bust was under way. It was thought that the decline during the 1960s was simply a temporary downward fluctuation in what would turn out to be a long-term, three-child-average trend. So the educational expansion kept right on going. And, of course, so did the fertility decline.

During the 1970s and 1980s, society again paid the price for uneven cohorts, this time in the form of empty classrooms, unemployed teachers, devastated schools of education, and retrenched faculty. The objective damage in terms of social, economic, and personal costs has been astronomical. Billions of dollars worth of school buildings have been sold at a small fraction of their value, and hundreds of thousands of careers have been ruined. While this extended example focused on educational problems, uneven cohorts have adversely affected other areas of American life in recent decades. This is particularly true for you baby boomers. In part because you have found the going exceptionally tough, you have scored alarmingly high on all the indexes of social distress, such as suicide, crime, illegitimacy, and divorce (Easterlin, 1980).

The presence of a large baby boom cohort surrounded by small cohorts will continue to pose problems for United States society well into the future. For example, even though the baby boom cohort is now having very small families and probably will continue to do so, there are so many parents that the total number of annual births will be large. Indeed, annual births rose by 600,000 between 1976 and 1985. You might call what we are now experiencing a baby "boomlet," an echo of the parent boom.

Within the next ten years, school enrollments will increase again, leading to a renewed demand for teachers and school buildings at a time when these things will be in short supply.

Parenthetically, this points up another reason why it is advantageous for societies to avoid booms and busts. These phenomena are not discrete, but tend to contain the seeds of echo boomlets and "bustlets" and, consequently, of another series of problems. When the emerging baby boomlet starts playing havoc with the school system, the number of individuals aged 18 to 21 will be relatively small. One ramification of this is that the pool for military service will be 25 percent smaller in, say, 1990 then in 1970, which might strengthen support for the reinstitution of the draft. This may occur soon enough to affect many of you or your younger brothers and perhaps even your sisters. In any event, the increased chance of being drafted into military service is one of the few drawbacks to being a member of a small cohort.

The scarcity of housing has already been alluded to as a problem related to cohort size, and it will continue to be a trouble spot in the future. Housing construction in the United States during the early 1980s was in a lull due to a variety of nondemographic factors. At the same time, housing demand was skyrocketing because of the millions of baby boomers searching for living quarters and the trend toward smaller household size (see Chapter 5). Ironically, whatever society is able to do to alleviate this problem will work to its disadvantage two decades from now when the baby bust generation reaches adulthood and the demand for housing sharply declines.

The baby boomers will create and suffer their last set of problems during their old age, which will begin to occur in the second decade of the twenty-first century. By 2030, there will be 60 million people aged 65 and older, a number which will probably account for 20 percent of the entire United States population.

These figures are 27 million and 11 percent today. Health costs, which over the last three decades have doubled as a proportion of the nation's gross national product, will undoubtedly continue their staggering ascent as the proportion of the population over age 65 increases. This group already is responsible for about one-third of the nation's health expenditures. Altogether, as much as 30 percent of the current federal budget is devoted to the elderly. No other budget category receives more, not even defense. And this proportion also will undoubtedly rise as the baby boomers become elderly. As if this were not enough, these problems will be compounded by the fact that a relatively smaller proportion of the population will be providing the financial resources for this large group of elderly baby boomers. You can clearly see in this situation the germ of generational conflict and the potential for problems—hence another source of difficulties stemming from uneven sized cohorts.

We have already noted that once the demographic pond has been disturbed by an unusual sized cohort, there is a ripple effect—that booms and busts give rise to echo boomlets and bustlets. These boomlets and bustlets are either already under way or inevitable. So that die is cast! But what about the future? Will there be any more full-scale booms and busts (not just echo boomlets and bustlets)?

The answer to that question is uncertain. Certainly, given the negative consequences just outlined, you would think society would try to avoid them. But society does not have the last say; individuals do. And some demographers, most notably Richard Easterlin (1980), predict that we will have another full-scale baby boom in the 1990s, as the small baby bust cohort of the 1970s enters the childbearing ages and—like the small cohort of the 1930s which produced the 1950s baby boom—finds more jobs, better jobs, and more available housing. However, the majority of demographers believe that the rising cost of children, the growing participation of women in the labor force, the improvement in birth control, and the other forces responsible for the current low fertility are simply too strong to permit another full-scale boom (McFalls, 1981). We will certainly be better off if that majority is correct, but only time will tell.

One other factor must be considered while peering into the future. There is the possibility that the United States will develop an overall population policy. Not only is it likely that this policy would call for low fertility over the long term, but it would probably call for as little temporal and cohort variation as possible. If so, the United States could implement such a policy by developing a set of social and economic incentives to dampen childbearing during periods of incipient boom, and to encourage it during periods of incipient bust.

MORTALITY PROBLEMS

Mortality is a problem in itself, one that transcends the boundaries of demography and of this chapter. You have been reading about mortality throughout this book, because it is an important objective outcome of many social problems. Indeed, mortality is such an important measure of well-being that it is a major factor in the calculation of virtually all composite indexes of the quality of life.

Death is dissimilar from many of the other problems discussed in this book in that it is inevitable. Wars won against one cause of death simply unleash another to take its place. The United Nations has grouped the many causes of death into five major categories. These are:

Group 1: infectious, parasitic, and respiratory diseases
Group 2: cancer
Group 3: diseases of the circulatory system
Group 4: deaths from violence (including accidents)
Group 5: other causes, including gastrointestinal diseases, diabetes, and birth injuries

Our success in reducing deaths due to causes in groups 1 and 5 has been almost exactly offset by increasing deaths due to groups 2 and 3. The bright side of this trade-off, however, is that the now prevalent causes of death strike primarily after age 50, and consequently, life expectancy at birth has increased. Thus, although death cannot be conquered, it can be postponed. The overriding problem, therefore, is not mortality itself, but premature mortality.

The Level of Mortality

The greatest authenticated age in the world, 114 years, was recorded in Japan. (The oldest American ever, died in 1981 at an age of 113 years and 215 days.) Obviously, few individuals live to anywhere near that age. Only about 1 in 10,000 persons in industrial countries lives beyond the age of 100. It is becoming increasingly clear that most human beings have a biologically fixed life span of about eighty-five years. One piece of evidence supporting this is that even though life expectancy has been increasing rapidly, the relative proportion of exceedingly old people has not. Therefore, the mean age at death would be about 85 years under ideal societal conditions. The difference between this age and an individual's life expectancy at birth is a good indicator of the extent of premature death in a society (Fries, 1980).

The United States, like other industrial societies, has come a long way in reducing premature mortality. Progress has been so rapid that it is difficult for us to appreciate how fortunate we are. Humans have lived under the fear of premature death for almost all of human history, with the specter of death hovering over the activities of everyday life. Life expectancy rarely rose above 20 years of age, due principally to high levels of infant mortality, which in some areas claimed up to one-third of all babies during the first year of life. And this awful toll was higher yet during epidemics. The ineffable anguish of losing infants and children used to be a normal experience for most men and women.

Next to this, many of our present concerns and social problems seem objectively trivial.

Only within this century have many of the major causes of early mortality been brought under control to the extent that the majority of Americans can now take a long life for granted. Our success in drastically reducing premature death may indeed be our greatest achievement. But, parenthetically, it has not come without a cost. In Chapter 1 it was noted that the attenuation of one social problem sometimes causes the expansion of another, and this is the case here. The reduction of premature mortality is the fundamental cause of the world population explosion discussed in Chapter 12.

Life expectancy at birth in the United States in 1985 was 75 years, up spectacularly from 47 years in 1900. It is one of the highest in the world, the lowest being that of Sierra Leone (34 years). Despite the United States' relatively high life expectancy, there is a subjective dissatisfaction for two reasons. First, there are seven countries with higher life expectancies. Second, given a biologically fixed average life span of 85 years, the average American is still being deprived of ten years of life, or about 12 percent of maximum life span. So there is still considerable room for improvement, and much of this potential improvement is social in nature. Violent deaths alone account, on the average, for three of the years by which we fall short of the limit (Fries, 1980); and cigarette smoking would certainly account for several more. Other socially controlled lifestyle changes such as better diets and regular exercise would also help retrieve more lost years.

Group Differences in Mortality

Another way to raise the life expectancy in the United States would be to remove the social causes of higher mortality in certain population subgroups. We will now examine some important factors associated with different levels of mortality: social class, race, sex, and age.

Social Class Differentials Differences in mortality by social class are among the most pervasive inequalities in modern society. Indeed, all major indexes of social status—occupation, income, and education—indicate that social status is inversely related to mortality; that is, the lower the status, the higher the death rate.

There are, for instance, marked differences in the risk of death by occupational group. Mortality rates for professionals are 20 percent below average, while laborers' rates are 19 percent above average. More generally, the mortality rate for blue-collar workers is 7 percent higher than the average, while that for white-collar workers is 8 percent lower than the average (Kitagawa and Hauser, 1973). Occupational differences reflect in part the nature of the work being performed. But they also reflect differences in income, access to existing health facilities, environmental surroundings, personal stress levels, and other mortality-related correlates of a given social class. The tip-off is that the mortality levels of wives who are not exposed to the hazards of the job or workplace generally follow the pattern of their husbands (Benjamin, 1969).

In short, social status is an important factor in premature mortality. These socioeconomic variations in mortality will diminish only if there is substantial social change—change which makes "death control" more accessible to all social strata in the United States.

Race Differentials There are tremendous differences in mortality by race in the United States. White female life expectancy at birth in 1983 was 78.7 years, 5.1 years higher than that of black women. Similarly, white male life expectancy was 71.7 years, 6.3 years above that of black males. While these differentials have been narrowing since 1900, when the overall gap between whites and blacks was more than fifteen years, the differentials are still very large. These differences in life expectancy are due to the fact that blacks die in proportionately greater numbers than whites at every age under 85. The biggest difference occurs between ages 25 and 44, when blacks die at more than twice the rate whites do. The lower death rates of blacks compared to whites after age 84 are due in part to age-reporting errors, but also to the possibility that blacks surviving that long are particularly hardy—much more so as a group than whites at those ages, proportionately more of whom are probably weaker but survived due to greater access to expensive health services.

This last idea gives you a glimpse of the most important cause of the overall racial difference in mortality. It is the fact that blacks have on the average lower incomes, less education, and lower status occupations than the white majority. All of these factors are related to high mortality, but social status differences do not provide the whole explanation. A comparison of whites and blacks within the same social strata found that mortality rates were still at least 20 percent higher for blacks (Kitagawa and Hauser, 1973). A variety of cultural and environmental factors account for the residual difference. Regardless of social status, blacks are less likely than whites to seek medical care early or to get the most modern treatment.

But not all nonwhite groups in the United States have higher death rates than whites. For instance, life expectancy at birth of Japanese-American males has been about seven years longer than that of white males in recent decades; the pattern has been similar for females. This mortality advantage is due in part to the higher family income of Japanese-Americans compared to their white counterparts, and no doubt to cultural differences such as a tightly knit family structure. The gap between Japanese-Americans and whites, and especially blacks, indicates clearly that the problem of premature mortality in the United States has sharp racial features and that even the white population suffers substantially from it.

Sex Differentials   In the above discussion of white/black differences in life expectancy, it probably did not escape your attention that there are striking sex differentials in mortality. White female life expectancy at birth in 1983 was 7.6 years greater than that of white males, and black female life expectancy was 8.2 years greater than that of black males. You will also notice that black females are now living 1.9 years longer than white males. It is sometimes argued that black women are at the bottom of the social totem pole because they face dual discrimination due to their race and sex. But as we have already mentioned, mortality is the paramount determinant of quality of life. Thus it is possible to argue that black men, rather than black women, are the most disadvantaged race/sex subgroup.

In the United States, men have higher death rates than females at every age. Even prenatally, many more male than female fetuses are spontaneously aborted. One reason for this lifelong differential is that females are physiologically superior to males from conception to old age. It is impossible to determine just how much additional life expectancy this biological superiority gives to women, since there is no way to separate its effects from medical and sociocultural factors which also produce life expectancy differentials. In some societies such as India, these medical and sociocultural forces are so great that they completely offset the biological forces, and men actually live longer than women. This generally occurs in societies where women bear many children and where there is intense discrimination against women in terms of access to health services and to food. But in developed societies like the United States, medical and sociocultural factors have tended to add to rather than subtract from the basic biological differential in life expectancy favoring women. Men have more hazardous occupations, have more accidents (especially in automobiles), smoke more, drink more, seek medical care later and less, and generally lead more stressful lives.

But the importance of these medical and sociocultural factors should not be overemphasized. When differences in living habits, stress, self-care, and the like are roughly controlled, or held constant, it is still found that females live longer. Madigan (1957) showed this clearly in his classic study of the mortality patterns of religious teaching orders of brothers and sisters. These men and women had very similar demographic backgrounds and lifestyles. Both groups were composed of white native-born Americans, whose religion was Roman Catholic. The men were not likely to engage in heavy drinking, or other forms of illicit behavior, and did not serve in the armed forces. The women's occupations were no less stressful than those of men, and they did not undergo the rigors of bearing children. The time allotted for work, study, recreation, and sleep was the same for men and women, and so were diet, medical care, and housing. If these sociocultural and medical factors were responsible for the difference in life expectancy by sex, then the life expectancies of the nuns and brothers should have been similar since many of these factors were nearly identical. However, Madigan found that nuns had higher life expectancies than brothers at every age. Moreover, while both nuns and brothers lived longer than their counterparts in the general population, the life expectancy gap was just about the same. This is evidence that there is a fundamental biological basis for sex differences in mortality.

It is clear then that the mortality gap between males and females is due to both biological and social factors. The crux of our problem is to diminish the social factors causing more premature mortality among men, keeping in mind that even if this were accomplished, a biological differential would still persist. Whether we will be able to substantially narrow the overall mortality differential in the future in this way is uncertain, though it is not likely in the immediate future.

If the differential does narrow substantially in the immediate future, it is more likely that it will be due to an increase in socially preventable premature mortality in women rather than a reduction of the same in men. For instance, female cigarette smoking has increased dramatically since World War II, and women with a history of smoking are now moving into the older ages, where smoking deaths are concentrated, in much larger numbers than ever before. During the 1970s, the death rate from lung cancer for ages 55 to 64 rose about 60 percent for women compared to only about 5 percent for men (National Center for Health Statistics, 1978a). By 1985, lung cancer surpassed breast cancer as the top killer of women. Moreover, one price of success for women entering the work force in unprecedented numbers has been a surge in stress-related illnesses and exposure to substances linked to cancer and heart disease. In recent years, for instance, the men to women ratio for peptic and duodenal ulcers has been 2 to 1, a dramatic narrowing from the 1960 ratio of up to 10 to 1.

Premature mortality is an important social problem in its own right, but so too is the sex differential itself. This differential makes it virtually inevitable that most women who read this book will spend a substantial portion of their lives as widows, suffering the economic, social, and personal problems which disproportionately plague this marital status. As lamentable as this is, it is not as problematic as the prospect of premature death which most men face.

Age Differentials   Death rates vary tremendously by age, being relatively high in the first few years of life and after age 44. Despite a remarkable reduction of the death rate at every age over the past century, there is still a good deal of unnecessary and preventable death at each age, and this, of course, is a serious problem. Here we have space to discuss preventable death only during infancy and young adulthood.

Infant Mortality   Infant mortality refers to deaths that occur during the first year of life. The amount of socially preventable infant mortality in the world is staggering. In 1985 the infant mortality rate exceeded 10 percent in the less-developed world, excluding China, and topped 20 percent in such countries as Afghanistan and Sierra Leone. By contrast, the lowest infant mortality rate in the world was in Finland, where only 0.6 percent of the babies died during their first year of life. These figures give you some idea of the extent of preventable infant death in the world. Countries able to achieve low infant mortality rates share two attributes—high levels of income and education (Weeks, 1981). High income allows a nutritious, sanitary diet for the child and the nursing mother, and adequate medical protection from disease and other health hazards. High education provides knowledge of what health hazards to avoid and how to do so, as well as how to respond should avoidance of health hazards be impossible.

Infant mortality in the United States has fallen tremendously during the twentieth century. The rate was about 1 percent in 1985, low by world standards but still about twice as high as that of Finland. The fact that many infant deaths occurring in the United States are preventable represents a genuine objective problem.

In the United States low-birth-weight babies (those weighing less than 5.5 pounds) account for the majority of infant deaths. Their probability of dying during the first month of life is forty times greater than that of normal-weight infants, and is five times greater during the balance of their first year of life. Infant death and low birth weight are often socially preventable by improving the prenatal medical care and nutrition of mothers, and by encouraging them to abstain from smoking, alcohol, and most drugs. Because inadequate medical care, mal-

nutrition, and drug use are more common among teenage women, unmarried mothers, lower-class women, and black women, these groups have the highest rates of infant mortality. For instance, black babies are nearly twice as likely to die as white babies in the first year of life (Bouvier and van der Tak, 1976).

Mortality in Young Adulthood   Young adults 15 to 24 years of age have a relatively low risk of death in the United States. There is only about 1 chance in 100 that those of you in this age bracket will die during this period. However, since in recent years about 4 million persons turn 15 years of age each year, that 1 percent probability of death means that 40,000 individuals in each group of 15-year-olds will die before their twenty-fifth birthday. What is particularly tragic about these deaths in the prime of life is that most are socially rather than biologically determined.

In 1983 the chief causes of death among young people in the 15 to 24 age group were, in order of importance, motor vehicle accidents, other kinds of accidents, murder, and suicide (which is up 300 percent since 1960). Murder is by far the chief cause of death for black youths, while automobile accidents are the major cause of death for white youths. Many of these deaths are also linked to drug use and alcohol. More than 8000 teenagers and young adults die in drinking-related accidents alone every year. The problem of socially preventable young adult mortality is an especially irksome one, because the death rate among young adults has remained about the same since 1950, while that of Americans as a whole has been cut in half.

INTERNAL MIGRATION PROBLEMS

Americans have always been a highly mobile population. Historically there have been several major migration streams. The first was from the eastern seaboard states westward, a demographic process that ultimately pushed the American frontier into the Pacific Ocean. This western movement has yet to completely ebb. The second stream was the movement from rural to urban areas. By 1980, about 73 percent of the United States population resided in urban areas. The third major stream was the movement from the South to the Northeast and North Central states, especially among blacks. In recent decades, however, more people, including blacks, have moved into rather than out of the South. This is part of the fourth and now dominant regional migration stream, the movement from the Snowbelt states to the Sunbelt states (see Figure 7-2). Another important type of movement is that within a neighborhood, community, city, or county. This local movement constitutes about half of all movement. Although this movement does not cross a county line and, therefore, is not technically migration according to some definitions, it is considered migration here.

Migration, of course, is not a problem in itself. In a modern industrial society a certain amount of migration is necessary to, for example, redistribute the labor force. Migration becomes a problem when there is too much of it, or when it has strong adverse effects on the places of origin or destination. Migration often constitutes a problem for society even when it is in the best interests of the individual migrants. It can also cause problems at the place of origin while it benefits the place of destination, or vice versa. These competing interests make migration problems difficult to solve.

The Level of Migration

During the 1980s, about 1 out of every 6 Americans moved each year. At this rate, if everyone took a turn moving, the entire population would change residences every six years. However, about half the population does not take a turn,

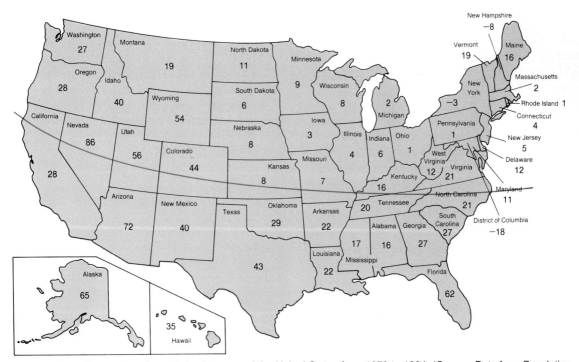

FIGURE 7-2 Percentage of population increase of the United States from 1970 to 1984. (*Source:* Data from Population Reference Bureau (1981; 1985a).)

so the other half actually averages two moves during the six-year period. Moreover, a sizable fraction of this latter group moves even more than twice in the six-year period. Thus, the United States population as a whole is a highly mobile one, and there are sizable subgroups that are extremely mobile, moving two or more times every six years. Some experts believe that this level is too high and that it leads to a deterioration of the quality of life (Weeks, 1981). Toffler (1970), for instance, worries that industrial nations like the United States are "breeding a new race of nomads," people who are forced to make and break social ties too rapidly. Similarly, Packard (1972) expresses the concern that the high level of migration is turning America into "a nation of strangers," and others (Keyes, 1973; Gordon, 1975) believe Americans are gradually becoming alienated, lonely people because of their growing lack of social roots.

There is certainly some basis for these concerns. For instance, frequent migration can cause problems for families and individuals. Migration tears the family loose from its roots in the community. Family members must give up their familiar home and usually their network of relatives and lifelong friends who often provide valuable financial, health, and other benefits. They also must relinquish established relationships with neighbors, businesses, churches, and other institutions. Children are pulled out of their schools, sometimes in mid-semester, and forced to adjust to new school systems. They may lose academic credit, social standing, and the opportunity to fully participate in extracurricular activities. Moreover, if the family moves frequently, it may never make a wholehearted attempt to sink social roots into new communities. Since the family knows it will probably be moving again soon, it has no stake in the welfare of the community, and the community itself has little interest in the welfare of transient families. High mobility, therefore, can be detrimental to the individual, the

family, and the community (Horton and Leslie, 1981).

Effects on Places of Origin and Destination

Rural to Urban Migration Migration affects the demographic composition and social structure of both the place of origin and destination. The demographic composition is altered principally because young adults migrate more than any other group. The social structure is influenced because extended family relationships are disturbed, and educational, political, economic, religious, recreational, and other institutions must change to accommodate dwindling or expanding local populations.

Rural areas typically have lost not only overall population but most of their young people as well. This has had a profound negative effect on the vitality of rural communities, and on the ability of their local institutions to service the remaining (largely aging) population. Sometimes this migration has also had a negative impact on the urban destination areas as well. Undereducated and underskilled rural people often increase the unemployment and welfare problems of the cities to which they move.

The problems posed by rural to urban migration are summed up nicely in this United States Senate finding which appeared in the *Congressional Record* (1970):

> The devastating consequences of the population shift are evident everywhere—in both urban and rural America. Countless rural communities, once thriving and prosperous, are facing social and economic bankruptcy because too few residents remain to support essential public services and civic institutions. On the other hand, our large cities are facing gradual strangulation. Our giant cities are finding themselves increasingly unable to deal with the large influx of uneducated rural migrants who are ill-prepared for urban living. The congested traffic arteries, and pollution of the water and the air, the soaring crime rates, the housing blight, and the simple lack of adequate

elbow room are rapidly making our larger cities unlivable as well as ungovernable.

Partially because of these urban conditions, there was a reversal of this flow in the 1970s; urban to rural migration actually exceeded rural to urban migration during that decade. However, this remarkable phenomenon was just temporary, and by the 1980s rural to urban migration reestablished its dominance. By the year 2000, 75 to 85 percent of the United States population will probably reside in just twenty-five urban regions. Over 70 percent of these urban dwellers will live in just four vast concentrations of people: the Northern Atlantic Seaboard region, the Great Lakes region, California, and Florida. Thus, the problems caused by rural to urban migration will remain for many decades and may even grow worse. Although the President, the Congress, both major political parties, the nation's governors, and many others have recognized and spoken out against the problems of urban concentration, the United States, unlike all other advanced industrial countries of the world, has failed to devise or implement a policy for dispersing its population (Sundquist, 1975).

Central City to Suburban Migration After World War II, suburban living became increasingly popular, and there was a significant movement of the cities' population into the suburban rings. This was predominantly a movement of the middle and upper classes. Those left behind and those moving into the cities tended to be members of minority groups, the elderly, the unemployed, welfare recipients, and other disproportionately poor groups. Thus there was (and still is) a concentration of relatively well-off people in the suburbs and of disadvantaged people in the cities.

Because these disadvantaged people are disproportionately black, there is a concept in demography, like astronomy, known as a "black hole." It refers to the poor black hole within the surrounding affluent white doughnut now typical of deteriorating cities in the North. However, even the once less-segregated Sunbelt cities may soon develop their own black holes if growth there continues to be concentrated in suburbs. Atlanta and New Orleans already exhibit the characteristics of doughnut cities (Biggar, 1979).

The movement of the middle and upper classes to the suburbs creates a variety of problems for the central city. There is a loss of wealth and a shrinking tax base, as well as a loss of the best educated and trained people. The departure of these people not only means they are not available to help solve present problems but also contributes to further economic stagnation. Meanwhile, the accumulation of low-income disadvantaged people in the central city requires increased appropriations for police protection against street crime, for fire protection against the increased risks posed by deteriorating housing, and for a variety of other social services. Thus, suburbanization not only increases racial segregation but also raises the cost of city services while shrinking the tax base for funding them.

Migration to the Sunbelt States The Sunbelt states are now the most rapidly growing region of the United States because they have the nation's highest levels of fertility and, even more important, net migration. Since 1970, the Sunbelt states have absorbed about two-thirds of the nation's total growth (see Figure 7-2). The movement of large numbers of people from the Snowbelt to the Sunbelt has caused problems in both areas.

The Snowbelt states have severe social and economic problems already. They are full of large old cities that are difficult to administer; their industrial infrastructure is outdated; their tax base is shrinking; their rail system has deteriorated; their labor costs are high and inflexible; their winter fuel costs are expensive and growing rapidly; their unemployment and

New Orleans has grown rapidly as a result of the Sunbelt boom and now exhibits the symptoms of a "doughnut city" with a "black hole." Its central city, which has a black majority, is surrounded by affluent white suburbs. (Georg Gerster/Photo Researchers, Inc.)

crime rates are high; and their environment is often ugly and unhealthy, especially within metropolitan areas. As a result, the Snowbelt states no longer attract as many in-migrants as in the past, and much of their own population is moving to the Sunbelt. This out-migration is beneficial for the nation as a whole because it redistributes the labor force to where it is most needed. Indeed, the controversial urban report of President Carter's Commission for a National Agenda for the 80s recommended that Washington actually encourage migration of northern urban dwellers to the Sunbelt by opposing federal aid programs that seek to restore northern industrial cities. (Carter rejected this recommendation before leaving office.) But this out-migration is also problematic because it

carries away the younger, more qualified people who are most likely to provide the ideas and leadership required to solve the Snowbelt's problems.

The huge numbers of in-migrants also pose problems for the Sunbelt states. These states must rapidly expand their educational, housing, welfare, and other services. Take Arizona, for example. Its population grew by 72 percent between 1970 and 1984. This means that for every two persons requiring services in 1970, there were more than three by 1984. While it is hard to keep pace with such growth under ordinary circumstances, it is even more difficult in this era of a Proposition 13 type of fiscal accountability, and of citizen groups vehemently opposed to increased taxes and state spending (Biggar, 1979). In response to the problems associated with rapid and unplanned growth, some Sunbelt communities are attempting to limit their size by making immigration difficult. Tactics include restricting the number of new and/or total housing units, and discouraging the settlement of labor-intensive industry.

INTERNATIONAL MIGRATION PROBLEMS

There are two types of immigrants in the United States: legal immigrants and illegal immigrants. *Legal immigrants* include persons admitted to the United States to reside here permanently. Also included in this category are political refugees, who are conditionally allowed to remain in the United States for an indefinite period and who almost invariably become permanent residents. *Illegal immigrants* are undocumented migrants who are illegally living in the United States through entry without permission, improper use of visa privileges (e.g., overstaying), or use of false documents.

Throughout the history of the United States, immigrants have contributed enormously to the nation's arts, science, and political life. However, immigration also causes or contributes to many problems. The lack of comprehensive data makes it hard to evaluate the significance of these problems, since it is not even known how many immigrants reside in the United States or in individual states or communities. But it is clear that these problems exist. Immigration problems are related, for example, to society's ability to achieve zero population growth; to the cost of providing a whole range of public services including welfare, medical care, education, public housing, fire and police protection, sanitation, transportation, and recreation; to the depression of wages and working conditions and the displacement of native workers from their jobs; to the difficulties, stresses, and strains caused by unsuccessful assimilation; and to the exploitation of illegal aliens by

unscrupulous businesspeople (Murphy and Cancellier, 1982).

Some of these problems are discussed in different contexts in other chapters. Here we will focus on just four points. First, regardless of the actual objective damage caused by immigration, subjective concern about it varies enormously. While it is true that a few conservative, environmental, and population action groups steadfastly support restrictive immigration laws, such groups represent only a small minority of the population. In general, when our economy is expanding, the public is largely indifferent to immigration, and the influx of foreign labor is welcomed by business. In times of recession, however, public concern about immigration and its attendant problems rises dramatically. Thus, the economic uncertainties of the early 1980s led to a high level of subjective concern about immigration. Large majorities of Americans supported slashes in immigration quotas and crackdowns on illegal entrants.

Second, while illegal aliens cause or contribute to many immigration problems, the objective damage they produce is often exaggerated. For instance, the adverse impact of immigration on the welfare system is caused primarily by legal rather than illegal immigrants (Select Committee on Population, 1978). Despite popular belief, illegal immigrants apparently do not place a heavy burden on government social service programs. In fact, they are more likely to pay taxes than to use tax-supported programs—another example of how subjective concern can be out of line with objective reality.

Third, immigration problems are very difficult to solve and create many policy dilemmas. For instance, medical care is the one public service heavily utilized by illegal immigrants, and this has a considerable economic impact on hospitals and on government medical programs, since illegal aliens are frequently unable to pay for these services. The government could develop policies designed to dissuade illegal aliens from seeking medical help. But such policies would create potentially serious health hazards in the communities in which the immigrants have settled because the illegal alien population has a high prevalence of infectious diseases. Such a policy would also violate humanitarian values.

As another example of value trade-offs, policies aimed at restricting immigration, especially illegal immigration, might force the closing of small businesses and farms unable to pay higher wages to Americans. And other firms might move to foreign countries where they can still find inexpensive labor. As a final example, policies which deny the noncitizen children of illegal aliens educational opportunities or other public services would result in a situation in which their skills would not be commensurate with their aspirations of upward mobility. Needless to say, such frustrated achievement could lead to a generation of alienated and embittered young people and, consequently, to serious social problems and political pressures in the future. These dilemmas illustrate the linkages among social problems as discussed in the opening chapter, and they clearly show the value trade-offs of immigration policy.

The final point we will make here is that three demographic aspects of immigration—overall level, ethnic and racial composition, and residential distribution—either cause or intensify immigration problems. Let us examine each of these in turn.

The Level of Immigration

The United States has traditionally received more immigrants than any other country in the world. We do not know exactly how many immigrants enter the United States each year, largely because illegal immigration is inadequately documented. But it is certain that in recent years well over 1 million newcomers have annually immigrated to the United States, the highest level since the mass migration of Europeans at the turn of the century. In the early 1980s, net legal immigration averaged about 600,000 persons a year, and many observers estimated that the net inflow of illegal immigrants was an additional 500,000 persons per year. The United States is now receiving twice as many immigrants as all the other countries of the world combined. Moreover, with population levels, political strife, and economic hard times increasing around the world, the level of immigration threatens to climb beyond its present dizzying height.

The important point is that when the level of immigration is very high, as it is presently in the United States, the problems related to immigration noted above generally increase in number and scope. Later in this chapter we will show in detail how this flood of immigrants makes the desirable goal of zero population growth almost impossible to attain.

Ethnic and Racial Composition

The United States was initially settled by immigrants from northern and western Europe and their descendants. For the first 100 years after Independence, the large majority of immigrants still came from northern and western Europe. During that time, there were few problems associated with immigration and virtually no laws governing it.

However, toward the end of the nineteenth century, there was a pronounced shift in the ethnic and racial composition of immigrants. The Irish, southern and eastern Europeans, and Asians began arriving in great numbers, and soon accounted for the majority of immigrants. The presence of these immigrants in America led to hostility, discrimination, and other problems. Many of these conflicts were related to language barriers, the development of ethnically segregated communities, and the fact that most of these immigrants were Catholic while the population as a whole was predominantly Protestant. The new immigrants were rapidly changing the racial and ethnic composition of the United States population, much to the dismay of many Americans. Consequently, strong social and political pressures were marshaled against the influx. This opposition produced a series of restrictive and racist laws which were successful in reducing immigration from Asia and southern and eastern Europe.

Legislation over the last twenty years and the upsurge of illegal immigration have once again led to a racial and ethnic composition of immigrants very different from the composition of the United States population. About 81 percent of legal immigrants and almost all illegal immigrants come from Latin America or Asia. Because the level of immigration is so high, it is now rapidly changing the ethnic and racial makeup of the United States population. As a result, the objective problems and subjective concerns that greeted earlier waves of immigrants and which produced restrictive laws are surfacing again today.

Obviously, much of this concern has overtones of racism and ethnic prejudice. But much is also due to the subjective fear that these immigrants, particularly the Hispanics, may not assimilate as rapidly into the main culture as the largely European immigrant groups of the past. Of particular concern is the fact that the vast majority of immigrants speak a single foreign language—Spanish—contrary to the immigration laws' intent, which is to encourage cultural diversity. Some Hispanics view the Spanish language as a source of cultural unity and power, and have fought hard for bilingualism in education and in government services. However, many other Americans fear that the huge influx of Spanish-speaking immigrants (and these efforts to make the United States a bilingual society) could lead to the kind of divisive factionalism that exists between French-speaking Quebec and the English-speaking parts of Canada. While some temporary bilingual measures are probably necessary to speed up the assimilation of Spanish-speaking immigrants into the main American culture, there is presently no agreement on what the nature and extent of these measures should be.

As has happened with many other ethnic groups in America, the Hispanics' growing numbers and their increased assertiveness have generated growing intergroup hostility. The antipathy is becoming more intense and pervasive as the Hispanics grow more insistent on their rights and more visible in their attempts to achieve them. Their visibility is high in part because much of their struggle to improve their situation has been well-documented by the media. As we discussed in the opening chapter, the media-heightened drama of movements like this often exaggerates the objective significance of the problems involved. One reason why the fears of an Hispanic takeover are subjectively overrated is that despite their common language, these immigrants come from a wide variety of countries and races. Differences among them are probably as important as the common thread of language (Murphy and Cancellier, 1982).

Residential Distribution

The impact of immigration problems is not distributed evenly throughout the United States, since immigrants settle disproportionately in certain states and communities. In the early 1980s over 70 percent of the aliens resided in just six states: California, New York, Texas, Florida, Illinois, and New Jersey. The first four states mentioned receive three-fourths of all Hispanic immigrants. In general, immigrants flock to the same Sunbelt areas that draw internal migrants. Thus, immigration problems and the cost of their solution are not burdens shared equally by all Americans.

GROWTH OF RACIAL AND ETHNIC GROUPS

In the last section we saw that the racial and ethnic composition of immigrants can alter that of the United States population as a whole. The other prime factor that can change the ethnic and racial makeup of the population is fertility—specifically, the *differential fertility* of various groups. Differential mortality can also have an effect, but it is usually much smaller than that of immigration or differential fertility.

As also noted earlier, shifts in the racial and ethnic composition of a population can lead or contribute to a variety of racial and ethnic problems. Whatever their objective reality, at the bottom of these problems is often the subjective fear that some other group will grow faster than one's own and, consequently, increase not only its share of the population but also its political (and even military) power.

This differential growth problem is immensely important in many parts of the world. For instance, the Israeli Arab population is growing much faster than that of the Israeli Jews, mostly because the Arab couples are averaging 6.1 children while the Jewish couples are averaging only 2.8 children. If this continues, the Arabs will constitute the majority population in Israel by the year 2000, and could take political control of that nation (Calib, 1981). The same situation exists in the Soviet Union, where the Russians' low birthrate will reduce their share of the total population to less than half by the end of the century, and the non-Russian minorities will become the majority (Feshbach, 1982). Another example can be found in South Africa, where blacks, already the overwhelming majority, are having so many more children than whites that the latter are on the verge of becoming a demographically negligible minority. And Catholics are outbreeding Protestants in Northern Ireland and will eventually become the majority there.

Compared to these foreign examples, differential growth problems in the United States have been relatively minor. But they have existed. In the early twentieth century, many white native-born Americans became concerned not only about the huge number of southern and eastern European and Asian immigrants flowing into the country, as noted earlier, but also about their relatively high fertility. In addition, they were concerned

about the relatively high fertility of blacks. Their fear was that white native-born Americans, who were mostly Protestant and descendants of northern and western Europeans, would constitute an increasingly smaller proportion of future United States generations because of their comparatively lower fertility and immigration.

This loss of share in future generations was viewed with alarm because native-born whites, especially those in the upper classes, were convinced they possessed the most desirable hereditary qualities (e.g., higher intelligence). Thus they contended their loss of share meant the population as a whole was losing quality. Those who subscribed to these ideas formed the eugenics movement, and they were successful in restricting immigration from countries outside northern and western Europe. The eugenicists' fears of societal deterioration declined with the passage of restrictive immigration laws and also with the observation that the fertility rates of most religious, ethnic, and racial groups tended to eventually converge toward the overall United States average, a tendency which the eugenicists helped foster through their support of the newly emerging birth control movement.

As we approach the twenty-first century, there is reason to believe that two issues concerning population composition may again confront the nation. The first issue relates to differences in the growth rates of the white and black populations. The second issue involves the increasing share of the population gained by Hispanics.

Growth of the Black Population

The United States is a racially divided society, with the two principal racial groups being the white population and the black population. One of the key concerns in a racially divided society is the relative size and growth of racial groups. Fertility is therefore a vital concern. Since Emancipation, blacks have always had higher fertility than whites, and this has been viewed as problematic by the more race-conscious elements of the white population.

Despite the higher fertility of blacks, their proportion of the population has actually been declining throughout most of United States history. Their proportion fell from 19 percent in 1790, the year of the first census, to 10 percent in the 1930s. This happened for two reasons. First, the black death rate has always been higher than that of the white population. Second, there has been little immigration of blacks from Africa since the slave trade was abolished in 1808, while there have been high levels of white immigration through most of the nation's history.

Although it is still only about 60 percent as high as it was 200 years ago, the black proportion has rebounded significantly in recent decades. The 1980 census enumerated 26.5 million blacks, 11.7 percent of the total population. This upsurge in the black proportion is primarily due to their higher rate of natural increase (births minus deaths). Black fertility (2.2 children per woman) was still about 30 percent higher than white fertility (1.7) in 1983 (National Center for Health Statistics, 1985c).

The black population will almost certainly increase its share of the population in the future. Bouvier and Davis (1982) have calculated that even if the black birthrate gradually falls to 1.8 (the United States rate in the 1980s) by 2030, the black proportion of the population will still increase to about 15 percent by 2080 (see Figure 7-3). This would occur as long as immigration remains at or below its current level and the racial and ethnic composition of the immigrants does not change.

Growth of the Hispanic Population

Hispanics are the country's fastest-growing minority. The 1980 census counted 14.6 million Hispanics, which represents 6.5 percent of the population. This figure does not take into account the enormous number of Hispanics who are living and working in the United States illegally. If illegal aliens were included, the actual total could be as high as 22 million, or 10 percent of the population.

The most important reason for this growth is Hispanic immigration (legal and illegal), which is running at an estimated rate of almost 1 million people a year. The other reason is their high fertility which, at about 2.9 children per couple in 1982, was 71 percent higher than that of whites and 32 percent higher than that of blacks (National Center for Health Statistics, 1985f). If this continues, Hispanics will move past blacks as the nation's largest minority around the turn of the century. Beyond that, their proportion will continue to grow rapidly. Bouvier and Davis (1982) have calculated that even if the Hispanic birthrate gradually falls to 1.8 by 2030, the Hispanic proportion of the population will increase to 29 percent by 2080 if the average annual level of overall immigration is 1.5 million; to 23 percent if immigration averages 1 million; and to 16 percent if it averages 0.5 million (Figure 7-3).

Growth of the White, Non-Hispanic Population

In 1980, Native Americans—Indians, Aleuts, and Eskimos—constituted 0.6 percent of the population, and Asians and Pacific Islanders accounted for another 1.5 percent. These groups taken together represented about 2 percent of the population. According to Bouvier and Davis (1982), these groups will also increase their share of the United States population to as much as 13 percent (remember this is greater than the proportion of blacks in the United States today) by 2080, depending on the overall level of future immigration (see Figure 7-3). The Asians will account for the lion's share of this growth due mostly to high levels of immigration.

Since blacks, Hispanics, Asians, and other minorities are presently increasing their share of the United States population, and are likely to continue to do so if substantial immigration continues, the white non-Hispanic share will

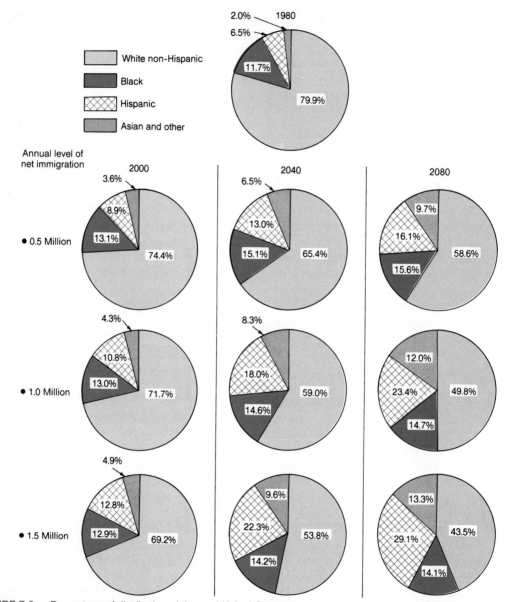

FIGURE 7-3   Percentage of distribution of the total United States population, 1980-2080, by annual level of net immigration and race. (Numbers do not always total to 100 percent because of rounding off.) (*Source:* Reprinted from Bouvier and Davis (1982: 40). By permission of the publisher.)

continue to decline. Bouvier and Davis (1982) estimate that if present levels of immigration persist, the white non-Hispanic share will decrease from 80 percent in 1980 to 49.8 percent in 2080. The 2080 share would be 43 per-cent with annual immigration at 1.5 million, and 59 percent at 0.5 million. Thus, by the year 2080—in less than a century—white non-Hispanics could be a minority group in the United States!

The population share projections discussed in this section are based on certain assumptions about fertility and immigration which may not actually occur. But one thing is certain: The racial composition of the nation will be substantially altered over the next century.

How the various ethnic and racial groups will react to these changes is also unknown. If a strong national consensus forms in favor of the continuation of the existing racial and ethnic composition, serious disturbances will likely result. And this turmoil will not simply be between whites and present minorities. Many blacks view the rapid growth of the Hispanic population with alarm: the two groups are already competing fiercely for the same jobs and government aid, and, of course, the consensus discussed above would have deep subjective roots in ethnic and racial prejudice. A consensus to maintain a racial and ethnic status quo in the United States has already grown to the point that restrictive immigration policy aimed principally at reducing the inflow of Hispanics was passed in 1986. However, this type of policy will at most only diminish the trends discussed in this section.

On the other hand, it is possible that the United States will experience a more peaceful transition to a true multicultural society. Much will depend on the manner in which cultural assimilation takes place in the nation's social institutions—particularly in the family, the schools, and the workplace (Bouvier and Davis, 1982). It will also depend on the progress we make as a nation in working out the problems of prejudice and discrimination. College students today will have a large say in determining how the nation will respond to this formidable challenge.

ZERO POPULATION GROWTH

Problems Posed by Positive Growth

The effect of population growth on the well-being of society has been debated for several hundred years. Experts now agree that population growth must cease sooner or later, because infinite growth cannot occur in a finite world. One demographer (Coale, 1974) calculated that at the current rate of world population growth, there would be one individual for every square foot on the earth's surface in 700 years. Though the experts agree that population growth must ultimately stop, there is disagreement about when this should occur. A few analysts hold that population growth can proceed, at least at a low rate, almost indefinitely, because additional resources will be discovered when existing supplies are exhausted or, better yet, substitutes will be developed. Most experts believe, however, that population growth must come to a halt within 100 years. Indeed, some argue that growth must stop almost immediately if the current world population, and future populations of similar size, are to be able to subsist on the world's resources (see Chapter 12 and 13).

An even more hotly debated issue is whether an affluent nation like the United States should cease its population growth, and this issue has been the focus of much debate among the experts over the last fifteen years. Rising subjective concern about United States population growth was expressed by the public during the 1960s. At that time, the stresses caused by the baby boom generation were mounting, and many people became anxious about the objective problems society would face if the baby boom generation itself had large families. During that decade, *zero population growth* turned into a household phrase. Public concern about future population growth was so great that it led President Nixon to create the President's Commission on Population Growth and the American Future.

However, this public concern dissipated rapidly in the 1970s when it became clear that the baby boomers were reproducing at such record-low levels that they were not even having enough children to take their place in the population. Both the media and the public thought that this meant zero population growth had been achieved. But this was not true because the number of births and immigrants still exceeded the number of deaths and emigrants by a wide margin (see Box 7-1). Indeed, more people were added to the United States population during the 1970s than in any other decade. This is an especially good example of the principle that the objective reality and subjective perception of a problem can move in opposite directions from each other.

Despite the atrophy of public concern, most demographers and a variety of organizations such as Zero Population Growth, Inc., have continued to advocate policies to terminate United States population growth. Among the most prominent bodies supporting this position was the Commission on Population Growth and the American Future. The commission concluded that population growth threatens severe problems for American society—and for the rest of the world—and "found no convincing argument for continued population growth." It recommended that the United States adopt the attainment of zero population growth as its national policy. We have already noted earlier in this chapter the sorts of problems posed by continued population growth. Its major negative effect is its tendency to intensify or aggravate other types of problems (Commission on Population Growth and the American Future, 1972). It leads to more congestion and crowding in metropolitan areas; increases pollution of the air, water, and land; places a great demand on energy resources; requires the development of new sources of food, minerals, lumber, and other raw materials; increases demand for water which is even now running short in many states; requires the duplication rather than the improvement of existing facilities such as nursing homes, hospitals, schools, and roads; leads to the destruction of agricultural land through urban and industrial expansion; and intensifies pressure on the fragile ecosystem.

The Commission on Population Growth and the American Future searched for the economic benefits of continued population growth but was unable to find any. Rather, it found that in the absence of population growth, the overall quality of life would improve and many of our domestic problems would be easier to solve. More generally, the commission concluded:

> [Zero population growth] can contribute to the nation's ability to solve its problems...by providing an opportunity to devote resources to the quality of life rather than its quantity, and by "buying time"—that is, slowing the pace at which problems accumulate so as to provide opportunity for the development of orderly and democratic solutions (1972:25).

In considering the desirability of continued population growth in the United States, we must also take into account its impact on the rest of the world. An additional American—like you—consumes and pollutes far more than an additional person in a poor country. Consequently, an American's impact on the well-being of the planet is much more adverse. Even though the United States makes up only about 5 percent of the world's population, it uses up about 35 percent of the world's natural resources and creates about 50 percent of its pollution. Indeed, on the basis of the threat the United States poses to the ecology of the planet, some people contend that the United States is, for all intents and purposes, already the most overpopulated country in the world (Weller and Bouvier, 1981). According to Miller (1975), the United States' population is now equivalent to a pollution population of somewhere between 5 and 10 billion, due to an environmental impact factor twenty-five to fifty times that of poorer countries. This is one reason why our population growth problem is also the world's problem.

Population growth in the United States also increases our dependence on other countries for raw materials. In 1940 the United States was a net exporter of raw materials, but now we import more than half of the raw materials necessary to maintain our current standard of living. If present trends continue, within twenty-five years the United States will be dependent on developing countries for most essential raw materials (Mumford, 1977). This dependence makes us economically and politically vulnerable, as we have already experienced in our relations with oil-producing countries. Perhaps you have already suffered from this personally by waiting in long lines for gasoline. But more important, it is extremely risky to rely on poor nations for our raw materials when they themselves have rapidly growing populations which may need most or all of these resources in the future. By the same token, many nations of the world rely on us for our agricultural surplus. If we continue to expand our population to the point where this surplus disappears, these nations would not be able to obtain needed food, and the United States would have fewer assets to trade for needed resources.

It is important to stress that the elimination of population growth in the United States will not eradicate the problems that it intensifies. It just makes their solutions easier and less costly. A nongrowing population only makes the good life more attainable; it does not, in itself, produce it (Day, 1978).

Problems Posed by Negative Growth

To this point we have been concentrating on the problems associated with positive population growth, largely because this is the actual problem faced by the vast majority of the nations of the world, including the United States. However, once positive population growth is eliminated and zero population growth (ZPG) is achieved, there is no homeostatic mechanism that keeps a society at ZPG. It can easily slip back into a positive growth mode or into a negative one.

A variety of things happen to a society that is experiencing negative population growth. One

is that the proportion of older people increases markedly. Another is that shortages develop in the labor force. Consequently, there are strains on systems such as social security. Most demographers agree that if a nation declines in size very gradually, the objective damage of such problems is minimal. But if the decline is rapid, it can produce severe economic and social dislocations.

Nevertheless, regardless of the actual objective damage caused by negative population growth, there is tremendous subjective concern about it. The few European countries that are at or near negative growth are already giving signs of being very uncomfortable with it. In West Germany, where there have been more deaths than births since the mid-1970s, the growing subjective concern was evidenced by a television show entitled "Are the Germans Dying Out?" According to the program, the answer to this question is yes. Indeed, one German demographer has remarked: "Beneath the blankets we are a dying people." Similarly, in France, where fears of losing population have long been of concern as a matter of both national prestige and national security, population growth is now the theme of a national debate. Former president Giscard d'Estaing cautioned that France could not aspire to grandeur if it were losing population. And France's former premier Michel Debré regards a declining population as a national peril (Westoff, 1978a).

Such subjective concerns are understandable in a world in which population size has traditionally been correlated, though not perfectly, with military power and security. Although this correlation has lost some significance in the nuclear age, it still has some meaning in the face of nuclear equivalency and deterrence. It would regain strength if nuclear disarmament becomes a reality.

The United States is not immune to the fears about negative growth prevalent in European countries. Consider for a moment what your reaction might be if the population (and armies)

of our enemies continued to grow while ours
declined—particularly if our nuclear armaments
were strategically neutralized or dismantled.
Would you be among the many American citizens and military leaders who would almost
certainly call for increased population growth?

Thus, both positive and negative growth
pose many, though different, objective and subjective problems for society.

The Attainment of Zero Population Growth

The demographic equation for the United
States for 1984 is presented in Box 7-2. It shows
that the United States is presently nowhere
near zero population growth. The population
grew by nearly 2.7 million individuals, because
the number of births and immigrants exceeded
the number of deaths and emigrants by that
amount. As we noted earlier, ZPG occurs only

when the quantity of births and immigrants is
equal to the quantity of deaths and emigrants.
How can this be achieved in the United States?

Before answering that question it should be
pointed out that it is not practical to try to
achieve ZPG in the near future. Such an objective would require drastic alterations in our
average family size even if immigration were
halted altogether. For example, couples would
have to limit themselves to only about one child
for the next twenty years or so (Frejka, 1968).
Obviously, most couples would view that requirement as a greater problem than the negative effects of population growth. The reason
that such drastic requirements would be necessary now is that the United States population
already has built-in momentum for growth resulting from its relatively young population.
The United States has a relatively young pop-

BOX 7-2

THE U.S. DEMOGRAPHIC EQUATION, 1984

The demographic equation* for the United States during 1984 is calculated below. Approximations are used where exact
data are unavailable.

Population size, Dec. 31, 1984	237,839,000
Population size, Jan. 1, 1984	235,671,000
Population growth 1984	2,168,000
Births 1984 (B)	3,704,000
Deaths 1984 (D)	2,055,000
Natural increase 1984 (B − D)	1,649,000
Legal immigrants 1984 (I)	619,000
Emigration 1984 (O)	100,000
Net migration (I − O)	519,000

(a) Population growth = natural increase + net migration

    2,168,000 = 1,649,000 + 519,000

Note, however, that the above equation does not take into account net illegal migration, which is currently estimated to
be about 500,000 persons a year. So the real equation for 1984 is closer to (b).

(b) Population growth = natural increase + net migration

    2,668,000 = 1,649,000 + 1,019,000

*See Box 7-1 for discussion of the demographic equation.

ulation because of the post-World War II baby boom and the baby boomlet that generation is now parenting. However, once these large cohorts grow old, they will yield a relatively large number of deaths, making ZPG easier to attain in the future—all things being equal.

It is more realistic to think of achieving ZPG gradually over the next fifty to one hundred years. Population growth would of course continue over this interval, but at least the goal of ZPG would ultimately be attained. Moreover, the problems posed by growth during this time span would be less troublesome than those caused by the unusually small cohorts resulting from trying to achieve ZPG immediately.

To achieve ZPG in the future, the United States must keep fertility and net immigration relatively low. Just how low can be seen in Table 7-1. This table presents projected United States population size and growth rates for various combinations of fertility and net immigration. It also assumes that life expectancy continues to increase over the period, although at a slower rate than in recent decades. The fertility measure used is the total fertility rate (TFR), an indicator of average number of children per couple. These fascinating projections were prepared by Leon Bouvier (1981).

The Level of Fertility   Panel A of Table 7-1 permits us to observe the impact on growth of different levels of fertility if no immigration were allowed. Two points stand out. First, the seemingly small four-tenths of a child difference between two low fertility rates, 1.8 and 2.2, leads to an enormous difference in total population in the future. A TFR of 1.8 will result in a population of only 201 million by the year 2080, while a TFR of 2.2 will produce a population of 341 million, a difference of 140 million persons. In addition, the demographic and social profiles of the two populations would be radically dissimilar. The first population (TFR 1.8) would be declining rapidly in size, dropping, for instance, by 76 million people in the

thirty years between 2050 and 2080. If this rate were to remain the same, this population would continue to attenuate and would eventually flicker out. The second population would still be growing, and although this growth would be slow, it would never end.

The point is, therefore, that slight differences in the level of fertility in an advanced society like the United States are profoundly consequential in terms of resultant population growth. (If such a small difference in the TFR can have such a profound effect on the rate of population growth, it is easy to understand why the much larger differences in the TFRs of the major racial and ethnic groups in the United States—whites 1.7, blacks 2.2, Hispanics 2.9—would, if they were to persist, result in widely disproportionate rates of growth between the three population subgroups and a radically different admixture of racial and ethnic types in the United States in the future.)

The second point that can be drawn from panel A is this: Even in the absence of immigration, a low average number of children of only 2.2, just one-tenth of a child above the 2.1 rate needed for population replacement, will lead to massive population growth over the next 100 years. Thus, the achievement of ZPG is not just a matter of avoiding a return to high fertility on the scale the United States experienced 200 years ago (TFR = 8.0) or on the scale which is being experienced today in the developing nations (average TFR excluding China = 5.0). It is not even a question of avoiding a return to the moderate level (TFR = 3.7) the United States experienced during the post-World War II baby boom. Achieving ZPG is a matter of avoiding a return to a level not much higher than the United States rate during the early 1980s (TFR = 1.8), which was less than one-tenth higher than the nation's all time low of 1.74 in 1976. Hence, in order to achieve ZPG, the United States must avoid a return to a level of *low* fertility that is *too high*.

TABLE 7-1   PROJECTED U.S. POPULATION SIZE AND GROWTH RATE, 2000 TO 2080, BY LEVEL OF ANNUAL IMMIGRATION AND TOTAL FERTILITY RATE *

	Year							
	2000		**2030**		**2050**		**2080**	
Total fertility rate	Total population (1000s)	Pop. growth rate (%)	Total population (1000s)	Pop. growth rate (%)	Total population (1000s)	Pop. growth rate (%)	Total population (1000s)	Pop. growth rate (%)
(A) Annual net immigration = 0								
1.8	243,677	0.3	244,835	−0.2	277,315	−0.4	201,563	−0.4
2.0	250,348	0.4	267,797	0.03	264,851	−0.06	260,790	−0.05
2.2	257,722	0.5	295,010	0.3	311,603	0.3	341,266	0.3
(B) Annual net immigration = 250,000								
1.8	249,539	0.4	261,219	−0.07	250,720	−0.2	234,870	−0.2
2.0	256,318	0.5	284,928	0.2	289,904	0.08	297,927	0.1
2.2	263,809	0.6	312,998	0.4	338,612	0.4	383,209	0.4
(C) Annual net immigration = 500,000								
1.8	255,402	0.5	277,603	0.06	274,125	−0.08	268,177	−0.06
2.0	262,287	0.6	302,059	0.3	314,957	0.2	335,066	0.2
2.2	269,896	0.8	330,986	0.5	365,620	0.5	425,149	0.5
(D) Annual net immigration = 750,000								
1.8	261,265	0.6	293,987	0.2	297,530	0.04	301,485	0.05
2.0	268,257	0.7	319,190	0.4	340,009	0.3	372,204	0.3
2.2	275,983	0.9	348,974	0.6	392,631	0.6	467,096	0.6
(E) Annual net immigration = 1,000,000								
1.8	267,127	0.7	310,371	0.3	320,935	0.1	334,792	0.1
2.0	274,226	0.8	336,321	0.5	365,063	0.4	409,343	0.4
2.2	282,070	1.0	366,962	0.7	419,641	0.7	509,039	0.6
(F) Annual net immigration = 2,000,000								
1.8	290,578	1.1	375,907	0.6	414,555	0.5	468,022	0.4
2.0	298,104	1.2	404,844	0.8	466,305	0.7	558,011	0.6
2.2	306,419	1.4	438,915	1.0	527,677	0.9	676,806ll	0.8

* The total fertility rate (TFR) indicates how many children women would average during their lifetimes if the rate of childbearing in a given year persisted. For example, the TFR in the United States in 1985 was 1.8 children. This means that if the rate at which women were having children in 1985 does not change, teenagers just entering the childbearing ages in that year would average 1.8 children during their lifetimes. The TFR is our best answer to the question: How many children are women having nowadays?

Source: From Leon F. Bouvier, *The Impact of Immigration on U.S. Population Size,* Washington, D.C., Population Reference Bureau, 1981, Table 2, p. 4.

Fortunately, there is not much chance that the United States will permanently return to high or even moderate fertility levels in the foreseeable future. Women report in surveys that they intend to continue to have low fertility. And the reasons for the current low fertility level would also hinder any movement toward moderate or large families. These reasons include (1) the increasing cost of bearing and raising children; (2) the fact that individuals are spending increasingly fewer of their prime reproductive years in a stable marital union, the place where most childbearing occurs; (3) the growing economic independence of women from men, which means women now have more practical and viable alternatives to marriage and motherhood; (4) the availability of sophisticated and versatile birth control, especially the pill, induced abortion, and sterilization; and (5) the decline in religious authority and the expansion of education for women, both trends being powerful antifertility forces. For the birthrate to rise to high or moderate levels in the future, many of these trends would have to be reversed, but there seems little likelihood of that (McFalls, 1981).

Though the factors above are probably strong enough to prevent a return to moderate or high fertility, they are not necessarily strong enough to ward off a return to "too high" low fertility, that is, fertility in the 2.2 to 2.6 TFR range. This means that massive population growth is still quite possible even in the absence of immigration. However, there is reason to believe that future fertility will remain very low, as it has since 1971, or fall even lower. The reason for this is that the trends discussed above, rather than reversing or just holding steady, are more likely to continue. Contraception, for instance, will be even more sophisticated and versatile in the future, with available methods including long-term pills or injections.

It is difficult to predict fertility, but it is probably fair to say that the chances that the birthrate will fall to an extremely low level, let us say 1.5, are probably as good as the chances that it will rise to 2.6. If the birthrate did fall to 1.5 in the absence of immigration, the United States population would stop growing early in the twenty-first century, and if this rate persisted, the population would then begin a rapid decline toward extinction.

The Level of Net Immigration Thus, in the absence of immigration, a birthrate above 2.1 would lead to substantial population growth; a rate of 2.1 would yield ZPG; and one lower than 2.1 would result in negative growth. Therefore, if ZPG is society's goal, the fertility level must be kept at or below 2.1 children per woman. If it is below 2.1, the difference between the actual birthrate and 2.1 determines the number

of immigrants that can be admitted if ZPG is to be attained.

Table 7-1 shows roughly how many net immigrants the United States could accept while still achieving ZPG. If our fertility rate remains at 1.8, we could accept 750,000 net immigrants a year and still achieve a growth rate near zero (i.e., 0.05) by the year 2080 (panel D). If our birthrate increases to and remains at 2.0, we would have to accept fewer than 250,000 net immigrants in order to achieve ZPG in 100 years (panel B). And, of course, if our fertility rate stabilizes at 2.2, we would not be able to achieve ZPG without substantial net emigration (panel A). It is clear from this analysis that fertility is the major determinant of zero population growth. Very slight changes in fertility result in large differences in the number of net immigrants that can be accepted.

Table 7-1 also permits us to observe how much population growth results from combinations of fertility and net immigration which do not produce ZPG. For instance, a birthrate of 2.2 and net immigration of 2 million per year would dramatically increase the United States population from 232 million in 1982 to 677 million in less than 100 years (see panel F). Net immigration of 2 million per year is admittedly almost twice the current 1.1 million record level, but it is by no means inconceivable, given that the demand for immigration to the United States is building up in the developing world. And, of course, a TFR of 2.2 is still a low birthrate, one which we could very easily adopt as a long-term average.

If you are a young college student in the early childbearing years, the number of children you have will directly affect our ability to achieve ZPG in the future. Your generation must average two or fewer children to get the ball rolling. This does not mean that you all must have two or fewer children. It simply means that as a generation, you must *average* two or fewer children. Some of you can have none; others one, two—even fifteen children. Also, regardless of your age, it is almost certain that you will have a say in the development of our immigration policy by choosing between politicians with different views on what the level of immigration should be. So you will help determine whether or not we achieve ZPG in the future.

SOCIAL POLICY: ZERO POPULATION GROWTH

Strategies for Solution

After a comprehensive evaluation of the pros and cons of positive, negative, and zero population growth, the Commission on Population Growth and the American Future concluded that the achievement of ZPG is in the best interest of the United States. However, the United States does not have zero population growth now, and our current demographic behavior will not lead us to it in the future. If our present annual levels of fertility (1.8) and net immigration (1.1 million) continue, the United States population will rise dramatically from 232 million in 1982 to nearly 400 million by the year 2080, an increase of about 70 percent. Moreover, the population would still be growing rapidly in 2080. Thus, if the United States is going to attain ZPG in the next 100 years, our demographic behavior must change. This could happen in two ways. First, the United States could adopt an overall population growth policy designed to achieve ZPG. Or second, United States demographic behavior could change spontaneously in such a way that ZPG is achieved. These two possibilities form the bases of two competing policies related to the achievement of ZPG in the United States: (1) a regulated growth policy and (2) an unregulated growth policy.

Regulated Growth Policy A regulated growth policy would recognize that it is impractical to try to reach ZPG immediately. Its goal would be to attain ZPG at a particular time in the future, recognizing that the size of the population then will be substantially larger than it is today. Given the United States' present built-in momentum for population growth, the lowest realistic goal to aim for at this time is a constant sized population of about 300 million to be reached within the next fifty to one hundred years (Bouvier, 1981). This goal would then determine the combinations of fertility and net immigration levels that would be necessary to achieve ZPG by that time. (These combinations would also be based on the usual mortality assumption that life expectancy will continue its gradual increase over the period.)

Obviously, under this policy, the levels of fertility and net immigration would be inversely related—the higher the level of fertility, the lower the level of net immigration, and vice versa. The levels of fertility and net immigration would have to be monitored throughout the transition period to make sure they did not collectively exceed or fall short of the intermediate growth goals. If they threatened to do so, then fertility and/or net immigration levels would be raised or lowered.

Unregulated Growth Policy The unregulated growth policy simply favors a continuation of the present system in which the government does not try to influence the fertility level, and in which immigration policy is not necessarily subordinated to an overall population growth policy. The unregulated growth policy recognizes that there is at least a chance that the United States will attain ZPG in the future without a formal overall growth policy. This is because United States fertility may resume its long-term decline, and net immigration may be reduced anyway due to a variety of reasons not necessarily, or at least not primarily, related to the attainment of ZPG at some time in the future.

Policies into Practice

Regulated Growth Policies This policy would work by permitting the birthrate to seek its own level as long as it did not exceed 2.1. If it settled at 2.1, than there would be no net immigration allowed. If the birthrate rose above 2.1, then programs would be introduced to lower it. If it fell below 2.1, then net immigration would be permitted to fill in the gap between the actual birthrate and 2.1. Or programs to encourage individuals to have more children could be introduced in place of, or in tandem with, increases in net immigration. Thus, this policy would regulate fertility and/or net immigration depending upon the circumstances prevailing at any given time during the transition to ZPG.

A likely future scenario is that the birthrate will hover between 1.7 and 2.1. If this does occur, the government could pursue its ZPG goal by manipulating its legal immigration quotas to make up the deficit in the number of births. This is certainly technically feasible, because the United States has manipulated quotas in the past. Indeed, the concept of adjusting legal immigration to suit our national interests—demographic or otherwise—already exists in our immigration law.

It is also possible to severely curtail the flow of illegal immigration. Illegal aliens cannot be prevented from entering the country at remote border points, but much of the incentive to do so is eliminated if there are no jobs. One effective regulatory measure would be to hold employers strictly accountable for hiring "undocumented" workers. Recent immigration bills before Congress have included this approach. Another measure that would probably work is the adoption of a counterfeit-resistant worker identification card, a tactic most Americans now favor.

While it is possible to regulate net immigration, the process would not be problem-free, especially if it led to substantial cuts in customary levels of legal and even illegal immigration.

There are several reasons for this. One is that a severe curtailment of immigration would violate the humanitarian pro-immigration values of many Americans. These values are symbolized by the oft-quoted inscription on the Statue of Liberty, and are particularly common among immigrants and the descendants of recent immigrants. However, most Americans are discontent with current immigration levels and favor reducing immigration of all kinds. So there are bound to be value conflicts. As with most policies, immigration policy will probably be determined ultimately by the values of the most powerful interest groups; and in this case, those groups are not opposed to substantial immigration cuts. Another social segment which would be against curbing immigration is the businesspeople who presently find it profitable to hire immigrants.

Finally, any major action by the United States to curb immigration will impose hardships and inconvenience on the principal countries from which the immigrants come. Since most of these source countries are neighbors of the United States, Mexico being by far the largest source, any severe adverse effects on them would have negative repercussions on United States foreign policy interests in the western hemisphere.

However, it must be remembered that immigration would be only terminated when the birthrate is 2.1 or greater. Much of the time the birthrate may be below this, and at those times large numbers of legal immigrants could be admitted. A birthrate of 1.8, for instance, would leave room for about 500,000 immigrants per year.

To this point, the discussion has focused on the practical problems of implementing an immigration cut when fertility is relatively high. But there are also practical problems involved in expanding immigration when fertility is relatively low. As Westoff (1978a:57) notes:

Immigrants...arrive in various colors and nationalities and speaking different languages. Any country with substantial immigration seems sooner or later to experience problems, arising from differences in language, customs, religion or race, that tend to offset many of the economic and long-term cultural advantages.

As we discussed, the United States has experienced many of these problems, and they may be sufficient to keep the public from accepting a high level of immigration as a means of attaining ZPG. It is especially noteworthy that none of the European nations presently at or below ZPG have yet opted for immigration to increase their growth rate. They have all chosen to try to boost the birthrate instead. The United States public might prefer this path also.

The European nations noted above are trying many ways to encourage couples to have more children, including interest-free credit of 10,000 dollars excused entirely on the birth of the third child; reduction of a mother's workweek, but not her pay; preference in housing; child bonuses; paid maternity and paternity leave; supplementary income for working mothers; child, marriage, and housing allowances; free maternity and child health services; free day-care centers and school lunches; and guaranteed job security for women workers who marry and become pregnant. In Sweden, despite many of these programs, the birthrate for citizens fell below replacement in the 1970s, and deaths have exceeded births since 1975. These programs have been more successful in eastern Europe, however, where there has also been a tightening of abortion laws, a powerful pro-natalist tactic.

So, the results have been mixed, leaving most sociologists convinced that most governments will be forced either to raise the financial ante substantially and/or wipe out legal and illegal induced abortion. The force of the latter tactic cannot be underestimated, for some societies presently have more induced abortions than births. It is estimated that the Soviet Union, for instance, has had years when abortions have outnumbered live births by 4 to 1. Thus, while it is apparently practical to boost the birthrate, there are heavy costs and value trade-offs involved. However, if the time should come that the United States wants to increase its birthrate, by then European countries will have worked out the most cost-effective formula and the United States can profit from their experience (McFalls, 1981).

Finally, if the birthrate exceeds 2.1, there are three basic methods that can be used to reduce it. One is family planning, which includes programs to teach birth control and to provide contraceptive services. These programs could be targeted mainly at those age groups or cultural subgroups which have especially high fertility. While these programs are practical and often effective, sometimes they face opposition from religious, racial, and other groups who fear they are either a form of genocide or a plot to decrease their share of the population.

The second method of reducing the birthrate is the use of financial and other incentives to encourage people to voluntarily limit their fertility. These incentives are often just the reverse of those used to boost fertility. For instance, China's ZPG-oriented program to bring down the birthrate is based on a system of rewards and penalties designed to encourage couples to have only one child (see Chapter 13). These incentives work fairly well. Incentives would probably also work in the United States, but like those aimed at boosting fertility, they would be very costly and would involve many value trade-offs.

The third method of reducing fertility is outright coercion of parents to limit their family size. This method simply would not work in the United States, because it would clash with many of our values, especially those related to freedom.

Unregulated Growth Policy This policy's chances of success hinge in part on the continuation of the present trends which depress fertility. If these forces remain at their current strength, the birthrate could hold at its present 1.8 level. If they increase in number and intensity, a not unlikely possibility, then the birthrate could fall even lower. Such low birthrates would make ZPG possible, provided immigration just happened to be at the right level.

One problem with this policy is that we cannot be confident that the birth rate will remain at or below current levels. Despite the prevailing forces, baby booms are still possible and so is a return to a long-term fertility level in the 2.2 to 2.6 range. In fact, factors which boost fertility may gain ascendancy over the fertility depressing factors from time to time or for long periods without a fertility control program to suppress them. These fertility enhancing factors include the United States' ideological addiction to growth per se; the deliberate and inadvertent pro-natalist influences of our social institutions, (e.g., tax deductions for children); the failure of our society to bring minorities and the poor rapidly into the mainstream of American life, thus postponing their adoption of small-family goals; and the fear of negative growth. This last factor is an important one. The historical record shows that many nations get cold feet as they approach ZPG (and negative growth) due to anxieties over national prosperity, security, virility, and "race suicide." Without a formal ZPG policy, a return to substantial positive growth could result.

The second problem with the unregulated policy is that there is no synchronization of fertility and immigration in either the short or the long run. Immigration reform bills in the early 1980s set a somewhat arbitrary quota of 425,000 immigrants per year. Assuming that illegal immigration is sharply curtailed, this quota would yield ZPG in the long run *only* if fertility averages about 1.8. But this is far from certain or even likely, and so are the chances that the United States will just "happen on" ZPG.

Thus, the unregulated growth policy is simply not practical in the real world. It is too much to expect that fertility and immigration will stabilize at exactly those rates which would yield ZPG. Nevertheless, the reason this policy might have substantial support is that it is more in keeping with traditional American values like personal freedom and autonomy. Many Americans would find a regulated policy unsettling. It would conjure up images in their minds of Uncle Sam in their bedrooms.

Evaluating the Evidence

In this section we will confine ourselves to remarks concerning possible broad social changes which might bear on the future functioning of these policies. In looking into the future, we must keep uppermost in our minds that the world of the next hundred years will be immensely different from that of the last hundred years (Population Reference Bureau, 1982). Political and economic turmoil in Third World nations, due in part to their population explosions and the pressures of development, will almost certainly swell the numbers of refugees and immigrants seeking a new home. Our decisions about how to manage our own population size in light of our prevailing fertility rate and the possibly large numbers of immigrants and refugees seeking entry into the United States will not be made in a vacuum, considering only the interests of the United States.

The increasing economic interdependence of the world economy could radically affect our population policies. An overpopulated nation with a precious resource could demand that the United States admit part of its population overflow. And the expansion of nuclear capability of more and more countries, some of whom are already overpopulated, introduces the threat of nuclear blackmail for space on this planet. Even in the absence of such economic and military tyranny, the world is changing such that more and more countries will make their presence felt in international relations and will have the power to influence our population policies. The time has passed when the United States could make demographic and other decisions independently and unilaterally, relying on the cover of geographic isolation and a robust economic system.

SUMMARY

1 The size, composition, and distribution of a population and the forces which determine their characteristics—fertility, mortality, and migration—are powerful causes of or contributors to many social problems.

2 In addition to the problem of too much or too little population growth in the long term, society must deal with problems associated with short-term fluctuations in the sizes of generations.

3 Life expectancy has almost doubled in the United States over the last century, due largely to the control of infectious diseases responsible for early death. However, life expectancy still varies sharply by social class, race, sex and age.

4 Americans are a highly mobile population.

Although there are benefits to be derived from this mobility, there are considerable costs, too, in both the places of origin and destination.

5 Immigration causes or contributes to many problems. Subjective concern about these problems varies enormously over time. Many of these problems are often exaggerated, and they create many policy dilemmas.

6 The racial and ethnic composition of the United States will be radically different in the future because of differences between blacks, whites, and Hispanics in their rates of growth.

7 Positive and negative population growth pose a variety of problems. To achieve ZPG in the future, the United States must keep fertility low and curb immigration.

8 Two long-term policies may lead the United States to zero population growth. One policy would regulate the levels of fertility and immigration so that together they would equal the number necessary for ZPG. The other policy would simply rely on the hope that the United States would arrive and remain at ZPG automatically without government regulations.

CHAPTER 8

Poverty: The Other Side of Affluence

Throughout my childhood, the private ownership of anything seemed to me a crude artificiality....For instance, we were keen for our favorite sleds, but it never occurred to me that I could possess a sled to the exclusion of the other boys.

—Pierrepont Noyes,
My Father's House: An Oneida Boyhood

Like most people, sociologists are trying to understand what is happening in their lives. Unlike most people, making sense of everyday social living is also our business. The professional as well as personal compulsion to figure out what is really going on explains the enormous attention that has been paid to society's inequalities by sociologists. Issues of who gets what and how they get it are a major—perhaps *the* major—concern of the discipline. A computerized literature review conducted by the authors uncovered over 2300 books on social inequality published in the last fifteen years. The number of professional articles written by sociologists on this topic would make a small mountain.

What have we learned from such a mass of theory and research? While the specific lessons fill this chapter, one general sociological truth should be stated here: The inequality in our everyday lives is *socially structured*. Given the power they have over us, it is natural to think of such things as banks, colleges, and corporations as omnipotent organizations that dispense rewards to individuals according to inhuman laws. This is a mistake. Despite its size and grandeur, the whole edifice of the American class system is a human social pattern, a structure designed and maintained by the individuals who live inside it.

To highlight the act of social creation, consider the quotation above. It comes from a personal account of life in the Oneida community, a utopian group that invented a system of distributing and valuing goods nothing like ours. Oneida males did not have exclusive sexual rights to a female (i.e., no husband-wife monogamy), because that would have implied property ownership. The fact that the Oneida abolition of private property is so outlandishly different from the system we are used to makes it clear they collectively invented their own class system. So it is with us. Inequality in the United States is a human order, a set of man-made rules for dividing up the goodies. That the

rules are often taken for granted does not change the fact that they are an invention of, by, and, presumably, for the people.

This sociological insight provides a unique and powerful vantage point for viewing everyday inequality. Accounts of fortune or misfortune are no longer to be seen only as matters of personal luck or effort. Individual inequality is controlled by an organized social pattern, a structure which sorts out those who get to eat cake from those who do not.

Among those going without cake (or, for that matter, bread) are the poor. Poverty is the most problematic aspect of the structure of inequality. Given its linkage to so many problems throughout this book, one can even make the case that it is *the* American social problem. In advance of the objective details about poverty, however, we would call your attention to the title of this chapter. Its implication is that the poor, the rich—and the middle class—are all part of the same system of social inequality.

OBJECTIVE DIMENSIONS OF INCOME INEQUALITY

Poverty amid Affluence

Riches are all around us. A walk down any main street may reveal luxury cars, palatial buildings, lavish jewelry—all features of our social landscape which we see without surprise. It can be surprising, however, to see such material bounty in its sociological light. A first ray of illumination concerns the degree of riches owned by the very rich. Consider the staggering fact that at least a dozen individuals in the United States each have a total worth topping 1 billion dollars, an amount which translates to an income of 3 million a day for nearly a year! Several of the very richest families in this country control fortunes greater than the gross national product of the *country* of Nepal (U.S. Bureau of the Census, 1980a). *Forbes* magazine's most recent listing of the 400 richest people in America (1985) included no one possessing less than 150 million dollars. Even that paltry sum is enough to pay well over 8 million American workers their average annual salaries!

Lottery winners to the contrary, these enormous rewards of personal wealth are rarely produced by a haphazard process of striking it rich. Some of the most potent forces for getting and keeping megabucks involve well-researched social structures. The most reliable path to the end of the rainbow is inheritance, which travels along the interpersonal bonds of kinship to deposit "about half of the great American fortunes" (Wilensky, 1978:93–94). Study after study has documented the operation of interlocking directorates, networks of relations tying together a tiny elite of executives and allowing them to pull the strings in the corporate structure of the United States (see Mintz and Schwartz, 1981).

Poverty amid affluence: Slum demolition in the shadow of opulent skyscrapers (Detroit). (*McDonald/The Picture Cube*).

Despite the well-known reluctance of the rich to open their private lives (or bankbooks) to public scrutiny, sociological research has painted a fascinating picture of the social habits of the very rich. Outside their business offices, the economic elite seclude themselves—together—in an exclusive handful of schools, clubs, and political organizations. This circle-the-wagons style of association is an informal device drawing the very rich closer as a class; not incidentally, it also promotes the accumulation of riches and the exercise of societal influence by the "inner circle" (Domhoff, 1970; Baltzell, 1964). Clearly, the Midas touch involves social contact.

How rich is rich? The definition of the wealthy—like the definition of the poor—ultimately depends on social standards. Nevertheless, the top 1 percent can be used as a cutoff point to estimate how much of society's wealth is appropriated by the truly wealthy. Using the term *wealth* in its technical sense, which excludes earnings from employment, the richest percentile of Americans owns over 40 percent of all stocks and bonds and over 80 percent of all trust fund moneys (U.S. Bureau of the Census, 1984*b*). This high concentration of wealth, by the way, was actually higher at the time Thomas Jefferson declared that "all men are created equal" (Williamson and Lindert, 1980).

Such statistics about the superrich are interesting, but you may be wondering what they have to do with a social problem. Consider the use of wealth percentages. In relative terms, they tell the size of the slice going to the affluent few. Since the cake can only be so big, the huge piece going to the rich means that many of the nonrich can get only crumbs. As the twin stories in the box below suggest, the excessive luxury at the top has its mirror image in wretched deprivation at the bottom.

The essential point is that rich and poor alike are parts of the same income system. While the popular culture enthralls us with get-rich-quick (or get-poor-quick) stories of individuals, an underlying social pattern is steadily separating the "successes" from the "failures." The reality of this social system is apparent in Table 8-1, which includes nonwealth income such as earnings from employment and transfer payments (e.g., welfare), but excludes income from stocks, bonds, etc. (which are even more concentrated at the top). Income recipients are sorted into fifths, with the best-paid 20 percent in the top row, the next-best-paid 20 percent in the second row, and so forth.

Obviously, in a system of perfectly equal income distribution (of which we have no actual example), each one-fifth of all households would get one-fifth of all available income. The numbers in the columns of the table show how far the United States deviates from the equality ideal. Note that in 1964, the highest fifth of the income distribution received over twice its proportionate share (41.2 versus 20 percent). At the other end of the system, the bottom fifth got only 5.1 percent of total moneys, about one-quarter of what they would have received in an equal distribution. All men may be created equal, but in 1964 in the United States, people were being paid very unequally.

In the ensuing decade, there were major changes in the American economy. Notably,

the gross national product doubled in size. This meant twice as large a cake to be sliced among the quintiles of the population. Even more pointed, there was a political assault launched against the income inequality shown in the first column of Table 8-1. In March of 1964, Lyndon Johnson declared his so-called War on Poverty, which involved redistribution of income shares from the top to the lower fifths. The effects of these changes are numerically summarized in the 1974 column, and can be verbally summarized in three words: almost nothing happened.

Although the dollar amounts received by each fifth did increase, *in no case did their relative shares change by as much as 1 percent!* About the same occurred in the 1974–1984 period, during which the poorest quintile actually lost a few tenths of a percent. The durability of this income ledger is quite amazing. Despite the growth of the economy, massive shifts in the labor force, and even billion-dollar federal programs to change it, the pattern of income distribution continues to deliver precisely the same portion of cake to each segment of the population. Who can doubt that the authors' present and your future salaries are all part of a larger social system?

Two concluding points should be made about this system of ironclad inequality. The first is

TABLE 8-1   THE DISTRIBUTION OF INCOME IN THE UNITED STATES

Income quintile	Percent distribution of family income*		
	1964	1974	1984
Highest fifth	41.2	41.0	42.7
Fourth fifth	24.0	24.1	24.4
Middle fifth	17.7	17.6	17.1
Second fifth	12.0	12.0	11.1
Poorest fifth	5.1	5.4	4.7

* Income includes earnings from employment and transfer payments (such as Social Security and welfare) but excludes wealth (such as stocks and bonds).

Sources: Adapted from United States Bureau of the Census, "Money Income of Households, Families, and Persons in the United States: 1980," *Current Population Reports,* Series P-60, No. 132, Washington, D.C., U.S. Government Printing Office, July 1982, p. 58; and *Current Population Reports,* Series P-60, No. 149, Washington, D.C., U.S. Government Printing Office, March 1985.

that it is incompatible with the "trickle down" theory of income redistribution. According to this popular notion, prosperity and profits dropping into the laps of those at the top of the income structure will overflow, gradually redistributing riches to the classes below. Table 8-1 shows virtually no downward trickle at all over a twenty-year period, merely a maintenance of each segment's relative share (although absolute dollar amounts in each segment did rise). A second key point about the income structure is its universal relevance to all of the people. Inequality is a problem not only for the unfortunate lowest fifth or for people living below the poverty line. Income shares affect everybody, a fact presently felt in your ability (or inability) to afford college tuition, and a fact which will make itself felt in your postgraduation living plans.

Only a relatively small minority of the American population can afford to buy a typical new house (average price in 1985: over 100,000 dollars). Moreover, the affordability gap—the difference between home prices and what a typical family can afford—has been rising steadily since 1960. This disturbing trend means that only the fortunate few can expect to realize an American dream of the many: owning a family home. Residential patterns are also revealing in the glaring contrasts between families from the top and bottom rungs of the income ladder, who may face each other within the same community (see Box 8-1). Housing is only one of a multitude of ways in which the social structure of income inequality touches each individual in each category of Table 8-1.

Types of Social Rewards

Inequality is a fact of everyone's life. Even among your peers, differences in looks, intelligence, sense of humor, and myriad other personal traits are self-evident. Such individual inequalities can cause some envy, but are not necessarily problematic in themselves. Whatever our personal differences, it is extremely hard for most people to swallow the fact that not all people are *treated* equally by society. One major dimension of unequal treatment is the process for allocating social rewards.

Think of society as a raffle. On the one hand, there is a mass of individuals with a stake in the outcome; on the other hand, there is a pile of prizes to be somehow awarded to those with tickets. The rules of the raffle determine which people get which prizes. This analogy is useful in highlighting the distributional problem facing any society, a problem "solved" in the United States by a system of concrete rules. The raffle comparison is also instructive in that the individual does not really matter: what counts is the number on the ticket.

Similarly, societies do not reward persons, they reward the social positions that persons occupy (Wright and Perrone, 1977). A prince will live in the lap of luxury regardless of who wears the crown at the moment; a pauper sweeping out the palace will get measly rewards even if he is an ex-prince. In a real sense, all of these social positions (known as *statuses*) are stamped with numbers telling how big a winner the individual who holds them will be. But the analogy between society and the unequal rewards of a raffle is misleading in a major sense. While society's rules for dividing up the prizes may seem capricious to the losers, they are not based on the randomness of a raffle. Social rewards are allocated in a consistent, predictable, almost monotonous way.

The phrase has not yet been defined, but *social rewards* undoubtedly suggests one thing to you: money. As the previous section amply demonstrated, income disparities are indeed an important dimension of inequality in the United States. But money is by no means the only prize systematically distributed to individuals. An illuminating insight into the reward patterns of modern societies came with Max Weber's classic distinction of prestige and power as logically separate from income. Although it may seem natural that a rich person be prestigious, these

BOX 8-1

THE OPPOSITE ENDS OF THE EARTH

Philadelphia, like any city, is many things to people, but nowhere is it so different as in two specific areas about seven miles—yet light years—apart. The two cities within a city are census tracts, groupings of many blocks drawn by the U.S. Census Bureau for comparisons from decade to decade. The two tracts...have a few common aspects: both have potholes, neither has a supermarket, and both are almost wholly residential. Tract 132 is the rock-bottom poorest census tract in the city. The median family income there, $4,359, was the lowest in the city. Tract 229 is among the most serene and idyllic spots in any American city. As in the 1970 and 1960 censuses, median family income reported in the 1980 census for Tract 229 was Philadelphia's highest, $75,001.

There are not just a few wealthy families or a few poor families in these tracts, however. There are many wealthy families in one, many poor families in the other. The two tracts are united only by Philadelphia and the dollar—the abundance or the lack of it. From behind the doors of the old red-brick row houses and subsidized projects in West Poplar, from behind the portals of the mansions in Chestnut Hill, additional census data provide a textbook portrait of wealth and poverty, or, as one city official put it, "the opposite ends of the earth." The data show that:

- The richest tract in Philadelphia was a large area with only 87 families, and 1980 figures show that among them, only three were headed by females.
- The poorest tract in Philadelphia was a smaller area

with 1,087 families. More than half were headed by females when the census was taken. And women generally make less money than men in the United States.

- The richest tract in Philadelphia had homes worth a median of $196,400 when the census was taken. Owner-occupied homes in the poorest tract were worth a median of $9,900—$186,500 less than in the Chestnut Hill neighborhood.
- In the richest tract, about 22 percent of the residents were under 20. A little more than 48 percent of the residents in the poorest tract were under 20, and most were black. As a group, blacks under age 20 suffer the worst unemployment in the current national economy.
- Only 8 percent of all structures in the richest tract in Philadelphia contained more than one household. More than 72 percent of all buildings in the poorest tract were apartments or rooms to let.
- Census statisticians found it simple to tabulate figures for the percentage of overcrowded homes (there is a federally defined formula for overcrowding), of homes lacking complete plumbing and of vacant and boarded structures in the richest tract in Philadelphia. For each category, the number was zero. In the poorest tract, 15.2 percent of all households were found to be overcrowded; almost 4 percent lacked complete plumbing, and more than 16 percent were vacant and boarded.

Source: The Philadelphia Inquirer, Dec. 27, 1983.

---

are, in fact, two different prizes in the reward system.

Prestige is highly valued in its own right, a kind of social honor that "stands in sharp opposition to the pretensions of sheer property" (Weber in Gerth and Mills, 1958:187–188). Weber illustrates the point through his observations in this country of would-be gentlemen buying houses on certain streets and wearing certain clothes because they hope to be invited to "society" parties. These social climbers already have high income rewards and are

eagerly seeking higher levels of prestige. Power also is a highly valued reward often mistakenly equated with income. While the rich may be quite powerful, money is not the only source of social control. A big-city mayor, for example, may hold an enormous amount of clout over business executives earning many times the politician's salary. Like income, prestige and power attach to one's social position. If the college president is coming to your house for dinner, that status carries an aura of prestige and power that will fill your family with anticipation regardless of what the person in the status is really like.

As the above examples suggest, a concrete way to compare and contrast the various types of social rewards is to look at specific occupations. Table 8-2 presents a list selected from the approximately 29,000 separate job titles defined by the U.S. Bureau of the Census. Note that each occupational role has a separate rank (in relation to the others on the list) for income and prestige. Whereas income figures are available from the census, how can one derive a score for something as intangible as prestige? The ranks in the right-hand column of Table 8-2 come from cross-sectional surveys of the American public in which people are asked to indicate their level of respect for each job. These studies (and there have been dozens of them) are thus based on subjective opinion, but they are startlingly stable. People across the whole spectrum of occupations have an almost perfect consensus about just how much social honor each job deserves. Moreover, this common prestige rating has remained virtually

unchanged since 1925 (Vanfossen, 1977) and is firmly entrenched in the heads of most students by the time they reach high school (Treiman, 1979).

A glance across the row for each occupation reveals two things. First, the reward ratings are not identical. Insurance agents receive a much higher income than prestige rank. The college professor teaching your course reverses this situation, with relatively higher prestige than income. Differences in occupational rank across the columns prove Weber's point about the differentiation of social rewards. A second point is proved by the general consistency of reward ranks. While all occupations do not receive the uniform treatment of physicians (highest income, highest prestige) or shoeshiners (lowest income, lowest prestige), the over-all reward pattern is a remarkably close match in the amount of income and prestige received. Exceptions such as pimps and professors (see Figure 8-1) prove the general rule of similarity in social reward, a phenomenon neo-Weberians call "status crystallization."[1]

TABLE 8-2 REWARD RANKINGS OF ASSORTED JOBS

Occupational category	Social rewards	
	Income	Prestige
Physician	1	1
Engineer	2	3
Professor	3	2
Insurance agent	4	7
Accountant	5	4
Undertaker	6	5
Electrician	7	6
Construction worker	8	9
Cashier	9	8
Food service worker	10	11
Farm laborer	11	10
Shoeshiner	12	12

Sources: Donald J. Treiman, *Occupational Prestige in Comparative Perspective*, New York, Academic Press, 1977, pp. 318–329; United States Bureau of the Census, "Earnings by Occupation and Education," *1980 Census of Population*, PC 80-2-8B, Washington, D.C., Government Printing Office, 1984; U.S. Bureau of Labor Statistics, *Occupational Outlook Handbook: 1982–83*, Washington, D.C., U.S. Government Printing Office, April 1982.

Stratification and Mobility

The sociological spotlight so far has been on how individuals are treated within society. This perspective has allowed us to observe not just that people are rewarded unequally but that the inequality tends to be mysteriously matched across the several types of social reward defined by Weber. Researchers have compounded the mystery by showing that one's social rank is suspiciously the same in terms of education, reputation, parent's occupation, property rights—the list is seemingly endless (Matras, 1980). Consider the enormity of the coincidence! In a society of at least 240 million individuals, most of us have a ticket with the same number for *all* of these different prizes.

[1] This term has been popularized by Gerhard Lenski, "Status Crystallization: A Non-vertical Dimension of Social Status," *American Sociological Review*, 27, 1962:469–480.

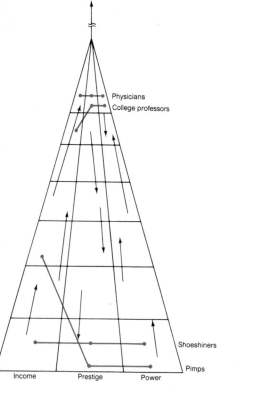

FIGURE 8-1   Social stratification and mobility in the United States.

How is this possible when there is no supreme agency evaluating individuals and doling out the goods? In Weber's terms, how does status get "crystallized"?

The answer lies in the framework known as social structure. A simple way to introduce this idea involves an everyday phrase: the ladder of success. The conventional wisdom holds that each higher rung stashes more and more of the makings of the good life. Sociologists have shown not only that this popular notion is true for many measures of life quality, but also that the ladder itself is a social pattern. The rungs on which individuals perch are commonly called *social classes,* and there are various theories

for how they are forged. Some have argued that prestige is the primary material of the class system, while income, power, and the other perks are secondary (Warner, 1949). Others contend that "differences in power engender differences in privilege (i.e., income); and differences in power and privilege create differences in prestige" (Treiman, 1977:223).

Many contemporary investigations provide support for Karl Marx's famous dictum that "political power...is merely the organized power of one class for oppressing another." The latter view, in short, is that the rungs of the ladder are first cast from economic control, and then the other social rewards are welded on (see Wright, 1979). Whatever the formula for alloying the various elements of the class system, it is clear that they have hardened into a solid social structure.

In addition to the issue of how individuals get similar social rewards within a class level, it is also important to consider the vertical dimension of the success ladder. The crystallized pattern of each class is related to the others in a very orderly way: they are piled atop one another. To help visualize this multidimensional, hierarchical structure, look at the simplified diagram in Figure 8-1. Note first the three tracks representing Weber's reward types of income, prestige, and power. Individuals will tend to be at the same level in each column, as is indicated by the more typical straight lines (representing crystallized status) connecting the dots for some occupations. Imagine that such lines were drawn for every one of us in the United States. What would emerge is an aggregation of people (a concentration of lines) *within* each of the vertical rungs. Note also how the shape of the diagram roughly approximates the number of Americans at a given reward level. The point at the top signifies a tiny elite; the flare in the middle, a relatively large middle class; and the broad base, a sizable class of persons lacking not only income but also prestige and power.

Structured inequality such as that pictured here is often called *social stratification*. The term is borrowed from geologic descriptions of the earth's crust divided into separate layers, or strata. The analogy is apt because of the commonality of this kind of layering in human societies. An extreme example is the caste system of India, in which one's social rank is strictly fixed at the level of one's parents. The differences in status are so great that merely being brushed by the shadow of a low-caste "untouchable" is enough to defile a high-caste person. This most hierarchical of systems is even religiously legitimated, in that attempts to escape from one's assigned caste duties are believed to lead to incarnation into a lower level of the social order in the next life. Obviously, there are dramatic differences between the stratification systems of India and the United States, but the very existence of strata here raises a serious question of values. Can the structured hierarchy in Figure 8-1 be reconciled with the solemn phrase "all men are created equal"?

The answer to this question depends on just what is meant by equality. Our situation portrayed in Figure 8-1 is called *inequality of condition* because, quite simply, reward conditions are unequal: those at the top are getting more of the good life than those below. Another dimension of the diagram—and of the meaning of equality—is suggested by the arrows penetrating its levels. They represent the potential for movement of individuals up and down the success ladder; the more restricted that movement, the greater the *inequality of opportunity*.[2] While extreme inequality of condition may be viewed as a social problem per se, American values seem to find the second kind of inequal-

ity more problematic. We judge our system of social stratification more by whether it rewards merit than by the merit of its rewards: "The American equalitarian ethic is in one sense an inequalitarian ethic, because it values the opportunity to become unequal" (Vanfossen, 1979:210).

Redefining the issue in this way by no means abolishes the social problem implied in the Declaration of Independence. Instead, it transforms "all men are created equal" into an assertion of equitable chances for achievement. To see how well this stirring statement reflects reality, we must assess the process of upward and downward movement—known as social mobility—throughout our contemporary stratification system. The arrows in Figure 8-1 are among the most heavily studied phenomena in modern social science. The multitude of mobility studies, in fact, suggests the almost obsessive importance our culture places on success. In words that still ring true, French sociologist Alexis de Tocqueville characterized the need to succeed in America in 1840:

> It is strange to see with what feverish ardour the Americans pursue their own welfare....The desire of acquiring the comforts of the world haunts the imagination of the poor, and the dread of losing them that of the rich....At first sight there is something surprising in this strange unrest of so many happy men, uneasy in the midst of abundance. The spectacle is, however, as old as the world; the novelty is to see a whole people furnish an example of it. (Tocqueville, 1961: xxxvii–xxxviii).

One of the reasons for reading this book so carefully is your own burning desire to achieve good grades and then, in turn, a favored rung on the success ladder. Is that rung within your reach?

There have been many attempts to answer this surprisingly complex question. Perhaps the best-known study of mobility patterns is Blau and Duncan's *The American Occupational*

---

[2] The conceptual distinction between the two types of inequality does not deny the fact (to be discussed below) that unequal conditions bear heavily upon an individual's opportunity for advancement. Obviously, an individual raised in a slum has little access to premium schools or country clubs in which to make elite social contacts.

TABLE 8-3   OCCUPATIONAL MOBILITY IN THE UNITED STATES

	Son's occupation, percent								
Father's occupation	Profes-sionals	Managers	Clerical and sales workers	Artisans	Operatives	Service workers	Laborers	Farmers and farm managers	Total
Professionals	15.3	5.2	6.5	2.0	2.7	2.7	1.4	1.0	4.7
Managers	19.8	24.7	16.2	7.9	5.4	5.4	3.4	2.0	11.6
Clerical and sales workers	13.5	11.1	12.2	5.1	3.9	6.2	2.9	1.5	7.4
Artisans	18.7	18.8	19.6	26.1	17.3	17.4	13.6	2.8	18.5
Operatives	14.0	11.6	14.5	17.7	21.4	16.7	17.8	3.7	15.5
Service workers	3.7	4.2	6.2	4.8	5.4	9.7	4.6	0.8	4.7
Laborers	3.0	3.2	6.4	7.1	9.2	10.8	14.1	2.0	6.5
Farmers and farm managers	12.0	21.2	18.4	29.3	34.7	31.1	42.2	86.2	31.1
Total (%)	100.0	100.0	100.0	100.0	100.0	100.0	100.0	100.0	100.0
Total (number in thousands)	4,370	5,517	4,000	7,067	6,331	1,857	2,220	2,622	33,972

Source: Peter M. Blau and O. Dudley Duncan, The American Occupational Structure, New York, Wiley, 1967.

Structure (1967), from which we have excerpted the key findings in Table 8-3. Each column corresponds to one occupational level of sons, and the percentages represent those in each column whose fathers were at a given occupational level on the left.[3] About 25 percent of the managers in column 2, for example, also had manager fathers, whereas only about 3 of every 100 in the managerial class had fathers who were laborers. A stratification system with no mobility opportunities would have all sons working at their fathers' occupational levels, which would produce a table with 100 percent of the sons along the main diagonal (the line stretching from the upper left to the lower right).

Table 8-3 shows that America deviates considerably from this immobile extreme, but there are more subtle patterns underlying the degree of inequality of opportunity. For one thing, much of the intergenerational movement displayed in the table is a result of changes in the distribution of occupations. In the postwar period, there has been a marked contraction in the

number of low-status blue-collar and farming jobs and a corresponding expansion in white-collar jobs higher on the class ladder.

This is *structural mobility*, a phenomenon forming a certain amount of upward occupational movement due to the changing size of the rungs on the ladder.

While these structural changes highlight the reality of class as a living social structure, the likely object of your ambitions is *circulation mobility*. This is the usual meaning of opportunity: the possibility of climbing up—or being bumped down—the rungs of the ladder. A central issue in assessing the level of inequality of this kind of opportunity is finding a baseline, in other words, inequality compared to what? One intriguing basis of comparison is international studies of occupational mobility. Given the obvious difficulties of matching up whole societies (with different kinds of occupational ladders), comparisons must be rough, but they generally find the United States to have an opportunity structure about as open as those in most other advanced industrial societies (Szymanski, 1983; Tyree, Semyonov, and Moore, 1979). Another baseline for gauging equality of opportunity is the past. Studies quantifying

[3] For reasons that are made abundantly clear in Chapter 10 on sex roles, there have been precious few large-scale studies of the mobility patterns of American women.

circulation mobility in the United States have concluded that the rate of passage up and down the ladder has changed little, if at all, over the past fifty years (Vanfossen, 1979).

These data add useful depth to the numbers in Table 8-3 and to the drawing in Figure 8-1. In terms of the latter, the "arrows" penetrating America's social strata appear to permit at least as much opportunity for occupational mobility as in similar societies worldwide. Existing inequalities of opportunity, however, are not dissolving over time. Such statements provide an objective scorecard for equality within the whole social system, but they seem too distant to relate to the aspirations of any particular individual. There is still the question of which rung on the ladder you may reach and, more pointed, *how* you may go about reaching it.

Education, Status, and the American Dream

The reading habits of Americans reveal a passionate search for secrets of personal success. Dozens of get-rich-quick manuals were best-sellers in the 1800s, and they regularly appear on the nonfiction book lists today. Horatio Alger's stories of rags to riches mobility fired the national imagination and are still a reliable theme to make novelists rich. Despite this popular interest in distilling success secrets, our everyday behavior as a society betrays a deep-seated belief in a simple formula: To get a good job, get a good education. There is objective evidence supporting the subjective belief in education as an elevator up the success ladder. According to the most recent estimates of the U.S. Census Bureau, a person with a college degree has expected average lifetime earnings of 1,109,000 dollars compared to 861,000 dollars for high school graduates. Not surprisingly, these figures are paralleled for occupational status. Over two-thirds of all professional and technical workers have graduated from college, whereas 19 of every 20 laborers lack that diploma (Hacker, 1983). Even with these data and your parents' constant nagging to get good

grades, you know there is more to the success formula than completing school. Everyone has heard stories of uneducated millionaires and taxi drivers with Ph.D.s.

Over the past twenty years, American sociologists have conducted an intensive search for the solution to the success formula. *Status attainment* researchers have moved beyond the commonsensical education equals success equation to compute the relative contribution of numerous individual traits to individual accomplishment. One illustrative model of the process through which you will attain status is displayed in Figure 8-2. Following the top arrows, you can see that family background (one major element of which is parents' occupational level) first of all exerts a direct effect on the individual's educational level; years of schooling then affect one's placement on the occupational ladder. The lower arrow suggests that your parents may bear on your success not only by influencing your schooling but also by a direct influence of their occupational standing on yours.

For more detail about these arrows of the success formula, consider an overview of the status attainment literature analyzing eight national samples. Fleshing out the model in Figure 8-2 with additional individual traits—such as IQ, personal motivation, etc.—these researchers are able to predict about 50 percent of individual income (Jencks et al., 1979). The status attainment approach can thus account for

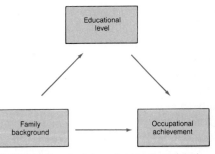

FIGURE 8-2 A status attainment model of individual achievement.

half of your future earnings, but where does the other 50 cents on the dollar come from? Is it luck?

A recent approach in sociological studies of achievement looks beyond the assumption that we succeed—or fail—alone. Instead of viewing you as a bundle of individual strengths and weaknesses about to scale the ladder, this approach starts with a seemingly obvious assumption: There are other people you know on the rungs. The individualism of the American dream blinds us to the social world within which we each "pull ourselves up by our own bootstraps." The *structural* approach corrects this oversight (Spilerman, 1977), and even offers you some practical tips for success. One study of the lower class found that males' occupational success can be predicted from the socioeconomic characteristics of their friends and nonparental relatives (Jones, 1979).

Analysis of mobility patterns within a broader sample of classes has shown that a major source of job information leading to upward movement is individual social contacts (Lin, Ensel, and Vaughn, 1981). This sociological "secret" is more complex than the cliché "It's who you know." The analysts also discovered that *weak ties*—i.e., relationships with acquaintances rather than strong ties with close friends or family members—are generally the most useful source of ladder-climbing information! Such findings support two clear implications. First, the structure of interpersonal relationships is a key coefficient in the success formula. The second implication follows from the first: when job seeking, contact *all* of your social contacts.

Let us be honest. Most people's interest in the subject does not concern objective achievement patterns, but rather individual success. Far less passion is sparked by thousands moving from blue-collar to white-collar occupations than by one individual who makes it to the very top of the heap. What is the formula for entering the elite, for attaining the pinnacle of Figure

8-1? The answer is surprisingly simple: Pick parents who are already there. The American Leadership Study drew a sample of 545 of the most elite position holders in United States society and determined that the overwhelming majority (85 percent) had fathers who had owned or managed businesses (Moore and Alba, 1982). More general studies of the occupational structure find the very top to be bounded by a barrier severely restricting mobility into or out of the elite (Featherman and Hauser, 1978:179). The best working estimate of Horatio Alger style upward movement is that about 3.4 percent of the children of manual occupation parents make it to the elite occupational level (Szymanski, 1983).

The unlikelihood of rags to riches mobility dramatizes a truth at the center of this maze of statistics on equality of opportunity. Clearly, the American dream is still just that. The class system does permit movement up and down the ladder, but mobility is not simply a matter of individual merit, skill, or chance. Achievement may be a race up the ladder, but we do not all start from the same rung.

THE SUBJECTIVE DIMENSION OF INEQUALITY

Learning to Live with Inequality

Undoubtedly, many of these details about your present and future rung on the class ladder are news to you. Despite a burning desire to "make it," most Americans know surprisingly little about the objective situation of inequality. As a first test of your IPO (inequality perception quotient) consider the cutoff points within Table 8-1. In order to reach the top quintile (20 percent), your family earnings must be about 40,000 dollars. If that figure does not seem unexpectedly low, how about estimating the percentile in the national income distribution if family earnings are 100,000 dollars? Answer: the top percentile; i.e., 99 percent of all families in America earn less than that seemingly moderate amount (U.S. Bureau of the Census, 1982*b*). These simple questions suggest the gap between the objective reality of the class system and our fuzzy subjective perception of it.

But the previous pages of this chapter should have closed a good deal of this perceptual gap. Given that you have just seen a sketch of actual reward inequities in the United States, *why aren't you angry?* To summarize the extent of objective inequality in a slightly different way than above, picture 1000 dollars of income as a child's block; if each American family piles up its blocks, the vast majority of us are within a yard of the ground, while some privileged families could look over the top of the Eiffel Tower.[4] Again, how can such published facts not trigger outrage, particularly if one adds the knowledge (as you now have) that we do not all have an equal chance for the pinnacle? Somehow, the American public has been reconciled to the incredibly rich looming above the moderately well-off and the desperately deprived.

The subjective acceptance of such dramatic inequities in the good life is especially peculiar since *egalitarianism* (the high value placed on equality) is such a well-known theme in American culture. To introduce an explanation of how such resignation is possible, consider the parallel problem in the USSR, a society culturally committed to the abolition of private property. Recent studies by Soviet sociologists document the existence of distinct classes which are unequally ranked by income, prestige, power, and many other concomitants of the Russian good life (such as separate living quarters). Clear class divisions are accepted by a society devoted to becoming classless because of the recognized need to reward highly educated personnel so that they can promote economic

development (Hahn, 1982). The social system of the United States is radically different from that of the USSR, but the problem is fundamentally the same: How can gross inequality be made palatable to a nation founded on a principle of equality?

As in the Soviet case where some communist ideals are sacrificed for growth, the answer begins with competing values. Americans prize equality, but we also hold dear the ideal of individual achievement. The latter value drastically alters the subjective perception of inequality. We have noted above the popular notion that people climb the ladder alone. Although the facts dispute this, the idea that individuals are responsible for their own success or failure is deeply ingrained. What follows is a composite of the attitudes toward achievement expressed by working-class people in an interview study:

> I see this man, who I know is no better than I, being treated better by others—even I treat him that way. Much as I know it isn't right, much as I rebel against his putting on airs and trying to act superior, there is a secret self-accusation implanted in me by my very belief in our basic equality. Even though we may have been born in different stations, the fact that he is getting more means that somehow he had the power in him, the character...to earn his superiority (Sennett and Cobb, 1973:255–256).

A high value placed on individual achievement conditions one to see society as a banquet in which those at the head tables get more and better food because they are harder-working, smarter—in short, better people. While this they-get-more-because-they-deserve-it view is understandably attractive to those getting more, the preceding quotation suggests that those getting less come to accept it as well. Recent research has confirmed this suggestion: Poorer Americans actually feel deserving of their deprived positions in a society they see as unequal but fair (Stolte, 1983).

---

[4] This architectural analogy was proposed by Paul A. Samuelson twenty years ago (*Economics*, New York, McGraw-Hill, 1964), and therefore could have the altitude adjusted upward for inflation.

A powerful image in the public mind is America as a *meritocracy,* a term characterizing a society which offers equal chances for unequal rewards based on merit.[5] Some have argued that the image is reality, that individuals achieve their wide disparities in reward due to wide disparities in talent, especially IQ (Herrnstein, 1980). Although we very much want to believe in such a meritocracy, statistical analyses controlling other factors have shown only modest effects of intelligence test scores on educational attainment, and relatively tiny effects on occupational success (Jencks et al., 1979). As the director of the Center for Educational Policy Research at Harvard has put it, "Being stupid is not what is responsible for being poor in America" (Cohen, 1974:134).

Despite these studies and the overwhelming sociological evidence that social class affects mobility (see above), public opinion opposes the restructuring of our achievement system to attain equality. In a New England survey, over three-fourths of the respondents disagreed (most of them strongly) with this statement: "It would be a good thing if Congress and the President decided to distribute all the money in the United States equally among all the population" (Bell and Robinson, 1978:249). While such a policy would be the most radical step toward our egalitarian ideals, the myth of the meritocracy makes much more moderate proposals similarly unpopular. A national poll proposed that "there should be a top limit on income so that no one can earn more than $100,000 a year" (Ladd, 1981). As you already know, this income cap would redistribute some moneys from only the top percentile to the other 99 percent of the population. Nevertheless, three-fourths of those polled rejected this limit on individual opportunity, including majorities in every occupational and educational group. Even respondents with the most to gain from any

income redistribution—those with annual incomes of 5000 dollars a year or less—opposed the income cap by nearly a 2 to 1 margin.

It is not that Americans do not care about equality; cross-cultural studies have documented the high value placed on egalitarianism in the United States compared to other nations (Bell and Robinson, 1978). Subjective acceptance of objective inequities is not simple apathy, but rather a result of caring deeply for other values such as individual achievement.

The Discovery of Poverty

Learning to accept one's own place in a social hierarchy is one facet of the subjective dimension of inequality. Another key—and related—issue is coming to accept the placements of other people, notably those at the lower rungs of the ladder. While the bounty of those at the top may be excused by the glory of their achievements, what is the alibi for the grinding misery at the bottom? How can a society with *trillions* of dollars and a genuine concern for equality sleep at night with the reality of poverty?

Although America subjectively awakened to the poverty problem in the 1960s, the poor have traditionally left the public's dreams untroubled. Around the beginning of this century, with immigrants literally pouring onto our shores, poverty tended to be viewed moralistically. Sociologist William Graham Sumner branded the poor as "the shiftless, the imprudent...the idle, the extravagant and the vicious" (1934:476). The Protestant work ethic of diligence and thrift sanctified the successful as God's favored ones and, by implication, vilified the unsuccessful as sinners. Contemporary attitudes toward the poor may be less religious, but they are no less judgmental:

> The average American is strongly of the opinion that, leaving the physically handicapped aside, there really is no reason for anyone in the lowest quintile of the income distribution to interpret his condition as permanent, since opportunities for "bettering one's condition" will and do exist (Kristol, 1984:197).

---

[5] For a fascinating fictional account of a society actually based on meritocratic principles, see Michael Young, *The Rise of the Meritocracy*, Baltimore, Penguin, 1958.

So what does it mean if an individual remains in that bottom quintile of Table 8-1? Since the opportunities for advancement are believed to be there for the taking, those who do not advance must be lazy or stupid or both (Vanfossen, 1979). Opinion polls have consistently reflected such negative stereotypes of the poor, with the public in effect viewing the deficiency of money as caused by a deficiency of character (Jones, 1984). The flip side of the value of individual achievement which praises the rich for their success is to blame the poor for their failure. This explains much about the traditionally low subjective concern about the poverty problem in the United States. It is natural to be untroubled by the poor if poverty is seen as their own fault.

Nevertheless, Americans suddenly opened their eyes to the shocking reality of poverty in the 1960s. An extensive study of opinion trends since the thirties found that the first year poverty was consistently identified by the public as a social problem was 1965 (Lauer, 1976). This outpouring of outrage was not the result of an abrupt increase in deprivation. Amazingly enough, the actual number of the poor had been *dropping* steadily since World War II, with a net 6 million people moving out of poverty between 1959 and 1965 (U.S. Bureau of the Census, 1982a). Poverty literally burst into the public's consciousness after a decade of objective improvement, attaining a level of subjective significance that this problem had not attained even during the Great Depression.[6] Why?

Begin with the *visibility* of the social problem. For large segments of the American population, the poor had been kept out of sight, and therefore out of mind. Sequestered in their rapidly growing suburbs, the middle class had little reason to see the poor in Appalachia or in the local slum. The mass exodus of poor blacks from the rural South to the metropolitan North continued through the 1950s, however, so that by the end of the decade a very large and very deprived population had been deposited on the doorstep of the nonpoor.

As it grew under the nose of the upper classes, the problem of deprivation in this subpopulation was gradually coming to national notice, but one factor really grabbed public attention: the riots. It is striking that the first appearance of poverty as a social problem in the polls (1965) came the year after the first major civil disorder by the black poor, namely the Harlem riot in July of 1964. Such violent outbursts are intrinsically dramatic events, particularly when mass media exposure runs to seemingly endless scenes of cities (sometimes one's own) in flames. Since the conventional wisdom was that material misery had driven the poor to rioting, the social problem of poverty quickly had Americans' full attention.

Additionally, more deep-seated cultural processes were at work. Remember that the objective and subjective dimensions are linked, and that people were generally aware of things going very well indeed for American society in the early sixties. An expanding economy with minimal inflation and unemployment meant not only the escape of millions from poverty, but also a rapidly rising general standard of living for the nonpoor majority. Consequently, those left in poverty were swimming along, with the ship of affluence pulling farther and farther away.[7] This objective situation was subjectively inflammatory both to those who had missed the boat and to those who had caught it. In a time when *expectations* about bettering

---

[6] Americans were, of course, greatly concerned about the causes and consequences of the Depression, but the polls show the subjective conceptualization of the problem to have been in terms of unemployment, not poverty (*Gallup Report,* March 1982).

[7] The described situation is not inconsistent with the stable income shares displayed in Table 8-1. Those in the bottom quintile were receiving about the same proportional piece of a bigger and bigger economic pie, thus supporting the movement of some above the poverty line.

one's economic fate ran high, individuals whose fate was continued poverty were in a state of "relative deprivation," feeling deprived relative to the prosperous persons they had expected to join.

This simmering sense of injustice made the previously accepted state of poverty newly problematic (Pettigrew, 1971). It is interesting to note that frustration flared into large-scale rioting in Watts, a section of Los Angeles which had been rated by the Urban League as the best city in the United States in its treatment of poor blacks (Banfield, 1974). There are historical parallels:

> It was precisely in those parts of France (before the Revolution) where there had been most improvements that popular discontent ran highest.... For the mere fact that certain abuses have been remedied draws attention to the others and they now appear more galling (de Tocqueville, 1955).

Due to the heightened expectations, many people at the bottom of our income ladder in the early 1960s were objectively doing better but subjectively feeling worse.

Violated expectations also heightened sensitivity to the plight of the poor among those on the ship of affluence. Reinforcing the general sense of societal progress created by recent economic and technological triumphs was the formal declaration of a War on Poverty in 1964. Just as President Kennedy had publicly challenged the nation to a (victorious) space race after the Russian launching of Sputnik, President Johnson likened poverty to another beachhead to be taken by American ingenuity and resources. The enormous public relations campaign launching the War on Poverty highlighted the visibility of the poor, and led the citizenry to expect that deprivation would shortly be wiped out. It is an oversimplification to say that the public was just "led," though, since changes in popular *values* formed part of the political base for the new policy.

We have discussed the complex balance in the American mind between achievement and equality, a balance that seems to have tipped toward the latter value before the debut of poverty in the public opinion polls. Many signs showed the rising evaluation of equality. Books such as John Kenneth Galbraith's *The Affluent Society* and Michael Harrington's *The Other America* stressed the paradox of poverty amid affluence, and were best-sellers in the early sixties. In 1963, "race relations" was at the top of the Gallup survey in response to the question: "What do you think is the most important problem facing this country today?" The following year the Civil Rights Act was passed, further evidence of rising public sentiment against societal inequities. Sociologist Herbert Gans of Harvard speaks of "The Equality Revolution" during this period:

> Someday, when future historians write the history of the 1960's, they may describe it as the decade when America rediscovered the poverty still in its midst and when social protest, ranging from demonstrations to violent uprisings, reappeared on the American scene. But these historians may also note a curious fact, that the social protestor had very little to do with poverty. Most of the demonstrators and marchers who followed Martin Luther King were not poor; the college students who protested and sat-in on campus were well-to-do.... The social protest that began in the 1960's has to do with *inequality* (Gans, 1973:7).

Clearly, a cultural ground swell in favor of equality turned the public—even many passengers on the ship of affluence—against poverty. The high visibility and expectations associated with the War on Poverty combined with the change in values to create the sudden antipoverty tidal wave in the opinion polls. As we will consider later in the discussion of social policy, the course of that War is now stirring new currents in our concern about this social problem.

UNDERSTANDING POVERTY

How Many Poor?

"The very poor are different from you and me."
"Yes, they have less money."[8]

What amount of money must one have to qualify as poor? The difficulties of defining deprivation in a society with billionaires and beggars are suggested by the following exercise. Assume for a moment that you are the head of the household in a nonfarm family of four (yourself, your spouse, and two children living in a metropolitan area). The task is to estimate the *absolute minimum income your family would require for each of the physical needs on the list.* Calculate the smallest monthly dollar total that would provide adequate nutrition, a livable apartment (with utilities), and enough clothes to keep your family warm:

Personal Poverty Budget (nonfarm family of four)

Food
Rent
Clothing   +   _____
                        Monthly total
Multiply x 12   _____
                        Annual total

Check the estimate against those of other students in your class who, hypothetically, have exactly the same family needs as you. Student to student variations in calculating the personal poverty budget indicate that identifying even the truly needy is a complex matter: "Poverty, like beauty, lies in the eye of the beholder...it is not something you can verify or demonstrate, except by inference and suggestion, even with a

[8] This is a paraphrase of a famous exchange between Ernest Hemingway and F. Scott Fitzgerald about the very rich.

measure of error. To say who is poor is to use all sorts of value judgments." These hedging comments were made by no less of an authority than Mollie Orshansky (1974:81), who drew up the first generally accepted federal poverty line. The FPL is often used as the upper boundary for *absolute poverty,* a state in which families cannot provide for even minimal physical necessities; we say "often used" because many experts believe that the current poverty line—about 10,000 dollars a year, calculated by updating Orshansky's formula—simply is not enough money to feed, house, and clothe four people. The original formula was based on the U.S. Department of Agriculture's economy food plan for temporary emergencies, which their own studies estimated could provide a nutritionally adequate diet for only about 10 percent of the population on a day-to-day basis (Orshansky, 1974).

Moreover, economic studies of purchasing power show that the poor actually pay *more* for the necessities of life—due to "ghetto gouging" by local merchants who overcharge those trapped in the slum (Caplovitz, 1979). Whether one accepts the assumptions of the formula or not, the FPL is surely a strict measure of real need.

So how many poor are there in America? Using the conservative FPL benchmark of absolute poverty for 1985, the answer is about 33 million people. One reason this is an approximation is that the IRS does not stand guard at the poverty line and hold families out for twelve months; millions dip into absolute poverty for part of the year, and many more hover just above it.

But accepting the 33 million figure as a rough estimate of the truly needy, let us now consider several objective facets of absolute poverty. There are more poor Americans than the combined *populations* of Denmark, Sweden, Finland, Norway, and Israel (Blumberg, 1980). In terms of our own population, 14 percent of all American citizens—about 3 out of every 20 men, women, and children on the street—are truly deprived. Although this issue will be discussed more fully in the policy section, it is germane in overviewing objective trends to note that absolute poverty has reversed its long-term decline. Between 1978 and 1983, about 10 million people were added to the ranks of the poor, contributing to the highest proportion of Americans below the poverty line since 1965! Given that deprivation is widespread and now spreading further, just how deeply deprived are these people? Government statistics show the poor are not just missing an occasional meal. The *average* family below the poverty line is over 3000 dollars a year short of the minimum they need to keep body and soul together.

Note that the personal poverty budget does not contain an entry for any of the basic comforts of American life. No church dona-tions, no car, no gift for sister's wedding—unless these "luxuries" come out of the grocery money. Would you be poor if you could not afford a telephone or a television? The problem is defining the standard below which you would see yourself as poor. For the Franciscan friars of the twelfth century, the lowest standard of living was prized: "Their glorification of poverty was boundless; every day they wooed anew their beloved [deprivation] with the full fervour of nuptial passion" (Simmel, 1978:254). On the other hand, a rock star who cannot afford at least one Mercedes may view himself as poor relative to his high-rolling friends. The point is that want is experienced relative to some socially defined standard. Between the atypical extremes of monks and musicians, what is a reasonable standard of *relative poverty* under which most

Eight of the millions of Americans caught in the low-visibility, high-deprivation state of rural poverty. (J. P. Laffont/Sygma)

Americans would feel comparatively deprived?

The answer is complicated by the fact that the living standards of the society do not hold still. As the ship of affluence sails, there tends to be an increase in the *median family income* (the dollar amount at which half of all families receive more and half receive less income) from year to year.[9] Taking into account this shifting social standard, economist Victor R. Fuchs has proposed that the threshold of relative poverty be set at half the median income (1967). His notion that families earning less than this standard will feel poor is supported by the results of a study of twenty-three years of Gallup polls in which respondents were asked: "What is the smallest amount of money a family of four needs to get along in this community?" (Rainwater, 1973). "Getting along" would seem to have a subjective meaning very close to relative poverty, and indeed, the study does show that the "get along" point tends to be set at a stable percentage of an increasing median income.

Applying the Fuchs definition to 1983 living standards, a family of four would have to earn about 14,000 dollars to escape relative poverty. About 45 million Americans—that is, 1 person in 5—are caught in this state of felt deprivation, lacking amenities that most of us take for granted. Despite the very real suffering of being excluded from the good life, and despite the opinion of experts that relative deprivation generates much of the antisocial behavior associated with the poor, policymakers rarely discuss programs for combating relative poverty. There are two immediate implications. First, we are not committed as a society to ending the subjective deprivation of relative poverty, to providing, in the words of Adam Smith, those

things "the custom of the century renders it indecent for creditable people, even of the lowest order, to be without...."[10] The concept of relative deprivation also adds a second human dimension to absolute poverty. People living below the poverty line are haunted not only by the specter of physical want but also by the spectacle of others getting more and more of what they want.

Who Are the Poor?

We view the poor through a cultural prism, through lenses colored by the value placed on individual achievement. As noted above, the public image of the poor is tarnished by the belief that affluence is the reward for hard work, and hence, poverty must be the punishment for idleness. This explains a consistent finding in public opinion polls concerning the poor: they are widely perceived as "lazy and unreliable...the little money they do make is spent on liquor and nonnecessities rather than for economic advancement" (Lauer, 1971:8).

Regardless of the improbability of such a success-obsessed society being so heavily stocked with loafers, the subjective dimension of poverty suggests that the "deserving" poor are outweighed by the "disreputable" poor, who deserve little concern and less aid. This view is not only improbable, it is clearly false. Perhaps because of a cultural curiosity about just who these supposed failures are, we have excellent objective statistics counting, measuring, and pigeonholing the poor. These data are a revelation. As displayed in Figure 8-3, the largest single subgroup of individuals below the poverty line is children. One-third of all persons in absolute poverty are too young to work (under 15), and the diagram also shows that more than 1 in 10 is too old to have to work (over 65). Are those of in-between ages able-bodied bums? Not many. Roughly 8 percent of

---

[9] The distance the median income of Americans has come since 1960 does not mean a steady voyage to affluence. Since 1979, in fact, this figure has stagnated and even dropped, if one considers the effects of inflation (Hacker, 1983:159). For purposes of personal comparison, 1984's median family income was about 26,000 dollars.

[10] From *The Wealth of Nations*, quoted in Paul Blumberg, *Inequality in an Age of Decline, p. 101.*

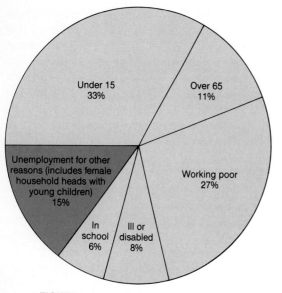

FIGURE 8-3 Who the poor are.

poor people suffer limited employment due to illness or disability, and 6 percent are in school, presumably improving their chances to pull themselves up by their own bootstraps.

The major subjective surprise is how many poor are working and how hard they work. Over one-quarter of the absolutely poor worked last year (40 percent of those over the age of 15), and the majority of the working poor were employed full-time. Figure it out yourself: A male head of family earning the minimum wage and missing no work at all over fifty-two weeks cannot earn nearly enough money to bring his wife and children above the poverty line. Notice how small the remaining crosshatched area of Figure 8-3 is. That is the portion of the poverty pie potentially containing impoverished loafers. According to the Bureau of Labor Statistics, many of these people are "actively seeking employment"—i.e., unemployed—not too difficult to believe in a society that did not have jobs for some 10 million of its people in some recent years. Of the remainder, a substantial proportion are female household

heads, most of whom are taking care of young children.[11]

As the previous section documented, there has been a recent surge in the total number of people below the poverty line. This means the size of the pie in Figure 8-3 has been expanding, but is the social character of poverty (i.e., the size of the slices) changing? The mass media have presented glimpses of the objective rise of poverty, a sampler of which is contained in these actual newspaper headlines: "Poverty Is Growing among Elderly," "Money Crisis in Female-Headed Homes," "Demands of Young Indigents Straining Shelters." The media spotlight has been especially bright on the *new poor*. Their poverty is called new essentially because they do not fit the subjective stereotype, the traditional conception of who the poor are supposed to be. They are young adults, established artisans, unemployed college professors—they are people who have suddenly dropped below the poverty line from higher rungs on the success ladder.

Despite all the publicity, the objective statistics indicate the novelty has been overstated. In any year of the last several decades, millions of people unceremoniously plummeted into poverty. In 1979, for example, before the poor had been labeled new and old, nearly 1 million families living below the poverty line were headed by individuals who had had professional/managerial occupations, some college education, or both (U.S. Bureau of the Census, 1982a). Although its likelihood obviously varies depending on one's rung of the class ladder, the threat of dropping into poverty has always been a real one for every American. An objective increase in poverty simply makes more of those threats a reality.

Part of the connotation of the term *old poor* is that these are people who have lived in

---

[11] Documenting links to Chapters 10 and 5 on sex roles and the family is the fact that more than one-third of the female-headed households in the United States live below the poverty line. The percentages displayed in Figure 8-3 were developed from U.S. Bureau of the Census documents (1984b, 1983a, and 1983b).

absolute poverty for quite a while. The phrase fits the subjective stereotype of impoverished individuals who lack the ambition to work their way out, and thus pass poverty on to their children. This notion of families living on the dole over the long term is not simply a product of negative attitudes toward the poor. One of the concepts emerging from public discussion about this social problem in the 1960s was the "cycle of poverty." According to the policy analysts who formulated the idea, the poor were not necessarily shiftless, they simply lacked the personal resources for success and could not provide them for their children. Hence, a vicious cycle was thought to operate in which poverty persists from generation to generation.

In terms of applicability to a substantial number of the poor, neither the public nor the professional perception of persistent poverty and welfare dependency appears to have much basis in objective fact. A recently concluded study following a sample of families for fifteen years found that blacks from welfare-dependent families were no more likely to receive welfare as adults than blacks from nonwelfare families. Analyses of both races revealed that only 10 percent of all families on welfare have been receiving a significant share of their income from that source for at least nine years.[12] Poverty is widespread and has recently been growing, but it is not populated by permanent freeloaders.

Why Are There Poor?

Whoever they are, how come the American poor are poor? We have posed the paradox before: In a society with a high enough gross national product to give every man, woman, and child some 12,500 dollars a year, millions of whole families are receiving less than half that amount. Why?

The answers to this question of objective causation are proposed on two levels. *Macro theories* are concerned with the very existence of poverty in society. Begin with an anthropological note: "The world's most primitive people have few possessions, but they are not poor. Poverty is a social status. As such, it is the invention of civilization" (Sahlins, 1972:37–38). Moreover, it persists and has, in fact, been multiplying in the most advanced industrial civilization on earth. The functionalist sociologists assert that inequality of social rewards is necessary for our kind of society to run smoothly:

> Occupations are not equally pleasant, nor are they equally important or difficult. In order to guarantee the complete and frictionless allocation of all positions, certain rewards have to be associated with them...the importance of different positions to the society and the market value of the required qualifications determine the unequal distribution of income, prestige and power (Dahrendorf, 1974: 44).[13]

Training for a physician takes long years in school, and working as one demands long hours, so society needs to dangle social rewards as "carrots" to attract talent to that crucial occupation. The occupational roles of the working poor, on the other hand, can be done by anyone, so they bring few rewards. Moreover, the fear of ending up in an unrewarding dishwasher job (or losing such a job and starving) may be a "stick" driving individuals to work harder. In these respects, both wealth and poverty serve positive functions for society. One of the major criticisms of this macrosocial view of inequality concerns the relative functional importance of various occupations (Tumin, 1953). If you are certain that physicians perform a more vital public service than garbage collecter, consider what would happen to

---

[12] Both data come from the Panel Study of Income Dynamics, which has been tracking a national longitudinal sample of 10,000 American adults. See Hill and Ponza (1983).

[13] This is Ralf Dahrendorf's summary of the classic functionalist statement by Kingsley Davis and Wilbert E. Moore, "Some Principles of Stratification," *American Sociological Review*, 10, 1945:242–249.

the health of your community if the garbage piled up in the streets. One also must consider the enormous negative consequences—or dysfunctions—of inequality for people's lives, a matter we will turn to shortly.

Conflict theorists offer no such elaborate explanations for the existence of poverty. Given their basic assumption that society is a set of groups competing for rewards rather than a benign system serving everyone, the rich and poor are simply winners and losers. Adopting the conflict perspective reshapes one's view of the success ladder. It is not some abstract arrangement of rewards for individual merit. The rungs form a hierarchy in the truest sense, with those on the upper rungs getting more by taking it from those on the lower rungs. Proponents of this perspective argue that the concept of class should be defined in terms of the relations of production, through the structured ways members of one class dominate another class in the running of the economic system. Evidence for the conflict theory of inequality emerges from studies showing that the degree of control exerted over others at work is a better predictor of one's income than a simple measure of individual occupational status (Wright, 1979); position is nice, but power pays.

Extending this logic to the very top of the ladder, we discern not an assortment of individuals who have earned the highest achievements but a favored class with a common interest in exploiting those on the rungs below. C. Wright Mills called occupants of this highest perch the "power elite," and ascribed to them the ability to "determine the size and shape of the national economy" (Mills, 1956a:125). Sociological studies suggest that a tiny, socially connected group of extremely powerful individuals does exist in the contemporary United States (Alba and Moore, 1983), a group which the conflict theorists say has an interest in actually *promoting* poverty. According to this neo-Marxist view, the owners of industrial capital underpay the working poor to extract more profits for themselves; the economic elite also benefit from a "reserve army of the unemployed," whose destitution will cow poor workers into accepting lower wages. Box 8-2 suggests that keeping poor people around also benefits those of us in less elevated social classes.

The essence of conflict theory is class exploiting class, but there is an obvious question: Why do people, especially the poor, put up with being robbed? Karl Marx's response was that the exploitees labor under a "false consciousness" preventing them from seeing the hand of the exploiter. The American achievement ethic pinning success/failure solely on the individual persuades rich and poor alike of the justice of existing inequalities (Lewis, 1978). If the poor are convinced that poverty is their own fault, this also justifies the privileges of the ruling class as the rewards of merit. The view of the conflict theorist is that the achievement ideology produces a subjective smoke screen hiding the fact that the haves are emptying the pockets of the have-nots. Those questioning this view note that the haves do give political support to welfare programs for the have-nots, an issue to be raised below.

Both functionalist and conflict explanations are macro theories of poverty. Whether deprivation is viewed as necessitated by efficiency or exploitation, it is by either account a necessary part of contemporary United States society. Knowing the reason behind the biblical injunction, "The poor shall be with you always," however, does not explain who will be the "poor" and who will be the "you" in the quotation.

Micro theories of poverty offer reasons why particular people are poor or nonpoor. Two such theories were developed in and around the War on Poverty. The first of these has received much public press, and it posits the existence of a separate culture of poverty. Aside from having less money, the poor are seen as different from everybody else in their basic attitudes and values. One of these differences concerns the cultural importance of planning for the future:

BOX 8-2

SOME POSITIVE FUNCTIONS OF POVERTY

1   The existence of poverty makes sure that "dirty work" is done—work that is physically dirty and dangerous, temporary, dead-end and underpaid, undignified, and menial.

2   Poverty creates jobs for a number of occupations: penologists, police, the numbers rackets, drug dealers, faith healers, prostitutes, pawnbrokers, and the peacetime army.

3   The poor buy goods that others do not want and thus prolong their economic usefulness, such as day-old bread, secondhand clothes, and deteriorating automobiles and buildings. They also provide jobs for doctors, lawyers, teachers, and others who are too old, poorly trained, or incompetent to attract more affluent clients.

4   The poor who are disabled or suffering from bad luck provide the rest of the population with the emotional satisfactions of compassion, pity, and charity.

5   The poor, being powerless, can be made to absorb the economic and political costs of change and growth in American society. During the nineteenth century, they did the work that built the cities; today, they are pushed out of their neighborhoods to make room for middle-class stores in the city and for expressways to enable suburbanites to commute downtown. The poor have also paid a large share of the human cost of the growth of American power overseas, for they have provided many of the foot soldiers for Vietnam and other wars.

Source: Adapted from Herbert J. Gans, "The Positive Functions of Poverty," *American Journal of Sociology,* 78, September 1972: 275–388.

The lower class forms of all problems are at bottom a single problem: the existence of an outlook and a style of life which is radically present-oriented and which attaches no value to work, sacrifice, self-improvement, or service to friends, family or community. Extreme present-orientedness, not lack of income or wealth, is the principal cause of poverty (Banfield, 1974:87).

Present orientation and other attitudes leading to irresponsible behavior—notably, lack of employment—are supposedly instilled in a poor person by the same learning processes that teach middle-class college students to be responsibly future oriented; the poor simply learn different cultural lessons. According to Oscar Lewis, author of the culture of poverty concept and several best-sellers about it in the sixties, an individual is socialized to a life of deprivation by others sharing that lifestyle (Lewis, 1966).

The alternative micro theory is called situationism because, logically, it emphasizes the rotten situation facing a lower-class individual (Spilerman and Elesh, 1971). By this account, poor people do not catch the disease of irrationality from their poor contacts who are carriers of an infected culture. Poor individuals quite rationally assess their life chances, correctly perceive that the chances for success are slim, and then abandon the value of success striving as they abandon hope. Why break one's back and save every penny when one may starve next week?

While both micro theories have been somewhat attractive to an American public suspicious of the poor, there has been a major scientific stumbling block to accepting either explanation: The achievement attitudes of the poor do not appear to be very different from those of the nonpoor. In a careful study published under the title *Do the Poor Want to Work?* Leonard Goodwin (1972) showed that even the most deprived people—those who should be crushed by their situation or apathetic because of their culture—are spurred by a work ethic every bit as rigorous as that of workers above the poverty line.

For decades, social scientific investigations have sifted for poor-nonpoor differences in the attitudes central to culturist and situationist theories—such as present orientation, fatalism, and impulsiveness—and essentially have come up empty (see Covello, 1980; and Rossi and Blum, 1969). Although there have been recent attempts to refine these concepts by focusing on the social relations of poor people, there presently is no accepted micro theory for why individuals fall or do not fall below the poverty line (Granovetter, 1983).

Of course it is necessary—and perhaps refreshing to you—for a body of knowledge to admit what it does *not* know, but more is at stake here than the aspirations of scientific sociology. While we busily gather data and argue over what they mean, poor babies are dying in the night. It is certainly important to find the theoretical reasons why the poor are poor, not only for the glory of science but also because knowing the objective causes of poverty will improve the efficiency of antipoverty policy (see Chapter 1). In the meantime, however, it would seem eminently sensible to direct our national will to rescuing people from drowning in poverty, regardless of exactly *why* they fell in.

THE CONSEQUENCES OF SOCIAL CLASS: MONEY MATTERS

"She's got an indiscreet voice," I remarked.
"It's full of—," I hesitated.
"Her voice is full of money," he said suddenly.
That was it. I'd never understood before. It was full of money—that was the inexhaustible charm that rose and fell in it, the jingle of it, the cymbals' song of it.

—F. Scott Fitzgerald, *The Great Gatsby*

This chapter is not just about poverty. It is, rather, about inequality, about the social structure we have devised for giving some untold riches, giving some a comfortable living standard, and giving all too many next to nothing. A major theme is that those in the latter category are not a problem separate from the American stratification system. The wealthy businessperson who lays off working poor to improve profits is no less a part of the problem than the unemployed poor person who must now wonder how to feed the children. Looming above the circumstances of these individuals is the so-called system within which they each find their place—and you find yours.

This section is concerned with the social structure of inequality and the difference it makes to people. As the Fitzgerald quote suggests, there is much, much more to class than the size of one's bank account. While the focus will be on the problematic effects of living at the bottom of the class ladder, an incredibly deep and diverse body of sociological literature shows how many facets of your life are touched by whatever rung you are on. The facts will be presented in terms of the fundamental American rights to life, liberty, and the pursuit of happiness. These data are a vivid testimony to C. Wright Mills' statement that sociology is concerned with "the imperial reach of social structure into the most intimate parts of our very selves" (Mills, 1956b).

Life

Chapters 3 and 7 paint a detailed picture of how income level affects one's level of health. The crudest—and most chilling—evidence concerns how much life you can expect. By definition, the poor get the least money, and by insurance company statistics, they get the least years to live. The poverty line, however, is not the only dividing line between life and death. The same statistics show that life expectancy rises at each higher rung of the income ladder. Lifetimes are parceled out to the income levels of Figure 8-1 just as surely as prestige and power.

Since the many facets of the health-income relationship are dealt with elsewhere, we will spotlight here only a single issue: *hunger*. The availability of adequate food obviously depends on the availability of money, and just as obviously, nutrition affects physical health. What may not be so obvious to you is the objective extent of hunger in America. Some subjective confusion is to be expected because this issue has been the source of much controversy in recent years, with some politicians actually calling the hunger problem a hoax. While the previous discussion of the poverty food budget (and the sharply increased numbers of people forced to use it) suggests the absurdity of this belief, there is ample direct evidence that Americans are starving as you read this book. Study after study has indicated that millions are hungry and that uncounted thousands actually starve to death in the Land of Plenty.

Moreover, the recent rise in poverty has been threatening to turn the disease of hunger into an epidemic. Separate national surveys by the U.S. Department of Agriculture, the General Accounting Office, and the Center on Budget and Policy Priorities found skyrocketing demands at emergency food centers between 1981 and 1983; according to the latter study "a significant number of [agencies] reported that need among those they serve had grown by over 200% in one year" (1983).

The reality of so many lives deprived of even enough to eat is unsettling to those of us with full stomachs, but the suffering of starving children can turn one's stomach. Maternal malnutrition significantly increases the chance of having a low-birth-weight baby, who faces thirty times the normal likelihood of dying before the age of 1. Those underfed babies that do survive face elevated risks of mental retardation, learning disabilities, and behavioral disorders (Citizens' Commission on Hunger in New England, 1984). There is little question that all of this human damage has a direct *problem linkage* to low income. The higher the rung on the family income ladder, the lower the risk of infant mortality, abnormal head circumference (an indicator of neurological damage),

and stunted growth (Schwartz-Nobel, 1981). In all likelihood, these ghastly results of keeping food out of the mouths of babes are actually going to get worse through the remainder of this decade. Federal food budgets have been slashed steadily from 1981 to 1985, with big cuts coming out of child nutrition programs.

The irony of hunger in America would test the powers of a poet. Poverty amid plenty is compounded by starvation in the Breadbasket of the Earth—and many of those starving are farmers! At the time of this writing, there are 26 pounds of cheese and 62 pounds of rice for every poor person in America just sitting there in U.S. Department of Agriculture warehouses at a storage cost of over 1 million dollars a day. A Florida senator recently held an 1800 dollars a plate luncheon in a private Capitol meeting room to announce plans to fight food stamp fraud. The contrast of the stuffed and the starving is almost funny. It is also a tragic demonstration that the same social system which unequally distributes income also selectively doles out the staff of life.

Liberty

By definition, poverty means that an individual is deprived of freedom from want. There are less obvious infringements of income—especially the lack of it—on personal liberty.

"Poverty is one of the most potent stressors known to social science" (Belle, 1983:93). This conclusion is based on a review of the recent literature relating low income to stress risk factors, and the evidence borders on the overwhelming. Compared to the nonpoor, poor people have more of the psychological and physical symptoms of stress, and their personal strain appears to be entirely sensible. Aside from an impoverished individual's immediate worries about just having enough to eat, the objective statistics give good reason for living in fear. An in-depth study of crime victimization in an urban housing project found that almost half of the

surveyed households had experienced a robbery, burglary, or assault against one of their
members (Merry, 1981). Numerous investigations of family violence have identified low
income as a risk factor (Straus, 1980; Garbarino and Sherman, 1980). Impoverished individuals thus live under the real and present
danger of violence both outside and inside the
home.

Speaking of homes, the poor are anything
but pleased about housing, with both adults and
children expressing negative attitudes toward
the blocks and communities in which they currently live (Belle, 1983). But given economic
circumstances, people in poor neighborhoods
are stuck where they are. Living in poverty
means living in fear and lacking the freedom to
flee to a better neighborhood. Such liberty is
not bounded only by the poverty line. More and
more middle-class families have not been free
to pursue that cornerstone of the American
dream: a new house. We noted above how the
long-term widening of the affordability gap
seems to be taking home ownership out of the
reach of many, and the predictions of this
financing formula are borne out by real estate
statistics. About 3 out of every 5 new houses
are being purchased by upper-class families,
apparently by outbidding middle-income buyers
whose purchases have been slipping by 15
percent over a decade (Friedan and Solomon,
1977). This pall over your family's future
proves again that social inequality is not just a
problem for the poor. Some liberty to choose
where to live is lost at each lower rung of the
stratification ladder.

The sociological point is that your freedom is
a function of class position; the many manifestations of liberty vary neatly across the many
levels of the inequality system. This social
structure not only applies financial pressure
upon individual decisions but also reaches inside people. Consider the results of a survey
directly relating mental strain to income (Caplovitz, 1979):

	Under $7,000	$7,000– $12,999	$13,000– $19,999	$20,000 and over
Percent undergoing high mental strain due to financial pressures:	44%	32%	18%	10%

Clearly, financial pressures are like chains
around the mind. Just as clearly, each higher
income level provides a key to liberation from
some sources of this personal strain. Aside
from these psychological bonds, class position
also alters attitudes affecting the liberty of
others. In a massive study compiling data from
some 20,000 respondents over an eight-year
period, class measures were found to be related
to 96 percent of the opinions polled! (Davis,
1982).[14] Included in this grab bag of attitudes
were questions tapping the individual's appro-
val/disapproval of the following: wives working, free speech for Communists, interracial
marriage, gay sex, the death penalty, and open
housing. All of these items concern civil rights
issues, and all vary by class. Americans are
fond of thinking of themselves as making up
their own minds. Be that as it may, lots of
individual opinions somehow are made up in
rows reflecting the structure of inequality.
These collective attitudes, moreover, determine how much liberty should be granted to
people elsewhere in the class structure.

The Pursuit of Happiness

Does money buy happiness? The most straightforward answer involves a list of the stuff of the
good life available for cash. Aside from consumer goods such as luxury housing, designer
clothing, and fancy cars that the rich can (and

[14] To keep these data in their proper context, James A.
Davis uses them to argue that the separate dimensions of
class (notably, education and occupation) are not all uniformly related to public attitudes. For an alternative interpretation, refer to Peter Knapp and Brian J. Jones, "Methodological Individualism and Model Specification in
Stratification Research," forthcoming.

do) buy in abundance, there are less obvious links between the quantity of money and the quality of life. About 7 out of 10 Broadway theatergoers come from the highest-income occupational groups (*Playbill*, 1978). In a recent recession which forced many families to cut out their yearly vacation, travel agents specializing in rich clients reported that business was better than ever for trips costing up to 8000 dollars! According to a consumer poll, the same recession led lower-income families to drastically cut back their consumption of steak, even as many upper-income family dinner tables were being set with more steak (Blumberg, 1980). If happiness is defined as the finer things in life, relatively few people can afford it.

You might reasonably object to such a materialistic definition, arguing that happiness cannot be reduced to the things one has. How about personal relationships? A wealth of sociological data has indicated the importance of social relations for personal well-being, but do they vary by class? Yes, and in a variety of ways. From rung to rung up the stratification ladder, there is a clear tendency to be involved with more people and, especially, to have more friends (Knapp and Jones, forthcoming). Aside from the ladder's effect on the raw amount of associates, each of us strongly tends to pick friends from our own rung. As a college graduate, you will be about four times as likely to invite another college graduate into your social circle as someone from another educational level (Fischer et al., 1977).

The actual content of relationships also varies across income categories. The lives of the very poor are so dominated by want that they use their relatives and friends as an economic defense, forming social circles bound by the obligation to share whatever meager resources are available (Stack, 1974). Poverty seems particularly corrosive to marriage, which research has shown to be a major factor in the pursuit of happiness (Fernandez and Kulik, 1981). Unstable family income is associated with unstable

marriages (Cherlin, 1979), and parents living below the poverty line are less likely to be happily married than those above it (Zill, 1978). People do seem to need people to be happy, but the lower one's income level, the harder it gets to fill those needs.

In answering the money-happiness question, there is an alternative to counting material pleasures or satisfying relationships: measure happiness directly. A number of surveys have polled individuals about various aspects of their life satisfaction, and generally found a positive income-happiness association across many rungs of the class ladder (Campbell, Converse, and Rodgers, 1976; Easterlin, 1974). By this point, such a finding can hardly be a surprise. Given that people with higher incomes live longer, are better fed and housed, are freer from stress, and get more of the finer things along with the intimates to share them, there is small wonder they are happier than low-income people. What is wondrous is the width and depth of class effects on individuals in the United States. The social structure of inequality controls your life, liberty, and pursuit of happiness in ways too numerous to discuss in this section, generally by increasing your problems as you decrease your class position. Perhaps out of exasperation at a seemingly endless recitation of income effects, a student recently challenged one of the authors in class by asking, "So what is *not* influenced by class?" His answer was very short.

SOCIAL POLICY

In a letter to a friend, Madame de Sevigne writes about a hanging she witnessed one morning. It was striking, she records, to see the condemned man trembling during the preliminaries of the execution, when he was only a common peasant. He groaned and wailed incessantly, causing some amusement among the ladies and gentlemen come to see the spectacle.

—Sennett and Cobb,
The Hidden Injuries of Class

In light of the array of evidence presented in the preceding sections, the injuries of the class system in America can hardly be called "hidden." The general public may not be apprised of all of these sociological details, but neither is there the blood-curdling callousness described in prerevolutionary France, where the suffering of the lower classes was viewed as the amusing antics of a subhuman species. The cultural ideal of equality has attuned Americans to doing something about the lot of others less fortunate, including the least fortunate of all: the poor. A study examining trends in public opinion over a forty-year period revealed remarkably consistent support for the federal government taking care of the truly needy. Since the Depression, about 7 out of 10 Americans have been in favor of providing the basic necessities of life to the poor (Montero, 1978). This impressive consensus that something should be done about poverty breaks down, however, when it comes to choosing the way to do it. Subjective support for the principle of aiding the poor has persisted amid heated debates over strategy. These arguments have centered on the merits of the two policy alternatives to which we now turn.

Strategies for Solution

The present system of antipoverty programs in the United States is not easy to describe. It is a complex whole with many loosely fitting parts, lacking the coordination that the term *system* implies. One major reason for the patchwork nature of the programs displayed in Table 8-4 is that they have been the object of political tinkering for nearly fifty years. Before the 1930s, the antipoverty policy in the United States was modeled along the lines of the Elizabethan poor laws, which officially treated deprivation as deviant behavior.[15] Starting with Franklin D. Roosevelt's New Deal policy devised during the Depression (a historical event

which rammed home the fact that individuals are not always responsible for their own poverty), the federal government began to systematically provide income benefits to people who could not provide their own. The largest single component of the new welfare state was—and is—Old-Age, Survivors, Disability, and Health Insurance (OASDHI), also known as Social Security. This massive program is a way of insuring those *in the labor force* against the rainy days of old age, death, or illness. Quite clearly, OASDHI ensures the many poor people who have not already had stable, long-term work histories (see Figure 8-3) of absolutely nothing.

In the main, the programs pictured in Table 8-4 are a safety net designed to catch individuals who drop through the cracks of the labor force/Social Security structure. Why so many programs? Part of the answer is the progressive effort to patch up previous program deficiencies, and part is the related effort to zero in on specific packages of benefits to specific subtypes of poor persons; for instance, Aid to Families with Dependent Children (AFDC) gives cash mainly to poor mothers supporting children in the household.

Despite this multifaceted attempt to target benefits to the particular needs of the poor, the present strategy remains a mixed bag of programs with no coherent rationale tying the system together. The only common thread appears to be the institutionalized belief that the poor have some personal deficiency. This view is most apparent in "curative" programs aimed at the so-called causes rather than symptoms of poverty (Dye, 1981:131). Manpower training, for example, presumes the poor are poor because individuals lack skills, and therefore it provides resources to "cure" them. It is a plausible notion which often leaves poverty's real symptoms untreated because there are not enough jobs even for some of the most skilled individuals in a lagging economy. Remarkably, the most skilled and seemingly deserving individuals of all—the working poor—have no spe-

---

[15] This treatment sometimes included whippings and de facto imprisonment in community workhouses. See Gale Miller, *It's a Living*, New York, St. Martin's, 1981, p. 13.

TABLE 8-4   PROGRAMS IN THE CATEGORICAL ANTIPOVERTY SYSTEM

Program	Average monthly recipients (1000) 1984	Expenditures (mil. dol.) 1984
Cash aid	(x)	24,229
AFDC	10,868	8,583
Supplemental security income (SSI)	4,042	9,085
Pensions for needy veterans	2,102	3,874
Earned income tax credit	18,300	1,731
General assistance	1,350	0
Food benefits	(x)	18,624
Food stamps	22,400	12,500
School lunch program	12,100	2,576
Women, infants, and children	3,044	1,360
Nutrition program for elderly	3,500	389
Jobs and training	(x)	3,962
Public service employment	(na)	(na)
Employment and training services	1,192	1,886
Youth employment demonstration program	(na)	(na)
Summer youth employment program	122	825
Job corps	41	599
Work incentive program	1,016	271
Medical care	(x)	26,521
Medicaid	21,915	20,094
Veterans	68	4,712
General assistance	(na)	0
Indian health services	937	840
Community health centers	5,000	351
Maternal and child health centers	(na)	339
Housing benefits	(x)	12,724
Rural housing loans	44	1,844
Lower-income housing asst. (sect. 8)	1,910	6,030
Low-rent public housing	1,332	2,821
Rural rental housing loans	27	919
Interest reduction payments	531	658

Source: Library of Congress, Congressional Research Service, "Cash and Non-Cash Benefits for Persons with Limited Income: Eligibility Rules, Recipient and Expenditure Data, FY 1982–84," Report No. 83-194 EPW, September 1985; and prior reports.

cial program, largely because of the suspicion they would stop working (Garfinkel, 1982). The still controversial culture of poverty and situationist theories that emerged in the 1960s (see above) have generally supported this popular approach of dividing up the poor and aiding separate categories of individual need (Jones, 1984). This antipoverty policy is known as the *categorical strategy.*Whatever the historical

and philosophical sources of the system, how much help do present programs actually give? By any measure, the answer is quite a lot. The first set of program categories in the table provide: direct cash grants totaling over 24 billion dollars to low-income individuals. Much more than that amount is spent through in-kind programs, so-called because they directly deliver goods and services to the poor rather than giving them the money to buy their own. Table 8-4 is by no means a comprehensive list of *all* antipoverty aid, yet it is a record of substantial societal effort to help the impoverished. A measure of the increasing scale of this effort is the number of recipients of aid. In the two major cash programs alone (AFDC and SSI), there has been a doubling of the number of poor people receiving monetary grants since 1965.

Although over time we have woven a larger and more closely meshed safety net to catch the poor, all too many slip through unaided. As you run your eye down the recipients column in the table, note that *in no case* does a program even come close to aiding the total number of individuals below the poverty line (about 33 million). Less than half of the poor get a nickel of the billions spent in cash aid, and 4 out of 10 of them get nothing from food stamps, Medicaid, housing subsidies, and school lunches (U.S. Bureau of the Census, 1982*b*)! Those falling into absolute poverty who *are* caught by the net of programs are treated very differently depending on where they land. Because the states have discretion over the amount to be paid AFDC recipients, a poor Californian receives nearly five times as much as a poor Mississippian (Hacker, 1983).[16] Aside from the fact that family address is more important than family needs in determining the level of aid, there is also a built-in bias against intact families. In about half of the states, a poor family cannot receive AFDC payments if a male adult is living in the household—even if he is working.

The search for a policy to fill in these gaps and inequities in the present categorical system has led some to recommend the alternative strategy of a *negative income tax*. Generally, the rationale of the proposed system is absurdly simple: If people are poor, just give them mon-

ey. Instead of classifying the many types of poverty and trying to funnel different aid packages to each, why not fill the one need they all share: too little income?

As is the case with most welfare policies, the complexities multiply when it comes down to the brass tacks of designing an actual program. Consider one version of a negative income tax (NIT) scheme presented in Table 8-5.[17] Its central feature is a guaranteed income which would assure each American at least enough money to purchase adequate food, clothing, and shelter. Guaranteeing everyone enough income to cross the poverty line would immediately aid all the unaided poor who do not fit any of today's neatly drawn categories; also, such a universal program necessarily eliminates geographic inequities because all poor everywhere would receive the same real incomes (note the cost of living adjustment) on the basis of financial need. Money would be paid out through a mirror image of the present progressive (or "positive") income tax structure. Just as we currently pay out a higher percentage of income *to* the IRS for each higher tax bracket, the NIT would pay out more *from* the IRS the further a family income fell below the minimum guarantee level—hence, a "negative" income tax.

The principle underlying the proposed program is that we the people of the United States should have a right to life's necessities. Escape from absolute poverty is to be put on the same footing as escape from ignorance, which all Americans are guaranteed in their right to a publicly supported education. But putting this noble principle into practice raises a number of practical questions, many of which may have

---

[16] This quintupling of Mississippi's payments by California is greatly in excess of the actual cost of living differences between the states.

[17] Many other NIT plans have been proposed by professors and politicians. Milton Friedman of the University of Chicago presented his much-discussed version in 1962, and numerous more elaborate plans have been put forth by academic researchers over the past twenty years (see Garfinkel, 1982:6–9). Three separate federal commissions have studied the NIT idea since 1967, and Presidents Nixon and Carter both formally proposed legislation with elements of an income guarantee.

TABLE 8-5   A PROPOSED NEGATIVE INCOME TAX SYSTEM FOR GUARANTEEING A MINIMUM FAMILY INCOME

I. *Income allocation:* Every American would be guaranteed a minimum income equal to the federal poverty line (currently 10,000 dollars for a family of four).

(a) Recipients would be paid a 50-cent work incentive on each additional dollar of earned income up to the earning limit:

Work incentive example

Earned income	NIT income	Total income
$ 0	$10,000	$10,000
$ 5,000	$ 7,500	$12,500
$15,000 (earnings limit)	$ 0	$15,000

(b) Payments would be uniform for families of comparable need throughout the United States, except for adjustments due to the local cost of living.

II. *Administration:* It would be assumed by the Internal Revenue Service and implemented as a negative income tax.

(a) The NIT administration would supersede all current federal cash and in-kind welfare programs, with the exception of Medicare/Medicaid.

(b) Applicants for the program would file quarterly income statements with the IRS, which would average their income over the previous year to determine family needs.

Payments would be in the form of biweekly checks delivered to recipients.

III. *Funding:* Moneys for the program would be drawn from the federal tax system, and would incorporate the budgets of all eliminated programs.

already occurred to you. The real issue in this—or any—policy comparison is not whether the categorical or NIT alternative is flawless, but rather which strategy minimizes the objective costs to society.

Policies into Practice

Because welfare policy touches some of our deepest values and political interests, both the present (categorical) and proposed (NIT) strategies have been heavily studied. One product of these studies is some surprises about the success of current welfare policy. While the various programs in Table 8-4 have been evolving for generations, the most rapid development occurred during the 1965–1975 period. The programs that were expanded, modified, and invented to fight the War on Poverty are widely regarded to have been failures. A recent CBS-*New York Times* poll found that 62 percent of the public believed that the antipoverty programs of the 1960s (many of which are still operating) either had little impact on the poor or made things worse for them.

This subjective perception of the War on Poverty as an outright defeat is flatly wrong. According to U.S. Census Bureau definitions, 39.5 million Americans were living in poverty in 1959. Despite a substantial rise in population, as of 1980 there were fully 10 million fewer people below the poverty line than before "war" was declared (U.S. Bureau of the Census, 1982:11). In some respects, these measures of victory are too conservative because they consider only cash income. A recent study traced the decline in the prevalence of poverty since 1965, when the cash/in-kind antipoverty campaign was first fully mounted. In this analysis, the "prewelfare poor"—the percentage of Americans in poverty not counting any form of categorical aid—showed very little change from the late 1960s through the late 1970s. By contrast, the "full aid poor"—counted after including cash welfare *and* in-kind benefits—dropped throughout this period, marking the steady retreat of poverty before the diversified forces of the present system (Danziger and Plotnick, 1982).

While this trend has reversed since 1980, current antipoverty programs still have a substantial antipoverty impact. Without any government support programs, expert estimates indicate that about 58 million Americans—1 in 4—would be below the poverty line! Despite the optimism with which Lyndon Johnson declared the War on Poverty, the present welfare system has not yet reached the "end to poverty to which we are totally committed in our time." It has, however, marched a long way toward that end.

Advocates of the negative income tax system do not deny these real victories, but do question the effectiveness of the basic strategy. As a measure of how efficiently the War on Poverty has been waged, consider the concept of the poverty gap. This dollar figure is a simple measure of the enemy's forces, an estimate of the total dollar figure that would wipe out impoverishment by bringing every man, woman, and child above the poverty line. The poverty gap was recently calculated to be 137 billion dollars, in a year when the United States was spending *over 350 percent of that amount in transfer programs!*

Despite such massive overkill, about 12 million poor got no cash and at least 10 million got no in-kind benefits. Proponents of an NIT argue that the categorical strategy misfires so badly precisely because all of this economic ammunition is being aimed at so many targeted populations. By definition, each category which is targeted must exclude many types of poor people, so separate bureaucracies have to be set up to determine eligibility. It is not unusual to be processed through a dozen forms for only *one* of the programs in Table 8-4. Investigations of welfare fraud have found over half of the payment errors to be made by welfare officials, apparently themselves confused by the tangle of red tape (Huttman, 1981). Is it any wonder that the

benefits millions of poor people have coming to them get lost in the bureaucratic maze? There is also a steep price tag for all of this bureaucracy. The officials checking the rules have to be paid salaries and supplied with filing cabinets, desks, computers—all expenses multiplied many times over for the many separate programs. Couldn't this antipoverty money better serve the practical needs of the poor if *they* spent it?

Critics of the NIT system correctly contend that no antipoverty program implemented in the real world can make administrative procedures disappear. The IRS will have to develop specialized forms to determine income eligibility, and then file, process and evaluate them for each family four times a year. NIT advocates respond that the snarl of red tape should be smaller because many of the other cash and in-kind programs would be collapsed into a single bureaucracy, thus streamlining administration. The proposed substitution of NIT cash for food stamps has been attacked as inhumane due to the questionable spending habits of the poor. The evidence, however, shows the poor to be no more likely than the rest of us to fritter away their money on nonnecessities such as liquor and gambling (Vanfossen, 1979); besides, inspectors of the U.S. Department of Agriculture report that food stamps are now a spendable currency which can be used to buy everything from clothes to cocaine. The contention of pro-NIT planners is that in-kind transfers such as food stamps are inefficient care packages to the poor, delivering only about 31 cents of antipoverty effect per dollar of program cost (Smeeding, 1977). Direct NIT cash grants would allow the poor to purchase more necessities because more of the money will be in their pockets instead of in bureaucratic budgets.

Evaluating the Evidence

How would you vote in the categorical versus NIT debate? In keeping score of the arguments back and forth, it is instructive to consider the policy dilemmas posed in Chapter 1. Picking the right antipoverty alternative is, first, a matter of minimizing *value trade-offs*. Defenders of the present system may admit the inefficiency of the categorical approach at getting money to the poor, but are unwilling to compromise the American value of hard work. Guaranteeing an adequate income would provide an incentive for laziness, they argue, trading off too much of our prized work ethic. The result could be an abandonment of the labor force by millions of the working poor. Advocates of the NIT system point directly to the work incentive feature, which would encourage employment by subtracting only 50 cents of each additional dollar earned by a recipient family from their original grant (for an example, refer to Table 8-5). This may not sound like much of an incentive, but it seems to be at least as pro-work as the present system, which until recently took well over half of each additional dollar of wages away in cash and in-kind benefits.

Whatever the precise impact of an NIT on hours worked, those for and against the proposed system are presenting evidence for and against different values. The anti-NIT group puts a premium on the work ethic, whereas those pro-NIT are willing to risk trading off this value in return for more efficient pursuit of income equality.

Aside from the clash of values, the poor's work response to a guaranteed income bears directly on program costs, one of the most crucial *implementation issues* for any real-world policy. If the many millions of the working poor *do* quit their jobs, the increase in recipients could bust the system. As we noted at the outset, there are ample nuts-and-bolts data about both alternative policies. The federal government has invested over 100 million dollars to test the effects of the negative income tax approach in what has been called "the most extensive social experimentation ever conducted" (Neubeck and Roach, 1981:308). Although the results of this massive set of studies are still

being debated by social scientists,[18] the most recent analysis of the University of Wisconsin's Institute for Research on Poverty drew this conclusion: "Most of the empirical evidence suggests that reductions in the work effort of male [family] heads would be quite small" (Garfinkel, 1982:8). It seems clear that some reduction in hours worked would occur, but not enough to wreck the economy or swamp the program budget.

Even with the real savings in tax dollars that would undoubtedly occur from the bureaucratic streamlining of welfare, it is possible that the NIT proposal would carry a higher price tag than the categorical system. The major reasons are that millions of unaided working poor families would immediately qualify for aid, and most other poor families would receive an across-the-board boost in spendable income. The billion-dollar question is whether the proposed form of income redistribution is worth its cost to society. After all, this book is packed with other objectively worthy social problems having expensive solutions.

As you prepare to cast your final ballot for or against the NIT alternative, it is important to see that antipoverty programs do more than fill the pockets of people at the bottom of the income ladder. The sociological evidence summarized above has related low levels of income to high levels of hunger, marital instability, crime victimization, and on and on. Since impoverishment seems to be a key link in the *linkages of social problems,* your vote for the categorical or NIT system is a choice which can affect every aspect of the human condition below the poverty line. Looking at these alter-

---

[18] Some researchers project severe reductions in employment by the working poor (e.g., Michael C. Keeley, "A Review of the Evidence on Labor-Supply Response from the Income Maintenance Experiments," *The Social Science Review,* 4, 1982:23–38); other analysts have criticized these projections on sociological grounds (see Brian J. Jones, "Social Networks, Poverty Research and Poverty Policy," forthcoming), predicting instead little or no decline in work effort by male family heads.

native policies in terms of contesting for your vote is not just some textbook rhetorical game. Welfare reform has been a hot issue in every presidential campaign since 1960, and current political events are boiling around antipoverty programs. You will probably get many real-world chances to decide what to do with the poor.

Clear policy choices have been made about the poor in recent years. The secular surge in the objective extent of poverty since 1978 has coincided with deep recent cuts in the federal antipoverty budget. The Congressional Budget Office estimates that funding of programs targeted mainly toward the poor was slashed over 57 billion dollars between 1982 and 1985 (O'Hare, 1985). To date, 1 million people have lost their eligibility for food stamps, and hundreds of thousands of families with children have been dropped from the AFDC rolls. The quantitative effect is reflected in a dramatic reversal of the progress against poverty. The number of "full aid" poor in the United States (i.e., the number of poor *after* considering the effect of all cash and in-kind benefits) has rocketed to an increase of 51.6 percent in just the first three years of the eighties (Danziger and Plotnick, 1982). Calculating the qualitative effect of aid cuts on the life quality of the poor is more difficult. A chilling thought is that most of the evidence presented to show the pains of poverty was gathered *before* the full force of the budget cuts.

Conflict theorists project these current events into the past as well as into the future. Their response to the finding that a lower-income family (under 10,000 dollars) lost an average of 270 dollars a year while the typical rich household (over 80,000 dollars) gained 7070 dollars under Reagan administration policies (Congressional Budget Office, 1983) is, essentially, so what else is new? They contend that a tiny power elite has persistently controlled American domestic policy, particularly as it bears on the distribution of income (Domhoff, 1970). More specifically, the conflict approach points to "welfare for the rich," which generates very little controversy about undermining

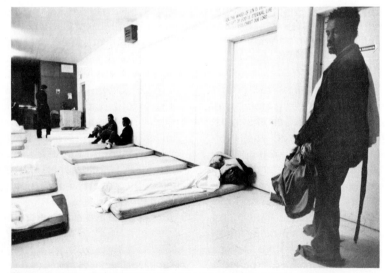

The beds in this shelter for the homeless poor might be empty because of deaths. According to a newspaper report, some forty-two homeless people died in Philadelphia from 1985 to 1986 because of exposure, violent crime, accidents, and untreated illnesses. (© *Alon Reininger/Contact 1984*)

the work ethic of upper-class recipients. For example, billions of dollars have been given to large farmers to keep land *out* of food production while millions of poor people went hungry. If one totaled all the federal funds distributed through Social Security, welfare, unemployment benefits, workers' compensation, veterans' disability, and railroad retirement benefits, it has been calculated—even before the current poverty crunch—that middle-income individuals get over *four times* as big a "handout" as poor people (Komisar, 1977:139).

The conflict theory school even maintains that the wealthy's short-lived support of the War on Poverty was an attempt to protect their disproportionate slice of the pie. Piven and Cloward (1971) contend that AFDC budgets rose *after* the violent rioting, reflecting the efforts of the haves to buy off the anger of the have-nots. Welfare spending cuts after things have quieted down are in the self-serving tradition of the rich continuing to exploit the poor.

There are, of course, other theoretical perspectives interpreting the facts about welfare policy. Whether or not you buy the conflict explanation, it is instructive in that it raises the prospect of welfare reform if such reform is perceived as serving the interests of the individual and/or society. Polling public perceptions yields a cloudy picture at this moment. While heavy majorities of the American public favor retaining existing categorical programs, only a few percentage points in some polls have separated those for and against a guaranteed minimum income like the proposed NIT policy. Longer-term studies of subjective trends indicate that a substantial majority of Americans can accept the idea of an NIT if it is combined with mandatory training or employment of the recipient, and that younger college educated individuals in particular favor pro-poor spending (Davis, 1980). Hazy as it is, the subjective dimension seems to predict that the very structure of social inequality in America will be personally shaped by the person reading this book.

SUMMARY

1 The distribution of income in the United States presents startling contrasts of deprivation and opulence. These extremes—and the income shares of individuals in between—are best understood as parts of a structured, durable social system.

2 The inequality of condition in the social stratification system of the United States must be viewed together with the degree of inequality of opportunity as assessed by sociological studies of class mobility.

3 The subjective dimension of poverty exploded in the 1960s despite reductions in the objective numbers of the poor over previous years. Societal changes triggering the subjective factors—visibility, expectations, and values—are analyzed.

4 Absolute poverty is defined as an income level below which a family cannot even purchase the physical necessities of life, whereas relative poverty is a state of deprivation in which the family income falls below some general societal standard of living.

5 The present system of categorical aid (i.e., eligibility of only selected poor individuals for specific benefit categories) is contrasted with a proposed negative income tax system which would establish a minimum income guarantee at the federal poverty line.

CHAPTER 9

Prejudice and Discrimination: Causes and Consequences

I will say, then, that I am not, nor have ever been, in favor of bringing about in any way the social and political equality of the white and black races; and that I am not, nor ever have been, in favor of making voters or jurors of negroes, nor of qualifying them to hold office, nor to intermarry with white people; and I will say, in addition to this, that there is a physical difference between the white and black races which I believe will forever forbid the two races living together on terms of social and political equality. And inasmuch as they cannot so live, while they do remain together there must be the position of superior and inferior, and I as much as any other man am in favor of having the superior position assigned to the white race.

Although these are the words you would expect to hear from a member of the Ku Klux Klan, the quote is actually from a speech that Abraham Lincoln gave at Charleston, Illinois, in 1858. Many people have come to think of Lincoln as an early proponent of blacks' rights, yet even the man who freed the slaves harbored prejudice toward blacks. This should give you some idea of how widespread the problem between the races has been. Certainly there has been some progress made in controlling racial conflict since Lincoln's speech, but it still remains as one of our country's most threatening and uncontrollable situations. It is so pervasive that it jeopardizes the health, happiness, and economic well-being of millions of Americans. It is also a problem not simply limited to conflict between blacks and whites. There are many recurring forms of tension which separate groups, including Jews from Christians and Hispanics from Anglos. This chapter deals with the dimensions and causes of these intergroup conflicts and evaluates what can be done about them.

PREJUDICE AND DISCRIMINATION

The Nature of Prejudice

Prejudice literally means *prejudgment,* but it would be foolish to think of prejudice as an operation of the mind involving logic, comparison, and good sense. Prejudice is a rigid predisposition to respond to a certain group in a specific way, a way which emphasizes only selective "facts" and ignores others. Since prejudice almost always involves negative feelings (hatred, aversion, etc.), it is actually the same as antipathy. Unfortunately, it is easy to find many examples of prejudice in American society. It manifests itself in such notions as the oversexed black male, the pushy Jew, the dirty Chicano, and the dumb Pollack. Many people are emotionally committed to these stereotypes and resist changing their attitudes.

The Nature of Discrimination

Prejudice is an attitude. It does not involve overt action. Discrimination does. To dislike a group of people is one thing (prejudice), but to treat those people in a less than equal way is another (discrimination). The distinction between attitude and action is important from a social policy perspective, since it is possible to pass laws to prevent discrimination without necessarily reducing prejudice. However, from a psychological perspective, prejudice and discrimination are highly interrelated. Prejudice typically causes discrimination, which in turn can increase prejudice.

The relationship between prejudice and discrimination is complex and varies considerably from person to person and from group to group. Robert Merton (1949) described four types of people in terms of the way they express prejudice and discrimination: prejudiced and discriminatory ("active bigots"), unprejudiced and nondiscriminatory ("all-weather liberals"), unprejudiced and discriminatory ("fair-weather liberals"), and prejudiced and nondiscriminatory ("timid bigots"). Active bigots and all-weather liberals require little explanation; they are simply individuals who act on their beliefs. Many people fall somewhere between these two extremes and act against their feelings, whether bigoted or not, when faced with countervailing social pressures. An example of a fair-weather liberal is a real estate agent who does not dislike Jews but refuses to sell to them because the agent feels it can hurt business. Conversely, realtors who hate blacks but do business with them for fear of legal reprisal are timid bigots.

Forms of Discrimination

Discrimination can take many forms, from a Jewish joke to a racially motivated murder. There is also a distinction between verbal and behavioral discrimination. This was first noted in a classic study by La Piere in 1934.

He traveled with a Chinese couple as they stopped at some 250 restaurants and hotels across the United States. They were refused service only once. Later, La Piere sent letters to each of the establishments, asking whether they would serve "members of the Chinese race." Half did not reply, but over 90 percent of those that did claimed they did not accommodate Chinese guests. While many *said* they would discriminate against Chinese people, almost none *actually* did. Apparently it is more difficult to discriminate against someone in a face-to-face situation than through the mail.

Clearly violence is a more extreme form of discrimination than simple verbal abuse or avoiding interaction with members of a minority group. Over time, minority group members have been beaten, whipped, hanged, burned at the stake, or desexed simply because they belonged to a hated group. Although violence has diminished, instances still occur today. In Beverly Hills, for example, there have been recent reports of wealthy couples forcing illegal Indonesian aliens into slavery and then beating them for failure to obey orders! In 1986, Mexican Border Patrol agents discovered a paramilitary group whose sole purpose was to capture and harass aliens. Some of the current violence against minorities is sponsored by the Ku Klux Klan, an organization which is treated sepa-

rately later in this chapter. Unfortunately, hate groups of all kinds have become increasingly common in the 1980s. People in these groups are extremists who will use robbery, violence, and smear campaigns to lash out at the nation's minorities.

Prejudice and discrimination are widespread objective national problems which have been with us for a long time. However, there are some notable regional differences in the prevalence of these problems. As most people believe, white southerners are especially likely to be prejudiced, particularly in terms of accepting blacks in equal status positions. Like alcoholism among the Irish, bigotry among white southerners is a popular subjective stereotype that happens to fit the objective facts. In fact, some parts of the South have been such hotbeds of antiblack feelings that the American Nazi Party, a lunatic fringe element, recently declared the time was ripe to set aside North Carolina as a Caroline Free State, a country for white people only. Today, regional variations in prejudice and discrimination are diminishing. As the data in Table 9-1 indicate, discriminatory attitudes toward blacks have declined significantly in the South over time. Some believe that southerners are no longer more prejudiced than other Americans, as evidenced by strong antiblack attitudes in northern areas such as South Boston.

TABLE 9-1   WHAT SOUTHERN WHITES THINK OF BLACKS

Here are some statements people sometimes make about black people. For each statement please tell me whether you personally tend to agree or disagree with that statement.

	Percent of whites who agreed					
	1963	1966	1967	1971	1976	1978
Blacks tend to have less ambition than whites	66	65	70	52	50	49
Blacks want to live off the handout	41	43	52	39	37	36
Blacks breed crime	35	33	32	27	31	29
Blacks have less native intelligence than whites	39	36	46	37	28	25
Blacks care less for the family than whites	31	33	34	26	22	18
Blacks are inferior to white people	31	26	29	22	15	15

Source: National Conference of Christians and Jews, *A Study of Attitudes toward Racial and Religious Minorities and toward Women,* conducted by Louis Harris and Associates, Inc., November 1978. By permission of the publisher.

RACE AND RACISM

The Meaning of Race

The term *race* is ambiguous and has been used in many ways. One concept of race is biological and refers to people who have interbred over a long period of time and, as a result, share distinctive physical features. These include skin color, hair texture, nose structure, head form, brain size, lip form, facial shape, and stature. The problem with the biological approach to defining race is that it is very arbitrary. The factors used to distinguish among races vary considerably within a given group of people. Skin coloring, for instance, differs greatly within races. A wide variety of human groups are commonly referred to as races, including the English, French, Arabs, Jews, Gypsies, Irish, Scots, Welsh, Basques, Indians, Nordics, Eskimos, blacks, Hindus, Latins, and Celts. The term race is applied in a general way to the following kinds of groups and categories: those who speak a certain language; a religious group, such as the Hindus; an isolated local population, such as the Cornish people; a hypothetical "pure type" that is assumed to have existed in the past, such as the Germanic; a recognizable type, such as the American Indian or the Eskimo.

Race has also been defined administratively by establishing racial categories through laws or bureaucratic practice. Here social definitions outweigh biological definitions. While the criterion might imply biological factors, there was really a social basis to the U.S. Census Bureau's definition of a Negro as anyone having "any trace of black blood." This also proved to be a highly subjective and useless approach to identifying race. Nevertheless, some states still use such arbitrary rules. In Louisiana, for instance, individuals are classified as black if they have more than $\frac{1}{32}$ part of Negro blood. As of this writing, the Louisiana legislature, embarrassed over the standard, is acting to repeal the nation's only racial classification law.

There are probably as many definitions of race as there are people defining it. This is because race is a social rather than a scientific category; in essence, race is what people say it is. Racial categories are established through the highly subjective impressions by which some people define themselves and others. Whether distinct races objectively exist or not, the everyday experience of most Americans makes it clear that the social concept of race frequently materializes as prejudice and discrimination against nonwhites.[1]

Forms of Racism

Our society has long been characterized by a dilemma between the objective principles of the American creed of justice for all and the racist reality of everyday life. This problem is compounded by the fact that many white Americans do not care about the dilemma but only about the troubles it has created (Silberman, 1964). Racism is prejudice or discrimination based on perceived racial characteristics. Essentially, racism takes three forms. One form is *individual racism,* a term often used interchangeably with *race prejudice*. It refers to negative racial attitudes which are ungrounded. People who put all blacks into one category and harbor hostile attitudes toward them suffer from race prejudice. Sexual racism, for instance, is one of the subjective components of racism. It is partly based on the idea that black males are expressively sexual, promiscuous, and preoccupied with white women. Objectively, it is white men who have historically enjoyed free sexual rein with black women, but their misdeeds (or guilt over them) have been projected onto black males.

Despite the objective facts, the myth of the supersexual black "beast" (the superstud) is widely circulated. This serves as a pillar of

[1] Today many American Negroes reject the label *Negro* and prefer the term *black*. In rejecting the term Negro they are rejecting the attempt of white people to assign blacks to a rigidly conceived racial category. Interestingly enough, "Negro" is the Spanish word for "black," but the substitution of the terms is symbolically important to blacks.

white racism which is really racial possessiveness challenged by interest in the women of one race by the men of another. Part of this interest is imaginary and part of it stems from public statements by black militants, such as Eldridge Cleaver and Dick Gregory, who claim that all of American society is programmed toward idealizing white women (especially blondes). Consider what Dick Gregory tells white audiences about the excessive desire for the majority female:

> Nothing upsets you more than to see a nigger with a white woman and you might find out why we want one and might find out it's your fault. You can't advertise a brand new automobile without putting a blonde in it to make my gear shift right. You keep that bitch in my face 24 hours a day, every time I open a magazine and then you wonder why I want one of them...you programming me to this white lady. (Gregory, 1968)

Another component of sexual racism, the myth of mongrelization, is also the product of a highly subjective set of beliefs about interracial sex. It centers on the idea that interracial marriages will produce children who are biologically and culturally inferior people. There is a widespread prohibition of sexual relations between black men and white women, while relations between white men and black women are not as stigmatized. The reason is that in sexist society's view, children belong to the women, and the child of a union between a white man and a black woman is still black; but the child born to a black man and a white woman renders the white race less pure.[2] This myth exerts a strong influence against interracial marriage, traditionally the least acceptable form of interracial contact. A 1983 Gallup poll disclosed that Americans are becoming more tolerant of interracial marriages, although there are still many people who disapprove—about 50 percent in

the Gallup study. Recently, in Wilkes-Barre, Pennsylvania, a black man with a white common-law wife was much tormented by his white bigoted neighbors. Subsequently, he engaged in a berserk outbreak during which he killed thirteen people, some of whom were his own children.

Inappropriate thinking about blacks is most typical of those segments of the white population that have the least. Race prejudice is closely linked to social class; individuals from the lower classes are typically more prejudiced than those from higher classes. Certainly the limited educational attainment of lower-class people is related to such a simplistic, stereotypic view of the world. They are also more frustrated than other people, and many need someone to whom they can feel superior. In addition, lower-class whites often find themselves in direct competition for jobs with blacks, many of whom are also lower-class.

A second form of racism is *institutional racism,* which involves sources of discrimination found outside the individual. It includes all the direct and hidden ways in which society's institutions work against the interests of minority groups. Institutional racism has a long history in the United States. Because it is the most widespread form of discrimination, examples abound. In the South, it used to be illegal to teach blacks how to read and write. During World War II, the Red Cross separated white blood from black blood. In the 1970s, it was discovered that the United States Public Health Service had approved of a medical experiment in which 425 poor black males were allowed to go untreated for syphilis in order for researchers to understand the long-term effects of the disease. These historical examples are relatively insignificant compared to the widespread institutional discrimination blacks currently face in education, housing, and employment. Much institutional discrimination may be unfair, but it is not illegal. For example, admission to a prestigious private school may be based on

---

[2] One extreme example of this attitude occurred in 1982 in Tampa, Florida, where a judge removed the child of a white woman after she married a black man.

ability to pay and personal recommendations. However, if nearly everyone who has the money and influential friends to write the recommendations is white, blacks will have a difficult time gaining admission.

The third form of racism, *cultural racism,* contains elements of both individual and institutional racism. It is the expression of the superiority of the cultural heritage of one's race over another. Cultural racism is at work, for instance, when the achievements of a race are ignored in classroom textbooks. Another example of cultural racism is the controversial research on intelligence differences between blacks and whites. Often the reported "intelligence deficiencies" of black people merely reflect their lack of knowledge of white culture, upon which the tests are based. Yet the test scores are taken at face value and become an instrument of institutional discrimination by which blacks are placed in less demanding curricula in school.

Consequences of Racism

From the perspective of the dominant group, there are a number of rewards afforded by racially discriminatory behavior. On the personal level, discrimination may enhance people's feelings of self-worth because they feel they are better than other people. On the societal level, racism allows the powerful to remain in power because racist beliefs (such as blacks being lazy, untrustworthy, and the like) justify keeping blacks "in their place" and maintain existing inequalities in society.

While a functionalist view may find some positive purpose in racism (such as keeping those on top in power), the list of dysfunctions of racism is almost endless. Consider these few: Not only are blacks more likely to starve because of poverty, but they also feel so inferior that they develop attitudes of self-worthlessness which seriously curtail their chances for rewarding lives. One example of this is that some blacks view their lower-class status as

fixed and never aspire to improve their position (Coleman and Rainwater, 1978). The self-esteem of some blacks is so low that many are ashamed of their physical characteristics (Clark and Clark, 1980).[3] Blacks in the South are especially likely to accept the doctrines of innate black inferiority and white domination. Some conform to the racist stereotypes by becoming obedient and contented "good niggers." These unhealthy attitudes are evident among black school children who have been subjected to overt discrimination and prejudice. There are reports that twisted self-concepts begin to develop among black children who are only 3 years old![4] However, at least one study reports that ethnic minorities in the United States may not suffer from low self-esteem relative to whites if they compare themselves to whites with low self-esteem (Jensen, White, and Galliher, 1982).

The consequences of racism are not limited to damaged personalities. For instance, although infant mortality rates are declining nationwide, the gap between the rates for black and white babies is widening. Another consequence is the large economic drain to the country of denying a whole group of people the opportunity to contribute to society and to fully utilize their talents. Parts of this chapter enumerate the massive costs and problems of discrimination in the areas of income, occupation, education, housing, politics, and social justice.

Before getting into these areas, it is important to note that racism appears to have de-

---

[3] Bachman and O'Malley (1984) report that black-white differences in self-esteem may be the result of blacks responding in extreme ways to the scoring methods used to calculate self-esteem rather than actual differences in self-esteem.

[4] The reports of negative self-esteem among black children refer to situations in which the children were raised in a racist atmosphere. This is not the experience of *all* blacks growing up in the United States. Those who do not regularly encounter prejudice and discrimination have levels of self-esteem comparable to and sometimes higher than whites (Simmons, Brown, Bush, and Blyth, 1978).

Interracial couples face a long, uphill battle for public acceptance. In some American cities their houses have been firebombed by bigots. (*Frank Siteman/ Taurus Photos*)

clined in recent decades. Harris polls show a steady reduction in prejudice on the part of whites from 1963 to today. Studies made since the Second World War by the National Opinion Research Center also reveal a distinct trend toward reduction of racial prejudice and approval of integration. A 1978 *New York Times*-CBS News poll found that 66 percent of whites would not be disturbed if a black with income and education comparable to theirs moved into their block. In 1968, only 46 percent felt that way. Reduction in prejudicial views toward blacks has been evident in a number of attitudinal areas, as the data in Table 9-1 indicate. The improvement in the objective conditions of blacks is documented in other sections of this chapter.

Additionally, there has been a *perceived* improvement; the reduction of riots and media coverage of such has reduced visibility of the race problem; expectations are not overshadowing actual improvement, as was true in the beginning of the civil rights movement; egalitarian values have become more common. As a consequence, race relations are no longer considered by the public to be one of the most pressing issues of our time. The substantial liberalization of white racial attitudes in recent decades is largely responsible.

THE SUBJECTIVE DIMENSION OF PREJUDICE AND DISCRIMINATION

The topic of the present chapter is highly controversial. Attitudes and actions toward other groups in society are tied up with some of our deepest feelings, and no doubt have been the subject of arguments among your own family and friends. Given the amount of emotional heat generated by the topic, it is essential to shed sociological light on the dual dimensions of this social problem.

As subsequent sections will show in detail, the objective substance of the problem has apparently been shrinking. While still wide-spread and pernicious, prejudiced attitudes seem to have weakened considerably over the past generation. Similarly, discrimination is an imposing problem which appears less imposing now than it did decades ago (Schuman, 1978:374). We will emphasize below the continuing reality of prejudice and discrimination, but would note here that the general direction of change has been a decrease rather than an increase in the objective scale of the problem.

Aside from the concrete evidence of social indicators (such as gains in income and schooling), improving conditions for minorities are reflected in popular perceptions. More than 3 out of 4 people—and a majority of nonwhites—in a 1981 Gallup survey thought that the quality of life of blacks in the United States has gotten better over the last ten years. This assessment of the past and present is consistent with the more specific subjective evidence of social problems opinion polls. For instance, only about 1 percent of Americans consider race relations to be a "main problem of concern" (Yankelovich, 1982b). Such a low subjective rating has not always been the case. In 1957 and for a three-year period between 1963 and 1965, race relations was rated as "the most important problem facing the country today" (Gallup, 1982:27). Charting the rise and fall of interracial concern is an instructive lesson in the importance of the subjective factors.

Not coincidentally, the peaks of concern about prejudice and discrimination in the fifties and sixties happened to coincide with public protests, some of which were openly violent. The Montgomery bus boycott of 1955–56 and the riots of the mid-sixties were intrinsically dramatic events whose media coverage created extraordinarily high *visibility*. Some analysts of these outbursts place partial responsibility on a widespread frustration about the objective treatment of minorities in society (Spilerman, 1970), a frustration fanned by unrealized

expectations.[5] Another sociological view highlights the importance of equality as a *value* in American life. As the value of egalitarianism gains strength—which appears to have occurred during the sixties—the continued unequal treatment of one's cocitizens seems all the more outrageous (Gans, 1973). That outrage may be expressed both by college student protests and by the cresting of public opinion about the problem. It is crucial to see these sudden rises and falls in subjective concern against the background of gradual—some would say too gradual—objective improvement in prejudice and discrimination.

THE OBJECTIVE DIMENSION OF PREJUDICE AND DISCRIMINATION

Income Discrimination

One of the most telling indices of discrimination in the United States is the sharp income difference between white and minority families. The median income for black and Hispanic families is only a fraction of that for whites. In 1984, the median income for white families was 27,686 dollars, and for blacks, 15,432 dollars. About one-third of black families and one-quarter of Hispanic families were below the poverty level (see Figure 9-1). A prejudiced individual would maintain that blacks earn substantially less than whites because they are lazy and less ambitious. However, the objective reality is that about 90 percent of the income gap can be attributed to racial discrimination—blacks earning less than whites with comparable levels of education (Willie, 1982).[6]

---

[5] A general sense of frustrated expectations does not imply general approval of rioting. At no time did a majority of blacks approve of violent protest (Goldman, 1970).

[6] Some contend that a significant factor in income differences between blacks and whites is a higher prevalence of broken families and female-headed families among blacks. Indeed, the National Urban League reports the proportion of fatherless black families has tripled since the 1960s.

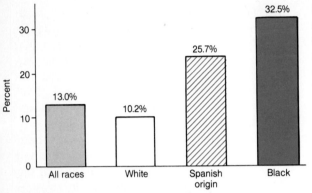

FIGURE 9-1   Percent of persons below the poverty level by race. (*Source:* Bureau of the Census, "Characteristics of the Population below the Poverty Level: 1980," *Current Population Reports,* Series P-60, no. 133, Washington, D.C., U.S. Government Printing Office, July, 1982, p. 2.)

Unemployment   Unemployment is also much greater among blacks than among whites. In 1982, the unemployment rate for whites was about 9 percent, and for blacks, 20 percent. But these statistics are misleading because they do not count those who are so disillusioned with fruitless job seeking that they have dropped out of the labor force entirely. In reality, the unemployment percentage among blacks may be three or four times greater than that of whites. The gap is greatest among teenagers seeking employment: in 1979, 16 percent of all 16- to 19-year-olds seeking work were unemployed, compared to 34 percent of black teenagers (U.S. Department of Labor, 1979). Unemployment among black youth has since worsened. In some cities, such as Philadelphia, it ran as high as 80 percent in 1982. This means that a significant number of black youths in the 1980s will enter adulthood without ever having had a meaningful work experience. The objective costs in terms of wasted talent and personal frustration are enormous.

The Black Bourgeoisie and the Black Underclass   It is important to remember that the relative income of black families is an average over hundreds of thousands of families. Obvi-

ously, some families are much better off than others. Class has always been important in determining black access to privilege and power. This is evident in the growing number of educated blacks now entering prestigious and well-paying occupations. The size of this black middle class (also known as the black bourgeoisie) has expanded, but the situation among lower-class blacks (also known as the black underclass) has deteriorated.

Blacks are going in two directions: one group is doing better and one is doing worse. Unfortunately, the black middle class constitutes only about 10 percent of the total number of blacks. These are well-educated people with substantial incomes and attractive housing who have broken from the cultural traditions of the bulk of black America. They tend to be intact families headed by young males. Members of the underclass are typically elderly or in female-headed households. To a limited degree, economic discrimination among blacks has declined, since economic subordination now centers on the underclass. However, this progress is overrated for two reasons: first, a significant number of blacks still live in the squalor of poverty; and second, the black middle class may be better off financially, but its members still suffer many forms of racism. Additionally, Collins (1983) argues that the black middle class is not as stable as it appears.

Recent Gains in Income   There is considerable controversy among social scientists as to whether racial discrimination in income has declined. Some feel discrimination is no longer a problem and optimistically claim half of American blacks are now middle class (Wilson, 1980). Others feel income discrimination has worsened as evidenced by reports that since the 1960s, occupational and income gains of blacks have been insignificant compared to those of whites (Oliver and Glick, 1982). Farley (1984) reports that if the growth rates of 1959 to 1982 persist without interruption, the median income of black and white families in the United States will be equal in about three centuries! Like most extreme positions, each of these is wide of the mark; clearly there is not full economic equality between the races, but there have been some gains since the advent of the civil rights movement.

While the economic status of blacks has undeniably improved, the improvement has been limited. Between 1947 and 1974, the average income of black families increased from 51 to 65 percent of the average white family income. A black middle class may be emerging, but it is only a minority of the black population and far less affluent than the white middle class. Despite limited financial gains, black unemployment rates are still double those of whites. The unemployment situation of black youths grew markedly worse in the 1970s, but since 1978 it has shown some modest improvement. Although these gains were not enough to restore losses sustained earlier in the decade, a growing proportion of black youths appear to be getting better jobs. This may be because younger blacks experience less discrimination than older blacks (Mindiola, 1979). Each new generation of blacks appears to be starting its labor force career in a more favorable position than previous generations. As gains among

blacks occur, Massey and Denton (1985) report that they enjoy better residential locations, which in turn affects such barometers of social well-being as improved health and decreased exposure to crime.

Occupational Discrimination

Another approach to understanding the socio-economic plight of blacks is to examine the occupational distribution of those who do have jobs. Blacks traditionally have been overrepresented in low prestige, low-paying jobs. Until recently, occupational discrimination was so powerful that blacks were almost completely denied access to prestigious positions. Latest figures from the U.S. Bureau of the Census show that blacks are more likely to be service workers and farm workers than whites, who are more likely to have professional, managerial, and sales jobs (see Table 9-2).

There is even discrimination *within* occupational groups; blacks, for instance, are especially likely to have the least desirable blue-collar jobs (Roner and Leon, 1979). This is partly the result of the hostile attitudes trade unions harbor toward blacks, another example of discriminatory practices restricting access to better jobs. Blacks are underrepresented in almost every union except those representing

TABLE 9-2 OCCUPATIONAL DISTRIBUTION (PERCENTAGE) OF EMPLOYED WORKERS, BY RACE

Occupation	Race	
	White	Blacks and others
Professional and technical workers	11.8	4.1
Managerial and administrative workers	11.7	2.4
Sales workers	6.9	1.2
Clerical workers	15.4	6.1
Artisans	14.3	5.9
Other blue-collar workers	22.3	34.8
Service workers	9.5	33.0
Farm workers	8.0	12.5
Total	100.0	100.0

Source: Bureau of the Census, *Social Indicators III: Selected Data on Social Conditions and Trends in the United States*, 1980, p. 355.

workers in unattractive, low-paying work. Within the professions, blacks are disproportionately concentrated in primary and secondary teaching and social service fields. They are rarely found in the ranks of lawyers, physicians, and college professors. The professions, like the unions, have their own ways of keeping blacks out, such as discriminatory entrance examination procedures.[7] The business world is no better. It is not uncommon for a corporation to have a large number of black employees concentrated in low-level jobs while most of the managers are white. Such firms have been likened to "corporate plantations."[8] Minority representation on the boards of directors of major American corporations is significantly less than that of whites. A 1982 national survey reported that only 6 percent of companies had a black, Hispanic, or Asian director.

Beliefs about Black Workers   One reason for the discrimination blacks have faced in employment is a set of inappropriate attitudes based on racist thinking. One such attitude is the idea that blacks are inherently lazy and therefore have no desire for better jobs. This is a classic case of blaming the victim, a self-fulfilling prophecy by which blacks are seen as worthless workers and therefore are not hired. Whites are considered less of a gamble. Another unfounded attitude toward blacks is the myth of the income cushion, the idea that taxes are high because the money is handed out to blacks on the dole. Thus blacks are seen as less interested

in work because the government supports them. In a 1981 national survey of over 8000 supervisors conducted by the Center for Supervisory Research at the School of Business at James Madison University, blacks were largely perceived as being treated with favoritism on the job.

The attitudes some whites have about blacks being lazy, on welfare, and basically inferior are examples of the groundless impressions some people perpetuate out of ignorance and malice. The objective facts are quite to the contrary. Blacks want to work and, in fact, have the same occupational values as whites (Goodwin, 1972).

Recent Gains in Occupation   Gains in black employment were made during the 1960s, although progress slowed during a recession in the 1970s. In 1964, fewer than 1 in 5 blacks had a white-collar job; today about 1 in 3 blacks has such a job. The representation of blacks in trade unions has also improved. In earlier years, blacks were prevented from joining. Now they constitute about 15 percent of total trade union membership. Although their numbers have increased, blacks are still underrepresented in business and the professions. Blacks may not be likely to own restaurants, but at least things have improved since earlier years when they could not even sit in them. An important exception to improvements in the relative socioeconomic status of blacks is increased levels of joblessness among black youths relative to whites (Mare and Winship, 1984). Additionally, there are pronounced city differences in racial occupational inequality (Fossett and Swicegood, 1982). Pomer (1986) reports that occupational discrimination against blacks is still a widespread problem, although they do have substantial rates of upward mobility to *nonmanagerial* positions within the public sector.

In the 1980s blacks are expected to significantly improve their position as professionals, managers, clerical workers, and skilled artisans (Anderson, 1979). Specifically, blacks are ex-

---

[7] In 1972, all black law school graduates who took the Georgia bar examination failed. Over 50 percent of the whites passed the exam. In many instances the blacks had academic records comparable to those of the whites (Parker and Stelman, 1973).

[8] There are some examples of blacks doing *better* financially than whites in the professional and business world. Black scientists and engineers earn slightly more than their white counterparts. On college faculties, blacks with top credentials outearn whites. Black MBAs often receive higher starting salaries than whites, but they climb the corporate ladder more slowly.

pected to make gains in engineering, accounting, nursing, health, and teaching and to show a continued decline in the proportion employed as service workers and laborers. What will the twenty-first century bring? In 1980, *Ebony Magazine* predicted racism will be wiped away by the year 2015, blacks will be an integral part of the corporate world, and a black vice president and black state governors will be commonplace. At this writing, it is certain that blacks have made gains but no triumphs. Sports, however, may be a special exception (see Box 9-1).

Educational Discrimination

Black America's economic plight is not entirely the result of racial discrimination in employment and pay. Much of it is the direct result of educational deprivation: blacks receive fewer

years and an inferior quality of education compared to whites. A 1980 study commissioned by the Joint Center for Political Studies reported that racial segregation in schools has increased since 1968. This is an important reason why so many blacks spend their lives unemployed or underemployed.

Blacks are keenly aware of this problem. In fact, more blacks (46 percent) than whites (35 percent) feel a college education is important today (U.S. Bureau of the Census, 1980). But blacks have much less chance of attaining a high school or college degree. In 1978, 32 percent of whites 25 years of age or older had not finished high school, while 52 percent of blacks had failed to do so. On the college level, the differences are also striking: 10 percent of whites 25 years of age or older had completed

---

BOX 9-1

BLACKS IN SPORTS

Because many occupational areas are limited to them, blacks have devoted a disproportionate amount of their talent and energy to sports. Many black youths dream of making it to the professional leagues, and those who do make it provide ample fuel for these dreams. Although it is widely believed that sports are the realm of equal opportunity, blacks dominate in certain sports. In fact, blacks have come to dominate some major United States sports as no other minority group ever has. For example, 65 percent of National Basketball Association players are black; in the National Football League, 42 percent of the players are black; 19 percent of baseball's major leaguers are black. As a point of comparison, remember that blacks constitute about 12 percent of the general population. Black dominance in sports is also evident at the amateur level. Blacks dominate the same sports in college that they do at the professional ranks, and a disproportionate share of the medals won by American track and field athletes in the Olympic Games are now gathered by black athletes, who win virtually all the United States medals in boxing as well.

Sports have traditionally been used by minorities to fight their way out of poverty and into the mainstream of American society. Blacks have been especially visible in taking this route. Part of their success may be due to physical advantages they have over whites. Blacks tend to have longer limbs, smaller calves, narrower hips, and less fat than whites, a combination which may lead to superior agility and speed. Blacks also have marked superiority in hyper-extensibility (capacity for double-jointedness) and general looseness of joints. This may be because they have more tendon and less muscle.

As in other fields of endeavor, the potential achievements of blacks in professional sports are limited, in part, by the racial prejudices of white managers and owners who place black athletes in positions where leadership is generally not required. In professional football, 96 percent of the quarterbacks are white; 77 percent of the defensive cornerbacks are black. In professional baseball, over 90 percent of the pitchers are white; yet in the outfield, far from responsibility for central decisions, almost 50 percent of the players are black. There is also racism in the National Basketball Association, particularly among the fans, who often give white players special attention.

For every black who "makes it" in sports, there are thousands of others who wasted their time pursuing the athletic dream. Sports can be a "jock trap" for blacks. In devoting so much energy to sports, they fail to develop academic aptitudes which are vital for other career possibilities.

college in 1978, but only 4 percent of blacks had done so. The underrepresentation of blacks is especially noticeable in graduate school programs. According to the latest figures available, blacks, who constituted 12 percent of the overall United States population, earned less than 1 percent of all the Ph.D.s conferred (Kronus, 1978:207). The statistics are similar for degrees in medicine and law. Although the statistics on blacks' relative educational attainment are discouraging, it is important to note that blacks have made substantial strides during the 1970s.

Blacks' Performance in School   Although, from a statistical point of view, the educational gap between blacks and whites is closing, blacks still receive a qualitatively inferior education compared to whites. Part of this is due to blacks attending understaffed and underfinanced inner-city schools. The type of education offered in these schools is simply not an adequate preparation for the challenges of college or a meaningful job. According to the famous Coleman (1966) report, the longer blacks remain in school, the larger the gap between blacks and whites on standardized tests. Black college-bound students typically do not fare as well on the Scholastic Aptitude Test (SAT) as white students. In 1982, blacks averaged 341 on the verbal section of the SAT and 355 on the math section, for a total of 696 (of a possible 1600). Whites averaged 444 in verbal and 483 in math, for a combined 927. That left whites 231 points higher on the combined scores than blacks. This gap is certainly significant, but it is declining over time, as black scores have been improving faster than white scores. For instance, in 1985, SAT results showed whites with an average score of 940; Mexican Americans scored 808, Puerto Ricans 777, and blacks 722.

Some feel black-white differences in SAT scores result from cultural biases in the test which favor whites. Others feel the unstable family structures of poor blacks produce frustrated children who do not do well in school. However, some of the blame must be placed on the poor quality of the schools many blacks attend. There are reports that blacks are often taught by minority teachers who fail teacher competency tests at an extraordinary rate. Additionally, there are numerous reports that teachers (both black and white) view black students as having less interest and ability than white students. As a consequence, perhaps they do! One example of this is the widespread subjective belief that black students are not interested in science. A 1980 report by the National Assessment of Educational Progress shows that objectively this is far from the truth; black students have more interest in science than white students, but the common experience of poverty among many blacks has made them less aware of the nature of science.

Blacks have traditionally fared less well than whites in school for many reasons. The textbooks, for instance, often portray blacks in derogatory ways. Some books used in grade schools and high schools ignore blacks completely; others suggest they deserve to be treated as inferiors. College textbooks are no exception. Even some sociology texts on marriage and the family further negative stereotypes toward blacks by depicting them as lazy, without a male head of the household, and as "deviant" if they marry interracially (Peters, 1974).

Social relationships among students can also affect happiness and adjustment in school. Perhaps as the result of discriminatory treatment, blacks are known to feel more alienated from their classmates than whites. In segregated schools blacks have higher self-esteem because they are surrounded by other blacks and are therefore insulated from the negative effects of societal prejudice and discrimination (St. John, 1975). In a 1981 study, Roberts concluded that the races interact well as long as blacks constitute a majority or a significant minority of the school population, but when the number of black students shrinks below one-quarter of the school population, they feel threatened and band together. The interracial climate also depends on whether the racial composition of a school is changing. The most negative interracial climates exist in schools where the racial composition is undergoing change (Davidson, Hofmann, and Brown, 1978), especially *rapid* change such as that fostered by integration policies whose only goal is racial balance without consideration for the unsettling effects of placing children in schools with strangers of both races.

Achieving Educational Equality Clearly many problems prevent blacks from having the same educational opportunities as whites, but at least programs are being tested to deal with some of them. In 1980, a federal district court in Michigan addressed the question of "black English" by ruling that a school system must take a child's spoken dialect into account in its instructional program. How? Possibly by teaching standard English to black students as though it were a foreign language.

Most programs designed to end educational discrimination are directed toward ending school segregation. In 1955, the Supreme Court mandated integration "with all deliberate speed." Yet, although it is required by law, other racial problems such as discrimination in housing, income, and occupation have made school integration a practically difficult goal to achieve. As a result, poor blacks still largely attend schools with other poor blacks.

The common remedy to school segregation has been to transport students from their local schools to other schools to achieve a racial balance within a school system. This policy, commonly referred to as busing, is designed to help overcome the problem of separation from mainstream culture, which can so severely limit blacks' educational attainment. Unfortunately, busing has proved to be riddled with difficulties, chief of which is a phenomenon called

"white flight." Many white parents, possibly fearing integration of schools will lower educational standards, have moved out of heavily integrated districts or sent their children to private schools.

Busing has also fostered other problems, such as the weakened local control over schools that occurs when children attend schools not easily accessible to their parents. In places like Boston, busing has been a factor in racial violence. Perhaps no other issue in black-white relations provokes emotions as much as busing. Even people in favor of desegregation are often opposed to it. One study found that 86 percent of white liberals (many of whom would qualify as fair-weather liberals in Merton's terms) expressed reservations about busing (Caditz, 1976). A 1982 Gallup report found that 72 percent of the overall population clearly oppose busing.

Police escort black students to all-white South Boston High School on the first day of court-ordered desegregation. (*Ellis Herwig/The Picture Cube*)

Desegregation is particularly difficult to implement, especially in the South where tough standards of desegregation are often met with strong opposition.[9] Jackson, Mississippi, is a case in point. When the federal courts ordered desegregation of Mississippi's public schools, the Wilkinson County Board of Education cut its school tax rate by more than one-half, and the school's superintendent took his children out of public school and enrolled them in a private academy hastily set up in a church. Many other whites followed his lead.

Presently the studies on the effects of desegregation on academic achievement are inconclusive, as are those on the effect of interracial contact on racial attitudes and behavior. However, the bulk of the evidence indicates that black and white children achieve more in predominantly white schools than in predominantly black schools, and that social contact between black and white students improves interracial attitudes and behavior. Curiously, one survey found that community conflict early in the desegregation process is associated with lower racial tension in school later (Crain and Mahard, 1982). This may be because conflict causes more cohesion among blacks, which in turn leads to greater support for desegregation among them.

The benefits and costs of desegregation vary from one situation to another. In integrated schools with tracking (homogeneous grouping by ability), racial separation may still be maintained. In other schools, desegregation may mean black students have less opportunity for leadership than they did in all-black schools. In smaller cities, racial balance can be attained by redesigning attendance boundaries without extensive busing. In larger cities, widespread busing (with the inevitable resistance to it) is the only available way to desegregate.

Desegregation does not always have the same result because its effectiveness depends partly on the amount of disruption it causes in people's lives. It also depends on the ages of those being directly affected. In studies of children of kindergarten age, desegregation appears to have the most positive effects. High school students, with more deeply entrenched racial attitudes, react more negatively (St. John, 1975). Apparently desegregation must be introduced early in life, does not work well among people with hardened attitudes, and will help bring about true racial equality only over a period of generations.

Racism in College Although some blacks may not even aspire to college because of oppressive experiences during early school years, those who do enroll often find college life to be far from a social utopia. There are reports that black college students feel depressed and alienated, and see colleges as hostile places overpopulated by white students and professors. See Box 9-2 for a report of some of the racist experiences of federal judge A. Leon Higginbotham, Jr., when he was a student at Purdue University. Several college presidents consider race relations the most pressing problem on American campuses today. University of Missouri president James Olson admits that the atmosphere at Missouri is marred by "covert racism." Similar problems are reported at the University of Texas and other southern schools. In 1980, a number of ugly racial incidents occurred on campuses throughout the country (see Box 9-3).

Black students encounter a variety of hostile behavior, ranging from white students who believe the blacks are all special admissions to campus security police who frequently stop them and require them to produce identification cards while making no such demands of white students. One prominent objective problem among black college students is the poor aca-

---

[9] A 1980 Gallup report found that 22 percent of northern white parents and 27 percent of southern white parents objected to sending their children to a school where half of the students are black. This is a significant improvement in the South, where 78 percent were opposed in 1963 compared to 28 percent in the North.

BOX 9-2

FEDERAL JUDGE HIGGINBOTHAM'S RACIST TREATMENT AS A STUDENT AT PURDUE UNIVERSITY

In 1944, I was a 16-year-old freshman at Purdue University—one of twelve black civilian students. If we wanted to live in West Lafayette, Indiana, where the University was located, solely because of our color the twelve of us at Purdue were forced to live in a crowded private house rather than, as did most of our white classmates, in the university campus dormitories. We slept barracks-style in an unheated attic.

One night, as the temperature was close to zero, I felt that I could suffer the personal indignities and denigration no longer. The United States was more than two years into the Second World War, a war our government had promised would "make the world safe for democracy." Surely there was room enough in that world, I told myself that night, for twelve black students in a northern university in the United States to be given a small corner of the on-campus heated dormitories for their quarters. Perhaps all that was needed was for one of us to speak up, to make sure the administration knew exactly how a small group of its students had been treated by those charged with assigning student housing.

The next morning, I went to the office of Edward Charles Elliot, president of Purdue University, and asked to see him. I was given an appointment.

At the scheduled time I arrived at President Elliot's office, neatly (but not elegantly) dressed, shoes polished, fingernails clean, hair cut short. Why was it, I asked him, that blacks—and blacks alone—had been subjected to this special ignominy? Though there were larger issues I might have raised with the president of an American University (this was but ten years before Brown v. Board of Education) I had not come that morning to move mountains, only to get myself and eleven friends out of the cold. Forcefully, but nonetheless deferentially, I put forth my modest request: that the black students of Purdue be allowed to stay in some section of the state-owned dormitories; segregated, if necessary, but at least not humiliated.

Perhaps if President Elliot had talked with me sympathetically that morning, explaining his own impotence to change things but his willingness to take up the problem with those who could, I might not have felt as I did. Perhaps if he had communicated with some word or gesture, or even a sigh, that I had caused him to review his own commitment to things as they were, I might have felt I had won a small victory. But President Elliot, with directness and with no apparent qualms, answered, "Higginbotham, the law doesn't require us to let colored students in the dorm, and you either accept things as they are or leave the University immediately."

As I walked back to the house that afternoon, I reflected on the ambiguity of the day's events. I had heard, on that morning, an eloquent lecture on the history of the Declaration of Independence, and of the genius of the founding fathers. That afternoon I had been told that under the law the black civilian students at Purdue University could be treated differently from their 6,000 white classmates. Yet I knew that by nightfall hundreds of black soldiers would be injured, maimed, and some even killed on far flung battlefields to make the world safe for democracy. Almost like a mystical experience, a thousand thoughts raced through my mind as I walked across campus. I knew then I had been touched in a way I had never been touched before, and that one day I would have to return to the most disturbing element in this incident—how a legal system that proclaims "equal justice for all" could simultaneously deny even a semblance of dignity to a 16-year-old boy who had committed no wrong. Shortly thereafter, I left Purdue University and transferred to Antioch College. Ultimately, I chose the law as my vocation, and in 1952 I graduated from Yale Law School.

A. Leon Higginbotham, Jr., *In the Matter of Color: Race and the American Legal Process,* New York, Oxford University Press, 1978, pp. VII–IX. By permission of the publisher.

demic performance of black college athletes relative to all others (Purdy, Eitzen, and Hufnagel, 1982). This can affect people's subjective perception of all black college students.

These problems are not limited to southern schools. Blacks at eastern colleges complain that their ideas are either ignored in the classroom or dismissed as irrelevant (Poinsett, 1980). In 1981, a Harvard report stated that black students do not perform well at the university and might be better off at "slightly lesser institutions." Almost half the black students at Harvard report that "being at Harvard has influenced my attitude about whites negative-

BOX 9-3

RACISM FLARES ON CAMPUS

The ugly message called for the elimination of "stinking black monkeys" from "a white society." It was mailed from Cleveland, signed K.K.K., and addressed to a black senior at Williams College in Williamstown, Mass., part of a spate of hate mail and threatening phone calls to blacks on campus. A similar letter was sent to Williams President John Chandler.

The wave of antiblack attacks began in early November. During homecoming, two figures in white sheets planted a wooden cross on campus. Few took any notice until the pair doused the cross with gasoline, ignited it and escaped. Williams, a small liberal arts college in a rural corner of Northwestern Massachusetts, is not the only school in the Northeast where racial incidents have occurred.

- At Harvard, Lydia Jackson, president of the university's Black Student Association, found her office calendar defaced with racist slogans, including TEN DAYS TO KILL and K.K.K. UNITE. She also received several frightening phone calls, one of which threatened her with rape if she did not "stop creating trouble and making noise on campus."
- At Cornell University in upstate New York, a gang of ten white youths jostled and harassed a young black student on Election Night. Six weeks before, someone had hurled a rock through a window of Ujamaa Hall, a residence predominantly for blacks.
- At Wesleyan University in Middletown, Conn., Associate Professor Jerome Long, director of the Afro-American Studies Center, got a letter addressed to all residents of Malcolm X House, a black student dormitory. "I have a dream," it read, of "wiping all goddamn niggers off the face of the earth."
- There have also been incidents in the Midwest. Earlier

this semester two cross burnings occurred at Purdue University in Indiana. One, made of wood, was planted on the lawn of a black fraternity house; the other, shaped of computer cards, was taped to the dormitory window of two black students and set afire. At Ohio's Kent State University, black student organization material on campus bulletin boards was defaced.

- The incidents have spurred students and faculty members to look anew at long simmering problems between the races both on campus and off. Acknowledges one white Williams senior: "There has been apprehension about relations between minorities and whites." Another white Williams student wonders why "each group seems to stick together, without reaching out to each other." A black senior who is president of the Williams student council says: "There is really nothing different here from the world outside. These incidents have just shown that Williams does not exist in a vacuum." Says Harvard's Jackson: "Until we sit down and talk to each other about what's really going on in this country that makes people lash out against blacks, Third World people, gay people and poor people, I think the problem will exist."
- The incidents and the resulting rallies, prayers and discussions appear to have brought blacks and whites on campus closer together. Says Wesleyan Professor Long: "In the nine years that I have been here, this is the first time the university has coalesced to speak to a common concern." Concluded Wesleyan President Colin Campbell: "Despite the cruelty of its motivation and the pain it has caused, this latest incident may yet serve a beneficial purpose by reminding us how far we have come and how far we still have to go."

ly" (Skerry, 1981). The fact that race relations are a problem at Harvard, a hotbed of liberalism, demonstrates how deeply ingrained racism may be.

Racial tensions are so bad on some college campuses that a *Black Student's Guide to Colleges*, published in 1983, provides black students with ratings of the racial climate of 114 campuses. It gives low marks to some of

the nation's most prestigious schools. Black-white student relations at the University of Michigan, for example, are described as "the pits." Radcliffe is termed "impersonal," and black students at the University of Arizona are "disenchanted and unhappy." Rave notices are given to the University of Iowa and Oberlin College, which, unfortunately, do not typify race relations at most American colleges and universities. In fact, some college campuses now harbor chapters of the Ku Klux Klan. The rise in Klan membership in the 1980s may be primarily due to an increase in the North.

Recent Gains in Education Despite all the problems enumerated above, blacks have made considerable gains in education. In the early 1980s, school enrollment rates were virtually the same for blacks and whites. Moreover, the percentage of blacks aged 18 to 24 in college nearly doubled, from 10.3 percent in 1965 to 19.4 percent in 1981. The proportion of blacks with a high school or college education rose sixfold from 1940 to 1980: 51 percent of blacks had high school degrees in 1980 and 8 percent had college degrees; but the figures for whites remain higher, 71 percent (high school) and 18 percent (college). On the other hand, a 1983 study by the Joint Center for Political Studies reported that racial segregation in the nation's schools has increased significantly since 1968.

Discrimination in Housing

Racial discrimination in income, education, and occupation severely cripples the chances for blacks to have happy lives. This is yet another example of the interrelationships of social problems. Consider how discrimination affects shelter, one of the most fundamental human needs. The national racial housing pattern is well known: in 1973, 3 out of 5 whites lived in suburbs, while 4 out of every 5 blacks lived in central cities (U.S. Bureau of the Census, 1973). In Chicago today, an estimated 1.1 million people live in areas that are at least 75 percent black. Other cities exhibit the same pattern. Within cities, blacks (and other minorities) are typically relegated to the least desirable neighborhoods with the worst housing. In addition, blacks are forced to pay what some call a "color tax"—an increase of

This Harvard graduate was fortunate enough to avoid many of the barriers to black advancement. (*Charles Gatewood/The Image Works*)

over 10 percent more than whites pay for the same housing.[10]

The Role of Real Estate Agents Real estate agents are partly to blame for these discriminatory practices. They are known to treat black and white clients quite differently, making their decision as to *whether* to show a home and *where* to show one based on their client's race.

---

[10] A similar thing occurs with apartment rentals. Blacks have fewer apartments made available to them than whites, and they also pay higher rents.

The chances of seeing a house on the first visit to a real estate agent (most of whom are white) are almost 3 out of 4 if you are white, but only 1 out of 4 if you are black (Pearce, 1979). The agents are quite adept at hiding their feelings by giving black home seekers such reasonable-sounding excuses as "no key" or "need to make an appointment ahead of time."

One stereotypic view holds that blacks live in city housing because suburban life does not appeal to them. However, the truth is that most blacks would like the opportunity to move to the suburbs, where the housing is better (Huttman, 1981:318). Another myth about black home buyers is that housing prices go down when black families move into a neighborhood. In fact, the prices typically remain the same or increase (Huttman, 1981:318). Also untrue is that white sellers will sell only to white buyers. Actually, middle-class owners prefer middle-class black neighbors to lower-class neighbors of any racial or ethnic group (Huttman, 1981:319). Real estate agents like to perpetuate these myths because they can use them to their own advantage by blockbusting, a practice in which they warn of a "black invasion" and of lowered property values to force white home owners into selling their houses to the agents at cheap prices. The agents then sell the homes to blacks at inflated prices. Because whites *believe* blacks lower property values, then the prices can actually decline through the mechanisms of a self-fulfilling prophecy.

Institutional Discrimination in Housing Banks and other lending institutions contribute to racial discrimination in housing through a practice known as redlining. Neighborhoods undergoing racial transition are often designated for special (unfair) treatment as "bad risks." People find they either cannot get mortgages for homes in these neighborhoods or must repay their loans in a shorter time period than would apply to similar houses in other neighborhoods.

For a long time, federal policy (or the lack of it) was one of the largest contributors to racial discrimination in housing. It was not until President Kennedy's 1962 executive order that the government attempted to control the problem. But the changes sought by the order, the 1968 Fair Housing Act, and massive ghetto housing programs (also begun in the sixties) never fully materialized. Open housing laws have, so to speak, affected a few trees but missed the forest. In some ways, current housing programs may encourage segregation rather than reduce it. Urban renewal programs, for instance, typically destroy more black housing than they build, and local resistance to federally subsidized housing for the poor generally results in placing houses for blacks in black neighborhoods. Housing discrimination is an enormous problem in itself, but it is especially problematic because without housing desegregation, school desegregation may never be effectively achieved.

Discrimination in Politics and Criminal Justice

Politics In the political arena, blacks and other minorities face unjust treatment even at the voting booth, where harassment and exclusion of minorities are commonplace. Some minorities are shortchanged at the polls because they do not have an adequate command of the English language. In 1975, an extension of the Voting Rights Act was passed which mandated bilingual elections in cities with a large "language minority."

The questionable state of black voting power and the token number of blacks in political office partly account for the low level of confidence blacks have in the federal government (now down to a fraction of the 83 percent of blacks who expressed confidence in the Kennedy administration). Although there has been a significant increase in the number of voters in the black voting-age population, there has not been a commensurate rise in the number of blacks in office. Today, fewer than 1 percent of the nation's elected officials are black. According to a 1983 *Washington Post*-ABC News poll, more than 1 in 6 Americans would not vote for a black candidate for president. On the brighter side, blacks have become the mayors of such major cities as Washington, New Orleans, Atlanta, Los Angeles, Cleveland, Cincinnati, Chicago, and Philadelphia. They have also made slight gains in the House of Representatives and the Senate, but to date, no state has had a black governor.

Criminal Justice Although blacks constitute only a small fraction of the population, they constitute 50 percent of the state prison population and about 50 percent of all people killed by police. Some of this may reflect the elevated crime rate among poor people in general (see Chapter 11 on crime), but some of it occurs because society values black lives less than those of whites. Indeed, a 1983 Rand Corporation study found that blacks and Hispanics are sentenced to prison more often and serve longer terms than whites convicted of similar crimes. There was a time in Texas when the customary penalty for a black rapist was a small fine if the victim were black, but death if the victim were white. Those days are gone, but parallels remain. In 1986, for instance, the NAACP Legal Defense Fund cited studies concluding that killers of whites are eleven times more likely to receive the death penalty in Georgia than killers of blacks. Capital punishment probably would not have been abolished if it did not blatantly constitute cruel and unusual punishment *for blacks*. Of the 3859 prisoners executed between 1930 and 1971, over 50 percent were black. Remember, only 12 percent of the population is black. On a more positive side, there are reports of a gradual trend toward equality in American criminal sentencing (Peterson and Hagan, 1984).

The bail system is also discriminatory. Since judges do not consider a person's financial status when setting bail, and since many blacks are poor, bail usually means jail to a black accused of a crime. Studies have shown that defendants who cannot raise bail and consequently stay in jail are more likely to be seen as deviant and therefore adjudged guilty. What this all boils down to is that black (and other poor minority) defendants are treated as if they are guilty because they are poor—a vicious circle that sadistically exploits the disadvantaged and one that further demonstrates the interrelations of social problems.

CAUSES OF PREJUDICE

What causes prejudice? Why do some whites, blacks, Jews, and other minority groups have such prejudicial attitudes toward one another? There are many theories. Because prejudice has been a widespread problem throughout history, many reputable researchers used to believe it was an inborn, instinctive human characteristic. Today it is apparent that prejudice is acquired. Evidence for this takes different forms. First, there was a time when European whites rarely displayed prejudice toward blacks. Most problems between blacks and whites began with slavery in the United States. Second, prejudice is unevenly distributed throughout the world, strongly suggesting that psychosocial forces cause prejudice rather than any set of natural tendencies. Of course, bigots see prejudice as natural and necessary. When questioned about their feelings, they usually offer such rationalizations as the need for the dominant group to defend itself or the biological inferiority of the minority group.

As is implied by the ambiguity of the concept of race, the real roots of prejudice are psychosocial. Some theories emphasize psychological forces, and others stress social forces. Some account for only a particular kind of prejudice, such as antiblack attitudes or anti-Semitism. No one theory can explain all instances of bigotry. For example, most of the theories reviewed here attempt to explain individual cases of prejudice as opposed to the broad social forces that can lead to institutional forms of prejudice and discrimination. Among the psychological theories are the following three: symbolic theory, frustration-aggression theory, and the theory of the authoritarian personality.

Symbolic Theory

Many people have traits, thoughts, or urges of which they are ashamed because they are socially unacceptable. The traits may be so deep-rooted in the personality that they cannot easily be eliminated. Some people are not even consciously aware of their undesirable traits because they are hidden in the recesses of the unconscious. Unwanted traits can be the source of considerable anxiety. To reduce the anxiety, some people unconsciously employ a psychological mechanism known as *projection*. These individuals can deny their unwanted traits by finding them in other people rather than in themselves. Thus, they can condemn the traits without condemning themselves.

According to symbolic theory, bigots see in certain racial and ethnic groups symbols of that which they fear within themselves or of something they envy. Some whites may hate blacks because to them blacks symbolize uninhibited sexual activity, something forbidden by the harsh constraints of a puritanical moral code. Other whites accuse blacks of being lazy because they really are lazy themselves. There is also evidence that those most appalled by homosexuals are gay themselves but cannot accept it. Symbolic theories have been offered most frequently to explain anti-Semitism. Jews are seen as having traits which some fear and others envy. Among them are pushiness, a preoccupation with power, and a good business sense. Those who stigmatize Jews in these ways are themselves often preoccupied with the very same traits.

Frustration-Aggression Theory

A second psychological theory holds that prejudice may stem from frustration, the tension that results from being unable to achieve a desired goal. This may lead to feelings of anger and aggression, which can be expressed in a number of ways. Because people are often unable to strike back at the actual source of their frustration (such as a boss or parent), they will vent their aggression on a safer, more convenient target. This psychological process is known as *displacement*. The target is known as a *scapegoat*.[11] Sometimes the scapegoat is a particular person, but when aggression is displaced onto a group of people, it constitutes prejudice. According to this theory, this is one of the things that occurred in Nazi Germany. The Jews were blamed for a host of societal problems, from the loss of World War I to the economic decline of the country. Hitler used the Jews as a scapegoat to unify the Nazi movement against a common enemy—the convenient Jew. Poor whites in the contemporary United States, unable to express anger directly to the landlords who drain their few dollars or the employers who underpay them, will often vent their hostilities on blacks.

Blacks, Jews, Hispanics, American Indians, and other minorities also provide convenient and reasonably safe substitute targets for majority members. Minority racial and ethnic groups are especially suited to this role because they are visible, not in a position to retaliate, readily accessible, previous objects of blame, and the personification of some undesirable trait (Allport, 1959). These are the ingredients for a good scapegoat—a group that is also a *safe goat* for the persecutor.

---

[11] During the days of atonement in ancient Israel, a priest would place his hands on the head of a goat while reciting the sins of the people. This symbolically transferred the sin from the people to the goat. The goat was freed in the wilderness, thus clearing the community of sin. The animal was called a scapegoat.

The Authoritarian Personality

A third psychological theory of prejudice was initiated in 1950 when Theodore Adorno headed a research team at the University of California at Berkeley to discover the roots of anti-Semitism. The research was spurred by the enormous amount of anti-Jewish feeling prevailing during World War II, feelings so extreme that death fell to millions of Jews. The Berkeley researchers found that people prejudiced against Jews were also likely to be prejudiced against other minority groups, especially blacks, intellectual liberals, and sexual nonconformists. They called this psychological syndrome the *authoritarian personality*.

Part of the syndrome is anti-intraception, an inability to look inside oneself and understand one's own feelings. This is consistent with both the frustration-aggression and symbolic theories: authoritarians may have been raised by brutal parents whom they despised; yet they cannot deal with aggressive feelings toward their parents, so they project them onto a safer target. The Berkeley researchers found that authoritarians were raised by parents (particularly fathers) who were unduly harsh. The psychological result is that authoritarians do not realize they harbor hatred within themselves but instead believe that hatred abounds in the outside, dangerous world.

Authoritarians are people who view the world in a rigid good-bad fashion. They idealize those they see as authorities with legitimate power over them (such as military leaders) and reject those they see as beneath them in status (such as poor blacks). They believe people can be simply divided into two distinct classes: the weak and the strong.

What is particularly curious about authoritarians is that despite their simplistic world view, their thinking is confused and inconsistent. They feel quite comfortable conceiving of minority groups in contradictory ways. For instance, the Berkeley researchers found that authoritarians believe Jews are seclusive, are clannish, and have a desire to keep apart from other groups. At the same time, they describe Jews as intrusive, as evidenced by a supposed desire to move into neighborhoods where they are not wanted! Apparently, prejudiced people see the world in ways consistent with their prejudice but not with logic. Consider the following dialogue with an anti-Semite, reported by Gordon Allport in his classic book *The Nature of Prejudice* (1954).

Mr. X The trouble with the Jews is that they only take care of their own group.

Mr. Y But the record of the Community Chest campaign shows that they give more generously, in proportion to their numbers, to the general charities of the community, than do non-Jews.

Mr. X That shows they are always trying to buy favor and intrude into Christian affairs. They think of nothing but money; that is why there are so many Jewish bankers.

Mr. Y But a recent study shows that the percentage of Jews in the banking business is negligible, far smaller than the percentage of non-Jews.

Mr. X That's just it; they don't go in for respectable business; they are only in the movie business or run night clubs.

There are two main social theories of prejudice: economic exploitation and social modeling.

Economic Exploitation

The economic exploitation theory of prejudice is helpful in understanding the origin of institutional forms of discrimination. Competition over ownership of economic goods and material wealth has traditionally resulted in the dominance of one group over others. This competition ultimately involves a struggle for power and results in the economic exploitation of the subordinate groups by the dominant one. As Marx noted long ago, this occurs in capitalistic societies where exploitation of less powerful social classes is a fact of life. In stratified societies, conflict between the haves and the have-nots is really class conflict expressed as racial conflict.

Why are certain groups the objects of economic exploitation? The explanation for Hispanics may be that the most recent group to enter the country is most likely to end up at the bottom of the pile. This was certainly true in earlier years for a number of immigrant groups, including the Irish, Poles, and Italians. If this is true, we should expect to find less discrimination against Hispanics in the future and more opportunity for better jobs. But what about the blacks? They have been and continue to be economically exploited. Blacks are a special case because of the unique way they entered the country: as indentured servants or slaves. White supremacy was used as a political issue (particularly in the South) to keep poor blacks and poor whites from discovering their common interests in overcoming poverty. This created a deep-seated ideology of black inferiority that is difficult to eradicate.

Whites gain in a number of ways through antiblack prejudice, aside from a feeling of superiority. Whites in power who hire blacks can pay them less. Since prejudice also makes it difficult for blacks to compete with whites for jobs, they are forced to accept whatever jobs are left over, regardless of how unpleasant or low-paying they may be. The economic advantages of racial discrimination are especially evident in the success trade unions have had in denying membership to blacks, thus keeping blacks out of relatively high-paying occupations controlled by whites. Economic exploitation theory is also supported by the observation that all of the economic problems blacks experience become especially intense, relative to others, during times when money and jobs are scarce.

Social Modeling

A second social theory of prejudice asserts that Americans who hold prejudicial beliefs and act in discriminatory ways are not necessarily authoritarian personalities, frustrated individuals, or people who project their own problems onto others. Many may have racist views and behavior because they are conforming to social norms. "Conforming bigots" become antiblack (or antianyone) as a way of belonging. This process begins early in life if children are raised in an environment (at home, at school, and in the neighborhood) where prejudice and discriminatory behavior against certain minorities are the norm. These children come to view those prejudices and behaviors as normal and natural. Some parents reward and punish their children on the basis of their attitudes toward various racial and ethnic groups. Some white parents spank their children for playing with black children. Some teachers subtly, and sometimes overtly, express prejudicial views and display discriminatory behavior to their students.

Contact with prejudiced people conditions children toward bigotry through modeling and imitation of adult role models. Many widespread prejudices are learned as supposed facts, such as "Pollacks are dumb" and "Blacks are oversexed." Social modeling also accounts for regional variations in prejudice, which reflect the predominant societal norms of an area.

Perhaps the most dramatic demonstration of prejudice stemming from contact with prejudiced people rather than from contact with members of minority groups was conducted in an experiment by Hartley (1964). He gave test subjects a long list of races and nationalities for comment. Prejudicial subjects recommended discriminatory action against Jews and blacks. They also recommended that the Danireans, Wallonians, and Pireneans be refused admission to the United States or be expelled if they are already living here. In actuality, the Danireans, Wallonians, and Pireneans are mythical! Hartley made them up to see if prejudiced people (who had prejudiced parents) are also prejudiced against groups that do not even exist.

Some of the blame for socializing children toward prejudice can be placed on the media. As mentioned earlier, the media often play a large role in the way people subjectively view social issues and groups of people. The press has given very selective coverage of black people by describing them in biased ways. Small black militant groups, such as the Black Panthers, receive more coverage than large moderate groups, such as the National Association for the Advancement of Colored People (NAACP). Blacks are also frequently portrayed as living on welfare in homes which the father has deserted, even though most are not living in deserted homes on welfare. Further unrealistic treatment of blacks is especially apparent in the film industry, which typically places them in stereotypical roles (as drug pushers, pimps, and the like). Rarely are they placed in roles as schoolteachers, bankers, police officers, or cab drivers, roles which reflect the reality of American life.

Perhaps there is no larger culprit in distorting the image of blacks than television (MacDonald, 1983). Regular television fare for children and many adults portrays all the "genetically perfect people" as whites with blue eyes and blonde hair. There are no strong, intelligent black figures on television, with the possible exception of *The Cosby Show*. Too many of the mothers are fat and jolly, a residual white image of Aunt Jemima. The fathers are portrayed as shiftless, rather than strong and intelligent. The children tend to be cutups, strutting around as superflies. Family life is screaming turmoil with the air full of insults. There are few images of success through education and accomplishment. These are the models of black people that are beamed to the world. It is no small wonder that children come to view these highly subjec-

tive misinterpretations of blacks as if they were objective reality.

THE CIVIL RIGHTS MOVEMENT

Protest Movements

During the last decades, widespread reaction to discrimination has been unification through organization and public protest. No one individual played a larger role in this movement than the late Dr. Martin Luther King, Jr. For a while, the civil rights movement accomplished some substantive gains in peaceful ways. With these gains, the expectations of black people grew to the point where their achievements did not meet their rising expectations. In this situation, the objective position of black people may have been improving, but they subjectively perceived that things were getting worse.

Because of the growing gap between expectations and achievements, black frustration grew in the 1960s and protest sometimes took violent forms. In Montgomery, Alabama, groups of whites attacked black Freedom Riders protesting against being forced to sit in a designated area of public buses, and then burned the bus the Freedom Riders had occupied. Southern civil rights workers used confrontation tactics fused with the Black Muslims' ideology of black pride to seek equality through political, economic, and quasimilitary means. In Oakland, California, in 1966, Bobby Seale and Huey P. Newton organized the Black Panther Party, essentially a vigilante group to protect blacks from the growing hostility of whites toward blacks' demands for equality.

Eventually, feelings of frustration and rage detonated the powder keg of the black ghettos—Philadelphia and New York in 1964; Chicago and Los Angeles in 1965; Omaha and Cleveland in 1966; Buffalo, Detroit, Newark, and Cincinnati in 1967. Scores of other riots occurred after Dr. King was assassinated in 1968. The large movement of blacks to the cities was a factor in these riots; blacks were physically concentrated, and urbanization made them a more sophisticated people capable of effective protest. Earlier confrontations between the races were usually one-sided conflicts like lynchings. In a riot, however, the opposing forces are more evenly matched; the minority fights back and feels it has some hope of defending itself. Riots are frequently triggered by the arrest of blacks by white police officers, who symbolize the status quo. Although young, unmarried, and unemployed males are the typical participants in a riot, the race riots of the sixties and seventies had proportionately more women and employed people than in the past. This may be an index of the great amount of rage and frustration that permeated the black community—the feeling that the only way "to make whitey listen" was to burn, loot, and riot.

Organized protest can be an effective weapon in achieving minorities' rights, but when change comes slowly, patience can be exhausted and nonviolent protest is replaced by violent demonstrations. The obvious limitations of violence contributed to a decline in this form of protest in the mid-1970s. There was also a noticeable decline in the unity and direction of the civil rights movement, a phenomenon consistent with the life cycle of social movements as explained in Chapter 1 (see Figure 1-2). The civil rights movement appeared to be in the fragmentation stage, but it never reached the stage of complete demise as recent events have demonstrated. In the early 1980s the deepening recession of the economy, skyrocketing unemployment, and sharp cutbacks in social services led to one of the worst outbreaks of racial violence in history. Three days of social fury in Miami left fifteen persons dead and took a financial toll of close to 200 million dollars, leaving much of the country wondering whether the vicious rioting was an omen.

Miami may very well be an indication of what lies ahead, since the civil rights movement has certainly failed to equalize the status of whites and minorities. The black power movement, directed at the cultural identity of blacks, was a more successful enterprise in some ways. It occasioned a number of normative changes in the relations between blacks and whites. "Nigger" jokes are now viewed as signs of ignorance.[12] In fact, it has become fashionable to be accepting of blacks. Hispanics and American Indians also command more respect now, but they are still saddled with problems of inequality not shared by other groups.

LEGISLATION AGAINST DISCRIMINATION

Major Laws

In the 1860s and 1870s, the legal foundations for minority rights were laid with the passage of the Thirteenth, Fourteenth, and Fifteenth Amendments to the Constitution. However, it was almost a hundred years later that minorities began to effectively claim their legal rights. The turning point occurred in 1954 in the famous *Brown v. Board of Education* decision, in which a unanimous ruling against de jure racial segregation in public schools eliminated the "separate but equal" doctrine and ruled that "separate educational facilities are inherently unequal."[13] This decision resulted partly from some twenty years of campaigning by the NAACP to show that the notion of separate but equal facilities was inherently wrong since it promoted, among other things, the feeling among black children that they were inferior and had no right to compete with white children.

Eventually the new "separate cannot be equal" doctrine was extended to theaters, beaches, golf courses, public pools, and the like. In the 1960s a number of laws were passed

---

[12] Even white comedians rarely make jokes about blacks, although it is quite acceptable for black comedians, such as Flip Wilson and Richard Pryor, to poke fun at the idiosyncrasies of whites.

[13] This was the first time the government asked social scientists for their advice on the civil rights issue.

to end specific forms of discrimination. The most sweeping was the Civil Rights Act of 1964. It outlawed discrimination in public facilities and employment and stipulated that federal funds be withdrawn from any institution practicing racial discrimination. In 1965, a Voting Rights Act was passed. State laws banning interracial marriage were declared unconstitutional in 1967, and in 1968, the first federal law against housing discrimination was passed. In 1976, the Supreme Court, in an attempt to undo the injustice of past discrimination, ordered that special seniority rights be given to blacks previously denied jobs because of their race.

Despite the passage of many civil rights laws, loopholes still legally permit discrimination. A private club, for instance, can discriminate on the basis of race as long as its corporate charter does not require it to do so, since therefore the state has not sanctioned the discrimination. This rule has led to confusion and anguish. Recently, the American Bar Association proposed that clubs which discriminate (by sex, ethnicity, or race) should be required to prove they are purely social by showing that less than 20 percent of their revenues have been treated as business expenses for tax purposes.

The Effect of Laws on Attitudes

Clearly the law has the limited ability to guarantee equal rights, but does it affect the way people think? Do civil rights laws help reduce prejudice? Some blacks may see these laws as mere tokenism since discrimination still exists, but changing racial attitudes show that laws can affect the hearts and minds of people.

When behavior is changed through laws, people's attitudes generally change to be consistent with the new required behavior. When whites find themselves sitting in classrooms with blacks, they tend to view school integration more positively. The same formula holds true for other areas of prejudice, such as housing and racial attitudes, as shown by early studies in integrated housing projects in New York City and segregated projects in Newark (Deutsch and Collins, 1951). The feelings of whites toward blacks became more positive in the integrated projects and did not change at all in the segregated projects. From a social policy perspective, it is useful to know that people's attitudes may be changed through legislation. From the perspective of the subjective-objective dimensions of social problems, the studies demonstrate that objective factors (new laws) can also affect the subjective dimension (prejudice).

OTHER MINORITY PROBLEMS

Anti-Semitism

Discrimination and prejudice are directed at many minority groups besides blacks. Bigotry directed toward women is an enormous problem which constitutes a separate chapter of this book (Chapter 10). Jews, Hispanics, and American Indians have also been traditional targets of the prejudiced. Jews have been discriminated against in some of the ways blacks have experienced.

Anti-Semitism often takes subtle forms, but sometimes it is overt, such as the exclusion of Jews from certain college fraternities and sororities. There have even been so-called scientific studies which have concluded that Jews are feebleminded and physically inferior to other groups (Gould, 1980). Recently, the president of the Southern Baptist Convention (a well-known "Christian") declared that God does not hear the prayers of a Jew! No one should ever forget the Holocaust in Nazi Germany. What is not widely known, however, is that an American World War II research report raised the possibility of rocketing wartime refugees—most of whom were Jews—to Venus or Mars for resettlement! Apparently, anti-Semitism knows no bounds.

Anti-Semitism declined after the widely publicized atrocities of the Second World War. Today it is reportedly on the rise, partly because of the open action by such groups as the Ku Klux Klan and the American Nazi Party. One white supremacist group (the Institute for Historical Review in Torrance, California) has offered 50,000 dollars to anyone who can prove Jews were gassed at Auschwitz! Consistent with the theory that frustration underlies prejudice and discrimination, attacks against Jews increased in the late 1970s and early 1980s as the United States economy worsened. The Anti-Defamation League of B'nai B'rith reported over 1000 anti-Semitic incidents in 1981. These included fire bombings, swastika daubings, bomb threats, cross burnings, telephone threats, graffiti, cemetery desecration, and other forms of vandalism in thirty-one states, chiefly New York, California, and New Jersey. This was the third straight year acts of anti-Semitism more than doubled despite new state laws against antireligious acts and new procedures for investigating them. In 1982, there was a reported decrease in anti-Semitic acts, but the decline was halted by the massacre of Palestinian civilians in Beirut, coinciding with a new wave of anti-Semitism in the United States. In 1983, reported assaults, threats, and harassments of Jews in the United States declined by 41 percent.

Jews have not reacted to anti-Semitism impassively. In the late 1960s, the Jewish Defense League (JDL) made the news because of its militant approach to protecting Jews' rights. The JDL believes that anti-Semitism has arisen because Jews are misunderstood and unfairly stigmatized. There are many ungrounded subjective beliefs about Jews. Blacks see them as slumlords, midwestern crusaders see them as atheists, leftists see them as capitalists, and rednecks see them as Communists. The JDL has been trying to get Jews to organize themselves into bands that patrol local areas, fight harassment by other groups (especially other minorities), and take pride in their Jewish identity.

Hispanics

Hispanics are a diverse group that includes immigrants from Mexico, Puerto Rico, Cuba, and the Dominican Republic. It has been difficult for these people to realize the promise of American equality, in part because they face occupational and educational discrimination similar to that confronting blacks. Their unemployment rate is one-third higher than that of whites, and those who are employed often work at extremely undesirable jobs, such as migrant farm work. Despite the highly publicized efforts of Cesar Chavez, the head of the United Farm Workers' Union, and others to improve conditions for migrant Hispanic workers, it was reported as recently as 1982 that thousands are enslaved and physically held against their will. Like blacks, Hispanics have many health problems, including short life expectancy, high infant mortality, and high mortality rates from pneumonia, tuberculosis, and influenza.

Economically, Hispanics are worse off than blacks because their larger families drop their per capita income below that of blacks. This results in a lower economic "investment" per child and a perpetuation of inadequate education and underemployment. In terms of pure prejudice, Hispanics may be better or worse off than blacks, depending on their skin color. Dark-skinned Hispanics invoke stereotypical thinking similar to that facing blacks. Light-skinned Hispanics are a partial minority insofar as they can pass for white. This is one reason some Hispanics feel their situation is significantly better than that of blacks, and also possibly why they report less psychological distress than blacks (Roberts, 1980). However, there is some evidence that discrimination against blacks is declining while discrimination against Hispanics is growing (Mindiola, 1979). Tienda (1983) reports that as much as 50 percent of the earnings gap between Hispanic and white men may be attributable to discrimination.

Stereotypical thinking about Hispanics, as with blacks, is inappropriate and damaging. Frequently Hispanic youths are defined as ignorant because they lack educational skills and motivation. Hispanic children come to define themselves in the same way and consequently have high dropout rates and/or poor school records, confirming and perpetuating the stereotype. A 1979 *New York Times*-CBS News poll uncovered a widespread subjective belief that Hispanics (particularly illegal immigrants) will do jobs that most Americans will not. This is one of the few stereotypical views of a group of people which actually matches the objective facts. Hispanics are so exploited occupationally that they have no choice but to work in undesirable jobs. Most stereotypical thinking about Hispanics, however, is ungrounded. There are some widely shared stereotypes about Mexican-Americans which have found their way into the mass communication messages of our society. Included are the notions that Mexicans are overweight, lazy, sneaky thieves who are disinterested in improving themselves, have body odor, and are always sleeping.

The Hispanic population is growing very fast. Currently, there are approximately 19 million Hispanics (including illegal aliens) in the United States. The Hispanic proportion of the United States population is around 9 percent versus 12 percent for blacks. If present trends continue, Hispanics will outnumber blacks within the next decade. A major reason for this rapid growth is the vast difference in quality of life between their Latin American homelands and the United States. Even the American slums look affluent when compared with Latin American barrios. For further discussion of the population problems of Hispanics in the United States, see Chapter 7.

American Indians

Today there are about 800,000 American Indians, over half of whom live on approximately 200 reservations. The rest live in cities or are scattered through the eastern United States. Although they constitute less than 0.5 percent of the total population, Indians are a significant minority in the United States.

American Indians suffer many forms of discrimination. Educational attainment, for instance, is extremely low, especially on reservations. Nationally, the median level of American Indian education is only 5.3 years. Moreover, the quality of education is often inferior, mainly because reservation schools are poorly staffed and generally underfinanced. On the Navajo reservation, over half the adults are unemployed or working only part-time, while virtually all the residents live lives of poverty in substandard housing. Indians also have severe health problems, including high rates of diabetes, tuberculosis, and alcoholism. The infant mortality rate among Indians is about 20 percent above that for the total United States population.

Unlike the other minority groups considered here, the Indians were colonized by nonnative American society. This historical fact adds an extra dimension to contemporary discrimination against Native Americans, and it helps to explain their extra measure of social problems. Even compared to other deprived groups, Indians suffer exceedingly high rates of a whole spectrum of problematic conditions, including suicide, crime, and alcoholism. This interrelated web of problems has been traced to a common sociological source: anomie (Bahr, Chadwick, and Day, 1972). The demoralization of conquest and the forced adaption of the survivors to the foreign culture have had a disastrous effect on traditional Indian culture. Since they are understandably reluctant to assimilate into the invading society, many Native Americans are left without any firm cultural roots: hence, the tragic consequences of anomie.

Underlying the discriminatory treatment of Indians is a set of highly prejudicial beliefs. One concept, that of the Indian as a "noble savage," defies logic. On the one hand, Indians are viewed

American Indians rallying for their civil rights in Washington, D.C. (*Gianfranco Gorgoni/Contact*)

Hostility between Minorities

Prejudice is not an attitude held only by members of the dominant group toward members of a minority group. There is also much ill feeling among minorities, especially between blacks and Jews. Since the early 1970s, intense anti-Jewish attitudes have been expressed by a number of black leaders, including Jesse Jackson and Reverend Joseph Lowery of the Southern Christian Leadership Conference. This came as a shock to many people who had assumed there was a natural alliance between blacks and Jews in this country. In fact, a number of Harris surveys throughout the 1970s showed a sharp increase in black anti-Semitism. Recently it was reported that blacks are even more anti-Semitic than whites (Martire and Clark, 1982). Blacks are especially likely to believe Jews choose money over people, are unethical in business, constitute the largest number of slumlords, and have too much power and influence.[14]

There has also been an increase in antiblack feelings among Jews. The Harris surveys showed that Jews are less willing than other whites to send their children to schools with blacks or to have blacks move into their neighborhoods. Ironically, since Jews are politically more liberal than any other white group and are ideologically opposed to racism, they are the closest social and political allies blacks have. Yet inappropriate feelings and misunderstandings prevent the two groups from working together to fight prejudice and discrimination.

Jews and blacks do not have a monopoly on hostility between minorities. Asians have also been regularly victimized. In 1986, for example, Philadelphia was the scene of numerous attacks against Hmong refugees. Many of the reported incidents involved blacks.

as uncorrupted by urban vice. At the same time, they are seen as vicious barbarians. Another common notion is that Indians on reservations are lazy and incompetent. Yet apparent Indian incompetence is actually the result of the inefficient way in which reservations are run by the government. Most federal expenditures for Indian programs are absorbed by the Bureau of Indian Affairs before they even reach the reservations. Cities like Chicago allocate ten times more funds for the Boy Scouts than they do for Indians. Recently, Indians have been protesting their economic and social powerlessness in such places as Alcatraz and Wounded Knee. But it will be forever before "red power" movements restore Indians to their rightful place in American society.

[14] Similar tensions exist in many American cities between Asian merchants and the black communities they serve and between blacks and Puerto Ricans living near each other.

SOCIAL POLICY: AFFIRMATIVE ACTION

Strategies for Solution

When antidiscrimination policies were first implemented in the 1960s, it appeared a rather simple matter to effect equality through legislation. But some strategies later brought on fierce debates and protests of their own. Although there has been limited success in achieving certain civil rights objectives, such as voter registration and school desegregation, there is clearly no easy solution or quick fix for such a deeply rooted problem as discrimination.

Probably no form of discrimination is more important than discrimination in occupation. Attaining real equality in people's chances to gain meaningful employment would greatly reduce other forms of discrimination. For instance, educational discrimination is tied to occupational (and therefore income) discrimination since it is partly the result of minorities being unable to *afford* college training. A number of social policy goals are directed toward occupational discrimination, including equal treatment of minorities and whites (or preferred treatment for minorities) with regard to hiring, promotion, fringe benefits, tenure status, training, and layoffs. Two policy alternatives that have emerged over the years are *assimilation* and *affirmative action*.

Assimilation is consistent with the immigrant analogy, a line of thinking becoming increasingly popular (Oliver and Glick, 1982). Essentially, it claims that since blacks are recent immigrants to urban America,[15] they must wait in line for their turn to gain economic success. Just like the Poles, Irish, and others before them, blacks will eventually make it by being patient and sharing a piece of the pie as it becomes available. Social policy directed toward helping blacks and other minorities would

be unnecessary. In fact, it would be unfair to other groups who have already made it through patience and hard work. Assimilation appeals to the conservative element in our society, people who believe that doing nothing is the right approach because nature will take its course. Neidert and Farley (1985) report that the assimilation process appears to work for some immigrant groups by the third generation, although there are important exceptions, namely blacks and Mexicans.

One conservative favoring this no-action approach is Thomas Sowell, a well-known black intellectual. Sowell (1981) believes blacks could measure their progress as if they were recently arrived immigrants. He disagrees with blacks who feel they should be given special treatment; their standard of living has significantly improved since they migrated from Africa. Every ethnic group has encountered obstacles to its progress in the United States, but any suffering they experienced here was small in comparison to their lifestyles in their native country. Jews, for instance, were destitute when they first set foot on American soil, yet they became one of the most economically successful ethnic groups in American history.

If blacks play by the rules of the American free enterprise system, Sowell believes financial rewards will eventually "trickle down" to them as they have to others before them. Wilson (1980) says this is already happening, as race has reportedly declined in significance in the economic sector throughout this century. Wilson argues that the gains in employment and occupational status that blacks made during the 1960s bred *social class* cleavages that did not exist within the black population prior to 1960. Previous research showed that as of 1962, blacks were poor not because they were born into poverty but because they were born black. Wilson does not deny the results of prior research. He argues that the balance of class and race effects changed after 1962. Hout (1984) tested Wilson's hypothesis that class has re-

---

[15] Some argue that blacks should not be counted as immigrants from Africa but as immigrants from the rural areas in the 1940s, thus making them the most recent immigrants.

placed race as the arbiter of economic opportunities for blacks in the United States and found strong support for Wilson's contentions.

Affirmative action was initiated by the Civil Rights Act of 1964 and established as government policy by Lyndon Johnson's Executive Order of 1965. Affirmative action is a set of government programs designed to increase the participation of minorities in industry, business, education, and service agencies by ending discrimination and actively recruiting minorities, including women. It includes hard quotas of minority people who must be hired, regardless of qualifications, and it makes the "last hired, first fired" rules of many companies illegal so that minorities can maintain all their gains of the last two decades.

The courts and administrations prior to Reagan's have enforced a stern standard of affirmative action: employers have had to set numerical goals and timetables for hiring and promoting minorities. If the employer fails to comply, grants and federal funds are withheld until the company shows it is actively recruiting minorities and women for available positions. The Department of Health, Education and Welfare (HEW) withheld millions of dollars from the nation's twenty largest universities until they demonstrated compliance. Universities have also had to make special programs for students with test scores and grades lower than those of the average entrant. Many universities, consequently, provide financial help and work-study opportunities to those from low-income minority families.

Affirmative action is based on the belief that to compensate for the historical preference for white males, preference for minorities is necessary. It is a hard-nosed policy under which the employer has the burden of proof to show it is *not* guilty of discrimination and is making a real effort to recruit minorities. During the Reagan administration, however, the rules were relaxed. Companies no longer have to draw up written affirmative action plans unless they have at least 250 employees and government

contracts worth 1 million dollars a year. Previously, the standard had been 50 employees and 50,000 dollars in government contracts. The exempted employers constitute 75 percent of the 200,000 companies that do federally paid work. In 1986, the Supreme Court took action on the long-standing debate over the legality of court-ordered racial goals and timetables by coming out on the side of affirmative action proponents.

Policies into Practice

It is difficult to evaluate the effectiveness of the assimilationist approach because as a passive policy, it cannot be clearly linked with any specific accomplishments. While it is true that the position of minorities has improved over time, no one can be certain what factors are responsible. It is interesting to note that most minority gains occurred in recent decades, the exact time when affirmative action programs were in effect. Overall, affirmative action programs appear to have achieved some success in promoting equality of opportunity for minorities. Some report they have significantly helped to improve the socioeconomic position of minorities in the United States (Kluegel and Smith, 1982). Economic and occupational discrimination still remains, but no policy can be expected to cure overnight what has been going on for 200 years. Essentially, there are two practical problems with affirmative action. One is the issue of reverse discrimination, and the other is uneven support for the policy by different administrations.[16]

Reverse discrimination is an example of an intended solution to a problem leading to a new problem, what some call a value trade-off. A number of lawsuits and a large segment of the white public object to affirmative action be-

---

[16] Another problem with affirmative action is that it does not directly deal with the fact that blacks lack job skills because of the numerous forms of institutional discrimination they faced over the years.

cause it discriminates against white males. They are also against it because jobs and college admissions are now distributed by race or sex rather than on the basis of qualifications. Advocates of affirmative action argue this is necessary to compensate for past discrimination against minorities. Opponents claim that blacks who were discriminated against in the past are now 40 years of age or older and are not being helped by affirmative action. Young blacks, who have not faced occupational discrimination in the past, are the ones getting preferential treatment. Young whites, who are not responsible for past discrimination, are the ones now facing discrimination.

Should social policy to end discrimination move from color blindness to color consciousness? Supporters of reverse discrimination argue further in the affirmative by noting that discrimination has forced minorities to be better qualified for jobs than the dominant group. Affirmative action alleviates that problem and is really no different from other laws which give preference to certain groups, such as veterans for civil service jobs. Opponents of affirmative action contend that this is a privilege earned through military service and through the fact that when veterans returned to civilian life, they were occupationally behind those not in the service. They say more generally that reverse discrimination is an unconstitutional quota system that disregards ability and talent. Past discrimination may have been wrong, but two wrongs do not make a right, especially if the present generation is being asked to pay for the wrongdoings of past generations.

Wide opposition to affirmative action was revealed in 1978 when the Supreme Court heard a landmark case, *Regents of the University of California v. Bakke*. Alan Bakke, a white applicant to the medical school, claimed he was the victim of reverse discrimination since he was not admitted, while minority applicants with lower test scores were admitted to slots specifically reserved for them. By a 5 to 4 margin, the Supreme Court supported Bakke and ordered that he be admitted. The court was not opposed to affirmative action per se but to the specific policy of strict quotas. Incidentally, the close vote demonstrates the value trade-offs on this complicated issue. Similar suits have occurred throughout the country, especially among academics who have been less pro-affirmative action recently as their jobs have been threatened by shrinking student enrollments.

Presently, there is growing opinion that affirmative action imposes an unjust burden on the white majority. Clearly, social policies have subjective dimensions just like social problems. In 1980, for instance, a Gallup poll reported that only 7 percent of whites felt minority group members should be given preferential treatment in getting jobs and places in colleges. About 86 percent of college students polled felt ability should be the main consideration. Garcia and his colleagues (1981) report that minority applicants to college are seen by others as less qualified when the college is committed to an affirmative action program. This suggests that affirmative action has a negative influence on the subjective perception of minorities' abilities. It can also have a negative influence on the membership of the Democratic party, which has always supported domestic programs such as affirmative action. A 1985 analysis of the growing number of defectors from that party found that almost all who are leaving party ranks are whites who are dissatisfied with affirmative action and similar programs.

Another problem with successful implementation of affirmative action policies is the level of federal involvement in promoting equal opportunity for minorities. Differences in the philosophy of federal administrations can affect the implementation of civil rights programs, particularly affirmative action. Since 1980 there has been a dramatic turnabout in Washington's enforcement of equal employment laws. President Reagan's attorney general claimed that justice does not mean treating every race or class in the same manner, and in 1982 the Justice Department decided to stop denying tax exempt status to private schools which discriminate against minorities. The Heritage Foundation, an influential New Right group, recommended that the Reagan administration dismantle hundreds of existing affirmative action agreements designed to remedy discrimination.

Not only has there been an all-out attack on affirmative action, but there have also been deep cuts made in public programs that especially benefit black people. By 1984, publicly assisted housing was cut by 54 billion dollars; 400,000 households were removed from the Aid to Families with Dependent Children program; 1 of 4 black families previously eligible for food stamps was declared ineligible; and payments for extended unemployment were cut by 15.4 percent (Bush, 1982). The Reagan administration has actually fought to dismantle affirmative action. In 1982, for instance, that administration joined white Boston police and fire fighters in a reverse discrimination case challenging court-ordered affirmative action. This was the first time the government sided with whites in a major racial discrimination case. More recently, the Reagan administration asked a federal appellate court to overturn a judicially approved agreement under which the city of New Orleans would have to promote equal numbers of black and white police officers. Additionally, efforts to increase the number of minority faculty in predominantly white colleges and universities in the United States have been less successful than is commonly supposed (Exum, 1983).

It is difficult to evaluate the efficiency of a policy to control discrimination when there is uneven support for it by different administrations. When affirmative action programs are not actively supported, assimilation becomes the chosen policy to achieve equality. However, while assimilation may lead to improvements in the lives of blacks, there is still a large income gap between them and whites. As Sowell and Wilson predict, this may shrink as blacks become more integrated into mainstream culture, like other groups before them. Wilson's argument that affirmative action and related antidiscrimination programs will not touch the underclass black because of a basic shortage of jobs is an important issue. Policies simply based on the premise that racism is the enemy may be doomed to failure since lessening discrimination will not create jobs, nor will it increase the wages of menial jobs.

Evaluations of the efficiency of the two policies in the mid-1980s have been inconclusive. Feinberg (1985) reports that affirmative action has the advantage of speeding equality, but assimilation can have the compensating benefit of establishing more jobs that are available to the disadvantaged.

Evaluating the Evidence

Programs such as affirmative action are specifically designed to end discrimination in a particular realm, in this case employment. They represent a shift from an attack on prejudice to an attack on segregation and discrimination. Is it possible to develop programs that effectively deal with the root of the problem—prejudicial thinking? Some feel it is not because racism is so deeply rooted in Western society, particularly in capitalist societies like the United States, where, they believe, racism is simply a manifestation of class exploitation. Through institutional forms of discrimination, the powerful exploit the disadvantaged, who presently happen to be black. Racism, some claim, is part and parcel of capitalism and will always be a problem as long as we live in a stratified society. To them, social revolution is the only answer. Others feel prejudice can be eliminated (or at least reduced) through the addition of programs to the present system. At one time, information campaigns like the "16-millimeter film approach" were in vogue. If, for instance, prejudiced people believe blacks are shiftless and lazy, show them a movie depicting blacks as decent, hard-working people. Unfortunately, approaches like this have not proved very effective, although much depends on the people involved and how hardened their attitudes are. Urban dwellers, for instance, are known to be more tolerant of minority groups than rural dwellers (Wilson, 1985).

Another approach to rooting out prejudice is to arrange for majority and minority group members to have contact with one another so they can learn from their own experiences that racist attitudes are ignorant attitudes. This approach is known to work only under certain conditions, such as when the minority group person is of equal or higher status than the majority group person and when the contact is socially approved and directed toward a mutual goal. This would be very difficult to formulate into a concrete social policy, for logistical reasons. Additionally, since intergroup contact alleviates prejudice only when the minority group is from a class similar to the majority group, it certainly would not be of much help to the millions of blacks who are economically deprived relative to whites.

Perhaps the best way to control prejudice is not through programs directed at people who are already bigoted but through educational programs aimed at children. If such programs worked, after-the-fact policies like affirmative action would be unnecessary. Can it be done? Yes, with the right kind of educational programs, programs which integrate values into a curriculum and help students identify and challenge prejudice and discrimination. They could include involving students in social analyses aimed at increasing their understanding of the different forms of discrimination which pervade the nation. Children's personalities are not fixed. They are particularly receptive to attempts to change their attitudes and perceptions of other people, especially during late childhood and the early teens. Later in adolescence their views of the world become more rigid. If certain analytical skills, such as the ability to distinguish between fact and stereotype, are learned at the right age, we may be able to minimize prejudice. Until that day comes, Band-Aid policies like affirmative action are the only feasible ways to control discriminatory behavior.

SUMMARY

1 Prejudice (a hostile attitude) and discrimination (an exclusionary act) take many forms and are directed at a number of different minority groups in the United States, including blacks, Jews, Hispanics, and American Indians.

2 Individual, institutional, and cultural racism may satisfy the psychological needs and social standing of members of the majority groups. However, the costs are enormous to minority group members, who develop negative self-images and are denied equal access to such things as employment and education. Because of widespread discrimination in income, minorities often live near the poverty line, are unemployed, and suffer a number of health problems.

3 There are three psychological theories of prejudice: symbolic theory, frustration-aggression theory, and authoritarian personality theory. Social theories of prejudice include economic exploitation theory and social modeling theory.

4 Blacks, Jews, Hispanics, and American Indians face such great hostility from mainstream society that they develop hostile feelings toward one another as well. This is particularly true in the case of blacks and Jews.

5 Two competing social policies to end discrimination are assimilation and affirmative action. Assimilation holds that all minorities will eventually get their fair share if they are patient enough. Affirmative action centers on giving preferential treatment to minorities in employment and education to make up for past inequities.

CHAPTER 10

Sex Roles: Between Men and Women

A child is injured in an accident and rushed to the hospital. The surgeon takes one look at the child and says: "I can't treat him, that's my son." The surgeon is not the child's father. How do you explain this?

SEX AND GENDER: AN OVERVIEW

In 1873, a Harvard medical school professor expressed the opinion that women should not be trained as physicians. The reason? They would, he said, develop monstrous brains and puny bodies. Such a statement may seem patently ridiculous to us today, when about 40 percent of incoming medical students and about 30 percent of all physicians in the United States are women. They have not, as a group, shown any sign of abnormally overgrown heads or abnormally undergrown bodies.

In spite of such changes, attitudes like the one expressed above are by no means extinct today, or are they without effect. They are manifested in problems such as job discrimination, sexual harassment, and domestic abuse. They may be more subtly expressed in lingering stereotypes such as the "dumb blonde" and the "strong, silent type." You are confronted by them if, as a female student, you find yourself called on less frequently than the male members of your class, or if, as a male student, you find yourself required to register for the draft while your female classmates are not.

Sex roles have been differentiated by societies for as long as societies have existed. They pervade every aspect of American life, and they determine far more than who will go to work and who will raise the children. In the United States, the phenomenon of sex roles has been associated with social problems as diverse as poverty, mental illness, drug abuse, discrimination, sexual variance, crime, physical illness, the breakdown of the family, and even the waging of war. The extent to which your problems and your self have been affected by your assigned sex role may not be fully apparent. But beginning with the day you were handed either a pink or a blue rattle, the accident of your sex has had an influence on the way you think, the way you feel, your career aspirations and opportunities, your choice of friends, the courses on your class schedule, and even how often you get lost when you drive your car. And all of these things must be fitted into a social framework based on one fundamental fact: The relationship between men and women in the United States is one of *inequality.*

We all have notions as to what it means to be male rather than female, or what feminine rather than masculine behavior is. But exactly what do these terms mean? To answer that question, a distinction must first be drawn between *sex* and *gender*. *Sex* refers to those biological attributes that determine whether a person is male or female. *Gender* is defined by attitudinal and behavioral characteristics deemed by a society to be appropriate to males and females, and measured in terms of masculinity and femininity (Richardson, 1981).

With this definition in mind, think: What do the concepts of masculinity and femininity mean to you? Whatever your personal opinions, you have been taught throughout your life that certain characteristics constitute appropriate male behavior, and certain characteristics constitute appropriate female behavior. If you made a list of such characteristics, your listing would undoubtedly include many of the terms in Table 10-1, which was compiled from the responses of university students in the United States, England, and Ireland. The students were asked to consider a number of adjectives and indicate which were more frequently associated with women and which with men (Williams, Giles, Edwards, Best, and Daws, 1977). Note that the list resembles one of those tests you had in grammar school in which you were asked to draw a line going from each word in the first column to its opposite in the second column. A surprising number of matches can be found, showing that use of the term *opposite sex* is no mere accident.

Another notable feature of such masculinity-femininity distinctions was uncovered in a similar study creating a male-female list (Broverman, 1970). This list showed that desirable qualities associated with men far outnumbered

TABLE 10-1 ADJECTIVES HIGHLY ASSOCIATED WITH MEN AND WITH WOMEN IN ENGLAND, IRELAND, AND THE UNITED STATES

Adjectives associated with men	Adjectives associated with women
Active	Affectionate
Adventurous	Appreciative
Aggressive	Attractive
Assertive	Changeable
Autocratic	Dreamy
Boastful	Emotional
Coarse	Excitable
Confident	Feminine
Courageous	Frivolous
Cruel	Fussy
Daring	Gentle
Dominant	High-strung
Enterprising	Mild
Forceful	Nagging
Handsome	Poised
Humorous	Sensitive
Inventive	Sentimental
Lazy	Softhearted
Logical	Sophisticated
Masculine	Submissive
Rational	Sympathetic
Reckless	Talkative
Robust	Timid
Rude	Warm
Severe	Weak
Stern	Whiny
Strong	Worrying
Tough	
Unemotional	
Unexcitable	

Source: John E. Williams and Deborah L. Best, *Measuring Sex Stereotypes: A Thirty-Nation Study,* Beverly Hills, Sage, 1982, p. 28. By permission of the publisher.

those associated with women. Some personality traits identical in literal meaning carry different connotations depending upon which sex they are assigned to. *Assertiveness* in a man might be considered *shrewishness* in a woman; a woman's passivity could be a man's cowardice. Here, then, are two dimensions of the cultural distinctions long drawn between socially appropriate male and female attributes: Masculine and feminine characteristics are *complementary* to each other; qualities consid-

ered male are valued more highly (in males) than those considered female.

Nature versus Nurture

The problematic question is: Are these distinctions valid? Are such sex differences real? Are they preordained facts of life that determine some grand design, or does some grand design determine them?

These are not simple questions to answer. Notions of sexual identity are so deeply ingrained that even the most rational scientific approach can wind up tainted; in one study, the results were questioned because the male experimenters smiled more often at their women subjects than at the men, possibly influencing the subjects' responses (Rosenthal, 1966). The most central questions regarding male and female work roles, male and female political roles, male and female family roles—all boil down to *how* men and women differ, and *why* they differ. Posing the questions this way leads us to the scientific debate on whether gender differences emerge from within individuals *or* are imposed on them by society. This debate, commonly referred to as the nature versus nurture question, is a central issue in the study of sex roles as a social problem.

One oft-cited study that favors a cultural explanation for sex differences is Margaret Mead's famous work *Sex and Temperament in Three Primitive Societies*. In it, Mead examines three primitive tribes in New Guinea. Among the Arapesh, both men and women behave in ways we would consider "feminine"; they are "cooperative, unaggressive, and responsive to the needs and demands of others" (Mead, 1969:55). By contrast, Mundugumor women are as "ruthless, aggressive, [and] positively sexed" as Mundugumor men (Mead, 1969:190). The Tchambuli actually reverse what we label as traditional sex roles; although the tribe is patrilineal in terms of property inheritance, the women are dominant economically, sexually, and emotionally, and the men are dependent upon them. Men are observed to be quarrelsome, jealous, and—as is said of females in our society—catty. From her observation of the New Guinea groups, Mead concludes that "the personalities of the two sexes are socially produced" (Mead, 1969:209).

Supporting the biological position in this debate are studies that report physiological bases for apparent gender differences. Much research has been done, for instance, on the effects of androgens (male hormones) on levels of aggres-

sion. While some relationship has been demonstrated in primates, studies of human males have generally shown no correlation for most individuals (Doering, 1974). More recent research on sex differences has investigated brain lateralization. Neurological findings indicate that there is a difference in the way the right and left hemispheres of the brain are organized in men and women, and in how the two halves communicate with each other. It has been suggested that these differences may account for, among other things, the apparent superiority of women in language and the apparent superiority of men in math (McGuinness, 1976; Durden-Smith and DeSimone, 1983).

The research—and the controversy—over the nature-nurture question has been far more intensive and far more heated than these illustrations indicate. As is the case for many scientific debates with societal implications, this one tends to degenerate into attacks on the opposite position. A few examples may show the folly of looking at the complex issue of sex differences as wholly produced by *either* nature *or* nurture. Take the well-established superiority of females in sensing and interpreting sounds. Women pick up nuances of voice and music more readily, and are six times as likely to sing in tune as men. This might simply reflect differences in brain hemispheres, or it might be entirely caused by mothers talking and singing more to girls. Very probably, it is influenced by both factors. Males generally outscore females in tests involving manipulation of objects and spatial visualization (an aspect of your sense of direction), a difference which could be wired into brain tissue, but which is certainly affected by being taught to play football rather than house. The cultural choice of gender-specific games, toys, and activities also nurtures male-female differences in aggressiveness, whatever the natural hormonal differences.[1]

[1] The examples discussed in this section have been adapted from Alice S. Rossi's literature review in "Gender and parenthood," *American Sociological Review*, 49, February 1984: 1–19.

The point is twofold. First, nature and nurture are connected in the real social world. One of the distinguishing characteristics of human beings—male and female—is the genetic capacity to respond to and learn from the environment. In other words, it is in our species' *nature* to be *nurtured*. A second, and related, point is the undeniable effect of the social environment. Margaret Mead's study illustrates the fact that cultural forces can overrule whatever inborn differences divide the sexes. Biology may build in male and female tendencies, but this chapter presents case by case evidence that much of the social problem of sex roles is, if you will excuse the expression, man-made.

THEORIES OF SEX ROLE SOCIALIZATION

Psychoanalytic Theory

Sigmund Freud, the founder of psychoanalysis, postulated that the human personality, including sex-role acquisition, is the end result of specific experiences during various stages of infancy, childhood, and adolescence. Freud believed that male and female infants at first identify with the mother because she is nurturing and the father is remote. The strong attachment the boy has for his mother is combined with feelings of jealousy and contempt toward the father, who has prior sexual rights to the mother. The boy, realizing his love for his mother is inappropriate, fears his father will discover his feelings and castrate him. This conflict, called the Oedipus complex (after the tragic Greek hero who killed his father and married his mother), is resolved only when the boy represses his love for his mother. Then he identifies with his father and internalizes the father's attitudes and behaviors, including those involving norms of masculinity.

Freud suggested a parallel process—the Electra complex—for the girl, although development is less complex for her because she begins life with an identification with the same-sex parent. Part of the theory involves the concept of penis envy on the part of the small girl. This leads her to identify with the father to some extent. Once she realizes these feelings are futile, she develops her own female sex role, modeled largely after her mother.

The notion of penis envy is not only difficult to prove but also very unpopular in some circles, not only among feminists but also among mental health professionals, including psychoanalysts. Equally unpopular is the psychoanalytic perspective that women's tendency to nurture and self-sacrifice is masochistic. However, these ideas do exemplify a principle emphasized by conflict theorists, that of the attitude of a dominant social group—men—toward a subordinate one.

Social Learning Theory

This perspective is based on principles of the behaviorist school of psychology, which holds that learning takes place through *conditioning,* a process of rewards and punishments. A child who does something gender-inappropriate (like a little girl fistfighting) may be punished (perhaps by ridicule) and, as a result, is less likely to repeat the behavior. The child who conforms to "proper" sex-role behavior is rewarded, and the behavior is likely to be repeated.

Social learning theorists believe sex-role socialization can also take place through *modeling,* a process by which children learn behaviors simply by observing them in significant others, such as parents. Modeling does not involve direct rewards or punishments. If children identify with same-sex role models, they will imitate the behavior of these models. Part of the imitation process is internalizing the sex-appropriate behavior of the model. Boys raised by fathers who are competitive, career-oriented, and nonromantic will become the same themselves. Role models, however, are not limited to parents, but can include any person who makes an impression on the young child, such as an older sibling or a teacher at school.

Cognitive Development Theory

Lawrence Kohlberg has propounded the idea that people differ from one another in terms of their development along a hierarchy of moral maturity. Young children, for instance, are likely to respond to actions which lead to external rewards. More sophisticated adults, on the other hand, may be motivated by abstract principles, such as justice.

The difference between the cognitive development and social learning theories of sex-role socialization lies in the role of rewards. Kohlberg believes children actively construct their own sex roles rather than being passively conditioned into them. After the child makes a cognitive judgment that he or she is a boy or girl, the child seeks values and activities that conform to that self-image. These then become the source of rewards. The social learning approach, on the other hand, assumes that rewards precede the self-image.

The idea that a child takes cues from the surrounding world and then actively constructs his or her own sex-role image is unique to Kohlberg's theory. However, there are further specifications of the theory which some people charge are sexist. Kohlberg's data seem to show that the moral development of women is stunted: they tend to progress only partway up the hierarchy of development. They get to the point where they make judgments based on caring about others but not on the higher level that involves abstract principles. Since Kohlberg's work is based on research with males, their development should not necessarily become the accepted pattern against which women are judged. The sexes may be different, but that does not make one morally superior to the other, although it is possible that women's development may be stunted by their socialization.

THE SUBJECTIVE DIMENSION OF SEX ROLES

You do not have to be a history major to know that the world today is an almost unrecogniz-able place compared to 2000 or 500 or even 100 years ago. Yet through all of history—and even prehistory—one fact of life has remained steadfastly the same. From the time when men were the hunters and women the gatherers, roles have been assigned to people according to their sex. And with very few (some say no) societal exceptions, men have taken the dominant role. While an occasional Queen Elizabeth I or Joan of Arc has emerged over the millenia, she has represented an isolated occurrence, not a trend, and the influential figures surrounding her have all been male.

Since most history is presented as "his story," overwhelmingly disregarding the accomplishments and even the existence of women, it is difficult to say how most females have felt about their subordinate position in the world. Only relatively recently has discontent on their part come to the forefront of the public's consciousness in the form of the women's movement.

While most people tend to think of the women's movement as the agitation for equal rights that began in the 1960s, this most recent and ongoing phenomenon is actually the crest of a wave that started to swell over a century ago. There have been, in all, three periods of intense activity by women working for their rights in the United States. These three periods had one important thing in common: Each came on the heels of a time in which social protest lent *visibility* to the problems of inequality, and social reform raised women's *expectations* as to their place in society. The first phase of the women's movement began in the 1830s in conjunction with the movement to free the slaves. Women abolitionists such as Lucy Stone and Sarah and Angelina Grimke who were publicly (and sometimes physically) attacked for stepping outside the socially acceptable feminine sphere to speak out against slavery soon realized the irony in seeking freedom for the slaves without seeking freedom for themselves. The awareness of what they could accomplish if barriers to equality were dropped raised their expectations for their own equality. They and other female abolitionists began to alternate their antislavery activities with feminist ones (Hole and Levine, 1971). In this early movement, women fought for legal rights, including their rights to property and children, and many gains were made before the movement declined in the conservative post-Civil War period.

The second wave of the movement, which began around 1890, took its momentum from the prevailing social winds of the Progressive Era. Women working for national reform once again became aware of their own powerlessness in society. This time the struggle was for the right to vote; and in 1920, with the passage of the Nineteenth Amendment, the battle was won. Afterward, in the face of another conservative reaction to a time of reform, the women's movement declined once more.

A few sociological props will be useful in setting the stage for discussion of the most recent—and powerful—phase of the women's movement, with a life cycle extending over the past two decades. In the first place, the feminist message of female devaluation and exploitation is certainly not news. As we have already seen, sexism[2] has been a societal reality on American soil as far back as the Mayflower and, in fact, before Columbus in the societies of Native Americans. To use more recent social history as a baseline, things had actually been looking up. Between the end of the 1890–1920 cycle and the middle sixties, the percentage of the female population in the labor force roughly *doubled,* and millions more women were working in 1965 than in 1950. Granted, these figures are a crude indicator of women's status, but few would argue that women in the United States were materially worse off than they ever had been.

[2] *The Encyclopedia of Sociology* defines sexism as "the exploitation of one sex by the other. The term is usually used to mean the subordination of women by men through ideology, stereotyping, family structures, and unfair legislation."

Against this objective backdrop suddenly entered widespread subjective concern about sex roles. American women—and men—seemed to look around, see their familiar gender inequality, and now perceive it as a social problem.

Why did this problem suddenly reappear in the public mind when it had been in the public's experience all along? Consider how subjective *visibility* bears on the case. The intrinsic drama attached to the unequal status of women has generally been quite low. The insults and indignities, the denials of self-worth, the doors slamming in one's face—these everyday events keeping women "in their place" have been unspectacular forms of persecution. Sexual inequality is quite like Chinese water torture in its ability to crush the spirit while no single droplet of discrimination seems all that outrageous to observers.

Betty Friedan's runaway best-seller *The Feminine Mystique* (1963) called this (then) invisible situation the "problem with no name," and thus began to name the problem of sex roles in the mass media. A major objective of feminist interest groups such as the National Organization for Women (NOW), formed in 1966 with Friedan as the first president, has been consciousness-raising, fanning the subjective spark about women's place in society. While their contributions to real social change are dubious, media events such as the Billie Jean King–Bobby Riggs tennis match, bra burnings, and demonstrations by radical feminists have certainly focused public attention on the sex-roles issue. The media spotlight on these once shocking events has been focused to project a steady glow on mainstream discussions of the problem in magazines, talk shows, and college courses.

The newly taken-for-granted status of sex roles as a social problem is a classic case of the independent operation of the objective and subjective dimensions, but it is not a simple case. Currents of social change in the attitudes and behavior of both sexes have been swirling beneath the surface of the sexual inequality problem in opinion polls. As we suggested above, the wide employment gap between the sexes had been narrowing before NOW's first convention; millions and millions of women then entered the labor force in the 1970s, in part because of fewer child-rearing responsibilities after the tapering off of the baby boom. Reinforcing these societal tides were the waves created by new legislation such as the Civil Rights Act of 1964 and Affirmative Action (see Chapter 9). Their rising status relative to men undoubtedly led many women to expect true equality, and to be outraged when it did not arrive. This is the familiar cycle of objective improvements raising *expectations,* and failed expectations raising the subjective dimension of a social problem.

It would be a mistake to suggest, however, that the unfairness of sex roles has occurred only to frustrated women. A well-charted shift in the *value* placed on equality by both sexes started to build in America in the 1960s. Men as well as women became markedly less tolerant of the less than equal treatment of blacks, Jews, homosexuals, the poor—and women (Gans, 1973). In fact, the rising tide of egalitarianism may have reached a high-water mark with regard to sexual inequality. Analysts of changing sex-role attitudes over the 1962–1978 period have documented a "tremendous shift" toward more egalitarian perceptions of women (Thornton, Alwin, and Camburn, 1983).

Here is the immediate point: If the right of women to equal treatment is valued more highly, continued denial of such treatment will seem more problematic. And, in fact, the trend toward egalitarian sex-role attitudes is paralleled by the growing sense that something should be done. According to Harris polls, only about 42 percent of Americans supported efforts "to strengthen and change women's status in society" in 1970; by 1980 about two-thirds supported such efforts, a true landslide in public opinion about a social problem.

SEX ROLES AND SOCIAL CHANGE

Social Structure and Individual Personality

Nothing seems more private than the self. The image that appears in your mind when you say "me" is a composite of one's most intimate experiences and deeply personal traits. It is especially difficult in a culture as individualistic as ours to shake the sense that this self is a self-contained package, a very private piece of human nature. And, in fact, mountains of studies within American culture have unearthed a staggering amount of individual variation in personality. While it would not deny that you are different from other people, the sociological perspective sees that not all of these differences arise from within. Social structure is viewed as reaching down to the very core of your self—even as deeply as sexual identity. Despite the unresolved status of the nature versus nurture debate, even the most doctrinaire biologist would not rule out the influences of social environment on what men and women are like.

The scientific consensus about the existence (if not the extent) of the culture-gender connection has a number of implications. In the first place, it alters the age-old fantasy of exchanging sexes. If a wizard could temporarily change you to the opposite sex, the transformation could not be complete if your unchanged personality were simply wrapped in a new set of gonads. To really experience life as a full-fledged man or woman in a society, the "you" underneath would have to submit to the complex process of praising, punishing, nagging, and imitating that society uses to create its sex roles. The intrusion of the social environment means that males and females really *are* different all the way down to the center of their selves. Rather than trading abstract arguments about nature and nurture, let us look directly at the impressive machinery society uses to process sexual selves for their adult roles.

The process begins at the moment of birth. Regardless of whatever biological differences actually exist, most parents have preset ideas as to what to expect of their baby girl or baby boy. In one study mothers and fathers were asked, within twenty-four hours of their babies' births, to describe the newborn by selecting adjectives from a list. Consistently, the boys were described as stronger, better coordinated, firmer, and more alert than the girls—even though all the babies were of the same average length, weight, and Apgar scores (a scale rating reflexes, heart rate, respiration, and color; Rubin, Provenzano, and Luria, 1974). Numerous other reports have documented differential parental treatment of boys and girls in the first six months of life. In various experimental settings, fathers have displayed more punitive behavior toward 12-month-old boys than toward 12-month-old girls; they were also less likely to hold their sons and more likely to engage in toy play with their daughters (Snow, Jacklin, and Maccoby, 1983). In another study two groups of mothers described babies Adam and Beth in terms of their appropriate masculine and feminine characteristics, and offered toy trains to Adam and dolls to Beth—even though, unknown to the adults, Adam and Beth were actually the same 6-month-old child (Williams, Giles, Edwards, Best, and Daus, 1977).

This last study illustrates an important point: In taking the first steps in socializing their children into sex roles, parents may not even be aware that they themselves are being directed by their own lifelong patterns of sex-role socialization. They unconsciously react to what they perceive in their children as gender-appropriate characteristics, and then reinforce those perceived characteristics. Through this self-fulfilling prophecy, parents experience what they expect.

By the time a child is ready to begin school, an outwardly imposed gender identity is firmly in place. We can safely assume that 6-month-old "Adam"—whose blue overalls established him in adult minds as being stronger, more aggressive, and more independent than his fe-

male counterpart—will probably spend the next 4½ years surrounded by toy trains, wagons, sports equipment, building toys, military accessories, and other items which lead him toward an active life away from home. "Beth," identified as sweeter and softer by her frilly pink dress, will likely be given dolls, doll accessories, toy kitchen appliances, and other items directing her toward a domestic life or a wifelike job (Rheingold and Cook, 1975). By the time they reach kindergarten, it will no longer matter that Adam and Beth started out as the same 6-month-old child. By age 5 they have been socialized to be two very different children: one masculine, one feminine. (Some countries have attempted to reduce male chauvinism. In 1986, for example, Switzerland abolished the once widespread practice of training girls at special schools to become good housewives.)

Once children begin school, the differences are usually further reinforced. The picture books (even those winning prestigious awards) in which male characters outnumber females by a ratio of 11 to 1 and in which males have adventures while females cook and clean for them have now been outgrown (Weitzman et al., 1972). They give way to readers, social studies texts, science books, and even math books in which women are underrepresented and portrayed, along with men, in stereotypical roles (Weitzman and Rizzo, 1974). And although progress has been made as a result of Title IX of the Education Amendments Act, which prohibits sex discrimination in federally funded educational programs and activities, boys' play still emphasizes competitive team sports while girls are steered toward noncompetitive or turn-taking activities, such as jump rope and hopscotch. More is at stake here than who will be on the professional teams of the 1990s. Evidence suggests that the more complex, team-oriented character of boys' play teaches them leadership ability, organizational skills, and strategic thinking, while the less structured, small group aspects of girls' play deemphasize leadership, competition, and goal seeking (Lever, 1978).

Through elementary, junior high, and high school, barely a day goes by that does not hold some form of sex-role differentiation, be it separate lines for boys and girls, tryouts for cheerleading squads, or senior prom rituals (and this is not to mention the matter of curriculum and career counseling that will be analyzed later in this chapter). The point is that these sex-divided aspects of school—and life—have been institutionalized, becoming familiar and unnoticed features of the social landscape.

The social messages about gender are indeed everywhere. A survey of print advertisements found women overwhelmingly represented in domestic roles. They are portrayed as dependent on men, unable to make important decisions, behaving as sex objects, and more likely than men to need mood-altering drugs; men are portrayed with the reverse stereotypes (Courtney and Whipple, 1983). In television commercials, a woman is most likely to be found bewildered in the kitchen or bathroom while an authoritative male voice tells her how to solve her cooking or cleaning crisis; the percentage of male voice-overs has actually *increased* in daytime television since the mid-1970s (Pesch, 1981). On network newscasts women, who constitute 51 percent of the population, appear less than 15 percent of the time (Forrest, 1983). In television drama, male characters outnumber females 3 to 1, and women are considered too old for romantic roles at a much earlier age than men. It is not surprising that a positive correlation has been found between television watching and traditional beliefs about women's roles (Gerbner and Signorielli, 1979).

Even in everyday language, sexism is so deeply entrenched that professors writing textbooks (like this one) not only need to be told by their publishers to avoid sexist language but also must be given strict guidelines as to what

constitutes sexist language (see Box 10-1). Even casual conversation betrays sex-role differences. There is no doubt that it is the norm in our society for men to dominate conversation while women behave in a supportive manner (Kollock, Blumstein, and Schwartz, 1985). According to studies of taped conversations, two men will interrupt each other's talk with about equal frequency; similarly, two women talking will butt in on each other on a half-and-half basis. When a man is speaking to a woman, however, his interruptions outnumber hers by over 9 to 1 (Kramarae, 1981)!

The people exposed to these and an infinite variety of other influences are not shaped by them in isolation. We learn to see the world in a certain way, accept it because it is the only way we have ever known, and go on to perpetuate it through interpersonal influences on one another. In intricate but powerful ways, the patterns of our personal lives reinforce the cultural patterns of sex-role socialization.

People Playing Changing Roles
Clearly, sex roles are more than a matter of personal opinion. Gender identity and inequality cannot be expected to disappear if feminists simply exhort people to change their minds about sexual stereotypes. Too many of our experiences have constructed individuals who do fit the stereotypical specifications. Adult roles such as nurse or naval commander impose responsibilities that are gender-specific, thus daily hardening the mold set by earlier socialization. Traditional parenting patterns encourage little girls to play with dolls. These little girls then have their "maternal instinct" celebrated when mothering infants of their own. Little boys rewarded for their competitiveness by fathers and friends receive further reinforcement for this trait as adult businessmen. Sex roles are not some sort of illusion supported only by chauvinistic attitudes. They are a very real construct within our personalities, built upon the foundation of social structure.

BOX 10-1

GUIDELINES FOR EQUAL TREATMENT OF THE SEXES IN McGRAW-HILL BOOK COMPANY PUBLICATIONS (EXCERPTS)

Members of both sexes should be represented as whole *human* beings with human strengths and weaknesses, not masculine or feminine ones.

Description of Men and Women

Women and men should be treated with the same respect, dignity, and seriousness. Neither should be trivialized or stereotyped, either in text or in illustrations. Women should not be described by physical attributes when men are being described by mental attributes or professional position. Instead, both sexes should be dealt with in the same terms.

No	Yes
the girls or *the ladies* (when adult females are meant)	*the women*
girl, as in: I'll have my *girl* check that.	I'll have my *secretary* (or my *assistant*) check that. (Or use the person's name.)
lady used as a modifier, as in *lady* lawyer	*lawyer* (A woman may be identified simply through the choice of pronouns, as in: *The lawyer made her summation to the jury.* Try to avoid gender modifiers altogether. When you must modify, use *woman* or *female,* as in: *a course on women writers,* or *the airline's first female pilot.*)
female-gender or diminutive word forms, such as *suffragette, usherette, aviatrix*	*suffragist, usher, aviator* (or *pilot*)
libber (a put-down)	*feminist; liberationist*
coed (as a noun)	*student*

(*Note:* Logically, *coed* should refer to any student at a coeducational college or university. Since it does not, it is a sexist term.) In descriptions of men, especially men in the home, references to general ineptness should be avoided. Men should not be characterized as dependent on women for meals, as clumsy in household maintenance, or as foolish in self care. To be avoided: characterizations that stress men's dependence on women for advice on what to wear and what to eat, the inability of men to care for themselves in times of illness, and men as objects of fun (the henpecked husband).

The intricate interweaving of sex roles with other societal roles is a key insight into the contemporary phenomenon loosely known as "women's liberation." Buried under the millions of words written about this emotionally charged topic in the popular press are social scientific studies showing the United States changing its collective mind about what men and women can do. Consider public opinion about a role at the apex of our social structure: the presidency. For nearly fifty years, Gallup polls have charted the responses of random samples of American adults to this question: If your party nominated a woman for President, would you vote for her if she were qualified for the job? In 1969, only 54 percent answered in the affirmative, whereas in 1983, a Gallup poll revealed that a full 80 percent would have accepted a qualified woman in the Oval Office. Interestingly, more men than women appear willing to vote for a female President (Cherlin and Walters, 1981).

The swing in public opinion about high political office reflects attitudinal doors opening for women in their everyday roles as workers, wives, and mothers. One particularly revealing study of the decay of traditional sex roles attitudes employed a *panel design.* People in the sample were questioned repeatedly over an eighteen-year period, thus highlighting patterns of change. The conclusion: "A definite trend toward more egalitarian conceptions of women's roles is observed through the mid-1970's and into the 1980's" (Thornton, Alwin, and Comburn, 1983:211).

Given the possibility that the sexes-are-equal survey responses could be nothing more than lip service (you might doubt that in the privacy of the polling booth, men really would choose a woman for President), have there been real changes in the roles played by the sexes? Yes. Figure 10-1 shows a steeply increasing trend for women to be in the labor force (over half of them were in 1980 compared to less than one-third in 1960), and the parallel trend specifically for married women. The most precipitous rise has been in the proportion of women with children under age 6 who work (19 to 45 percent, not shown). The employment trend within the latter subgroup is particularly notable be-

cause it means the demise of traditional role restrictions for wives to work at caring only for husband, house, and—most hallowed of all—young children.

Figure 10-1 also projects these changes in sex roles into the future. National samples of women polled since the mid-seventies indicate a movement toward an ideal lifestyle *combining* the three roles of wife, mother, and full-time worker. A 1982 Gallup poll reported that this movement is most pronounced among college-age females who will soon be assuming their adult roles. Quite obviously, the continuing shift in sex-role attitudes is being paralleled by changes in the places women want—and get—in the American social structure.

Despite the evidence that minds and opportunities seem to be opening to women, objective equality between the sexes is not at hand in the United States. The following major section details continuing gender discrimination in many institutional spheres. The mandate of the present section is to put the changes that are occurring in their proper sociological context. Keep in mind that the trends traced above are not just ripples of numbers; they are counts of real people who have accepted—or not accepted—new ways of life for men and women. Note that the ideal lifestyle figure shows that the numbers of women who want (40 percent) or do not want (39 percent) a full-time job are still almost equal.

The general liberalization of sex-role attitudes has been anything but universal. According to the polls, college students have among the most liberal views of gender, and yet you probably have antifeminist classmates and maybe even some qualms of your own about changing sex roles. One study of college students found strengthening overall support for occupational and educational equality, but a slight recent shift toward traditional roles among *female* students (Helmreich, Spence, and Gibson, 1982). Such resistance to egalitarian change cannot be expected just to evaporate

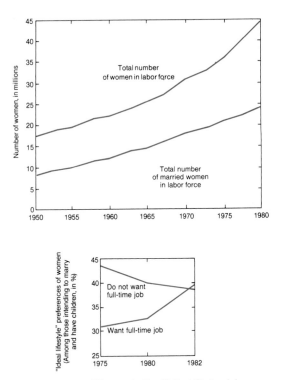

FIGURE 10-1   Women in the United States labor force: 1950-1980. (*Source:* U.S. Department of Labor and the Gallup Report, August 1982, p. 27.)

over time. A national survey of high school seniors indicates that over two-thirds of them oppose wives working when there are children to take care of (Herzog, Bachman, and Johnston, 1979).

Also indicative of deep-seated sex-role traditionalism are studies of the families of working women. While such households are more and more common and are likely to share decision making between spouses, they still organize the family division of labor in unequal ways. Employed women average twice as much time with their children and devote 2½ times as much time to housework as employed men (Staines and Peck, 1983). Here is a sociological interpretation: Changing attitudes about working women are the melting tip of an iceberg of sex-role traditionalism. Especially inside the home, we observe behavior patterns frozen by gender socialization that have yet to thaw for men *or* women. Consequently, many contemporary women are afflicted by

role conflict, caught between rising demands of occupational roles and the continuing responsibilities of home management.

As you will see below in the section Sex Roles and Mental Health, the shifting sexual division of labor even produces conflicts among women who prefer to keep the traditional full-time homemaker role. What we have here is a textbook case of the *social change* theory presented in Chapter 1. The relative position of males and females is changing gradually and unevenly across the social structure, a source of some strain for both those who embrace and those who do not embrace the changes.

This theoretical perspective on contemporary sex roles provides the insight that social change has its human costs. Moreover, it suggests that "playing" the newly changed roles will not be all fun and games. Return to the wizard who opened this section, and imagine that she (were you expecting a he?) could conjure a society with full equality in its sex

Sex-role changes have sometimes led to role reversals as in the case of the working wife and the househusband. (*Hannah Schreiber/Photo Researchers*)

roles. Bypassing all of the transitional costs of change with a wave of her sociological wand, the wizard inspects a society transformed right down to the gender socialization training of men and women for their respective—and equal—places in the social structure. The benefits to both sexes are clear.

Closer inspection, however, would reveal a price to be paid for women assuming traditional male roles. Consider the principle of *problem linkage* as it applies to sexual inequality. Nearly every chapter in this book describes some difference in problem prevalence by sex. Dubious demonstrations of male superiority appear in their dominance of the objective statistics on premature death, drug use, and criminality. To read these wide differences as only a reflection of sex hormones would be as simpleminded (and sexist) as the claim that occupational inequality is caused by menstruation. An equal place for women implies an equalization of the distribution of problems tied to social roles. Although the gender gap in life expectancy has not narrowed significantly in recent years, there has been a sudden and dramatic upsurge in cigarette smoking specifically among young females, the very group making the strongest claims to sex-role equality—and equality in lung cancer deaths (see Chapter 3). This example is not part of an argument against social changes leading to gender equality. Our intent, rather, is to face unmagical sociological reality. Egalitarian sex roles would reduce many of the objective ills about to be described, but would bring the sexes nearer to parity in other social problems that women and society would rather do without.

THE OBJECTIVE DIMENSION OF SEXUAL DISCRIMINATION

Discrimination under the Law

One reason the law often looks unfavorably upon women is that they have traditionally had little influence in public life. They make up 53 percent of the nation's voters but hold only 5 percent of the elective positions. It was not that long ago that women were formally barred from jury duty in certain states. On the other hand, some state laws have clearly discriminated against men. Until 1976, Oklahoma prohibited selling "3.2" beer to men under 21 but allowed sales to women over 18. And until 1975, girls in Utah were no longer minors after 18, but boys were until 21. The Supreme Court has taken a strict approach to striking down virtually all gender-based statutes.

Since the early 1970s, military laws have been revised to permit women entry into branches of the service previously closed to them, such as allowing them to be Navy pilots and admitting them to service academies. However, women are still excluded from draft registration and are significantly underrepresented in the military. As a result, they are denied smooth access to government jobs, since both the federal and state governments give veterans preference over other public job seekers.

Women's rights in marriage are especially limited. Married women are sometimes barred from acquiring credit cards or entering contracts without their husbands' signed consent. The most egregious form of discrimination is the discounting of a woman's income in considering all loans, particularly mortgage loans. The Equal Credit Opportunity Act, passed in 1977, prohibits denial of credit on the basis of sex or marital status, but not all problems are solved by the law. Women often find themselves caught in a credit bind since credit worthiness is usually based on level of income and length of employment. Divorced or widowed women are likely to have low-paying jobs, and when credit is tight, such women are the first to be denied.

Although many people do not see the law as having very much to do with the intimacy of marriage and the family, each state has its own laws which determine when we may marry, when and if we may divorce, and how property settlement and child custody will be established if the marriage dissolves. Overall, men have more rights than their wives. Power relationships in most marriages are dominated by men because they have more resources than their wives. The fact that women have been socialized to function less autonomously also contributes to male dominance, a dominance supported by the legal system. For instance, because of the legal principle of *merger of identities* which occurs in marriage, women lose and men gain. At one time, the wife was denied the right to manage real estate, to sue or be sued, to make a will, or even to keep her wages if she worked outside the home. The customary loss of a woman's surname at marriage seriously curtails her ability to get credit after divorce. Additionally, if a husband moves for occupational reasons and his wife refuses to go with him, in a number of states she is guilty of desertion.

Although some exceptions have been carved out in recent years, the general rule persists that a married woman loses her domicile and acquires that of her husband, no matter where she resides. If she marries a man who lives in a different state, she cannot vote or run for office in the state where she has lived. The list of similar legal injustices is rather lengthy, but there is a glimmer of hope for equity within marriage. An independent commission has drafted the Uniform Marriage and Divorce Act and offered it to state legislatures as a model. It is a distinct move toward a partnership model of marriage and has already been adopted, at least in part, by several states.

Social Security is another area in which the law has institutionalized discrimination by sex. Homemakers, for instance, are not recognized as job holders and receive neither wages nor Social Security benefits. Women in paying jobs receive only 61 percent of the earnings of their male counterparts. Thus, women receive only a fraction of men's Social Security benefits (which are determined by past income). Moreover, 1985 figures show that the survivor's

benefit for a two-salary couple is 35 percent lower than that for a one-salary family earning the same income. Since women live longer, they are thus likely to be penalized by Social Security after their husbands die.

Sexual discrimination also exists within the criminal justice system. Typically, men are more likely to be convicted and given longer sentences than women. The most popular interpretation of this preferential treatment attributes it to chivalry; male judges and prosecutors treat females more leniently, it is argued, because society has taught them to approach females in a fatherly, protective manner. A recent study by Kruttschnitt and Green (1984) found that women receive preferential treatment largely because they are more likely to obtain pretrial freedom than men. Occasionally, punitive treatment is greater toward females if they commit "manly" crimes such as robbery. Additionally, some states convict girls under juvenile delinquency laws for acts for which boys are not punished. Connecticut makes it a crime to be an unmarried girl between 16 and 21 who is in "manifest danger of falling into habits of vice." No boy can be convicted of this. Often the practice is simply a result of the attitudes of social workers and judges. If girls disobey their parents, run away from home, have a child without marrying, or are promiscuous, they are branded as juvenile delinquents. Boys engaged in the same conduct are seldom even referred to juvenile court, although, unlike girls, they are liable for statutory rape.

Perhaps no other area of the law is as riddled with sex-based statutes as divorce and child custody. Here men do not fare well, often losing the house, car, and children to their wives. Awarding child custody to the wife is an old practice based on stereotyped notions about the relationships of male and female parents with their children. For years, courts have followed a legal rule called the *tender years doctrine* under which the mother was presumed

Nursing, one of many female-dominated occupations, is now attracting more males. (*George Gardner/Stock, Boston*)

to be the better custodian for children of tender years (usually under age 7). A husband could obtain custody only if he could show that his wife was unfit, a principle which led to nasty courtroom battles.

Custody decisions are often not decisions at all but simply legal proceedings based on the preconceived notion that women have an automatic right to custody of children. The issue of maternal preference in custody cases has provoked extremely varied responses: the Utah Supreme Court found it wise that children should be in the care of their mother; Maryland permits the use of maternal preference as a tiebreaker; but in New York, a court held that the maternal preference rule violated the Fourteenth Amendment. Despite the controversy, women still obtain custody of their children over 90 percent of the time.

Women and Work

Equality in Work For many, work is the very heart of the social problem of sex roles in the United States. The rightful place of women in the occupational world has been passionately argued in the boardroom, in the courtroom, and, quite possibly, in your classroom. "Equal pay for equal work" was the slogan that launched the National Organization for Women in 1966, and the self-evident fairness of the sentiment helped to inflame a public opinion already simmering about unequal treatment of minorities (though females are, ironically, a numerical majority). The issue of women and work has generated so much subjective heat that one can easily be blinded to the objective light. Below are data which provide the proper illumination, and highlight the fact that women's place in the occupational structure is only part of the larger issue of women's place in the social structure.

Subjective support for the ideal of occupational equality is overwhelming. National surveys indicate that nearly 9 of every 10 Americans "feel that women should have equal job opportunities with men." However, the same 1982 Gallup polls reveal only 4 in 10 believing that sexual parity in work opportunities does exist. In this case, the weight of subjective

BOX 10-2

SUBJECTIVE MYTHS AND OBJECTIVE FACTS ABOUT WORKING WOMEN

The Myth: Women Don't Need Their Salaries; They Work for Pin Money

The notion that you don't have to pay a woman as much as a man is the result of certain myths about women in the workplace. These include the notions that women don't really need to work as much as men do, that they aren't as well trained, that they are less dependable workers, and that their personalities and physical capabilities are not suited to the rigors of certain types of work.

The facts: Most women work because of financial need. About two-thirds of working women are single, widowed, divorced, separated, or are married to men who earn less than $10,000 annually.

The Myth: Women Have High Absenteeism and High Turnover and Thus Are Not Dependable Employees

The facts: The Public Health Service reports that women miss 5.6 days of work per year due to illness or injury—only slightly more than the 5.2 days missed by men.

Nor are women significantly more likely to leave jobs than are men. An analysis of turnover rates in manufacturing found that 5.2 percent of female employees left—as compared with 4.4 percent of men. In other segments of the work force, women are likely to stay on the job longer than men.

Blau comments that "workers in higher-wage and more challenging jobs are less likely to quit than those in lower-wage, more boring jobs. In the same types of jobs, women are no more likely to quit than men."

The Myth: Women Aren't Physically Capable of Holding Certain Jobs

The facts: "Women have consistently been discouraged from even applying for positions because of personnel directors' subjective data that women could not possibly have the strength to do the particular job in question," write David Gloss and Miriam Wardle in the journal *Occupational Health and Safety.*

But the experiences of Rosie the Riveter and women shipfitters during World War II—and more recent research on women's stamina—show that women do have the capacity to undertake physically demanding tasks for extended periods.

More important, most jobs today require brains, not brawn. A person in an office job rarely needs to slay dragons or move mountains to get ahead, and even jobs in heavy industry do not rely on brute strength.

Some employers use rigorous tests of physical strength to exclude women from certain jobs, but such tests are discriminatory—and thus illegal—if they do not relate to skills that will actually be used on the job.

Women, stereotyped as the weaker sex, have been denied jobs because of assumptions about their physical abilities. But recent tests of stamina often find that women excel. Research on potential astronauts found that women can more readily endure the tumbling and disorientation of space without showing signs of shock than men can. And when tasks that involve mental ability are added to the test, women really blossom.

Lori B. Andrews, "Myths and Facts about Working Women," *Parents,* July 1983. By permission of the publisher.

opinion is clearly correct. Equal pay for equal work is still just a slogan.

In 1970, when this battle cry of the newborn feminist movement was first being uttered, a woman working full-time earned a median income that was only 60 percent of the male median. Now that the slogan has become a cliché, the comparable figure is a whopping 65 percent! Even though the gap is narrower for selected subgroups of women workers, the diamond-hard resistance to change of the overall sex-earnings ratio is quite remarkable. It is

even more remarkable considering the enormity of the objective changes swirling around unequal salaries. The storm of statutes stirred up since 1963 (see Box 10-3) constitutes an impressive legal force which has been hurled against sex barriers to employment. Both a cause and an effect of these changes in official policy is the cascade of women into the labor market. Nearly 1 million additional women a year have entered employment over the last decade; the current majority (52 percent) of women over the age of 16 working is projected to gain percent-

---

BOX 10-3

STRESSING THE RIGHTS OF WORKING WOMEN

NEW YORK—Working women should know their legal rights, especially those key laws that were designed to protect them against sex discrimination. But most of them don't, says Sandra Porter, executive director of the National Commission on Working Women in Washington.

At a seminar in New York titled "The New American Woman," sponsored by Women in Communications Inc. and *House Beautiful* magazine, Porter sketched those basic laws as follows:

The 1963 Equal Pay Act, which states that workers, male and female, can expect to be paid equally for equal work.

Title VII of the 1964 Civil Rights Act, which states that, in employment and training, it is against the law to discriminate on the basis of sex, race or national origin.

Title IX, among 1972 amendments to the Higher Education Act, which protects women from discrimination in educational institutions and covers employment, student services, enrollment and participation in athletics.

EEOC-Sexual Harassment Guidelines, issued in 1981, which forbid verbal or physical abuse on the job and make employers responsible for assuring workers a harassment-free environment. Workers can file grievances with the Equal Employment Opportunity Commission.

The Equal Credit Opportunity Act, which protects women against discrimination in consumer credit. It is the law that guarantees women the right to get credit cards, bank loans and mortgages in their own names. When the law is violated, women can file grievances through Consumer Credit Bureaus.

The Vocational Education Amendments, which contain strong sex-equity protections and promote the entry of women into vocational education schools.

The Philadelphia Inquirer, Jan. 6, 1983. By permission of the publisher.

---

age points in the decade ahead. Despite this rising flood of working women with new legal rights, the sex-earnings ratio has remained high and dry. How is such stable inequality possible?

This is not a simple question. Begin with some perfectly good reasons why women should be paid less than men. In the first place, their educational qualifications are not as good. While the existing education gap between the sexes may itself be viewed as problematic (see below), it is certainly part of the explanation for the earnings gap. Education is also not the whole story. Female college graduates are now earning less than male high school dropouts. Although such figures are probably in the process of change, the sex-earnings ratio is worse than the overall 0.65 when directly comparing male and female college graduates (Saxton, 1983). How about job experience? Since it is well established that having children reduces females' labor force participation (Smith-Lovin and Tickamyer, 1978), and also well established that years in the job are related to earnings

(U.S. Bureau of the Census, 1984), does not fairness require women to be paid less? Yes and no, but mostly no. A typical female spends less than 3 percent of her lifetime pregnant and/or nursing, and recent studies suggest that women are planning their children in order to minimize any interruption to their careers (Rexroat and Shehan, 1984). Besides, single women who have been in the work force continuously do not earn substantially more than married women (Waite, 1981).

Even though males do get paid more than females with identical job experience, one hopeful sign for the future is the fact that so many millions of women have so recently entered the labor market; as they gain experience, there should be some closing of the earnings gap. Given all these arguments back and forth, how important are individual qualifications in preserving sexual inequality in pay? Careful analyses have concluded that only about half of the earnings gap can be accounted for by sex differences in education and experience (National Academy of Sciences, 1981; MacKinnon, 1979). One small encouraging sign of improvement in the earnings gap was registered in 1986. At that time, women who earned the master's degree in business administration (MBA) at the prestigious Wharton School of the University of Pennsylvania reported receiving higher average starting salaries than men.

Sex and Job Type   It is tempting to assign the remaining pay differential to sex discrimination, pure and simple. The devil's advocate would correctly argue, however, that more is involved than male chauvinist bosses denying raises to "the girls." One of the realities hidden within the national sex-earnings ratio is an obvious one: Men and women do not work at the same jobs. The first two columns of Table 10-2 present a sample of jobs whose occupants are dominated by one sex. The figures are lopsided indeed. As you can see, females are highly segregated in occupations that involve cleaning, nurturing dependents, performing support activities for males—in short, wifelike jobs. Not incidentally, they tend to pay less than the traditionally male occupations. Even

women professionals tend to be concentrated in the so-called college women's ghetto of teachers, nurses, social workers, and librarians—all jobs that have lower average salaries than other professional occupations (Blau, 1978).

It is a truism that these traditional patterns are undergoing change, a notion supported by highly publicized cases of females becoming judges, coal miners, and sportswriters. The third column of Table 10-2 indicates such cases are not isolated. Numerous occupations are experiencing a rocketing rise in female entry rates, and interestingly, several jobs once dominated by women are being filled by more and more men (e.g., nurses, dietitians, and stenographers; Hacker, 1983).

The sociological sense you have developed in reading this book may lead you to expect such changes to have been uneven. That expectation is correct. The two left-hand columns of Table 10-2 were compiled at the same time as the right-hand column, thus showing pronounced sex segregation in spite of scattered change. To cite an example very close to home, only about 1 in 4 college sociology professors is a woman, very nearly the same percentage as in

TABLE 10-2   SEX SEGREGATION BY OCCUPATION

Female dominated occupations		Male dominated occupations		Female entry rates, 1970–1980	
Occupation	Percentage female	Occupation	Percentage male	Occupation	Female percentage increase
Secretaries	99.1	Stonemasons	99.9	Lawyers	166.7
Dental assistants	98.6	Auto mechanics	99.3	Computer operators	104.8
Nursery and kindergarten teachers	98.4	Electricians	98.8	Bank and financial managers	90.9
Child care providers	97.4	Fire fighters	98.7	Social scientists	87.5
Practical nurses	97.5	Truck drivers	97.8	Stock and bond sales agents	80.2
Dressmakers	97.2	Engineers	96.0	Bus drivers	60.4
Chambermaids	97.0	Clergy	95.8	Real estate agents	58.9
Typists	96.9	Dentists	95.7	Shipping clerks	49.0
Receptionists	96.3	Police officers	94.5	Educational administrators	40.5
Telephone operators	91.8	Architects	93.3	Accountants	39.2

Source: U/S: A Statistical Portrait of the American People, New York, Viking, 1983, pp. 127, 128, 133. By permission of the publisher.

1972, when the federal government specifically outlawed discrimination in education (American Sociological Association, 1984). This highlights the fact that gender barriers in occupations are not supported by—or dissolved by—legislation alone. People, after all, do not just randomly end up in occupations. Differing experiences in school, family, and other institutions prepare a boy or girl for different kinds of work experiences. Consequently, lots of individuals will want jobs traditional for their sex. The point is a familiar one: Sexual inequality has its roots throughout the social structure. If the riddle on the first page of this chapter about the surgeon and the boy in the hospital gave you pause, that is because the surgeon was the boy's mother. Many have come to assume that "surgeon" means "male." That is not necessarily the way things are—another example of sex stereotyping in the world of work.

The larger point concerns the male-female earnings gap. Job segregation does account for a substantial portion of the pay differential (Waite, 1981), but still another piece remains to be fitted into this complex puzzle. Despite our emphasis and the wider sources of discrimination, bosses do unfairly deny advancement to females. To assess the significance of this form of discrimination, it is necessary to look at the relative movement of the sexes on the ladder of success. Sophisticated studies of career paths show that men have not only entered the labor force at a higher rung than females (reflecting the occupational segregation discussed in the previous paragraph) but also advanced much more quickly through job grades (Rosenfeld, 1980).

Like most everything about working women, there is evidence that these traditional career patterns have been shaken. In 1970, less than 1 in 5 management jobs was occupied by a woman; now, the figure is approaching 1 in 3 (U.S. Bureau of the Census, 1984b). Like most everything about working women, such changes must be seen in context. Females still get promotions

at a slower rate than males doing the same job, and the biggest gains for women have come in the lower-paying executive positions, such as retail sales managers and bank officials. Men, quite literally, monopolize the positions exercising the greatest control over the workplace (Hachen, Costello, and Sprague, 1982). A Fortune magazine survey of the 6400 most highly paid officers and directors of United States companies found that only ten of them are women; 99.84 percent of the Captains of Industry are men.

The picture is now complete. Viewed from any analytical angle, working women are in the economic background. (See Box 10-4 on the feminization of poverty.) Statistical snapshots taken over the last fifteen years have shown females to be moving forward, but males still dominate the occupational scene. Perhaps the best way to put the sexual inequality at work in contemporary perspective is to focus on *female* dominated occupations. Fewer than 1 in 1000 registered nurses is a man. Despite this overwhelming numerical superiority, female nurses are currently paid over 5000 dollars a year *less* than the rare male nurse. This imbalance between women's high numbers and low pay is the rule rather than the exception: receptionists, stewardesses (now called flight attendants because of the entry of males), typists, librarians—all are paid more if they happen to be men.

As the previous paragraph suggests, one force behind these pay differentials is promotions: men actually advance into the administrative grades of certain "female professions" faster than women (Parcel and Mueller, 1983). If you find this puzzling, ask yourself who you would rather have as a boss: a man or a woman? That very question was addressed to a national sample in a 1982 Gallup poll with striking results. Even at that late date, over *half* of the females said they would prefer to be bossed by a male; in fact, many more women expressed this preference than men!

BOX 10-4

THE FEMINIZATION OF POVERTY

WASHINGTON—The U.S. Commission on Civil Rights said yesterday that the rapid increase in the number of poor families headed by women was a "time bomb" in American society.

In a report titled "A Growing Crisis: Disadvantaged Women and Their Children," the commission said it was "alarmed about the increasing income disparities for women, particularly minority women, heading households."

"Disproportionate numbers of America's poor in the early 1980's are women," the report concluded. "The demographic data that reflect these trends suggest that more of the same may lie ahead."

In 1960, the median income for families with two incomes was $10,516, compared with $5,093 for female-headed families, according to Census Bureau data cited by the commission.

By 1981, income levels for both groups had risen, but the differences still were wide—$25,065 for husband-wife families and $10,960 for female-headed families. The median income for families with a female head declined between 1970 and 1981 from 41.4 percent of that for two-earner families to 37.4 percent.

The commission also found that a family's economic status was likely to be worse if the family were not white. The overall poverty rate for female-headed households in 1981 was 34.6 percent. For white female-headed families, the rate was 27.4 percent. But for black female-headed families it was 52.9 percent, and for Hispanic female-headed families it was 53.2 percent.

The commission report said American women, especially those who were not white, faced an interrelated set of obstacles to financial stability: increases in the number of divorces, a growing number of out-of-wedlock births, and employment discrimination and socialization that combine to funnel women into low-paying jobs and pay them less than men with comparable training.

"Sex-stereotyped education, biased vocational counseling, sex-segregated jobs and wage discrimination, although against the law, continue to influence the employment and earnings of women," the commission's report said.

Commission vice chairwoman Mary Louise Smith said: "What this points out is the disproportionate burden that is going to be borne by women. The burden of poverty is going to fall upon those families where there are women heads of households."

Authors' note: Current statistics reinforce the U.S. Commission on Civil Rights' grim predictions. The most recent available data (O'Hare, 1985) find female-headed families to be *four times* as likely to be below the poverty line as male-headed families.

The Philadelphia Inquirer, Apr. 12, 1983, p. A3. By permission of the publisher.

The voices in this survey echo a familiar sociological theme. Even in occupations numerically dominated by women, men do the dominating. Even with the consciousness-raising of recent decades, women generally are comfortable taking orders from men. The point is *not* that women bring subordination upon themselves. Despite the lowering of formal sex barriers in the work arena, the job is only one role in a complex social structure. Individuals live in societies, not at their desks. What happened when growing up, what was learned at school, what friends think—all of these social forces shape one's expectations and behavior while sitting behind the desk. A woman typically has to work about eight days to earn what a man earns in five because while the differences may be narrowing, males and females are made into different people by a still sexist United States society.

Sexual Harassment Although the single largest issue concerning sex roles and work is pay inequity, other emotionally charged problems arise from the still uneasy coexistence of men and women in the workplace. One of the ugliest of these problems is sexual harassment on the job.

According to the Equal Employment Opportunity Commission, sexual harassment exists if

(1) an employee must submit to sexual demands in order to keep a job, (2) an employee's submission to or rejection of such demands is a basis of employment decisions, such as promotions or working conditions, or (3) such conduct "has the purpose or effect of substantially interfering with an individual's work performance or creating an intimidating, hostile or offensive working environment." Falling within the broad area covered by this definition is conduct ranging from sexual innuendo to outright rape. Although both men and women can be subjected to it, sexual harassment is less a matter of sex than a matter of power. Consequently, the great majority of victims are women. The ingredients that go into sexual harassment have to do with the sociocultural position of the sexes, including beliefs about male dominance in sexual relations, women as sex objects, and the subordinate position of women in the occupational world.

Although subjective awareness of the problem of sexual harassment has increased greatly in the last few years, some people still find it difficult to take the problem seriously. To the victims, however, it is anything but funny; their reactions include anger, fear, shame, sleeplessness, impaired job performance, and physical stress symptoms (Crull, 1980). As in the case of rape, they may not be believed or, worse, are blamed for the act. Many feel the only way of dealing with the problem is to quit their jobs or suffer in silence. In 1981 the Merit System Protection Board, a federal agency, reported that sexual harassment of civil service workers that year had cost the federal government 188,700,000 dollars in time lost because of emotional and physical stress, high job turnover, and increased use of health benefit plans. About 42 percent of all female and 15 percent of all male civil servants reported having been sexually harassed—all of this *inside* the walls of government, where citizen protections are supposed to be guaranteed (Hacker, 1983).

Homemaker Role   In 1974, a New York jury awarded 56,000 dollars to a man whose wife was injured in a car accident. The money was to compensate him for having to do all the housework for the two months his wife was incapacitated. *Newsweek* observed at the time that not even the women's movement had ever valued housework at 336,000 dollars a year (Tavris and Offir, 1977).

The fact is, no one can agree on the worth of the homemaker role. The work is obligatory and unpaid. Its monetary value is absent from the gross national product. The person (almost always the woman) who does it is likely to say that, no, she does not work; she is "just a housewife." The very inclusion of the homemaker role in a discussion of work such as this one is still a rather unusual presentation.

There was a time when the homemaker role as we know it today did not exist. Before the nineteenth century, work, family, and home were all one unit. The wife who spun the thread and the husband who wove it into cloth were both considered vital to the family's economic survival. All that changed with industrialization, which took the income-earning work out of the home, distinctly divided the two sexes' working worlds, and devalued both the housework and the women who were left home to do it (Miller, 1981).

Although many women now have careers of their own outside the home, the devaluation of the work they do inside it continues. For example, the Labor Department's *Dictionary of Occupational Titles*, which rates occupations on a scale from 1 (highly skilled) to 887 (unskilled), lists homemakers at a skill level of 878. Not only is there little appreciation for their efforts, but homemakers also have to deal with monotonous and repetitive tasks, isolation, and a lack of generally shared clear-cut standards by which they can judge their own work (Dabley, 1974). In a survey of housewives, married professional women, and single professional women, the housewives ranked themselves lowest

Women in politics—one visible sign of female progress. It was not that long ago that the notion of a female candidate for Vice President was unthinkable. In 1984, Geraldine Ferraro made it a reality. (*Robert Ginn/EKM-Nepenthe*)

of the three groups in self-esteem, competence, and attractiveness (Birnbaum, 1975).

Does this devaluation of housework reflect a general devaluation of women? One simple fact attests to it: On the whole, men will not do it. Even the husbands of employed women spend much less time on housework and child care than their wives (Staines and Peck, 1983). The contemptuous phrase "That's woman's work" is a revealing figure of speech. But do not place all the blame on the men; the majority of the women in a national sample said they did not want more help from their husbands (Waite, 1981). No matter how uneven the burden, the majority of American men and women believe housework is the woman's responsibility (Osmond and Martin, 1975). Such beliefs are not surprising from a sociological perspective; after all, they were socialized that way by parents who lived that way.

Education

Earlier in this chapter, we touched upon some of the ways in which experiences encountered

by boys and girls in school help to shape their masculine and feminine identities. Here we will go to the heart of the issue of sex roles in school: sex-role distinction in the formal educational process itself.

Americans place an extremely high premium on education. The Land of Opportunity offers more of its opportunity to those with diplomas. Succeeding generations of each ethnic and minority group have in turn celebrated the first high school diploma in the family, the first college graduate, the first professional degree.

A more tangible indicator of the value placed on a good education is the thickness of the wallet; not surprisingly, people completing four years of college can expect average lifetime earnings at least 40 percent higher than those of high school graduates (U.S. Bureau of the Census, 1983*d*). A closer examination of the figures, however, reveals a more startling state of affairs: although women's average expected lifetime earnings increase at roughly the same rate as men's according to amount of education, the men earn substantially more at every educational level (see Figure 10-2).

Some reasons for this gap have already been discussed in the Women and Work section of this chapter. They deal with the work half of the work-education relationship. All these factors are vital in explaining the disparities in Figure 10-2, but the part played by education itself bears close scrutiny.

To begin at the end, consider doctoral degrees. In 1980, women earned only 28 percent of all Ph.D.'s awarded. While this figure is low, it does reflect a gain over the previous decade. To understand the overall situation, however, it is necessary to examine the distribution of those degrees; and the fact is that women are heavily concentrated in a few traditionally female areas such as education, psychology, and literature, while their numbers remain low in the more technical and higher-paying fields such as engineering and computer science.

The roots of this circumstance are complex, and they sprout from seeds planted many years before professional studies commence. To highlight one perspective, consider that most college majors leading to prestigious occupations—in fields such as engineering, medicine, or the sciences—require students to take advanced-level mathematics (Weitzman, 1984). Yet one study showed that only 8 percent of female students entering the University of California at Berkeley in 1972 had taken enough math in high school to enable them to begin advanced math courses in college (as compared to 57 percent of the men) (Sells, 1978).

The verdict is not yet in on whether males and females differ in "natural ability" in math; the findings of numerous studies on this questions are contradictory. What is clear, however, is that a boy and a girl of the same age, studying the same subject, in the same class, in the same school will not share the same educational experience. Although equal percentages of the sexes express a liking for math, for example, fewer girls than boys are still doing well in it by the time they reach high school. Possible explanations are varied. One is that math is labeled a male subject, which may cause female students to fear they will be less popular if they excel in it. It has been demonstrated that girls are steered away from math by teachers, parents, and guidance counselors who perceive math as a male domain.

Other forces in American schooling direct students into what are virtually two separate achievement tracks, segregated by sex. In the lower grades, girls receive negative criticism on the *content* of their work, while boys are more likely to be chided for sloppiness or lack of effort. The result is that girls believe they lack ability, while boys think they only need to try harder (Jacklin, 1983). One investigation in which junior high school teachers were asked to

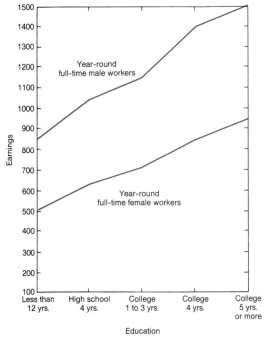

FIGURE 10-2 How much money will you earn? Expected average lifetime earnings in thousands of 1981 dollars for 18-year-olds. (*Source:* United States Bureau of the Census, 1984.)

select adjectives describing good male and good female students produced lists of sex stereotypes like those in Table 10-1 (Sadker and Sadker, 1974). Given the effects of educators' own schooling and socialization, it is not surprising to find teachers, guidance counselors, and parents supporting traditional sex-segregated educational goals. Boys take woodworking shop, while girls take home economics; sex-segregated vocational training programs offer girls cosmetology (hairdressing) and secretarial skills, while boys learn auto mechanics and industrial arts (Richardson, 1981). A girl who excels in science may be guided toward teaching, while her male counterpart is encouraged to apply to medical school. Boys are discouraged from becoming nurses, secretaries, or preschool teachers (Pleck and Brannon, 1978).

The cumulative result is the production of female adults who may find it difficult to take themselves seriously as students, since many of the people around them did not take them seriously in that role. Even some women with high aspirations may feel that earning anything less than A's in college confirms their professors' lower expectations of them, and so they may opt for "safe" majors. They learn from college faculties that are only 25.5 percent female, an imbalance that deprives women students of the role models and mentors so necessary and so readily available to the male students. A woman who pursues her education to the graduate school level may actually be considered deviant. She is, in fact, statistically deviant because the minority of which she is a part is extremely small.

It would seem, on the surface, that men reap all the advantages of this particular sex-roles coin, but their side of it is not without its disadvantages. Men are under extreme pressure to perform well in career-oriented studies to enable them to fulfill their future roles as breadwinners. They often cannot afford the luxury of taking elective courses purely out of personal interest. They may be ridiculed if they choose to go into such fields as literature, education, and nursing, because these majors lead to less lucrative and "unmanly" pursuits. For both men and women, the academic world from kindergarten through college remains a vital element in helping to bring about and reinforce sex-role differences in attitudes and lifelong achievement.

Sex Roles and Mental Health

For decades, the literature on sex differences and mental health consistently reported that women were more frequently mentally disordered than men. Now, as research methods improve, that situtation is changing (Veroff, Douvon, and Kukla, 1981). A 1984 National Institute of Mental Health study concluded that the traditional impression that women have higher rates of mental disorder than men is erroneous. Past research often covered only selected disorders, such as depression and anxiety, which are more common among women. The 1984 NIMH study also included drug and alcohol abuse as well as antisocial behavior, all of which are more common among men. Past research also reported that the emotional impact of undesirable life events is greater among women than among men, a presumed reflection of the greater vulnerability of the "weaker sex." Now there is evidence that the greater vulnerability of women to life stress is actually due to their greater involvement in the lives of those around them (Kessler and McLeod, 1984).

Despite recent evidence to the contrary, some still feel that that women are more mentally disordered than men because of the growing stress placed on women in the post-World War II period. Some studies indicate that the increased labor force participation of women in recent decades may have reduced psychosomatic symptoms among women (Kessler and McRae, 1981). However, rates of other types of mental health problems (such as depression) among women are high.

Recently, the sex-role hypothesis has developed as a way of understanding the high reported rates of psychological distress among women. This perspective predicts that the relationship between sex and distress will decline as sex roles become more comparable. The findings of the 1984 NIMH study suggest this may already be happening. Perhaps past studies have consistently reported rates of certain disorders among women because it has been more acceptable in our society for women to express their problems. Consequently, women may be more likely than men to *admit* to feelings and behaviors that lead to a psychiatric diagnosis. At least one study found that women seek psychiatric help at a higher rate than men with comparable emotional problems (Kessler, Brown, and Broman, 1981).

Closely related are the heavy negative sanctions men receive for abnormal behaviors; they suffer more stigmatization than women because the culturally defined male role tolerates less abnormal behavior than the female role (Broverman, 1970). Consequently, men may *admit*

to fewer psychological problems and are underreported as cases. Perhaps men are reported to have more problems with drug addiction and antisocial conduct and fewer problems with depression and anxiety because antisocial and drug-related problems are more likely to be reported by others, such as legal authorities.

The most widely researched aspect of the relationship between mental disorder and sex concerns sex and depression. Numerous studies have confirmed that women have a higher prevalence of depression than men (Aneshensel, Fredericks, and Clark, 1981). Why? Some believe women are more biologically vulnerable to depression, while others contend that the sex roles they fill are responsible. Recent data indicate there is a sex-role basis for sex differences in these rates. (Rosenfeld, 1980). Look at the patterns of depression for men and women shown in Figure 10-3.

Although some feel that the happiest women are married and working, the impact of a wife's employment on her own and on her husband's depression depends on whether it is consistent

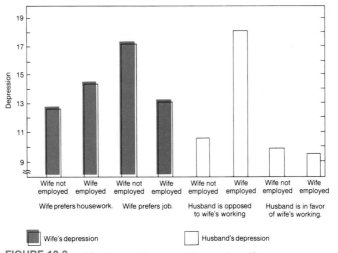

FIGURE 10-3   Marriage patterns and depression. (*Source:* Catherine E. Ross, John Mirowsky, and Joan Huber, "Dividing Work, Shaping Work, and In-between: Marriage Patterns and Depression," *American Sociological Review,* 48, (1983), p. 817. By permission of the publisher.)

with their preferences. For instance, unemployed wives who want to work have high rates of depression, as do husbands who are opposed to their employed wives working.

No discussion of this topic would be complete without mention of menopausal depression. Some women during their "change of life" experience a sudden breakdown and feel that their lives are not worth living. The traditional explanation is that biological changes are responsible for the change in mood. But it is more likely that these women react to menopause with depression because of the limited definition of the female sex role in American culture. If women have based their lives on a narrow range of fulfilling experiences, such as childbearing and child rearing, they have few alternative channels through which to gain satisfaction when childbearing is no longer possible and the children are grown up (Gallagher, 1981). Particularly vulnerable is the woman who believes she is attractive to others largely because of her appearance and figure, which she finds are suddenly giving way to wrinkles and middle-age spread. This woman will be more threatened by such changes than the woman in a nontraditional role in which she sees herself admired for her intellect and occupational success.

Depressive problems also occur among men later in life. The causes are similar to the causes of depression among women, usually a *loss*, particularly the loss of one's job through forced retirement. This is especially threatening to the man whose life centered on his work. Now he has nothing fulfilling left, unless he had developed outside interests and hobbies earlier in life.

One indirect measure of depression is suicidal behavior. Although many sociologists view suicide as the result of social influences, there are many psychiatrists who consider it the unadulterated expression of depression. Numerous studies report that females *attempt* suicide more than males, although male rates of *completed* suicide are much higher than those for females. This may indicate a greater tendency for women to use suicidal gestures, such as drug overdoses, to call attention to their problems. Men, on the other hand, are apparently less interested in changing the stressful aspects of their lives. As a consequence, they employ more certain means, such as a gunshot wound to the head or a jump from a tall building. At least one study reports that the female to male ratio of attempted suicide has declined in the last two decades, as sex roles have started to become more homogeneous (Kessler and McRae, 1983).

Important differences between the mental health patterns of males and females emerge when marital status is taken into consideration. Married women have much higher rates of reported disorder than their husbands, perhaps because the housewife role has fewer sources of gratification than the role of the married man in the work force. Consistently, Kessler and McRae (1982) found that mental health is greater among married women who are employed outside the home. Labor force participation of married women may yield some definite mental health advantages to the wives, but the cost of these nontraditional marriages is an increase in depression among husbands who oppose their wives working (refer to Figure 10-3). Additionally, recent studies show that declines in men's employment are as important as increases in women's employment in accounting for differences in psychological distress (McLanahan and Glass, 1985).

Contrary to the popular stereotypes of the carefree bachelor and the unhappy spinster, mental health studies regularly show single men to be more frequently disordered than single women (Gallagher, 1987). This is possibly because single men, as a result of their socialization, are more introverted and socially isolated than single women, who have closer interpersonal ties. Single women may be happier than bachelors because they are better able to form attachments with others and avoid the anguish of social isolation.

Nowhere is this more apparent than among divorced and widowed men—the once married who are severely stressed by the loss of their most important link to the social network of life (Gallagher, 1987).

SOCIAL POLICY: COMPARABLE WORTH

Looking at sex roles as a social problem necessarily slants one's view. A focus on the existing inequality between the sexes draws attention away from the larger picture showing real improvement in every objective sphere of society. Our purpose here is not merely to weigh the good news with the bad but rather to highlight the social forces producing both. What instrument of public policy can most effectively dissect sex-role inequality in the United States? What are the sociological sources of resistance to equality between the sexes? Since the "ideal" policy will be implemented in a real society, the answers to these qustions must be sought together.

A glance back over the topic headings for this chapter will underscore the fact that the problem of sex roles is multifaceted, touching just about every corner of social life. The pervasive character of sexism means that policy panaceas—i.e., all-purpose solutions to every form of the problem—had best be left to the role-changing wizard mentioned earlier. The

Women, like many groups facing discrimination, have become increasingly vocal in their attempts to achieve meaningful social change. (*Esaisas Baitel/Photo Researchers*)

more realistic transformation to be analyzed here concerns parity in only one social arena: the workplace. Before we consider the alternative policies for balancing sexes and jobs, it is worth emphasizing what is *not* true of the present imbalance.

It has already been stated that unequal treatment of women at work is not a simple reflection of sexist attitudes. There are males who consider women to be inferior workers, and there is evidence that female raises and promotions suffer as a result of such prejudice. If personal prejudice were the primary source of sex discrimination at work, however, one would expect a rapid closing of the earnings gap to have paralleled the rapid egalitarian movement in sex-role attitude polls. The lack of parallelism between attitudes toward and treatment of working women points to the more complex institutional sources of discrimination.

Consider this: "Work" is not confined to the job. Women carry the burden of responsibility for household drudgery and, especially, the labor associated with child rearing. There is no escaping the fact that a child's illnesses, school schedule, and simple needs for everyday care can conflict with a woman's occupational role. Other social institutions have just not adapted quickly enough to support the dual role of working mothers. Only about 4 percent of 3-to 6-year-old children whose mothers are employed attend an organized day-care center (Scanzoni and Scanzoni, 1981). In lieu of available or affordable day care (current costs for one child range up to 6500 dollars a year), 1 in 11 mothers actually brings her children to work (Hacker, 1983), a situation which is ideal for no one. While day-care centers are expanding, and husbands are helping more with family tasks, the cultural lag in the adaptation of nonbusiness institutions to women's changing work demands forces uncounted numbers to seek part-time employment or less demanding career paths. Unequal treatment of working women thus arises in substantial degree from the social

structure beyond the realm of male chauvinist bosses. Such complex patterns of institutional discrimination suggest how nearly everyone's attitudes can favor an earnings equality which very few women attain.

If every woman currently in the labor force were paid dollar for dollar what similarly qualified men at the same job receive, there would still be a sizable earnings gap by sex. We have confronted the reason before: Women are in different jobs than men. Since a 1981 National Academy of Sciences study found that for each 1 percent increase in the number of women working at an occupation, the average pay drops by $42 a year, why don't women just get out of sex-segregated occupations? Turn the question on yourself. By your selection of major courses, you are preparing over a period of years for a career you may have chosen way back in childhood. Consider, first, that picking another career is more than a matter of filling out a different job application and, second, that your choice of what to be when you grow up reflects a lifetime of the influences of parents, teachers, and friends.

Even if such deep-seated personal orientations could be discarded in order to conquer male dominated occupations, sexual integration of the workplace would require an invasion more massive than D-Day. About 6 out of every 10 working women—an estimated 26 million people—would have to strike out into male occupational terrain, with a similar number of males retreating into female territory. While we have taken pains to point out that the triumph of women's work equality is not opposed only by on-the-job attitudes, let there be no doubt that integration on this scale would encounter active sexist resistance. The reality of the office chauvinist, in fact, underscores the present point about the wider sources of work inequality. As Chapter 9 explains, bigots are made, not born. The same socialization processes in home and school that channel the sexes into jobs likewise channel opinions about what women and men should do. Public policies must face the socio-logical fact that the war between the sexes at work is mobilized by forces throughout the social structure.

Strategies for Solution

Return to the opening point that substantial gains have been won for working women. The weaponry for these successful battles has been built around the strategy of *equal pay for equal work,* formally enshrined as a national policy by the Equal Pay Act of 1963 and attendant legis-lation (see Box 10-4 and Box 10-5). The basic thrust of this policy has been simple: Take legal action whenever females are being paid less than males for the same job, or whenever females are unfairly barred from entering those same jobs.

The case by case tactics have won some highly visible victories. In 1981, a suit brought by the Equal Employment Opportunity Com-mission (the EEOC is the federal agency estab-lished as the enforcement arm of the Civil Rights Act of 1964, also currently empowered to enforce the Equal Pay Act of 1963) led to a 5 million dollar settlement for sex discrimination to be paid to some 6000 National Biscuit Co. employees. That same year, the FBI, ironically enough, was found guilty of discrimination against over 2000 women; the ruling called for back pay and the elimination of certain physical training requirements for potential agents. Dis-crimination in promotions was specifically at-tacked in the case of *Hishon v. King and Spalding,* which resulted in a Supreme Court

---

BOX 10-5

PROSPECTS FOR THE EQUAL RIGHTS AMENDMENT

Equality of rights under the law shall not be denied or abridged by the United States or by any state on account of sex.

This simple statement has been the focal point of complex sociological forces. Although some form of equal rights amendment to the Constitution had been brought before every Congress since 1923 (Lee, 1980), the House and Senate did pass the above version in 1972. Over the next seven years, the ERA was signed by all but three of the states required for the three-fourths majority leading to ratification. In response to the swirl of interest groups around this controversial statement, Congress extended the usual time limit for ratification to June 30, 1982. The necessary number of states was not added by that date, however, in large part because five states had voted to rescind their earlier ratification.

Why all of the sound and fury about such a simple statement? The political limbo in which the ERA now rests may be a consequence of the wild predictions made by activist groups for and against the amendment. Oppo-nents have conjured images of men entering women's rest rooms and females being drafted into male military bar-racks. Feminist supporters have asserted that real progress toward sexual equality is impossible without such a conditional amendment. The exaggerations of both positions have confused a plain truth: We just do not know the objective effects of an ERA. Pennsylvania has had

a state ERA since 1971, and still officially evaluates its impact as "currently being implemented." The reason is that the state—and the proposed federal—amendment is worded so broadly that specific applications have to be laboriously decided by administrative and court decisions.

The passion play over the ERA that has been per-formed in the mass media raises questions about its subjective status. Public opinion polls do not reflect the current constitutional deadlock. The most recent available survey showed a 61 versus 39 percent split in *favor* of the amendment. For the typical college age range, 7 out of every 10 respondents were pro-ERA (Gallup, 1982:7). These data are portents of the eventual passage of an equal rights amendment, and there is another sociological sign supporting this prediction. A study in the journal *Sex Roles* (Jackson, 1983) reports the following conclusion: "When people are given the actual text of E.R.A., but not told what it is, they display more positive attitudes toward it than people who respond to the term 'E.R.A.' without being informed of its actual text." If the roar of controversy gives way to quieter, more objective analysis of content, the underlying attitudes of the voting public may soon make an ERA a constitutional reality.

decision enjoining admission of women to law firm partnerships and, by implication, the upper echelon of other professions.

Court rulings have frequently utilized the Affirmative Action (see Chapter 9) approach of *quotas,* requiring a stipulated proportion of females to be hired or promoted over a given period. The FBI case, for example, called for 41 percent of all new agents each year to be women. Opponents of quotas cite a number of value trade-offs. Percentage requirements may force firms to pass over better-qualified males to comply with the law, thus treating one inequity with another by so-called reverse discrimination. If this devaluation of qualifications does occur (the FBI, after all, had to change its physical standards), talent and merit become secondary to simply having a woman in the job. The objection is that legal quotas trade societal efficiency for sexual equality. The rebuttal, of course, is that societal efficiency is currently compromised by the exclusion of talented women from responsible positions.

The most telling criticism of the policy of the present system visualizes its ultimate success. Will sexual equality at work be achieved if every woman is paid the same as a man doing her job, and all discriminatory barriers to employment are struck down? You already know the answer is negative. The massive sex segregation of the United States economy (again, over 50 million men and women would have to switch occupational categories) guarantees a continued earnings gap. This sociological reality has generated increasing support for a very different policy approach. The alternative strategy emphasizes *equal pay for comparable worth* instead of equal pay for equal work. The difference is crucial. Over and above unfair barriers to female entry into male-typed occupations, comparable worth would reward women more equitably right where they are. In response to the National Academy of Sciences' finding that female dominated jobs are underpaid, the new strategy would see that jobs of comparable skill, effort, and responsibility would command comparable salaries.

Comparable worth is no longer just a textbook idea. Recent court decisions have led Linda Chavez, staff director of the U.S. Commission on Civil Rights, to call comparable worth "the civil rights issue of the 1980's."[3] A 1981 strike in San Jose, California, ended when the city agreed, among other examples, to pay female recreation supervisors as much as male gardeners. Minnesota is spending 22 million dollars to raise women's pay, based on a 1982 study showing that, for instance, the work of female stenographers was comparable to that of male laborers. The most significant single case so far has emerged from a federal judge's original decision that the State of Washington must raise the wages of thousands of its women employees on the basis of a comparable worth evaluation performed for the state by an independent consulting firm. This study assigned 573 "worth points" to a registered nurse with experience, compared to a score of 97 for a *better-paid* beginning truck driver. The Washington case ultimately resulted in a binding settlement requiring the state to begin to redress the 20 percent underpayment of female employees relative to males at the same worth point levels (*New York Times,* Jan. 2, 1986).

In its sweeping strategy of closing the gap between the sexes right in their present jobs, comparable worth bypasses the cumbersome process of finding a woman who is (or ought to be) in the same job as a man, and then bringing suit. This alternative policy can cut right through the case by case approach to discrimination, but its critics contend that the widespread implications of comparable worth make it a double-edged sword.

[3] It should be noted that Linda Chavez is an appointee of the Reagan administration, which is opposed to the principle of comparable worth. This label was first attached to the comparable worth issue by Eleanor Holmes Norton, chair of the EEOC under President Carter.

In the real world of social problems, one must always consider the price tag of a policy. Implementation of comparable worth will not be cheap, as is indicated by the original Washington state settlement estimated to cost up to 1 billion dollars. Such enormous sums could mean linkages to other problems, such as inflation caused by higher salaries, higher taxes, and/or cutbacks to public services. Opponents of comparable worth also note that it interferes with setting wages through supply and demand in labor markets. Consequently, occupations such as computer specialists, which are in hot current demand, will be paid no more than economically marginal jobs with similar levels of skill, effort, and responsibility. Critics also see comparable worth as tending toward rigid salary schedules, paying people in terms of general occupational requirements rather than rewarding individual initiative or performance.

Policies into Practice

Public opinion polls and surveys of sex-role attitudes reveal a collective concern that *something* should be done about occupational discrimination by sex. As we learned in the War on Poverty, however, seemingly overwhelming subjective support for the conquest of a social problem can bog down in the practical—or impractical—execution of a policy solution. Hence, our attention now turns to the nuts and bolts operation of the alternative strategies.

The equal pay for equal work strategy operates on a search and destroy basis, seeking out illegal discrimination and then striking at it with governmental and private lawsuits. These tactics obviously require that the inequities be located, no easy task in an economy with some 29,000 occupational titles which employers may even use to disguise discrimination (in one case, the same job was called Assembler I for the women and Assembler II for the men). This case by case approach has meant step by step progress. Professor Derrick Bell, Jr., of the Harvard Law School makes this pessimistic

assessment: "Even the most wildly optimistic of us cannot reasonably hope that reliance on this complex and uncertain process will close the wide gap in...male and female salaries" (1977:681). An analysis of employment policy spanning the United States, Canada, and western Europe noted that our society has probably brought more cases of sex discrimination than all the rest of these countries combined (Ratner, 1980). The fact that the gender gap in earnings is smaller in several other advanced industrial democracies is a cross-cultural comment on the difficulties of implementing equal pay for equal work through the courts.

The equal pay through comparable worth strategy is proposed, in part, because of the maddeningly slow progress of the present system. This alternative to the status quo would attempt to cut through the Gordian knot[4] of employment discrimination by a large-scale invasion, sweeping across pay scales in whole state governments and industries instead of seeking out pockets of sexist resistance. Like a large-scale military operation, comparable worth has imposing logistical problems. The concept of a worth index to be applied to occupations as the basis for pay seems eminently fair, but who would you want estimating the value of your future job? There is a technical question as well: *Can* various kinds of jobs be reduced to a numeric scale?

Proponents of the policy answer that business has been using job point evaluations as a management tool for over fifty years. Assuming that technical issues such as the skill level of various kinds of work can be ironed out, be clear on the fact that the evaluation scales convert directly into pay scales. A conflict theorist would predict a tug-of-war among professionals, management, and unions, all fighting to establish the worth

[4] This term refers to a knot of incredible complexity which, according to legend, would be untied by the future ruler of Asia. Alexander the Great solved the puzzle by cutting the Gordian knot with a single stroke of his sword.

of their vocations in the scale. From this perspective, the worth index could easily end up as a numeric weapon of the more powerful interest groups, namely, those representing already well-paid male occupations.

A final consideration in implementing the comparable worth strategy is the size of the stakes. An article in *Labor Law Journal* (Soel-foegel, 1980) called the proposed policy an idea "of cyclonic proportions which, if left unchecked, may soon rip through the American economy, costing untold millions of dollars." Such emotional statements may reflect the subjective hesitancy of the public about a policy change of such scale, but they also suggest a key difference between the two policies. Equal pay for equal work has been a relatively cautious march of incremental progress. Implementation of equal pay for comparable worth would carry the higher risks—and higher potential benefits in equality—of a blitzkrieg policy.

Evaluating the Evidence

In many respects, the entire Women and Work section was an evaluation of the present policy against employment discrimination. The many facets of sexual inequality all reflect this essential truth: Despite some evidence of progress, females can expect fewer rewards of the work world than males.

Consider now two additional bodies of data sharpening this basic insight. The first exhibit for your consideration is a formal evaluation study which attempted to determine the direct impact of equal pay for equal work enforcement activities on the earnings gap. Using a sophisticated statistical model that incorporated general social changes in sex-role attitudes, the researcher was unable to detect a substantial effect of EEOC enforcement on the relative earnings of white females (Burstein, 1979). Obviously the present policy has helped women. But despite breakthrough cases such as those cited above, and despite indications that the earnings gap has closed more in the occupations

where the EEOC has been the most active, evidence of across-the-board success of equal pay for equal work is less than compelling.

A second data set relevant to both policies comes out of the backyard of the present system: the federal civil service. Although equal pay has been the law for national government jobs since 1923, male and female earnings are still far apart. The reason is sex segregation. About 4 of every 10 men on the payroll are at civil service grade GS 12 or higher, compared to only 1 of every 20 women. This is a vivid reminder of the limits of present policy, but how does it bear on comparable worth?

Even though some eighteen states considered its implementation in 1984, comparable worth is a policy of the future for the United States. We may parenthetically note that worth indexes have been developed and applied on a large scale in West Germany, and that the United Kingdom and Canada have comparable worth laws, but this is evidence of an indirect kind (Ratner, 1980). Despite the caution sociology preaches about generalizing across the boundaries of societies, these cases reinforce the lesson to be learned in our own civil service. No policy or combination of policies will equalize working men and women unless there are changes in those regions of the social structure where you make your career choice.

SUMMARY

1 Sex roles have been with us for as long as societies have existed. There is much debate as to whether the attitudinal and behavioral characteristics of masculinity and femininity are valid as well as whether gender differences emerge from within individuals (nature) or are imposed on them by society (nurture).

2 Growing subjective awareness about sex roles by both American men and women is partly due to the consciousness-raising of women's groups. Despite evidence that minds and opportunities seem to be opening for women, objective equality between the sexes does not exist.

3 In employment, objective discrimination against women takes many forms, including unequal pay, sex typing of jobs, and sexual harassment at work.

4 There are three major theories of sex-role socialization. The psychoanalytic view rests on unconscious processes. Social learning theory emphasizes conditioning and mod-

eling; and cognitive developmental theory hinges on the concept of a hierarchy of moral development.

5 There are two major social policies designed to control sexual discrimination in the workplace: (1) equal pay for equal work and (2) equal pay for comparable worth. Both policies are limited by deeply entrenched attitudes about appropriate career choices for men and women, as well as by practical problems of implementation.

CHAPTER 11

Crime and Delinquency: Causes and Consequences

Why do I rob banks for a living? Well, that's where the money is.

—Willie Sutton

THE UNIVERSAL NATURE OF CRIME

Crime in Society

Look at the Table of Contents. As is traditional for textbooks of this kind, it neatly divides the material on social problems into separate, subdivided chapters. This practice makes educational sense in organizing the professor's lectures and your studying, but important lessons can be lost in the cracks between the chapters.

One truth that the study of social problems teaches again and again is the importance of their intimate links to one another. Chapter outlines tend to force apart problems that really need to be understood together. To introduce this point in the discussion of criminal behavior, consider a research project the authors have been working on while writing this book. We have applied for a research grant to evaluate a residential treatment center for adolescent (ages 13 to 21) drug abusers in the Philadelphia area. Preliminary studies paint the following portrait of a typical client of that facility: He is a male (see Chapter 10 on sex roles) with an unstable family history (see Chapter 5 on the family), abusing several substances (see Chapter 2 on drug abuse) and relatively likely to have engaged in some criminal behavior (see the present chapter).

In designing the study, we had to directly confront the reality of problem linkages. Analyzing these adolescents as though they were one-dimensional individuals with *only* a drug problem would have been downright silly. Much can be learned by the study of separate social problems, but much can be missed as well. How can you properly understand a youth's pattern of petty theft apart from the fact that he is addicted to expensive illegal drugs?

The principle of problem linkages is indispensable to a sociological discussion of crime and delinquency. So too is the related principle that social problems are rooted in the structure of a particular society. It seems natural to think of crime as self-evident evil, a kind of intrinsic

defect of human nature. The commonsensical perception of criminal behavior as individual evil is exploded by cross-cultural studies. What you have to do to commit a crime and the numbers of people who do it both vary enormously across national boundaries. Consider even a crime as basic as murder. All societies have rules against killing, but the rules are very different in different cultures. We permit police officers discharging their duty to kill without guilt of a crime; in some societies, not only would such a killing by a stranger be a crime but their culture would actually require family members to kill the killer.

Too exotic? Rather than qualitative differences in the definition of crimes, let us consider quantitative differences in individual evildoers among societies like ours. According to the most recent cross-cultural study by the World Health Organization (see U.S. Bureau of the Census, 1984b), the homicide *rate* (i.e., number of victims per 100,000 people) in the United States was nearly eight times as high as in England and West Germany, and over ten times the rate in Norway and the Netherlands. Despite the waging of an undeclared civil war, one's chances of death by homicide in Northern Ireland were 39 percent *less* than the chances of being murdered here.

It is too much to believe that the United States is one of the more murderous societies on earth because we somehow have gathered the most evil individuals into our society. Similarly, Canada's population cannot have so much less risk of violent killing simply because more peaceful people have decided to settle north of our border. As one surveys the staggering cross-cultural variety in the types and amounts of crime, a sociological truth becomes crystal clear: Patterns of criminal behavior grow out of the structure of the society rather than from the souls of individuals.[1]

[1] This is not to deny the relevance of factors such as conscience, motivation, and responsibility to individual

Despite the wild diversity of crimes and criminals, a cross-cultural survey does find uniformities. There is the datum that every society has some behaviors which are treated as criminal. This point can be stated even more broadly in terms of *deviance,* simply defined as behavior violating social norms. Not only societies but all groups—corporations, families, drinking buddies—create the rules we call norms, and *in all such groups these social rules are broken.* Can you think of a single norm, anything from mailing birthday cards to not sending explosives through the mail, for which you do not know of a violation?

To personalize the point a bit, consider the universality of deviance in the college setting. A series of surveys conducted since the mid-sixties (when the authors were in school) have indicated the widespread willingness of students to cheat on exams, thus breaking one of the most hallowed norms of higher education. The Carnegie Council's studies suggest that about half of all undergraduates have cheated, some through such devious means as infiltrating the campus computer to change grades or slipping lecture tapes into a Walkman. This is not meant to give you deviant ideas but rather to give some idea of the prevalence of deviant behavior.

If not among the cream of American youth, where can a deviance-free group be found? Certainly not in the pristine wilderness of our national parks. Although viewed by many as refuges from crime-haunted urban areas, official statistics show federal lands to contain more pressing dangers from the human animal than from grizzly bears. Outlaw motorcycle gangs, timber thieves, marijuana growers, and survivalists conducting paramilitary maneuvers with automatic weapons have brought crime to Mother Nature. Even monasteries, with hand-picked individuals of high character and social routines devised to promote religious conformi-

ty, can be wracked with controversy due to acts which we might consider trivial but which the monks treat as serious offenses (Sampson, 1969). Here is the point: Neither the ivy-covered halls of academia, nor the mountain majesties of national parks, nor sanctified religious monasteries house people who do not "sin" against their norms. Deviance is universally abhorred but universally endured by human groups.

Macro Theories of Crime

Why? There is irony in the fact that all groups produce both rules and rule breakers, but there is also a question to be answered by sociological analysis. Emile Durkheim, one of the founders of sociology, proposed an answer in 1893 in his classic essay "Rules for Distinguishing between the Normal and the Pathological." Those rules, according to Durkheim, are not as simple as deviance equals pathology. The universal nature of crime means to Durkheim that "it is a factor in public health, an integral part of all healthy societies" (1964:67).

Despite the obvious negative consequences of crime for the victim, a heinous criminal act may actually serve the rest of the society by drawing its people together in their collective outrage. A famous application of this argument is presented in Kai T. Erikson's book *Wayward Puritans* (1966), in which he develops a sociological explanation for the seemingly inexplicable case of the Massachusetts witch hysteria. During 1692, hundreds of people were arrested and dozens were actually executed for the crime of witchcraft. Erikson observes that the witches were "discovered" in the midst of a community that had recently experienced much dissension and upheaval.[2] Noting the irony of

---

actions. The focus here is on the broader differences across societies within which individual free will is exercised.

[2] Witch crazes have been observed before during periods of social unrest. Half a million people may have been burned for this crime in Europe between the fifteenth and seventeenth centuries (Harris, 1974). In Erikson's words, "Perhaps no other form of crime in history has been a better index to social disruption and change" (1966:153).

such deviants appearing in just the kind of religiously based society which loathes them most, Erikson points out that the heat of the earlier community disputes seemed to be quenched in the flood of antiwitch feeling.

The heart of the idea is that deviants—whether witches or muggers—may have quite the same unifying effect on a society as declaring war, but without the threat of annihilation. Criminals are a kind of domesticated enemy who do damage to society but who provide the public service of reinforcing the common culture.

This unusual perspective on criminal behavior is drawn from *functionalism,* a theoretical approach analyzing aspects of everyday life in terms of the functions they serve in the overall social pattern (see Chapter 1). Durkheim's functionalist theorem suggests why all groups need a certain amount of rule breaking, and why front page crime news satisfies deeper public needs than a thirst for blood. For another application of the functionalist perspective, consider the phenomenon of ''Saturnalia.'' The term comes from festivals in the ancient world held in honor of the Roman god Saturn which were, to say the least, festive. Here is a description of the revelry by Cronus, mythical ruler of a Roman Golden Age:

> The serious is barred, no business allowed. Drinking and being drunk, noise and games of dice, appointing of kings and feasting of slaves, singing naked, clapping of tremulous hands, an occasional dunking of corked faces in icy water—these are the functions over which I preside (Bourbolis, 1964:10).

Such regularly scheduled rule breaking may be intriguing, but what has it got to do with contemporary American life? Consider the connotations of the term weekend. If the truth be told, we must confess that these regular occasions in our society contain more rule breaking than the whole rest of the week combined; statistics on drug use and morals arrests bear out this confession. A functionalist theorist would look at

these cases of culturally scheduled deviant behavior and draw two conclusions. First, the periodic deviance serves the function of blowing off steam so that people can follow the letter of the law most of the time. Second, the regulated timing and predictable types of rule breaking shift attention away from the individual rule breaker. Deviance and even criminality seem to be built-in parts of the social system.

Looking at crime at the level of whole societies, a *conflict theorist* sees something very different. While conceding to the functionalist that crime's universality needs to be explained, the conflict approach objects to the vision of society as one big happy family which condones occasional naughtiness. Another of Durkheim's seminal insights was that there can be no lawbreaker without a law; in a real sense, society creates criminals by declaring certain human actions to be crimes. Proceeding from Durkheim's observation, the conflict theorists wonder: Who gets to make the laws?

Their response to this rhetorical question is, quite simply, the rich. Given the theoretical assumption that societies consist of groups contending for power, and given the clear advantages of economic resources in this struggle, control of the criminal justice system is part of the spoils of victory for the upper classes. Even in democratic societies such as our own, the conflict perspective sees the so-called ruling classes as steering the machinery of government in the direction of a legal code that will serve their best interests.

Again consider the seemingly self-evident crime of murder. Within our society, conflict theorists ask: Why is it that a death resulting from an impassioned street brawl is a criminal homicide, whereas cold-blooded corporate neglect of safety standards killing thousands of people a year is not murder under the law (Box, 1983)? Their answer is that the former makes the streets unsafe for the rich as well as the poor, but the latter is just too profitable to the rich to be defined as a serious crime.

The conflict approach offers class-based explanations for law enforcement as well as lawmaking. In fact, the need to control growing working-class populations in the cities of nineteenth-century America is viewed as a major reason for upper-class sponsorship of the first real municipal police forces (Harring, 1983). Current arrest statistics for poor burglars compared to wealthy tax evaders tell a similar story of class dominance. The central point here concerns the very presence of crime and criminals in societies. Conflict theory explains the universality of this phenomenon not in terms of depraved human nature or hidden functions performed by the criminal but rather as the result of upper-class economic and political control from society to society (Calvin and Pauly, 1983). The haves direct the behavior of the have-nots by declaring anti-have acts illegal.

One of the most generally useful insights of the conflict perspective stems from its attention to the law as a product of human groups. Enshrinement in marble buildings and gold-bound books makes it natural to think of the law as some sort of eternal, inhuman monument. But even the fabled Code of Hammurabi—the first formalized law "published" on an 8-foot stone column—was, so to speak, hammered out by the real people of Mesopotamia. While the stone column has endured since 1800 B.C., the law chiseled upon it has no reality outside of the living society which created the code.

The immediate point is that criminal codes *must* be viewed in societal context, as sensitive to the many sociological forces boiling outside the courtroom. One key application of this sociological principle views laws as only part of the larger cultural system of norms. Generally, legislators select the most important, deeply revered popular rules—called the *mores*—and write them into the legal code. Rape, for example, is widely considered to be a heinous act and is also a matter for criminal prosecution.

All laws, however, do not so neatly mirror the popular mores. A well-studied case of the breaking of this mirror is Prohibition. The so-called temperance movement was propelled by a rather small, religiously based WASP political core whose abstinent values were not shared by growing Catholic immigrant populations (Gusfield, 1963). Although this politically mobilized interest group did succeed in outlawing alcohol, per capita consumption actually increased while the Eighteenth Amendment was in effect! Not only did the passage of this amendment immediately create a new class of criminals out of people just drinking as before, but the law also provided an enormous funding base for organized crime in the new black market.

A primary reason for the spectacular failure of Prohibition was the lack of support for the policy in everyday social life. If one's friends, relatives, and coworkers do not apply moral pressure about the "crime," police efforts are likely to be futile. This historical case has immediate relevance to contemporary legal issues such as marijuana, gambling, and prostitution. Unless laws are rooted in the lifestyle of society, the following ancient phrase will still ring true: "Leges sinae moribus venae" (laws without the mores are in vain).

While a criminal statute may be imposed on an inhospitable culture by a powerful interest group, another reason for a law being out of step with popular mores is *social change*. When society moves forward, the old criminal code does not automatically keep pace. As illustrations of this type of cultural lag, consider the following laws recently "on the books":

- Women in Oxford, Ohio, are forbidden to undress in front of a man's picture.
- Florida law requires keeping on your clothing while bathing.
- It is prohibited in Minnesota to hang male and female undergarments on the same clothesline.

Clearly, changing sexual mores have transformed such "blue laws" into humorous anachronisms throughout most of American society.

To spotlight social change in norms applying to college students, we offer a historical instance from Villanova College (now University) where your authors currently teach. In the 1850s, students were actually imprisoned for lateness and "disrespect to prefect" (Sack, 1961:265). Although some professors may think of these penalties with nostalgia today, more permissive public attitudes mean that such punishments no longer fit the crime. Enforceable laws and the popular culture are in a delicate balance that can be readily upset by social change.

On the other hand, changes in the law can also express new shifts in public opinion. Take the well-publicized case of Mothers Against Drunk Drivers (MADD). Through an inspired blend of emotional appeals ("People like Pat Owens lost two daughters and two nieces, with a third niece paralyzed for life [all to drunk drivers]") and official statistics ("In the last ten years, more than 250,000 people have been killed in alcohol-related crashes—more than were killed in Vietnam"; MADD pamphlet: 2–3), this highly organized interest group has been instrumental in changing laws in California, New York, Pennsylvania, and numerous other states. From a situation in which an individual convicted of driving drunk could often pay a charge less than that for killing a deer out of season, even first-time offenders may now face mandatory jail sentences and/or fines in the thousands of dollars. In terms of both public perception and enforcement, drunk driving is now being treated as a *crime*.

This case is an apt conclusion for the present section. In the first place, the changing legal status of drunk driving illustrates how the law may be called into tune with changing popular mores by the prodding of a

Through its masterful public relations campaigns, Mothers Against Drunk Drivers (MADD) has succeeded in mobilizing subjective opinion to support changes in the law. (*Michael Silnk/EKM-Nepenthe*)

determined interest group. The case also illustrates, in turn, the broader point of the linkage of social problems (alcohol and accidents) and, more broadly yet, the societal sources of crime as a social problem. Both the differences across societies and the differences across time in our society in defining crime show that it does not just result from individual bad guys. MADD's activities also nicely demonstrate the classic dimensions of a social problem. Through mass mailings, public service spots, and even television movies publicizing the objective consequences of drunk driving, MADD massively increased the visibility of the problem. A subjectively aroused public has been instrumental in

TABLE 11-1   ADMITTED CRIMINALITY DURING THE PAST TWELVE MONTHS

Illegal act	Self (check)	Sample (%)
Engaged in fistfighting	_____	43.0
Fought with a weapon	_____	7.6
Used force to steal	_____	4.3
Used marijuana	_____	49.5
Used downers	_____	9.2
Used cocaine	_____	4.8
Stole car	_____	5.7
Engaged in drunk driving	_____	17.9
Destroyed property	_____	27.0
Theft over $20	_____	20.4

Source: Adapted from a study by Larry Siegel and Spencer Rathus presented in Larry J. Siegel and Joseph J. Senna, *Juvenile Delinquency*, St. Paul, Minnesota, West Publishing, 1985, pp. 53–54.

pressing legislators for new policies which appear to have met some objective success.[3] All of these sociological themes apparent in the MADD case are to be woven around the *general* social problem of crime in the sections that follow.

COUNTING CRIME: THE OBJECTIVE DIMENSION

The working of social forces to define what is illegal does not imply that crime is some figment of our collective imagination. Every day there are individuals who bleed real blood because of the social problem of crime. Although the evidence of this problem is all around, and even though it is likely to victimize each of us, objective measurement of crime is no simple matter. As the sociological subdiscipline of criminology has emerged, so have several approaches to quantifying criminal behavior.

Counting Criminals

One vantage point on the significance of the crime problem looks at the numbers of individuals who have perpetrated illegal acts. Are you a criminal? Please cover the right-hand column of Table 11-1

[3] Under a stiff new Pennsylvania law, drunken driving arrests increased 26 percent and alcohol-related traffic deaths dropped 9.5 percent over 1983–1984.

and place a check next to any of the listed offenses you have committed in the past year. Even a single check marks you as a lawbreaker, but you have plenty of company. Uncovering the column on the right shows the substantial percentages of young people polled who admitted engaging in each illegal act over the previous twelve months. If detected by the police and prosecuted, all of these lawbreakers would swamp the jails of the upper middle class neighborhood in which the study was conducted.

There is excellent evidence that the guilt you share with this studied community is not atypical. As early as 1947, a survey in the New York City metropolitan area revealed that nearly everyone sometimes breaks the law. In Wallerstein and Wyle's classic study, 1681 out of 1698 individuals polled—that is 99 percent—checked off at least one offense sufficiently serious to draw a maximum jail sentence of not less than one year under the New York penal code. Three decades of studies in a variety of communities, states, and regions confirm this basic finding: Everyman—and Everywoman—contributes to the social problem of crime by breaking the law.

While it does undermine popular misconceptions about the nature of the criminal, the statistical fact that both you the reader and we the authors have very probably committed crimes oversimplifies the objective picture of the problem. In the first place, *prevalence* statistics suggesting that nearly everyone breaks the law must be distinguished from measures of *incidence,* which count the frequency of lawbreaking. Much data support the view that the majority of offenses are committed by a relatively small minority of chronic offenders (see below).

But a two-group characterization of criminal incidence as bad guys versus most-of-the-time good guys is likewise too simple. One complication is the extent to which criminality exclusively involves guys. The results of the National Youth Study (Elliot and Ageton, 1980) shake sugar and spice stereotypes of the female noncriminal. But while the prevalence pattern shows that females break many different laws in abundant numbers, the gender gap in incidence looms large for more serious offenses (e.g., the ratio of boys to girls admitting to larceny over $50 is 11 to 1).

Another key to the pattern of criminal incidence is age. While there are no national surveys enumerating illegal acts across the entire life course, the National Youth Study uncovers important trends up to the age of 17. Simply, juveniles report committing a lot of crime, much of it while they are quite young; the incidence of some serious violent and property offenses actually peaks among 13- to 15-year-olds (Ageton and Elliot, 1978)!

Studies comparing black and white youth show the races to be about equally likely to report commission of a delinquent act over the previous year, but there is a greater incidence of violent offenses among black adolescents and more offenses involving cars (auto theft, reckless driving, etc.) among whites (Empey, 1982). Complicating black-white comparisons is the fact of educational, occupational, and income differences across the races.

On this issue of social class differences in criminality, the scientific jury is still out. In an article entitled "The Myth of Social Class and Criminality," several criminologists concluded from their review of thirty-five separate studies of the subject that lower-class youth are no more delinquent than those at higher rungs on the class ladder (Tittle, Villemez, and Smith, 1978). A number of their criticisms of previous studies, however, have been met by the National Youth Study. The latter data tell a story of somewhat greater overall incidence and much greater incidence of more serious crimes against persons and property for respondents lower on the class ladder.[4] It is still necessary to reserve judgment on the precise nature of the class-criminality relationship, but one general ruling meets no objection in the criminological literature: The likelihood of lawbreaking is a variable, and it varies by the social characteristics of individuals.

All of the findings used so far in the section Counting Criminals have been drawn from self-report studies, so-called because they ask the respondent to check off the types and amounts of offenses admitted by that person. Such an approach brings all of the weaknesses as well as the strengths of survey research (refer to Chapter 1) to the measurement of criminality. Obvious methodological problems such as unrepresentative samples of respondents and unwillingness to truthfully confess crimes are progressively being solved in later studies (through national probability surveys including lie scales), and in any case are biases that compare favorably with the built-in distortions of the only other available counting of criminals: official arrest statistics. The most glaring flaw of the latter is that most of us get away with it. Moreover, individuals caught in the act may not be treated equally by criminal justice agents, thus inflating the arrest statistics for some social categories (e.g., poor black males) and undercounting real incidence for others released before official arrest (e.g., rich white females).

---

[4] By contrast, middle-class youth register a *higher* incidence of hard drug use and status offenses than those in the lower or working classes (Elliot and Ageton, 1980).

Although the selective treatment of the Saints and Roughnecks presented in Box 11-1 gives credence to such social selection, current scientific opinion accepts a rough correspondence between self-report and official arrest counts of crime (Hindelang, Hirschi, and Weis, 1981). The main difference is in the *scale* of the problem sketched by the two techniques; arrest statistics present the same objective outline as self-reports, but in miniature. Using the ominous phrase coined by the National Commission on the Causes and Prevention of Violence in 1969, the "dark figure" of actual crime may loom nine times as large as the official count of crime!

Counting Victimizations

The second major strategy for measurement of the objective dimension has been counting the number of times individuals are touched by the crime problem. Here again, estimates are derived both by scientific surveys and by official statistics.

Let us open the discussion with the latter, since these records include one of the best known enumerations of any American social

---

BOX 11-1

THE SAINTS AND THE ROUGHNECKS

By midnight on Fridays and Saturdays the Saints were usually thoroughly high, and one or two of them were often so drunk they had to be carried to the cars. Then the boys drove around town, calling obscenities to women and girls; and driving recklessly through red lights and at high speeds with their lights out. Occasionally they played "chicken." Construction sites and road repair areas were the special province of the Saints' mischief. A soon-to-be-repaired hole in the road inevitably invited the Saints to remove lanterns and wooden barricades and put them in the car, leaving the hole unprotected. The boys would find a safe vantage point and wait for an unsuspecting motorist to drive into the hole. Often, though not always, the boys would go up to the motorist and commiserate with him about the dreadful way the city protected its citizenry.

Leaving the scene of the open hole and the motorist, the boys would then go searching for an appropriate place to erect the stolen barricade. An "appropriate place" was often a spot on a highway near a curve in the road where the barricade would not be seen by an oncoming motorist. The boys would wait to watch an unsuspecting motorist attempt to stop and (usually) crash into the wooden barricade. With saintly bearing the boys might offer help.

The local police saw the Saints as good boys who were among the leaders of the youth in the community. Rarely, the boys might be stopped in town for speeding or for running a stop sign. When this happened the boys were always polite, contrite and pled for mercy.... None ever received a ticket or was taken into the precinct by the local police.

Hannibal townspeople never perceived the Saints' high level of delinquency. The Saints were good boys who just went in for an occasional prank. The Roughnecks were a different story. Although the two gangs of boys were the same age, and both groups engaged in an equal amount of wild-oat sowing, everyone agreed that the not-so-well-dressed, not-so-well-mannered, not-so-rich boys were heading for trouble.

The fighting activities of the (Roughnecks) were fairly readily and accurately perceived by almost everyone. At least once a month, the boys would get into some sort of fight, although most fights were scraps between members of the group or involved only one member of the group and some peripheral hanger-on.

Over the period that the group was under observation by the author, each member was arrested at least once. Several of the boys were arrested a number of times and spent at least one night in jail. While most were never taken to court, two of the boys were sentenced to six months' incarceration in boys' schools.

Selective perception and labeling—finding, processing and punishing some kinds of criminality and not others—means that visible, poor, nonmobile, outspoken, undiplomatic "tough" kids will be noticed, whether their actions are seriously delinquent or not. Other kids, who have established a reputation for being bright (even though underachieving), disciplined and involved in respectable activities, who are mobile and monied, will be invisible when they deviate from sanctioned activities.

William J. Chambliss, "The Saints and the Roughnecks," *Society*, November 1973:24–31.

problem: the Federal Bureau of Investigation's Uniform Crime Reports. This source is the basis for the annual headlines about national increases or decreases in the crime rate. Most of the media attention is focused on only the eight crimes which constitute the so-called Index Offenses listed on Figure 11-1. Aggregate numbers of these offenses are taken mainly from citizens' reports of victimization to local law enforcement agencies, who pass the totals, in turn, to the FBI. In the latest year for which the national statistics are available (Federal Bureau of Investigation, 1985), about 12 million offenses were recorded. Since the crime problem is often gauged in terms of an individual's risk of victimization, the totals are usually converted to reported rates per 100,000 population.

Figure 11-1 displays FBI Index crime rates over the past two decades, and the long-term trend is clear: Things have been getting riskier. In 1980, a typical person's chances of being an official victim were about 1 in 17, obviously a substantial increase in risk over 1960. The steeply rising curves are visible evidence of a true, sustained crime wave. As you can see, there has been a slight drop-off in the total rate (as well as the rates for both property and violent crimes) in the early 1980s.

While sections to follow will spotlight individual differences in victimization by type of offense, the concern here with the aggregate amount of victims calls for a breakdown of official crime rates by type of community. The risk of violence varies enormously depending on where you live. In fact, if you were to move from an SMSA (standard metropolitan statistical area containing a city with at least 50,000 inhabitants) to a smaller city, and then on to a rural small town, your likelihood of being a violence victim would be cut about in half with each change of address. This objective facet of the crime problem is singled out for presentation because it uncovers the broad social factors looming above individual criminals and their victims. Just as cultural differences across societies materially alter the nature of crime, so do community differences *within* American so-

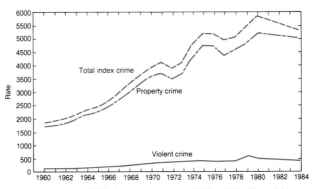

FIGURE 11-1 FBI Index crime rates, 1960–1984. The eight FBI Index Offenses are criminal homicide, forcible rape, robbery, aggravated assault, burglary, larceny-theft, motor vehicle theft, and arson. (*Source:* U.S. Dept. of Justice, FBI, *Crime in the United States, 1975*, p. 49, table 2; 1981, p. 39, table 2 (Washington, D.C.: U.S. Government Printing Office). It should be noted that the inclusion of an increasing proportion of local law enforcement agencies in the FBI totals accounts for part of the upward trend. The authors have extended the graph through 1984 to reflect the current downward trend.

ciety condition your chances of being robbed, raped, or even rubbed out.

Although they are an invaluable and well-known source of information about the distribution of lawbreaking behavior, the FBI Uniform Crime Reports blur the objective picture of crime in America. In the first place, the highly publicized totals for the Index offenses contain no information at all about dozens of other serious kinds of crime, such as extortion, child abuse, and tax evasion, each of which is often more harmful than the Index crimes (arson was only added to the index in 1983).

Second, local law enforcement agencies have the discretion to classify offenses. Since people calling in a crime simply report what happened, police must often render subtle judgments about whether a fistfight was an aggravated assault, or whether a wallet snatched in anger in a family argument should be listed as a larceny-theft. Such recording decisions by the "village watchman" are affected both by the professionalization of police procedure (McCleary, Nienstedt, and Erven, 1982) and by not-so-subtle local political pressures to keep the official crime rate down.

The third and final question mark over the FBI figures is suggested just above: In the vast majority of cases, citizens must call the police. It is not unlikely that a member of your family has been recently victimized by one of these offenses, and yet no one picked up the phone and reported the crime. Lack of confidence in the police to catch the criminal or to protect the victim who speaks up means no official record of a very real crime.

These known biases in the FBI Uniform Crime Reports (UCR) led the Commission on Law Enforcement and Administration of Justice to recommend to President Johnson that a household survey be conducted to provide an alternative measure of criminal victimization. Subsequently, the National Crime Survey (NCS) has interviewed samples of over 125,000 individuals twice a year. The findings generated by this rich data source have more than justified the Commission's recommendation.

The NCS estimate is that about 35 million serious crimes were perpetrated in 1984, a number roughly *tripling* the FBI official total. Just as was the case for criminals, breakdowns of the social characteristics of victims can yield surprising clues about the objective nature of the crime problem. At the cost of some detail, the essential demographic picture is this: To be young, male, nonwhite, and poor is to be at high risk for serious criminal victimization (U.S. Department of Justice, 1984). There is a perverse statistical justice in this statement. Check the paragraphs above and you will find that the very factors (age, sex, race, social class) which seem associated with increased commission of crimes are also risk factors for potential victims; the crime-prone and the victim-prone in the population are the same social types (although not necessarily the same individuals).

Consider a few concrete—and chilling—illustrations of the levels of risk: Roughly 1 out of every 8 of our white female readers (ages 20 to 24) can expect to be a victim of larceny-theft within a year of reading this sentence; about 6 percent of white males in the 12 to 15 age group are victims of violence in a typical year; and there is 1 chance in 21—not too much better than Russian roulette—that a black male will eventually be a homicide victim!

What is the final tally in the counting of crimes in America? Our matching of official and survey statistics has produced some obvious differences and some striking similarities. To be succinct, the FBI Uniform Crime Reports view crime through a methodological microscope. The NCS shows the underreporting of serious offenses to be quite substantial; for example, only about half of all robberies and rapes end up on the police blotter. Despite the contrast in scale, UCR and NCS sketch the same statistical profile of most likely victims. Both sources are also in parallel in tracing a key recent trend: less crime. The official total of UCR offenses dropped 7 percent in 1983, the largest one-year decline in the history of the Index and part of the first ever two-year drop. It is notable that the NCS total also slipped 7 percent over 1982–1983, including a 10 percent decline in violent crime. Both statistical sources traced a continuation of this downward trend into 1984 (although they differed on the 1985 trend).

Despite recent policy shifts such as mandatory jail sentences and anticareer criminal programs, deeper demographic forces might bear much of the credit for the crime decline in the 1980s. It is a statistical fact that young males commit a disproportionate share of all serious crimes. As is outlined in Chapter 7, the raw number of young males is now eroding fast with the aging of the baby boomers. Back in the 1960s, your coauthors were told as graduate students to expect the end of the crime wave with the end of the seventies, and also to expect politicians, wardens, and judges to be falling over themselves to claim credit. While this prophetic demographic analysis suggests the relevance of sociological explanations to the social problem of crime, it is only a preface to other crucial questions. Blaming much criminal behavior on one demographic slice of the population does not explain *why* they do it, or why the majority of you (even you young males) are *not* chronic offenders.

Counting the Cost

Assessing the social damage of the crime problem involves more than totaling up the number of offenses. While lawbreaking might be considered an evil in itself from a moralistic perspective, it is instructive to directly weigh the suffering and human losses occasioned by criminal acts. Begin with the obvious: Homicide is responsible for about 20,000 deaths a year, and is a leading cause of death among college students.[5] This amount is suf-

ficient for our society to be among the world leaders in murder, but it is less than the annual number of suicides and far less than the number of motor vehicle fatalities each year in the United States (U.S. Bureau of the Census, 1984*b*).

One may quite properly object that mortality is too simple an index of crime's harm, so consider damage to physical and mental health. About 3 of every 10 violent crimes result in some physical injury to the victim; only 7 percent of all victimizations lead to hospitalization (Reiss, 1981). Of course, these figures still add up to carnage for millions and death or maiming for tens of thousands. Besides, a beating not requiring stitches or a brain scan is still unwarranted physical suffering for the assaultee. The same point should be emphasized when assessing psychic harm, which is intrinsically more difficult to measure. Violent crime may trigger immediate and incapacitating mental trauma; also, mental health researchers are currently detecting a delayed reaction in some victims analogous to the "post-traumatic stress syndrome" which afflicts Vietnam veterans. Again, even if there is no subsequent pathology, the sense of personal violation and the outrage of harm to loved ones mean real, if unmeasured, harm to society.

Somewhat more amenable to measurement are the dollars and cents costs of crime. According to FBI statistics, the typical burglary victim loses about 1000 dollars compared to 665 dollars for a victim of robbery; motor vehicle theft is the most costly Index crime (average loss 3173 dollars), but also the most recoverable through insurance or police returning the vehicle (Federal Bureau of Investigation, 1982). These figures do not include indirect costs such as the loss of at least six days of work reported by 1 in 5 rape, robbery, or assault victims (Reiss, 1981). The fact that murder is associated with an average loss of only 59 dollars preaches caution in developing purely economic measures of crime's harms.

---

[5] This total does not include deaths incurred by white-collar crimes, a topic addressed in some detail below.

Care in the measurement process is also well-advised for societal-level estimates of the economic costs of crime, which often number in the hundreds of billions of dollars. Such estimates vary widely and are rapidly dated by inflation, but they reveal a reality that transcends all quibbles about measurement: The objective cost of crime to society is enormous.

THE SUBJECTIVE DIMENSION OF CRIME AND DELINQUENCY

If you ask people to name social problems, most will have trouble thinking of some of the topics covered in this book. We would bet money, though, that anyone you ask will quickly think of crime. Unlike mental illness or overpopulation, criminality is widely viewed as a deliberate problem inflicted by one person on others, the antisocial act par excellence. This view is enshrined in the ancient legal principle of mens rea ("the evil mind"), which defines evil intent as "the very essence of crime."[6]

Another reason for the high profile of crime as a social problem is its status as a real and present danger in everyday life. Most of us have been or will be victimized by crime (watch it: about 6 percent of all assaults occur in schools), and most people take daily precautions against it (did you lock your car? About 23 percent of all 18- to 24-year-olds had their property or car vandalized in the past year; U.S. Department of Justice, 1984). Criminal behavior is well recognized as a social problem of immediate relevance to our personal lives.

Given that virtually everyone accepts crime's status as a social problem, how high is the level of public concern on this particular issue? That is another way of asking about the

subjective dimension of the crime problem, and Figure 11-2 offers several answers. The lowest line traces the percentage of respondents to national Gallup polls who chose crime as "the most important problem facing this country today"; as you can see, 2 to 5 percent of the public have listed crime as the No.1 problem through the early eighties (crime has never been the consensus leading problem since the poll was first taken in 1935). Americans do not view crime as *the* most serious issue, but they usually list it as *one* of the most serious.

The middle line in the figure graphs the proportion naming crime and lawlessness as one of the "two or three [issues] you personally are most concerned with today." Generally, around one-third of the public lists crime as among the several most serious problems, placing it second among all issues named (behind inflation) for this series of Roper polls.

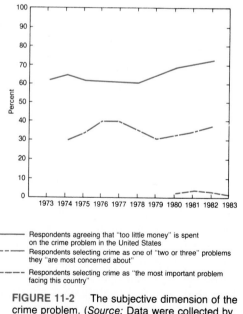

FIGURE 11-2   The subjective dimension of the crime problem. (*Source:* Data were collected by the National Opinion Research Center, the Roper Public Opinion Research Center, *The Gallup Report,* and The Gallup Poll. These data were aggregated into graphic form by the authors.)

---

[6] The quotation is from the 1878 case *State v. Blue* 53, pp. 978, 980. Interestingly, many of the offenses in the FBI's Uniform Crime Reports are attempted rather than completed offenses in which the offender is guilty in terms of mens rea.

Finally, the uppermost line in Figure 11-2 depicts the percentage of Americans who think that "we are spending too little on halting the rising crime rate." Although this question is a bit loaded (it pronounces the rate to be rising whether it is or not), the General Social Survey indicates that about two-thirds of the public consider the problem serious enough to devote more money to anticrime policy. Throughout the 1970s and well into the 1980s, subjective concern about crime has registered at a high and relatively stable level (see also Davis, 1980).

The widespread recognition of and concern about crime as a social problem has made it one of the most studied subjects in modern social science. Some of those studies focus on the predatory and exploitative nature of criminal behavior and an emotion it elicits: fear. Just as student test anxiety varies by subject and time of the semester, citizen fear of crime depends on the situation. About 1 of every 6 Americans feels unsafe in the home at night, while nearly half report fear of walking alone at night (*The Gallup Report*, 1983a). Even with their variations, these figures show the sinister presence of a social problem haunting some corner of the personal lives of tens of millions of individuals.

For certain kinds of individuals, moreover, the specter of crime fear looms much larger. Depending on the situation described in the survey question, the ratio of fearful females to fearful males is between 2 to 1 and 3 to 1. Age is another personal factor which conditions the emotional response to crime. Most research indicates that the elderly are highly fearful of victimization, and some surveys suggest that those over 65 consider crime to be their most serious social problem (Harris and Associates, 1975; The Select Committee on Aging, 1977). Furthermore, having that fear has been linked to other problems of the elderly, such as low morale and involuntary isolation (Yin, 1982).

Money may not buy happiness, but it is associated with a sense of security from crime:

For many elderly Americans, fear of victimization makes them prisoners of crime. (*Carlin/The Picture Cube*)

the higher the family income, the smaller the percentage of respondents who worry about victimization. Cutting across all of these personal traits is the social character of the community in which one lives. The more urban the area (as measured by total population size), the greater the fear of crime (U.S. Department of Justice, 1984). The various individual and social factors can combine to make some people virtual prisoners of the fear of crime, as illustrated in this photograph of an elderly woman in a poor urban area.

The data on crime fear reveal a whole new level of the subjective dimension. General views about the seriousness of crime in the

United States here find their reflection in the individual's terrors about being touched by this social problem. The reflection is, however, strangely distorted. In terms of the objective statistics on victimization rates, upper-class and rural respondents are correct to be less worried than their lower-class, urban counterparts. While the fears of females and the elderly are far from groundless, all of the objective sources scrutinized above show much less fearful young males to be much more likely to have their fears come true. Why do personal perceptions not match the objective realities of crime?

To resolve this so-called fear-victimization paradox, it is necessary to seek the subjective forces shaping the image of criminal behavior in our minds. As was noted in the opening of this section, crime is publicly and legally viewed as a predatory act of person against person. Traditional religious notions of crime as sin and everyday examples of heartbreaking harm to victims contribute to making all crime seem pathological (remember, Durkheim proposed a certain amount of lawbreaking to be "normal"). As opposed to other social problems such as poverty and mental illness for which some societal level is accepted as natural, any and every criminal behavior is felt to be a violation against the social order.

Crime is especially outrageous to the public conscience because of the criminal's personal decision to ignore the urgings of his or her conscience. Robbing the old lady in the apartment upstairs is a personal act in which the individual's guilty hand is clearly evident as the cause of her suffering; contrast this cold-blooded case with the more mysterious ways in which one person may contribute to the unemployment or emotional disturbances of a homeless stranger. This individual-creates-problem aspect of crime explains why public *expectations* about it run so high.

Since criminal acts are perceived to be patently evil and are apparently caused by choices inside each of us, why can't we stop them? The individualistic roots of this expectation run deep in American culture and help to explain the historically high level of subjective concern about this social problem. The power to end criminality seems to be right in our personal and societal grasp, even as crime rates maddeningly climb above our grasping fingers.

A key piece in the subjective puzzle of the crime problem is society's *value* system. In general, laws enshrine fundamental values of a people in official rules (see the discussion of mores above); deviation from the law is therefore viewed as a desecration of the cultural shrine. In particular, criminal acts trespass against the hallowed American values of life, liberty, and property. The point is straightforward: More so than other problematic behaviors, crime appears to be a frontal attack on the very heart of society. This unique cultural position of criminality makes it seem all the more serious, and steadily props up concern about the issue in public opinion.

The special reasons that crime violates our expectations and values help to explain the height of the curves in Figure 11-2. In addition to their overall relevance to the subjective dimension of the crime problem, these factors also hold clues to the still unsolved fear-victimization paradox. Begin with the basic human value of protecting the weak and helpless or, if you prefer, "Blessed are the meek." A rape and killing of a 78-year-old woman seems especially savage precisely because of this value of compassion. Given the view that the individual freely chooses to commit crimes, one would expect that the criminal should at least be civilized enough to spare women, children, and the elderly. Similarly, the general expectation that we should be able to control our own citizens' viciousness applies with particular force to those whose protection we value most: Can't we even expect our policies to defend those who are defenseless?

Crimes against females and the elderly are especially outrageous, an outrage which is readily transformed into fear for these potential victims. Whatever the statistics say, the public outcry suggests that women and the elderly *should* be afraid, particularly when their plight as victims is trumpeted from national news magazines.

The subject of the mass media arrives right on cue. Consider the general point that one rarely gets to observe social problems in the flesh. While the evidence in this chapter shows that the odds of such observation of crime do vary by neighborhood, and that one's own victimization will probably be experienced at least once, exposure to the crime problem comes overwhelmingly from a secondhand source: the "news." The quotation marks have been added to make the point that crime reporting is not some direct, computer-sensed image that replicates the objective dimension. Lots of crimes happening outside our doors right now will remain subjectively unknown to us while other, objectively similar, events cause gasps of disbelief because they make the morning edition.

In introducing the concept of the subjective dimension, Chapter 1 discussed a classic study of metropolitan newspapers which revealed that the amount of news coverage was unrelated to the amount of officially recorded crime (Davis, 1952). More recent and detailed research has looked at the actual social processes by which news people sort through piles of potential stories to select some few that are newsworthy (Lester, 1980). Not surprisingly, newsworthiness is rarely bestowed on commonplace criminal events such as larcenies and embezzlements (unless the victim is a celebrity). Study after study has shown that violent crime gets a disproportionate share of both ink and airtime (Humphries, 1981; Bennett, 1985). In-depth coverage, moreover, is related to the level of brutality of the violent crime. A really gory ax murder is likely to generate a picture of the body on the cover of the local tabloid and on-camera personal interviews with relatives of both the murdered and the murderer.

Although the studies also show that the amount of crime coverage increases as newspaper circulation declines, the essential issue is not the media pandering to our basest instincts. Public interest in crime stories is less a matter of thirst for blood than a matter of thirst for justice. Real or fictional[7] accounts of violent crimes are a source of horrified fascination in large part because the criminal rejects the most deep-seated demands of our culture. Whether or not Durkheim is correct in suggesting that reading about such depraved deviance promotes cultural conformity in the rest of us, it is certainly true that violent crime piques the public interest and sells papers.

Print and electronic images of the criminal subtly shape both levels of the subjective dimension of the crime problem. In addition to the high *visibility* the media eye casts on crime compared to other social issues (10 to 20 percent of news programming is crime-related), this subjective factor acts as a catalyst on cultural values and expectations. By spotlighting the sensational cases that are most outrageous to popular culture, the mass media trigger the subjective impact of these two factors. Ten news specials on the Manson killings mean ten times we can all see how antithetical these acts are to our values and expectations. The selective visibility of the most antisocial crimes illuminates the great level of general concern in Figure 11-2.

Concern for personal safety is the second subjective level, and fear-victimization differences now appear to be less of a paradox. Who are the victims in the most infamous crimes? While there are no hard data covering every news station and police beat, the question seems almost rhetorical: The publicized victims of violence are disproportionately old and/or

---

[7] Police and detective shows are one of the staples of television programming. Consider how often the criminal character is a psychotic killer or crazed drug addict with no semblance of a social conscience and how rarely he or she is a garden-variety burglar or tax evader.

female. It is little wonder that these subgroups have an emotional response to the crime problem that exceeds the cold objective statistics. Interestingly, relatively high percentages of women and people over 65 do think that "television gives too much attention to stories about crime" (U.S. Department of Justice, 1984:205), and yet they appear to be susceptible to its fearsome picture of the crime problem.

THE VARIETIES OF CRIME: SELECTED TOPICS

As we have remarked before, criminal behavior is one of the most thoroughly analyzed and widely surveyed of all social problems. The *Sourcebook of Criminal Justice Statistics* (U.S. Department of Justice, 1984) is only one of the reference works to which we have repeatedly referred, and it consists of some 700 pages of hard data (i.e., all numbers, no text). Part of the reason for the embarrassment of riches of crime information is our cultural hypersensitivity to it, and part of the reason is that rule breaking is a very common and complex human activity—like sex or politics. The present section will illuminate the human complexity of criminal behavior at a more concrete level. Within the broad strokes painting the panorama of the crime problem above, more descriptive details will now be filled in for three areas of major sociological significance.

Suite Crime

Given the theoretical themes of the book, your authors have hardly been able to contain themselves in getting to this topic. *Suite crime* is a play on the words *street crime*, a much more familiar phrase for reasons about to be explored. Suite crime (so-called for the executive suites where the lawbreaking occurs) is more commonly called *white-collar crime*. It was defined as "crime committed by a person of respectability and high social status in the course of his occupation" by Edwin H. Sutherland (1971:9), the famous criminologist who

coined the term. According to most expert estimates, the largest single portion of the economic damage done by the crime problem is inflicted by white-collar criminals.

Now a personal question: When is the last time you worried about being victimized by corporate or governmental employees? To more broadly suggest the low subjective visibility of this class of crimes, consider the fact that the voluminous *Sourcebook of Criminal Justice Statistics* presents over 100 pages of data on public attitudes toward various aspects of crime, with not a single poll concentrating on the white-collar criminal! Part of our enthusiasm to present this topic is the classic fashion in which it illustrates the distinction between the objective and subjective dimensions of a social problem.

The point is not that people are unaware of the existence of white-collar criminals; E. F. Hutton, ABSCAM, and other well-publicized fraud schemes have put suite crime in the public eye. It is just that, with rare exceptions, people seem to see no serious evil there. Your lack of concern may reflect the widespread perception that at least nobody is badly hurt by white-collar crime. This is a gross misperception. Although they may be less dramatic and obvious than a street criminal putting a gun to your head and pulling the trigger, the effects of white-collar crime are no less lethal.

Consider the Buffalo Creek disaster in which a dam of coal wastes burst, killing 125 people and leaving some 5000 homeless in the flooded towns; the disaster was a result of the irresponsible corporate decisions of the Buffalo Mining Company (owned by the Pittston Corporation), later found culpable by the courts. Or consider the case of "Pinto Madness" in which the car was marketed despite dangers documented by Ford studies. According to an internal company memo, the total costs of installing a plastic piece which would prevent the car from exploding on rear-end impact (11 dollars per car, 137 million dollars total) were balanced against the corporate costs of the estimated 180 burn deaths a year (200,000 dollars per death, 49.5 million dollars total), and a decision was reached: Put profits ahead of safety.

Whether or not you would call these cases cold-blooded mass murder, they are certainly clear instances of the real and present dangers caused by people wearing white collars. Isolated instances? No: "Corporate crime is exceedingly violent, killing and maiming thousands of people each year" (Kramer, 1983:181).

The case convicting white-collar criminals of serious economic harm is even better documented. In one study focusing on 300 white-collar felons, the upper level of the studied group were involved in frauds averaging *over 22 million dollars* (and their prison sentences averaged less than a single year; Bequai, 1978)! White-collar criminals do not all wear blue-flannel suits. A Senate subcommittee investigating Medifraud abuses estimated that up to 10 percent of the funds of the Medicaid program (that is one-tenth of about 35 billion dollars) are spent on fraudulent payments to physicians.

To bring the point even closer to home—perhaps your own home—take the case of income tax evasion. In the aggregate, Americans now cheat their own government of 120 billion dollars a year; that averages out to a 500 dollar offense for every man, woman, and child in the United States (the average larceny-theft involves a property loss of only 340 dollars).[8] Lest this lead to holier-than-thou thoughts about the moral decay of the older generation, about 4 billion dollars has been stolen from the government (and, thus, from other taxpayers) by students defaulting on college loans.

Widespread willingness to commit white-collar crimes does not explain the lack of con-

cern about them. Many of us, after all, have committed one of the street crimes we find so outrageous (see above). How is it possible for people to be shocked that some perpetrators of the Great Electrical Conspiracy (a price-fixing scheme that took over 1 *billion* dollars from rich and poor alike) did time while feeling a warm sense of justice when the local junkie goes to the penitentiary for a purse snatching?

Our previous discussion on the overpublicizing of violent crime is part of the story, although big-time white-collar defendants have lately attained a certain notoriety (e.g., Spiro T. Agnew, the E. F. Hutton executives, etc.). The heightened media visibility of the issue may have contributed to some closing of the objective-subjective gap on white-collar crime (and to some increase in its enforcement; see Cullen, Link, and Planzi, 1982), but the major factor shaping our response to crime news is the value system. To put it simply, white-collar officials benefit by a cultural halo effect that glows around their social positions. Government agencies and, especially, corporations are revered institutions in this society ("The business of America is business"). An upper-level white-collar position, moreover, is viewed as a prize the individual has won fair and square through the valued qualities of ability and hard work (see Chapter 8 on learning to live with inequality). These deep-seated values in the American cultural system may not keep the public from flinching at the damage done by suite crime, but they do tranquilize the subjective outcry.

Street Crime

A reassessment of the seriousness of white-collar criminality does not diminish the damage done by street crime. Such crimes are many, they are harmful, and they are part of everyday life. Since this is familiar ground, the present section will expand the discussion in answer to two specific questions about FBI Index crime perpetrators: Who and how?

---

[8] This is not meant to encourage illegality but rather to reinforce the point about society's orientation toward white-collar crime: in 1982, only 1624 people were prosecuted for income tax evasion and just 717 were sentenced to jail (*Time,* Mar. 28, 1983).

BOX 11-2

RAPE

Rape, like murder or drug dealing, is a criminal act, a felony punishable by prison sentences. Rape is something more than one item in a category of felonies, however. As a crime involving a sexual act, it would seem to be linked to the broader societal patterns encompassing sex roles (see Chapter 10). The relatively recent concept of the "rape culture" (Herman, 1984) examines the social roots of this crime through cross-cultural analysis. One study comparing ninety-five tribal societies found that those classified as rape-free were characterized by sexual equality and the belief that each sex makes important contributions to the well-being of the other (Sanday, 1981).

As the objective evidence on victimization would suggest, the United States does not fit the rape-free pattern. Chapter 10 detailed the many dimensions of sexual inequality and their deep (if changing) sources in American culture. Notions that men are "natural" sexual aggressors or that women "bring it on themselves" by deliberate enticement fit traditional stereotypes. This sociological background dramatizes the fact that rape is *not* a random act; in the foreground we now present a fictionalized account of a rape victim's experience in a major urban center:

"Good morning, Ms. Atkins. May I call you Sheila? I'm Mr. Cramer, the prosecutor assigned to this case." Sheila nods.

"O.K. What can you tell me about what happened?"

"Well, I was raped. That's about all."

" 'Rape' is a legal term, Sheila. It's not a description of what happened. I'll need to know what he did and what you did."

"I took the subway home from work about 7:30 at night. Then, I stopped at a place in the neighborhood for awhile before heading home."

Cramer interrupts, "This place, was it a restaurant? A bar?"

"Yeah, I had a drink, what about it? Well, this here guy Leroy offered to buy me a drink but I said no. I made for

the door and heard Leroy say he was leaving too. I could tell he was drunk and he tried to get 'friendly.' Then he got mean. He pulled me into the alley and raped me."

"Now, Sheila, I'll need to know exactly what he did."

"So, he dragged me into an alley and pointed a knife at me. Then he made me touch him all over and he sucked my tits and spread my legs and did it, O.K."

"Did what?"

"He put his fuckin' penis in my pussy."

"Your vagina?"

"Yeah, damn it."

"Then what?"

"He left and I put my clothes on and ran home to take a shower. God, I felt so dirty."

"O.K. Let's go over it again…"

"Sheila's" case is excruciating to read, but very revealing. It shows both the brutality of the crime and the often brutal questioning of the victim which the criminal justice system may require. Until very recently, that system had institutionalized procedures for processing rape cases that were patently sexist. A victim could be questioned about her prior sexual history and moral habits even though a defendant's prior rape convictions could be withheld from the jury! Some states even required the *victim* to undergo a psychiatric examination (Tong, 1984).

Although such tests are still permitted in some jurisdictions, there has been considerable reform in the treatment of rape victims. As of 1984, some twenty-two states had restricted the use of evidence concerning the victim's history and reputation. Police are now being trained in how to question raped women more sensitively, and support groups are available to help victims through the still-grueling trial process. Despite the reforms, rape is still shockingly common (a woman stands about a 1 in 15 chance of being raped in the United States) and—perhaps understandably given "Sheila's" ordeal—still has one of the lowest conviction rates of any major crime.

Source of dialogue: Karen Reardon, J.D., provided this fictionalized account based on her experiences in the district attorney's office of a major American city.

On the who-victimizes-you question, consider the pervasive public image of the predatory stranger, the faceless thug who takes what he wants from the innocent and then disappears. He or she exists in abundance, but many common crimes are committed by the devil you know. According to the National Crime Survey (NCS), about one-third of all robberies and rapes are committed by nonstrangers to the victim; FBI statistics (UCR) indicate that in well over half of all recorded homicides, the killer was a member of the deceased's social network (U.S. Department of Justice, 1984). The sociological significance of these unsettling data extends to later sections which deal with the myth of the crazed criminal. If criminals are, in fact, just wild-eyed, irrational beings, one has to question the taste of millions of victims in their social choice of friends, relatives, and acquaintances.

On the issue of how street crimes are committed, consider now the modus operandi in our collective image of the criminal; in the mind's eye, he usually has a gun in his hand. Such is often the case in the eye of official statistics as well, particularly for homicides. Having compiled data for officially recorded homicides over a seventeen-year period, the U.S. Department of Justice reports that over 60 percent of all murders and nonnegligent manslaughters are committed with a firearm (1984). That works out to an appalling number of deaths per year, but a number that needs to be further multiplied by the principle of problem linkages. If one includes firearm fatalities resulting from suicides and accidents as well as homicides, about 30,000 deaths a year are notched into the barrels of guns. All told, there are an estimated 1 million incidents a year in which firearms are present, brandished (as in a robbery), or fired. The researchers who arrived at these statistics pose the issue sharply:

> The amount of death, injury, destruction, and generalized terror inflicted in the United States with firearms is a national disgrace—of that, there is no serious question. The serious question is whether the amount of death, injury, destruction and generalized terror would be any less if fewer firearms were available (Wright, Rossi, and Daly, 1983:313).

How available are firearms in America? The question is almost rhetorical. The authors quoted above estimate roughly 120 million guns are in private hands—that is 1 gun for every 2 Americans. Any local gun shop's window highlights their ready availability. Even a semiautomatic weapon can be purchased for about the price of a portable television.

These facts and their implications for crime are very controversial. Anti-gun-control interest groups such as the Institute for Legislative Action (the lobbying arm of the National Rifle Association) contend that this is a case of correlation being confused with causality. An individual with violent intent may kill, rob, or maim with a broken bottle if no gun is available. Besides, they argue, in Switzerland nearly everyone is an armed member of the national militia, and yet gun fatality rates are only a tiny fraction of ours; the United States has lots of guns and lots of violence, but the former need not necessarily be the cause of the latter.

Interest groups propounding stricter gun control legislation (there are already some 20,000 statutes on the books) also cite cross-cultural fatality figures. According to a widely circulated pro-gun-control pamphlet ("A Shooting Gallery Called America"), the annual number of gun deaths in the United States exceeds the total number of gun deaths in all the countries of the world combined. This is powerful circumstantial evidence. To the anticontrol groups' point that "it is people who kill, not guns," pro-control groups respond that this argument cuts both ways. Putting a killing machine as efficient as a gun into the hands of a people with a well-established cultural streak of violence seems to guarantee an inflated body count for street crime.

At its base, the anticontrol versus procontrol debate is not a legislative struggle between people who do and people who do not like guns. The tug-of-war over firearms is really a conflict of values. Any law controlling guns trades off the right to bear arms and defend one's privacy against the value of freedom from readily armed street criminals. This and related value conflicts will be further examined in the Social Policy section.

Juvenile Delinquency

The spotlight on selected crime issues has swung from the upperworld to the underworld, and now to the younger world. It would be illuminating to begin with a definition of the phrase *juvenile delinquency.* Unfortunately, we cannot. Even *juvenile,* seemingly a commonsense term for an adolescent, has no common legal meaning in this country. Many jurisdictions officially decree adulthood to begin at 18, but upper age limits for the juvenile offender vary between 15 and 21. As little agreement as there is on what constitutes a juvenile, there is even less certainty regarding the definition of *delinquency.* One-third of the states do not even have a statutory definition; among those states that do, a survey of statutes has found some twenty-five separate acts or conditions defining delinquency (Eldefonso, 1978).

There is one commonality in this bewildering array of legal definitions: a young person convicted of "any act which, if committed by an adult, would be a crime" is officially a delinquent (Frank, 1981:79). In the National Youth Study (see Counting Crime), extraordinary numbers of individuals under the age of 17 confessed to committing such "adult" crimes; these self-report data showed that the commission of some such offenses peaks between 13 and 15, well under anyone's definition of adulthood. The NCS reports provide confirmation from another angle. Since these annual surveys

question victims, detailed information on perception of assailants is available. Data examined for selected FBI Index crimes committed over the 1973–1981 period indicate that the amount of serious street crime perpetrated by 12-to 17-year-olds remained relatively stable over the nine years, with a slight dip in aggregate victimization by youths at the end of this period.

The good news is that no explosion occurred in serious youth crime in recent years. The bad news is that commission of grown-up crime by youths simply remained stable at an already very high level. Even in 1980 when the crime trend line had dipped, there were over 1 million reported victimizations by juveniles; in 1981, these delinquents committed 11 percent of the rapes, 19 percent of the robberies, 15 percent of the aggravated assaults, and 21 percent of the personal larcenies reported to the NCS (Siegel and Senna, 1985).

The heavy involvement of youths in adult crime further blurs the meaning of juvenile delinquency. While it by no means dissolves all of the ambiguities, one clear distinction of delinquents from criminals involves so-called status offenses. These are various—and we do mean various—acts not defined as illegal if committed by adults. Juveniles can be picked up by the police for being runaways or truants (imagine your cutting class being against the law), or even for such vague sins as being "incorrigible," "wayward," or "stubborn." In California alone, an average of 100,000 status offenders are arrested annually (Eldefonso, 1978). On the face of it, such selective enforcement against youth seems patently unfair and, more formally, seems to be an open-and-shut case of age discrimination. To understand anything about juvenile delinquency, however, its face must be understood as firmly connected to the changing body of society.

The very term *status offense* is highly suggestive. It closely reflects the sociological term *status,* which means a recognized position in a group. Difficult though it may be to believe, the very existence of childhood as a distinctly recognized phase of the life cycle is historically recent. In part because of their staggeringly high death rates, infants in preindustrial societies were rarely the subjects of doting attachment. Even children who survived to adolescence were thought of as miniature, if inadequate, adults who were expected to serve utilitarian purposes:

> The modern notion that growing up requires careful guidance through a series of physical, moral, and intellectual stages, in fact, has been totally alien to most people throughout Western history. It did not even occur to them (Empey, 1982:8).

Gradually, children came to be viewed as both blessings and beneficiaries of society's sacred duty to nurture and protect them well into what used to be considered adulthood. Although some of the legal principles supporting the differential treatment of child criminals were already part of English common law, the first institutional recognition of delinquents appeared in this country in the Illinois Juvenile Court Act of 1899. The creation of a parallel legal structure specifically for delinquents was propelled in the United States by the so-called child savers (Platt, 1969), a social movement which sought to rescue juveniles from a life of crime and from premature, overly severe punishment in adult courts.[9]

Building on historical trends redefining the status of childhood, this coalition of middle-and upper-class interest groups converted the state, in effect, into a superparent. Judges in the juvenile justice system were to have wide, parentlike discretion in dealing with young offenders. Status offenses limited the personal freedoms of juveniles, but were viewed as de-

[9] Some conflict criminologists have contended that the child savers' reforms actually served capitalist-class interests by attempting to train a more disciplined labor force (Platt, 1974). See John Hagan and Jeffrey Leon (1977) for an opposing view.

vices for derailing deviance before it followed the track leading to adult criminality.

In recent years, societal pressure has been building to overhaul the juvenile justice system and dismantle the concept of the status offense. Some experts have argued that the dubious benefits of "kiddie courts" in preventing future crimes are not worth the value trade-off in juveniles' constitutional rights. Due in part to well-publicized episodes of youth violence, there has been a rising public perception of both the seriousness of delinquency and the leniency of juvenile courts; this subjective dimension of youthful deviance has provided political support for the increasing numbers of juveniles who are being diverted into the adult criminal system (U.S. Department of Justice, 1984).

THEORIES: THE CAUSES OF LAWBREAKING

Where do crime and delinquency come from? Although the shuffling of statistics on perpetrators and victims yields indispensable information about the problem, it is not fully satisfying. In paging through the volumes of data, some version of this question becomes more and more insistent: *Why do people break the law?*

There is no shortage of proposed answers to the nagging question of causation. Just about everyone has an opinion about what makes a criminal a criminal, and social scientists have produced dozens of their own more formal explanations. Untangling this dense thicket of theories is beyond the scope of the present chapter. However, some discussion of scientific theory is a must in analyzing this social problem, and not just because of curiosity about deviants.

Consider the truism that "knowledge is power." While experts would agree we do not now have a finished, all-purpose explanation of lawbreaking behavior, such an intellectual device would permit much more efficient societal work to grind down crime's objective dimension; if it becomes known that lawbreaking is caused by low self-esteem, for example, society has the power to reduce the problem by devoting resources to positive-thinking seminars. There is danger in this truism as well. If enough people are convinced of an incorrect theory, their knowledge may give them the power to fund programs which are unproductive or even counterproductive (criminals given more self-esteem may become audacious enough to plan bigger bank heists).

Meanwhile, we are forced to forge *some* anticrime policy from imperfect—but not equally imperfect—theories. Here is the point: A basic familiarity with theorizing about crime and delinquency is a prerequisite to a serious discussion of public policy.

Given the profusion of crimogenic (i.e., crime causation) theories, presentation of even a preliminary sketch is a daunting task. Rather than attempting a superficial in-text discussion of every theory, this section will follow a three-point approach that is both more selective and more concrete. Point one is the compendium of crimogenic theories exhibited in Table 11-2. Each concept is classified according to its "family of explanations" (e.g., all in the biological group view crime as caused by defects within the individual's physical nature), briefly summarized under "specific cause," then further elaborated under "specific effect" (i.e., type of crime resulting from the cause) and "policy implications."

This table serves as a reference source for point two in the presentation, in which selected substantive issues will be overviewed. Theories will be compared and evaluated in terms of their ability to explain the chosen issues of chronic offenders and organized crime.

The final point in the application of crimogenic theories to criminal behavior will consider their synergy. Instead of a scientific debate arguing the merits of one theoretical idea over all others, we will draw what we can from each theory in hopes that the combined comprehension of the issue will be greater than the sum of its theoretical parts. Just as an architectural feature is better understood when viewed from several different angles, the sources of law-breaking behavior may grow clearer from the complementary insights of several theoretical perspectives.

Chronic Offenders

While most people have committed a crime, few make a habit of it. Those few, moreover, are likely to engage in the more serious and objectively damaging forms of crime. These generalizations are based on the survey evidence in the Counting Crime section, and their basis has been further reinforced in a series of classic studies conducted by Marvin Wolfgang and associates.

The first project traced the official careers of 9945 males born in 1945, all of whom lived in Philadelphia from their tenth to eighteenth birthdays. This approach was original in its attempt to use an entire *cohort* (i.e., all male juveniles of the same age) instead of a sample, and in its longitudinal design following cohort members over an eight-year period down the official trail of hospital, school, and police records. At the end of that trail is the statistical portrait of the chronic offender. About one-third of the males (3475) had had at least one recorded arrest, but nearly half of this number never committed another officially processed crime during their juvenile years. A small subgroup of delinquents committed the lion's share of the crime—627 individuals (6.3 percent of the cohort, 18 percent of the delinquents) accounted for over half of all offenses and some two-thirds of the violent crimes (Wolfgang, Figlio, and Sellin, 1972).

A follow-up study scrutinizing a cohort of 28,000 youths born in 1958 strengthened these conclusions. The hard core of chronic offenders expanded slightly to 7.5 percent, and they committed an even greater proportion of offenses than in the previous cohort (61 percent compared to 52 percent; Wolfgang, 1983). To put it simply, the second study found a few more monsters and a good bit more monstrous behavior by these chronic offenders.

Clearly, there are real criminals to be explained. The general observation that everyone breaks the law yields to the more useful finding that all lawbreakers are not equal. This is the precise question to be answered by theory: *Why are these few who commit most of the street crimes different from the many who are mere dabblers?*

The use of terms like "monster" by professionals and public alike suggests that chronic offenders are virtually a different species. Such thinking has stimulated biological theories, which probe for causes in the protoplasm of the hard-core criminal. One of the earliest formal attempts to explain crime naturalistically—i.e., as other than sin or demonic possession—was devised by nineteenth-century Italian criminologist Cesare Lombroso, a leading figure in the *positive school*. Here he describes the revelation that struck as he was performing a postmortem on the skull of Villela, a notorious criminal of Lombroso's day:

> At the sight of that skull, I seemed to see all of a sudden, lighted up as a vast plain under a flaming sky, the problem of the nature of the criminal—an atavistic being who reproduces in his person the ferocious instincts of primitive humanity and the inferior animals. Thus were explained anatomically the enormous jaws, high cheek-bones, prominent superciliary arches...and the irresistible craving for evil for its own sake, the desire not only to extinguish life in the victim, but to mutilate the corpse, tear its flesh and drink its blood (Lombroso, 1911:xiv–xv).

The dark nature of the criminal is thus inherited, and clues to this personality are to be found in specific physical traits such as high cheek-bones and beady little eyes.

A more current theory from the same family of explanations also posits a built-in criminal nature for some people, but the physical evidence is buried deeper. In the late 1960s several published studies of very violent, institutionalized offenders reported that a suspiciously high percentage had a rare cellular condition. Typically, a male's cells contain one X and one Y chromosome, and the latter produces primary and secondary sexual characteristics that distinguish him from a (XX) female. XYY males have received an extra dose of maleness in their genes and, presumably, an exaggerated tendency toward aggressive and violent behavior. The appeal of this theory has been considerable, with several XYYs offering their chromosomal state as evidence of temporary insanity in criminal cases.

Although the mark of Cain is to be sought with an electron microscope rather than with measuring calipers, the underlying source of criminogenesis is the same as in Lombroso's theory: an inherited criminal constitution. Both theories have also failed to meet acceptable standards of scientific evidence. Minuscule samples, lack of adequate comparison groups, and conflicting findings have kept the jury out on the conclusion that some offenders have a built-in reason to be chronic (Inciardi, 1978). Nevertheless, such theories may be real in their consequences if believed (why try to rehabilitate a genetic defective?), and the continuing interest in unproven biological explanations indicates that many do want to believe. Particularly in an individualistic culture like that of the United States, there is something seductive about the notion that the chronic offender is an individual whose evil comes from inside rather than from outside sources—like society.

Another set of theories seeking criminogenesis inside the chronic offender begins with personality rather than protoplasm. The popular view that brutal criminals must be somehow "sick" finds formal statement in the psychological explanations. Richard L. Jenkins applies the Freudian concepts of the id (primitive antisocial impulses inherited by all human beings) and the superego (internalized social restraints

TABLE 11-2   MICROTHEORIES OF CRIMINAL CAUSATION

Family of explanations	Specific cause(s)	Specific effect(s)	Policy implications
Biological	*Positive school* (Cesare Lombroso): Many lawbreakers have inherited a primitive biological constitution which is revealed through anthropometric measurements (e.g., slanting forehead, peculiarities of the eyes, etc.).	A generalized predisposition toward crime, but especially violent offenses.	Discover and control the born criminals. Apply indeterminate prison sentences depending on the degree of the individual's impairment.
	Somatotype (William H. Sheldon): Individuals inherit one of three basic body structures: ectomorph (naturally thin), endomorph (naturally fat), and mesomorph (naturally muscular). Each somatotype has associated personality traits, with the mesomorph's built-in vigor, impulsiveness, and aggressiveness making him a likely lawbreaker.	Predatory offenses such as assault, robbery, and rape.	Control mesomorphs either by selective breeding or by providing alternatives for positive action for this body type (e.g., war).
	Chromosomal theory: Males genetically endowed with an extra Y chromosome (i.e., giving them an XYY constitution) are predisposed to exaggerated male traits such as hyperaggressiveness and sexual deviation.	Highly violent crimes such as aggravated assault, sexual psychopathy, and even multiple murder.	Selective breeding and/or special attention to the known XYY individual by the criminal justice system.
Psychological	*Freudian theory* (Sigmund Freud): All individuals are natural criminals in their inheritance of the id (inborn antisocial urges centering on sex and violence). If the internalized social restraints of the superego do not develop normally, the individual is likely to express these urges and commit crimes.	Generalized deviance from social norms, but in particular offenses involving sex and violence.	Psychoanalytic therapy for criminals and, since basic personality pattern is set very early in childhood, social programs providing skills and motivation to parents in their child rearing.
	The socialized delinquent (Richard L. Jenkins): Some individuals develop normal inhibitions about releasing id impulses toward relatives and friends (the in-group), but lack sufficient superego controls toward strangers (the out-group).	Predatory behavior toward out-group members along the lines of the delinquent gang.	Same as above, with special emphasis on bolstering superego restraints toward people outside the social network.

The names in parentheses usually following the title of each theory are criminologists most closely associated with that approach toward criminal causation.

388

TABLE 11-2   MICROTHEORIES OF CRIMINAL CAUSATION *Cont.*

Family of explanations	Specific cause(s)	Specific effect(s)	Policy implications
	Neoclassical school (James Q. Wilson): The decision to break the law emerges from a rational consideration of potential costs and benefits by the person; therefore crime is a utilitarian choice made within the individual psyche.	Offenses from which the individual might realize some sort of personal gain.	Appropriate punishments for each offense in considering its costs and benefits—i.e., the punishment should fit the crime.
Social structural	*Strain theory* (Robert K. Merton): When there is a gap in the social structure between cultural goals (widely shared aspirations such as material success) and the institutionalized means (culturally approved ways to achieve those goals such as education and occupation), anomie is created. A common result will be "innovation," in which illegal techniques are used to attain the cultural goals.	Anomie implies a generalized state of lawbreaking, but the primary goal of "innovation" is material gain as in property offenses like robbery and organized crime.	Extend educational and occupational opportunities to those segments of the social structure—mainly, the lower class—currently caught in the gap between cultural goals and institutionalized means.
	Control theory (Travis Hirschi): Generally, several social controls operate to restrain an individual's impulse to break the law: attachment (ties of affection and respect to law-abiding persons), commitment (motivation to perform socially approved activities), involvement (actually performing approved activities such as schoolwork and sports) and beliefs (acceptance of the morality of the law). If these bonds of the individual to society are broken—as may occur in a broken home—lawbreaking becomes more likely.	A generalized disposition to delinquency and crime.	Reattach criminals and delinquents to social control mechanisms such as law-abiding friends and the promise of a future career. Such restraints give the individual(s) a stake in conformity.
	Differential opportunity (Richard Cloward and Lloyd Ohlin): The structural positions of individuals must be viewed not only in terms of the strain of blocked legitimate opportunities but also in terms of illegitimate opportunities available to individuals in specific social settings.	The type of crime depends on the specific criminal group one joins; criminal subcultures are organized, systematic operations with professional criminals; conflict subcultures are oriented toward street violence (as in gangs) and are often found in disorganized, transient areas; retreatist subcultures are heavily involved in drug use.	Provide more legitimate opportunities (primarily to the lower class) to render socially available illegitimate opportunities for success relatively less attractive.

TABLE 11-2   MICROTHEORIES OF CRIMINAL CAUSATION *Cont.*

Family of explanations	Specific cause(s)	Specific effect(s)	Policy implications
	Labeling theory (Edwin M. Lemert): Individuals are selectively caught and convicted of criminal acts, a selection process that is guided by social structural variables such as class, sex, and age. Once an individual is officially labeled a criminal by the justice system, that person will be more likely to commit illegal acts (secondary deviance) because of the social stigma.	A generalized tendency to violate the law as a kind of self-fulfilling prophecy.	Decriminalize (i.e., remove official criminal penalties from) as many offenses as possible, especially for victimless crimes such as drug use and illicit sexual behavior.
Cultural	*Differential association* (Edwin H. Sutherland): "A person becomes delinquent because of an excess of definitions favorable to the violation of the law over definitions unfavorable to the violation of the law." Individuals are exposed to these cultural definitions through personal relationships which vary in frequency, duration, priority, and intensity. Becoming a criminal is a social learning process involving language, motivations, and skills.	The specific criminal acts depend on the cultural influences and training applied by one's criminal associates.	Reduce personal contact with criminals and increase association with law-abiding social contacts, perhaps by using community halfway houses rather than prisons ("schools for crime").
	Techniques of neutralization (Gresham M. Sykes and David Matza): Noncriminals and criminals alike have cultural commitments to conventional society, but the latter are more influenced by a patterned set of excuses which may release—i.e., neutralize—guilt about breaking the law. Techniques such as denial of injury (it didn't really hurt anyone) reduce inhibitions about crime.	Permissible crimes are those which the group recognizes as relevant to its available rationalizations (e.g., a group of males who regularly employ the denial of responsibility to excuse brawling because they were drunk and, therefore, could not help it).	Reduce cultural exposure to the techniques of rationalization, and restrict the social situations in which they may operate unobserved.
	The delinquent subculture (Albert K. Cohen): Lower-class boys aspire to mainstream goals of educational and occupational success, but they enter school at a disadvantage because of middle-class children's prior socialization for academic achievement. Consequently, lower-class boys tend to fall behind in school and suffer from a sense of failure. The delinquent gang subculture arises as an alternative source of status and an indirect attack on mainstream society.	Delinquent acts are consistent with the basic values of the subculture, which are nonutilitarian (stealing for "kicks" rather than for any rational purpose), malicious (committing deviant acts precisely because they outrage others), and hedonistic (seeking momentary pleasures such as drugs and sex).	Improve the educational preparation of lower-class children and reduce requirements for poor students to stay in academic programs in which their sense of failure is magnified.

BOX 11-3

REMARKS OF A SERIAL MURDERER

The United States has witnessed many unusual and violent crimes during the last 25 years. Most recently, serial murderers have reared their ugly heads. David Berkowitz, popularly known as the "Son of Sam," went on a rampage of blasting young couples with a 44-Magnum pistol in New York City. John Wayne Gacy tortured, sexually assaulted and sadistically murdered at least 33 young men and boys. Outwardly, Gacy displayed a mask of sanity, dressing up as "Pogo the Clown" and making the rounds of children's wards in hospitals and by serving as chaplain in the Jaycees. Ted Bundy roamed the country, periodically killing as many as 33 women, all pretty, small and dark-haired. But to date, no one has approached the macabre level of Henry Lee Lucas who claims to have murdered 360 people in 36 states and three different countries. What makes people like this tick? It is likely that they suffer from a mental disorder known as the antisocial personality (originally known as the psychopath or sociopath). These are people who are basically unsocialized and consequently have no conscience. They can rape, rob and murder and not feel an ounce of remorse. No one knows for sure how this sickness develops. Theories include bad genes, physical brain abnormalities, an extra Y chromosome (almost all antisocials are reportedly male), a biochemical need for vicious thrills and lack of proper parenting.

One leading expert thinks there may be as many as a hundred serial murders on the loose right now. Below are some quotes from Henry Lee Lucas. They will allow you to appreciate from a safe distance the chilling make-up of a murderer without a conscience.

I've got 360 people. I've got 36 states and three different countries. My victims never knew what was gonna happen. I've had shootings, knifings, strangulations, beatings, and I've participated in actual crucifixions of humans. All across the country there's people just like me who's set out to destroy human life. I was death on women. I didn't—didn't feel they—they need to exist. I hated them, and I wanted to destroy every one I could find. And I was doing a good job of it. I've tracked them from all over the United States almost. Just do it out of spite, you know. I want to torment 'em. Every time they'd stop or go someplace, I'd be there. I'd follow them on the highway, I'd go around them, play with 'em, back up and let them go by me. A woman alone ain't safe at all.

When I grew up I would watch my mom have sexual acts. She wouldn't go into a different room, she'd make sure I was in the room before she started anything, and she would do it deliberately, to make me watch her, you know. And I got so I hated it. I'd even leave the house and go out and hide in the woods and wouldn't even go home. And when I'd go home I'd get beat for not coming home. And I can't say that—you know, I don't blame Mom for what she done, I don't blame her for that. It's the idea of the way she done it. I don't think any child out there should be brought up in that type of an environment. And I can—in the past, I've hated it. It's just inside hate, and I can't get away from it.

Authors' note: Presently, there is some confusion as to how many people Lucas actually murdered, since he may have lied about many killings for his own sick reasons. It is a fact that he has murdered, although the extent of his macabre acts remains a mystery.

ABC News, *20/20*, July 5, 1984, transcript, New York, Journal Graphics, Inc., excerpts pp. 2–4.

---

that control the id in normal human beings) to several kinds of chronic offenders (Jenkins, no date). The unsocialized aggressive type simply has not developed a normal superego, and is likely to engage in conscience-less killing, raping, and maiming at any time. Interviews with the associates of some perpetrators express shock at the brutality of an otherwise "nice kid." Jenkins calls such an individual the *socialized delinquent*. This personality type has superego restraints against victimizing relatives, friends, and other members of the in-group (including those in the same gang); because of the selectivity of the superego, out-group members (i.e., everybody else, including members of other gangs) are fair game for remorseless attacks.

As Table 11-2 shows, the psychological theories share the limits of the biological approaches in the relatively few kinds of lawbreaking they purport to explain. A theoretical limitation is also implicit in explanations of how personalities get malformed. By tracing today's chronic offender to yesterday's defective socialization of the child—especially by parents—the psychological theories strongly suggest the significance of social processes outside the individual.

The social structural and cultural theories put these very processes at center stage in the story of the chronic offender. It is a story that is more than biography. Instead of telling the tale of an individual who becomes a criminal, these approaches focus on the general circumstances bearing on the lives of whole collectivities of individuals. Even with this common point of departure, the theories within each family of explanations emphasize different causal themes.

Strain theory takes its name from criminogenic strains placed on people by their structural position in society. In its classic formulation by Robert K. Merton (1938), this theory abstracts two key elements of a society. The cultural goals are widely shared aspirations instilled in individuals as they are socialized; institutionalized means are the culturally approved courses to follow in achieving those aspirations. While the culture conditions all Americans to seek the goal of material success (e.g., everyone watches the same television commercials associating money with happiness), all do not have equal access to the institutionalized means of good schools and good jobs. The proposed chain of criminal causality is linked in this way: Society creates a gap between goals and means for the poor, which leads to a personal strain corroding commitments to cultural norms (anomie), which leads to crime. Specifically, the individual caught in this societally created niche may adapt by innovation, that is, by beating novel but illegal paths to the cultural goals, such as robbing one's way to a house in the suburbs.

Strain theory does account for the apparent overdistribution of chronic offenders at the lower rungs of the class ladder, but there are other sociological explanations equally consistent with these data. Rather than highlighting the distribution of criminal motivation in society (i.e., there is more at the bottom), the key variable for *control theory* is the distribution of social restraints on people's behavior. Assuming that "we are all animals and thus naturally capable of committing criminal acts" (Hirschi, 1969:31), those with the weakest social ties to conventional society will be most likely to release such vicious tendencies. Commonplace activities such as joining sports teams or doing homework with friends are important because they bind individuals to their present and future places in the social order. Social ties are anticrime restraints, and of particular importance are the bonds of family. When these bonds are severed (a "broken" home), a criminal nature may be unleashed. Since family instability is relatively common (see Chapter 5) and some other forms of societal attachment are relatively uncommon in the lower class (see Chapter 8), chronic offenders should be concentrated there.

They are, but this interpretation leaves us in a theoretical bind: Since strain theory and control theory both render identical predictions about which social status will tend to be criminogenic, and since both theories appear to be supported by the same data, how do we choose between them?

The answer is, we do not. In a real world in which chronic offenders kill every day, we cannot wait for criminological research to pick the perfect theory. Some of the gaps in current theories can be plugged by a complementary approach. To begin putting the pieces together, few experts would deny that psychopathology, blocked opportunities, and unstable social ties all contribute to the development of some chronic offenders. The question of which factor is predominant may be unanswerable because they are so intricately interrelated. As the name of the theory states, poverty undoubtedly creates strain for the poor seeking to climb the status ladder, but it also generates an everyday hardship that strains the very family relationships so critical for the development of normal personality. Additionally, *labeling theory* would posit that economic deprivation increases the risk of arrest and conviction for those deprived, thus forging a deviant self-concept and making hardened criminals.

The joint picture that emerges from these mixed theories of the chronic offender suggests that public policy need not be paralyzed until the ultimate criminogenic theory arrives. What we know about problem linkages indicates that extending opportunities to the lower class will not only relieve status strain but also bolster the antilabeling resources (e.g., a lawyer's fee), the external social controls (e.g., conformist co-workers), and the internal personality controls (e.g., a normal conscience) emphasized by the various theories.

Organized Crime

At several points in this chapter, pains have been taken to make the point that all lawbreaking is not spontaneous, irrational activity. While there are indeed many crimes of passion, there are also patterns of illegal activity that are at least as planned and regular as the United States mail. Individuals pursuing careers in organized criminal operations may openly scorn the wild, uncontrollable street criminal and may themselves emulate the straitlaced behavior expected of any aspiring young business executive. This is not to say, however, that criminal operations are the bureaucratic equivalent of IBM. Although direct evidence has been scanty (for obvious reasons), the popular image of the Mafia as a nationwide entity enforcing its uniform corporate policy with violence appears to be grossly exaggerated (Morash, 1984).

Nevertheless, illegal enterprise syndicates furnishing prohibited goods and services do attain quite respectable levels of organizational sophistication, and more than respectable levels of profit; some experts estimate that the net income of organized crime exceeds that of any other single industry in the United States (Simon and Eitzen, 1982). The roots of these organizations straddle both sides of the law. Studies have shown that their illegal activities are supported by accommodating ties to court administrators, politicians, and law enforcement officials (Block, 1980; Chambliss, 1978), and that syndicates seek to diversify their holdings by involvement in legitimate businesses (Abadinsky, 1981).

Working at a lower level of social organization but well above the street fighter or rapist is the "professional thief." As the title implies, this is not just someone who chronically steals things. Professional thieves are distinguished by highly developed skills sharpened through selection into a social circle that provides training, consultation, and support much like that of any other professional society (Inciardi, 1984).[10] Members of this criminal elite scorn unpolished street criminals ("amateurs") and themselves display personality traits that seem distinctly uncriminal:

> Chic Conwell was an attractive person. He could have passed readily as a lawyer, a banker, or a merchant so far as personal appearance and casual conversation were concerned. He had the initiative, ingenuity, and abilities that are characteristic of leaders. He was near the top of his profession (Sutherland, 1956:vii).

Chic Conwell's profession, of course, was thief, and the author characterizing him developed a theory which explains how this type of person could become a career criminal. Edwin Sutherland's conception of *differential association* focused on the interpersonal influences exerted

---

[10] Inciardi observes that this particular form of criminal activity is in decline but that professional thievery has structural similarities to several virulent forms of lawbreaking, notably white-collar crime (Inciardi, 1984).

by relatives, friends, coworkers—one's "different associates." Why does a member of a well-to-do, respectable family (like Chic) choose a life of crime? Sutherland would answer by looking beyond family ties to the whole pattern of social contacts. If the preponderance of one's associates define the violation of the law as desirable—and can help one to "learn the ropes" of lawbreaking—they emanate a powerful social field attracting an individual to the lifestyle of the professional criminal.

As Table 11-2 indicates, there is more to the differential association concept than the advice your mother gave you about the effects of hanging out in bad company. Sutherland's theory points to the whole pattern of personal relationships, but it has little to say about who happens to meet the bad apples that can spoil a law-abiding bunch.

Cloward and Ohlin's *differential opportunity* approach to criminogenesis plugs this gap and also attempts to complement strain theory. Accepting Merton's basic proposition about cultural goals and institutionalized means, they begin by noting that "innovators" generally do not start from scratch. As Sutherland suggests, criminals—especially professionals—tend to follow in the footsteps of other criminals they already know. Even if one is predisposed to lawbreaking due to some generalized sense of strain, there is the need for role models who may or may not be socially available. One cannot simply look in the Yellow Pages under "crook." Paralleling the legitimate opportunity structure is an unequal distribution of counterfeiters, bookies, and pimps across different neighborhoods. Cloward and Ohlin further note that individuals under strain (in general, the poor) who have local access to organized criminal institutions may become the professionals of the underworld; those who lack such access may express their strain in mindless street violence or drug abuse (Cloward and Ohlin, 1960).

Although it is not a comprehensive theory (most poor people in neighborhoods with bad schools and good crime syndicates still do not become organized criminals), Cloward and Ohlin's propositions do add finishing touches to the other theories. The concept of illegitimate opportunities distributed throughout society complements Merton's social structural view, and fills in some of Sutherland's blanks concerning the location of bad guys who may lurk among one's different associates.

SOCIAL POLICY: CORRECTIONAL CHOICES

The sociological themes so painstakingly threaded throughout this chapter will not unravel here. They weave a tapestry of real complexity, but this intricacy imitates the reality of crime in America. And crime is truly in America, as much a part of the fabric of society as the elaborate social institutions we have spun to deal with the problem.

Perhaps it is best to introduce the policy issues by beginning in simpler times. Part of the reason for our continued fascination with the wild, wild West is its representation of classic American values such as independence, aggressiveness, and self-reliance. These values were often called into play in the unsettled frontier society, which lacked a reliable system of law enforcement. In this storied social environment, vigilante groups flourished. These nonlegal, voluntary associations have killed no fewer than 700 people in our history through their attempts to enforce social order (Brown, 1975). Two conclusions are immediately relevant. First, their take-the-law-into-your-own-hands approach strikes a chord deep in American culture; in fact, even the villain of western fact and fiction is the object of grudging admiration because of his aggressive individualism. Second, the vigilantes' implementation of cultural values in such a violent manner was triggered by the perceived inadequacies of the criminal justice system.

Although the analogy of our current urban society to the pioneer West can be overdrawn, there are intriguing parallels. Vigilantism has been modernized into *self-help*, a term encompassing a wide variety of private citizens' strategies for dealing with twentieth century criminals. One strategy is to bolster one's anticrime defenses, hence, the booming sales in home protection devices (including computerized alarm systems), self-defense courses (see your neighborhood shopping mall), and guns (see the section on street crime). At a higher level of organization are quasi-vigilante groups such as the Guardian Angels who patrol the subways of metropolitan centers, and private (i.e., for hire) security forces which actually command more workers and money than all local, state, and federal law enforcement agencies combined!

As in the earlier era, these are typically American attempts to do something about a fear of crime that is not much reassured by the everyday operation of the criminal justice system, despite the impressiveness of the official machinery built to control the crime problem in the United States. The multileveled governmental system costs around 30 billion dollars, employs over 1 million people, and makes over 10 million arrests each year (U.S. Department of Justice, 1984). While selected features of this system will be spotlighted below, these statistics make clear the extent of our societal investment in stopping crime. Given the public policy structure and the private reinforcements called in by self-help efforts, *why is crime not being stopped?*

The answer lies in the very nature of United States society. Consider the principle of value trade-offs as it applies to the rights of the accused. Elimination of all of these "legal technicalities" would undoubtedly cause an objective drop in crimes committed; it is just as certain that more innocent individuals would be convicted and all of us would have less personal privacy. The legal rights of the criminal are not simply humanitarian protections for those about to be incarcerated. Criminal law is a compromise between basic but conflicting values that apply to all of us through the Bill of Rights. Recent Supreme Court decisions liberalizing search and seizure powers have resulted in some major criminal convictions, but they imply a minor increase in everyone's chances of having the door kicked in by the police. If you approve of the new rules, you have accepted this value trade-off.

Without further embellishment, here is the point: Every aspect of the crime problem can be traced to the heart of American culture. Criminal motivation is fed by popular values such as aggressiveness and materialism; an aggressive attack on crime is restrained by civil liberties we hold sacred; self-help efforts conjure the image of a Minuteman defending his family's doorway. The same uniquely American stamp is on the official system which processes people who have been declared criminal.

Strategies for Solution

Whatever the wider sources of crime and the response to crime in the United States, there is the immediate practical problem of what to do with those who have been convicted of committing it. The dilemma is ancient enough to be posed in biblical terms. Should society take vengeance for the victim by extracting "an eye for an eye" in retribution, or instead have "the lion lie down with the lamb" in order to reform the lion? In evaluating this dilemma for our contemporary criminal justice system, it is not a simple either/or proposition. Since the present system contains elements of both punishment and rehabilitation, the real issue—and it is a real issue now—is which element to emphasize.

Punishment is the more traditional answer. Of the three major rationales for getting tougher on criminals (Reid, 1976), the simplest is the moral argument of *retribution* for the evildoer. From this perspective, punishment restores the scales of justice for the wronged victim. A second rationale is termed *incapacitation* in reference to the removal of the criminal's capacity to harm the rest of us. Given that punitive policies severely restrict the contact of the convicts with the rest of society, society is shielded from their predations as long as the cell door remains locked.

The final and pivotal argument concerns *deterrence*. In theory (see the neoclassical school in Table 11-2), an eye-for-an-eye policy makes crime seem more costly and conformity more attractive. Both the punished person and the mass public of potential criminals may thus be deterred from breaking the law. If valid, this theory of punishment would mean staggering reductions in the objective dimension of crime. Since about 80 percent of all felonies are committed by *recidivists* (criminals who have had prior contact with the criminal justice system), the chastening effects of stiffer punishment could be very substantial indeed. Moreover, the vast majority of uncaught criminals out there (only 20 percent of FBI Index crimes reported to police are cleared by arrest each year) might be similarly deterred from further lawbreaking.

Advocates of a policy thrust toward rehabilitation also advance both moral and practical arguments. One of the former is that warehousing criminals in a degrading environment breeds brutality and despair rather than personal reformation. They offer capital punishment as a case in point. Despite the trend toward increased executions, more inmates on death row were murdered or committed suicide than were legally killed in 1982. Besides perpetrating human misery, such cruel punishment teaches the morally questionable lesson that violence is the way to handle perceived wrongs. This is all the more unsettling because of evidence that many violent crimes are actually a form of self-help in which criminals feel they are righting a wrong (killing an adulterer, robbing back an unpaid debt, etc.; Black, 1983); many others are crimes of passion in which probabilities of jail sentences are not rationally calculated and weighed.

Typically, pro-rehabilitation interests characterize criminals as sick and punishment advocates as offering only symptomatic treat-

ment. To effect a cure, the criminal justice system must find the source of the deviant infection and surgically repair it by providing psychological counseling, job skills, or whatever is necessary. Otherwise, self-respecting recidivists with unchanged motivation will still believe they can evade the law no matter how stiff the penalties. Worse yet, stiffer sentencing means that convicts spend a longer time in a "total institution" (Goffman, 1961) in which they must submit to authoritarian control of their lives while being deprived of contact with mainstream society. How can their coping with society's pressures be expected to improve after the prison door slams shut behind them?

Counterarguments have been highly refined in this long running debate. While the pro-punishment side may generally contend that the pains visited upon the criminal are far less "cruel and unusual" than the punishment inflicted on the victim, they also make a case for the personal rights of the perpetrator. The very term *rehabilitate* comes from a Latin root meaning "to make suitable." Of necessity, rehabilitation programs intrude on the personal space of criminals by creating conditions designed to remake their personalities in society's image. Whether the treatment involves in-depth therapy probing one's relationship with mother or provision of the job skills the vocational counselor thinks one needs, the rehabilitant must surrender some individual privacy and autonomy.

The pro-rehabilitation position has also noted some surprising value trade-offs. To the common charge that criminals do not deserve lavish treatment services at state expense, they respond that cold, spare prisons are an extravagance. At current prices, building a cell costs 50,000 dollars; keeping a prisoner in a cell runs between 1000 dollars and 2000 dollars a month, well above what it would cost to buy the criminal a house on a mortgage (Cressey, 1982). An increasingly punitive corrections policy will carry a whopping price tag and increasing fiscal pressure to divert funds from other essential public services.

Policies into Practice

The social costs of a get-tough sentencing policy have been making headlines in the 1980s. With the recent trend toward mandatory sentencing (in the last several years, some thirty-seven states have legislated fixed prison terms for certain offenses), cells in the United States are bursting at their metal-reinforced seams. New records for numbers of inmates have already been broken every year in this decade, with nearly 500,000 people (about 1 of every 500 Americans) now behind bars. To comply with the stiffer sentencing procedures, 4 billion to 6 billion dollars in prison and jail construction funds are to be set aside over the next ten years.

Meanwhile, prisons across the nation are ominously overcrowded. Because of this inhumane—and potentially explosive—situation, individual prisons or entire prison systems in thirty-nine states are under court order to upgrade living conditions. Attica's prison population has been permitted to exceed the legal residence limit set after the infamous 1971 riot in which forty-three people were killed. Matters are so desperate that more than 17,000 inmates were actually released in 1984 due to overcrowding.

The latter datum is particularly ironic given the rationale of the stiffer punishment policy. In part, this policy was a reaction against the accusations of the public and professionals alike that the criminal justice system had become a revolving door for lawbreakers. There is

Stiffer punishment of criminals implemented through new mandatory sentencing laws has produced ominous overcrowding in many prisons. (*Tony O'Brien/Frost Publishing*)

objective evidence behind that image. About 2 out of every 3 recipients of life sentences actually serve time for seven years or less; a typical convicted rapist spends less than three years and an average robber just over two years in prison! Major factors in these reduced sentences are *parole* (premature release of a prisoner based on evidence of good behavior), *probation* (sentencing offenders to be monitored by probation officers in the community instead of prison), and *plea bargaining* (in which the accused offers information or a guilty plea in return for a reduced sentence).

Traditionally, each of these mechanisms had been wielded with wide discretion by judges, prosecutors, and prison authorities. First offenders, cooperative informants, and penitent felons would be dealt with less harshly to hasten their return to society's good graces. Of course such discretion, as the pro-punishment faction has argued, means not only shorter sentences but also grossly unequal punishments for the same crime. As these sources of discretion are locked up by unbending mandatory sentencing laws, however, carrot-and-stick tools used for rehabilitation are lost.

Implementation of a larger-scale rehabilitation policy would not be without its own real-world problems. Training a convict to be an electrician cannot be expected to be rehabilitative unless there are jobs for electricians—and broad-minded employers who trust ex-cons. In the present system, over 10,000 inmates are taking college classes. Using your own tuition as a base, multiply times a number of prisoners, say, twice that large to estimate the dollar costs of an expanded policy.

A more complex implementation issue arises from the fact that the systems of punishment and rehabilitation are not distinct. Those college classes are usually offered right inside maximum security facilities rather than on idyllic ivy-covered campuses. Moreover, a cynical con wanting to beat the punishment system knows that enrolling in a social problems class

may impress prison authorities and speed parole. To have a real chance, rehabilitative programs may have to be separated from the prison setting. This would imply a radical change from the status quo in which both are funded together in the "corrections" budget.

Despite the surge of support for stiffer sentencing, rehabilitation has been a persistently attractive idea in a society beguiled by self-improvement and helping those who help themselves. The gangster movies of the 1930s expressed the widespread sentiment that criminals had been scarred by the hard knocks of life but could be cured by the balm of opportunity. A recent national survey reveals that such sentiments are still widespread (Humphrey Institute of Public Affairs, 1982). More than 6 of every 10 people polled thought that not enough money and resources are being spent to prevent juvenile crime. Should it be spent to punish or rehabilitate? While 78 percent of the respondents agreed that the juvenile courts are too lenient with those committing serious crimes, 73 percent also agreed that the main purpose of the system should be to treat and rehabilitate rather than to punish. The two strategies under consideration here are not mutually exclusive options in the public mind. There appears to be subjective support for *both* more punishment *and* more rehabilitation.

Evaluating the Evidence

Given popular ambivalence about these policy alternatives, which position is best supported by social science? Consider first the theoretical implications drawn in Table 11-2. The right-hand column contains much support for rehabilitation programs. Halfway houses and work release programs would allow the criminal to cultivate personal ties to the community; these would be positive differential associates and social controls, according to Sutherland and Hirschi, respectively. By the lights of labeling theory, rehabilitation programs may effectively reduce recidivism because they are less stigmatizing to the labelee than being locked up.

In theory, though, severely restrictive punishment should also be effective. Individuals with inadequate internal controls (as discussed in the psychological theories section of Table 11-2) should cause less objective damage if they are denied free access to victims; such unscrupulous characters on the outside may also be deterred by the prospect of more severe penalties, even if they are not deterred by the promptings of conscience. Theory parallels public opinion in finding both alternatives to be eminently desirable.

This is precisely the sort of policy situation in which empirical research may serve as a tiebreaker. Does punishment reduce crime? The scientific consensus is yes and no. Longer sentences certainly mean less victimization of citizens outside the prison walls (through incapacitation), although ample victims of violence are found among inmates. In some studies, higher levels of both *certainty* (e.g., the ratio of persons actually serving time to the total number of reported robberies) and *severity* (e.g., the average amount of time served for robbery) of sentencing have been associated with lower offense rates; other studies have uncovered no relationship at all between these factors and crime, and still others have actually indicated a positive correlation in which stiffer and more certain sentences are associated with higher rates of crime (Reid, 1976).

The jury is also out on the impact of rehabilitation programs. If not the last word, certainly the most influential word on this case was uttered by researcher Robert Martinson. After screening a vast literature to find those evaluation studies of rehabilitation projects which meet social scientific standards, he distilled from the 231 acceptable reports the following conclusion: "With few and isolated exceptions, the rehabilitative efforts that have been reported so far have had no appreciable effect on recidivism" (1974:25). Martinson took pains to point out, however, that rehabilitation is cheaper, more humane, and no *more* likely to produce recidivists despite its apparent leniency.

Clearly, the empirical evidence to date offers no easy answers to resolve the present debate. The research may not allow us to broadly choose between the punishment and rehabilitation models, but it does facilitate specific choices within each policy alternative. Punishment appears to be efficacious in deterring crimes in which the criminal has an established stake in society, such as domestic assault (Sherman and Berk, 1984) and, significantly, white-collar crime (Chambliss, 1969). Key data on deterrence should emerge in the immediate future as the effects of mandatory sentencing are assessed. Even Martinson's largely negative generalizations about rehabilitation found some successful exceptions that should serve as pilot projects for further development and evaluation. Particularly promising are non-punishment programs that recognize the linkage of crime to other social problems such as poverty (Berk, Lenihan, and Rossi, 1980) and drugs (Simpson and Sells, 1982). Fittingly, both sets of suggestions are a capstone to *the* theme of this chapter: Crime is rooted in social structures.

SUMMARY

1 According to Durkheim's functionalist perspective, rule breaking is a necessary aspect of all healthy societies. Conflict theorists, on the other hand, see crime as a result of upper-class economic and political control over lower classes. The social change perspective sees law as rooted in the changing activities of human groups.

2 There are two basic approaches to quantifying criminal behavior. *Counting criminals* records the number of lawbreakers and their relative distribution in various social categories. *Counting victims* is accomplished both by official records and by mass surveys polling the victimized. Despite the uncertainties in measurement of both methods, it is clear that the objective costs of crime to society are enormous.

3 Throughout the 1970s and well into the 1980s, subjective concern about crime has registered at a high level. Expectations, visibility, and especially values trigger a strong subjective response to the problem of crime in United States society.

4 Micro theories of crime causation fall into several broad categories: biological, psychological, social structural, and cultural. Chronic offenders, organized criminals, and, indeed, all forms of law breaking are presently best understood by a complementary blend of theoretical approaches.

5 A current policy dilemma concerns the relative emphasis on punishment versus rehabilitation within the criminal justice system. One of the central issues is social scientific evidence concerning the effectiveness of deterrence and personal reform of the lawbreaker.

Megaproblems: American Society in the World

The issues that are the focus of this segment are often excluded from treatment as traditional social problems. In our view, recent historical events such as the oil crisis and worldwide terrorism make it shortsighted in the extreme to pretend that social problems in the United States are self-contained. Each of the following three chapters sociologically examines global issues which are intimately linked to present and future problems within our borders.

CHAPTER 12

Megaproblems Introduction and World Population Growth

Just for a moment, imagine that you are a first-class passenger on a huge spaceship traveling at a speed of 100,000 kilometers per hour. You discover that the ship's environmental system is faulty. Some passengers are dying due to poisonous gases in their oxygen supply. Also, there is a serious shortage of provisions—food supplies are being used up and the water supply is rapidly becoming polluted due to breakdowns in the waste and propulsion systems.

In the economy sections passengers are crowded together. Conditions are bad, especially for children. Many are seriously ill. The ship's medical officers are able to help few of the sick and medicines are in short supply.

Mutinies and fighting have been reported in some sections. Hopefully this conflict can be contained, but there is fear that the violence may spread into the other compartments.

The spacecraft has an overall destruct system, with the controls carefully guarded by a special technical crew. Unfortunately, the number of technologists who know how to set off the destruct system has increased, and there is great concern over what might happen if the fighting does spread.

We could go on, but the point is: What would you do if you were on that spaceship? Now that you have "imagined," are you ready to face reality? You are on such a spaceship right now— Spaceship Earth!

Donald Morris (1971)

INTRODUCTION

The earth has been constructing and destroying continents for at least 2500 million years. About 330 million years ago, all the then-existing continents came together to form a single colossal landmass: Pangea. Pangea ultimately broke apart, yielding the continents we know today. This process of landmass change continues due to the incessant movement and alteration of the earth's tectonic plates. Africa is currently moving clockwise and will eventually choke off the Mediterranean Sea and smash into southern Europe, creating great new mountain ranges in the process. The floor of the Atlantic Ocean will pass under the eastern coast of the United States, and present-day New York City and Philadelphia may eventually stand in the midst of a vast volcanic range. And the now-balmy Los Angeles area, situated on the Pacific plate, will become increasingly colder as it moves relentlessly northwest toward Alaska. Thus, the continents we know today will eventually cease to exist.

Continental transience is not an anomaly. *Nothing* endures. Not continents, not nations, not planets, not suns, not even the present universe itself. And certainly not humanity. There will come a day when our last descendant perishes. Our species is doomed. Only the date and the manner of our demise are uncertain. The outer limit of humankind's existence on earth (or on nearby planets) is roughly known because it is determined by the predictable behavior of the sun. Several billion years from now, the sun will swell, the earth will heat, the oceans will evaporate, and the atmosphere will escape into space (Sagan, 1980). All life forms, including humanity, will be extinguished in the process. The sun will then continue to expand and probably someday engulf the very place where you are reading this book. It is almost certain, however, that the human race will be gone long before the sun begins to die.

The doomsday question—When and how will humankind die out?—is a matter of serious controversy among astronomers, geophysicists, biologists, sociologists, paleontologists, environmentalists, demographers, health experts, and other scholars (Browne, 1978). Most of these scientists believe that human extinction is probably not very likely in the near future, though they caution that it may not be as distant as commonly thought. Some believe the possibility of not-too-distant extinction is so real, however, that society (and science) should devote considerable resources to projects designed to minimize the risks. Some of these projects are already under way. For instance, scientists are increasing their efforts to understand why the dinosaurs abruptly vanished after having thrived for 140 million years. The hope is that humanity, which has existed a mere several million years, can learn something about the dinosaurs' demise that will help forestall its own.

The extinction of the human species will probably come about in one of the following ways (Browne, 1978):

- By the explosion of a nearby star which would vaporize the earth
- By the earth being struck by a celestial body such as a large comet or asteroid
- By an increase in solar radiation resulting from a lowering of the earth's magnetic field defense
- By a new disease (that either attacks humans directly or exterminates an organism vital to our food chain) resulting from genetic mutation or genetic engineering
- By environmental degradation such as a severe ''greenhouse effect'' situation (a warming of the earth due to atmospheric pollution)
- By depletion of resources which humanity depends upon for existence and which are limited (just as they are in the imaginary spaceship above)
- By the long-term effects of nuclear war

Not all these routes to extinction are social problems in the traditional sense since some—

i.e., supernovas, collisions, and changes in the earth's magnetic field—either do not have social origins or are not amenable to social control. But some are social problems. In this and the following two chapters we will focus only on those ways in which the human race is jeopardizing its own existence through known social processes. These include overpopulation, environmental degradation, resource depletion, and nuclear war—the internal problems that confront Spaceship Earth. (A full chapter on another threat—genetic engineering—is included in the *Study Guide*.) These problems are increasingly being studied by sociologists, as evidenced by the fact that they were a theme of the 1984 Annual Meeting of the Society for the Study of Social Problems.

In earlier chapters we dealt with the domestic social problems of the United States, problems such as mental illness, crime, drug abuse, and poverty. As important as these problems are in the United States (and elsewhere), they are dwarfed by the world problems discussed in these last three chapters. Overpopulation, environmental degradation, resource depletion, and nuclear war (and possibly genetic engineering) are social *megaproblems*. They are the problems that scientists (e.g., physicist-novelist C. P. Snow) and world leaders (e.g., former President Jimmy Carter) almost always list as the major menaces confronting humankind because they threaten its very survival. While the specter of doomsday looms over us, it is unlikely to occur during our lifetimes or for some time thereafter (unless nuclear war with its feared geophysical consequences occurs). However, if present trends continue, we and succeeding generations will have to face more immediate problems, such as the gradual deterioration of the planet's basic life support systems and the colossal objective problems associated with them. The balance of this book will focus mostly on these more immediate and chronic problems rather than on ultra-long-range consequences such as extinction.

We will first examine the problem of world population growth, the underlying cause of the overpopulation megaproblem. Population growth is arguably the central social megaproblem, since the product of population times per capita rates of consumption determines the *scale* of economic activity, total consumption, food and agricultural needs, energy requirements, and concomitant environmental problems. And the dimensions of these factors are often related to the probability of social unrest and war. Consequently, population growth also affects any effort to reconcile the need for improved living standards with the carrying capacity of the earth (L. Grant, 1982). In short, population growth is an especially important problem because it contributes in some degree to all the other megaproblems. It is a multiplier; population increases intensify the damage created by the other problems.

POPULATION GROWTH

Population Explosion

In the early 1980s a British television series was broadcast in the United States called *UXB*, an acronym for unexploded bomb. It was the remarkable story of heroic young men whose job it was to defuse unexploded bombs which fell on England during World War II. Most of these men were selected for this task solely because they were then college engineering majors and presumably knew something about how bomb fuses worked. But in reality they knew virtually nothing about fuses and received only brief and inadequate training. Because of this and the fact that the Germans kept changing the fuse design and frequently booby-trapped the fuses of bombs intentionally rigged not to explode on impact, the life expectancy of these men once they entered this service was a matter of weeks. The series began with a young soldier straddling a bomb called a "blockbuster," which was about the size of a horse. All was quiet as he tinkered with the fuse, trying to extract it. Suddenly, the fuse began to tick, and horror swept across the man's face. Several seconds later the bomb exploded. His body was rocketed upward in thousands of tiny pieces which birds would ultimately find and consume. In one instant the soldier, the bomb, and the city block were there, and in the next instant they were gone.

Writers have used the metaphors population "bomb" and population "explosion" to characterize what has been happening to population growth in recent history. While watching this opening scene from *UXB*, it somehow occurred to us just how apt these expressions really are. What is happening now to population growth is just as explosive—just as much a departure from the preexplosion status quo. We are now in the midst of that explosion and really have been since about 1650 (see Figure 12-1).

We cannot begin to understand the gravity of the population growth problem without placing it in historical perspective. Homo sapiens evolved as a species between 2 million and 5 million years ago. During most of this time, the rate of population growth was scarcely above zero, and the world population remained below 10 million. Just as an atomic bomb of the size exploded at Hiroshima is used to detonate today's far more powerful hydrogen bomb, a relatively small population explosion ignited the current much larger one. The smaller explosion occurred around 8000 B.C. with the initiation of agriculture and the domestication of animals. This smaller explosion petered out around 1650, but in the process world population had expanded about fifty times from 10 million to 500 million. Then came the big explosion. Another 500 million people were added in just 150 years, and world population reached its first *billion* around 1800. But the big explosion had only just begun. The second billion people were added by 1930, in just 130 years; the third billion by 1960, in just 30 years; and the fourth billion by 1975, in just 15 years.

Today, the explosion is still building toward its peak. The world registered its biggest twelve-month population increase in history (82 million people) during 1985 when it reached 4.85 billion people. World population is growing

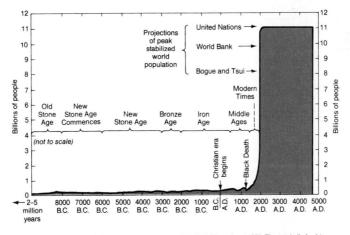

Human numbers took 2 to 5 million years to reach half a billion, about 1650. The total climbed to 2 billion by 1930, doubled to 4 billion by 1975, and is projected to be up to 6 billion by the year 2000. Current projections of the world's peak stabilized population are: 8 billion, reached about 2050 (University of Chicago demographers Donald Bogue and Amy Ong Tsui); about 10 billion, around 2090 (World Bank); or 11 billion about 2125 (United Nations).

FIGURE 12-1   World population growth. (*Source:* Reprinted from van der Tak et al., 1983: 198.)

so quickly now that the addition of the next three years alone will equal the population of the United States. The world population will reach 5 billion by 1987 and 6 billion before the year 2000.

Consider for a moment the awesome dimensions of this ongoing population explosion. It took humankind 2 million to 5 million years to reach a population of 1 billion. We now add 1 billion people in just twelve years. Figure 12-1 depicts what is happening. The population growth trend is now going almost straight up. But this often depicted exhibit, dramatic as it is, tremendously understates the unprecedented, explosive character of the recent trend because the period from 5 million B.C. to 8000 B.C. is not drawn to scale. If it were, the low, flat part of the trend would extend more than 200 feet to the left of the 8000 B.C. mark, and would show that the explosion is an even more radical departure from humanity's historical experience than illustrated in Figure 12-1.

Demographic Transition

Why is this population explosion taking place? The explanation has to do with the change in the ratio of births to deaths. Before the explosion took place, both birthrates and death rates fluctuated at a relatively high level. This is stage one of the demographic transition (see Figure 12-2). Mortality was high in preexplosion societies because of harsh living conditions. Indeed, for much of the period prior to the population explosion,

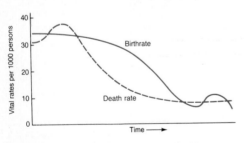

FIGURE 12-2   The demographic transition. (*Source:* Reprinted from Weeks, 1981: 37. By permission of the publisher.)

average life expectancy was less than thirty years, due mostly to very high infant mortality. To offset this mortality, women had to average at least six children or the society would simply die out. So traditional societies developed cultures which encouraged individuals to have many children. For instance, a woman's value and a man's virility were often determined by the number of children they had, and religious institutions urged people to "be fruitful and multiply." But offsetting mortality was not the only reason large families and growing populations were favored in preexplosion societies. Large families served many other important functions, such as providing parents with an economical labor force to work the family farm and with guaranteed care during old age. And growing populations were deemed functional for a variety of economic and political reasons such as military security.

Stage two of the demographic transition was set into motion by the improved living conditions and the control over disease engendered by modernization. These changes caused death rates to drop. But birthrates remained at or near their previous levels, leading to a dramatic rise in population growth. Thus, stage two of the demographic transition ignited the population explosion.

Technological innovations, and other advances which lower death rates, are rapidly adopted by traditional societies not only because of their obvious utility but also because these societies do not have values supporting high mortality. But because pro-natalist values are deeply entrenched in the social system (and often remain functional for other reasons such as providing for old-age security), positive attitudes toward large families are not easily or rapidly changed. People in traditional societies have a difficult time appreciating that the demographic circumstances of their lives have changed in just a few decades. This whole phenomenon is a classic example of cultural lag, with birthrate changes lagging well behind death rate changes.

In the final stage of the demographic transition, the birthrate declines as the death rate remains low. The rate of population growth remains relatively high during the early part of this stage, but declines to near zero in the latter part. The birthrate falls because large families gradually come to be seen as problematic in nontraditional societies. The birthrate of some countries that have completed the demographic transition may even fall below replacement level and remain there, which, in the absence of net immigration, ultimately results in an actual decline in the population's absolute size.

Most of today's developed nations such as the United States have nearly completed the demographic transition, and are now contributing far less to the ongoing world population explosion than the developing nations, which are still in the midst of the transition. Even including net immigration, the developed countries are growing at only 0.6 percent annually, compared to 2.0 percent for the developing countries (see Box 12-1). The latter are growing so rapidly that by the year 2000 their population will outnumber that of the developed countries by 4 to 1, up from just 2 to 1 in 1950. According to the UN's medium series of projections (which include a decline in Third World fertility), this ratio will balloon to a staggering 18 to 1 by the year 2100. By the year 2033, the populations of such countries as Nigeria and Brazil could rush past that of the United States. The population explosion is still building in intensity because the growth rate in the developing world is being applied each year to a huge and still-increasing population base.

Nevertheless, like any explosion, the population explosion will eventually fizzle out probably sometime near the end of the twenty-first century. The rate of growth (although not absolute growth) is already declining in the developing countries, falling from about 2.4 percent annually during 1965 to 1970 to 2.0 percent in 1985. This decline is due largely to the fact that

---

BOX 12-1

ARITHMETIC AND POPULATION POLICY

TABLE 12-1

WHAT ANNUAL GROWTH RATES MEAN WITH RESPECT TO THE TIME IT TAKES FOR A POPULATION TO DOUBLE IN SIZE; AND WHAT THEY MEAN WITH RESPECT TO GROWTH PER CENTURY

Annual growth rate (percent)	Doubling time (years)	Growth per century (percent)
1	70	270
2	35	724
3	23	1,922
4	17	5,050
5	14	13,150

An appreciation for the true objective dimensions of population problems and, consequently, population policy-making has long been hindered by a lack of understanding of basic arithmetic. Many national political leaders do not realize what an annual population growth of, say, 3 percent, relatively innocuous in the near term, will add up to in the long run (Brown, Chandler, Flavin, Postel, Starke, and Wolf, 1984). A common fallacy is that a 3 percent growth rate is merely three times as great as a 1 percent rate. While this is true the first year, it is untrue over longer periods as the rate compounds. A 1 percent annual rate will not even triple the population in a century, but a 3 percent rate will increase it almost twenty times. When you come upon a growth rate in this chapter, consulting this table will give you a quick idea of just how significant it is.

fertility has begun to fall in the developing societies as a whole. But it is also due to a slowdown in their mortality decline. This lamentable slowdown is occurring because some causes of death like dysentery and diarrhea cannot be fully controlled by modern medicines and clinic-based health services. Their eradication requires improved living conditions, especially more and better food and education. But rapid population growth in developing countries has undermined this possibility by eating away at gains in per capita economic resources (van der Tak, Haub, and Murphy, 1983).

There is the real possibility that developing countries will not pass all the way through the classic demographic transition. Rather, they may stall and stabilize at moderate birth and death rates rather than low ones. As demographers frequently caution, the grim reaper is ever poised to use death control in those places which need, but are too slow in applying, birth control.

THE SUBJECTIVE DIMENSION OF WORLD POPULATION GROWTH

Today the population growth problem has a relatively low subjective dimension in the United States because many articles have appeared in major newspapers in the 1980s announcing the *end* of the population explosion. This shift in the public's perception of the problem came about because many journalists thought the aforementioned decline in the *rate* of world population growth meant that the explosion itself had subsided. You know now that this is not true. While there has been dramatic progress in lowering the *rate* of population growth in developing countries, it is worth restating that the population explosion is still continuing and adding unprecedented numbers to the world population each year. Indeed, the net increase in world population in the year 2000 (i.e., 92 million) will be 13 percent higher than the record levels of the mid-1980s. More-

over, the fastest expansion is occurring by far in those places that can afford it least: the poor developing nations where food, housing, sanitation, and economic opportunity are in shortest supply.

In the late 1960s and early 1970s, the American public and the media became very concerned about the population explosion in the United States and the world and tended to exaggerate its objective consequences. Rapid population growth was blamed for virtually every present and future natural, economic, and ecological disaster. It was believed that if the world could reduce its rate of population growth to zero immediately, this alone would save it from a variety of global catastrophes. Since that time, popular interest in the population explosion and, consequently, its subjective dimension as a social problem has greatly diminished. Indeed, a few scholars (e.g., Simon, 1981) and journalists have recently taken this trend to its extreme. They contend that population growth poses little, if any, threat to the economy, environment, or individual welfare. On the contrary, they claim it is actually more beneficial than problematic. But this view has few adherents among population experts and government leaders.

The consensus view among population experts is that continued rapid population growth in a finite world is a major social problem in its own right. As noted in Chapter 7, at the current rate of growth, there would be one individual for every square foot on the earth's surface in 700 years. With respect to the present and more immediate future, there is also almost unanimous agreement among population experts that population growth contributes to and exacerbates many other problems such as environmental degradation, resource depletion, and undernutrition. However, it is also recognized that population growth cannot be held *solely* responsible for these other social problems. We now realize that the reduction of rapid population growth alone would contribute to, but

There is almost unanimous agreement among population experts that population growth contributes to and exacerbates many other problems such as undernutrition. Both mother and child in this photograph show the effects of undernourishment. (*UNICEF/Adrian Clark*)

certainly would not be sufficient to ensure, their satisfactory solution.

OBJECTIVE CONSEQUENCES OF RAPID POPULATION GROWTH

The objective damage that rapid population growth causes occurs across the entire spectrum of human, animal, and plant life in both developing and developed societies. The developing countries are already unable to provide their present populations with tolerable living conditions, and in some cases even subsistence, and the inevitable continued growth will make circumstances even more dire. Rapid population growth in developed countries also threatens severe problems for those societies and for the rest of the world. Indeed, you may recall from Chapter 7 that based on the threat the United States poses to the welfare of the planet, it can already be viewed as the most overpopulated country in the world. Thus, additional growth in developed countries, albeit slow relative to that in developing ones, is also a major social problem. In the next two chapters you will see the critical role population growth plays in exacerbating the megaproblems of environmental degradation, resource depletion, and nuclear war. Here we will briefly review the objective damage it causes with respect to economic development, unemployment, urban growth, and international migration.

Economic Development and Unemployment

The World Bank estimates that about 1 billion people in developing countries are living in absolute poverty. This is not the kind of poverty we discussed in Chapter 8 on United States poverty. Absolute poverty is living on the edge of subsistence, and is beyond a dollar definition. It is a condition of life so limited that it prevents the realization of human potential: a condition so degrading as to insult human dignity (Peccei, 1977). One goal of developing societies, therefore, has been to improve living conditions through economic development. To do so, economic growth must significantly exceed population growth. While many developing countries were able to grow economically over the last two decades, their simultaneous rapid population growth severely diminished their overall gain in income per capita, and thus in their standard of living. Eighteen nations actually experienced a decline in per capita income during the 1970s. We have already noted how this unfortunate situation has led to a slowdown in the mortality decline in these countries.

Extreme poverty has many dire consequences. Take health care, for instance, a factor in the mortality decline slowdown. Health conditions are extremely poor in most developing nations, particularly for the most impoverished groups and especially for children. Almost 1 billion of the inhabitants of these societies still have no access to any health care at all, and more than 80 percent have no access to any permanent form of health care. Not only are there few physicians compared to the United States, but those present are concentrated in the cities, especially the capital cities. Nevertheless, medical care even in the cities is grossly inadequate by Western standards. In Cali, Colombia, for instance, the patient to doctor ratio is 900 to 1; 17 percent of the children never see a physician during their fatal illness, and an additional 19 percent do not see one during the forty-eight hours preceding death.

African nations have by far the poorest ratios of health personnel and facilities to population of any continent. This is particularly true of the forty-nine sub-Saharan countries, which contain about four-fifths of Africa's 500 million people. These nations average only 4 physicians per 100,000 people. But because physicians are concentrated in the urban areas, even these extremely low ratios greatly exaggerate actual availability. In the rural areas, where about 80 percent of African populations reside, the ratio is less than 1 physician per 100,000 people (McFalls and McFalls, 1984).

Another consequence of diminished economic development is rising unemployment. By the end of this century there will probably be between 500 million and 1 billion unemployed and underemployed people in the developing world outside China. A large proportion of these individuals will be urban youths aged 15 to 24. Needless to say, the potential for social and political unrest in this situation is gigantic.

It is difficult for us to appreciate the extent of poverty in some developing societies and the tragic dilemmas it forces upon individuals and families. Consider, for instance, the poor rural woman with eight children who must choose between the possible death of one of her children and the sale of the family milk cow, which nourishes them all, in order to buy health care for the sick child (*Popline,* 1983). These are the kinds of heartbreaking decisions that parents often face. By multiplying this story millions of times you get the grim picture of life in many developing countries. Poverty in the United States, as harsh as it is, pales by comparison.

If people in developing countries see little hope for personal economic advancement, they are less likely to limit the size of their families. Thus, developing countries find themselves in a vicious cycle. Rapid population growth retards development, and continued poverty leads to high birthrates and continued rapid population growth. This dismaying cycle can be broken by well-coordinated policies aimed at the various causes of poverty. One of the most important of these policies is the rapid reduction of population growth (van der Tak et al., 1983).

Urbanization and Urban Growth Trends

One conspicuous consequence of the population explosion in the Third World is urban growth. The urban population of developing nations shot up from 275 million to 972 million between 1950 and 1980, and will approach 2 billion by the year 2000.

Urban growth has three components. The least important is the reclassification of previously rural areas to urban areas. The two important components are migration and natural increase (the difference between the numbers of births and deaths of current city dwellers, both those born in the city and those who have migrated there in the past). About 60 percent of all urban growth in developing countries is caused by natural increase. Most of the remainder is the result of rural to urban migration. But these percentages vary from country to country and from city to city. Migration has been credited with up to two-thirds of urban growth in some of the largest and fastest growing cities. Thus, urban growth is due mainly to demographic factors, the same ones that determine overall population growth (see the demographic equation in Chapter 7). Indeed, urban growth closely parallels national population growth.

Consequences of Urban Growth If you had taken a social problems course during the 1950s or early 1960s, you would have learned that this rapid urban growth was viewed by sociologists on balance as a positive trend. As noted earlier, economic development has been a goal of Third World societies, and urban growth was considered a necessary and beneficial step toward this desired modernization. At least this had been the role urban growth played in the development of the already industrialized countries.

However, during the late 1960s and 1970s most social scientists changed their overall appraisal. If you had taken the course then, you would have learned that rather than being a benefit, urban growth in the Third World was considered a major social problem. Textbooks of that era focused on some of the highly *visible* negative impacts of urban growth: crowding, squatter settlements, wretched housing, polluted air and water, traffic congestion, and unstable social conditions. But most important, the fear was that there simply were too few productive jobs in urban places for the ever-expanding work force. Population growth was thought to be outpacing economic growth in the cities, something that had not happened in the urban growth experiences of the developed world. This negative perspective on urban growth found expression in the 1974 World Population Conference's *Plan of Action*, which noted:

Urbanization in most countries is characterized by a number of adverse factors: drain from rural areas through migration of individuals who cannot be absorbed by productive employment in urban areas, serious disequilibrium in the growth of urban centres, contamination of the environment, inadequate housing and services and social and psychological stress (World Population Conference, 1976).

However, today many social scientists, perhaps even the majority, are changing their professional judgment again, and swinging back to the view that urban growth is beneficial for development in the Third World at least in the long run. Key to this view is the objective finding that despite the cities' many problems, income and productivity are still higher there than in rural areas, which, incidentally, are full of their own problems. Urban residents also have access to superior schooling, to better health care, and to a variety of other services, and their lower fertility helps the country reduce its overall population growth. Despite unemployment, underemployment, and exploitation in the cities, the urban population—and the country as a whole—seems to be better off than if there were no migration and all population growth occurred in rural areas, where both income and the chance for upward mobility are even lower.

This current more positive judgment about urban growth is reconciled to the fact that there are and will continue to be for quite some time the highly visible and serious urban problems emphasized during the late 1960s and 1970s. As Calvin Goldscheider notes:

In one sense, the problems of urban growth and urbanization are necessary costs that accompany development and modernization. These costs may be high and, in developing nations, higher than ever before in modern history. Nevertheless, the rapid rate at which developing nations are entering the process of social and economic development cannot be expected to occur without conspicuous social and economic strains and tensions. The transformation of societies and persons toward greater urban concentration and urban life is a revolution in social structure and processes. Even silent revolutions have disorganizing implications as part of societal and personal readjustment and realignment (Goldscheider, 1983).

In short, there is presently no consensus among experts concerning whether massive urban growth is largely beneficial or harmful to Third World countries. One group argues that current urban problems are growing pains these nations must endure during their quest for economic development, and this is the dominant view today. The other group contends that these current problems are or may become so severe that they will ultimately scuttle that development. Both groups agree, however, that these current urban problems are grave.

Squatter Settlements One of the most serious urban problems is the inability of many Third World cities to provide decent public services and housing to their residents. Housing is already the most visible shortage, and new construction often lags hopelessly behind pent-up and still-growing demand. In Bangkok, for instance, 120,000 additional housing units are required each year, but less than half that number are built. As a result, huge numbers of desperate urban dwellers in the Third World squat illegally on unoccupied public and private land. Houses are built helter-skelter from shipping crates, cardboard, tin, and other scrap material, and almost overnight empty lots become neighborhoods. In some of these squatter settlements, people live ten to a room, forty to a house, sleeping in shifts. Many settlements lack running water, sewer systems, electricity, and garbage collection. And major public health problems abound due to such conditions as the frequent contamination of water by raw sewage and garbage. Squatters constitute more than 25 percent of the inhabitants of most large cities in Third World countries, but this percentage is as high as 50 to 70 percent in some cities such as Cartagena (Colombia), Colombo (Sri Lanka), and Kinshasa (Zaire). In short, great masses of people live in horrid, subsistence-level conditions in sprawling urban shantytowns.

A carpet of humanity spreads outward from Manila's high-rise inner city. More than a third of the Philippine capital's population consists of impoverished squatters. The nation has begun serious efforts to bring population growth under control. (*AP/Wide World Photos*)

Gigantic Cities Another current problem facing developing countries is that a large segment of their urban growth is concentrated in jumbo-sized cities. In 1950, Shanghai was the only Third World city with a population of more than 5 million. If current growth rates continue, there will be forty-five such cities by the year 2000, mostly in Asia, and twenty cities with more than 10 million people. You may never have heard of Curitiba, Jos, Lanchow, and Surabaja—unless you are familiar with the geography of Brazil, Nigeria, China, and Indonesia. But you will in the future, for these are among the forty-five Third World cities whose populations will have exploded through the 5 million mark by the turn of the century. One of the major problems with these gigantic cities is the gigantic shantytowns they contain. (See Box 12-2 on Mexico City.)

Conflict and Unrest In reading about the horrid conditions in the Third World's ubiquitous and mammoth shantytowns, you may have been shocked and/or sympathetic, but you may also have felt detached from it all, living as you do in affluent America. But you are not detached from it. You have already been affected by the conditions in these places and will increasingly be so in the future. Third World urban growth, fueled by its underlying cause, population growth, negatively influences international relations, helps foster conflict and terrorism, and leads to frustrations exploitable by groups willing to trade peace and development for their own political objectives.

Teeming shantytowns are the natural spawning grounds of alienation and frustration, particularly among young people who are disproportionately unemployed and who increasingly

---

BOX 12-2

MEXICO CITY

For years, doomsayers have forecasted gloomy scenarios for the Third World's megacities and their sprawling ghettos. For Mexico City, with nearly 20 million inhabitants, those grim scenarios are already a reality. It is a city plagued with seemingly unsolvable problems. Here is a short list of some of its mammoth troubles:

- Traffic jams which slow the average speed to less than 3 miles per hour downtown and raise the average noise level to 90 decibels, which is like standing near a jackhammer.
- Poor distribution of fresh food, leading to frequent shortages of milk, eggs, and vegetables.
- Blinding, disease transmitting dust storms which sweep across downtown in the dry season, carrying pollution from a lake bed used as a drying rack for raw sewage. (During the hottest months, the dawn sun faintly shines through a huge hanging bubble of brown air. Visibility during the morning rush hour is less than 100 yards.)
- Chemical pollutants from 80,000 factories and businesses which darken the sky. (Though Mexico's

antipollution laws are strict, the laws are not enforced. Officials prefer to make the trade-off that most Third World nations make, that is, encourage development at the expense of the environment.)
- Air contaminated with dried airborne refuse from 3000 tons of garbage left daily on the streets and never picked up. (In some neighborhoods the middle of the street is stacked with piles of rotting garbage.)
- Dust, smog, and airborne refuse which combine to foul the air with an estimated 11,000 tons of solid-particle pollution every day. (Breathing Mexico City's air is the equivalent of smoking two packs of cigarettes a day.)

The above is not a complete list of Mexico City's woes, but it does give you an idea of what life is like there. Even the city's leaders acknowledge that its future appears hopeless. They recognize that the city cannot build roads, houses, and public utilities fast enough to cope with its 5 percent annual growth rate. By the year 2000, Mexico City will have a staggering 31 million inhabitants, and by 2025, 37 million. And even then the city will still be growing.

Adapted from Mott (1983).

resent their own intolerable living conditions, which contrast sharply with the highly visible wealth of the cities' elite. As discussed elsewhere in this book, revolutions and other forms of social unrest generally occur when social conditions are improving rather than when things are stagnant. This is because rising aspirations for positive social change, which are engendered by past progress, often exceed the society's ability to produce the desired improvements. The gap between rising aspirations and actual progress leads to frustration and unrest. It is in Third World cities that the slow progress in living standards is being made, and it is there that the unrest is occurring. In addition, unlike in rural areas where the population is scattered, people are concentrated in cities and have power by virtue of their sheer numbers. They may also be more susceptible to the manipulation and control of extremist groups (Green, 1981).

Unrest in the Third World's cities has already had serious international impacts, some of which have been felt in the United States. Consider, for instance, the upheaval in Iran which occurred in the late 1970s, with its American hostages, its negative effect on the availability and cost of oil, and a variety of other untoward effects. Analyses of the causes of that serious international problem pointed not only to the Shah's spendthrift and corrupt government but also to the country's massive urban growth (and, incidentally, to its population growth in general). George Lencgowski, in his analysis which appeared in *Foreign Affairs,* noted that Iran's rural to urban migration produced "a new city proletariat, clustering in shantytown slums, increasing by leaps and bounds and providing typical 'cannon fodder' for any skilled agitator with a demagogic appeal" (cited in Green, 1981).

Finally, as noted in Chapter 14, one of the catalysts of nuclear war may be political turmoil in the cities of one or more Third World nations. Obviously, this potentiality alone means no one on the earth is really detached from the consequences of population and urban growth in the Third World.

Urban Growth Policies   Policymakers in the Third World are extremely concerned about the social, economic, and political problems produced by rapid urban growth and the formation of gigantic cities. Various policies have been tried to cut down on rural to urban migration, including (1) development programs in rural areas to improve the quality of rural life and to create more jobs, (2) restrictions on employment and housing in urban areas, and (3) the use of passes and permits to impede the movement of individuals to the cities. In addition to these policies, others have been aimed at slowing the growth of giant cities. These include (1) the creation of new capital cities, (2) the development of smaller cities through incentives for workers and industry to relocate there, and (3) the founding and support of new rural or frontier settlements through colonization policies.

By and large these policies have been unsuccessful for a number of reasons. One is that they demand long-term political commitment, substantial economic resources, and administrative efficiency—factors that are frequently in short supply in Third World nations. Another reason is that some of these policies have the latent effect of fostering urban growth. Better education and improvements in transportation services in rural areas provide inhabitants with the motivation and means to migrate to urban areas. Moreover, other national or city policies which are not primarily concerned with urban growth often have countervailing effects on the negative urban growth policies. For example, high minimum wage levels or artificially low food prices in urban areas may encourage movement from rural areas to the major cities (*Population Reports*, 1983).

Because these urban growth trends are fueled in large part by population growth, a reduction in that growth is bound to slow them.

Policies aimed at lowering the birthrate, if successful, would diminish the supply of potential rural to urban migrants, and would also decrease the natural increase of urban dwellers.

International Migration

The Migration Explosion Another major consequence of the population explosion is international migration. The reader has probably already anticipated this consequence by putting together two phenomena already discussed. First, the population of the Third World, which is situated largely in the southern hemisphere, now outnumbers by 3 to 1 that of the developed countries, which are mostly located in the northern hemisphere. Because the population explosion is now occurring primarily in the Third World, this ratio will balloon to a staggering 18 to 1 by the year 2100. The second phenomenon is the appalling conditions of life in much of the Third World: the dehumanizing poverty, massive unemployment, squalid housing, chronic hunger, devastating infant mortality, and other conditions that add up to almost unimaginable privation and misery. The sum of these two phenomena, of course, is pressure to get out—to move across international borders in search of a better life. Kingsley Davis (1948) aptly described this potentially explosive situation as early as 1948 when he noted:

> Demographically the potential migration pent up in today's world is enormous.... What more natural than to expect the destitute masses of the underprivileged regions to swarm across international and continental boundaries into the better regions? Like the atmosphere, the earth's population is characterized by high and low pressure areas, and one expects an inevitable current of migration from one to the other. Actual migration, however, is not governed solely by high and low pressure. It is governed by economic costs, political barriers, ethnic attitudes, and limited horizons. These barriers have slowed down migration to a snail's pace. One wonders how long the

inequalities of growth between major regions can continue without an explosion.

The world has already felt the first tremors of this migration explosion. Including the movement of legal and illegal migrants and the flight of refugees, international migration is now at an all-time high. Few people leave the wealthiest countries like the United States, although there is substantial movement from the less affluent to the more affluent developed nations (e.g., from Portugal to France or from Italy to West Germany). Movement also occurs within the Third World from the most destitute nations to the relatively more prosperous ones (e.g., from Egypt to Saudi Arabia or from Colombia to Venezuela) (Bouvier, 1984). But the most important movement now and in the future is that from Third World nations to developed nations.

Though international migration is at an all-time high, it is presently just a trickle compared to its torrent potential. Only about 1 percent of the Third World's population growth—just the *growth*, not the population itself—is absorbed by the developed nations today. As the Third World to developed world population ratio expands toward the 18 to 1 figure in the year 2100, population pressure in the Third World will grow enormously, perhaps to the point where it will overwhelm the barriers to migration erected by the developed nations. It is certainly conceivable that the scenario envisioned by Jean Raspail (1982) in his novel *Camp of Saints* could become reality—that is, that the inhabitants of the Third World eventually will swarm across international and continental boundaries and inundate the relatively sparsely populated developed nations. Indeed, the late President Boumedienne of Algeria has already predicted this, stating:

> No quantity of atomic bombs could stem the tide of billions who will someday leave the poor southern part of the world to erupt into the relatively accessible spaces of the rich northern hemisphere looking for survival (Population Action Council, 1983).

Once again we can see clear links between the consequences of the population explosion, world stability, and our own national interests and security.

Why don't the developed nations voluntarily open their borders and permit the redistribution of the world's population? The reason is that these countries believe that accepting huge numbers of migrants would place enormous strains on existing political, social, and economic structures, and that it would lead to a lower standard of living, racial and religious animosities, and many other social problems. It would also make the attainment of zero population growth, a goal in many developed nations, all but impossible. You may recall the problems discussed in Chapter 7 that even current levels of immigration are posing for the United States. These problems would surely become more intractable if immigration increased. But massive immigration does not simply pose problems for wealthy nations like the United States. It also threatens to wipe out social, economic, and demographic progress in less affluent developed nations and in those Third World nations most likely to succeed in their development efforts. Venezuela is one such country which has a serious problem with illegal immigrants who come mostly from much poorer Colombia. About 1 out of every 8 inhabitants of Venezuela is an illegal alien, compared to only 1 in about 40 in the United States.

Many experts believe that international migration will become the most critical population issue of the future, once population growth itself subsides (Bouvier, 1984).

International Migration Policy During World War II, a United States research group under the direction of President Franklin Roosevelt raised the possibility of rocketing wartime refugees—most of whom were Jews—to Venus or Mars for resettlement. Although this idea now strikes us as preposterous, it is indicative of the reluctance nations have to accommodate large numbers of aliens. In general, international migration policies have had little more success than this space resettlement policy would have had. Restrictive policies on immigration, common in the United States and other developed nations, have not halted illegal entries or stopped temporary migrants from settling. Many observers believe that as long as there is a huge chasm between the standards of living of rich and poor nations, these kinds of policies have little real chance for success. Clearly, policies aimed at minimizing international migration cannot ignore its source: galloping population growth in the poor nations. Reductions in fertility can help ease the pressure for emigration there. As the relationship between population growth policies and international migration policies becomes better understood, family planning programs increasingly will be seen as an essential part of both fertility and international migration policy (*Population Reports*, 1983).

POPULATION GROWTH AND POLICY IN CHINA: A CASE STUDY

China has over one-fifth of the world's population and nearly one-third of that of the developing world. What happens to China therefore has an enormous bearing on the future size and growth rate of the world's population. It is worthwhile then for us to examine China's population problems and policies in some depth. You will also notice that this case study, which is based largely on the work of Tien (1983) with a minor assist from several other sources (*Interchange*, 1983; *Time*, 1982; and Song et al., 1985), provides cogent examples of many of the principles discussed in this chapter.

Demographic Billionaire and Nightmare

It is a very good thing that China has a big population. Even if China's population multiplies many times, she is fully capable of finding a solution. (Mao Tse-tung, 1949)

The Chinese now concede that Mao's failure to appreciate the need for population control was a disastrous mistake. When he made this statement in 1949, the year his Communist Party came to power, China contained about 550 million people. Today, China has become the world's first "demographic billionaire." Its 1982 population stood at 1,008,180,000. To help you understand just how many people that is, consider this: If all Chinese stood in a row, 6 feet apart, and marched through Peking's Gate of Heavenly Peace at a steady pace of 3 miles per hour, it would take more than sixty years for them to pass. In fact, there are as many people in China today as lived in the entire world not much more than a century ago. And China is still growing—rapidly. Its 1982 crude birthrate of 21 per 1000 population and crude death rate of 6.6 per 1000 population yielded a population growth rate of 1.5 percent. China's population would double to more than 2 billion people in just forty-six years if these rates persisted. The nation is now growing by more than 15 million people annually, a number equal to the entire population of Australia.

Because of its huge population and its population growth, China has experienced many of the Third World problems discussed in this chapter on a colossal scale. Population growth, for instance, has seriously delayed the country's ambitious economic development program. Indeed, about 60 percent of the nation's economic growth over the last thirty years had to be used to support the newborn rather than increase the standard of living of the impoverished masses. Per capita income in 1983 remained only 290 dollars. Mao's disastrous population policy is a classic example of a policymaker relying more on the tenets of a political ideology than on the advice of population policy experts.

Early Population Views

Between 1949 and 1970 China's population grew dramatically. Annual growth rates during this period rose as high as 3.4 percent (doubling time equals twenty years). At first this growth was greeted with optimism, and population policy actually encouraged births by, for instance, providing economic incentives for each child born to government workers. But gradually more pessimistic views of population growth began to proliferate. A strident debate on the role of population numbers in China's socioeconomic development was carried on during the 1950s and 1960s by the optimistic supply-siders (those who viewed each person primarily as a producer) and the pessimistic demand-siders (those who viewed each person primarily as a consumer). In general, the demand-siders—those who wanted to limit population growth—became more influential throughout the period. Abortion was legalized in 1953, and several modest family planning campaigns were launched in the two decades. But these programs were undermined by supply-siders and were eventually terminated by political events such as the Great Leap Forward in 1958 to 1959 and the Cultural Revolution in 1966 to 1969.

By 1970 the population had risen to 830 million, and it was growing at a rate of 2.6 percent. It was then that the Chinese as a whole first saw the handwriting on the wall. Economic progress since the Communists took power had fallen far short of expectations, and subjective concern about their exploding population rose sharply. It was calculated then that if the 1970 growth rate of 2.6 percent continued indefinitely, China's population would reach 1.7 billion by 1997, 3.3 billion by 2024, and about 25 billion before the end of the twenty-first century. Clearly, China then realized it had no choice but to slam on the demographic brakes. So in 1971 an ambitious national family planning program was launched.

The Two-Child Campaign

This program had two objectives during the 1970s. The first was getting Chinese couples to have only two children. The second objective, designed to help achieve the first, was to postpone the age at marriage to the mid-twenties for women and the late twenties for men. But unlike Western-style programs, China did not rely on the decision making of individual couples. The program was based more on state-set goals with which individuals were expected to comply. Population growth policy was set at the national level, but officials at every bureaucratic level were held responsible for the attainment of their portion of these goals. The goals were ultimately implemented at the grass-roots level. Couples who complied with these goals were rewarded. Those who did not were continuously encouraged, and harassed, to do so; sometimes they were coerced into "voluntary" compliance or penalized for noncompliance.

These programs were extremely well organized at the local level. Birth planning leadership groups oversaw paramedics and others who distributed birth control devices to households. The paramedics also personally escorted individuals to clinics for birth control procedures. These procedures included sterilization (tubectomy for women, vasectomy for men), IUD insertion, and induced abortion. The birth planning groups also met with individuals to encourage compliance with birth quotas, drew up birth plans for the coming year, and issued planned birth certificates to couples authorized to have a child (which had to be presented at all prenatal health visits), and provided incentives to people complying with the local family planning objectives. The work of the birth planning group was reinforced by many other social groups. Indeed, it seemed as if the whole society assumed the task of campaigning against population growth: the Communist Party, the police, the school systems, the Women's Federation, and the health professionals. Strong peer group pressure to comply with family planning goals was also mobilized.

This program was extraordinarily successful. During the 1970s the growth rate fell from 2.6 to 1.2 percent, a drop of more than 50 percent, and the expected average number of children per couple dipped below three. But as impressive as this decline is, it became apparent to the Chinese by the late 1970s that even their two-child family goal would result in continued population growth for at least another fifty years. This was deemed unacceptable because the population would grow by a huge amount in the interim. Rather than endure that, China set out to do the virtually impossible: to achieve zero population growth by the end of this century. If this audacious goal could be achieved, China's population would peak in the year 2000 at about 1.2 billion people. The plan then would be to permit a period of negative growth and to eventually stabilize the population's size at some lower level. To achieve these goals, greater individual sacrifices were required. What was necessary was the one-child family, and this objective became the new centerpiece of the country's family planning program in 1978.

The One-Child Campaign

Like most Third World nations, China's traditions favor large families, and the society had been sorely taxed just to get the average number of children below three. Many segments of Chinese society were strongly opposed to the one-child family, especially the rural population where almost 80 percent of the people live. To deal with this opposition, a system of rewards and penalties for compliance and noncompliance was installed. Parents who pledge to have only one child receive certificates which entitle them to benefits such as free medical care and tuition for their child, monthly allowances or extra food and supplies, preferential treatment in housing, and extra old-age pensions and other financial assistance. Only children when they mature will also be given favorite status in job assignments. Only children are also frequently given preference in nonroutine matters. For instance, in Canton an orthopedic group

实行计划生育是我国的一项基本国策

To encourage Chinese couples to have just one child and to combat traditional preference for male children, billboards like this one invariably show adoring parents with a single, happy daughter. (*Bruce Rosenblum/The Picture Cube*)

performs surgery on only-child polio victims first. And during the northern China drought in 1982, only children received limited vitamins and powdered milk first when there was too little for other famished children.

In contrast, those who break their pledge by having a second child not only lose these benefits but must pay back those already received. Families with more than two children commonly have 10 percent of their monthly wages confiscated, are given inadequate housing, and suffer other financial penalties. Rural dissenters face the possible loss of part of their land.

In some areas of China, another tactic used against those who are unwilling or unable to conform to the one-child family goal is forced abortion. In 1982 in Guangdong province, for

instance, it was announced by the Communist Party leader that at least 47,000 of the 100,000 pregnant women who already had one child would have to undergo abortions. Many of these women were seven, eight, and even nine months pregnant. An American anthropologist working in the province at the time noted that "it is just as hard for a Chinese woman to go through an abortion she does not want as it would be for an American woman." Some women desperately try to protect their unborn babies by moving away from their home districts for the final months of pregnancy. But like something out of an Orwellian nightmare, they are usually tracked down and forced to have the abortion.

A recent film made by the United Kingdom's BBC entitled *China's Only Child* shows how the totalitarian state accomplished this in the case of a typical factory worker (WGBH, 1984). Factory workers need permission from the factory to become pregnant, and there is usually 1 employee for every 16 women who keeps the authorities informed about "unapproved" pregnancies. In the words of one informer:

> We watch for women who start to eat less or who get morning sickness. If a woman isn't as active as she usually is—that's a sign of pregnancy. It's very difficult to escape...the attention of us family planning workers. No one has ever become pregnant without one of us finding out.

Another family planning worker relates:

> There was a pregnant woman in Wazan factory. We persuaded her to have an abortion. We took her to the hospital. That night she changed her mind and escaped. She ran off to Shanghai. The Shanghai people helped us find her...and we brought her back...to the hospital for the abortion.

A substantial number of abortions that are labeled "voluntary" are in fact forced. Many women who initially refuse abortions agree to have them only after being forced to participate in exhausting round-the-clock "study courses," where they are browbeaten and berated for their lack of patriotism.

Obstacles to the One-Child Family

By 1982, four years after the one-child family goal was established, about 15 percent of eligible couples had taken the pledge. This is a remarkable feat for a Third World country, but one that has fallen far short of that necessary to achieve China's goal of zero population growth by the year 2000. The one-child family has not been widely accepted in China for many reasons. The most important is that many Chinese couples still favor large families and are willing to suffer the penalties for having them. In 1982, for instance, nearly 25 percent of all babies were born into families that already had at least two children. Another obstacle to the one-child family is the persistent male preference in Chinese society. About half of all couples would not have their treasured son under the one-child system. The one-child goal is also threatened by the absence of an old-age pension system for 90 percent of the population. Traditionally, the elderly depend on their children to support them, and until they are convinced that the government will perform this function adequately, there will still be strong motivation to have at least two children. Also discouraging one-child compliance is the fact that the cost of the rewards for having one child noted above must currently be borne by local organizations, whose ability and even willingness to cover these costs is suspect, especially over the long term. If the one-child campaign is to succeed, the cost of these benefits will have to be absorbed by national organizations.

There is also evidence of goal incongruence or clashing policies in China. The birthrate goal has been undermined by policies allowing families direct responsibility for specific plots of farmland. This reform has helped revive the traditional notion that more children, who can help on the farm, will make the family more prosperous. Some localities have now begun to install new penalties for farmers who succumb to this temptation, such as heavy fines and confiscation of land.

Resistance to the one-child family is not the only reason China is unlikely to achieve zero population growth (ZPG) by the year 2000. Another major reason is the huge number of young people about to enter their childbearing years. The children of this extra-large group of young people will boost the growth rate even if they have few siblings, by virtue of their sheer numbers. China has also had problems with the other major strut of their family planning program, that is, restriction on the age at marriage. During the 1970s there were administrative rules prohibiting marriage before the mid-twenties for women and the late twenties for men. This policy created serious social frustration. Chinese couples sidestepped the policy by living together before marriage and by reviving the custom of gaining social recognition if not legal sanction for marriages by holding secret weddings among just family and friends. The average age of first intercourse—and the risk of pregnancy—was, therefore, substantially lower than the average age of marriage. Recognizing these sociodemographic realities, China lowered the legal age of marriage in 1981 to 20 for women and 22 for men, deciding to use birth control alone to achieve its population growth objectives. The Chinese experience with dictated late marriage clearly shows the limitations of such policies as long-term means of population control.

In sum, China is given little chance of reaching its ZPG goal by the year 2000. Indeed, since 1980 its population growth rate has actually begun to creep up. Chinese officials have responded to this situation by issuing new directives and threatening that further noncompliance would be met with additional disciplinary measures and administrative punishments. For instance, the Chinese government has escalated its control program by instituting forced sterilization and increasing the prevalence of forced abortion (*Intercom*, 1983 *b*). For the time being, both of these policies are aimed at couples with two or more children. But the government is serious about its one-child family goal, and few doubt that it is only a matter of time before these policies will be broadened to help achieve that goal also. The important question at this stage is: To what extent will local officials follow through on these policies, which are bound to be controversial among the people affected by them?

H. Yuan Tien, a China-born expert on the demography of China, believes that China's goal of attaining a ZPG population with no more than 1.2 billion by the year 2000 is now out of reach. The best it can probably hope for is 1.35 billion by that date. But even this figure will require that the country continue to zealously enforce its draconian birth control program.

Linkages to Other Problems

A general principle of social problems is that the solution to one problem often leads to or aggravates other problems. The attempt to reduce the population growth problem in China is a classic example. We have already seen how population growth policies have resulted in involuntary family size restrictions, forced sterilization and abortion, age at marriage restrictions, and other erosions of personal privacy and freedom. But there have been many other problems as well. By far the most gruesome and alarming has been the upsurge in the traditional practice of female infanticide (Haupt, 1983). Baby girl victims are typically drowned at birth or abandoned to die shortly thereafter. This practice has been indirectly encouraged by the government's policy of favoring two- and then one-child families. Girls are killed to make room for boys because of the strong traditional preference for sons. Moreover, in some localities mothers who bear daughters are persecuted and even shunned by other family members. A related problem is the use of sex-selective abortion. In this procedure, amniocentesis determines the sex of the fetus, and if it is female, an abortion is performed.

The full extent of these problems may never be known, but a study of the National Academy of Sciences concluded that more than 60,000 infant girls born during 1981 were missing from China's official population statistics in 1982 (*Population Today*, 1984*b*). Infanticide and/or nonreporting are the probable causes. In any event, infanticide and selective abortions are likely to become much more common as the Communist Party presses harder for the one-child family.

These practices of female infanticide and sex-selective abortion are heinous social problems in their own right, but they also lead to another problem, an imbalance in the ratio of males to females in a generation and in the overall population. China already has a moderate imbalance. Its sex ratio of 106 means that there are 106 males for every 100 females. Most countries have sex ratios below 100, and given the female's apparent inherited longevity advantage (see Chapter 7), a ratio substantially above 100 like China's is often a telltale sign of female infanticide (and other forms of female abuse). Since every major statement by a Chinese official on family planning contains a warning against female infanticide and sex-selective abortion, and the maltreatment of mothers who bear female children (Haupt, 1983), these officials must believe that these practices and subsequent sex ratio imbalances either are already occurring or are likely to occur in the future.

If an unbalanced sex ratio should develop in China, there would be a shortage of marriage partners for men, and a variety of other social problems might follow. These include increases in prostitution, homosexuality, and other substitutes for marital sexual relationships, and increases in crime (including rape) and other negative social factors related to unmarried men. These would, however, exert downward pressure on population growth.

Additional negative fallout from China's population growth policies is the apparent movement toward eugenics. Obviously if couples are limited to just one child, there is increased motivation for a "high quality" one. And if China is successful in getting couples to average two or fewer children, the resulting cohorts will be very small compared to older ones. Since the smaller cohorts will at some point be required to support the larger ones, it would be beneficial if the former had an unusually large proportion of super achievers. China is now flirting with the idea of a eugenics program (Intercom, 1980). The subject has been raised in the Communist Party's official newspaper. One article quoted a medical official as saying:

We have done a lot...in controlling [the quantity of the] population but very little to improve the quality of the population....Only by simultaneously grasping both quantity and quality can we reduce the birth rate and enhance the people's intelligence, physique, and life expectancy....It is necessary to promulgate the necessary laws and eliminate factors that endanger the quality of the population. Those who are suffering from congenital diseases must be dissuaded from getting married and giving birth to children.

Another article stated that the physically and mentally ill were a drain on society, and "from the point of view of genetics and eugenics, we should gradually reduce their number." Thus, in the future, a sizable proportion of Chinese may be forced to have no children at all.

China's population growth policies are also leading to massive generational problems. As noted above, Chinese birth cohorts are getting progressively smaller. If this continues, eventually their age structure will resemble an inverted pyramid. The population will be exceptionally old, and there will be relatively few producers compared to elderly dependents. The social and economic problems that this age structure imbalance will create will be truly stupendous. Given their other policies, it would not be surprising if the Communist Party were to give serious consideration to some form of massive elderly euthanasia program in the future—like something out of the science fiction movie Logan's Run.

Consider also some of the problematic social consequences of the one-child family. One is the elimination of many relatives. There would be no brothers, sisters, aunts, uncles, cousins, nieces, or nephews. Another might be the fact that every child will be an only child. If these children are unduly pampered by their child-crazy, child-starved parents, will China become a nation of spoiled brats? What kind of antisocial behavior might result from this treatment?

Conclusion

China's population story is both encouraging and discouraging. It is encouraging because despite the fact that the nation probably will not achieve its herculean objective of ZPG by the year 2000, it has been able to drastically reduce its population growth in a relatively short period. Since China represents more than 20 percent of the world's population, and 30 percent of the Third World's population, progress against massive population growth there is good news everywhere. It goes a long way to help ameliorate the problems discussed in this and the following two chapters, problems that affect the quality of life of everyone on this planet.

But at the same time China's population policies are profoundly disturbing. The country has moved from one horror to another—forced abortion, forced sterilization, female infanticide, and so on—in its no-holds-barred quest for population stabilization. One wonders whether the cures are, in fact, worse than the problem. What kind of precedents is China setting for humankind? Will global concepts of the value of human life and liberty be seriously downgraded?

China has painted itself into a population corner as a result of its past failures to stem its growth by voluntary means. It can be argued that China now has little choice but to use involuntary means, even if they are horrid. They may constitute the only realistic path open to China, given its population size, its resources, and its level of development. If so, China's predicament stands as a stark and ominous warning to other Third World nations, and to the world as a whole, of the costs of procrastination in confronting rapid population growth.

SOCIAL POLICY: RAPID POPULATION GROWTH

Strategies for Solution

Since the 1950s a debate has raged concerning how the population explosion and its negative consequences can best be stopped. On one side of the debate are the family planners; on the other, the development advocates. The family planners have always assumed that Third World people are having more children than they want, and are doing so because they do not know about or cannot obtain birth control. Their policy goals, therefore, involve teaching birth control techniques and providing birth control devices and services.

On the other hand, development advocates have always assumed that Third World people are not having more children than they want. They believe that the number of children born in Third World societies is a function of social values and institutions, and that fertility cannot be lowered without first changing the social structure. The policy goals of development advocates are aimed to do just that: to accelerate the passage of Third World nations along the development and modernization continuum. They argue that development is in fact the best birth control, and stress that many elements of development are particularly effective in lowering birthrates. These include reduction in infant and child mortality, enhancement of the status of women, expansion of basic education (especially for females), more equitable distribution of the benefits of economic growth, and an increase in the age at marriage.

Policies into Practice

Obviously, it is far easier to provide birth control knowledge and services than to change the nature of a society. The latter requires enormous social and financial resources, and efforts are hampered by suspicions of cultural imperialism. Also, cultural lag is a constant problem faced by development programs. No matter how good the program is, there are bound to be substantial delays before it takes full effect.

This disagreement between the policy experts (i.e., the family planners and the development advocates) posed a serious dilemma for policymakers in the Third World during the 1950s and 1960s. They had to decide how to deal with annual population growth rates of 3 percent and upward. Many of these politicians governed societies that were uneasy about or hostile toward family planning for ideological (often Marxist), nationalistic, or religious reasons. And well-designed national family planning programs were expensive and would strain already troubled economies. These politicians were also well aware that the benefits of family planning programs are long term in nature, and do not have the immediate political and economic visibility of building a road, school, hospital, or factory. Finally, development was a much more palatable policy option anyway since many Third World nations already had at least fledgling social and economic development programs. So throughout the 1950s and 1960s, most Third World nations concerned with population growth relied on development to bring it down rather than on family planning programs. Indeed, in 1960 only two countries— India and Pakistan—believed enough in family planning to support organized programs.

Evaluating the Evidence

Effectiveness of the Policies   During the late 1960s and early 1970s it became apparent that development was occurring much too slowly in most Third World nations, and consequently, the rapid population growth would persist far longer than had been expected. Politicians also became keenly aware that population growth was partially, and in some countries wholly, offsetting development itself. In the face of this objective policy failure, world subjective awareness of the immensity and complexity of the population growth problems rose sharply. Some pro-natalist countries tried policies and programs other than family planning to alleviate the problem, but these were generally short-lived and unsuccessful. Indonesia, for instance, tried to move people from densely populated Java to the sparsely populated outer islands. But they soon discovered that the resettlement flow was dwarfed by the number of births occurring in Java and elsewhere in the country. Thus, Indonesia joined much of the Third World in turning to family planning programs during the 1970s.

By 1978, thirty-five developing nations, containing 77 percent of the Third World's population, had official policies to decrease population growth. And another thirty countries containing 15 percent of Third World peoples supported family planning programs for reasons other than reducing population growth, such as maternal health. While sixty-six developing countries had no family planning activities, their combined populations included only 7 percent of the Third World's people (van der Tak et al., 1983). Indigenous support for family planning programs in the Third World is evidenced by the fact that developing countries now put up approximately $4 of their own resources for every $1 contributed by other nations and agencies (The Population Institute, 1984).

As noted earlier, fertility has begun to fall in the Third World. Between 1965 and 1975 there was a 13 percent decline in the birthrate of ninety-four developing nations containing 98 percent of the Third World's population. The decline varied from 10 to 40 percent in twenty-eight of these nations which altogether constitute over two-thirds of the entire world's population (Mauldin and Berelson, 1978). And these declines have since continued. Declining fertility in some Third World nations is due to development; in others, to family planning programs; and in many, to a combination of the two. As you would expect, family planning programs have had the most impact in nations that were also undergoing rapid development. South Korea, Singapore, Taiwan, and Hong Kong fall into this category (Tien, 1983; Leontief et al., 1977; and World Bank, 1983). All four have well-designed family planning programs, all have rapidly modernizing economies, and all have substantially reduced their birthrates.

However, because development has been proceeding slowly or not at all in many Third World countries (per capita gross national product in 1983 for these countries was still only 700 dollars), population experts have been anxiously awaiting the answer to the vital question: Can family planning programs succeed in countries that are not enjoying substantial economic progress? The preliminary answer to this question is encouraging. Several such nations or their subregions have begun to report substantial success.

The island of Bali, Indonesia, provides one example. Bali is an extremely poor and overpopulated island with a largely rural and illiterate population. Yet, after the government family planning program began in 1969, the birthrate dropped precipitously, falling 36 percent by 1976. Over the same period, the percentage of couples using modern contraceptives rose from virtually nil to over 50 percent.

Thailand provides another example. This rural, tradition-bound nation was able to reduce average family size from about 6.5 in the mid-1960s to about 3.9 by 1983 with the help of an increasingly influential government family planning program. The proportion of married, reproductive-aged women who were using contraception increased from only about 14 percent in 1970 to about 60 percent in 1981 (Kamnuansilpa, Chamratrithirong, and Knodel, 1982).

As we have seen, China is another example of a country whose family planning program has achieved considerable success in reducing the birthrate, despite sluggish economic development and a traditional social structure designed to generate large families. The hope is that these countries' successes can be duplicated in other countries experiencing development problems. If so, the population explosion will die out sooner than expected.

More encouraging news comes from the sixty-two nation World Fertility Survey, the largest global social science project ever undertaken. An important finding of the survey is that 50 percent of the Third World women of reproductive age interviewed desired no more children. Moreover, a large number of these women did not want either their last child or their current pregnancy. For instance, more than 40 percent of the women surveyed in Colombia and Peru felt this way (*Popline,* 1982). These new attitudes contrast sharply with those expressed in sayings such as, "I want as many as God (or Allah) will give me," attitudes which were nearly universal in many Third World nations just two or three decades ago. This shift in reproductive desires also augurs well for an accelerated end to the population explosion.

What explains this surprising popular interest in planning families and the willingness, and in some cases even eagerness, to take advantage of services when they become available? Were the family planners correct all along? Probably not. It is highly doubtful that family planning programs would have been as successful in the 1950s and 1960s as they have been since. The two programs that did exist back then—India's and Pakistan's—were not very effective. What changed dramatically between the onset of the population explosion and the 1970s was the attitude of many leaders and people. Decades of living with the population explosion and its grinding consequences had gradually convinced substantial numbers of people that the old ways were now dysfunctional.

In short, cultural lag may have simply run its course in many places as the people's subjective awareness of the population problem rose ever nearer to its objective level. Another reason for the current success is that the family planning programs have learned much from their past mistakes and have improved substantially. Earlier programs were often hampered by a misunderstanding of and/or an insensitivity to the local culture on the part of international sponsoring agencies. Today these programs are increasingly locally designed and responsive to the community's values, traditions, and needs (The Population Institute, 1984). Finally, these programs have benefited from the myriad influences of modernization which the Third World has been experiencing in varying degrees.

But despite increases in the quantity and quality of family planning programs and reductions in fertility and population growth in some Third World countries, there are surely no grounds for complacency. As noted above, the world has yet to reach the crest of the population explosion. Population growth rates in many developing countries have declined only slightly, and the already extremely high growth rates in some countries in sub-Saharan Africa and southwest Asia are actually climbing. Nearly sixty Third World countries have yet to reduce fertility to under six births per woman, and some thirty still have populations expanding at 3 percent or more annually (Population Reference Bureau, 1985*b*). Moreover, the governments of a substantial number of Third World countries have still not been convinced to dedicate adequate resources to population programs. Consequently, the actual delivery of family planning services is still woefully inadequate in most of these nations, especially in rural areas.

Even in those countries that have experienced significant progress in reducing population growth, the task remains formidable. Mexico provides a good example. In 1972 when Mexico launched its family planning program, its annual population growth rate was 3.5 percent—one of the highest in the world. During the next decade the rate fell to 2.6 percent, a dramatic improvement. But a 2.6 percent rate still means a doubling of the population in about twenty-seven years. Not only is this rate still far too rapid, but Mexico will be forced to try to reduce it in the face of an increasingly disadvantageous age structure. Over the rest of this century an enormous number of young people—the extremely large cohorts born before the family planning program took effect—will enter their child-bearing years. Thus Mexico could experience increased population growth even if it continues to have success in reducing average family size (Manautou, 1982).

Family planning practices will have to increase at a faster rate than they did during the 1970s and early 1980s if the world is to reach replacement level fertility by the middle of the next century and zero population growth by 2100. Yet even these goals would yield a stabilized world population of 15 billion people in 2100, a truly frightful figure. So much remains to be accomplished if we are to fend off an incredibly huge global population in the future.

Population Growth and the World Future In 1983, the earth's population grew by 1.7 percent, a rate with a population doubling time of forty-one years. If this rate continued indefinitely, the earth's population would increase to 10 billion by 2029, 20 billion by 2070, 40 billion by 2111, 80 billion by 2152, and so on. It is possible to continue such projections until people outweigh the earth and the solar system, events that would occur in remarkably short periods of time. Something has to give!

Zero population growth cannot be achieved immediately, in part because of the time it takes for fundamental social change to occur and in part because the world's current age structure favors massive growth even if relatively small family size is achieved. Nearly half of the Third World's population is now below age 15, and they will inevitably give birth to the largest birth cohorts in history. But the population explosion will eventually subside and zero population growth will be achieved. The issue is not whether population growth will stop; it is when and how the change will occur. Will it taper off before or after Spaceship Earth reaches its carrying capacity? Must unprecedented catastrophe be experienced, or can it be evaded? Will humankind act to control population growth, or will we succumb to the blind constraints of nature?

Experts differ in their estimates of how large the world population will actually be when it finally stops growing. As you can see from Figure 12-2, these estimates range from about 8 billion to about 11 billion people (see Bogue and Tsui, 1979; Zachariah and Vu, 1979; United Nations, 1979). But the vital question is: Can the earth accommodate such huge populations?

No one knows what the earth's ultimate carrying capacity is. One reason for this is that carrying capacity is a dynamic concept whose parameters are continually changing as discoveries are made, as new technologies are developed and implemented, and as resource management techniques are improved. Despite these estimation difficulties, the U.S. National Academy of Sciences studied the carrying capacity problem in 1969 and arrived at two estimates. One estimate was a largely theoretical one—i.e., how many people could the earth support by allocating to each person the fewest possible resources needed to merely sustain life. This estimate assumed, for example, near starvation diets and the total sacrifice of individual freedom. The academy concluded that the earth's ultimate population ceiling was about 30 billion (a figure we would reach at current growth rates prior to the year 2100).

The second estimate was much more realistic, taking into consideration humanity's needs for things other than mere sustenance. The academy concluded that a world population of 10 billion "is close to (if not above) the maximum that an intensively managed world might hope to support with some degree of comfort and individual freedom" (National Academy of Sciences, 1969). The Council on Environmental Quality and the U.S. Department of State (1980) generally concurred with this assessment in 1980, but stated that "if anything, data gathered over the past decade [the 1970s] suggest the Academy may have underestimated the extent of some problems," and hence overestimated the earth's carrying capacity.

The Worldwatch Institute and its founder Lester Brown are also highly skeptical of these carrying capacity figures (see Brown et al., 1984; Brown, 1979). Brown argues that the world's basic biological systems—croplands, grasslands, fisheries, and forests—and oil resources will not stretch far enough to ever permit a world population in the 11 billion range. He notes that these systems are already exhibiting severe strains even at our current 4.8 billion population (see Chapter 13), and that these pressures will expand into major systems failures well before the 11 billion range is reached. Thus, Brown believes that the earth's carrying capacity is substantially lower than 11 billion people, and is convinced that as societies collide with this lower figure, whatever it turns out to be, it will force them to restrict individual childbearing and to adopt policies to quickly stabilize population. If they are not successful at doing this, Brown warns that the earth's major biological systems may collapse. To avoid this, he urges that the world undertake a "concerted global effort to slam on the demographic brakes" *now* in order to bring population growth to a stop by about 2015. This would result in a world population of about 6 billion. But such an ambitious effort is unlikely to even be attempted, let alone succeed (van der Tak, Haub, and Murphy, 1979).

In any event, most estimates of peak stabilized world population either exceed or are uncomfortably close to most estimates of the earth's carrying capacity. This is probably no mere coincidence, since the carrying capacity constraints undoubtedly are prime determinants of the ultimate size of the human population. What seems to be happening is that the human race, like the aforementioned microbes in the culture dish, has decided to grow to its environmental limit (and perhaps temporarily beyond it) rather than stop well short of it. This is a pity since there are severe costs—ecological and human—in moving ever nearer to the earth's carrying capacity (see Chapter 13).

The earth's carrying capacity will continue to be a focus of debate. Some analysts will make optimistic assumptions about social and technological change and environmental resilience and conclude that the earth could support many tens of billions. Other experts will make more pessimistic assumptions about human and environmental adaptability and argue that the earth has already exceeded its sustainable carrying capacity. But in the final analysis, we have to ask ourselves what kind of a world we really want for ourselves and our descendants? Humanity may somehow find a way to survive the gross disruptions of the major biological systems that will accompany large increases in population. But we would be so much poorer, both economically and spiritually, than we could be if population did not approach the earth's carrying capacity.

Clearly, it is in the world's and especially in the high fertility Third World's best interests to do everything possible to reduce population growth as quickly as possible. As World Bank President McNamara (1979) notes: "For every decade of delay in achieving...replacement level fertility—the world's ultimate stabilized population will be about 11% greater." To accelerate the decline in population growth, Third World nations, with the help of other countries, should speed development, improve family planning services, and develop economic and social incentives to enhance motivation for smaller families. These latter incentives can include preference in housing, tax credits, health care, and a variety of other rewards for achieving small families (and penalties for achieving large ones).

Hopefully, an energetic commitment to this three-pronged approach will be sufficient to make unnecessary the kinds of involuntary birth control measures that have cropped up in China, India, and elsewhere. Such involuntary measures have included limits on family size, compulsory sterilization, and forced abortion. As lamentable as these measures are, if birth

rates are not reduced rapidly enough by voluntary means, involuntary measures may constitute a society's only remaining choice other than letting the death rate rise. In a sense, one social problem would be simply traded for another. Americans should have an interest in forestalling the necessity of this sort of forced totalitarianism.

Global Population Policy for the United States
The population problem must be brought under control not only because it undercuts the Third World's efforts to solve a broad range of environmental, resource, and economic problems but also because, as noted throughout this chapter, many important interests of the United States and other developed nations are at stake. These interests include maintaining the earth's carrying capacity and reducing the potential for social unrest, political instability, international conflict over control of land and resources, massive migration of ecological refugees, and deterioration of world prosperity and trade.

The United States already has a policy of providing international population assistance. Indeed, we are the world's leader in this activity, providing more than one-half of all governmental family planning aid. However, despite the continued objective explosion, United States population assistance has actually declined in real dollars since 1972, as it has for the industrialized world as a whole. Moreover, in the mid-1980s United States government support for international family planning had seriously eroded as the Reagan administration increasingly favored the development side of the development versus family planning argument. Judging from the contents of this chapter, this policy change is clearly imprudent. The United States should now substantially increase rather than decrease population assistance. Evidence increasingly suggests that this policy would be highly effective. Family planning programs are achieving excellent results in many countries, and the demand for United States assistance substantially exceeds the supply. At the same time the United States should encourage other developed nations to increase their contributions.

The United States must also substantially raise its assistance for overall economic development. Better nutrition and health, lowered infant mortality, and improved education and employment opportunities are powerful antidotes to population growth, and to other megaproblems as well.

Finally, more people throughout the world must be made mindful of the nature of current population problems and their political, economic, environmental, and resource consequences. In other words, we must raise worldwide subjective concern. The United States should place population issues at the forefront of the world's agenda whenever possible. By doing this, we can help create a strong and sustained international consensus which can influence and support national leaders in their longsighted efforts to solve their nations' population problems. And we will also further our own interests in reducing population problems that affect us.

SUMMARY

1 Inevitable human extinction could come about as the result of either overpopulation, environmental degradation, resource depletion, or nuclear war. These megaproblems are the major social menaces confronting humankind.

2 World population is increasing by enormous and unprecedented numbers. Population growth is an especially important problem because it contributes to all the other social megaproblems.

3 The population explosion is largely a product of the demographic transition, the period in which populations move from high to low birth and death rates.

4 Rapid population growth causes or intensifies retarded economic development, unemployment, urban growth, and international migration. Population policies which lower birthrates of Third World nations help diminish these problems as well.

5 China already contains more than one-fifth of the world's population and is still growing rapidly, despite recent impressive reductions in its birthrate brought about by vigorous and, in part, draconian population policies. The nation's population predicament stands as an ominous warning to the world of the costs of procrastination in confronting rapid population growth.

6 Two policies have evolved concerning how to stop rapid population growth in the Third World: one emphasizing family planning and the other, economic development. Each policy has been successful in some countries, but both are most successful when they are applied together.

CHAPTER 13

Resource Depletion and Environmental Degradation

INTRODUCTION

One million years ago the earth was characterized by a pervasive wilderness which we may call "nature." In the midst of this wild nature stood small enclaves of human habitation. Whether caves with artificial fire to keep men warm, or later cities with dwellings and artificial fields of cultivation, these enclaves were distinctly unnatural. In the succeeding millennia, the area of untouched nature surrounding artificial human enclaves progressively declined, although for centuries the trend remained invisible.

Even 300 years ago in France or England, the great cities of man were isolated by hectares of wilderness in which untamed beasts roamed, as they had for thousands of years before. And yet the expansion of man continued inexorably.

One hundred years ago, in the last days of the great European explorers, nature had so radically diminished that it was a novelty: it is for this reason that African explorations captured the imagination of nineteenth-century man. To enter a truly natural world was exotic, beyond the experience of most mankind, who lived from birth to death in entirely man-made circumstances.

In the twentieth century the balance has shifted so far that for all practical purposes one may say that nature has disappeared.... Today we are surrounded by man and his creations. Man is inescapable, everywhere on the globe, and nature is a fantasy, a dream of the past, long gone.

—Michael Crichton (1980)

Just as the population explosion could not be fully appreciated without placing it in historical perspective, so too the phenomenal changes in the earth's character escape us if we do not look to what the earth was like in the past. Crichton's passage above helps us to do that, showing us that the earth has been radically transformed by humanity from its natural state to an increasingly human-made one within just the past century or two, a period representing only the blink of an eye in the course of human history. We really have no clear idea what the objective consequences of this continuing transformation will be, but it is a matter that now gravely concerns scientists and laypersons alike. For there is a suspicion—one that is backed up by virtually every major world-model study—that these changes are fundamentally incompatible with the earth's capacity to support life. Alarming trends abound, including a steady loss of croplands, fisheries, forests, animal and plant species, and energy and mineral reserves, as well as increasing pollution of our water and atmosphere. In short, the earth is now experiencing a progressive depletion of its resources and degradation of its environment—two of the megaproblems introduced in the previous chapter.

WORLD HUNGER

Objective and Subjective Dimensions

Throughout this book, you have confronted a vast array of actual (and potential) social problems. Some of you may have wondered which of the existing problems is the most serious; that is, which has the greatest objective dimension? One possible answer to that question is world hunger. World hunger is not a potential problem like all-out nuclear war. It is a reality, and it has been humanity's overriding problem throughout history. Today, hunger is the world's No. 1 health problem (Berg, 1973) and the chief cause of premature death. Indeed, it has been noted that hunger "has accounted for

more deaths and suffering than all epidemics, wars, and natural disasters combined. During the last five years alone, more people have died as a consequence of hunger than from all the wars, revolutions, and murders of the past 150 years" (Erhard, 1982:4).

Because Third World nations do not have good statistics on the number of undernourished people, no one knows the exact number of hungry persons in the world today. But according to the Food and Agriculture Organization (FAO) of the United Nations, which probably has the best estimates, about half the world's population has an inadequate diet, including about 700 million seriously undernourished persons (*Population Today*, 1984c). The World Bank calculates that there are as many as 900 million seriously undernourished persons (U.S. Department of Agriculture, 1979), and still other experts (e.g., Peccei, 1977) say that even these fantastic numbers may substantially underestimate the objective dimension of this problem. The number of hungry people in the world has increased greatly in recent years, and the figure will continue to mount due in large part to rapid population growth. Hunger is a serious problem in the United States (see Chapter 8) and in many other developed countries, but it is extremely prevalent in the Third World, upon which this discussion is focused.

The term *undernutrition* is used here to refer to diets that lack either sufficient quantity (calories) or quality (nutrients). The most extreme form of population undernutrition is famine, a temporary regional shortage of food leading to starvation. Famine has been no stranger in recent decades. It has claimed the lives of hundreds of thousands of people in many countries. While this chapter was being written, almost 150 million people in twenty-four African countries faced starvation due to several consecutive years of drought.

The world often mobilizes to help check famines because famine generally has a high subjective profile. The gaunt faces of the starving are nightmarishly photogenic, and the intrinsic drama of famine rivets public attention both at the national and international level. Today, famine clenches its bony fist hardest in destitute and isolated areas, where it is able to elude early detection by national and international agencies.

In some ways, the high-profile horror of famine diverts attention from the more basic and widespread problem of chronic undernutrition. This global problem of chronic undernutrition has a low subjective dimension among persons in the developed world. Pervasive and ongoing, it is a low visibility crisis that does not make dramatic news copy. But its toll in human lives is many times that of occasional famines (Eckholm and Record, 1976).

Chronic undernutrition strikes young children hardest, especially in the Third World where about 25 percent of the children are affected. It slowly siphons off their energy, subtly retards their growth, and insidiously lowers their resistance to disease (Grant, 1982). Undernutrition is both a cause and a consequence of disease. That is, morbidity and mortality rates from disease are much higher among undernourished children—a malnourished child who contracts measles, for instance, is 400 times more likely to die than a well-nourished child—and the reduced food intake and utilization associated with disease lead to a worsening of the child's nutritional status and even greater susceptibility to disease. Thus, the undernutrition/disease relationship is a vicious cycle.

Undernutrition is a consummate killer of children. Each *day* 42,000 infants and children die from malnutrition and related illnesses. This amounts to more than 15 million young lives per year—about 30 percent of all world deaths—a number equal to the entire population of children under age 5 in the United States! Another way to grasp the towering objective dimension of this situation is to compare it to the death tolls at Hiroshima and Nagasaki. The nuclear bombs dropped on those cities killed an esti-

mated 105,000 people and injured another 94,000. If there were a Hiroshima and Nagasaki every three days, incinerating and permanently disabling like numbers of children, the world would be up in arms (because of the dramatic nature of these events and our subjective appreciation of the horrors of nuclear weapons). But this is the toll that world hunger is silently taking. In fact the toll is even higher: about 126,000 deaths and 126,000 permanent injuries (such as blindness and deafness) every three days. The world is experiencing a hunger holocaust day in and day out that dwarfs all others in history, including the Nazi genocide against Jews and other groups. Yet this unimaginable horror goes virtually unnoticed by most Americans.

This book is full of daunting statistics, and sometimes we have a difficult time comprehending the enormity of huge numbers and the ineffable pain and suffering of the many victims (and their families) who make them up. No statistic could begin to express what it is to see even one child die from undernutrition, let alone more than 15 million a year. James Grant (1982) gives us a heartrending glimpse of these tragedies in this passage from the United Nations Children's Fund (UNICEF) Annual Report:

> To see a mother sitting hour after anxious hour leaning her child's body against her own; to see the child's head turn on limbs which are unnaturally still, stiller than in sleep; to want to stop even that small movement because it is so obvious that there is so little energy left inside the child's life; to see the living pink at the roof of the child's mouth in shocking contrast to the already dead-looking greyness of the skin, the colours of its life and death; to see the uncomprehending panic in eyes which are still the clear and lucid eyes of a child; and then to know, in one endless moment, that life has gone.

The tragedy of child starvation is sometimes compounded by responses to it. One such re-

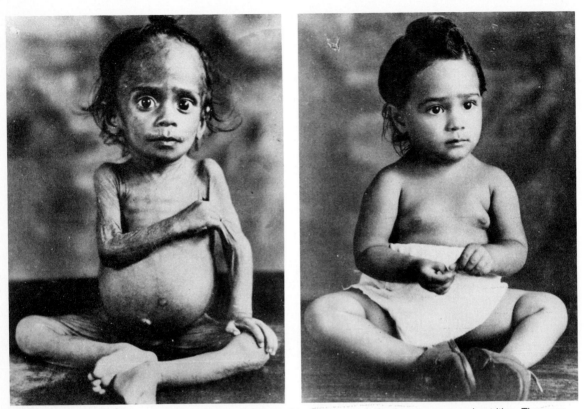

Photos of a 2-year-old girl from Venezuela before (left) and after (right) she received proper care and nutrition. There are tens of millions of hungry children in the Third World who would benefit from such treatment, but most never receive it. (*WHO photos, issued by FAO*)

action among Rwandan refugees was a mass suicide of adults, most of them aged and infirm, so that more food could be given to hungry children.

As noted above, chronic undernutrition, though much more serious than famine, has a much lower subjective profile among persons in the developed countries. This is particularly true of hunger among children. One reason for this is that only about 2 percent of child undernutrition is apparent to the eye. Indeed, so invisible is the problem that almost 60 percent of the mothers in one recent study thought their undernourished children were growing normally and developing well. Because of this invisibility, the United Nations is now urging

the world to jettison its skin and bones image of the starving child and to replace it with a better (subjective) understanding of what child undernutrition really means (Grant, 1982).

Child death rates in the Third World were reduced by half between the end of World War II and the beginning of the 1970s. However, in recent years that progress has slowed down in the Third World as a whole, and the situation is now actually deteriorating for children in many parts of Africa and in the poorest shantytowns of Asia and Latin America. If present trends continue, the proportion of children without adequate food will remain about the same between now and the end of this century. But because of inevitable population growth, the

BOX 13-1

COUPLE CHANGES LIFESTYLE TO HELP HAITIAN CHILDREN

How is it possible for the world and, in particular, relatively affluent Americans to go about their lives spending money on luxuries and frivolous things while that same money could be used to halt the agonizing deaths of millions of the world's children each year? Part of the explanation comes from the principle of *bystander apathy,* a sociological concept that helps us understand why human beings do not always come to the aid of others even in life-threatening situations. The most publicized example of bystander apathy is the case of Kitty Genovese, who was murdered over a half-hour period outside her home in New York City while thirty-eight neighbors watched. Not only did these neighbors fail to come to her aid, but none even bothered to call the police.

Common sense would suggest that Kitty Genovese's neighbors were callous and unfeeling, but sociological research has shown that these situations are far more complicated than that. Two factors are commonly involved. First, emergencies are often ambiguous, and people are reluctant to act until they have interpreted them. Second, to interpret the situation, individuals look for cues from others. If others do not act concerned, then the individual will not define the situation as an emergency. Moreover, each person in the group is hesitant to act because of fears of overreacting. The result of all this is that bystanders collectively mislead one another. Just as a crowd can panic when one individual defines a situation as dangerous, a crowd can also maintain a collective unconcern when no one makes such a definition. Only when one person takes the responsibility to do something do others do the same. But the more people there are, the less likely it is that any single person will assume responsibility. The moral responsibility to act is escapable at the individual level because it is diffused among the group. The tendency, therefore, is to wait for someone else to take the initiative (Robertson, 1981).

The situation of millions of hungry children perishing while relatively affluent Americans spend potentially life-saving money on many unnecessary things is in part a macro example of bystander apathy. If most of us were confronted on a one-to-one basis with a starving child, we would probably give up our luxuries and even some supposed necessities to keep that child alive. But we as a society, and most of us as individuals, have adopted a collective unconcern about hunger-related child mortality, and have evaded the moral responsibilities to halt it. As members of a vast crowd (i.e., the United States population), most of us either ignore the problem, make a small charitable financial contribution, or wait for someone else (perhaps the government) to take the initiative. We are, for the most part, apathetic bystanders.

But William Zuspan is no apathetic bystander. The Drexel University engineering professor and his wife shop for clothing at Goodwill Industries, sold their 100,000 dollar farm to move into a mobile home, and sold their two late-model cars. They plan to unload their television set, sell their dishwasher, and rid themselves of every other luxury that most middle-class Americans accept as a matter of course. The Zuspans are actively diminishing their lifestyle because they believe that by stripping their life to its necessities, they can save precious dollars that can be funneled into Haiti to keep alive children who otherwise would die.

"It became impossible for us to reconcile our affluent lifestyle with the fact that we knew that 30 cents a day would keep one Haitian child from starving to death. After we returned from a visit to Haiti, we simply realized, together, that there was no honest way to face our own affluence knowing what we did about these poor children," Zuspan said.

"This is no personal crusade or anything," he continued. "We are doing it solely because we were psychologically devastated by what we saw there. We were just overwhelmed by the grim fact that [real children would die] unless we were able to [send money]. Knowing this, we just couldn't do the usual thing—like putting money into an IRA.

"We're not heroes; this is just a private decision by the both of us to redirect our previous affluence. It may not be the right course for anyone else," Zuspan said. "But we just keep asking ourselves, 'Do we really need this?' And the answer is usually no."

Source: Adapted from Pothier (1983).

absolute number of children affected will increase by 30 percent (Grant, 1982).

Undernutrition injures and kills proportionately more females than males because of the ingrained cultural tradition of male preference in many Third World countries. In practical terms, this means that in food-short areas females are fed last. In a classic example of false consciousness (i.e, the oppressed believing in the legitimacy of an oppressive system), women deliberately deprive themselves and their daughters because they believe that the earning members of the group (adult males and male children, who are potential earners) are more valuable than those who do domestic work and rear children, which they consider to be devoid of economic value. This type of eating hierarchy is one of the major ways in which female infanticide operates in the Third World.

Third World women are also more often the victims of hunger because of other features of their lives. For millions of these women, teenage marriage is the beginning of several decades of uninterrupted pregnancy and lactation from which they never fully recuperate. During these taxing decades, moreover, they must perform much of the agricultural work and a variety of other strenuous tasks. The Third World is replete with women in their thirties with the haggard, wizened faces and bodies of the elderly. They are victims of maternal depletion syndrome. These women are undernourished, often anemic, and generally debilitated from excessive reproduction. They are increasingly vulnerable to death during childbirth or from the Third World's cavalcade of diseases, and their babies swell the infant mortality statistics discussed above (Eckholm and Newland, 1977).

Causes of World Hunger

Early explanations for world hunger were based on the idea that there were too few resources available, particularly arable land, with which to feed the entire world's population. But this simple explanation failed to hold up under scientific

scrutiny. Presently, the world has more than enough food to feed every individual in it. If the world's food supply were evenly divided, each person would receive more than the minimum number of nutrients and calories—and this has been true for at least several decades. So while population size and such resource factors as the amount of land play a role in world hunger, there are many other crucial determinants. These include miracle seeds, fertilizer, pesticide, water "inputs," modern farming machinery and techniques, the cost of oil, the availability of credit, the market price for products, the cost of importing food compared to export profits, patterns of land ownership, government investment in agriculture, the amount and nature of foreign aid, and population distribution (Murphy, 1983). Thus, the explanation for world hunger is anything but simple.

World hunger is inextricably bound up with several social problems discussed elsewhere in this book. For example, many of its causes are manifestations of the Third World's gripping poverty. The poor are the ones who are undernourished; the nonpoor can buy the necessary food. Hunger is often a problem of distribution and social power. In many nations where hunger is prevalent, up to half the cultivated land is devoted to crops which are exported to those who can afford them, rather than to foodstuffs for the country's hungry. In fact, thirty-six out of the forty poorest and hungriest nations export food to the United States. Thus, undernutrition is rooted in the political and economic institutions that engender economic deprivation, and its existence is testimony to the failure of these institutions to satisfy basic human needs.

Paradoxically, Third World governments often have policies which tend to decrease the amount of food produced for their people. For instance, to placate their urban population which demands subsidized food, many nations maintain food policies that retard domestic food production. One tactic is to manipulate markets so that farmers receive artificially low prices for their products. This discourages them from producing more food, although the potential is there. In other cases, some Third World nations overvalue their currency to make imported food cheaper. But this drives down the prices their own farmers get, and devitalizes domestic agriculture. Another common policy is to impose taxes, embargoes, and quotas on exports. While this tends to minimize the exportation of food, it too depresses farm prices and discourages production. Thus, neither the causes of nor the solutions to world hunger are simple, or can they be separated from social institutions.

Future Prospects

Hunger in the past and present has been largely a social phenomenon, caused by economics, politics, and social institutions rather than by biological limits to food production. There are biological limits to food production; we just have not reached them yet, at least not at the global level. But the world is moving ever closer to those limits. Two recent studies confirm this view. One study by Bernard Gilland (1983) assessed the capacity of the earth and concluded that the world will reach its food production limits just one generation from now, when the population will be about 7.5 billion.

The second and more important study was conducted by the FAO and the United Nations Fund for Population Activities (UNFPA) between 1973 and 1983. It is the most thorough and most scientifically sound effort yet undertaken to determine just how much food Third World lands are capable of producing and how many people they can feed at different technological levels of farming (Harrison, 1983). The results of this ten-year study show that by the year 2000 at least sixty-five countries, with a combined population exceeding 1 billion, will be unable to feed their people with low-technology farming methods (i.e., no fertilizer or chemicals, traditional seed varieties and cropping patterns, etc.). Between them, they

would have a population of 441 million in excess of their domestic food supply. By adopting intermediate-technology methods, thirty-six countries would still be unable to feed their people. Even with the most advanced farming methods, nineteen countries would remain unable to feed their year-2000 populations.

Bad as this scenario is, world population will not stop growing in the year 2000, the end point of the FAO/UNFPA study. It will probably double again before stabilizing toward the end of the next century, and the bulk of this growth will occur in those places already hard pressed to feed their populations. So the overall prospect for world hunger during the next century is ominous. It is conceivable that further breakthroughs in agricultural technology, such as biological nitrogen fixation by cereals, may increase crop yields. But such technological progress, including the Green Revolution (an effort to expand food production in the 1960s and 1970s based on new high-yield seeds), has come in the past with drawbacks such as the need for increasingly expensive energy-intensive products (e.g., tractors, fertilizer, herbicides, and pesticides) as well as environmental pollution and degradation. (These drawbacks are examples of social problem linkages.)

Many experts doubt that such new technology can be implemented rapidly and extensively enough to keep food supplies ahead of population growth. Moreover, optimistic predictions that the world's food supply can be expanded enormously in the future often point to the massive land areas that could be put into production. But the fact is most of this land is not now in production for a good reason; i.e., it is relatively poor land for agriculture. Most well-watered arable land is already under cultivation. The potentially tillable land remaining requires the special care of tropical soils or expensive and scarce energy and water inputs. In any event, the challenge facing new technology is a truly audacious one, and we cannot rely on it alone to solve the world hunger problem. Notes Norman Borlaug, winner of the Nobel

Peace Prize for his work in developing the Green Revolution:

> As the world population is expected to double by early in the 21st century, that means that within the next half century world food production must be increased by at least as much as was achieved during the 12,000-year period from the beginning of agriculture up to [the present]—just to maintain per capita food production at the inadequate [present] level (*Intercom*, 1981).

It should also be noted that the results of the FAO/UNFPA study, as disturbing as they are, substantially underestimate the future gap between population and land resources in the Third World for many reasons. For instance, the study is full of optimistic assumptions. One is that all cultivatable land will be used for growing staple food crops. The study ignores the fact that with the growth of population and the increase in scope and variety of economic activities, competition for this land will become increasingly keen. Land for residential, industrial, commercial, and recreational uses, mining and mineral extraction, transportation, and the preservation of natural habitats must be subtracted from the total amount of land before that available to agriculture and pasture can be calculated. Beyond this, the study makes no allowance for the land that must be used to grow firewood, fibers, tea, coffee, or even green vegetables. It also used the minimum recommended food intake, and very optimistically assumes that food supplies will be evenly distributed.

But perhaps most important, the study fails to incorporate the fact that the biological systems that support food production are decaying even now under the strain of the present world population, and that this deterioration is likely to accelerate in the future due to population growth.

Deterioration of the Earth's Food Producing Systems

Soil The most serious deterioration problem is the loss of productive soil due to erosion,

desertification, deforestation, and other causes. The equation of life is a simple one: Topsoil gained must exceed topsoil lost over the long run. When the amount of topsoil lost due to erosion is greater than that created through natural processes, the thin layer of life-sustaining topsoil diminishes, leading to a decline in inherent agricultural productivity and, hence, to a decline in the earth's human carrying capacity. This is exactly what is happening now. Due to the enormous population growth that has occurred during the last century and to rising affluence (and thus increased demand for food) in many parts of the world, the earth's soils have been put under more pressure than they can sustain. The topsoil over much of the earth's surface is only inches deep, and the intensive cultivation and the extension of cultivation to marginal lands resulting from the increased food demand have relentlessly accelerated soil erosion.

Soil erosion has attained colossal proportions. Each year nearly 23 billion tons of topsoil is stripped from the world's croplands in excess of new topsoil formation (Brown et al., 1984). The United States is one of the big losers. Indeed, the U.S. Department of Agriculture found that the inherent productivity of 34 percent of this nation's cropland is now withering due to the excessive loss of topsoil (van der Tak, 1981).

Desertification, the most serious form of soil erosion, is due to the destruction of vegetation caused by overcultivation, overgrazing, and the cutting and burning of trees. The United Nations reports that more than 20 percent of the world's land surface, nearly 20 million square miles, is threatened by desertification (Rosenthal, 1984). Particularly at risk are the world's arid and semiarid lands. A substantial fraction of United States land falls into this category.

But desertification is more than just a threat. All over the world desertlike areas are being created, and existing deserts are swallowing up adjacent fertile land. Desertification is most

This extensive soil erosion and gully formation is an example of the deterioration of the earth's food-producing system that is occurring throughout much of the world. (*USDA—Soil Conservation Service*)

serious in Africa. The Sahara is steadily moving southward at a rate of 4 miles per year, absorbing the nations in its path and threatening the people of these nations with greater depletion of already scarce resources. According to the U.S. Agency for International Development (1972), the Sahara gobbled up 650,000 square kilometers of productive land along its southern fringe over just the fifty years prior to 1972, and since then the pace of desertification has quickened. In addition, each year some 14 million acres of potentially productive grasslands is destroyed by livestock. Already the continent is 20 percent desert, but experts believe that the process of desertification could consume another 25 percent of Africa in just fifty years if present patterns of land use persist (Hoyle, 1984).

Desertification is also a major problem in the southwestern United States. One of the most dramatic examples of desertification is the Navaho Indian Reservation. The Navaho Indians were encouraged to become sheep farmers after subjugation, but their flocks multiplied without proper range management. In one area, for instance, they were trying to raise 140,000 sheep instead of the 16,000 that could safely be supported. This overgrazing turned lush meadows into a desolate terrain, with shifting sands and deep gullies. Thus, desertification can be added to the long list of social problems plaguing the American Indian (Eckholm and Brown, 1977).

Deforestation is another major threat to the earth's soil, particularly in tropical regions. In Central America, for instance, 4.4 million acres of forest is destroyed each year. Vast tracts are converted to pasture land and to single-crop agriculture under the control of huge plantations, many of which are owned by United States corporations. As impoverished peasants are forced to give up their traditional land to these plantations, they retreat into forested mountains, clearing away trees to make room for subsistence farming. The effect of this process on the environment is catastrophic. Massive soil erosion commences as soon as the mountainsides are denuded. And the fertility of the soil rapidly diminishes because its nutrients are not replenished by trees, and because the land can no longer retain water. So the peasants move higher and higher into the mountains, wreaking the same ecological havoc wherever they go (Golden, 1983).

Other serious problems affecting the food-producing ability of the earth's soil include an increase in salinity and alkalinity from irrigation; the rapid depeletion of almost irreplaceable groundwater needed for irrigation; the abuse of pesticides which leads to the contamination of soils and foods, the elimination of the natural predators of pests, damage to nonpest species, and the rise of pesticide-resistant pest strains; the increased use of dung and crop residues for fuel rather than fertilizer in impoverished areas; and the continuous growing of one crop (monoculture), which increases vulnerability to pests and disease and lowers the genetic diversity necessary to improve future plant varieties (Murphy, 1983).

The deterioration of the earth's soil is a true megaproblem in its own right. Several studies have concluded that if the factors just described continue, the world will lose one-third of its currently arable land by the end of this century (Murphy, 1983). Indeed, if erosion continues to exceed new soil formation by 23 billion tons per year, the earth's approximately 3.5 billion tons of food-producible topsoil will disappear in about 150 years, only a few decades after the exhaustion of ultimately recoverable oil.

However, this survival-threatening loss of topsoil has an exceedingly low subjective dimension in the United States. It is a quiet, humanmade crisis, one that is unfolding relatively slowly in comparison to earthquakes, volcanic eruptions, and other natural disasters. Although governments everywhere have responded to the growing scarcity of oil, they have done little to deal with soil depletion and its consequences. Differing levels of visibility and information help account for the contrasting awareness of oil and soil depletion. The oil crisis gained widespread attention because oil is widely traded, and most nations import it. The world keeps its fingers on oil's pulse, making regular estimates of reserves and constantly adjusting these to reflect production and new discoveries. Unfortunately, world soil reserves are not monitored in this way. Consequently, losses become apparent only when the topsoil has largely vanished and food shortages and famine have developed (Brown et al., 1984). Also, no one has ever had to wait in a topsoil line. Thus, no social problem in this book probably has a greater gap between its objective and subjective dimensions than the loss of the earth's productive soil. If this gap does not dissipate soon, many more countries (and eventually the world) will pass the limits of their land's carrying capacity, and environmental degradation will accelerate, lowering that capacity further still.

Fisheries   Human pressure on the world's basic biological systems can be seen most clearly in ocean fisheries. The opening passage of this chapter discusses the fact that for almost all of their existence on the earth, human communities were a dabbling of specks in the overwhelming vastness of nature. The idea that humankind could ever catch and consume virtually all the fish in the oceans would have been a preposterous notion during most of that time. The fact that this is now a real possibility should be a clear warning to us that the systems that have sustained human life on the earth for so long have been seriously tampered with.

As noted in the previous chapter, the population explosion began to intensify after World War II, and to satisfy the protein needs of burgeoning populations, the fish catch increased along with it. The world catch shot up from 22 million tons in 1950 to 70 million tons in

1970. In the process the fish catch per capita more than doubled (Table 13-1). Then the bottom dropped out. The population explosion kept on going—in fact, kept mounting in severity—but the world fish catch leveled off, and the per capita catch has declined since 1970 by about 13 percent (Table 13-1). Many of the major traditional fisheries are now in serious decline. Production from the leading fisheries in the North Atlantic, for instance, peaked around 1970 and has fallen substantially since then. And even some of the more recently exploited fisheries, like those in the Gulf of Thailand, have already seen their total production peak and then drop off (Brown et al., 1984).

One dramatic example of the real limits to the world's fisheries is provided by the Peruvian anchovy fishery. In 1970 the FAO calculated that the highest yield this fishery could sustain was 9.5 million tons annually. But the Peruvian government disregarded this advisory and permitted a catch of about 13 million tons annually in the early 1970s. Predictably, the fishery collapsed. The catch fell to less than 3 million tons per year, and remained at that level. This is the kind of economic and ecological catastrophe that overfishing can produce (Brown et al., 1984; Eckholm, 1976).

But overfishing is not the only reason why harvests of traditional fisheries have slackened off and may not even be sustainable at current levels. Other problems include urban and industrial development that destroys highly productive coastal wetlands and reef areas; chemical and radioactive pollutants washed from the land, discharged directly into the ocean, or deposited from the atmosphere; the choking of rivers and coastal waters with silt or mud from erosion (siltation); and uncontrolled exploitation of ocean resources.

Notice the links between problems and their possible solutions in the above list. A sizable fraction of the chemical pollutants that wash from the land come with soil erosion. Erosion is a major way by which chemicals like pesticides,

herbicides, and fertilizers reach rivers, lakes, and oceans. Pesticides and herbicides contaminate or kill fish, either outright or by affecting elements in their food chain. Fertilizers cause algae to grow, leading to a decline in fish and other aquatic organisms. Erosion is also the main cause of siltation, especially where deforestation is practiced. Once the mountainsides are denuded, the land can no longer hold water. Floodwaters surge off the mountains in the rainy season, carrying the soil and other debris into the rivers, lakes, and coastal waters. As this material is washed into coastal waters, the particles reduce the sea's transparency, blotting out sunlight and stifling coral reefs and valuable coastal sea grasses on which much marine life depends. Erosion and deforestation come about in many places due to efforts to wrest more food from the land to ease poverty and hunger. These efforts not only fail in the long run but reduce the fish catch as well. A policy aimed at minimizing soil degradation, therefore, would also improve the fish catch.

The other threats to the fish catch have similar links. One "solution" to the problem of pollutant disposal—dumping it in the oceans—contaminates and kills fish and thus contributes to the world food problem. One solution to energy and mineral scarcities—deep-sea mining and offshore oil production—is similarly counterproductive. For example, about 7 percent of the total offshore oil production spills into the oceans because of such mishaps as blowouts, platform fires, and other accidents, and thus exacerbates the pollution problem.

Aquaculture—the harvesting of fish and other types of aquatic protein under commercially controlled conditions—may eventually become an important future source of protein. But it has never been seriously proposed as a possible remedy for the world's food problems. One drawback is that fish must be fed cereals and other nutrients, and are thus in direct competition with humans for scarce food. This also makes aquaculture products costly, and experts doubt that they will ever be affordable to many of the world's poor.

In sum, production from the world's fisheries cannot be counted on to expand along with population in the future. Like the other major biological support systems—croplands, grasslands, and forests—the fisheries are already under tremendous pressure. They may not be able to even sustain present catch levels, let alone increase their yield.

Implications for the United States

If you as an American citizen are not sufficiently moved to consider effective solutions to world hunger by the haunting reality of stunted and starving children, perhaps you will be more personally concerned by the degradation of the earth's food-producing ability and by the hazards of world-destabilizing revolutions. The potential for political and social unrest where there is widespread hunger and starvation is well known. History is littered with peasant revolts and international conflicts due entirely or in part to inequitable land ownership patterns and to differential access to food, along with the political and economic repression that keeps such systems intact. The revolutions in Mexico, Russia, China, and Cuba are good examples, as are many of the revolts against colonial powers. More recently, hunger has played a role in causing widespread violence in Chile, Iran, Nicaragua, Guatemala, and El Salvador. Rioting erupted in Egypt in 1977 after prices for bread and other basics were boosted, and in Poland in 1980 due in part to meat prices and shortages.

If people in a semisubjugated country like Poland can move to the brink of revolution because of meat shortages, consider what mammoth social disruptions may confront the world as millions, or perhaps billions, of Third World poor become better informed subjectively, and thus angry and organized. From a humanitarian standpoint, hunger is a blight on the world's conscience that should be eradicated. But it is certainly in our national security interests as well to do as much as we can to solve the problem of world hunger.

However, as world hunger grows, the demand for United States–grown food will certainly grow. The United States will be called upon to increase food exports, and to raise food aid to poor countries. But just like the rest of the world, the United States has the problem of protecting its agricultural resource base. Overproduction, erosion, desertification, loss of soil fertility, and conversion to nonagricultural uses are just some of the menaces confronting our croplands now. The dilemma is that if the United States attempts to solve or ameliorate world hunger by expanding food production, we may further degrade our agricultural resources. Similarly, if food production capacity declines elsewhere in the world, the temptation is always great to expand our food exports to help our balance of payments, but this would be at the expense of our—and the world's—long-term production ability.

The United States also has an important stake in the productivity of the world's fisheries. We cannot afford the collapse of one of our major sources of protein for humans and domestic animals. And we would also be adversely affected by the conversion (to dry land) and pollution of coastal wetlands both in the United States and elsewhere. These wetlands are a resource base for fisheries and wildlife, and they assimilate waste, cleanse water, and buffer coasts from destructive storms.

The United States should expand its present efforts to help Third World nations increase their food output. But these nations must also do their part. They must examine their policies that directly or indirectly discourage long-term farming and fishing productivity. The issue of land ownership is of paramount importance and must be addressed effectively. As recently proved once again, this time by China, farmers work harder and produce more for everyone when they can fully profit from the benefits of their labor on land they control. Economic development is also crucial because it helps reduce poverty, which is often the major cause of hunger. Finally, and perhaps most important, Third World nations must reduce their population growth to buy time for agricultural reform and for all the other changes to occur. Slower population growth will also reduce pressure on the land from competing purposes (e.g., housing, mineral extraction, lumbering, etc.) (Murphy, 1983). And family planning programs with their associated general health services have a crucial part to play in improving the health of mothers and children and reducing the rate of infant mortality. Much of this infant mortality is due to undernutrition, and the sooner these programs are in the field, the sooner the Third World's child holocaust will be checked (*Popline*, 1984).

WATER SHORTAGES

Objective and Subjective Dimensions

Water, one of the basic building blocks of life, is a resource that most Americans take for granted. Consequently, there is also little awareness of or concern about water shortages, at least at the national or world level. This low subjective dimension stands in marked contrast to the towering objective dimension of this problem, both in the United States and globally. Water shortages are so severe that they have been labeled by a national news magazine as the resource crisis of the 1980s, a comparison to the energy crisis of the 1970s. One key difference between these two crises, however, is that, unlike oil, water is absolutely essential to human survival.

The amount of water on the earth has been roughly stable for millions of years. It is used and then recycled again and again. Some of the water molecules in your body (which is 70 percent water) almost certainly have been part of various bodies of water—from under-

ground aquifers to oceans—at one time or another. Nature cleanses water for reuse by filtering it underground or by evaporating it into the atmosphere and bringing it back through precipitation. The problem with this system, however, is that at any given time less than 3 percent of the world's water is kept as fresh water, and only 1 percent is drinkable (LaDuke and Brown, 1983). Thus, fresh, usable water is a finite resource, and the quantity available for human use is limited. It is quite possible for humanity to exhaust supplies of usable water faster than nature can replenish them. Indeed, many societies have done this in the past and have paid the inevitable penalty: extinction. Great ancient civilizations—in Mesopotamia, Persia, Egypt, India, China, Southeast Asia, and Latin America—have vanished, due in large part to the exhaustion of water resources.

Today, the world is in the process of repeating that scenario, but on a global scale. Many societies are depleting the earth's usable water by tapping available above-ground and underground supplies at rates far faster than nature is able to replace. Only about one-fifth of the world's population presently has access to processed drinking water, and in many places it is available for only a few hours a day. But restricted and even unrestricted consumption of drinking water is only a small part of the problem. Water is in short supply because it is a component of many things. It takes 100 gallons of water to grow a single orange, 4000 gallons to produce a pound of beef, about 40,000 gallons to produce a ton of steel or to refine a ton of oil, 250,000 gallons to grow a ton of wheat, and 1 million gallons to generate a single megawatt of electrical power. In the United States, industry uses about twice as much water as homes consume; agriculture (irrigation), five times as much; and energy production, six times as much. Thus, cutting down on home consumption of water would hardly make a dent in the shortage problem.

Because water is so basic to animal and plant life, and to human activities, water shortages lead to shortages elsewhere. Water shortages are, for instance, a major cause of the world food problem, and a serious impediment to industrial development in the Third World. And energy problems are, in part, water problems. For instance, prodigious amounts of water are needed to move coal in slurry pipelines, to produce synthetic fuels from coal and shale, and to cool both fossil and nuclear power plants. Thus, solutions to water shortages would help solve these other problems as well.

Unfortunately, such solutions are not in sight, and the objective dimension of the water shortage problems will become ever more serious in the future. Worldwide consumption is expected to increase fivefold by the year 2000 due to population growth, increased agricultural production, and industrialization. Much of the increased demand for water will occur in the Third World countries of Africa, south Asia, the Middle East, and Latin America, which are already suffering severe water shortages and droughts. During this period, some of these nations will come close to using their maximum retrievable water supply, and the cost of developing their last water resources will become extremely expensive. Moreover, less usable water will be collected and recycled because of the extensive loss of their forests to agricultural use and fuelwood (Council on Environmental Quality and the U.S. Department of State, 1980).

Water Shortages in the United States

The United States also has serious water shortage problems. One is the continued rapid depletion of precious subsurface water supplies. In the last three decades, withdrawals from these supplies have tripled, outstripping nature's capacity to refill the natural underground reservoirs of water (aquifers) in some areas. The most dramatic example is the Ogallala Aquifer which lies beneath the eight states of Kansas,

Nebraska, South Dakota, Colorado, Wyoming, Oklahoma, New Mexico, and Texas. In 1980 these states took three times as much water from this aquifer as they did in 1950. In some places, like western Kansas, the Ogallala is being drained twenty times faster than nature restores it. At the current rate of overdraft, the region will use up almost all its groundwater in less than forty years. This would have many deleterious effects, among them an enormous negative impact on the United States' agricultural productivity, which would worsen the food crisis both here and elsewhere.

Water shortages in the United States vary by region. The arid Southwest is water-poor as expected, a fact that is glaringly out of sync with its growing population. The Colorado River is so heavily used that it ends in puddles before reaching its natural delta. Arizona has so little water that it is forced to choose between agriculture and industry. The state is now in the process of removing agricultural land from production so more water will be available for industrial growth. Some analysts argue that cities such as Tucson and Phoenix should never have been built, and as water becomes increasingly scarce and dear, such cities may ultimately shrivel and turn into modern ghost towns. It is not implausible that today's migration from the Snowbelt states to the Sunbelt states may someday reverse itself and become a movement from the Parchbelt states to the Waterbelt states, that is, those comparatively rich in water resources.

Implications for the United States

The United States has much to gain by helping solve the global problem of water shortages. Successful solutions to many of the other megaproblems discussed in these last two chapters hinge on what happens to water problems. If water supplies are not managed successfully in the Third World, for instance, much of the United States' development assistance will be fruitless; the need for massive drought, famine, and other types of relief will soar; and pressures for mass migration to the developed world will intensify. Our national security interests are also very much at stake. There is great potential for conflict in water scarcity, and conflicts do exist within national boundaries and between adjacent countries over competing uses of water. Indeed, 148 major river basins are shared by two or more countries, and conflict over many of these basins is inevitable without water resources progress.

DEFORESTATION

Objective and Subjective Dimensions

Another basic biological system upon which humans depend heavily is the world's forests. Forests are obviously important economically. They supply the world with wood and wood products for the manufacture of housing, furniture, paper, plywood, fiberboard, chemicals, pharmaceuticals, and numerous other items. Also, about 40 percent of the world's population use wood as their primary fuel. In the Third World, 90 percent of wood consumption is devoted to heating and cooking, and wood is a necessity of life.

Forests are also important ecologically. We have already discussed two functions: the minimization of soil erosion and water shortages. Forests retain rainwater and allow it to seep slowly downward to replenish underground aquifers. When forests are leveled, this critical process is undermined. Rainwater runs off the land rapidly, water tables drop, and streams fluctuate between torrents and trickles. Soil erosion and sedimentation of streams and reservoirs also result. In addition, forests house thousands of important plant and animal species, sponge up tremendous amounts of carbon dioxide (thus retarding the greenhouse effect), and release precious oxygen through photosynthesis. Forests also retard desertification. Moreover, the loss of the rain forests could turn the tropics into desert and near-desert. This

would heat up the air in that region, changing global wind and cloud patterns. This could, for example, push the temperate climate required for growing wheat and corn—now a feature of the American and Canadian Midwest—farther north. Obviously, forests are an extremely valuable world resource.

Nevertheless, the world's forests, particularly its tropical rain forests, are being rapidly chopped down. As this chapter's introductory passage describes, almost all of the earth's land surface was once overlaid with forests. But by 1950 they covered only 25 percent of the land surface. Today, that figure is less than 20 percent, and the shrinkage is continuing at the annual rate of 1 percent. This means that every year the world is losing a forested area the size of Hungary (Brown and Shaw, 1982). Just in recent decades, Latin America has lost 37 percent of its rain forests; Southeast Asia, 38 percent; and Africa, 52 percent. Burgeoning populations have already outstripped the sustainable yield of forests in most developing countries. Worldwide wood production per capita peaked in 1964, and it has fallen continuously since then by a total of 11 percent.

There are many reasons why the world's forests are in full retreat, many of which are touched upon in other contexts in these mega-problems chapters. They include the rising cost of oil, inequitable land distribution which forces peasants into the forests, sheer poverty, and the developed world's demand for cheap timber and meat. (Produced on deforested lands, much of this meat goes to our fast-food restaurants.) But by far the greatest factor has been the population explosion in the Third World, which has driven up pressure for land and for fuel and other forest products. Because this enormous population growth is bound to continue for another century or more, the situation for the world's forests is grim. Indeed, experts predict that by the end of the century half of the world's jungles will have vanished, and by 2020, virtually all the physically accessible forests in the

Third World will have been cut down (Council on Environmental Quality and the U.S. Department of State, 1980). It is probable that someday jungles will become as fictional as Edgar Rice Burrough's Tarzan. Because of the forests' valuable economic and ecological functions, their sharp attenuation has been labeled the greatest environmental threat of modern times (Golden, 1983).

The United States is not immune to forest problems, although they are not nearly as grave here as in the Third World. Deforestation issues here include excessive harvesting of timber in the Pacific Northwest, increased pressure to harvest forests on publicly owned lands; the conversion of thousands of acres of privately owned forests to cropland; the damage to forests caused by acid rain (an insidious air pollutant that has been linked to the death of spruce stands in Vermont); the harvesting of timber from environmentally sensitive regions such as areas with steep slopes and highly erodible soils; the destruction of wildlife habitats; and inadequate reforestation. Although forests now cover about one-third of the United States, the nation's forestland is under increasing pressure and is decreasing slightly.

Subjective awareness of the plight of the world's forests is virtually nonexistent among the American public. There is little concern even about the pressure on United States forests. Fortunately, there is a heightened international awareness of the seriousness of current trends in world forests, due in part to such books as Norman Myers' *The Sinking Ark* (1979) and conferences on deforestation (U.S. Department of State, 1978). As the economic consequences of worldwide deforestation are increasingly brought to bear on the average American, our subjective awareness will almost certainly rise.

Implications for the United States

In most of the advanced industrial societies like that of the United States, the area in forests has either stabilized or declined slightly. This has been possible in part because these countries have imported relatively cheap wood products from the Third World. But as the forests of the Third World gradually disappear, the developed countries will be forced to consume more of their own forest resources. Stabilization of forest area may give way to renewed deforestation, but at the very least wood products will become more costly. Some of these trends have already been set in motion as evidenced, for example, by the steeply rising cost of lumber and other wood products (including textbooks, as you no doubt are aware) in the United States.

But deforestation in the Third World has many other serious costs for Americans. There is the tragic loss of forest-derived drugs and pharmaceuticals, the extinction at an unprecedented rate of plant and animal species, and the ominous risk of worldwide climactic change. There is also deforestation's negative impact on world hunger and water shortages to be concerned about, which undermine United States development assistance efforts and increase the need for disaster relief. Thus, the welfare of the United States is intimately affected by the consequences of deforestation. It is in our humanitarian and self-interest to help solve this problem.

DISAPPEARING SPECIES

Objective and Subjective Dimensions

In an age of plastics, transistors, microcomputers, artificial organs, and journeys to the moon, it is easy to overlook how dependent humanity is on animals and plants. The fact is that animal and plant products serve many crucial medical and industrial purposes in addition, of course, to their vital role in agriculture. Consider some of the medical drugs that come from plants and animals: quinine for malaria; digitalis for heart disease; painkillers such as morphine; anti-schistosomiasis drugs; penicillin and other antibiotics; oral contraceptives; drugs for Hodgkin's disease, leukemia, and other types of cancer; respiratory stimulants; blood pressure boosters; pupil dilators; muscle relaxants; and local anesthetics. All told, about 50 percent of modern medical drugs originated in nature rather than in chemists' laboratories.

And the search continues. Scientists are now investigating many hitherto unstudied plants and animals, looking for new wonder drugs. In addition, they are continuing to study ancient folk medicines and potions based on natural products, because these substances often turn out to be medically useful. For instance, such research in the past led to the discovery of curare, a plant-based arrow poison used by Amazon tribes, which is now widely used to paralyze muscles during surgery (Eckholm, 1978b). Similarly, a vast array of industrial (and agricultural) products come from plants, including cotton, wool, rubber, tobacco, gums, oils, pigments, dyes, and pesticides.

There are now an estimated 10 million plant and animal species living on the earth. Scientists have been able to identify only 1.5 million of these, but all this usually means is that the species' appearance and location have been noted in the scientific literature. Those organisms that have been carefully studied to ascertain their utility for humanity probably number only in the tens or hundreds of thousands. Thus, there are more than 9 million species yet to investigate. Within that collection there are certainly a large number of extremely valuable species, species that could contain the future's wonder drugs, food supply, and energy sources.

The problem is that humanity is now in the process of extinguishing these species at a rate without precedent in human history. It has been estimated that about 2 million species—fully 20 percent of all those existing in 1980—will become extinct by the end of this century, mainly because of loss of wild habitat but also because of pollution (Council on Environmental Quality and the U.S. Department of State, 1980). This means that a spe-

cies—usually an obscure tropical plant—is now becoming extinct every five minutes. And the rapid liquidation of the earth's species is almost certain to continue after the year 2000. This massive biological impoverishment will change the nature of life on the earth for all time. It will sweep away many of the world's most beautiful plants, unknown fruits and nuts, sources of pharmaceuticals and other chemicals, natural predators of pests, building materials, specialty woods, and fuels, which could have been boons for all humanity. And it will severely limit the tools and building blocks available for genetic engineering.

Perhaps as important as the loss of species is the extinction of subspecies and varieties of cereal grains. This is because fewer than two dozen animal and plant species form the basis of 80 percent of the world's food supply. To maximize production, the world has increasingly cultivated high-yield varieties, but it is necessary to routinely breed into these varieties wild and other domestic strains to maintain resistance to pests and pathogens. But many of these wild and domestic strains are rapidly being lost due to the destruction of their habitats or to their displacement by higher-yield varieties. The practice of monoculture—the cultivation of a single crop, such as wheat or corn, to the exclusion of other crops on the land—makes the situation even more critical. This is because monoculture makes crops more vulnerable to disease and pests, and this practice is increasing while the genetic resources to combat such disasters are being irretrievably squandered (Council on Environmental Quality and the U.S. Department of State, 1980).

In short, the extinction of much of the earth's life will mean the loss not only of a substantial part of the world's beauty but also of the potential for curing (present and future) disease and eliminating human suffering as well. Erik Eckholm (1978b) has this to say about this immense catastrophe:

Within sight is the destruction of plant and animal species, and of the genetic heritage of eons they embody, on a scale that dwarfs the combined natural and human-caused extinctions of the previous millions of years. Should this biological massacre take place, evolution will no doubt continue, but in a grossly distorted manner. Such a multitude of species losses would constitute a basic and irreversible alteration in the nature of the biosphere even before we understand its workings—an evolutionary Rubicon whose crossing Homo sapiens would do well to avoid.

Edward O. Wilson, a noted biologist and the founder of sociobiology, is also deeply concerned about this crisis. He suggests that this loss of species and genetic diversity may be our worst social problem, noting that it is the one process ongoing in the 1980s that will take millions of years to correct—the folly our descendants are least likely to forgive us (Russakoff, 1984).

But as unimaginably costly as these aesthetic, economic, medical, and other losses will be, there is an even more foreboding threat lurking in the wholesale destruction of many of the earth's life forms: human extinction. Again, no matter how sophisticated our technologies may seem, the human body and human activities are ultimately based on biological processes, entangled in ecological webs so complex that the consequences of cutting out huge numbers of these strands cannot be anticipated. But it is known that few species go to oblivion alone, that because of intricate biological interdependencies they usually take others with them. Scientists are not yet able to predict where the critical thresholds for humanity lie, at what level of species eradication the web of life will become so seriously weakened that it can no longer support humankind. But such thresholds do exist, and we are moving steadily toward them. As noted biologist George Woodwell put it, "The biota is humanity's ultimate resource, and we are destroying it" (Eckholm, 1978b). But you do not have to be an expert biologist to make such observations. Ask yourself this simple question: If humanity's behavior is making the planet unlivable for so many species, at what point will it become unlivable for people?

The American public is almost totally unaware of the immense objective dimensions of this problem. What little subjective awareness of endangered species exists is concentrated among animal lovers, bird watchers, and small groups of environmentalists, and usually pertains to a few hundred familiar and appealing birds and animals—such as elephants, wolves, tigers, cheetahs, whales, eagles, and whooping cranes. One reason for this awareness is that the fate of such animals is followed in the media. It is not unusual for the national news to carry a story, for instance, on a condor chick hatching in California. And, of course, there are international campaigns to "save the whales" or "save the tigers."

As laudable as this concern for higher-order species is, it is in a sense a form of vertebrate chauvinism. There is little concern about the millions of unsung species on the edge of extinction—including obscure small plants, shrubs, insects, and mollusks. Although the endangered vertebrates receive the greatest public attention, the extinction of the lower-order species may be vastly more significant ecologically and economically. The demise of a single plant species can lead to the extinction of as many as thirty dependent species, such as insects and other plants. And the aforementioned medical and other benefits offered by endangered species generally come from plants and lower-order animals.

Causes of Species Extinction

Humans extinguish other species primarily through pollution and the destruction of land and marine habitats. The effluents of society kill off species by contaminating the water, soil, and air. But the destruction of habitats is far and away the biggest cause of species extinction. Population and economic growth lead to the extension of human settlements with a concomitant shrinkage of wilderness. As wilderness is lost, the inhabiting species vanish.

The problem of habitat destruction is most serious in the tropics because that is where most species reside and where the population and economic pressures are the greatest. There are more woody plant species living on the slopes of one volcano in the Philippines, for instance, than in the whole United States. But biologically affluent nations tend to be economically poor. They also tend to be overpopulated. The pressures to exploit the remaining virgin territories are already enormous and building. In these nations deforestation, desertification, coral reef destruction, and other deleterious environmental practices are most prevalent. The foreign exchange: hungry governments and the land-hungry people of such nations are least likely to be able to forsake immediate (though ruinous) economic gains in favor of abstract long-term ecological goals. Multinational corporations and the inhabitants of developed nations like the United States contribute to the problem by consuming huge amounts of tropical wood and agriculture products (Eckholm, 1978b).

Although species extinction is most serious in the tropics, it is also a problem in the United States. Private and public funds have been able to rescue some species from the edge of extinction, such as the bald eagle. But a far greater number of species are on the brink of extinction or have already toppled over it. More than half of southern Florida's plant species, for example, are about to disappear due to the tripling of the region's population over the past three decades.

Developed countries like the United States face the same value trade-offs as the Third World, although the choices are not as limited or dire. The welfare of species often comes

into direct conflict with development projects, such as in the famous case of the snail darter and the Tellico Dam in Tennessee, which jeopardized the small fish's existence. One result of such conflicts during the early 1980s was that the United States government slowed down the process by which actually endangered species were added to the official list. Because being on the list gives a species the potential to disrupt development projects, this slowdown favored short-term economic and political interests over environmental ones.

Implications for the United States

The United States' best interest in minimizing species extinction goes far beyond our own borders. All of the untoward effects—the loss of medical, industrial, and agricultural products, as well as the threat of our own extinction—are global in nature. The United States already has policies to protect endangered species, although they are inadequate in both scope and enforcement. Nevertheless, a series of measures bespeak our concern in this area, including state wildlife conservation laws, the U.S. Endangered Species Act, the Convention on International Trade in Endangered Species of Wild Fauna and Flora, and the International Whaling Convention.

But ratifying international treaties, passing conservation laws, and providing funds for the creation and policing of national parks and conservation areas—as essential as these policies are—will not by themselves slow the loss of species. This is because these actions do little to lessen the social forces that are driving these species to extinction. Once again, population growth is the crucial factor. Rising numbers of people, many of whom are striving for ever more material goods, are placing staggering pressures on wildlife habitats everywhere. So especially are the Third World's rapidly increasing poor, who exterminate large numbers of species in their desperate quest to eke

BOX 13-2

MINERAL RESOURCES

Modern civilization relies heavily on minerals such as iron, copper, lead, and aluminum. They are essential for many activities including manufacturing, construction, transportation, and defense. The problem is that the mineral deposits in the earth's crust are finite, and they are being extracted and consumed in the twentieth century at rates which cannot be sustained indefinitely. Moreover, global consumption of minerals is projected to increase in the coming decades due to population growth and continued industrialization throughout the world. Consumption is expected to double just between now and the year 2000. If one assumes that demand for minerals will stay the same in the years to come, and that known reserves of the minerals will not increase, then one can calculate a life expectancy of those minerals. It turns out, for example, that iron and manganese will last only 200 years and that aluminum (in bauxite) and chromium will last only 300 years. Even less encouraging is the fact that several minerals—fluorine, silver, zinc, mercury, sulfur, and lead—have a life expectancy of less than 40 years.

Such estimates of low life span are alarming, but the situation is not without hope. Demand is flexible and could fall in the future; new reserves could be found; new technologies or higher prices (due to scarcity) could permit the extraction and processing of deposits that were impossible or uneconomical to exploit previously; recycling of minerals could become more efficient and prevalent; and substitutes could be developed. (For example, copper is already increasingly being replaced by fiber optics in communications systems.) But these activities—taken all together—are necessary actions, not options, if the developed world is going to sustain a reasonable standard of living and if the developing nations are to attain one. The boom times of cheap and easy-to-get minerals are over.

Aside from scarcities, there are a variety of other social problems associated with minerals. One is environmental problems. Since most mining operations are carried out at the surface, land use and restoration become critical problems. In addition, the impact of mining and processing on the atmosphere and water is extreme. Water, air, and noise pollution and solid waste disposal are persistent problems and expensive to solve. Mining of seabed minerals—a hope for the future—may pose the danger of significant oceanic deterioration with resulting damage to marine life.

Another social problem is the uneven distribution and consumption of mineral resources. In most cases, the countries which possess the mineral reserves or process them are not the chief consumers. The quarter of the world's population living in the developed countries will continue to consume three-quarters of the minerals produced in the next two decades. Even the United States, which is blessed by rich mineral resources, relies on imports for more than 50 percent of its mineral consumption. For Western developed nations, critical problems may arise because of dependency on many minerals from Communist eastern Europe, developing countries, and South Africa. Western industrial countries currently hold 44 percent of the twenty most important minerals; 23 percent are held by eastern European countries; and 33 percent, by the developing countries.

In addition, there are concentrations of certain important minerals in only a few countries. There are fifteen minerals of which 75 percent of their reserves are found in only five countries. To complicate things further, mining is dominated by multinational companies. In times of shortages, these countries and companies have enormous power to raise prices or to discriminate against some customers and favor others. Disruption of supplies due to political or economic discrimination is a real threat to the United States economy and to world peace—a tie-in to yet another megaproblem: nuclear war.

Source: Adapted in part from Murphy (1983).

out a living from the land. Consequently, the salvation of much life on the earth depends largely on the development and successful implementation of policies affecting population growth and the interrelated problems of consumption, employment, land tenure, and income distribution (Eckholm, 1978b). One function of United States population and development aid is to facilitate the development of such policies in the Third World, and thus this aid indirectly plays a role in minimizing species' extinction.

ENERGY SHORTAGES

Objective and Subjective Dimensions

Energy is another vital human resource, for it is energy that does society's work. For most of human history, the major energy sources were fires (fueled by wood) and human muscle power (fueled by food). Even the domestication of animals—by which humanity harnessed the muscle power of oxen, horses, camels, elephants, and other creatures—was a comparatively recent event in history. The energy sources of modern civilization—petroleum, natural gas, coal, hydropower, and nuclear fission—are last-minute appearances. Today, societies use different mixes of these energy sources. You may recall from the section on deforestation that 40 percent of the world's population still rely on wood as their primary fuel, and these individuals are concentrated largely in Third World societies. Industrial societies derive their power mostly from coal, petroleum, and natural gas.

The energy problem can be simply stated: The world is now in the process of using up the major current sources of energy in both the Third World and in industrialized societies. We have already discussed the fact that the world's forests are shrinking rapidly, and that once-plentiful fuelwood is becoming scarce. Here we will focus primarily on coal, petroleum, and natural gas. Of nonwood fuels, petroleum accounts for about 46 percent of the world's energy consumption, followed by coal (20 percent) and natural gas (17 percent). Nuclear fission, hydropower, and a variety of other sources make up the remaining 17 percent.

The world's supply of petroleum was produced over 100 million years by the transformation of solar energy into petroleum deposits by biological and geological processes. But this ancient endowment is being guzzled up by humanity in an incredibly brief time period. The depletion of the world's petroleum resources on a mammoth scale only really began in the early twentieth century. It has accelerated sharply since then, especially during the 1950s. Indeed, in that one decade, humankind devoured more petroleum than it had in all previous history! Then in both the 1960s and 1970s, the human race consumed twice as much as in the 1950s (Shinn, 1982). This rate of consumption means that we will exhaust the world's economically retrievable supply of petroleum, our current major source of energy, sometime during the first half of the next century. In just 100 years, then, humanity will have used up most of the oil it took nature millions of years to produce. Per capita production of oil already peaked in 1973, and has fallen 15 percent since then (Table 13-1). Total production should plummet by the end of this century, as the earth's oil reserves edge ever nearer to empty.

Oil is an extraordinarily valuable commodity. It is an exceptionally versatile energy source that can be employed in many different ways. It can be used as a fuel for powering cars and trucks, running machinery, heating homes, cooking meals, generating electricity, or making chemical feedstock, fertilizer, plastics, and other materials. It comes in liquid form, is highly concentrated, and is easy to store and transport. It is because of these valuable characteristics that the world has placed such enormous demands on petroleum in recent decades.

As noted above, those demands skyrocketed during the 1950s, in part because of the explosive population and economic growth which took place during that decade. Indeed, because of its extraordinary versatility, cheap oil ($2 a barrel in 1950 compared to $30 in 1984) eased many of the traditional resource constraints on population and economic growth. Petroleum-based fertilizer increased the productivity of croplands, petrochemical feedstocks improved livestock output, and oil-based synthetic fibers were substituted for natural ones, permitting more cropland to be devoted to food production rather than cotton, and more grassland to be used for meat, dairy, and other animal-based food products rather than wool. Similarly, kerosene was substituted for firewood, and as tractors and other farm machinery took the place of draft animals, gasoline and diesel fuel replaced forage and grain.

In a sense, cheap oil acted as a safety value, reducing pressure on other world resources (Brown et al., 1984). Oil depletion increased enormously, but such problems as poverty, world hunger, desertification, deforestation, and even the population explosion were not as severe as they otherwise would have been. This is a classic example of creating one social problem (accelerated oil depletion) in the process of trying to solve others. Conversely, the steeply rising cost of oil which began in the 1970s means that these substitutions are becoming ever more costly; and as the oil safety value closes, the problems that oil has been dampening are becoming more severe.

There are also finite supplies of the other two major energy sources: natural gas and coal. Like petroleum, the world's supply of natural gas will be exhausted during the first half of the next century. Reserves of coal are much larger and could last for several hundred years. But the world is already reeling from the environmental effects of coal (e.g., the greenhouse effect, acid rain, strip mining), and scientists have grave reservations about even maintaining the current level of coal consumption, let alone expanding it.

And a tremendous expansion would be necessary! World energy demand is expected to increase by more than 50 percent between now and the year 2000 due to population growth, industrialization, and rising standards of living, mostly in the Third World. And energy demand will continue to swell throughout the twenty-first century and probably beyond. World energy demand in the long-term future will probably be ten to fifteen times greater than the present demand (Murphy, 1983). Given the loss of petroleum and natural gas, the world's consumption of coal would have to increase many times to satisfy this rapidly expanding demand. This not only would hasten the exhaustion of coal reserves but could well deal the earth an environmental death blow.

The rapid depletion of two of the world's three major sources of energy, and the expanded use and ultimate exhaustion of the third, amounts to a problem of such immense objective importance that it certainly qualifies as a social megaproblem. Regardless of short-term ups and downs in energy prices and supplies, such as gasoline shortages and gluts, the energy crisis is authentic. It is not a sham creation of corporate treachery or government blundering. It is the real product of excess demand over supply, and represents one of the most serious problems facing the world. Energy is a vital human resource, for it is used in some of the most elemental processes of human life such as cooking, heating, manufacturing, and the securing of other resources. Plentiful energy is a sine qua non of industrial societies, which depend on it to drive industry itself, to support essential urban areas, to perform society's drudgery, and to power health technologies—to mention just a few of its crucial functions. But it is also a vital resource in the Third World, where it is needed not only for everyday living but also to help bring about the economic development which would alleviate so many of the staggering problems these nations currently endure. A long-term energy shortage would have almost unimaginably catastrophic consequences. Most societies would simply not survive it, including all of the advanced ones. Indeed, it would mean the end of the world as we know it.

Fortunately, the chances of avoiding a long-term energy shortage are good. There is an excellent possibility that humanity will eventually develop renewable forms of energy which have minimal effects on the environment. The earth is actually awash in solar, wind, tidal, geothermal, atomic, and other forms of energy which humanity's technological genius could ultimately harness satisfactorily. The energy crisis is the megaproblem probably most amenable to a technological fix. But as long as the problem remains unsolved, and until it becomes certain that the solution will come before the world runs out of usable (environmentally safe) energy, the crisis will continue to be an objective megaproblem.

In contrast to world hunger, water shortages, deforestation, species extinction, and even the population explosion, the energy crisis has a relatively high subjective dimension among the American public. Indeed, it was the public's top concern in 1974 and 1979 (*Gallup Report*, various years). Nevertheless, subjective concern about the energy crisis has been much lower in other years, both before and since. What explains these roller-coaster-like fluctuations in the energy crisis' subjective dimension given that there has been little change in its overall objective dimension?

The answer to that question is that the public attitude is geared more to the short-term rather than to the long-term dimensions of the problem. When energy is in short supply and people are forced to wait in long lines at gas stations, as was the case in 1974 and 1979, the subjective dimension of the problem soars. But when there is a seeming oil glut, concern diminishes. For instance, in 1978, just four years after the public labeled the energy crisis their top concern, the majority of Americans not only failed to rank the problem as serious but did not believe that the problem even existed. This subjective roller coaster is also abetted by the media, which magnify energy problems during the lean years.

But it is highly misleading to judge the objective seriousness of the energy crisis facing the world by what happens in the short run. Energy gluts and scarcities from year to year are due primarily to political and corporate decisions—the decisions by energy producers to speed up or slow down the rate at which their energy stocks are depleted, to fix prices, or to undercut their competitors. Energy-importing

countries can also influence the short-run energy situation by reducing consumption, by increasing domestic production, or through a variety of other energy policies (Murphy, 1983).

The reason subjective awareness was high in 1974 and 1979 is that these were the years of the twin oil shocks. The first shock occurred in 1973–1974, when the Organization of Petroleum Exporting Countries (OPEC) arbitrarily raised the price of oil from about $2 to more than $11 per barrel, and also cut off oil exports to the United States. The second oil shock occurred in 1979, following the overthrow of the Shah of Iran, when the price of OPEC oil rose as high as $40 per barrel. Both oil shocks produced reactions from energy consumers that affected the short-term supply situation. For example, after being staggered by the 1979 shock, consumers conserved fuel to an unprecedented degree. The consumption of electricity in the United States, for instance, actually shrank in 1982, the first decline since the end of World War II (Alexander, 1984).

Conservation is a partial solution to energy shortages in the short run. But conservation, like the solution to any social problem, is not without a downside. One thing that has been done to conserve energy is the tightening of homes and other buildings to reduce heat leakage. But this traps dangerous substances inside, including the radioactive gas radon. Radon is continuously produced in all rock, soil, bricks, cement, plaster, and other materials, and is therefore present in all buildings. It has been estimated that 10,000 people in the United States die each year from radon-related lung cancer. Radon is thought to account for as many as one-half of all lung cancer cases among nonsmokers, and a small percentage in smokers as well (Haney, 1984). Another energy-conserving tactic is driving small automobiles. But if everyone in the United States switched to them, there would be an additional 10,000 American lives lost each year in automobile accidents. Thus there are classic value trade-offs here: conservation of energy versus human health.

Transition Period

Although the world is running out of two of its three major sources of energy and faces grave environmental risks by continued and, especially, expanded consumption of the third, there is probably still time to develop the environmentally safe, renewable forms of energy mentioned above. The world is now in a transition period, moving from present sources of energy toward new forms. We have about fifty to seventy-five years to accomplish this task. Actually, OPEC probably did the world a real service with its two 1970s oil shocks. The economic damage they caused forced nations to curb wasteful energy habits, thus extending the transition period available to solve the long-term energy crisis. Before these shocks, oil and natural gas supplies were expected to be virtually exhausted by the end of the twentieth century.

But the transition period is not without its own serious problems. First, the time allotted to develop the new energy regimen may turn out to be too short due to any number of difficulties, delays, and technological and geological constraints. Second, even if the ultimate goal is achievable, the interim period is one of great uncertainties. A variety of energy crises with world-shattering consequences could easily emerge. Energy experts Daniel Yergin and Martin Hillenbrand (1982), for instance, warn that a devastating energy crisis could erupt at any time as long as the United States and other consuming nations remain addicted to petroleum from the explosive Middle East. This area contains about 60 percent of the non-Communist world's known petroleum reserves and provides 65 percent of the oil traded in international markets. One or more of the almost inevitable future conflicts in the Middle East could interfere with oil exports and plunge the world into a crisis.

Another oil shock would have a far more adverse effect than those of 1974 and 1979, because it would come on top of the lasting damage created by those setbacks. The Yergin and Hillenbrand study (1982) concludes that the previous shocks cost the United States and other major industrial nations a total of 1.2 trillion dollars in lost economic growth between 1974 and 1981. The jolts also doubled unemployment rates, tripled the inflation rate, and tripled the share of the gross national product spent on energy. A ruinous new energy crisis would probably double or triple oil prices again, pushing them up to $70 to $110 per barrel. Economies would be battered, governments around the world would topple, and it is grimly plausible that United States business would go into a slump that can be compared only with the Great Depression. According to Yergin, another such energy crisis "is probably the greatest direct danger to world peace."

Another transition period problem is the environmental and meteorological damage which will be caused by the continued use of the fossil fuels (i.e., petroleum, natural gas, and coal) and by the use of stopgap energy sources such as oil shale and nuclear fission. The environmental degradation brought about by the fossil fuels has already been noted (e.g., the greenhouse effect, acid rain, ozone depletion, air pollution). Not only does oil from shale present many of the same problems, but its production requires huge amounts of water, thus aggravating the water shortage problem. It also creates a great deal of waste, and like strip mining, it leaves the land scarred and desolate. The economic costs of extraction are also high, and likely to remain so.

Nuclear power will be used to a considerable extent during the transition period and perhaps beyond. Indeed, during the 1950s, 1960s, and much of the 1970s, nuclear power was widely seen as one of the major solutions not just to the short-term but to the long-term energy megaproblem. Nuclear power burst onto the American scene in the late 1940s, raising great expectations. The scientists and engineers who had demonstrated the monstrous power of the atom at Hiroshima and Nagasaki promised to harness its stupendous force to produce electricity so easily that it would be "too cheap to meter." Such inexpensive energy was supposed to utterly transform the economic basis of American life. Indeed, James Newman, a congressional counsel who wrote part of the Atomic Energy Act of 1946, noted at the time: "This new force offers enormous possibilities for improving public welfare, for revamping our industrial methods, and for increasing the standard of living."

But the ramifications of cheap energy extended well beyond the American consumer's pocketbook. Cheap energy was expected to not only help solve many world megaproblems (e.g., power to desalinize ocean water and power to replace fuelwood, thus easing deforestation and species extinction) but also defuse many world political problems as well through a battery of United States foreign policies known as the Atoms-for-Peace program. One aspect of this was expected to be a reduction in international struggles over energy itself. In this vein, David Deitz, author of the 1945 book *Atomic Energy in the Coming Era,* declared: "The day is gone when nations will fight for oil" (Alexander, 1984). In a way it was hopefully envisioned that the peace-promoting side of atomic power would remove the need for the future use of its darker, destructive side.

Unfortunately, that optimism is long gone. Today there are serious doubts about the survival of the nuclear power industry both in the United States and elsewhere. Nuclear power turned out to be plagued by many serious problems that are extremely difficult to resolve. These include plant safety, waste disposal, economic cost, and nuclear weapons proliferation. The first three problems are discussed briefly here, while the last problem is addressed in Chapter 14.

No one anticipated how difficult and complicated a task it is to build a safe nuclear power plant, and consequently, many of the first units were beset by problems. Publicity about these early problems raised fears about the plants' safety at least among a small minority of Americans. Then in 1975, an accident occurred at the Browns Ferry nuclear reactor in Alabama which heightened this subjective concern by showing that a potentially grave situation can develop as a result of a combination of human and mechanical errors. The Browns Ferry incident gave the fledgling antinuclear movement an enormous boost. The movement hurt the nuclear industry in many ways through demonstrations, through lobbying, and, most important, by tying up projects in legal battles which both increased their costs and delayed their completion.

Subjective concern reached a fevered pitch in 1979 when the nuclear power industry was staggered by the one-two punch of the Three Mile Island accident in Pennsylvania and the movie *The China Syndrome.* At Three Mile Island a series of mechanical and operator errors temporarily uncovered the nuclear reactor's radioactive core, and the reactor came very close to a meltdown (i.e., a situation in which the molten reactor core melts itself into the earth, with the subsequent release of radioactive gases and particulates into the atmosphere). The event was covered in minute detail by the media. The public not only became aware of the serious objective dimension of plant safety problems but also witnessed the publicly revealed ineptness of the industry and the Nuclear Regulatory Commission (NRC). As a result, the credibility of the industry and the NRC plummeted.

The China Syndrome, which in an extraordinary coincidence was released just two weeks before the accident, magnified public concern even more. The film depicted safety problems in a plant very similar to the one at Three Mile Island. Except for its dramatically exaggerated

Nuclear power plants like this one at Three Mile Island are plagued by many serious problems related to plant safety, waste disposal, and economic cost. (*Giannini/Sygma*)

assertion that a meltdown would render "an area the size of Pennsylvania uninhabitable for years," the film was surprisingly realistic and accurate. It showed a utility company with a cavalier attitude toward safety regulations suffer a near meltdown. According to most investigating agents, this scenario corresponds almost exactly to what happened at Three Mile Island. Every time *The China Syndrome* is rebroadcast on television, the public's concern about nuclear power is given a booster shot, and people in the power industry still blame Jack Lemmon and Jane Fonda for the intensity of the public's alarm over the real accident.

Waste disposal is another pressing problem. Spent nuclear fuel rods include such fission products as strontium 90, cesium 137, and plutonium 239. The latter is the most poisonous substance in existence. It is 324 million times as deadly as strychnine and 486 million times as lethal as arsenic. Less than 4 grains of plutonium, about the size of a pencil's eraser, is enough to kill the entire United States population; one-sixth of an ounce could wipe out the human race. Nuclear waste remains very dangerous for thousands of years, for it takes that long for the radioactivity to decay to safe levels. Nevertheless, some three decades after the first commercial plant went on line, there is still no acceptable permanent solution to this disposal problem. Deadly nuclear waste from power plants and many other sources is piling up in enormous quantities at unsafe, temporary sites, and some of it is deposited illegally in dumps, landfills, and waterways. There is little prospect that an adequate solution will be implemented during this century. One big stumbling block is that no one wants a nuclear graveyard in their neighborhood. Perhaps even more worrisome is the fact that we have lost track of some of this waste, including 4000 pounds of plutonium.

But nuclear power's most immediate and, perhaps, most insolvable problem is that contrary to the aforementioned beliefs, it is no longer economically attractive. A decade of catastrophic cost overruns has undermined the economic underpinnings of many completed plants as well as many of those currently under construction. In 1984 a nuclear plant cost almost three times as much to build as a coal-fired plant with state-of-the-art pollution control equipment, and the cost differential has been steadily widening (Alexander, 1984). Indeed, all indications suggest that the economic competitiveness for nuclear power continues to diminish, without even factoring in enormous postponed costs such as adequate long-term waste disposal and the decommissioning of worn-out nuclear plants.

Due to these multifaceted problems, the nuclear industry in the United States has been ailing since the early 1970s. In 1984 nuclear power from eighty-two plants supplied about 13 percent of the nation's electricity, and this will increase to about 20 percent by the mid-1990s as plants under construction in 1984 are put on line. But utilities have not placed an order for a nuclear plant since 1976, and 107 reactor orders have already been canceled, with more terminations probably in the offing. As a result, nuclear power in the United States may peak and then decline in the mid-1990s. Thus, the United States, which led the world into the nuclear power age, may well lead it out (Brown et al., 1984).

There is evidence that the world may already be following the United States' example. The Organization for Economic Co-operation and Development (OECD) predicted in 1970 that there would be 563,000 megawatts of nuclear generating capacity in its member nations by 1985. By 1978 the OECD projection had plunged to 214,000 megawatts, just over one-third the earlier figure. A 1983 Worldwatch Institute project placed the figure at an even lower 183,000 megawatts due to the cancellation of partially completed plants. As nuclear power expert Christopher Flavin noted in 1984: "Hard, cold economics is now doing to nuclear power what thousands of hot-blooded demonstrators never could. It is slowly, painfully shutting down the world's nuclear industries" (Flavin, 1984). Similarly, the *Financial Times Energy Economist* (1983), a publication of the international energy establishment itself, stated in 1983 that "the day when nuclear power will be the world's leading electricity source now seems to have been postponed indefinitely."

By 1984, Wall Street had all but abandoned the nuclear industry, and opponents and critics of nuclear power were ready to write the energy source's obituary. But as in the initial reports of Mark Twain's death, any present announcement of the demise of nuclear power may be premature and exaggerated. Nuclear energy's future may depend largely on the speed with which the new environmentally safe energy sources such as solar, wind, and geothermal energy are developed. If it becomes clear in the transition period that these sources can adequately replace oil, natural gas, and coal, then nuclear energy will not be resuscitated. But if it becomes apparent that these new sources will not be ready or able to satisfy all our energy needs, then nuclear energy may be revived. In the latter scenario, nuclear energy would compete with coal on the basis of economic and environmental criteria. Nuclear power may be more expensive than coal, but its environmental impact, though problematic in its own right, might prove to be more endurable than that of coal.

It is difficult enough to appraise the relative environmental impact of these two fuels now, let alone in the future when technologies will be different. But it is safe to say that then, as now, such appraisals will reflect not only objective but also subjective dimensions. The public is presently much more concerned about the risks posed by nuclear energy than by coal. Paradoxically, the evidence to date reveals that coal is far more dangerous to human life than nuclear power. Four major studies agree on this judgment (American Medical Association, 1978; Schurr, 1979; Inhaber, 1979; and Turner, 1979). The AMA study for instance reviewed the risks associated with the two fuels with respect to extraction, transportation, processing, pollution, release of radioactivity, and waste storage. It concluded that a coal-fired plant causes 48 to 285 times as many deaths as a nuclear plant of comparable capacity. Mining accidents, black lung disease, other coal-cycle occupational accidents, and pollution by combustion products account for the coal-related deaths.

There are also deaths throughout the production cycle of nuclear energy, such as cancer deaths among uranium miners. But these are negligible compared to those connected with coal (or petroleum) because of the smaller work forces involved (Shinn, 1982). (Incidentally, here is where the Navaho Indians, not coincidentally, are the victims of yet another social problem. Most of the uranium ore is mined by the Navaho in the United States, and the fatal illnesses associated with uranium mining have now reached epidemic proportions among this group.)

Opponents of nuclear energy argue that it would take just one major nuclear power plant accident to make these death ratios obsolete, and there are several studies which support this position. For instance, a 1982 United States government report found that if the worst-case accident took place at, for instance, the Salem, New Jersey, nuclear power plant, 102,000 individuals would suffer "early" deaths within a year of the accident. (The study also found that the greatest financial damage, 314 billion dollars, would take place at the Indian Point 3 reactor 25 miles north of New York City.) A worst-case accident would involve severe core damage, melting of uranium fuel, essential failure of all safety systems, and a major breach of the reactors containment vessel leading to a large release of radioactivity into the environment. This would be a far more severe accident than the one that occurred at Three Mile Island. According to the NRC, there is approximately a 2 percent chance of a worst-case accident occurring in the United States before the year 2000 (Benjamin, 1982).

Parenthetically, a major accident may have already occurred in the Soviet Union. The details are sketchy and controversial, but in 1958, a nuclear plant in the Ural Mountains may have experienced either a vast explosion of its wastes or a meltdown. Hundreds were reputedly killed and thousands suffered radiation sickness. And thirty small towns in the area have disappeared from Soviet maps (Medvedev, 1979; Koffler, 1984). Moreover, while this book was in press, another large-scale nuclear accident occurred in the Soviet Union, this time near Kiev. The Chernobyl power plant experienced a reactor meltdown and explosion, causing untold death and suffering. The catastrophe also raised the prospect of long-term health and environmental damage on a colossal scale, and served to reanimate the entire nuclear debate in western Europe and the United States.

The risk of worst-case and lesser accidents must somehow be incorporated into any truly comprehensive appraisal of the relative risks of using nuclear versus coal power. But by the same token, estimates of the health impact of coal must include the risk of its worst plausible scenarios, such as a severe greenhouse effect and one of its possible outcomes—human extinction. Thus, both power sources carry the risk of catastrophe.

Given the objective uncertainty about which is worse, why is nuclear energy so much more alarming to the public than coal? There are several reasons. First, while coal is ordinary and humdrum, the harnessing of the atom—from the bomb to the plant—is full of high drama and is highly visible. Intellectuals, newscasters, and filmmakers are not nearly as fascinated by commonplace coal, even though thousands of miners die each year from black lung disease. Second, nuclear power plants also contain the potential for the really big accident, which attracts attention and heightens public anxieties. Third, there is a certain mystique about radioactivity. It is imperceptible to any of the senses, yet treacherous; it hurts unsuspecting people, and causes genetic defects and cancer many years after exposure. People are especially intrigued and concerned about this insidious, hidden threat. Finally, unlike coal, nuclear energy is related to nuclear weapons, and the former could well lead to the proliferation of the latter throughout the world. This makes nuclear energy all the more foreboding.

There are other problems in the transition period to clean, renewable energy sources besides limited time for development, possible Middle East oil shocks, and the problems associated with coal, nuclear power, and other interim fuels like shale oil. One is that the present mammoth consumption gap among nations will continue through the transition period. Even though energy consumption will rise several times faster in the Third World than in the industrial world between the years 1975 and 2000, the rich countries will still consume seven times more energy per capita than the poor countries at the end of this period (Murphy, 1983). This will contribute to world instability and to other megaproblems.

Thus, the transition period will be a challenging one, full of social, political, economic, and technical hurdles. To successfully negotiate it, we will need extraordinary vision, planning, organization, and international cooperation.

The New Energy Era

The answer to the world's long-term energy needs appears increasingly to lie in the many forms of renewable energy. These include wind power, wood fuel, geothermal energy, photovoltaic solar cells, hydropower, methane generators, solar water heaters, and energy crops. Efforts to develop these power sources have proceeded at an unprecedented pace since the first OPEC oil shock in 1973, although government research and development funding has been far less than optimal. If wood fuel is included, renewables accounted for 18 percent of the world's energy in 1984, and rapid growth in this energy share is expected in the years ahead. The key to a viable renewable-energy future is the gradual phasing in of new fuels before the traditional ones run out. This will permit societies to make the necessary adjustments with a minimum of social disorganization. The whole process seems to be well under way (Flavin and Postel, 1984).

Renewable energy forms will offer society a variety of benefits in addition to energy itself. For instance, renewable resources are largely indigenous, which increases energy independence and decreases problematic outlays of foreign exchange. Another benefit is that these energy sources are virtually inflation proof. Once the system is in place, the operating cost of, say, a hydroelectric dam or a solar water heater is largely independent of rising fuel prices. Renewables are also extremely attractive in terms of employment. In contrast to fossil fuels and nuclear power, they demand less capital and generate more jobs. With massive worldwide unemployment and huge cohorts of young people entering the job market, the gradual switch-over to renewables will solve several social problems at once (i.e., energy shortage and unemployment).

But as you know by now, there is rarely a "free lunch" when it comes to solving social problems, and renewables are no exception. They certainly have their problems too. For instance, no renewable will be as versatile and convenient as oil, and many of oil's wonderful products may be lost forever. The cost involved in shifting from a fossil-fuel system to a renewable system—new types of machines, new methods of storage and transportation, and the like—will also be astronomical. And even the renewables, particularly hydropower dams and the burning of wood, have adverse effects on the environment. Nevertheless, the problems posed by renewables appear manageable, and are dwarfed by the problems posed by an energy shortage.

SOCIAL POLICY: ENVIRONMENTAL POLLUTION

Strategies for Solution

Despite the diversity of topics, this chapter is bound together by two unifying themes. First, each piece is part of the larger megaproblems puzzle. Viewing issues such as food shortage and deforestation as truly distinct from each other is as misguided as reading the odd-numbered pages of this book separately from the even-numbered pages. A second theme of the presentation has been, with the exception of energy shortages, the consistently low public profile of issues whose significance justifies the title "megaproblems." At times, we have strained to find the adjectives to describe the size of the gap between the subjective and objective dimensions. Repetition of this point from section to section may have suggested that once awareness of these problems spreads, they will solve themselves. This is a dangerous fallacy. If we have convinced you that these megaproblems are real and present dangers to the world—and the American college students who live in it—panaceas will not magically appear. Even with a much-heightened subjective dimension, there are imposing practical barriers to scale in reconciling humanity to the natural environment.

Some of these dilemmas have been mentioned in our analyses of the separate-but-related megaproblems. We will now turn up the focus on the complexities of environmental problems with an in-depth examination of pollution policy in the United States. As you have seen above, this topic follows familiar themes in its intimate interrelationship with other megaproblems, such as population growth and energy. But pollution, like energy shortages, differs from the other problems in this chapter in that it has been a matter of serious subjective concern to the American public. In a 1970 National Harris poll, air and water pollution was the majority choice as the most serious social problem facing the United States, outscoring even the Vietnamese war! In the political aftermath of this subjective peak has followed a set of institutional changes that crystallize present policy issues.

We will pose those broad issues in the form of a specific question: Should the United States significantly expand its efforts at pollution control? In these terms, the alternative strategies would simply implement a yes or a no answer, but the implications of that choice are anything but simple. Fundamental to both the affirmative and negative positions is a sketch of the objective dimension of pollution since 1970. That was the year of the first Earth Day and—no political coincidence—the year the Environmental Protection Agency (EPA) was established. Since that landmark date, there have been major legislative changes (notably, the Clean Air Act of 1970 and the Water Pollution Control Act of 1972), a major societal investment in pollution control (over 400 billion dollars spent in the last decade alone), and, as a consequence, major progress in reducing the quantities of air and water pollution. In 1970, the United States pumped about 204 million tons of pollutants into the atmosphere daily—nearly 1 ton per person per day! By 1981, the amount had dropped to 162 million tons.

Despite the fact that we are fouling our air at a slower rate, real problems remain. The ingredients of the corrosive brew known as acid rain continue to build up in our atmosphere, and several substances such as ozone and sulfates are proving to be serious health hazards (*Environmental Quality Index,* 1984). The picture for water pollution is similarly clouded, with clear gains mixed together with murky problems. Again substantial reductions have taken place since 1971, and the President's Council on Environmental Quality reports that the majority of United States surface waterways are meeting the Clean Water Act's 1983 goal of being "fishable and swimmable" (*Environmental Quality Index,* 1984). Despite real progress in reducing the amount of untreated municipal and industrial sewage poured into our waters, many of you live near rivers, lakes, and streams in which you should neither fish nor swim, and from which you certainly should not drink. Two good reasons are the buildup of toxic substances and the failure to control "nonpoint" pollution created by runoff from farms, city streets, and construction sites.

The objective report card on air and water pollution in the United States thus reads as follows: The overall grade-point average for antipollution programs has been improving since 1970, but there are still some subjects in which environmental quality is failing. The present question is whether it would be worth the societal effort to further improve those grades.

Policies into Practice

Everyone agrees that clean air and water are nice, that environmental quality is a positive value. Disputes arise from the fact that this value is part of a complex social system with many other values and social problems.

Those who speak in favor of more aggressive antipollution policy cite the benefits deriving from *problem linkages.* Their position is that additional gains in ambient air and water quality mean not only a prettier landscape but a better overall quality of life. Less pollution could improve America's health by limiting the short-term hazards of drinking water poisoned with toxic wastes, the intermediate-term hazards from substances which may be carcinogenic after years of exposure, and the long-term hazards of catastrophic destruction of basic biological systems such as the ozone layer or phytoplankton. In addition to these spillover benefits of pollution control on the social problem of public health, some contend that an expanded environmental policy would also improve the economic health of our society. The unemployment rate might drop because of jobs created for the engineers and construction workers developing pollution-control technologies, as well as for the administrators and field agents who would implement the stricter standards.

The words *ecology* and *economy* come from the same Greek word meaning "household management." According to those who oppose stricter antipollution standards, we have already invested too much in cleaning up our societal household at the expense of earning our collective living. Like pollution-control proponents, opponents also speak in terms of problem linkages—but not in such positive tones. More pollution control, they argue, means more unemployment since businesses will have to trim payrolls to afford expensive cleaning technologies. Moreover, firms which can afford such unproductive capital investments will contribute to the social problem of inflation by passing the bill on to consumers in higher prices. A final persuasive point of those against more control has already been raised above: Less pollution can translate into less energy. The tightening of societal standards around environmental contaminants would lock up sources such as coal and nuclear power, which could be vital in the transition period to renewable energy sources. By noting the interrelationship of all of these economic problems to pollution solutions, the anticontrol faction poses the issue as a classic trade-off between effluents and affluence.

Both sides in the debate argue their positions in terms of problem linkages, an idea already familiar to you as a reader. The immediate relevance of this principle is that implementation of a policy of stiffer pollution controls will have real-world reverberations on problems discussed throughout this book. Consider the contemporary issue of acid rain as an example. The seemingly biblical threat of poison falling from the sky is a direct result of human decisions about other social problems. Over half of the sulfur dioxide (SO_2 is the source of the acidity) emitted into our skies comes from the utility industry, which burns coal to generate electricity. This relatively dirty form of power production has been permitted because strict pollution standards could mean inflationary rates to utility customers, and possibly a worsening of energy and unemployment problems if plants had to close down. The balance of pollution control versus other practical problems implemented in the Clean Air Act was not achieved through dispassionate, objective analysis of problem linkages. Instead, a swirl of interest groups, such as utility shareholders and high-sulfur coal interests, struck the compromise which now brews acid rain.

Earlier, we noted that a surge in public opinion around 1970 provided political impetus for the present pollution control policy. Given the significance of the subjective dimension for program implementation, how does the public vote on the matter at issue here? A Gallup poll shed some light on this question by asking a sample of Americans whether they favor or oppose "reducing environmental regulations if needed to improve business conditions." While college educated adults would reject such measures by nearly a 2 to 1 margin, national opinion is very evenly divided, with 55 percent opposing and 45 percent in favor of sacrificing the environment to the economy (*Gallup Report*, 1982). Clearly, trading off ecological quality versus related social problems is a live issue in the public mind; just as clearly, objective evidence may be a key to swinging the subjective deadlock toward or away from pollution control.

Evaluating the Evidence

As we have said, the crux of the present issue is not whether a cleaner environment is desirable, but whether we desire it enough to pay the bill. There is now some empirical data on the price tag in terms of other social problems.

Several independent analyses have shown that current and projected pollution-control spending may increase the rate of inflation by 1 percent a year; more stringent (and expensive) standards would create even more inflationary pressure. There is no such neat summary figure for the energy costs of pollution control, but they are already considerable. We all pay higher prices for heat, light, and fuel thanks to environmental restrictions on coal and nuclear power. New pollution laws to protect public health could be lethal to those industries, incurring a higher cost in jobs and at the gas pump. Also on the pollution control debit sheet is, ironically enough, harm to the environment. Tough legal standards for sewage treatment have cleaned up many waterways but produced mountains of sludge, a by-product of the treatment process which sometimes is laced with toxic substances. Sewage sludge used to be dumped into the ocean, but now that that cheap escape valve has been closed by the courts, some EPA experts view sludge as one of our most serious waste disposal problems. Catalytic converters installed by manufacturers to meet the automobile emissions standards have effectively screened some pollutants out of car exhaust (carbon monoxide, hydrocarbons, and nitrogen oxides), but under certain conditions they have produced sulfuric acid mist, which is every bit as dangerous as it sounds. On balance, there is no question that America's antipollution policy has been a net benefit to the health of the society. These counterexamples do indicate, however, that the positive effect of new pollution controls on the social problem of health can easily be overstated; more generally, they remind us of the complexities of policy implementation, of how even successful policies can bring about further problems.

The real heart of the pollution versus other social problems issue really centers on one subject: jobs. In the public mind and in the political arena, there is widespread fear that a more active environmental cleanup will cause employment to dry up. Adding substance to the fear is the fact that each 1 percent increase in the unemployment rate costs United States society about 25 billion dollars a year in lost tax revenues and increased expenditures for linked social problems (e.g., infant mortality, welfare spending) (Kazis and Grossman, 1982), to say nothing of the human anguish of losing a job. Is there objective evidence for this fear? There have been plant closings occasioned by new environmental quality standards, especially in highly polluting industries like steel, paper, and chemicals.

However, other industries have directly benefited from the legislation, such as cement makers who have prospered due to new demand for waste treatment plants. According to the policy research organization Environmentalists for Full Employment, clean air and water laws have created roughly *ten times* as many jobs as they have eliminated (Kazis and Grossman, 1982). Indeed, a recent study by a private consulting firm found that pollution control was a 70 billion dollar industry in 1985, employing over 166,000 people. While such estimates strongly suggest that the pollution versus unemployment trade-off is subjectively misperceived *in aggregate,* they do not deny that stricter environmental standards may be deleterious to specific groups of firms and workers who must bear the brunt of solving this social problem.

The problem of balancing economic and environmental needs is not unique to the United States. Other industrialized nations, even Communist ones, face the same value trade-offs. For instance, although the Soviet Union has tough environmental laws, they are often given only lip service by bureaucrats anxious to meet economic goals. Consequently, there are still high levels of air and water pollution as well as other environmental problems in the country. Third World countries also face the same economic/environmental dilemma, as Box 12-2 on Mexico City illustrates. Many of these countries now have a difficult time providing the basic necessities of life to their inhabitants, and there are precious few resources remaining to support their quest for industrialization. Thus, pollution control has a very low priority; it is simply a luxury they cannot afford.

This, of course, is bad news for us because pollutants do not respect national boundaries. They cross them in air and water, in foods, in consumer products, as imported bulk chemicals, or as chemical wastes. And they can deleteriously affect the global climate. Thus, environmental pollution will increase in severity over the next several decades from sources outside our direct control. It is certainly in our best interests to work actively to build an international consensus on the seriousness of global pollution problems, and to do what we can to assist Third World nations in controlling their pollution.

SUMMARY

1 The earth has been radically transformed by humanity from its natural state to an increasingly human made one within just the past two centuries. There is increasing evidence that this transformation is incompatible with the planet's capacity to support human life.

2 Hunger is the world's No. 1 health problem. While hunger is largely a social phenomenon today, there are biological limits to food production and the world is moving ever closer to them.

3 Fresh usable water is a finite resource, and societies can exhaust supplies faster than nature can replenish them. Presently there is a global water shortage which threatens the existence of many societies.

4 Forests are important economically and ecologically. Nevertheless, the world's forests are rapidly being chopped down.

5 Animal and plant species provide many crucial medical, industrial, and agricultural products. We are now in the process of extinguishing these species, and changing the nature of life on the earth for all time.

6 The world is now in the process of using up the major current sources of energy. Humanity will eventually develop renewable forms of energy to replace these sources. But the present transition period is full of serious problems such as energy crises and environmental damage.

7 The problem of balancing economic and environmental needs is one that industrialized societies, both capitalist and Communist, must grapple with. It is also one that Third World nations must face.

CHAPTER 14

Nuclear War

INTRODUCTION

College and university teachers in this country are just beginning to wake up to their full responsibility in the age of nuclear armaments and potential nuclear war. Until very recently their sleep had been deep and undisturbed. True, a few of them sometimes had vexing dreams. Yale psychiatrist Robert Jay Lifton tells of receiving a letter from a college provost who confessed: "I have a minor nightmare that in the year 2050 there will be some hypothetical survivors looking in disbelief at our 1981 and 1982 catalogues. It's as if, living on the edge of the cliff, the Academy seemed not to care." ...Fortunately, all this has changed dramatically in the past two years....We are obviously long past the time when the nuclear subject was felt to be unacademic, unrespectable, or irrelevant.

—Dick Ringler (from Academe, *December 1983)*

In 1945 the United States detonated the first atomic bomb at Alamogordo, New Mexico. One of its creators, physicist J. Robert Oppenheimer, was astounded and filled with horror as he watched that first nuclear explosion. It reminded him of Vishnu's incantation as the Hindu god turned himself into the avatar of apocalypse: "I am become death, the destroyer of worlds." In the ensuing four decades, the major world powers have stockpiled more than 50,000 nuclear warheads, and Oppenheimer's prophetic fear of doomsday could well become a reality. For if these weapons were ever unleashed, the earth would briefly flicker back at the distant stars and then go out. And it may not just be the nuclear-born fires that die down. The planet's very ability to support human life could be extinguished as well, and that nightmare continues to haunt humankind with increasing regularity and intensity.

More than twenty-five years ago, the eminent sociologist C. Wright Mills turned his attention to nuclear war in his classic book *The Causes of World War Three* (1960). There he vigorously denounced "the rise of the cheerful robot, of the technological idiot, and of the crackpot realist" in both the United States and the Soviet Union, and outlined a strategy to stave off a nuclear holocaust. Unfortunately, the problem of nuclear war received scant attention from sociologists over the next quarter of a century. Indeed, *no* articles on the nuclear threat have appeared in the journal *Social Problems* since 1963! And an analysis of social problems textbooks found war and peace to be the *least*-discussed issue (Lauer, 1976). Given the blessed fact that nuclear war is not here yet, why should sociologists turn their attention to it, and why should we devote an entire chapter to the topic?

Once the question is directly posed in this way, it almost seems silly. Sociological forces bear on every facet of the nuclear threat, from the interpersonal influence used in Congress for military spending to the mental stability of the

military personnel controlling the attack computers. Even without mushroom clouds on the horizon, nuclear weapons are assessing a heartbreaking objective price in linked social problems that might be solved but for the lost resources. Shaped by political events and the subjective factors discussed below, the threat of nuclear war has been climbing to the top of social problems opinion polls to become our No. 1 national nightmare. The current objective and subjective significance of nuclear war seems to have jarred sociologists out of their professional slumber on the issue. In the thematic address to the 1986 convention of the Society for the Study of Social Problems, President Rudolfo Alvarez stated: "In my personal judgment conditions that increase the probability of nuclear holocaust constitute the major social problem confronting the world today" (1985). And a 1985 issue of *The Sociological Quarterly* was devoted to this topic. We applaud this scholarly attention, and we agree with one reviewer who noted after reading this chapter that the book's other social problems "seem so pedestrian" when compared to the sociological significance of nuclear war.

OBJECTIVE DIMENSIONS

Nuclear weapons are the greatest *immediate* threat to the health and welfare of humanity. We have no way of precisely gauging the objective dimensions of an all-out nuclear war, for nothing in human experience serves as a precedent for such immense destruction. However, several recent studies do provide assessments of the probable effects of nuclear war on human society. While such studies are based on many assumptions, they nevertheless furnish an approximate frame of reference for understanding the probable effects of nuclear conflict. These studies generally focus on one or both of two scenarios: the detonation of a single 1-megaton thermonuclear bomb on a large city (e.g., Geiger, 1982; Ilyin, 1982; Haines, 1982; Shohno and Akiba, 1982) and all-out nuclear warfare (e.g., Lown, 1982; Bergstrom, 1983).

Scenario 1: A Single 1-Megaton Bomb

The biggest conventional bombs of World War II contained 20 tons of TNT. Because they could lay waste an entire city block, they were nicknamed "blockbusters." The yield of the atomic bomb which the United States dropped on Hiroshima in 1945 was gigantic by comparison. Packing the equivalent of 13,000 tons (13 kilotons) of TNT, it was 650 times more powerful than a blockbuster. Yet that atomic bomb produced only a puny puff relative to the potential of the 50-megaton bombs in today's arsenals, bombs that are about 4000 times more potent than the Hiroshima bomb and 2.6 million times stronger than the fearsome blockbusters of World War II. A 1-megaton bomb is therefore just a medium-sized warhead in our present-day stockpiles, but a warhead 80 times more powerful than the bomb that flattened Hiroshima. It is monstrous compared to anything previously used in warfare. A megaton is the equivalent of 1 million tons of TNT. To help you comprehend what that means, consider this: If 1 million tons of TNT was transported by rail, it would fill a freight train more than 400 miles long.

The impact of a 1-megaton nuclear explosion on a city depends on many variables such as the location, range, and type of the weapon's physical effects (Geiger, 1982; U.S. Office of Technology Assessment, 1982). Where the bomb detonates is an important variable. A ground-burst concentrates the heat and blast effects around ground zero, decreases the outward spread of these effects, and yields a high level of radioactive fallout. An airburst results in far less fallout, but disperses heat and blast effects over a much larger area. If the enemy's objective is to maximize death and injury in the city, the most devastating explosion would result from an airburst at 6000 feet. Another important set of factors are local atmospheric conditions.

Clouds, fog, and smog lessen visibility and sponge up heat, thus reducing the number of burn victims. Other conditions, such as snow on the ground or low white clouds over nonpolluted air, extend the range of hazardous thermal radiation. The velocity and direction of the prevailing winds determine the prevalence of fire and the dissemination of fallout. And rain lowers fire damage while boosting fallout.

The amount of destruction also hinges upon whether a conflagration or a fire storm develops. A conflagration is a wall of fire that is spread by surface winds as far as there is combustible material to sustain it. A fire storm is a massive self-fanning stationary fire. It can cover 100 square miles, generate temperatures up to 2000 degrees Fahrenheit (enough to melt metal and set asphalt streets on fire), create howling 200-plus miles per hour winds capable of uprooting trees and flinging cars about, and burn for days (Tsipis, 1982). Both conflagrations and fire storms increase the number of burn deaths enormously. They also make fallout shelters worthless by consuming all the oxygen in the air and replacing it with toxic gases. Those inside shelters (and cellars) are first asphyxiated by these gases, and then dry roasted because the ground is heated to high temperature. Shelters become in effect gas chambers and crematorium ovens, as they did in such cities as Dresden and Hamburg which experienced fire storms due to conventional allied bombing during World War II. It is hard to accurately predict whether a given city will experience a conflagration or a fire storm. A conflagration swept through Nagasaki and a fire storm struck Hiroshima.

Finally, the number of fatalities and injuries caused by a 1-megaton nuclear explosion is also a function of social behavior. For example, an attack on a city would yield many more victims during the working hours of a weekday than at other times because cities are then jammed with additional thousands (or, in very large cities, millions) of people who commute to factories, offices, schools, and other urban institutions (U.S. Office of Technology Assessment, 1982). Similarly, a nuclear strike during the summer would maximize casualties because more people would be outdoors, lightly clothed, and likely to glance at the fireball. This would make them more vulnerable to the heat and blast effects.

The effects of a 1-megaton nuclear explosion are frequently set forth in a model of concentric circles around ground zero. Each circle represents a certain level of destruction, death, and injury, these effects decreasing with distance from the center. Here we will discuss what happens in each circle if a 1-megaton warhead were airbursted above the heart of downtown Detroit. This discussion applies to virtually all cities, although death and injury tolls would vary depending on population density and the features of the local terrain. The Detroit scenario is based largely on a study by Geiger (1982).

The first circle has a radius of 1.5 miles and covers 7 square miles of the city. Its center is ground zero, the place where the explosion's fireball touches down. The fireball is momentarily like a miniature star, hotter at its core than the sun itself. Its temperature approaches 30 million degrees Fahrenheit, causing everything nearby to simply vaporize to atoms and vanish. Humans would be instantaneously reduced to smoke, which would then be propelled away by 2000 miles per hour winds.

The nuclear explosion also triggers a 2-second flash of thermal radiation, i.e., heat and light. Rocketing outward at the speed of light, thermal radiation strikes well before the blast wave, just as lightening can be spotted seconds before thunder is heard. The heat from the 1-megaton bomb can burn individuals as far as 7 miles away; the light can flashblind persons at distances of 53 miles on a clear night (U.S. Office of Technology Assessment, 1982). In the middle of the first circle (but outside the fireball), thermal radiation would incinerate people to ashes before they could move. Only the shadows of some would endure, indelibly scorched onto the walls by which they were standing. The thermal radiation would then broil the area near the outer rim of the first circle. Steel would melt, concrete would explode, and humans would char.

In the split second after detonation, a second horror would commence: the effects of the explosive blast. The blast from large megaton nuclear weapons does the most damage to cities. The blast forces air outward from the explosion site, causing sudden alterations in air pressure called *static overpressure*. Overpressure is pressure in excess of normal atmospheric pressure. Unlike conventional explosives which deliver a swift slaplike shock, nuclear blast waves endure for several seconds and can encircle buildings, crushing them as though a giant fist had squeezed them on all sides. The overpressure can lift other buildings off their foundations and fling them outward along with other debris. The movement of air away from the explosion site also produces *dynamic pressure* (high winds) that can move buildings suddenly or knock them over. Overpressure in the first circle would range from 200 to 20 pounds per square inch (psi). It would flatten every building, including the strongest steel and reinforced concrete structures. Winds ranging from 2000 miles per hour at ground zero to 400 miles per hour near the circle's rim would also fire debris outward at lethal velocities. The air would be saturated with whirling matter, including screaming people writhing in agony as burning clothing and flesh whip from their frames.

Nuclear explosions generate radiation two ways: (1) direct radiation from the explosion, which has a limited range; and (2) fallout radiation from particles made radioactive by the explosion, which has a range determined by local weather conditions, particularly the wind. Radiation can kill people outright in the short term and the long term (via, e.g., cancer), and

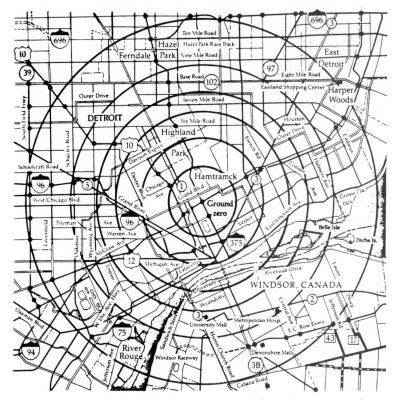

The six circles of a 1-megaton airburst over Detroit. For a 20-megaton explosion, the sixth circle would be the first circle. (*Courtesy of Office of Technology Assessment*)

can also weaken them so that they are more susceptible to death from other conditions (e.g., burns, infections, blast injuries).

A *rem*, or roentgen equivalent man, is a measure of damage to human health. A dose of 600 rems within, say, the first week after an explosion causes death within a few weeks in about 90 percent of otherwise healthy persons; 450 rems, in 50 percent; and 300 rems, in 10 percent. And the survivors would be at high risk of developing fatal cancers and suffering serious genetic effects later. Doses below 50 rems would not create any apparent short-term consequences, but nevertheless would do long-term damage (U.S. Office of Technology Assessment, 1982). In the Detroit scenario, fallout radiation would be minimal because the warhead would be airburst. Direct radiation is

another matter. For a 1-megaton explosion, the range of intense direct radiation is substantially less than the fireball and blast effects. But it would be slaughterous in the first circle, where it would exceed 10,000 rems at the core and 1000 rems at the edge.

In short, the first circle is one of certain death. Every human being would be either vaporized, crushed, charred, asphyxiated, or massively irradiated, and most would be simultaneously killed several times over by some combination of these fates.

The second circle has a radius of 2.9 miles from ground zero and adds 20 square miles to the area of damage. The heat there would be intense enough to spontaneously ignite combustible materials, and to evaporate materials like aluminum siding. All unshielded persons would receive third degree burns, the most severe type because of the destruction of skin tissues. Blast overpressures (10 to 20 psi) would be strong enough to demolish all but the sturdiest buildings, to strip the exterior walls from steel skyscrapers, and to suck out their interior walls, floors, furniture, and occupants. In the downtown areas of Detroit and other large cities, the streets are narrow chasms running between the buildings' towering walls. In much of ring two, the buildings would tumble and fill the streets several stories high with rubble. This avalanche would crush pedestrians and make rescue and evacuation all but impossible. Many people would be buried alive. Along with the overpressure would come 300 miles per hour winds, capable of throwing 200-pound adults the length of a football field and dashing them against objects at death-dealing speeds. About half of those caught in this zone would perish just from blast injuries: skull fractures, severed spinal cords, penetrating wounds of the chest and abdomen, rupture of the lungs and other organs, multiple lacerations, massive blood loss, and crushed chests, extremities, and vertebrae. Many others would die from burns and radiation.

The third circle extends 4.3 miles from ground zero and encompasses an additional 32 square miles. The heat there would still be high enough to ignite clothing, wood, and fabrics inside buildings and to melt asphalt paving. Those caught outdoors would suffer third degree burns from the fireball, and others would be burned by widespread secondary fires. Many would have difficulty scrambling to safety because of temporary flashblindness due to reflex glances at the fireball. Others would receive retinal burns, plunging them into partial or total blindness. The overpressure (5 psi) would crush ordinary buildings and inflict severe damage on heavily constructed factories and commercial buildings. Winds would still make lethal projectiles of debris, and would toss people around like bowling pins. The pres-

sure would rupture the eardrums of many persons, leaving them deaf. Thus, about half the inhabitants of the second and third rings would perish immediately, and another 40 percent would sustain serious and/or incapacitating injuries.

The fourth circle, with a radius of 4.9 miles from ground zero, includes an additional 18 square miles of Detroit. The heat here would still be sufficient to cause third degree burns and to ignite secondary fires. The overpressure (4 psi) and 125 miles per hour winds—greater than hurricane force—would flatten brick and frame houses and damage sturdier buildings. Massive secondary fires would break out as a result of downed electric lines, exploding gasoline stations and fuel tanks, broken natural gas mains, and damaged furnaces, stoves, water heaters, and electrical circuits.

Even at the outer edge of the fifth circle, 6.3 miles from ground zero, the effects of the nuclear explosion would be awesome. Overpressure (3 psi) and 100 miles per hour winds would be strong enough to blast away the exterior walls of buildings, and to blow humans and other objects out of them. Thermal radiation would give third degree burns to persons caught outside, and light combustibles like paper and leaves would ignite. Fires would likely occur throughout the zone.

The sixth and last ring has a radius of 9.5 miles from ground zero and covers an additional 100 square miles. The still-intense heat would deliver third degree burns to 20 percent of those caught outdoors, and extensive second degree burns (producing blisters which, if untreated, lead to infection and permanent scars) to another 70 percent. Overpressures (2 psi) and hurricane-force winds (80 miles per hour) would turn ordinary objects and debris into deadly projectiles. For example, windows would shatter into 100 miles per hour glass shards. These forces would also topple 30 percent of the utility poles and trees, clogging roads and blocking evacuation and rescue vehicles. Most homes

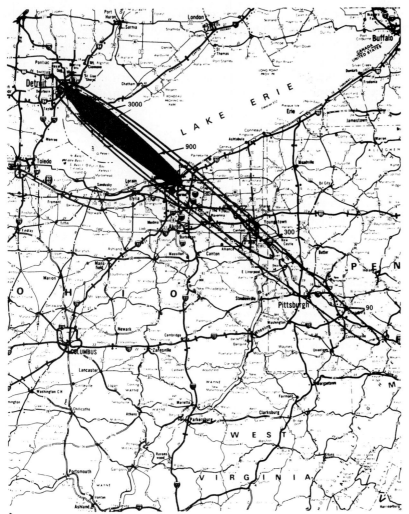

Main fallout pattern from a 1-megaton surface burst in Detroit, assuming a uniform 15-mph northwest wind. The contours represent seven-day accumulated doses (without shielding of 3000, 900, 300, and 90 rems). (*Courtesy of Office of Technology Assessment*)

would suffer moderate damage without considering the effects of possible secondary fires.

As the explosion wreaked its devastation on the six rings of Detroit, a dense mass of smoke and dust would cover the city like a shroud, and a mushroom cloud, the quintessence of Doomsday, would gush upward, spreading about 12 miles in diameter. If the attack occurred during the day, these phenomena would blot out the sun and plunge the city into inpenetrable dark-

ness. If it occurred at night, it would become darker still. But gradually the scene would be reilluminated by the secondary fires which would begin to rage, stoked by a strong, steady wind blowing toward ground zero. Eventually, the individual fires would grow together and turn into either a fire storm or a conflagration. And the horrors and agonies would continue unabated. Survivors in the inner circles would most likely be doomed by the giant fire, and those fleeing in the outer circles would be forced to leave behind blind and disabled family and friends, or else to perish in the flames with them. In general, the larger the city, the smaller the proportion of the population that has a chance of escaping. With a 1-megaton explosion, fires break out as far away as 10 miles from ground zero, and most streets are no longer serviceable (Schell, 1984).

Assuming that a fire storm developed, Geiger (1982) calculated that a single 1-megaton explosion would kill about 1 million (25 percent) of the nearly 4 million people in the Detroit metropolitan area. More than 1 million more would be seriously injured. Thus, about 54 percent of the population would be casualties. But even these figures severely underestimate the true totals, especially if the attack on Detroit is part of an all-out war, because help would not be forthcoming from elsewhere. For instance, many victims would be buried deep in the rubble of wrecked buildings, and there would be no social system with the necessary organization and equipment to rescue them. Fear of radiation exposure would also seriously delay the rescue efforts.

But rescue would be worthless for many persons anyway. Even the preexplosion medical institution, let alone its few shattered remnants, could not have dealt with more than 1 million profound and incapacitating injuries. For example, the 200,000 third degree burn victims in Detroit alone would be enough to fill all the present intensive-care burn beds in the United States—more than 100 times over! Thus, a sizable portion of the injured would eventually join the ranks of the dead. Moreover, there are whole classes of other kinds of casualties to consider. For example, in any large urban area there are tens of thousands of individuals whose lives are dependent upon modern medical technology and supplies. Many would become critically ill and die when supplies of such things as insulin, digitalis, and cortisone dried up; or when renal dialysis,

surgery, and other medical services were no longer available. Still other types of threats to health and life will be discussed below.

The above description of the effects of a 1-megaton explosion over Detroit is horrifying enough, but it is a minimum-damage scenario for such a city in an all-out nuclear war. Both the United States and the Soviet Union have warheads ranging up to 50 megatons, and some of the larger weapons would undoubtedly fall on major cities. If Detroit were struck by a 20-megaton warhead, for instance, the sixth circle in the scenario above would become the first circle. A single 20-megaton bomb—of which both the United States and the Soviet Union have more than 100—would unleash the equivalent of 1600 Hiroshima bombs. It would disintegrate or burn up every structure within 450 square miles and kill everything within a radius of 20 miles. Its fireball would be so powerful that it would flashblind individuals hundreds of miles away (Commager, 1984). If such a bomb exploded in the New York City area, it might kill as many as 20 million people in one fell swoop—almost 10 percent of the United States population (Schell, 1982).

To make matters worse, the most probable scenarios for nuclear war call for massive, multiweapon strikes. In such attacks, metropolitan areas like Detroit would be targeted at the rate of one nuclear weapon for every 200,000 to 500,000 inhabitants. (New York City alone would likely be hit with twenty to thirty-five airburst and groundburst nuclear explosions.) These explosions would be scattered about the cities, and their circles of destruction would interlock, forming a hellish tangle of overkill and rubble bouncing. The damage to metropolitan areas would be so immense that it would be virtually incalculable (Geiger, 1982).

Scenario 2: All-Out Nuclear War

Immediate Effects Weapons specialists reckon that the explosives detonated in all the wars until now add up to about 16 megatons. The combined arsenals of the United States, the USSR, and other countries currently exceed 20,000 megatons, or 5 tons of deadly power for every man, woman, and child on the earth. Nothing in all past history remotely approaches the holocaust that an all-out nuclear war would produce. A 10,000-megaton attack on the United States would be the equivalent of about 1 million Hiroshimas. According to Schell (1982) it would render more than one-sixth of the territory of the United States uninhabitable, and subject nearly three-quarters of it to incendiary fires. The physical structure of the country would be whisked away, like leaves in a strong wind. The Soviet Union and Europe would suffer similar fates.

When college students take a course in population studies, they are usually surprised to learn that World War II and other American wars have had only a negligible effect on the country's age and sex structure. Indeed, all the wars of the twentieth century are virtually indiscernible on a graph representing world population growth. The lesson here is that the direct impact of armed conflicts on population trends has been remarkably modest in all of recorded history.

But the development of nuclear weapons may change all that. In one likely scenario of all-out nuclear war developed by the World Health Organization, the United States and the Soviet Union would use about half of their nuclear arsenals. About 90 percent of this megatonnage would strike targets in North America, Europe, and Asia, and the remainder would hit Latin America, Africa, and Oceania. Half the bombs would be groundburst and half airburst, the latter over cities with 60,000 or more residents. This nuclear exchange would kill at least 1.1 billion people immediately, and *seriously* injure another 1.1 billion (Bergstrom, 1983). Such a war would result in about 140 million deaths in the United States (Lown, 1982). One reason for this especially high

United States death toll is that 65 percent of Americans would be within 20 miles of a prime military-industrial target at zero hour, and 95 percent would be within 100 miles of such targets (Miller, 1985). In sum, about half of humanity would be the *immediate* victims of an all-out nuclear war.

Short-Term Effects   As in the city scenario, many of the injured and the noninjured would be added to the world death toll in the first few weeks and months after a nuclear attack. This is not only because of the inadequate rescue and treatment of the injured but because of the breakdown of the social structure, the collapse of public health services, the scarcity of food, and the environmental damage. The absence of an administrative structure, the lack of energy, the destruction of communications, and possibly rampant social disturbances would make the situation even more precarious. Obtaining an adequate supply of uncontaminated water would be one of the most immediate and serious problems. Water systems would be partly or wholly destroyed, and many remaining sources of fresh water would be contaminated with radiation or with toxic chemicals from destroyed chemical plants and storage tanks. Much of the available food would be similarly contaminated. Indeed, the consumption of radioactive food and water, along with the inhalation of radioactive particles, would be major causes of internal (body) radiation. Thus, survivors would face the twin hazards of internal and external radiation (Bergstrom, 1983).

Disease would also be a scourge for survivors due to the destruction of public health, sanitary, and medical facilities. There would be a widespread lack of sewage treatment plants, waste disposal systems, and refrigeration; and disease-causing viruses and bacteria would contaminate available food and water. Billions of rotting human and animal corpses and ubiquitous accumulations of untreated waste and sewage would serve as breeding grounds for legions of insects which would spread malaria, typhus, and other deadly diseases. The population of flea-infested rats would also multiply, increasing the chance of bubonic plague, which alone could strike 12 percent of the survivors, killing half of them. A partial list of other diseases that would become epidemic throughout the world includes infectious hepatitis, tuberculosis, salmonellosis, amoebic dysentery, and streptococcal and staphylococcal infections.

Moreover, many survivors would have deficient immune systems because of exposure to sublethal doses of radiation. Not only would this make them more susceptible to the epidemic diseases, but such diseases would be more life threatening once contracted. Indeed, the immunodeficiency would render these individuals vulnerable to infection even from organisms residing in their own bodies which normally do not cause illness. Finally, secondary infection, which is ordinarily the principal cause of death in burn and radiation victims (and in many blast victims as well), would become an even more potent killer due to the immunodeficiency (Abrams, 1981; 1982).

Psychological factors would also lower the survival rate of the injured in the immediate aftermath of the war. In natural disasters, the initial shock and stupor are generally followed quickly by an ardent identification with the community and an eagerness to help others. But in Hiroshima and Nagasaki, the psychic problems were more persistent. Survivors experienced profound psychic numbing, a dissociation from reality, and a feeling of coexistence with the dead (Bergstrom 1983). In an all-out nuclear war, these psychic processes could be so extreme that they might well become irreversible (Lifton, 1982; Lifton and Erikson, 1982).

Long-Term Effects   The long-term effects of nuclear war would also be devastating. Many of the short-term health effects would persist for years because the reconstruction and operation

of public health, sanitation, and other important systems require a stable social organization and sophisticated manufacturing and distribution systems—things which may take decades to properly restore. The incidence of cancer and miscarriages would rise substantially, particularly among those directly exposed to the explosion or to local radioactive fallout. And about 20 percent of liveborn children would be afflicted with hereditary damage (Bergstrom, 1983). The psychological impact of threatened cancer and hereditary damage, as well as the knowledge that the nuclear war and all its dreadful horrors could have been prevented, would be deeply felt, and many would find it hard to live with such psychological baggage (Sagan, 1980).

One of the major long-term problems would be reviving agriculture. Fire and residual radioactivity would have laid waste much of the world's fertile lands, and accelerated desertification would claim even more. The atmospheric effects of nuclear war would also have deleterious effects on agriculture, negatively affecting plant growth and/or photosynthesis. And there would be persistent widespread shortages of seeds, fertilizers, pesticides, farm equipment, and fuel. The food distribution system—markets, refrigeration, transport, and so forth—would also be extremely limited, and much of the available food would never find its way to those who needed it. The destruction of the United States agricultural system and its distribution networks would be a catastrophe not only for Americans but for other industrial and Third World societies that rely heavily on food imports from the United States. Millions of survivors throughout the world would perish from starvation and undernutrition in the years following a nuclear war (Bergstrom, 1983).

One rarely considered but supremely important casualty of nuclear war would be modern society itself (Lenski and Lenski, 1982; Shinn, 1982; Bergstrom, 1983). The negative effects on the social and economic structures of advanced

Thousands of charred corpses lie in the street of Tokyo, Japan, after a March, 1945, fire raid by American planes. Nearly four weeks passed before survivors were able to dispose of the bodies. A nuclear war would kill at least 1.1 billion people immediately as well as billions of animals. Furthermore, the rotting human and animal corpses would serve as breeding grounds for legions of insects which would spread many diseases among survivors. (*Koyo Ishikawa/Morita Photo Laboratory*)

societies would be immense. The political institution, especially the central government authority, would vanish, and social and political anarchy would reign. Conflict would break out between individuals, families, groups, and communities over scarce food and other resources as the struggle for survival became all-consuming. The present world economy would revert to a more primitive one because industrial sites, sources of raw materials, and skilled labor would all be decimated by the war. Energy supplies needed to fuel industrial and domestic processes would be partially or completely lost, and communication and transport systems would be obliterated. Monetary systems would be nonexistent, and commerce would revert to the barter system. Technological and economic recovery would be severely retarded by the loss of the educational institution and the paucity of skilled workers.

But recovery—in the sense of a restored industrial civilization—might never occur (Boulding, 1964; Weisskopf, 1981). Indeed, the most likely outcome of an all-out nuclear war is the permanent regression of modern civilizations to the level of development typical of agrarian societies (Lenski and Lenski, 1982; Shinn, 1982). United States society might resemble that of the Middle Ages or those of classic postnuclear war science fiction movies like *The Road Warrior,* with scattered communities and roving bands fighting over scarce resources and territory. Reindustrialization could prove impossible because some circumstances that facilitated the first industrialization would no longer exist. For instance, the rich mineral beds close to the surface of the earth, the supplies of easily accessible petroleum, unexploited wilderness, and virgin continents are now either gone or seriously depleted (Chapter 13). To offset these losses, modern society over the centuries developed complex technological systems which now yield high living standards despite the fact that crucial resources are far harder to obtain. But these complex technologies (e.g., offshore oil rigs, sophisticated low-grade ore smelting) presuppose advanced industrialization. They cannot be resurrected and grafted onto the more primitive societies which would result from nuclear war. As geophysicist Harrison Brown (1954:114) puts it:

> Our present civilization, itself the result of a combination of no longer existent circumstances, is the only foundation on which it seems possible that a future civilization capable of utilizing the vast resources of energy now hidden in rocks and seawater, and unutilized in the sun, can be built. If this foundation is destroyed, in all probability [civilization] has "had it." Perhaps there is possible a sort of halfway station in which retrogression stops short of a complete extinction of civilization, but even this is not pleasant to contemplate.

Reflecting on this situation, Einstein remarked that "if the next war is fought with atomic weapons, the war after that will be fought with clubs."

Modern society may not be the only thing nuclear war makes extinct. Recent studies by American, European, and Soviet scientists (Turco, Toon, Ackerman, Pollack, and Sagan, 1983; Ehrlich, 1983) indicate that the long-term climactic effects of such a war would be much graver and more far-reaching than previous studies suggested. These new studies conclude that nuclear war would subject vast areas of the earth to unusually low temperatures, prolonged darkness, toxic smog, violent windstorms, and persistent fallout—a set of conditions known as *nuclear winter.* A number of biologists and ecologists now maintain that nuclear winter could lead to the extinction of many species including humanity. This grim view has been accepted after extensive study by the National Academy of Sciences, the nation's most prestigious scientific body, and by the U.S. Department of Defense (Ahern, 1985).

A nuclear-winter-type phenomenon did occur on a small scale in 1816. The Indonesian volcano Tambora erupted then, sending tons of smoke and particles into the atmosphere. As a result, there was no summer that year throughout the world, and snow fell during July in North America and Europe. Thus, the nuclear winter theory is by no means farfetched. But its underlying computer projections are based on a series of assumptions about such factors as the amount of smoke generated by nuclear war, and how long it takes before these particles are "rained out" of the atmosphere by moisture in the air. And these assumptions are uncertain and controversial. For instance, some scientists—including Edward Teller, the physicist who helped develop the hydrogen bomb—argue that the nuclear winter scientists overestimated the amount of smoke. Teller insists that temperature changes would be moderate. But other researchers are beginning to fashion even grimmer visions of nuclear winter than those referred to above. Their research indicates that the nuclear winter could last as long as five years, rather than the earlier six-months-to-a-year estimate. If so, the earth would become an empty arctic wasteland where little or no food would grow. And the worst-case consequence of the nuclear winter theory—the extinction of humanity—would become more likely (Bayles, 1984).

In sum, a large-scale nuclear war would probably kill from 50 to 75 percent of the world's population due to its immediate and short-term effects and the prolonged effects of radiation. In addition, much of the remaining population would be doomed by the war's long-term effects. It is also possible that in the sum of their arsenals, the superpowers have unwittingly created the fabled doomsday machine, a common theme in the science fiction literature (e.g., *Return to the Planet of the Apes*). The unleashing of such a potentiality would be, of course, the ultimate horror, one that Jonathan Schell contemplates in his consciousness-raising book *The Fate of the Earth* (1982). Reviewing that book, arms control expert Strobe Talbott (1982*b*:21) writes:

> Until now, most of those who have thought either occasionally or professionally about the unthinkable have tended to concentrate on the impact that nuclear war might have on a city or a nation. Schell looks beyond that particular horror to an even greater one and ponders the awful finality itself. If the worst comes true, after all, what more is there to think about? But Schell looks beyond the end, as it were, into the void. "Death lies at the core of each person's private existence, but part of death's meaning is to be found in the fact that it occurs in a biological and social world that survives." Were that world to perish, it would be "the second death"—the death of the species, not just of earth's population on doomsday, but of countless unborn generations. They would be spared literal death but would nonetheless be victims—in his view the most important victims—of a nuclear war.

Occasionally there is an offhand remark in the popular literature that a nuclear war might actually benefit humanity (albeit in a grisly way) in the long run because it would tremendously relieve pressure on some of the other megaproblems like runaway population growth and resource depletion. The notion is that it might give the human race some breathing time in which to find the solution to these survival threats. But given the long-term effects discussed above, it should be clear that such a problem linkage is a cruel mirage.

Economic, Social, and Psychological Costs of the Arms Race

The objective dimension of the nuclear weapons problem extends far beyond the consequences of their actual use. The production and testing of these weapons have already taken the lives of many soldiers, uranium miners, and nuclear industry workers (Wasserman and Solomon, 1982). Cancer rates among American civilians who lived downwind of atmospheric nuclear weapons test sites have also risen dramatically. For instance, Mormons who lived in southwestern Utah when the detonations occurred in Nevada suffered five times more cases of leukemia than expected between 1958 and 1966, and also endured higher rates of other cancers, despite the group's healthy lifestyle which under normal circumstances results in a 23 percent lower overall cancer rate than the national average. The residents of other test areas have also suffered greatly, including the inhabitants of the Marshall Islands. Those living on the Bikini atoll, for instance, were not only forced to leave their still-now radioactive homeland but have absorbed the largest amount of radiation of any known population.

Enormous military spending is another consequence of the arms race. The global defense budget in 1983 was 790 billion dollars (International Institute for Strategic Studies, 1984), an amount that far exceeds the combined income of the poorest half of humanity. The United States alone will probably spend more than 1.6 trillion dollars for military purposes between 1982 and 1987—a sum equal to a stack of dollar bills 107,000 miles high (Miller, 1985). These expenditures are so astronomical that some analysts believe they are affecting the stability and integrity of the international economic system (Brown et al., 1984).

There are conflicting views on the role nuclear weapons play in military budgets. One argument is that nuclear arms are relatively cheap compared to conventional weapons. This view posits that the current overreliance of the United States on nuclear weapons stems in large part from a past desire to reduce defense spending, and an unwillingness to match the vast armies, tank forces, and other conventional war capabilities of the Soviet Union and its Warsaw Pact allies. Instead, the United States decided to rely on its nuclear superiority, which has only recently melted away. As former Secretary of State John Foster Dulles put it in the 1950s, nuclear weapons offer "more bang for the buck" (Krauthammer, 1984). If this perspective is the right one, then a decline in reliance on nuclear weapons might require a radically enlarged conventional defense and, hence, military budget. (This might also lead to cuts in funds allocated for nonmilitary social problems such as poverty, given that the funds saved by emphasizing nuclear weapons were expended on these other problems.)

The competing argument is that the true cost of nuclear weapons includes the human resources that are invested in their design and construction, the funds and materials that are needed to produce the weapons themselves, the fantastically expensive delivery systems, the extraordinarily costly radar, satellite, and other systems used to monitor other nations' nuclear forces, and the extensive military support systems that are needed to service, maintain, defend, and use nuclear weapons. Thus, as Shinn (1982) notes, "nuclear weapons are at the center of a circle whose circumference reaches far into human affairs."

As we noted in Chapter 1, social policies must be assessed by a kind of value accounting, in which benefits are balanced against costs. A dollar spent in one program budget—in this case, the defense budget—means a dollar less to deal with some other form of human suffering, including many megaproblems. The world's (and the United States') enormous defense budget (1.5 million dollars per minute) siphons off financial, natural, and human resources that would be better applied to peaceful, constructive purposes.

Consider, for example, how much progress could be achieved if only a small portion of the world's defense budget were diverted to health projects. The World Health Organization eradicated smallpox, which as recently as 1970 was a dreaded disease endemic in thirty-three countries with 1.2 billion inhabitants, with an investment of just 300 million dollars—an amount equivalent to just three hours of the cost of military budgets. The funds consumed by the arms race in just two weeks would provide a sanitary water supply for the inhabitants of the entire world. What a boon this would be for humankind, since contaminated water is presently responsible for 80 percent of global illness and inflicts incalculable misery and degradation on more than half of humanity (Lown, 1982). Similarly, about one day's worth of the world's annual military expenditures would provide enough farm equipment to help food-deficit Third World countries approach self-sufficiency by the early 1990s (Shinn, 1982). And two days' worth would cover the cost of the world's family planning needs (Brown et al., 1984).

Another way to appreciate this value trade-off is to consider the deployment of scientific resources. About 22 percent (or 500,000) of the world's finest scientists and engineers—including 50 percent of the physical scientists and engineers—work exclusively on military research and development (Brown, et al., 1984). By contrast, only 8 percent devote their talents and skills to energy research and development (with the bulk working in the nuclear power industry), 7 percent to health, 5 percent to transportation, and 3 percent to agriculture. Nearly 50 percent of United States government research and development funds are earmarked for military-related projects (Miller, 1985).

Consider also the claims that militarization makes on the time of political leaders. If these leaders were not constantly absorbed in attempts to resolve conflict around the world, they would have more energy to devote to solving other problems. And if a confrontational world climate did not exist between the two superpowers, they could cooperate to help solve major world problems (Brown et al., 1984). Dwight Eisenhower, former United States president and commander of the allied forces in World War II, summed up this value trade-off situation aptly:

> Every gun that is made, every warship launched, every rocket fired, signifies in the final sense, a theft from those who hunger and are not fed, those who are cold and not clothed. This world in arms is not spending money alone. It is spending the sweat of its laborers, the genius of its scientists, the hopes of its children (cited in Miller, 1985).

But the cost of the arms race and the growth of nuclear weapons do not end there. There are profound and widespread psychological, social, and moral costs as well. Nuclear weapons have spawned a new reality for humankind with serious psychological effects. Living under the threat of nuclear war has bred a persistent fear in people throughout the world that they, their loved ones, and their total surroundings might be swept away at any moment (Chazov, 1982). This is particularly true of children who are aware of nuclear issues and harbor intense fears about them (Cook, 1984). The prospect of nuclear war also undermines individual confidence in the possibility of a meaningful personal future. And poised nuclear arsenals force people to live with the possibility of the total extinction of humanity (Lown, 1982). Psychiatrists have identified defense mechanisms—such as avoidance, perceptual distortion, and dehumanization—which people (including political leaders) use to deal with the fear and guilt arising from this new nuclear reality. Unfortunately and ironically, these defense mechanisms increase the possibility of nuclear war by distorting reality (Lown, 1981).

Like the psychological costs, the social costs of the nuclear arms race are difficult to calculate but are undoubtedly staggering. Huge defense budgets negatively affect social structure and social values both in capitalistic and Communist societies. Such arms buildups generate pressure for still more arms and tend to bolster the relative strength of the military-industrial complex at the expense of other institutions (Lown, 1981). Moreover, some experts argue that the awareness that civilization could come to a cataclysmic end has caused many adults to lose interest in handing their culture on to their children, and has caused many young people to lose interest in commitment, marriage, and children (Wallace, 1982). The threat of nuclear weapons has been linked in part to the exacerbation in recent decades of many social problems, including drug abuse, teenage suicide, and divorce.

Preparation for nuclear war can also have a deleterious effect on the moral strength of a society. Bertrand Russell was one of the first to recognize this, noting almost at the dawn of nuclear confrontation: "Our world has sprouted a weird conception of security and a warped sense of morality—weapons are sheltered like treasures, while children are exposed to incineration" (Lown, 1982).

With so many serious economic, psychological, social, and moral costs associated with the arms race, there are many leaders and people who advocate that the United States should either withdraw from the race or, at least, substantially reduce the defense budget. However, most Americans support a strong defense, and there are still many defenders of the present level of defense spending. These defenders argue correctly that in the 1980s the United States defense budget, as a percent of both the gross national product and the total federal budget, was relatively low compared to that of most years since World War II (Dye, 1981). They also maintain that strategic nuclear weapons consume only about 10 percent of the defense budget, and that nearly 50 percent goes for the routine support costs of the military's 3.2 million soldiers and civilian personnel. Finally, they argue that high levels of both nuclear weapons and the conventional forces are necessary to avoid nuclear war. Indeed, one function of the deployment of United States troops in many parts of the world is to help prevent minor clashes from mushrooming into global nuclear war (Miller, 1985).

However, it is possible to argue that this defense policy makes sense only in the short run. That is, if resources needed to solve the world's other megaproblems continue to be diverted to military uses, the strains from these other problems at some future point could well overwhelm these defensive strategies and plunge the world into nuclear war (Lown, 1981).

THE SUBJECTIVE DIMENSION OF NUCLEAR WAR

It is essential that not only governments but also the peoples of the world recognize and understand the dangers of the present situation....Removing the threat of world war—a nuclear war— is the most acute and urgent task of the present day.

—United Nations General Assembly (1978)

In the last chapter we noted that world hunger probably has the highest objective dimension of all actual social problems because it debilitates and kills more people than any other problem. But a major nuclear war would rocket to the top of that list if it were ever to become a reality. War in general—and nuclear war in particular— already has the highest subjective dimension of any problem. Concern about war has been named by the public as the most important problem facing Americans in thirty-one of the last fifty years (economic concerns rank second) (*Gallup Report,* various years). Other more thorough studies concerning what Americans value most of all report that world peace outranks everything else including freedom, happiness, and family security (Manis, 1984). This primacy of peace in our value system is an enduring reason for high subjective concern about the problem of war. As you learned in Chapter 1, public perceptions of a problem determine the resources that will be available for its solution. The huge military budgets just discussed should come as no surprise then, given the primacy of these war concerns.

Although war concerns have been traditionally high in the United States, their level has varied considerably from year to year. Much of the variation since World War II is due to change in the public's apprehension of nuclear war. Concern about nuclear war started off very high in the postwar years. The destruction of Hiroshima and Nagasaki by American atomic bombs terrified much of the world's population, including many Americans. People were fearful that these weapons would be used again in anger. Indeed, the authors of this book, as children during the 1950s, remember the regular air raid drills at school during which we climbed under our desks while teachers cautioned us to close our eyes to avoid being blinded by the fireballs. Fortunately those fireballs never came, although they did visit many children of that era in their dreams.

The nuclear-war shivers of the 1950s peaked in 1962, when the Soviet Union stationed missiles with nuclear warheads in Cuba. A petrified nation held its breath while President Kennedy moved to the brink of nuclear war to force the Russians to remove the missiles. Then in a classic example of how the objective and subjective dimensions of a problem can move in opposite directions, concern about nuclear war receded into the subconscious of civilization from the mid-1960s to the late-1970s, even though both sides increased their nuclear firepower by several orders of magnitude. This decline in concern was due in part to the superpowers' highly visible but only modestly successful efforts to pursue arms agreements that would lessen the chances of nuclear war (Talbott, 1982*a*).

In the late-1970s nuclear war's subjective dimension began to rise once again for several reasons. Technological developments led to the creation of nuclear weapons systems which were more powerful, more accurate, and more mobile than those which preceded them. *Détente* (the relaxation of international tension) and the promise of arms limitation gradually gave way to the politics of confrontation between the United States and the Soviet Union. The rush by other countries, including some trouble-plagued Third World nations, to become nuclear powers in their own right was another unsettling factor. Finally, and perhaps most significantly, strategic discussions in both the West and the East placed increased emphasis upon two concepts: namely (1) a winnable nuclear war, the notion that one superpower might be able to survive a nuclear war without terminal damage and emerge from it in much better shape than its adversary; and (2) the tactic of limited nuclear war, with "only" tens of millions of casualties.

Awareness of these phenomena expanded dramatically from the late-1970s to the mid-1980s, stimulated in no small part by the attention and visibility given to the nuclear predicament by academics, scientists, policymakers, politicians, and the mass media. Consequently, the prevention of nuclear war once again re-

This mural was painted on the side of a building in Berkeley, California, in 1983. The subjective dimension of nuclear war peaked in that year, and this mural was one manifestation of this deepening concern. Among other things it shows the leaders of the superpowers deciding the fate of humanity. It also shows two possible futures for humanity: The continuation of our present advanced civilization or a more primitive society which may result from nuclear war.

turned to the top of the global agenda, where it had been in the aftermath of Hiroshima and during the depths of the cold war (Kegley and Wittkopf, 1985).

The new peak in nuclear war's subjective dimension occurred in late 1983, when 37 percent of Americans polled labeled war-related concerns the nation's most important problem (unemployment finished second with 31 percent) (*Gallup Report,* 1984). This reawakened awareness of the dangers of nuclear war cut across traditional political, social, and demographic groups. Those concerned included archconservatives and diehard liberals, professionals with impeccable "establishment" credentials and peacenik activists, males and females, whites and nonwhites, and the college educated and the uneducated. College students were no exception to this subjective trend. When asked, "How likely do you think we are to get into a nuclear war within the next ten years?" 34 percent answered that is was "fairly" or "very likely" (*Gallup Report,* 1983*b*).

One force responsible for the heightened subjective dimension was the nuclear-freeze movement. This movement comprised a loose coalition of groups including such long-time disarmament organizations as the Union for Concerned Scientists and SANE, as well as a band of newer organizations. The latter included Physicians for Social Responsibility, International Physicians for the Prevention of Nuclear War (a group whose founders won the Nobel Peace Prize in 1985), Artists for Survival, the Business Alert to Nuclear War, and the Lawyers Alliance for Nuclear Arms Control. Altogether about 20,000 individuals were actively involved in the movement during 1983.

The primary objective of the nuclear-freeze movement was to raise public awareness about nuclear war. Such a war was viewed as an abstract, distant possibility during much of the 1960s and 1970s even by the educated members of society—something that, like taxes and death, had become simply an unavoidable and perma-

nent feature of postindustrial life. The movement tried to shock people out of these ostrichlike attitudes by painting for them a comprehensive, vivid, and often personal picture of the true horrors of nuclear war. To accomplish this, the movement used a highly visible array of public relations gimmicks, including media tours of hypothetical blast zones in major cities, newspaper articles showing maps with concentric circles radiating from ground zero in everyone's hometown, publication of grotesque pictures and haunting stories of Hiroshima victims, mass marches, and benefit rock concerts. By educating the public this way, the movement hoped to bring pressure on the United States and other governments to pursue policies that would diminish and ultimately eliminate the risks posed by these weapons.

Awareness of the nuclear predicament was also heightened by a variety of other social phenomena that occurred during this period. One was the explosion in the number of mass consumption books on nuclear weaponry. By 1983 there were some 250 such books, more than ten times as many as existed in 1973. Probably the most subjectively powerful of them all was Schell's *The Fate of the Earth,* referred to above. With *Fate,* Schell entered the select company of such scientific moralists as Rachel Carson, whose *Silent Spring* alerted many Americans to the growing threat to our environment. Similarly, films dramatizing the tragic consequences of nuclear war were more common during this period. The most famous of these was the much-publicized television movie *The Day After.* It was viewed in 46 percent of America's television households, making it the twelfth highest rated United States program ever.

In addition, groups of scientists held conferences on chilling topics like nuclear winter, and the media routinely gave these meetings extensive coverage. Organized religion also helped boost awareness. Leaders and groups within the Catholic, Protestant, and other religions began to proclaim the unambiguous immorality of nuclear weapons, and raised their voices against the nuclear arms buildup (Wohlstetter, 1985; National Conference of Catholic Bishops, 1985). The number of college and university courses on the arms race, the threat of nuclear war, and kindred matters also grew at an astonishing rate all across the nation (Ringler, 1983). In short, beginning in the late 1970s Americans got an unprecedented total-immersion course on the dangers of the nuclear age.

The subjective dimension of possible nuclear war, although still relatively high, has declined somewhat since its peak in late 1983. By 1985 it was no longer cited as the nation's most important problem. This decline was not due to any decrease in the problem's objective dimension, which, in fact, continued to rise sharply. Rather it was due to the same kind of cosmetic changes which helped smother concern in the late 1940s and early 1960s. Among these changes were more circumspect public pronouncements on nuclear issues by United States government officials, and a return to arms agreement talks between the superpowers.

It is possible to argue that the threat of nuclear war, with its nonpareil objective dimension, has never assumed its rightful place at the center of the social and political agenda—that even at the height of its subjective dimension concern was way too low, being only slightly higher than that of unemployment. What can account for this impressive apathy with which the vast majority of Americans, even those in the seats of power, have accepted this hellish situation? One explanation is that most humans can neither fully imagine nor truly comprehend the horrors of nuclear war, for it defies comparison—qualitatively and quantitatively—with anything we have ever known. This incomprehensibility is especially pertinent to the people of the United States, a nation which has not been ravaged even by conventional war since the Civil War over a century ago (Geiger, 1982). Another reason why we find the danger of nuclear weapons so difficult to grasp is the

natural tendency of the human mind to ward off thoughts that are too frightening to contemplate, particularly if the menacing situation can be made to seem remote. (In terms of the subjective factors, *expectations* about one's personal ability to do anything about nuclear Armageddon may be low, so why lose sleep over it.) Young people are better able than adults to look directly at the objective dimension of the nuclear danger, because the former's psychological defenses are probably less developed (Mack, 1982).

SOCIAL POLICY: NUCLEAR WAR

Strategic nuclear theory is a matter of mind-deadening complexity and ferocious ideological dispute. Consequently, understanding nuclear policy is akin to walking through a maze of mirrors. This is partly because nuclear policies are rife with paradoxes. Consider, for instance, those paradoxes implicit in the policy of nuclear deterrence. Weapons are produced in order never to be used. Defensive weapons such as antiballistic missile systems are greater menaces to peace than offensive weapons, such as manned bombers. And weapons trained on people reduce the risk of war, while those trained on weapons boost it (Krauthammer, 1984). In addition to such paradoxes, there is only one given in the debate over nuclear policy, namely, that nuclear weapons cannot be disinvented. Thus, we must find ways to ensure that they are never used.

After evaluating dozens of books and articles on nuclear policy, we find ourselves in agreement· with the discomforting yet compelling conclusion of the Harvard Nuclear Study Group: "Humanity has no alternative but to hold [the] threat [of infinitely destructive nuclear war] at bay and to learn to live…in the world we know: a world of nuclear weapons, international rivalries, recurring conflicts, and at least some risk of nuclear crisis…. Living with nuclear weapons is our only hope" (Carnesale, Doty, Hoffmann, Huntington, Nye, and

Sagan, 1983:19, 255). So we have decided to limit our policy discussion to two alternatives which do not presume the eradication of nuclear weapons. These include the traditional and present United States policy known by its acronyms—MAD, NUTS, and DEAD (MND); and a contrasting one called the Good Neighbor Policy (GNP). (If you are interested in reading about more utopian policies such as those associated with total nuclear disarmament, a good starting point would be Jonathan Schnell's book *The Abolition*, 1984.)

Mad, Nuts, and Dead: Policy 1

Strategy for Solution   Deterrence is the centerpiece of all policies which do not presume the eradication of nuclear weapons. United States strategists have traditionally regarded the capability to deter nuclear aggression as an indispensable element of our nuclear policy. Deterrence has been defined as a condition created when an aggressor's attack is stopped by threatening retaliation (Kegley and Wittkopf, 1985). Or as Rothschild (1983) describes it, "Deterrence ...consists of the following threat: 'Do not attack me because if you do, something unacceptably horrible will happen to you.' " Schnell (1984:36) summarizes the basic tenets of deterrence like this:

> that nuclear weapons offer nations effectively unlimited force; that winning a nuclear war is impossible; that it is imperative, therefore, to stop such a war from ever beginning; that the weapons themselves play a crucial role in that effort; that an invulnerable retaliatory force is of particular importance; that there is a special danger inherent in any capacity, on either side, for destroying the nuclear forces of the other side in a first strike; and that "perceptions" and "psychology" play an essential role in convincing the adversary that any aggression by him will lead only to his annihilation, and so in maintaining the "stability" of the whole arrangement.

This policy of deterrence has come to be known by the acronym MAD, which stands for mutually assured destruction. The "mutual" aspect of MAD indicates, significantly, that age-old military strategies aimed at providing unilateral national security are now obsolete. The chief purpose of a superpower's military in the era of MAD is no longer to win wars but to avert them. As Winston Churchill put it in 1955, MAD means that "safety will be the sturdy child of terror, and survival the twin brother of annihilation."

Policy into Practice   Since the beginning of the nuclear age, both the United States and the Soviet Union have in effect adopted essentially the same MAD strategy. Although MAD has succeeded in preventing nuclear war to date, there are a number of practical problems which could cause the policy to fail in the future. These problems include (1) nuclear imbalance, (2) technical or human error, (3) unauthorized or improper use, (4) brinkmanship, (5) proliferation, and (6) nuclear terrorism.

Nuclear Imbalance   MAD depends heavily on the maintenance of a stable balance between the nuclear arsenals of the United States and the USSR. This balance of terror ideally must be near-perfect or dangerous instabilities result. But nuclear strength and, hence, parity are very difficult to gauge. Strength is not merely a function of the numbers and sizes of weapons, but also includes such factors as the ability to find the enemy's weapons (and thus target and destroy them), and the ability to hide one's own weapons. The United States leads the USSR in these finding/hiding abilities—known formally as transparency technologies—and this is why the United States maintains parity vis-à-vis the USSR with fewer weapons and superiority with equal numbers. For example, the United States has fewer attack submarines than the USSR, but the Soviet submarines have a significant stealth disadvantage—they are noisier. Moreover, the United States submarines have superior underwater hearing. Consequently, American submarines have a decisive advantage in submarine warfare because they can detect (and target) Soviet submarines at four times the distance that Soviet crafts can spot American ones (Deudney, 1983). Similarly, civil defense programs have a bearing on the balance of terror. Since the USSR has embarked on an extensive civil defense program while the United States has not, the United States needs relatively more weapons to place the USSR in comparable jeopardy, all other things being equal.

Because nuclear strength is difficult to gauge accurately, neither the United States nor the USSR can be absolutely certain of parity. So each nation continues to design new weapons, especially ones that would limit damage to its homeland in the event deterrence failed. This situation triggers a vicious spiral: as one nation strives to defend itself, the other frets about imbalance and sets out to restore it. One nation's quest for parity invariably results in the other's actual or imagined vulnerability, and a stable balance of terror is never fully achieved (Kelly, 1982).

An imbalance can lead to nuclear war two ways. First, if one nation forges well ahead of the other in the nuclear arms race, it might be tempted to launch a first strike while the trailing nation is weak. The leading nation might theorize that it could knock out both the first strike potential and most of the retaliatory capability of the trailing nation with a sneak attack, while itself suffering "only" the loss of a few cities and a small fraction of its own population. Secretary of Defense Caspar Weinberger argued in 1981 that the Soviet Union had developed this "can win" attitude (Associated Press, 1981), and this is one reason why the Reagan administration pressed hard during the 1980s for increased defense expenditures.

But there is a twin hazard inherent in nuclear imbalance. Not only is the leading nation tempted to strike, but—what is undoubtedly even more dangerous—the trailing nation

might, in a crisis, feel compelled to launch hostilities itself rather than risk completely losing its forces. As Schelling (1960) puts it, once a significant imbalance occurs, both nations may reason as follows: "He, thinking I was about to kill him in self-defense, was about to kill me in self-defense, so I had to kill him in self-defense." Thus, under MAD, nuclear superiority is as menacing to the leading nation as it is to the trailing one (Schell, 1982). Indeed, it is worth noting that the most desperate and dangerous event of the nuclear era—the Cuban missile crisis of 1962—occurred at a time when the United States enjoyed an overwhelming nuclear advantage over the USSR.

The second way an imbalance can lead to nuclear war is the situation in which one nation is on the verge of a major weapons breakthrough or buildup. The other nation could decide to initiate a nuclear war before this occurred while its opponent is relatively weak. Because of its technological superiority, the United States regularly produces new, destabilizing weapons systems, such as missiles with multiple independently targeted nuclear warheads (MIRVs), the ingenious stealth bombers, and super-accurate cruise missiles. The Soviet Union eventually catches up one way or another, but the lag interval is rife with danger. Similarly, the overall United States military buildup during the 1980s is perilous not only because it is eroding some hard-won Soviet advantages but because the Soviet Union with its relatively weak economy will be hard-pressed to keep pace with the United States if the latter significantly escalates the arms race. This is one reason why the United States' Star Wars program, a space-based system to protect the United States against Soviet nuclear missiles, is so destabilizing. Star Wars is not just a major weapons breakthrough, one which, not incidentally, the Soviet Union ominously believes would also give the United States the capacity to strike first. It represents an across-the-board transfusion into all sorts of weapons research that will widen the technological gap. The Soviet Union's efforts to match such a program would bleed their economy white.

The idea of destroying the enemy while the enemy is relatively weak is a classic military strategy, one that is not farfetched even in the nuclear era. During the late 1940s, 1950s, and 1960s, for instance, many American citizens and some military leaders favored launching full-scale nuclear attacks on the Soviet Union and China before these nations were strong enough to do the same to us (Horton and Leslie, 1974). Indeed, the U.S. Strategic Air Command developed a battle plan in the 1950s which was intended to reduce the Soviet Union to "smoking, radiating ruin" in two hours, a plan that allegedly was suited more to a preemptive strike than to a retaliatory one (Rosenberg, 1982).

Technical or Human Error   The second problem with the MAD policy is that human or technical failure could accidentally cause a nuclear war (Lown, 1982). Accidental war is a recurrent theme in the popular culture of the nuclear age. Films like *Fail-Safe, Dr. Strangelove,* and *War Games* have played on humanity's—and sociology's—deep-seated understanding that no social organization can operate flawlessly. Indeed, history is replete with examples of the disastrous consequences of organizational infirmities. The near meltdown at Three Mile Island and the death-dealing gas leak at Bhopal, India, are just two that came readily to mind (Jackson, 1985).

Accidental nuclear war could happen in many ways. One possibility is that a human error or a technical failure might occur that would lead to a nuclear explosion(s) in a place or under circumstances that would cause a nation to think it was under attack. This would then lead that nation to launch a retaliatory attack. Nuclear mishaps are not rare. The Pentagon admits to thirty-two mishaps just between 1950 and 1960, although some experts state the true figure is probably four times that number.

And there have been some very close calls. For example, two 24-megaton nuclear bombs accidentally fell from a B-52 bomber over Goldsboro, North Carolina, in January 1961. One came within a whisker of detonating; parts of the other have never been recovered. Another so called broken arrow occurred off the coast of Palomares, Spain, in 1966. Two Air Force planes collided, four nuclear bombs dropped, and two bombs exploded on impact (Anderson, 1981). A more recent mishap occurred in 1985 in Stuttgart, West Germany. An unarmed Pershing 2 missile was accidentally ignited only 250 yards from a combat-ready battery of Pershing missiles armed with nuclear warheads. What would be the United States response, for instance, if one of its NATO military bases in a place like West Germany was suddenly obliterated by a nuclear explosion? Would we think this was the beginning of a nuclear attack by the Soviet Union, a plot popularized by the James Bond movie *Octopussy?*

Another way nuclear war could be started accidentally is if a nation responds too quickly to a warning system that falsely indicates that an enemy attack has been launched. Many such false alarms have already taken place. The North American Air Defense Command reported 151 false alarms in just one 18-month period, some of which led to the alerting of bomber and missiles units to prepare for possible action. One particularly serious false alert, which occurred when a training tape of a Soviet attack was mistakenly fed into an American military computer, was not squelched for an agonizing six minutes (time enough for Soviet submarines lying offshore to strike United States cities with nuclear missiles) (Miller, 1985). Another bizarre incident occurred when a brand new radar warning system mistook the rising of the moon for a full-fledged Soviet missile attack. Such errors would be catastrophic if a superpower were to adopt a "launch on warning" strategy, an option to launch missiles immediately upon warning of an attack, rather than awaiting further confirmation. Neither the

United States nor the USSR has renounced future use of this launch on warning strategy.

In general, the probability of accidental nuclear war is directly proportional not only to the number of weapons but to the number of people who are authorized to work with or around them. About 100,000 individuals in the United States hold such positions. Yet, despite careful screening, more than 15,000 of these people were banished from any access to nuclear weapons in just one 2-year period during the 1970s. The reasons for their exclusion include alcohol and drug abuse, aberrant mental behavior, negligence, and contemptuous attitudes toward authority (Miller, 1985). In one instance, an American soldier committed suicide with his M-16 rifle while on duty at a nuclear storage site in the Netherlands (Inquirer Washington Bureau, 1983). He might have decided in his deranged state to take his unit and the surrounding community with him.

Thus many social problems discussed in this book are linked ominously to the megaproblem of nuclear annihilation. And such harrowing problem linkages could extend all the way up to those who have responsibility for ordering the first use of nuclear weapons. Indeed, one recent American President allegedly was frequently drunk and incoherent in times of international crisis (Hersh, 1982). This is one reason why some American law groups have tried to get the President to share his awesome nuclear decision-making responsibilities with Congress (Baker, 1984).

Accidental war might also come about as a result of some unpredictable, freakish event. We have already briefly discussed such a happening in Chapter 12—the Tunguska Event in Siberia. The Tunguska Event was caused by a cometary fragment which collided with the earth in 1908. Its connection to possible nuclear war is outlined by Sagan (1980):

> If such an impact occurred today it might be mistaken...for a nuclear explosion. The come-

tary impact and fireball would simulate all effects of a one megaton nuclear burst, including the mushroom cloud, with two exceptions: there would be no gamma radiation or radioactive fallout. Could a rare but natural event, the impact of a sizeable cometary fragment, trigger a nuclear war? A strange scenario: a small comet hits the Earth...and the response of our civilization is promptly to self-destruct.

A similar situation occurred in 1979 when a United States satellite detected an intense double flash of light from the vicinity of the South Atlantic and Western Indian Ocean. At first it was thought that Israel or South Africa had secretly tested a nuclear weapon. But now it is speculated that the flash was really produced by the impact of a small asteroid or a cometary fragment.

The chances that any one human or technical error will lead to nuclear war are remote, though the sheer number of these incidents multiplies the odds substantially. But what might be more important is the timing of these events. If one were to happen during an already existing crisis—like the Cuban missile crisis or the Soviet invasion of Afghanistan, one nation might shoot first and ask questions later. MAD forces the superpowers to put their nuclear arsenals on hair trigger; the danger is that if a crisis and an accident coincide, one or both fingers could twitch.

Unauthorized or Improper Use The third problem with the MAD policy is that nuclear war could result from the unauthorized or improper use of nuclear weapons by heads of state; the military, and even civilians. We do not like to think about it, but fools, madmen, and megalomaniacs do exist and sometimes rise to power. It is certainly possible that a latter-day Nero, Attila, Genghis Khan, or Hitler could appear and see the chance to blackmail or eliminate most of humankind outright, even though this action might be contrary to the wishes and interests of the governed. Zbigniew Brzezinski, former President Carter's national security adviser, believes that the Soviet system is capable of producing this type of leader. He argues that Stalin, who presided over the slaughter of as many as 60 million of his own people, was such a person (Sidney, 1982).

The problem of possible improper use did rear its head in 1973 shortly before Richard Nixon's ignominious resignation. There was some concern about his emotional stability, and the possibility that he might instigate an international crisis to divert attention from his Watergate-based domestic problems. Nixon did put the country on full military alert during this period in response to, what many considered, insufficient Soviet provocation.

There is also the possibility that renegade military men who actually control nuclear weapons might become sufficiently disturbed or disordered to unleash them without authorization. The idea is that a determined officer—or even enlisted personnel—might penetrate or ingeniously circumvent safety precautions and send missiles winging on their way (Horton and Leslie, 1974). This possibility has been periodically riveted into the public's consciousness by such plausible films as *Seven Days in May, The Bedford Incident,* and *Twilight's Last Gleaming.* But renegade behavior is not just the stuff of fiction. One real-life incident happened in 1981 when two United States soldiers kidnapped their commanding officer and forced him, at gunpoint, to drive to a West German nuclear base and command the entry guard to admit the pair and their hostage to the nuclear weapons area. Their attempt failed and the two are now imprisoned at Fort Leavenworth, Kansas (Inquirer Washington Bureau, 1983). A nuclear submarine is particularly vulnerable to renegades because of its relatively small crew and autonomous mode of operation. Ominously, one missile-firing submarine carries at least sixteen missiles, each tipped with about ten independently targetable warheads, enough to destroy half of the major cities in the USSR.

Another way a military or even a civilian renegade could conceivably start a nuclear war is to enter information into the computers that man our defensive systems and strike forces. These data could cause ordinarily cautious officers to think that the circumstances had arisen to use their weapons (Horton and Leslie, 1974). This scenario is more than plausible because purportedly unbreakable computer-access codes are routinely foiled (Dolnick, 1984). Indeed, the media regularly run stories about computer hackers who illegally tap into restricted government systems. One college sophomore, for example, using a bare-bones 200 dollar home computer, broke into several such systems, including a Defense Department communications network. At last report he faced a possible six years in prison.

Brinkmanship Another problem with MAD is that the superpowers sometimes use the threat of nuclear war as a negotiating tool. The tactic is to move dangerously close to war in order to gain concessions from the opposition. The risk of advancing to the brink of war is that it is possible for one nation to inadvertently slip over the edge (Horton and Leslie, 1974). This global game of "chicken" has been played during many crises. During the Berlin crisis of 1959, the Eisenhower administration made it clear that it was prepared to hold Berlin at all costs, even if it meant using nuclear weapons. Both the United States and the Soviet Union moved to the brink during the Cuban missile crisis in the early 1960s. And the United States tried nuclear blackmail in efforts to end both the Korean conflict (successfully) and the Vietnamese war (unsuccessfully). It is also possible to argue that the hard-line posturing and saber rattling that characterize the 1980s are a form of brinkmanship. With their tough talk and increased military spending, both sides seem to be edging inexorably toward quasi-permanent positions on the brink of the abyss.

Another form of brinkmanship is the threat to use nuclear weapons to respond to nonnuclear attack. The United States has reserved the option to use nuclear weapons against Soviet conventional forces because the United States is not as strong as the Soviet Union in this respect. The United States has important interests in Europe, the Middle East, and elsewhere where it would be at an immense conventional disadvantage vis-à-vis the Soviet Union. Consequently, the United States relies on a nuclear trump card to prevent the Soviets from taking advantage of their conventional superiority. This policy of extending nuclear deterrence to conventional conflicts is considered exceedingly dangerous because it blurs the distinction between conventional and nuclear war. Indeed, the threat of "limited" nuclear war could easily precipitate a full-fledged nuclear war, because there is no guarantee that a limited nuclear war can be kept limited. Thus, it is probably necessary for the United States and its allies to right the conventional balance so that this kind of extended deterrence can be eliminated (Krauthammer, 1984).

The elimination of the policy of extended deterrence will almost certainly mean higher defense budgets and, perhaps even more important to you, the return of the military draft. But these costs are worth enduring because many experts (e.g., Talbott, 1982a; Krauthammer, 1984) believe that this form of brinkmanship poses the greatest risk of nuclear war. When discussing how a nuclear war is likely to begin, most experts downplay the old "bolt out of the blue" scenario. They argue that World War III will start not as World War II did, with a German blitzkrieg in the West and a Japanese sneak attack in the East, but as World War I began, with a mixture of blunders, oversights, bad fortune, and events getting out of control. World War III is most likely to come about as a result of a regional conflict between the superpowers (Talbott, 1982a). One side will start to lose the conventional battle, and will threaten the use of nuclear weapons to safeguard its "vital interests." There will be rival alerts—no one wanting to fight, but no one backing down—and a gradual losing of control. And at some point in the mounting confrontation, one side will go nuclear.

Proliferation Another practical problem posed by MAD is that it does not limit the spread of nuclear weapons—and, hence, the nuclear problem—to other nations. While the United States and the USSR have been busy checkmating each other, Great Britain, France, China, and India constructed and tested nuclear weapons. Another ten nations either already have nuclear weapons (probably Israel, South Africa, and Pakistan) or have the knowledge and wherewithal to build them. And it has been projected that as many as sixty nations—1 out of every 3 in the world—will be able to build nuclear weapons by the year 2000. The knowledge and materials necessary to permit these nations to join the "nuclear club" come directly from their experience with nuclear power plants and research nuclear reactors. These facilities were provided largely by the United States, the USSR, France, Italy, and West Germany (Miller, 1985). There is enough plutonium produced in the free world's 260 active power plants to make at least 6000 nuclear weapons a year.

Obviously, nuclear proliferation is an ominous development. The more nations that acquire nuclear weapons, the more that are able to use them. This fact has given rise to the nth nation theory: the theory that there is some unknown point (i.e., the nth nation to possess nuclear weapons) at which the use of nuclear weapons becomes more likely than their non-use. The risks posed by proliferation are frightening, especially when you contemplate the kinds of nations and leaders who will wield them in the future.

Consider for a moment what would have happened over the last twenty-five years if nuclear weapons had been in the hands of Idi Amin in Uganda, Pol Pot in Cambodia, Muammar Qaddafi in Libya, Ian Smith in Rhodesia, or Jean-Bedel Bokassa in the Central African

Republic. Consider also that there have been nearly 100 wars in the last twenty-five years, all fought in the less developed world. These wars—which incidentally are often fueled by the other megaproblems discussed in this book—may not seem important to you, but they are intensely important to the combatants. The next nuclear aggressor may well be a relatively isolated country, affluent enough to possess the bomb, which perceives its very survival to be endangered by some local dispute.

Another problem is that once other nations acquire nuclear weapons, they (and the world) face many of the practical MAD problems endured by the superpowers: maintaining balance between rivals, technical and human error, unauthorized or improper use, nuclear terrorism, and even brinkmanship. One instance of brinkmanship may have already occurred when Great Britain allegedly considered using nuclear weapons in the Falklands war against Argentina (*Time*, 1984b). The latter is now, not surprisingly, thought to be readying to join the nuclear club. And there are grave doubts that these nations can manage MAD problems as well as the superpowers have, even given the latter's admittedly poor record. Lack of experience and skill with high-tech weapons is the rule rather than the exception in much of the world. One example of weapons incompetence can be taken from the 1973 Middle East war. Arab forces fired 2100 Russian-made antiaircraft missiles, managing to shoot down 85 planes—40 Israeli jets and 45 of their own.

Moreover, a country with a small nuclear force could destabilize the balance of power between the United States and the USSR. It could disrupt United States strategic plans by threatening neighbors that furnish bases to United States forces, or it could even attack United States forces. But a bigger danger is that the United States and the USSR could be drawn into a conflict between smaller powers that have acquired nuclear weapons and that are allied to the superpowers. Six places in partic-

ular are potential crisis spots that could spawn conflict involving the United States, the USSR, or both: the Sino-Soviet border, Korea, eastern Europe, southern Africa, Mexico, and the Mideast.

The Non-Proliferation Treaty (NPT) of 1968 could have been the basis for counteracting this proliferation if the superpowers had lived up to their end of the bargain. The nonnuclear signers agreed not to develop nuclear weapons, while the nuclear nations agreed to negotiate "in good faith" toward the goal of disarmament "at an early date." But the superpowers failed to move toward disarmament, and consequently, the nonnuclear nations no longer feel obliged to comply with the agreement, and are that much more apt to cave in to the forces of national self-interest and sovereignty that propel them toward joining the nuclear club. Thus, the policy of deterrence rather than disarmament has directly contributed to proliferation.

Nuclear Terrorism Another problem with the nuclear status quo is the possibility that radical groups could steal or make a nuclear device and either detonate it or use it to force outrageous concessions from governments. A nuclear terrorist organization operating without a national base or even a political agenda could slay more Americans than were killed in all previous wars combined. And the United States is a likely target since the State Department reports that since 1975, almost 40 percent of all terrorist attacks were directed against Americans.

Nuclear devices and the materials needed to make them are within the reach of dedicated terrorists. Although security surrounding nuclear warheads is generally tight, some isolated warhead depots are guarded by relatively small forces which could easily be overwhelmed by larger, better trained, and more ferocious terrorist bands (Greve, 1983). There are also other weak links in the system, especially in the manufacturing and transportation stages. Nuclear fuels are an even more likely and vulnerable terrorist target. They can be stolen from nuclear weapons facilities or power plants by people working there or by intruders, and they can be rifled from shipments of these materials. By 1985, enough enriched uranium was missing from just one manufacturing plant in Oak Ridge, Tennessee, to make eighty-five nuclear bombs. No one knows whether it was stolen or whether it represents sloppy measuring techniques or bookkeeping. In any event there is little doubt that a small cadre of terrorist scientists could put together a nuclear weapon once they had the fissionable bomb-grade material.

Delivery of these weapons would be no problem either. They could be delivered by unconventional means, such as a truck crossing a border or a commercial ship anchored in a harbor. Indeed, some nuclear devices would be easier to smuggle into a country like the United States than a bale of marijuana. Unfortunately, there is not much that can be done to stop a skilled, determined, well-organized terrorist group from detonating a nuclear device on United States territory.

A particularly alarming scenario is one in which a roving mad-dog terrorist group like the Red Brigades (or even a small, impassioned, rogue nation) would use nuclear weapons catalytically to draw the superpowers into a major war (Jackson, 1985). Ask yourself these questions: What would the United States response be if a merchant ship secretly carrying a nuclear bomb were abandoned by terrorists in the port of New York and timed to explode hours later? What if this happened at the height of a United States/USSR crises? Would the United States' answer be to launch a massive counterattack or to at least knock out one Soviet city in retaliation for a presumed Soviet attack?

There are some political analysts who believe that this scenario is far from farfetched— that there are groups diabolical and dedicated enough to trigger global devastation (Sidney, 1982). These individuals would likely come from societies that do not have a stake in peace.

They may perceive that they have nothing to lose, and may be so desperate that they lose regard for their own survival. Universal destruction may be more acceptable to them than continuing in their angry despair. After all, violence is not always designed to achieve an end. As Rollo May puts it: "For no human being can stand the perpetually numbing experience of powerlessness.... Violence is the ultimate destructive substitute which surges in to fill the vacuum where there is no relatedness" (Shinn, 1982).

One of the most important social problems issues is inequality. In simple terms, the world contains the haves and the have-nots. The last several chapters have given you a glimpse of the appalling problems that plague much of the world: 40,000 pathetic children dying every day, grinding poverty, and the like. The wealthy nations have responded with aid amounting to well less than 1 percent of their collective gross national products, an amount bitterly viewed by the Third World as mere tokenism. Thus, for the most part, the wealthy nations traditionally have stood by apathetically, leaving the have-nots to their allotted fate. Although the inequity of this situation has enraged many have-nots, there was not much they could really do about it. But the possibility of nuclear terrorism changes all that. If the wealthy nations do not move in a dramatic way to somehow solve the world's megaproblems, thereby giving everybody a stake in peace, they now must risk becoming the victims of some have-nots' nuclear vengeance.

NUTS MAD's strength is that it tells nations what to do with nuclear weapons: nothing. Its major weakness—in addition to those just reviewed—is that it is constantly being outflanked by technological change. Military technology has continued to evolve since the invention of the atomic bomb. Suitcase size nuclear devices and faster, more accurate missiles, for example, make more plausible such strategies as a surprise attack against an enemy's nuclear weapons (as opposed to its population). There-fore, these weapons lose value as means of retaliation, and a symmetrical instability en-sues. There is both more temptation to attack and more inducement to preempt that attack (Lown, 1982). New weapons technologies also make more plausible the use of nuclear weap-ons for limited, coercive purposes.

In response, the superpowers have multi-plied and dispersed their forces in order to increase their ability to retaliate under these new, more complicated circumstances. But the MAD doctrine was simply not comprehensive enough to cope with the versatility, quickness, and accuracy of these new offensive and defen-sive weapons systems and strategies. It had to be supplemented by nuclear utilization theories (NUTS) (Gray, 1981). Examples of NUTS in-clude planning for limited nuclear war, pro-tracted nuclear war, and preemptive nuclear war. This discussion of NUTS (and subsequent ones on DEAD and GNP) is based largely on the work of Daniel Deudney (1983).

NUTS requires the ability to maintain com-plete control over dispersed nuclear forces once the war has begun. But this requirement turns out to be NUTS' Achilles' heel. Human psychology and technical limitations make it probable that a controlled or limited nuclear war will inevitably spin out of control. The world's most powerful combat simulator reveals that even veteran United States officers have the tendency to "go nuke" indiscriminately if their force is caught out of position and they wish to retrieve the battle (Faflick, 1982). Moreover, the most basic and irrational human fears—terror, self-preservation, and revenge—are likely to engulf even the most stable and informed leaders once nuclear weap-ons begin to cascade down on their homeland or forces (Alfven, 1985).

It would also be extremely difficult to keep command centers operating and lines of com-munications open against a determined oppo-nent, because the command and control system is the most militarily valuable and vulnerable

target. Thus, leaders attempting to limit an exchange or work out a cease-fire once the war has begun will almost certainly be stymied by a severely degraded or even nonexistent commu-nications systems. And once out of contact with national leaders and senior officers, and think-ing the worst has happened to their loved ones and homelands, soldiers manning mobile and dispersed nuclear forces are likely to choose as their target the enemy's most sensitive spot: cities and industrial centers (Ball, 1982).

Control of nuclear weapons will also slip away as the communications system becomes more sophisticated (Carter, 1985). Paradoxical-ly, control of a far-flung war machine is reduced rather than expanded as options multiply, as communication contacts expand, and as infor-mation becomes available as events are happen-ing. To deal with this loss of control, sophisti-cated computers are inserted between human operators and smarter, more versatile weapons. But this yields only the illusion of control. The sheer complexity of these expanded communi-cations systems nullifies any meaningful control (Arkin and Fieldhouse, 1985). In the mind-blowing "fog" of nuclear war, all it might take to make the difference between a limited nu-clear war of World War II proportions and the self-destruction of civilization is a single nu-clear military unit deviating from a controlled escalation or cease-fire plan (Miller, 1979).

NUTS also leads to a loss of control by exacerbating many of the practical problems of MAD. The miniaturization, multiplication, and dispersal of nuclear weapons increase the like-lihood of accidents, theft (i.e., diversion by third forces including terrorists), unauthorized launch, and mutiny. These problems not only become easier to accomplish under NUTS but are harder to detect and rectify (Frei, 1982).

NUTS has also gradually eroded tight civil-ian control over nuclear weapons. Both the United States and the Soviet Union at one time physically separated nuclear bombs and war-heads from delivery systems, and explicit civilian consent was required to join them. But given the speed with which nuclear war would now occur and the NUTS-based need to deploy mobile weapons worldwide (and in evermore exotic environments), this tight civilian control has given way to various electronic codes which are largely in the hands of the military (Quester, 1976).

In short, the main problem with NUTS is that the human institutions and technology created to control the utilization of nuclear weapons are likely to fail, increasing both the risk of war and the inability to limit or stop it once it has begun (Bracken, 1983).

DEAD MAD needed to be supplemented by NUTS because of the evolution of military technology. But this evolution has continued, making the MAD/NUTS amalgamation increasingly inadequate. What has happened in brief is that the speed of offensive weapons has increased enormously and will continue to do so in the future with the perfection of Star Wars technology and laser-beam weapons. There are also great advances being made in the detection and targetability of weapons. These phenomena place enormous pressure on military planners seeking to hedge against surprise attack. They are increasingly compelled to hand over the command of nuclear weapons to automatic devices and to delegate authority to use weapons as they see fit to a large number of military commanders around the globe.

To accomplish this, Deudney (1983) concludes that MAD and NUTS are gradually being supplemented by a new policy: the development and use of destruction-entrusted automatic devices (DEAD). DEAD strategies respond specifically to the evolution in both the command and control of nuclear armaments. As noted above, the major problem with NUTS is the unplanned but unavoidable loss of control. With DEAD the loss of control is clear and intentional. An inspection of some nuclear strategies and weapons will show how DEAD is operationalized.

As one U.S. Defense Department official notes, "Speed is the tightening noose around our neck" (Cox, 1982). Soviet submarines lying off the United States' Atlantic and Pacific coasts can strike United States cities in five to eight minutes; the United States can do the same to Soviet cities in like time from submarines and European-based missiles. The most hardened missile silos of both superpowers are also now vulnerable with the same lightening speed (and accuracy). With so little time to react before the barrage of attacking warheads arrives, the superpowers are now sorely tempted to adopt the aforementioned strategy of launch on warning. Both the United States and the USSR have publicly threatened to adopt this strategy in recent years. Launch on warning is a DEAD strategy. It gives military leaders the authority and the ability to launch nuclear missiles in response to nothing more than radar and computer signals that an attack has commenced. The President and the civilian leadership are no longer in the nuclear decision loop.

While vengeance is satisfying, retaliation is increasingly being seen as too modest a goal for our rapidly improving military technology. More and more military strategists are thinking in terms of creating defensive systems with this technology. One possibility is the creation of antiballistic missile systems (ABMs), i.e., missiles designed to shoot down incoming missiles. Such a system if it were to work would have to be controlled by machines. Indeed, it was this feature that helped fuel the bitter controversy surrounding the ABM system which the United States decided to construct in the late 1960s (which was later terminated by the 1972 Antiballistic Missile Treaty). That system entailed the firing of nuclear antimissiles without presidential authorization and, in the event of close-range attacks, without human intervention. Although ABMs have not been deployed, the United States has made major progress since the mid-1970s in perfecting this technology, and the increasing vulnerability of land-based missiles has revived interest in implementing it.

The aforementioned Star Wars strategy—the erection of a system of space-based battle stations armed with missiles, energy beams, and other weapons capable of shooting down attacking missiles—is another example of DEAD. There are conflicting arguments about the feasibility of this strategy, but there is no debate about one aspect: A Star Wars system would have to be controlled automatically by machines. Only machines could discover, target, and destroy missiles in the few precious minutes available. Humans would simply be passive observers—and perhaps, intentionally or unintentionally, prey—of these self-directing war machines (Bethe, Garwin, Gottfried, and Kendall, 1984).

Another DEAD stratagem that has been proposed and prophesied is the concealment of nuclear robots in the vastness of deep space, where they would be safe from preemptive attack. These robots would be programmed to come back and hit enemy cities either by the controller's direct order or by the absence of regular "don't come back" commands. This stratagem has been advanced as a fail-safe deterrent because a surprise attacker's annihilation would be assured. It also dovetails well with NUTS because the more unlimited the nuclear war becomes, the less likely it is that the avenging robots can be called off. The forfeiture of control in this strategy is the primary feature of these doomsday machines (Salkeld, 1970). But machines can malfunction, and what if some of these robots came back by mistake?

Thus, the technological innovation that underpins our present nuclear policy has actually attenuated rather than enhanced our security. Since the beginning of the atomic age, technological progress has steadily reduced the difference between offensive and defensive activities, and between peacetime preparedness and mobilization for imminent war. And it has gravely narrowed the margin of allowable error. We are now entering a frightful era in which the control of awesome weapons, perhaps even doomsday machines, is

gradually passing out of human hands. Box 14-1 gives us a preview of this fantastic and precarious military era, the inevitable product of MAD, NUTS, and DEAD.

Subjective factors also bear on the viability and effectiveness of the policy of deterrence. There are two groups in the United States with values opposed to MAD and to those of each other: namely, the military utopians and the antinuclearists. The military utopians have values in line with traditional military thinking. They rebel against the policy of assuring our own annihilation, and argue instead for a return to policies that aim for unilateral national security, military superiority, and victory in the event of war. These objectives are incompatible with deterrence.

The antinuclearists have values favoring complete disarmament or at least a substantial reduction in nuclear weapons. Many in this antinuclear group argue for the United States to begin unilateral disarmament in the hope that the Soviet Union will follow suit. It is possible to argue the relative merits of disarmament versus deterrence, but that is not the issue here. The issue is how do the activities of the antinuclearists affect the implementation and success of the present deterrence policy. Opponents of the antinuclear group answer that question this way: If the Soviet Union became convinced by the activities of disarmament groups that revulsion against, and rejection of, nuclear weapons had become commonplace in the United States, they might be tempted to strike or, at the very least, to wring concessions out of the United States using nuclear blackmail (Talbott, 1982a). The theory is that in a deterrence standoff, any signal that one side does not have the willpower to fight increases the likelihood of provocative and even aggressive action on the part of the other.

Evaluating the Evidence   MND has one singular achievement to its credit: It has prevented a nuclear World War III for more than forty years. This is an enormous accomplishment given that

BOX 14-1

THE HALF-HOUR WAR

For thirty years, military thinkers had been awed by intercontinental ballistic missiles. But [General] Martin said that "ICBMs are crude weapons. They do not begin to approach the theoretical limits imposed by physical laws. According to Einsteinian physics, nothing can happen faster than the speed of light, 186,000 miles a second. We are now developing high-energy pulsed lasers and particle beam weapons systems which operate *at the speed of light.* In the face of such weapons, ballistic missiles travelling a mere 17,000 miles an hour are slow-moving dinosaurs from a previous era, as inappropriate as cavalry in World War I, and as easily eliminated."

Speed-of-light weapons were best suited to space, and would first appear in satellites. Martin noted that the Russians had made a "kill" of the American spy satellite VV/02 as early as 1973; in 1975, Hughes Aircraft developed a rapid aiming and firing system which locked onto multiple targets, firing eight high-energy pulses in less than one second. By 1978, the Hughes team had reduced response time to fifty nanoseconds—fifty billionths of a second—and increased beam accuracy to five hundred missile knockdowns in less than one minute. Such developments presaged the end of the ICBM as a weapon.

"Without the gigantic missiles, miniature, high-speed computers will be vastly more important in future conflicts than nuclear bombs, and their speed of computation will be the single most important factor determining the outcome of World War III. Computer speed now stands at the center of the armament race, as megaton power once held the center twenty years ago."

Elliot recognized at once the most serious consequence of the speed-of-light weapons—they were much too fast for human comprehension. Men were accustomed to mechanized warfare, but a future war would be a war of machines in a startlingly new sense: machines would actually govern the moment-to-moment course of a conflict which lasted only minutes from start to finish.

In 1956, in the waning years of the strategic bomber, military thinkers imagined an all-out nuclear exchange lasting 12 hours. By 1963, ICBMs had shrunk the time course to 3 hours. By 1974, military theorists were predicting a war that lasted just 30 minutes, yet this "half-hour

war" was vastly more complex than any earlier war in human history.

In the 1950s, if the Americans and the Russians launched all the bombers and rockets at the same moment, there would still be no more than 10,000 weapons in the air, attacking and counterattacking. Total weapons in interaction events would peak at 15,000 in the second hour. This represented the impressive figure of 4 weapons interactions every second around the world.

But given diversified tactical warfare, the number of weapons and "systems elements" increased astronomically. Modern estimates imagined 400 million computers in the field, with total weapons interactions at more than 15 billion in the first half hour of war. This meant there would be 8 million weapons interactions every second, in a bewildering ultrafast conflict of aircraft, missiles, tanks, and ground troops.

Such a war was only manageable by machines; human response times were simply too slow. World War III would not be a push-button war because as General Martin said, "It takes too long for a man to push the button—at least 1.8 seconds, which is an eternity in modern warfare."

This fact created what Martin called the "rock problem." Human responses were geologically slow, compared to a highspeed computer. "A modern computer performs 2,000 calculations in the time it takes a man to blink. Therefore, from the point of view of computers fighting the next war, human beings will be essentially fixed and unchanging elements, like rocks. Human wars have never lasted long enough to take into account the rate of geological change. In the future, computer wars will not last long enough to take into account the rate of human change."

Since human beings responded too slowly, it was necessary for them to relinquish decision-making control of the war to the faster intelligence of computers. "In the coming war, we must abandon any hope of regulating the course of the conflict. If we decide to 'run' the war at human speed, we will almost surely lose. Our only hope is to put our trust in machines. This makes human judgment, human values, human thinking utterly superfluous. World War III will be war by proxy: a pure war of machines, over which we dare exert no influence for fear of so slowing the decision-making mechanism as to cause our defeat."

Source: Michael Crichton (1980)

the interval between the first two world wars was only twenty-one years, and given the animosity between the world's two superpowers (Shinn, 1982; Krauthammer, 1984).

One reason why deterrence might work indefinitely is based on the possible precedent-setting nonuse of poison gas in World War II. Poison gas was used in World War I (as nuclear weapons were used in World War II), and with all sides possessing it, Europeans fully expected it would be used again in World War II. But no combatant, not even genocidal megalomaniacs like Hitler and Stalin, used what was then the ultimate weapon, even when ignominious defeat became a certainty. Why? The answer is not that these leaders had any compunction about killing huge numbers of soldiers and civilians. The answer is that all parties were convinced that any first use of gas would have meant that similar canisters would have rained down on their own cities within hours. In short, mutually assured destruction worked then, has worked since, and may work in the future as well.

Some experts argue, however, that the notion that we have learned to live symbiotically with the bomb is a dangerous illusion, and that the stability MND has wrought so far is not necessarily permanent. Indeed, a host of political analysts, including many United States government and military officials, believe that there is a very good chance that nuclear war will occur eventually (e.g., David Gompert, director of the State Department's Office of International Security Policy; and Gene LaRocque, a retired admiral who is director of the Center for Defense Information).

Many scientists also agree with this pessimistic assessment. Indeed, in 1947 a group of nuclear scientists created a doomsday clock (with midnight symbolizing doomsday) to show graphically how close they believe the world is to a nuclear holocaust. In the mid-1980s forty-seven scientists (including eighteen Nobel prizewinners) set the clock at three minutes before midnight, the closest it has been in thirty

years. The United Nations is also on record against the long-term workability of deterrence in its present MND formulation: "So long as reliance continues to be placed upon the concept of the balance of nuclear deterrence as a method of maintaining peace, the prospects for the future will always remain dark, menacing, and as uncertain as the fragile assumptions upon which they are based" (United Nations, 1980:157).

The widespread pessimism about the prospects for nuclear war originates in the practical problems previously discussed. But in general there are three overriding reasons for such fears. First is humanity's propensity to use war to settle disputes. There have been more than 100 wars just since 1945. As Karl Marx put it, "War is the midwife of history." Second is the escalating nuclear arms race. History provides scant comfort for the position that preparation for war fosters peace. It can be argued that the arms race cannot be an endless contest, that its terminus is inevitable nuclear war. But one thing is not arguable: The risk of nuclear war increases as the number of nuclear weapons of any kind increases. And they are increasing rapidly. Finally, there is fear that the old expression "time devours all things" might have a new application in the nuclear age. For even if the chances of war are small in any given year, the probability of it ever happening becomes sizable and then large with the sheer accumulation of time. There is also the realization that the policy of deterrence must work better than any other social policy. It is the only one that is a total failure if it is successful 99.9 percent of the time.

In sum, if nuclear war is not inevitable, it is not unlikely and is an increasing danger (Talbott, 1982a). The MND policy has hardly been a problem-free one. It has not only exacerbated the very problem (i.e., nuclear insecurity) it was designed to solve but intensified a host of such linked problems as world hunger and international terrorism.

The Good Neighbor Policy: Policy 2

Strategy for Solution   Algebraically, MND equals deterrence, plus mutual hostility between the superpowers, plus an escalating arms race. The second policy, the good neighbor policy (GNP), equals deterrence, plus political reconciliation between the superpowers, minus the arms race. Deterrence is a common element in both policies, but there the similarities end. GNP takes as axiomatic the premise that superpower security is now indivisible, and that the United States and the USSR must join together to defeat their common foe: nuclear weapons. The arms race is abandoned because of the belief that more and better weapons actually decrease security rather than increase it.

Policy into Practice   Deudney (1983) has delineated the five basic elements of GNP: (1) the abolition of secrecy, (2) limits on weapons innovation, (3) cooperative science, (4) pacification of the commons, and (5) political reconciliation. These five struts of GNP are not an exhaustive plan or a cure-all for planetary insecurity. They are simply the main components of an alternative security system more limited in scope than world government, but more comprehensive than traditional arms control.

GNP will necessitate major changes in behavior both within and between the superpowers. Some of these changes are relatively easy to implement, like missile flight bans; others would have to be phased in gradually. But all are possible. Fortunately, GNP is not a radical proposal. It does not demand a transformation of human nature, the disestablishment of the nation state, or a universal outpouring of goodwill. It requires only that the superpowers act in their own best interests—that is, to more intelligently service their traditional and still hugely powerful desire for security.

Abolition of Secrecy   One of the main features of GNP is an end to the arms race. But even if nuclear weapons do not provide security, the superpowers will not stop the arms race unless they can be certain that the other side will do the same. Reducing present nuclear arsenals also depends on this kind of information. So what is needed is the abolition of secrecy. It was not true in past military eras, but in the nuclear age the exchange of information enhances rather than jeopardizes national security (Bok, 1982).

Information plays a central role in the construction of GNP's alternative security system. Just as in traditional arms control negotiations, verification is needed albeit on a larger scale to assure that cheating can be detected. There are three types of verification: (1) remote observation (e.g., by satellite, seismic stations, and aerial platforms), (2) on-site observation by mechanical means (e.g., by audio, video, and other sensing equipment), and (3) human on-site inspection. All three methods would be used simultaneously and extensively under GNP (Pieragostini, 1983).

The abolition of secrecy at first glance might seem like an impractical goal. But the technologies of remote information acquisition are so powerful that they have already stripped away most of the world's military secrets anyway. (For example, the United States has satellites that can show wave-height differences of an inch from a vantage point 500 miles away through thick clouds, infrared sensors that can detect body heat and resolve an object just a few degrees different from those surrounding it from hundreds of miles away, and telescopes and infrared sensors that can see inch-long objects in earth orbit.) On-site inspection is still necessary, however, and remains a thorny issue. But it is more acceptable now than it would have been in the past due to the breadth of this transparency revolution. In addition, the feasibility of each strut of GNP must be viewed within the context of the policy as a whole. Secrecy would be of little value anyway (and thus easier to relinquish) if there were a ban on weapons innovations, cooperation of United

States and USSR scientists on all major weapons-related technologies, and no place to put secret weapons without their detection.

Nevertheless, the above does not suggest that there are not serious real-world implementation problems that must be solved. Two come readily to mind. The first obstacle is the Soviet Union's traditional obsession with secrecy. The USSR is a far less open society than the United States, and the former has a long history of using secrecy and misinformation to further domestic and international objectives (Cohen, 1980). The second obstacle is the distaste many Americans have for anything that smacks of a Big Brother society like "eye in the sky" and a plethora of "commie" inspectors. Americans highly value privacy and independence, and some will strongly resist any policy that trades off these cherished values.

Limits on Weapons Innovation The second element of GNP is limits on innovation in weapons technology. In the past, both superpowers have hoped that some weapons innovation would give them a decisive lead in the arms race, a lead that could be exploited for political gain and which would lead to increased security. But every major weapons advance since World War II by either superpower has soon been matched or neutralized by the other. The result is that weapons innovation has served to elevate the nuclear standoff to ever more precarious heights at tremendous financial and opportunity costs (Morrison, 1983). Examples of this GNP strut would be comprehensive bans on the testing of nuclear weapons and missiles.

The practical implementation of such limits would not be without problems. The military would object because they value new and better weapons, and would insist that older weapons must be tested periodically to ensure that similar ones still work. But reducing confidence in the reliability of aging weapons would be a boon for humanity because it would make their use less likely. Other groups may complain that limits on weapons innovation and testing would

retard the advance of science and diminish the number of valuable nonmilitary spin-offs (Dyson, 1979). But the regulation of science is a legitimate although sometimes difficult task of society (see the chapter on genetic engineering in the *Study Guide*). And, of course, the industrial complex that invents and perfects new weapons would be devastated by GNP, and would fight ferociously against limits on weapons innovation. However, on the plus side, compliance with this GNP provision would be easier to verify with the abolition of secrecy. And the transparency revolution guarantees that any bomb or missile test would be detected.

Whereas secrecy is the strong suit of the Soviet Union, technological innovation is the forte of the United States. The United States leads the USSR in nineteen of the twenty basic war-making technologies, such as computers and submarine detection. Moreover, technological innovation is deeply rooted in the American value system, and plays a central role in our current arms strategy. Consequently, it would be particularly difficult to wean the United States from its cherished belief in the possibility of a technological fix for military insecurity.

Cooperative Science The third element of GNP is the institution of cooperative science. Science, as it is presently conducted, is the origin of technologies with war-making applications. Indeed, as noted above, much science has been deliberately channeled toward these ends. It is thus at the root of superpower insecurity. GNP would break this connection. All major research projects with potential military applications would be conducted jointly by scientists from the two superpowers. Neither the United States nor the USSR would have to dread—and hence hedge against—the important scientific advances of the other. Scientific cooperation would be facilitated by the abolition of secrecy, and would make the ban on weapons innovation more feasible. The sciences that would be most affected would be those involved with weapons, delivery systems, and the transparency revolution—in short, those that affect the strategic balance of power. These include such areas as high-energy physics, oceanography, aeronautics, and space sciences. Another good candidate for scientific cooperation would be the space program.

Scientific cooperation can be implemented. There is already a tradition in science to share knowledge, and there is a fraternal kinship among scientists that has an international character. And as already noted, many scientists on both sides have already expressed their apprehension about the consequences of present nuclear policy (Rotblat, 1982). Moreover, there have already been successful though limited instances of cooperation such as the joint Apollo-Soyuz space mission in 1975 (Ezell and Ezell, 1978).

Pacification of the Commons   The fourth part of GNP is the systematic pacification of the earth's commons—those vast, largely uninhabited realms of air, water, ice, and space. At one time, these commons were buffer zones and barriers between nations, but technology has gradually converted them into corridors of attack. Pacification of the commons would immensely increase the security of both superpowers (Brown, 1977).

The Antarctica Treaty serves as a good example of the practicality of pacification (Quigg, 1983). The continent of Antarctica was demilitarized in 1959, and has remained so ever since. Incidentally, the Antarctica situation bodes well for two other struts of GNP. First, to keep the continent demilitarized the thirteen nations (some who are enemies elsewhere) active in the region permit on-site, short-notice inspection of all facilities. And second, these nations dedicated the continent to open, cooperative scientific investigation. There are now ongoing efforts to keep space from being colonized by weapons, and to establish nuclear free zones in such places as Latin America, the Middle East, Scandinavia, the Balkans, the Indian Ocean, Africa, the central Pacific, and central Europe.

Probably the most difficult commons to demilitarize would be the oceans, which are now heavily militarized. One reason for this is that they house nuclear missile-carrying submarines, the least vulnerable and hence most stabilizing segment of the superpowers' forces. But as noted above, nuclear submarines lying off the superpowers' shores create an enormous security risk because they can strike so quickly. Consequently there have already been proposals urging the creation of submarine-free zones. If these proposals meet with success, they could serve as a starting point for gradually ridding the oceans of these and other nuclear menaces.

Political Reconciliation   GNP's first four parts cannot be accomplished unless the superpowers improve political relations with each other. This will require much effort, and substantial changes in social values and institutions, on both sides. But this reconciliation may be necessary if the common threat to their mutual survival is to be eliminated. Here are a few things that could be done to facilitate a rapprochement.

First, the superpowers should stop the propaganda and misinformation that obscure their common interests. Second, both nations should agree not to intervene militarily in the affairs of other nations. Or at the very least, they should resist the impulse to sour United States-Soviet relations generally in response to specific actions· on the part of one nation in its principal sphere of influence that do not meet with the approval of the other. Détente, an effort during the 1970s to improve superpower relations, was scuttled on this account (Barnet, 1981). Third, both nations must create long-term, stable institutions to ensure that political reconciliation and the other parts of GNP are pursued continuously, consistently, and relentlessly. The United States in particular can no longer afford the situation where each new administration sets off in new policy directions, and where the nature of the United States-Soviet relationship is constantly being challenged and changed (Krauthammer, 1984). Fourth, both nations should strive to build as many human bridges as possible between the two superpowers. The most important of these would be annual summit meetings between heads of state, regular get-togethers of military leaders, increased economic interdependence, and expanded cultural exchanges.

An example of the latter would be student exchange programs. One idea that has been proposed is a reciprocal "guestage" program in which about 25,000 young Soviets would live and attend schools and universities located in prime target areas in the United States; 25,000 young Americans would do the same in the Soviet Union. Children of political, military, and industrial leaders would make up the majority of these groups, so that each nation's leaders would be in effect killing their own offspring if they advocated, commanded, or executed a nuclear strike. Thus, this program would not only lead to better understanding between the populace and leaders of the two superpowers but also decrease the chances of nuclear war between the United States and the Soviet Union (Miller, 1985).

GNP will not be implemented or successful unless it gets the support of an informed and active public, probably in both countries, but especially in the United States. Moving away from MND, the arms race, and mutual hostility cannot be done without the aid of an intelligent, broad-based, and perpetual peace movement. Such a movement must press for GNP, even with its maintenance of some level of nuclear weapons well into the future, at least until complete nuclear disarmament becomes practical. A movement that pushes for unilateral disarmament in the interim is bound to fail for it will only weaken one superpower. This will diminish, not advance, the chances of peace

because it will create the same kind of nuclear imbalance that plagues present nuclear policy. The success of GNP would also depend heavily on the superpowers' willingness to challenge and alter axiomatic values regarding such things as science, technology, progress, competition, morality, and national sovereignty.

Evaluating the Evidence   Unlike MND, GNP has never been tried, so there are no data on its success or failure. MND has not worked well, but it almost goes without saying that any alternative to it will have a difficult time getting adopted, let alone succeeding. This is because the underlying social problem—nuclear insecurity—is so grave and complex. In the previous section we have listed the practical problems that GNP must face, and these are clearly formidable. But they are not necessarily insurmountable. Indeed, we were also able to list successful precedents for each of the elements of GNP: super sensors capable of stripping away secrecy, treaties banning ABMs and the testing of nuclear weapons everywhere but underground, joint space missions and the cooperative scientific investigation of Antarctica, agreements to keep weapons out of Antarctica and space, and détente. It is true that some of these successes have not endured and that some are now threatened. And it is also true that other visionary ideas have floundered almost immediately, such as the Baruch Plan to internationalize atomic energy and the Atoms for Peace plan to use atomic power to eliminate poverty as a cause of war (Oppenheimer, 1963a; 1963b). Nevertheless, the successful precedents provide models and starting points for GNP, while the failures provide valuable experience and knowledge about potential pitfalls.

Pessimists might argue that GNP will never succeed because the mutual hostility between the superpowers is so great that political reconciliation is impossible. But this is a historically naive belief. History is replete with former warring neighbors—even long-time, seemingly implacable enemies—joining together to face a new, bigger common threat. Who would have thought that the United States would presently enjoy friendly relations with Japan and West Germany, when less than a half century ago they were mortal enemies; or with Communist China, an even more recent foe. Thus, reconciliation with the Soviet Union is certainly a practical objective, particularly since it is in the best interests of both nations.

Another cause for optimism is the abundant evidence that fundamental social change is possible. Slavery, an institution stretching back thousands of years, has all but been banished from human societies. Women, who have been patronized and discriminated against for millenniums, are gradually assuming an equal status with men throughout the world (Sagan, 1980). Cannibalism, dueling, and human sacrifice are among the other onerous practices that humanity has abandoned. Perhaps nuclear weapons will someday be added to this list.

EPILOGUE

Nuclear weapons now confront Spaceship Earth with a choice that is both basic and stark: catastrophe, oppression, a perilous standoff, or accommodation (Deudney, 1983). It is we who must make this choice. In so doing, we will become one of the few landmark generations of all history. Hopefully, our descendants will remember us for our wisdom rather than our folly.

SUMMARY

1 A large-scale nuclear war would probably kill from 50 to 75 percent of the world's population due to its immediate and short-term effects and the prolonged effects of radiation. In addition, much of the remaining population would be doomed by the war's long-term effects. Even human extinction is a possibility.

2 Another casualty of nuclear war would be modern society itself.

3 The production and testing of nuclear weapons and, more generally, the arms race itself have important economic, social, and psychological costs for society. One of the most important of these is the fact that the arms race siphons off enormous financial, natural, and human resources that would be better applied to peaceful, constructive purposes.

4 Although war concerns have been traditionally high in the United States, their level has varied considerably from year to year. Nevertheless, nuclear war has never assumed its rightful place at the center of the social and political agenda.

5 Two policy alternatives—MND and GNP—are discussed, which do not presume the eradication of nuclear weapons.

6 MND equals deterrence, plus mutual hostility between the superpowers, plus an escalating arms race.

7 GNP equals deterrence, plus political reconciliation between the superpowers, minus the arms race.

8 Both policies have serious implementation problems. But GNP is our best hope to avoid nuclear war between the superpowers.

Glossary

abortion A term that refers to induced abortion; the voluntary and deliberate termination of a pregnancy.

absolute poverty An income level less than the minimum necessary to provide for physical necessities. The cutoff figure generally used is the federal poverty line, currently set at about 10,000 dollars for a nonfarm family of four.

acid rain Rain (and snow) that become acidic when the water vapor in the air reacts with air pollutants.

acute disease A short-term condition with rapid onset of symptom seriousness.

affirmative action A social policy to end discrimination through legislation such as hiring quotas.

alcoholism An addiction to alcohol, seen by some as a disease and by others as a mental disorder.

anomie A state of disorganization where the hold of norms over individual conduct has broken down. Anomie is closely associated with many aspects of social problems.

anti-Semitism The discrimination and/or prejudice directed toward Jews.

arms control Any measure reducing or limiting forces, regulating armaments, and/or restricting the deployment of weapons or troops that is intended to induce restrained behavior, or some other concession from another state(s).

assimilation The idea that discrimination will end on its own as different groups become more thoroughly integrated into society.

authoritarian personality People who view the world in rigid good-bad, weak-strong categories. Their thinking is confused, inconsistent, and likely to be directed toward many minority groups.

behaviorist theory A school of thought which holds that mental disorder results from learning, such as conditioning or modeling.

birth control The practices employed by couples that reduce the likelihood of conception (contraception) or deliberately terminate a pregnancy (abortion).

carrying capacity The maximum sustainable size of a resident population in a given ecosystem.

catastrophic illness A financially ruinous medical condition.

categorical strategy An antipoverty approach which defines separate categories of poor persons and provides different benefit packages for each category.

causation A condition that exists only when a change in one variable directly produces an associated change in another variable.

certainty The ratio of the number of persons actually punished to the number of crimes reported.

chronic disease A long-term condition with gradual onset of symptom seriousness.

circulation mobility The degree of movement of individuals across enduring statuses in an occupational structure (i.e., mobility up and down the ladder of success).

circumstantial-situational drug use A term that means restricted to specific circumstances.

civil defense Passive measures planned to minimize the impact of enemy action on all aspects of civilian life, especially to protect the population and the industrial base.

closet homosexuals Gay people who hide their sexual preferences from others.

cohabitation A couple living together in a sexual relationship outside of marriage.

comparable worth A strategy to eliminate pay inequities between traditionally male and female jobs by rating the jobs in terms of the skills required to perform them.

compulsive drug use Frequent use of a drug to the point of physiological and psychological dependence.

conflict theory A conceptualization of society as consisting of contending groups whose interests are in conflict.

correlation A statistical association between variables. Not to be confused with causation.

crime rate The number of crimes per a given unit of population (usually the unit is 100,000).

crime Any act which is prohibited by law in a given society.

criminal justice system The structure of official agencies which deal with aspects of the crime problem, including police, courts, prisons, etc.

cross addiction The simultaneous dependence on more than one drug.

cultural lag An uneven rate of social change such that, for example, technological innovation advances faster than related social institutions, which experience adjustment problems.

cultural racism The expression of the superiority of the cultural heritage of one's race over another.

culture of poverty A theory which stipulates that the unique beliefs and values passed on in poor communities prevent escape from poverty.

DEAD An acronym for destruction entrusted automatic devices, the technological basis for a nuclear policy in which the control of nuclear weapons passes out of human hands.

deinstitutionalization The release of the mentally disordered from mental hospitals for treatment in the community.

demographic transition The historical shift of birth and death rates from high to low levels in a population.

demography The study of human populations including their size, composition, and distribution, as well as the causes and consequences of changes in these factors.

depopulation The state of population decline.

desegregation Policies aimed at ending discrimination through such active approaches as busing.

deterrence The principle of reducing the desirability of criminal behavior by the punishment of convicted criminals.

developed nation A nation with a relatively high standard of living and level of industrial production, such as the United States and most Western nations. Also called industrial nations or MDCs.

developing nation A nation with a relatively low standard of living and level of industrial production, such as India, Haiti, and most African nations.

deviance Behavior violating social norms.

deviant behavior An approach to social problems' explanation focusing on individual violation of social norms.

disarmament The reduction of armaments or military forces, particularly to levels determined by international agreements.

discrimination An action whereby a group of people are treated in a less than equal way.

displacement See frustration-aggression theory.

drug abuse The improper use of drugs to the point where the individual and/or social group suffers.

drug addiction A severe form of abuse leading to drug dependence.

drug Any habit-forming chemical substance that affects perception, mood, or consciousness.

dysfunction According to functionalism, a problematic effect of some social practice.

dyshomophobia A psychological condition found among homosexuals who are troubled by or in conflict about their sexual orientation.

ecosystem A self-sustaining and self-regulating community of organisms interacting with one another and with their environment.

egalitarianism The high value placed on social equality.

energy crisis A shortage or catastrophic price rise in one or more forms of energy.

exhibitionism A sexual disorder involving the public display of one's genitals.

expectations The widely anticipated conditions in a society. One of the major sources of concern affecting public opinion about social problems.

experimental design A scientific strategy in which the researcher creates an artificial situation in order to allow a controlled observation of particular features of social problems.

experimental drug use A short-term trial use to experience a drug's effects.

extended family A family in which several generations such as grandparents, parents, and children live together. It may also include other relatives such as aunts and uncles.

fear-victimization paradox The greatest subjective fear of crime among population segments with a lesser objective risk of victimization.

fee for service A feature of the United States health care system in which payment increases for each additional service received by the patient.

feminization of poverty The increasing tendency for a disproportionate number of female-headed households to exist below the poverty line as compared to male-headed households.

fertility   The number of births, generally expressed as a yearly birthrate or as the average number of children born to a group of women.

fetal narcotic syndrome   The physical problems passed to newborns from drug-addicted mothers.

fixation   An arrest of personality development at a particular psychosexual stage.

frustration-aggression theory   The notion that prejudice stems from frustration which is alleviated through aggressive actions toward a target group (scapegoat).

functionalism   A conceptualization of society as consisting of various social elements, each of which serves purposes (or functions) in the larger social pattern.

gender   A term defined by attitudinal and behavioral characteristics deemed by a society to be appropriate to males and females. It is measured in terms of masculinity and femininity.

greenhouse effect   A condition in which carbon dioxide and other gases in the atmosphere allow the sun's warming rays to reach the earth but do not permit the heat to escape, thus making the earth's atmosphere increasingly warmer.

health care delivery   The social system for bringing services to the patient, as distinguished from health care itself.

Health Maintenance Organization(HMO)   A prepaid insurance plan in which a fixed monthly premium is charged no matter how many health services are consumed. The organization is designed to shift health care incentives toward disease prevention.

health   A term defined by the World Health Organization as ''a state of complete physical, mental, and social well-being and not merely the absence of disease or infirmity.''

hidden addiction   The unrecognized abuse of legal drugs, such as sleeping pills and tranquilizers.

homophobia   An ungrounded, intense fear of homosexuals.

homosexual behavior   Sexual relations between members of the same sex, not necessarily an indication of true homosexual orientation.

horizontal proliferation   The spread of nuclear capabilities from nuclear states to nonnuclear ones and/or nongovernmental political entities.

hypersexuality   Excessive sexual desire that cannot be satisfied.

hypotheses   Testable research questions drawn from theories.

iatrogenic disease   A health problem caused by the physician.

ideology   Beliefs justifying the interests of particular groups, especially classes.

illegitimacy   The birth by a mother not married to the father.

illness   A subjectively defined state based on perceived symptoms.

implementation issues   Factors bearing on the transformation of an ideal policy into a working social program. One of the dilemmas to the solution of social problems.

incapacitation   The principle of reducing victimization by keeping the convicted criminal locked away from the general population.

incest   Forbidden sexual relations between relatives who are not married.

incidence   The number of new cases affected by a condition during a given time period; the frequency of crimes committed.

individualism   The high value placed on independence and self-determination in American culture. One of its effects is the tendency to perceive social problems as created by defects in individual personalities (victim blaming).

inequality of condition   Unequal levels of social rewards actually received by the members of a society.

inequality of opportunity   The unequal access to the social positions providing unequal levels of social rewards.

infanticide   The act of killing an infant or young child.

insanity   The legal definition of mental incompetency based on such narrow concepts as the right-wrong principle of the M'Naghten rule.

institutional racism   Direct and hidden ways in which society's institutions work against the interests of minority groups.

intensified drug use   The long-term, habitual, and regular use of a drug.

internal migration   The population movement between different areas within a country.

international migration   The population movement between countries.

juvenile delinquency   Illegal acts committed by minors. Both the nature of the acts (with the exception of adult crimes) and the age defined as a "minor" vary by jurisdiction.

labeling theory An approach to deviant behavior that focuses on the causes and consequences of the selective application of rules and sanctions to particular individuals; a school of thought which holds that mental disorder results from being caught performing a deviant act and labeled as a deviant.

launch on warning Retaliatory nuclear attacks launched upon notification that an enemy attack has begun, but before enemy forces or armaments actually strike.

life cycle A term applied to the tendency of social problems movements to rise, peak, and then decline in public concern.

life expectancy An estimate of the average number of additional years people of a specified age can expect to live if current mortality trends were to continue.

life span The maximum age that human beings could reach under optimum conditions.

MAD An acronym for mutual assured destruction, a nuclear policy based on the ability of both the Soviet Union and the United States to inflict massive damage on each other after absorbing a full-scale nuclear attack from the other.

manic-depressive illness A common psychosis in which a person undergoes extreme mood swings involving excitement and/or depression.

marital disruption The temporary or permanent discontinuation of marriages due to divorce, separation, or the death of a spouse.

marriage cohort A group of individuals of various ages who marry during the same year.

masochism A sexual disorder found among people who achieve sexual pleasure by receiving pain.

median family income The dollar amount at which half of all families receive more and half receive less income.

Medicaid A federal program financing health care aid for the poor.

medical addiction An addiction to a drug prescribed by a physician in the course of medical treatment.

medical model An approach to health care which focuses on physicians' treatment of already-existing illnesses in patients.

medical students' disease The self-diagnosis of common symptoms as an exotic or fearsome disease being studied in medical school.

medicalization of mental disorder Defining abnormal behavior as a medical problem which should be treated by physicians only.

medicalization The trend toward socially defining various forms of behavior as "illness."

Medicare A federal program financing health care for the elderly.

megalopolis The growing together of urban areas into an interconnected metropolitan region.

mens rea ("the evil mind") The legal principle which defines intent as the essence of crime.

meritocracy A (fictional) society offering equal chances for unequal social rewards based on merit.

migration The movement of people across a specified territorial boundary for the purpose of changing residences.

morbidity The distribution of disease in a population.

mores Widely shared and important group rules, often made into laws.

mortality The number of deaths that occur in a specific time period, generally expressed as a yearly death rate or by life expectancy.

narcotic In pharmacological terms, opium and opiate derivatives or other drugs which kill pain and/or produce sleep. Subjectively, the term *narcotic* means almost any drug assumed to be habit-forming.

national health insurance A program in which the government guarantees payment of the medical costs of all of its citizens.

natural increase The difference between the total number of births and the total number of deaths in a population.

nature versus nurture The scientific debate on whether gender differences are inborn or imposed on individuals by society.

negative income tax A proposed antipoverty policy which would complement the current income tax system by guaranteeing individuals below the federal poverty line a minimum level of income.

net migration The difference between the total number of people migrating into an area and the total migrating out.

neurosis A milder form of mental disorder in which a person suffers from anxiety.

norms   Group-based rules for conduct.

nuclear family   A family consisting of wife, husband, and their children.

nuclear winter   The climatic aftermath of a major nuclear war in which the earth could be subjected to abnormally low temperatures, prolonged darkness, toxic smog, violent windstorms, and persistent radioactive fallout.

NUTS   An acronym for nuclear utilization theory, a body of strategic doctrine which gives nuclear weapons a practical war-fighting role.

objective dimension   The concrete, measurable human harm associated with a societal phenomenon.

opportunity theory   An approach to deviant behavior that focuses on the relationship between cultural goals and the socially approved means (opportunities) for achieving them.

organic therapy   Any biological form of treatment, such as drugs, electroconvulsive therapy, and brain surgery.

organized crime   A systematic, rationalized operation (including the Mafia and enterprise syndicates) for committing illegal acts.

overfishing   The harvesting of so many fish of one type that the species cannot repopulate for the next year's catch.

parole   The premature release of a prisoner based on evidence of good behavior.

participant observation   A scientific strategy in which the researcher participates in the activities of a real-world group in order to intimately observe its functioning.

pedophilia   The sexual contact between a child and an adult.

phobia   An intense fear of a specific object or situation.

plea bargain   A transaction in which the accused offers information or a guilty plea in return for a reduced sentence.

pollution   An undesirable change in the biological, chemical, or physical characteristics of the air, water, or land that can negatively affect the health, survival, or activities of living organisms, including humans.

population composition   The characteristics of a population, such as marital status, class, age, sex, and religion.

population distribution   How individuals and their population-related activites are spatially dispersed.

population growth rate   The rate at which a population is increasing (or decreasing) in a given year due to natural increase and net migration.

population pyramid   A special type of bar chart that shows the composition of a population by age and sex.

population   The total set of individuals or groups about which the researcher wants to generalize on the basis of a smaller sample.

power elite   A term coined by C. Wright Mills to refer to a tiny, socially connected set of individuals dominating societal institutions.

prejudice   A rigid predisposition to respond to a certain group in a specific way, emphasizing selective ''facts'' and ignoring others.

prestige   A social reward (distinguished from income and power) which consists of the honor and respect allocated to the occupants of various societal statuses.

prevalence   The total number in a population with a given condition; the proportion of a population committing crimes.

probation   The sentencing of offenders to be monitored by probation officers in the community instead of being incarcerated.

problem linkages   The interconnections of social problems. One of the dilemmas to the solution of social problems.

projection   A psychological mechanism found among people who deny their unwanted traits by finding them in other people.

psychoanalysis   A lengthy and intense talking-out approach between a patient and a therapist.

psychogenic view   The belief that mental disorder is caused by a disturbance in an individual's psychological state.

psychosis   A severe mental disorder involving loss of contact with reality.

psychotherapy   A form of treatment designed to change personalities through a talking-out technique whereby patients are helped to understand the nature of their problem(s).

punishment   An anticrime policy based on penalizing the offender.

race prejudice   Individual racism involving negative racial attitudes which are ungrounded.

race An ambiguous term based on such factors as biology, language, religion, or a bureaucratic practice.

random sample A technique for drawing a representative cross section of a population by giving each unit an equal chance of selection into the sample.

rape culture A view of society which holds that rape is an act of violence occurring because of the way men and women are socialized to the sexual aspect of their sex roles.

reactivity Research subjects changing their behavior due to awareness that they are being watched.

recidivist An offender who has had prior contact with the criminal justice system.

relative poverty The subjective sense of impoverishment relative to a general standard of living. Surveys suggest that the threshold in the United States is about half the median family income.

reverse discrimination An alleged result of Affirmative Action policies whereby members of majority groups (e.g., white males) have limited opportunities in areas like job promotions.

role conflict Contradictory social expectations applied to individuals performing their roles.

role The behavior expected of a person in a specific group position.

sadism A sexual disorder found among people who achieve sexual pleasure by inflicting pain on others.

safety valve theory The idea that pornography allows the private release of sexual fantasies and decreases sex crimes.

schizophrenia A common psychosis in which a person's thought processes become so disordered that fantasies, delusions, and/or hallucinations may result.

secondary deviance Additional rule breaking committed by persons already labeled as deviants by society for their acts of primary deviance.

sex ratio The number of males per 100 females in a population.

sex-role hypothesis The prediction that the relationship between sex and psychological distress will decline as sex roles become more comparable.

sex A term that refers to those biological attributes that determine whether a person is male or female.

sexism Prejudicial beliefs concerning sex roles that lead to discriminatory practices by one sex toward the other (in most cultures, by men toward women).

sexual disorder A sexual orientation which is heavily stigmatized and considered to be a psychological abnormality.

sexual harassment Unwelcome sexual advances made by an employer to an employee or by any superior to a subordinate which imply a threat to or create an unpleasant working environment for the recipient.

sexual lifestyle An action which is tolerated, though it is at variance with ideal norms of sexual conduct.

sexual variants People whose sexual orientation runs counter to accepted social norms.

sick role The pattern of expectations applied to individuals labeled ill. The expectations include exemption from usual social responsibilities and conformity to the recommendations of physicians.

situationism A theory which stipulates that the poor develop antiachievement attitudes because they confront a miserable life situation.

social change theory An approach to the causation of social problems which focuses on the effects of societal transformation.

social class A set of individuals receiving similar levels of social rewards, generally defined by their common relationship to the system of economic production.

social disorganization An approach to social problems' explanation focusing on the improper design of a social system.

social megaproblems The most severe social problems confronting humankind, ones that threaten its very survival.

social modeling A theory of prejudice based on the idea that bigotry stems from being socialized toward it.

social problem A social issue composed of concrete human harms (the objective dimension) and public opinion about those harms (the subjective dimension).

social recreational drug use The occasional indulgence among friends to share an experience or enhance interaction.

social stratification   A descriptive term applied to the broadly unequal conditions and opportunities facing the hierarchy of social classes in a society.

social structure   The pattern of formal and informal relationships connecting the members of a society.

social support   The interpersonal services provided by the members of one's social network that appear to reduce risk of morbidity and mortality.

somatogenic view   The belief that mental disorder is caused by biological problems.

statistical control   A technique for clarifying the relationship between two variables by holding constant the statistical effect of another variable with which they are correlated.

status attainment   A sociological research model focusing on the effect of parental and personal traits on individual achievement.

status crystallization   The receipt of similar levels of the various types of social rewards.

status offense   An act defined as illegal if committed by a member of a particular social status (usually a juvenile).

status   The social position occupied by an individual that is the basis for the allocation of social rewards.

STDs   An abbreviation for sexually transmitted diseases.

stigmatization   Inappropriate and negative views toward certain groups (e.g., the mentally disordered).

street crime   A term usually applied to the FBI index offenses of criminal homicide, forcible rape, robbery, aggravated assault, burglary, larceny-theft, motor vehicle theft, and arson.

structural mobility   An occupational movement occasioned by changes in the overall occupational structure of a society.

subculture theory   An approach to deviant behavior that focuses on the exposure of individuals to pro-deviance social standards.

subjective dimension   The general level of concern about a social problem as revealed in public opinion.

survey research   A scientific strategy in which representative samples of individuals are drawn from larger populations and their verbal responses are subjected to statistical analysis.

syndrome   Certain sets of symptoms which occur together.

tender years doctrine   A legal guideline used in child custody cases, under which the mother is presumed to be the better custodian for children of "tender years" (usually under age 7).

third party payments   The disbursements by insurers to physicians for the health care bills of patients.

tolerance   The ability of the body to adapt to progressively larger doses of the drug, making even larger amounts necessary to achieve the desired effects.

total institution   A place (like a prison) where individuals must submit to authoritarian control of their lives while being deprived of contact with mainstream society.

traditional American family   A family consisting of a breadwinning husband, a stay-at-home wife, and their dependent children.

transvestism   The sexual pleasure derived from wearing clothes of the opposite sex.

trickle-down theory   The idea that social rewards overflow from upper to lower groups.

trigger theory   The idea that pornography stimulates deviant drives and increases sex crimes.

true prevalence   The total number of treated and untreated cases of mental disorder at a particular time.

Type A personality   The hard-driving time-pressured personality type that has been linked in the literature to the risk of heart disease.

undernutrition   A term that refers to diets that lack either sufficient quantity (calories) or quality (nutrients).

value trade-offs   The cost in terms of other values of reducing a given social problem. One of the dilemmas to the solution of social problems.

value-free   The principle of scientific objectivity by which researchers minimize the intrusion of their own values into investigations by adhering to the rules of research methods.

value   A collective conception of the desirable. Values are one of the major sources of concern affecting public opinion about social problems.

vigilante   A member of a nonlegal voluntary group organized to enforce the law. They are often stimulated by the perceived failure of the criminal justice system.

visibility   The public profile of a social problem

based on its intrinsic drama and media exposure. One of the major sources of concern affecting public opinion about social problems.

voyeurism A sexual disorder found among people preoccupied with watching others nude, in a sexual act, and the like.

weak ties Social relations characterized by low levels of interpersonal contact which have been shown to be important sources of achievement information.

white-collar crime (suite crime) A term defined as "crime committed by a person of respectability and high social status in the course of his occupation" by Edwin H. Sutherland, the criminologist who coined the term.

withdrawal The unpleasant physical symptoms resulting from discontinuation of an abused drug.

zero population growth (ZPG) The condition of neither gaining nor losing population size.

REFERENCES

Abadinsky, H. 1981 *The Mafia in America: An Oral History*. New York: Praeger.

Abrahamsen, David 1967 *The Psychology of Crime*. New York: Columbia University Press.

Abrams, H. 1981 "Medical Problems of Survivors of Nuclear War." *New England Journal of Medicine,* 305:1226–1232. 1982 "Survivors of Nuclear War: Infection and the Spread of Disease," in E. Chivian et al, eds., *Last Aid,* 211–233. San Francisco: Freeman.

Adler, Patricia A., and Peter Adler 1978 "Tinydopers: A Case Study of Deviant Socialization." *Symbolic Interaction,* 1:90–105.

Adorno, T. W., Else Frenkel-Brunswik, D. J. Levinson, and R. N. Sanford 1950 *The Authoritarian Personality*. New York: Harper & Row.

Ageton, Suzanne S., and Delbert S. Elliot 1979 "The Incidence of Delinquent Behavior in a National Probability Sample of Adolescents." Project Report No. 3. Boulder, CO: Behavioral Research Institute.

Ahern, T. 1985 "Nuclear Winter and Arms Build-up." *Philadelphia Inquirer,* Mar. 15:A3.

Akers, Ronald L., Marvin D. Krohn, Lonn Lanza-Kaduce, and Marcia Radosevich 1979 "Social Learning and Deviant Behavior: A Specific Test of a General Theory." *American Sociological Review,* 44:636–655.

Alba, Richard D., and Gwen Moore 1983 "Elite Social Circles," in Ronald S. Burt and Michael J. Minor, *Applied Network Analysis*. Beverly Hills, CA: Sage.

Alexander, C. 1984 "Pulling the Nuclear Plug." *Time,* Feb. 2:34.

Alfven, H. 1985 "Nuclear War: The Worst Environmental Threat," in G. Miller, ed., *Living in the Environment,* E16–E17. Belmont, CA: Wadsworth.

Allport, Gordon 1954 *The Nature of Prejudice*. Cambridge, MA: Addison-Wesley. 1959 *ABCs of Scapegoating*. New York: Anti-Defamation League.

Altrocche, J. 1980 *Abnormal Behavior*. New York: Harcourt Brace Jovanovich.

American Cancer Society 1983 *Cancer Facts and Figures*. New York: American Cancer Society.

American Diabetes Association 1983 *American Diabetes Association 1981–1982 Report to the American People*.

American Humane Association 1984 *Report on Child Abuse*. Denver, CO.

American Psychiatric Association 1980 *Diagnostic and Statistical Manual of Mental Disorders,* 3d ed. Washington, DC: American Psychiatric Association.

American Public Health Association 1982 *Health of Minorities and Women Chart Book*. Washington, DC: U.S. Government Printing Office.

American Sociological Association 1984 "Incorporating Women Faculty into Sociology Departments during 80s." *Footnotes,* April: 4.

Anderson, Bernard E. 1979 "Minorities and Work: The Challenge for the Decade Ahead," in Clark Kerr and Jerome M. Rosow, eds., *Work in America: The Decade Ahead,* 92–110. New York: Van Nostrand.

Anderson, Elijah 1978 *A Place on the Corner*. Chicago: University of Chicago Press.

Anderson, J. 1981 "Are We Safe from Our Own Nuclear Weapons?" *Parade Magazine,* Oct. 18:12–15.

Andersen, K. 1983 "Private Violence." *Time,* Sept. 5:18–19; "Crashing on Cocaine." *Time,* Apr. 11:22-30.

Andrews, Lori B. 1983 "Myths and Facts about Working Women." *Parents,* July.

Aneshensel, Carol S., Ralph R. Frericks, and Virginia A. Clark 1981 "Family Roles and Sex Differences in Depression." *Journal of Health and Social Behavior,* 22:379–393.

Aneshensel, Carol S., Ralph R. Frericks, and George J. Huba 1984 "Depression and Physical Illness: A Multiwave, Nonrecursive Model." *Journal of Health and Social Behavior,* 25:350–371.

Antunes, George 1974 "Ethnicity, Socioeconomic Status, and the Etiology of Psychological Distress." *Sociology and Social Research: An International Journal,* 58:361–368.

Arensberg, Conrad M., and Arthur A. Niehoff 1964 *Introducing Social Change.* Chicago: Aldine.

Arkin, W., and R. Fieldhouse 1985 *Nuclear Battlefields—Global Links in the Arms Race.* Cambridge, MA: Ballinger.

Ash, P. 1949 "The Reliability of Psychiatric Diagnoses." *Journal of Abnormal and Social Psychology,* 44:271–276.

Associated Press 1981 "Russia Thinks It Could Win a Nuclear War." *The Bulletin* (Philadelphia), Nov. 4:A3.

Bachman, Jerald G., and Patrick M. O'Malley 1984 "Black-White Differences in Self-Esteem. Are They Affected by Response Styles?" *American Journal of Sociology,* 90:624–639.

Bachrach, C., and M. Horn 1985 "Marriage and First Intercourse, Marital Dissolution, and Remarriage." *NCHS Advanced Data,* Apr. 12:107.

Badinter, E. 1982 *Mother Love: Myth & Reality.* New York: Macmillan.

Bahr, Howard M., Bruce A. Chadwick, and Robert C. Day, eds. 1972 *Native Americans Today: Sociological Perspectives.* New York: Harper & Row.

Baker, S. 1984 "Curb Sought on Nuclear Authority." United Press International, Sept. 9.

Baldwin, W. 1980 "Adolescent Pregnancy and Childbearing—Growing Concerns for Americans." *Population Bulletin,* 31(2).

Ball, D. 1982 "Can Nuclear War Be Controlled?" *Adelphi Papers,* No. 196. London: International Institute for Strategic Studies.

Baltzell, E. Digby 1964 *The Protestant Establishment.* New York: Vintage.

Bane, M. 1976 *Here to Stay.* New York: Basic Books.

Banfield, Edward C. 1970 *The Unheavenly City.* Boston: Little, Brown.1974 *The Unheavenly City Revisited.* Boston: Little, Brown.

Banta, H. David, and Stephen B. Thacker 1979 "Policing toward Medical Technology: The Case of Electronic Fetal Monitoring." *American Journal of Public Health,* 69:931–935.

Barber, James 1975 *Clear and Present Dangers.* New York: Praeger.

Barker-Benfield, G. J. 1976 *The Horrors of the Half-Known Life: Male Attitudes toward Women and Sexuality in Nineteenth Century America.* New York: Harper & Row.

Barnet, R. 1981 *Real Security: Restoring American Power in a Dangerous Decade.* New York: Simon and Schuster.

Barnhouse, Ruth Tiffany 1977 *Homosexuality: A Symbolic Confusion.* New York: Seabury.

Bartell, Gilbert 1970 "Group Sex among the Mid-Americans." *Journal of Sex Research,* 6:113–130.

Bassis, M., R. Gelles, and A. Levine 1982 *Social Problems.* New York: Harcourt Brace Jovanovich.

Bayles, F. 1984 "Some Have a Newer, Colder Theory on the Aftermath of a Nuclear War." *Philadelphia Inquirer,* Nov. 22.

Beck, J. 1984 "Choosing Motherhood: Consider All the Options." *Chicago Tribune News Service,* Jan. 10.

Beck, M. 1985 "America's Abortion Dilemma." *Newsweek,* Jan. 14:20–25.

Becker, Howard S. 1953 "Becoming a Marihuana User." *American Journal of Sociology,* 59:235–242.

Beckman, P. L. 1971 "Life Stress and Psychological Well-Being." *Journal of Health and Social Behavior,* 12:35–45.

Bell, Alan P., and Martin S. Weinberg 1978 *Homosexuals: A Study of Diversity among Men and Women.* New York: Simon and Schuster.

Bell, Wendell, and Robert V. Robinson 1978 *Comparative Studies in Sociology,* vol. 1. Greenwich, CT: JAI Press.

Belle, Deborah E. 1983 "The Impact of Poverty on Social Networks and Supports," in Laura Lein and Marvin B. Sussman, eds., *The Ties That Bind: Men's and Women's Social Networks.* New York: Haworth.

Beneke, T. 1982 *Men on Rape.* New York: St. Martin's.

Benjamin, B. 1969 *Demographic Analysis.* New York: Praeger.

Benjamin, M. 1982 "Nuclear-Mishap Study Projects 100,000 Deaths." *Philadelphia Inquirer,* Nov. 3:1A.

Bequai, August 1978 *White-Collar Crime: A 20th Century Crisis.* Lexington, MA: Lexington Books.

Berg, A. 1973 "Nutrition, Development, and Population Growth." *Population Bulletin,* 29 (1).

Berg, Ivar 1970 *Education and Jobs: The Great Training Robbery.* New York: Praeger.

Berger, B., and P. Berger 1984 *The War over the Family: Capturing the Middle Ground.* New York: Doubleday.

Berger, Peter L., and Thomas Luckmann 1967 *The Social Construction of Reality.* New York: Anchor.

Bergstrom, S. 1983 *Effects of Nuclear War on Health and Health Services.* Report submitted to the World Health Organization Thirty-Sixth World Health Assembly, March. Geneva.

Berk, Richard A., Kenneth J. Lenihan, and Peter H. Rossi 1980 "Crime and Poverty: Some Experimental Evidence from Ex-Offenders." *American Sociological Review,* 45:766–786.

Berkman, L. F., and S. L. Syme 1979 "Social Networks, Lost Resistance, and Mortality—A Nine-Year Followup Study of Alameda County Residents." *American Journal of Epidemiology,* 109:186–204.

Bethe, Hand, Richard Garwin, Kurt Gottfried, and Henry Kendall 1984 "Space-Based Ballistic Missile Defense." *Scientific American,* 251:39–49.

Beulow, M. 1983 "Abortion Failures Stir Concern." Associated Press, Mar. 23.

Biggar, J. 1979 *The Sunning of America: Migration to the Sunbelt.* Population Bulletin, 34:1. Washington, DC: Population Reference Bureau.

Birnbaum, Judith Abelew 1975 "Life Patterns and Self-Esteem in Gifted Family-Oriented and Career Committed Women," in Martha T. Shuch Mednick, Sandra Schwartz Tangri, and Lois Wladis Hoffman, eds., *Women and Achievement: Social and Motivational Analyses.* New York: Holsted.

Black, Donald 1983 "Crime as Social Control." *American Sociological Review,* 48:34–45.

Blau, Francine 1978 "Women in the Labor Force," in Ann Stromberg and Shirley Harkess, eds., *Women Working: Theories and Facts in Perspective,* 29–62. Palo Alto, CA: Mayfield.

Block, A. A. 1980 *East Side, West Side: Organizing Crime in New York 1930–1950.* Cardiff, Great Britain: University College, Cardiff Press.

Bloom, David 1982 "What's Happening to the Age at First Birth in the United States? A Study of Recent Cohorts." *Demography,* 19:351–370.

Blumberg, Paul 1980 *Inequality in an Age of Decline.* New York: Oxford University Press.

Boffey, Philip 1985a "Top Health Official and Expert Seek Greater Rise in AIDS Money." *New York Times,* Sept. 27:C3. 1985b "U.S. Offers Goal to End Spread of Deadly AIDS." *New York Times,* Oct. 1:C1.

Bogue, Donald, and Amy Tsui 1979 "Zero World Population Growth." *The Public Interest,* Spring:99–113.

Bok, S. 1982 *Secrets: On the Ethics of Concealment and Revelation.* New York: Pantheon.

Bonham, Gordon Scott 1979 *Use Habits of Cigarettes, Coffee, Aspirin and Sleeping Pills, United States, 1976.* Washington, DC: National Center for Health Statistics.

Bott, Elizabeth 1971 *Family and Social Networks: Roles, Norms and Eternal Relationships in Ordinary Urban Families.* New York: Free Press.

Boulding, K. 1964 *The Meaning of the 20th Century.* New York: Harper and Row.

Bourbolis, Photeine P. 1964 *Ancient Festivals of "Saturnalia."* Thessalonike.

Bouvier, L. 1980 *America's Baby Boom Generation: The Fateful Bulge. Population Bulletin,* 35:1. Washington, DC: Population Reference Bureau. 1981 *The Impact of Immigration on U.S. Population Size.* Washington, DC: Population Reference Bureau. 1984 "Planet Earth 1984–2034: A Demographic Vision." *Population Bulletin,* 39(1).

Bouvier, L., and C. Davis 1982 *The Future Racial Composition of the United States.* Washington, DC: Population Reference Bureau.

Bouvier, L., and J. van der Tak 1976 *Infant Mortality—Progress and Problems. Population Bulletin,* 31:1. Washington, DC: Population Reference Bureau.

Box, Steven 1983 *Power, Crime and Mystification.* New York: Tevistock.

Bracken, P. 1983 *The Command and Control of Nuclear Forces.* New Haven: Yale University Press.

Brecher, Edward M., and the editors of *Consumer Reports* 1972 *Licit and Illicit Drugs.* Boston: Little, Brown.

Brenner, M. Harvey 1973 *Mental Illness and the Economy.* Cambridge, MA: Harvard University Press. 1978 "The Social Costs of Economic Distress." *Consultation on the Social Impact of Economic Distress.* New York: American Jewish Committee.

Breslan, Naomi, David Salkever, and Kathleen S. Staruch 1982 "Women's Labor Force Activity and Responsibilities for Disabled Dependents: A Study of Families with Disabled Children." *Journal of Health and Social Behavior,* 23:169–183.

Brewton, Berry, and Henry Tischler 1978 *Race and Ethnic Relations.* Boston: Houghton Mifflin.

Brinton, Crane 1960 *The Anatomy of Revolution.* New York: Random House.

Brodin, E. 1983 "The Family in the Welfare State." *The University Bookman,* 24(1):17–20.

Broverman, I. K. 1970 "Sex Role Stereotypes and Clinical Judgements of Mental Health." *Journal of Consulting and Clinical Psychology,* 34:1–7.

Brown, H. 1954 *The Challenge of Man's Future.* London: Secker and Warburg.

Brown, L. 1979 *Resource Trends and Population Policy: A Time for Reassessment.* Worldwatch Paper No. 29. Washington, DC: Worldwatch Institute.

Brown, L., and P. Shaw 1982 *Six Steps to a Sustainable Society.* Worldwatch Paper No. 48. Washington, DC: Worldwatch Institute.

Brown, L., W. Chandler, C. Flavin, S. Postel, L. Starke, and E. Wolf 1984 *State of the World 1984.* New York: Norton.

Brown, Richard Maxwell 1975 *Strain of Violence: Historical Studies of American Violence and Vigilantism.* New York: Oxford University Press.

Brown, S. 1977 *Regimens for the Oceans, Outer Space, and Weather.* Washington, DC: The Brookings Institution.

Browne, M. 1978 "Doomsday Debate: How Near Is the End?" *New York Times,* Nov. 14:C1.

Bryan, James H. 1966a "Apprenticeships in Prostitution." *Social Problems,* 12:287–297. 1966b "Occupational Ideologies and Individual Attitudes of Call Girls." *Social Problems,* 13:441–450.

Bryant, Clifton D. 1982 *Sexual Deviancy and Social Proscription: The Social Context of Carnal Behavior.* New York: Human Sciences Press.

Bullough, Vern L., and Sheila Groeger 1982 "Irving W. Potter and Internal Podalic Version: The Problems of Disciplining a Skilled but Heretical Doctor." *Social Problems,* 30:109–117.

Burstein, Paul 1979 "Equal Employment Opportunity Legislation and the Income of Women and Nonwhites." *American Sociological Review,* 44:367–391.

Bush, David F. 1983 "Interpersonal Dimensions of the Consultation: Recent Trends in American Research on Doctor-Patient Communication," to appear in D. A. Pendleton and D. F. Bush, eds., *Communication and the Consultation.* Oxford, England: Oxford University Press.

Bush, Rod 1982 "Class Analysis of the Right-Wing Attack on Racial and National Minorities." Paper presented at the Annual Meeting of the Society for the Study of Social Problems, San Francisco.

Byrd, Benjamin F., Jr. 1976 Quoted in *Cigarette Smoking and Disease, 1976,* hearings before the Subcommittee on Health, Committee on Labor and Public Welfare, U.S. Senate, Feb. 19, Mar. 24, May 27.

Caditz, Judith 1976 "Ethnic Identification, Interethnic Contact, and Belief in Integration." *Social Forces,* 31:630–638.

Cafferata, Geil Lee, Judith Kasper, and Amy Bernstein 1983 "Family Roles, Structure, and Stressors in Relation to Sex Differences in Obtaining Psychotrophic Drugs." *Journal of Health and Social Behavior,* 24:132–143.

Calabresi, Guido, and Philip Bobbitt 1978 *Tragic Choices.* New York: Norton.

Calib, A. 1981 "Israel's Demographic Cabala." *Intercom,* Oct. 8–9.

Califano, Joseph A., Jr. 1982 *Report on Drug Abuse and Alcoholism.* New York: Warner.

Callahan, D. 1984 "Changing Arguments in an Unending Controversy." *Family Planning Perspectives,* 16:96–98.

Campbell, Angus, Philip Converse, and Willard Rodgers 1976 *The Quality of American Life.* New York: The Russell Sage Foundation.

Caplan, Gerald 1981 "Mastery of Stress: Psychosocial Aspects." *American Journal of Psychiatry,* 138:413–420.

Caplovitz, David 1979 *Making Ends Meet: How Families Cope with Inflation and Recession.* Beverly Hills, CA: Sage.

Caplow, T., H. Bahr, B. Chadwick, R. Hill, and M. Williamson 1982 *Middletown Families: Fifty Years of Change and Continuity.* Minneapolis: University of Minnesota Press.

Carley, Michael 1980 *Rational Techniques in Policy Analysis*. London: Heinemann Educational Books.

Carnesale, Albert, Paul Doty, Stanley Hoffmann, Samuel Huntington, Joseph Nye, and Scott Sagan (The Harvard Nuclear Study Group) 1983 *Living with Nuclear Weapons*. Toronto: Bantam.

Carter, A. 1985 "The Command and Control of Nuclear War." *Scientific American*, 252:32–39.

Cattell, Raymond, and John H. Morony 1962 "The Use of the 16PF in Distinguishing Homosexuals, Normals, and General Criminals." *Journal of Consulting Psychology*, 26:531–540.

Cavanagh, John R. 1966 *Counseling the Invert*. Milwaukee: Bruce Publishing.

Center on Budget and Policy Priorities 1983 *Soup Lines and Food Baskets*. Washington, DC: U.S. Government Printing Office.

Chambliss, William J. 1969 *Crime and the Legal Process*. New York: McGraw-Hill. 1973 "The Saints and the Roughnecks." *Society*, 11:24–31. 1978 *On the Take*. Bloomington: Indiana University Press.

Champlin, Carole 1978 "Neo-oriental Religious Sects in America: Opiate of Impoverished Middle Class Youth." *The Social Science Forum: An Interdisciplinary Journal*, 2:1–27.

Chaplin, J. P. 1959 *Rumor, Fear and the Madness of Crowds*. New York: Ballantine.

Chappell, Duncan, Robley Geis, and Gilbert Geis 1977 *Forcible Rape: The Crime, the Victim and the Offender*. New York: Columbia University Press.

Chazou, E. 1982 "Physicians for Nuclear Disarmament," in E. Chivian et al., eds., *Last Aid*, 16–22. San Francisco: Freeman.

Cherlin, A. 1979 "Work Life and Marital Dissolution," in G. Levinger and O. Moles, eds., *Divorce and Separation: Context, Causes and Consequences*. New York: Basic Books.

Cherlin, Andrew, and Pamela Barnhouse Walters 1981 "Trends in United States Men's and Women's Sex Role Attitudes: 1972 to 1978." *American Sociological Review*, 46:453–460.

Chodoff, P. 1960 "The Problem of Psychiatric Diagnosis: Can Biochemistry and Neurophysiology Help?" *Psychiatry*, 23:185–191.

Christ Church Hospital Research Group 1983 Cited in "When Hard Times Hit Families." *Parents Magazine*, May:12.

Citizens' Commission on Hunger in New England 1984 *American Hunger Crisis*. Boston: Harvard School of Public Health.

Claassen, Alfred 1980 "The Policy Perspective: Social Problems as Investment Opportunities." *Social Problems*, 27:526–540.

Clark, Kenneth B., and Mamie Phipps Clark 1980 "What Do Blacks Think of Themselves?" *Ebony Magazine*, November:176–181.

Clinard, Marshall B. 1974 *The Sociology of Deviant Behavior*. New York: Holt, Rinehart and Winston.

Cloward, Richard A., and Lloyd E. Ohlin 1960 *Delinquency and Opportunity*. New York: Free Press.

Coale, A. 1974 "The History of the Human Population." *Scientific American*, 231:41–51.

Cobb, S. 1979 "Social Support and Health Through the Life Course," in Matilda White Riley, ed., *Aging From Birth to Death*. Boulder, CO: Westview Press.

Cohen, David K. 1974 "Schooling, I.Q. and Income," in Lee Rainwater, ed., *Social Problems and Public Policy*. Chicago: Aldine.

Cohen, S. 1980 "The Evolution of Soviet Views on SALT Verification: Implications for the Future," in W. Potter, ed., *The Challenge of Strategic Deception*. Boulder, CO: Westview.

Cohen, Wilbur J. 1976 "Policy Planning for National Health Insurance," in U.S. Department of Health, Education, and Welfare, *Health in America: 1776–1976*. Washington, DC: U.S. Government Printing Office.

Cohn, Steven F., and James E. Gallagher 1984 "Gay Movements and Legal Change: Some Aspects of the Dynamics of a Social Problem." *Social Problems*, 32:72–86.

Coleman, J. 1966 *Equality of Educational Opportunity*. Washington, DC: U.S. Government Printing Office.

Coleman, Richard P., and Lee Rainwater 1978 *Social Standing in America*. New York: Basic Books.

Collins, Sharon M. 1983 "The Making of the Black Middle Class." *Social Problems*, 30:369–382.

Colvin, Mark, and John Pauly 1983 "A Critique of Criminology: Toward an Integrated Structural Marxist Theory of Delinquency Production." *American Journal of Sociology*, 89 (3):513–551.

Commager, H. 1984 "A Message the Nation Must Heed to Halt Its Drift toward Doomsday." *Philadelphia Inquirer,* Apr. 11:1R.

Commission on Population Growth and the American Future 1972 *Population and the American Future.* Washington, DC: U.S. Government Printing Office.

Common Cause 1978 *How Money Talks in Congress: A Study of the Impact of Money on Congressional Decision-Making.* Washington, DC: Common Cause.

Comte, Auguste 1854 *System of Positive Policy.* New York: Burt Franklin Series.

Congressional Record 1970 Sept. 14, 116:31607.

Conrad, P., and Rochelle Kern, eds. 1981 *The Sociology of Health and Illness: Critical Perspectives.* New York: St. Martin's.

Conrad, Peter 1975 "The Discovery of Hyperkinesis." *Social Problems,* 23:12–21.

Conrad, Peter, and Joseph W. Schneider 1980 *Deviance and Medicalization: From Badness to Sickness.* St. Louis, MO: Mosby.

Consumers' Union of the United States, Inc. 1980 "The HMO Approach to Health Care." *Consumer Report,* May.

Conway, Terry L., Harold W. Ward, Ross R. Vickers, Jr., and Richard H. Rake 1981 "Occupational Stress and Variation in Cigarette, Coffee and Alcohol Consumption." *Journal of Health and Social Behavior,* 22:155–165.

Cook, B. 1984 "How the Specter of Nuclear War Affects Families." *Philadelphia Inquirer,* Sept. 2.

Coppen, A. 1967 "The Biochemistry of Affective Disorders." *British Journal of Psychiatry,* 113:185–191.

Council on Environmental Quality 1975 *Carcinogens in the Environment.* Washington, DC: United States Government Printing Office.

Council on Environmental Quality and the U.S. Department of State 1980 *The Global 2000 Report to the President.* Washington, DC: U.S. Government Printing Office. 1981 *Global Future: Time to Act.* Washington, DC: U.S. Government Printing Office.

Courtney, Alice E., and Thomas W. Whipple 1983 *Sex Stereotyping in Advertising.* Lexington, MA: Lexington Books, D.C. Heath.

Covello, V. T., ed. 1980 *Poverty and Public Policy:*

An Evaluation of Social Science Research. Cambridge: Schenkman.

Cox, A. 1982 "A War of Computers—For Nuclear Starters." *New York Times,* May 27.

Crain, Robert L., and Rita E. Mahard 1982 "The Consequences of Controversy Accompanying Institutional Change: The Case of School Desegregation." *American Sociological Review,* 47:697–708.

Cressey, Donald R. 1982 *Society,* 19(5), Transaction, Inc.

Crichton, M. 1980 *Congo.* New York: Avon.

Cronin, Denise M. 1974 "Coming Out among Lesbians," in Erich Goode and Richard Troiden, eds., *Sexual Deviance and Sexual Deviants.* New York: Morrow.

Crowell, M. J., and B. L. Hirst 1979 *Mortality Differences between Smokers and Nonsmokers.* State Mutual Life Assurance Company of America.

Crull, Peggy 1980 "The Impact of Sexual Harassment on the Job," in Dail A. Newgarten and Jay M. Shafritz, eds., *Sexuality in Organization.* Oak Park, IL: Moore.

Cullen, Francis T., Bruce G. Link, and Craig W. Planzi 1982 "The Seriousness of Crime Revisited: Have Attitudes toward White Collar Crime Changed?" *Criminology,* 20:83–102.

Cultural Information Service 1984 "The Burning Bed." New York.

Curtis, H. 1977 *Biology.* New York: Worth.

Dahrendorf, Ralf 1974 "On the Origin of Inequality among Men," in Lee Rainwater, ed., *Social Problems and Public Policy.* Chicago: Aldine.

Danziger, Sheldon, and Robert Plotnick 1982 "The War on Income Poverty: Achievements and Failures," in Paul M. Sommers, ed., *Welfare Reform in America,* 40. Boston: Kluwer-Nijhoff.

Darby, William J. 1978 "The Benefits of Drink." *Human Nature,* November:31–37.

Davidson, James D., Gerhard Hofmann, and William R. Brown 1978 "Measuring and Explaining High School Interracial Climates." *Social Problems,* 26:50–70.

Davidson, T. 1977 "Wifebeating: A Recurrent Phenomenon throughout History," in M. Roy, ed., *Battered Women: A Psychosociological Study of Domestic Violence,* 2–23. New York: Van Nostrand Reinhold.

Davis, F. James 1952 "Crime News in Colorado Newspapers." *American Journal of Sociology,* 57:325–330.

Davis, James A. 1980 "Conservative Weather in a Liberalizing Climate: Change in Selected NORC General Social Survey Items, 1972–78." *Social Forces,* 58(4):1129–1156. 1982 "Achievement Variables and Class Cultures: Family, Schooling, Job and Forty-Nine Dependent Variables in the GSS." *American Sociological Review,* 47:569–586.

Davis, James Allan, and Tom W. Smith 1985 *General Social Surveys 1972–1985.* [machine-readable data file]. Principal investigator, James A. Davis; senior study director, Tom W. Smith. NORC ed. Chicago: National Opinion Research Center, producer 1985; Storrs, CT: Roper Public Opinion Research Center, University of Connecticut, distributor. 1 data file (18586 logical records) and 1 codebook (554 pp.).

Davis, K. 1948 *Human Society.* New York: Macmillan. 1983 "The Future of Marriage." *Bulletin of the American Academy of Arts and Sciences,* 36:15–48.

Davis, K., and J. Blake 1956 "Social Structure and Fertility: An Analytical Framework." *Economic Development and Social Change,* 4:211.

Davis, Karen, and Cathy Schoen 1978 "Health, Use of Medical Care, and Income." *Health and the War on Poverty: A Ten-Year Appraisal,* Brookings Institution.

Davis, Kingsley, and Wilbert E. Moore 1945 "Some Principles of Stratification." *American Sociological Review,* 10:242–249.

Davis, Nanette J. 1978 "Prostitution: Identity, Career and Legal-Economic Enterprise," in James M. Hanslen and Edward Sagarin, eds., *The Sociology of Sex: An Introductory Reader.* New York: Schocken.

Davis, Neil M., and Michael R. Cohen 1981 *Medication Errors: Causes and Prevention.* Philadelphia: George F. Stickley.

Davison, Gerald C., and John M. Neale 1974 *Abnormal Psychology: An Experimental Clinical Approach.* New York: Wiley.

Day, L. 1978 *What Will a ZPG Society Be Like? Population Bulletin,* 33:3. Washington, DC: Population Reference Bureau.

Dean, A., and N. Lin 1977 "The Stress-Buffering Role of Social Support: Problems and Prospects for Systematic Investigation." *Journal of Nervous and Mental Disease,* 165:403–417.

DeJong, William 1980 "The Stigma of Obesity: The Consequences of Naive Assumptions Concerning the Causes of Physical Deviance." *Journal of Health and Social Behavior,* 21:75–87.

Deudney, D. 1983 *Whole Earth Security: A Geopolitics of Peace.* Worldwatch Paper 55. Washington, DC: Worldwatch Institute.

Deutsch, M., and M. E. Collins 1951 *Interracial Housing.* Minneapolis: University of Minneapolis Press.

Devereux, G. 1976 *A Study of Abortion in Primitive Societies.* New York: International Universities Press.

Diaz-Briquets, Sergio, and Lesandro Perez 1981 *Cuba: The Demography of Revolution. Population Bulletin,* 36:1. Washington, DC: Population Reference Bureau.

DiMatteo, M. Robin, and Ron Hays 1982 "Social Support and Serious Illness," in Benjamin H. Gottlieb, ed., *Social Networks and Social Support.* Beverly Hills, CA:Sage.

Dixon, Katherine N., L. Eugene Arnold, and Kenneth Calestro 1978 "Father-Son Incest: Unreported Psychiatric Problem?" *American Journal of Psychiatry,* 135:835–838.

Dobash, R., and R. Dobash 1981 "Community Response to Violence against Wives: Charivari, Abstract Justice, and Patriarchy." *Social Problems,* 28:563–581.

Doering, C. H. 1974 "Plasma Testosterone Levels and Psychologic Measures in Men over a 2-Month Period," in R. D. Friedman, ed., *Sex Differences in Behavior.* New York: Wiley.

Doering, Susan G., Doris R. Entwisle, and Daniel Quinlan 1980 "Modeling the Quality of Women's Birth Experience." *Journal of Health and Social Behavior,* 21:12–21.

Dohrenwend, Bruce P. 1975 "Sociocultural and Social-Psychological Factors in the Genesis of Mental Disorders." *Journal of Health and Social Behavior,* 16:368.

Dohrenwend, Bruce P., and Barbara Snell Dohrenwend 1974 "Social and Cultural Influences on Psychopathology." *Annual Review of Psychology,* 25:434–435.

Dolnick, E. 1984 "Code Unbreakable No Longer." *Philadelphia Inquirer,* Nov. 7.

Domhoff, G. William 1967 *Who Rules America?* Englewood Cliffs, NJ: Prentice-Hall. 1970 *The Higher Circles: The Governing Class in America.* New York: Vintage.

Dooley, David, and Ralph Catalano 1984 "Why the Economy Predicts Help-Seeking: A Test of Competing Explanations." *Journal of Health and Social Behavior,* 25:160–176.

Dorland's Medical Dictionary Various Years. Philadelphia: Saunders.

Dressler, William W. 1985 "Extended Family Relationships, Social Support, and Mental Health in a Southern Black Community." *Journal of Health and Social Behavior,* 26:39–48.

Duncan, Beverly, and Otis Dudley Duncan 1978 *Sex Typing and Social Roles: A Research Report.* New York: Academic Press.

Durden-Smith, J., and D. Desimone 1983 *Sex and the Brain.* New York: Arbor House.

Durkheim, Emile 1897 *Le Suicide.* Paris: F. Alcan. 1964 *The Rules of Sociological Method.* New York: Free Press.

Dye, T. 1981 *Understanding Public Policy.* Englewood Cliffs, NJ: Prentice-Hall.

Dyson, F. 1979 *Disturbing the Universe.* New York: Harper and Row.

Easterlin, R. 1974 "Does Economic Growth Improve the Human Lot? Some Empirical Evidence," in Paul A. David and Melvin Reder, eds., *Nations and Households in Economic Growth.* New York: Academic Press. 1980 *Birth and Fortune.* New York: Basic Books.

Eaton, W. W. 1978 "Life Events, Social Supports, and Psychiatric Symptoms: A Re-analysis of the New Haven Data." *Journal of Health and Social Behavior,* 19:230–234.

Eberle, Patricia 1982 "Alcohol Abusers and Non-users: A Discriminant Analysis of Differences between Two Subgroups of Barriers." *Journal of Health and Social Behavior,* 23:260–271.

Eckholm, E. 1976 *Losing Ground: Environmental Stress and World Food Prospects.* New York: Norton. 1978*a* "Cutting Tobacco's Toll." Worldwatch Paper No. 18, March. Worldwatch Institute. 1978*b* *Disappearing Species: The Social Challenge.* Worldwatch Paper No. 22. Washington, DC: Worldwatch Institute.

Eckholm, E., and L. Brown 1977 *Spreading Deserts—The Hand of Man.* Worldwatch Paper No. 13. Washington, DC: Worldwatch Institute.

Eckholm, E., and K. Newland 1977 *Health: The Family Planning Factor.* Worldwatch Paper No. 10. Washington, DC: Worldwatch Institute.

Eckholm, E., and F. Record 1976 *The Two Faces of Malnutrition.* Worldwatch Paper No. 9. Washington, DC: Worldwatch Institute.

Ehrenreich, B. 1983 *The Hearts of Men.* Garden City, NY: Anchor/Doubleday.

Ehrenreich, Barbara, and John Ehrenreich 1971 *The American Health Empire: Power, Politics and Profits.* New York: Vintage.

Ehrlich, Paul R., John Harte, Mark A. Harwell, Peter H. Raven, Carl Sagan, George M. Goodwell, Joseph Berry, Edward S. Ayensu, Anne M. Ehrlich, Thomas Eisner, Stephen J. Gould, Herbert D. Grover, Rafael Herrera, Robert M. May, Ernst Mayr, Christopher P. McKay, Harold A. Mooney, Norman Myers, David Pimentel, and John M. Teal 1983 "Long-Term Biological Consequences of Nuclear War." *Science,* 222:1293–1299.

Elliot, Delbert S., and Suzanne S. Ageton 1980 "Reconciling Race and Class Differences in Self-Reported and Official Estimates of Delinquency." *American Sociological Review,* 45:95–110.

Empey, Lamar T. 1982 *American Delinquency.* Homewood, IL: Dorsey.

Encyclopedia of Sociology, The 1981 Guilford, CT: DPG Reference Publishing.

Engels, F. 1942 *The Origin of the Family, Private Property and the State.* New York: International Publishers.

Engs, Ruth C., and David J. Hanson 1983 "Drinking Patterns and Drinking Problems of College Students." *Chronicle of Higher Education,* Jan. 19.

Environmental Quality Index 1984 Washington, DC: National Wildlife Federation.

Erhard, W. 1982 *The End of Starvation.* San Francisco: Hunger Project Press.

Erikson, Kai T. 1966 *Wayward Puritans.* New York: Wiley.

Erskine, Hazel 1972 "Polls: Pollution and Its Costs." *Public Opinion Quarterly,* 36:120–135.

Etzioni, A. 1982 *An Immodest Agenda: Rebuilding America before the 21st Century.* New York: McGraw-Hill.

Exum, William H. 1983 "Climbing the Crystal Stair: Values, Affirmative Action, and Minority Faculty." *Social Problems,* 30:383–399.

Eyer, Joseph 1975 "Hypertension as a Disease of Modern Society." *International Journal of Health Services,* 5(4):539.

Ezell, E., and L. Ezell 1978 *The Partnership: A History of the Apollo-Soyuz Test Project.* Washington, DC: NASA Scientific and Technical Information Office.

Faflick, P. 1982 "Brutal Game of Survival." *Time,* Aug. 16.

Family Planning Perspectives 1985 "American Adults' Approval of Legal Abortion Has Remained Virtually Unchanged since 1972," 17(4):181.

Family Service America 1984 *The State of Families.* New York.

Faris, R. E. L., and H. W. Dunham 1960 *Mental Disorders in Urban Areas.* New York: Hafner.

Farley, Reynolds 1984 *Blacks and Whites: Narrowing the Gap.* Cambridge: Harvard University Press.

Faux, M. 1984 *Childless by Choice: Choosing Childlessness in the Eighties.* Garden City, NY: Anchor/Doubleday.

Featherman, D. L., and R. M. Hauser 1978 *Opportunity and Change.* New York: Academic Press.

Feder, Judith, John Holahan, and Theodore Marmor 1980 *National Health Insurance: Conflicting Goals and Policy Choices.* Washington, DC: The Urban Institute.

Federal Bureau of Investigation 1982 *Uniform Crime Rates for United States—1982.* Washington, DC: U.S. Government Printing Office. 1983 *Uniform Crime Rates for United States—1983.* Washington, DC: U.S. Government Printing Office. 1984 *Uniform Crime Rates for United States—1984.* Washington, DC: U.S. Government Printing Office. 1985 *Uniform Crime Rates for United States—1985.* Washington, D.C.: U.S. Government Printing Office.

Feiberg, William F. 1985 "Are Affirmative Action and Economic Growth Alternative Paths to Racial Equality?" *American Sociological Review,* 50:561–576.

Feigelman, William 1980 *Prescriptions for Better Days.* Dubuque, IA: William C. Brown.

Fernandez, Roberto M., and Jane C. Kulik 1981 "A Multilevel Model of Life Satisfaction: Effects of Individual Characteristics and Neighborhood Composition." *American Sociological Review,* 46:840–851.

Ferraro, Geraldine 1985 Keynote address at the annual convention of the American Home Economics Association, June 24, Philadelphia.

Ferraro, K., and J. Johnson 1984 "How Women Experience Battering: The Process of Victimization," in D. Kelly, ed., *Deviant Behavior,* 277–294. New York: St. Martin's.

Feshbach, M. 1982 *The Soviet Union: Population Trends and Dilemmas. Population Bulletin,* 37:3. Washington, DC: Population Reference Bureau.

Financial Times Energy Economist 1983 "Nuclear Energy: World Status," January.

Finkelhor, D. 1979 *Sexually Victimized Children.* New York: Free Press. 1984 *Child Sexual Abuse: New Theory and Research.* New York: Free Press.

Finkelhor, D., and Yllo, K. 1985 *License to Rape: The Sexual Abuse of Wives.* New York: Holt, Rinehart, & Winston.

Fischer, Claude, et al. 1977 *Networks and Places: Social Relations in the Urban Setting.* New York: Free Press.

Fishburn, P. M., H. I. Abelson, and I. Cisin 1979 *National Survey on Drug Abuse: Main Findings.* Washington, DC: Department of Health and Human Services.

Flavin, C. 1984 "Reassessing the Economics of Nuclear Power," in L. Brown et al., eds., *State of the World, 1984.* New York: Norton.

Flavin, C., and S. Postel 1984 "Developing Renewable Energy," in L. Brown et al., eds., *State of the World, 1984.* New York: Norton.

Ford, Clellan S., and Frank A. Beach 1951 *Patterns of Sexual Behavior.* New York: Harper and Row.

Forrest, Thomas R. 1983 "Sex Role Imagery in Network News." Paper presented at the annual meeting of the Society for the Study of Social Problems, San Francisco.

Fossett, Mark, and Gray Swicegood 1982 "Rediscovering City Differences in Racial Occupational Inequality." *American Sociological Review,* 47:681–689.

Foster, George McClelland, and Barbara Gallatin Anderson 1978 *Medical Anthropology.* New York: Wiley.

Fox, Renee C. 1977 "The Medicalization and Demedicalization of American Society," in John H. Knowles, ed., *Doing Better and Feeling Worse.* New York: Norton.

Freeman, Howard E., Sol Levine, and Leo G. Reeder, eds. 1979 *Handbook of Medical Sociology.* Englewood Cliffs, NJ: Prentice-Hall.

Freeman, Howard E., Wyatt C. Jones, and Lynne G. Zucker 1979 *Social Problems: A Policy Perspective.* Chicago: Rand McNally.

Frei, D. 1982 *Risks of Unintentional Nuclear War.* Geneva: United Nations Institute for Disarmament Research.

Freidan, Bernard J., and Arthur P. Solomon 1977 *The Nation's Housing: 1975–1985.* Cambridge, MA: Joint Center for Urban Studies of MIT and Harvard University.

Frejka, T. 1968 "Reflections on the Demographic Conditions Needed to Establish a United States Stationary Population Growth." *Population Studies,* 22:379–397.

Friedan, Betty 1963 *The Feminine Mystique.* New York: Norton.

Friedman, Lawrence M. 1977 "The Social and Political Context of the War on Poverty: An Overview," in Robert H. Haveman, ed., *A Decade of Federal Antipoverty Programs.* New York: Academic Press.

Friedman, Mark 1975 "Homosexuals May Be Healthier Than Straights." *Psychology Today,* March:30.

Friedman, Meyer, and Ray H. Rosenman 1974 *Type A Behavior and Your Heart.* New York: Fawcett Columbine.

Friedrich, Otto 1983 "Cheating by the Millions." *Time,* March 28.

Friedson, Eliot 1970 *Professional Dominance: The Social Structure of Medical Care.* New York: Atherton.

Fries, J. 1980 "Aging, Natural Death, and the Compression of Morbidity." *New England Journal of Medicine,* 303:130–135.

Fromm, Erich 1965 *Escape from Freedom.* New York: Holt, Rinehart, and Winston.

Fuchs, Victor R. 1967 "Redefining Poverty and Redistributing Income." *The Public Interest,* 8:88–95. 1974 *Who Shall Live? Health, Economics and Social Choice.* New York: Basic Books.

Furstenberg, F., and P. Allison 1984 Unpublished results from their analysis of the National Survey of Children.

Furstenberg, F., and C. Nord 1982 "Parenting Apart: Patterns of Childrearing after Marital Disruption." Paper presented to the Annual Meeting of the American Sociological Association, San Francisco.

Gagnon, John H., and William Simon 1968 "Sexual Deviance in Contemporary America." *The Annals of the American Academy of Political and Social Sciences,* March: 116–117. 1973 *Sexual Conduct: The Social Origins of Human Sexuality.* Chicago: Aldine.

Galizio, Mark, and Stephen A. Maisto 1985 *Determinants of Substance Abuse: Biological, Psychological and Environmental Factors.* New York: Plenum.

Gallagher, Bernard J. III 1987 *The Sociology of Mental Illness.* Englewood Cliffs, NJ: Prentice-Hall.

Gallagher, Bernard J. III, Joseph A. McFalls, Jr., and Brian J. Jones 1983 "Racial Factors in Birth Seasonality among Schizophrenics: A Preliminary Analysis." *Journal of Abnormal Psychology,* 92:524–527.

Gallup, G. 1984 "What Americans Think about Their Lives and Families," in O. Pocs and R. Walsh, eds., *Marriage and Family 84/85,* annual ed., 10–11. Guilford, CT: Dushkin.

Gallup Organization 1985 Poll on abortion conducted for *Newsweek* magazine (results published in *Newsweek,* Jan. 14).

Gallup Report 1981 "Occupational Prestige of Physicians," September: 19; October: 43. 1982 "Most Important Problem Trend," March: 27; "Legalization of Marijuana," November: 12. 1983 "Crime," March: 3-9. 1983a "Ideal Number of Children," March:11. 1983b "Likelihood of Nuclear War," November:8. 1984 "Most Important Problem," June:17. 1985 "Premarital Sex," June:28.

Gans, Herbert J. 1973 *More Equality.* New York: Pantheon. 1979 *Deciding What's News.* New York: Praeger.

Garbarino, J., and D. Sherman 1980 "Identifying High Risk Neighborhoods," in J. Garbarino, S. H. Stocking, and Associates, *Protecting Children from Abuse and Neglect.* San Francisco: Jossey-Bass.

Garcia, Luis T., Nancy Erskine, Kathy Hawn, and Susanne R. Casmay 1981 "The Effect of Affirmative Action on Attributions about Minority Group Members." *Journal of Personality,* 49:427–437.

Garfinkel, Irwin 1982 *Income-Tested Transfer Programs.* New York: Academic Press.

Garmezy, Norman 1978 "New Approaches to a Developmental Overview of Schizophrenia." Paper presented at the annual meeting of the American Psychological Association, Toronto.

Gay, G. R., and C. W. Sheppard 1973 "Sex-Crazed Dope Fiends: Myths or Reality?" in E. Harms, ed., *Drugs and Youth: The Challenge of Today.* New York: Pergamon.

Gebhard, P. H. 1965 *Sex Offenders.* New York: Harper and Row.

Geiger, H. 1982 "The Medical Effects on a City in the United States," in E. Chivian et al., eds., *Last Aid,* 137–150. San Francisco: Freeman.

Geiss, Gilbert 1972 *Not the Law's Business?* Rockville, MD: National Institute of Mental Health.

Gelles, R. 1979 "The Myth of Battered Husbands and New Facts about Family Violence." *Journal of Marriage and the Family,* 42:873–885.

Gelles, R., and C. Cornell, eds. 1983 *International Perspectives on Family Violence.* Lexington, MA: Lexington Books.

Gerbner, George, and Nancy Signorielli 1979 "Women and Minorities in Television Drama 1969–1978." Philadelphia, PA: Annenberg School of Communications.

Gershan, E. S., S. D. Targum, and L. R. Kessler 1977 "Genetic Studies and Biologic Strategies in the Affective Disorders." *Progress in Medical Genetics,* 2:103–125.

Gerth, H. H., and C. Wright Mills 1958 *From Max Weber: Essays in Sociology.* New York: Oxford University Press.

Gilland, B. 1983 "Population and Food Supply." *Population and Development Review,* 9(2).

Ginsberg, Irving J., and James R. Greenley 1978 "Competing Theories of Marijuana Use: A Longitudinal Study." *Journal of Health and Social Behavior,* 19:22–34.

Ginzburg, Kenneth N. 1977 "The 'Meat-Rack': A Study of the Male Homosexual Prostitute," in Clifton D. Bryant, ed., *Sexual Deviancy in Social Context.* New York: New Viewpoints.

Glick, P. 1984 "American Household Structure in Transition." *Family Planning Perspectives,* 16:205–211.

Goffman, Erving 1961 *Asylums: Essays on the Social Situation of Mental Patients and Other Inmates.* New York: Doubleday.

Golden, F. 1983 "Fighting Blight in Paradise." *Time,* Apr. 4:68.

Goldman, Marion S. 1985 "Prostitution, Economic Exchange and the Unconscious." Paper presented at the Annual Meeting of the Society for the Study of Social Problems, Washington, DC.

Goldman, N., C. Westoff, and C. Hammerslough 1984 "Demography of the Marriage Market in the United States." *Population Index,* 50:5–25.

Goldman, Peter 1970 *Report from Black America.* New York: Simon and Schuster.

Goldscheider, C. 1983 "Modernization, Migration, and Urbanization," in P. Morrison, ed., *Population Movements.* Liège, Belgium: Ordina.

Goleman, D. 1984 "Traumatic Beginnings: Most Children Able to Recover." *The New York Times,* Mar. 13:C1.

Gooberman, Lawrence 1974 *Operation Intercept: The Multiple Consequences of Public Policy.* New York: Pergamon.

Goode, Erich 1978 *Deviant Behavior: An Interactionist Approach.* Englewood Cliffs, NJ: Prentice-Hall.

Goodman, E. 1985 "Women Are Telling Their Stories." *Philadelphia Inquirer,* May 24.

Goodwin, Leonard 1972 *Do the Poor Want to Work?* Washington, DC: The Brookings Institution.

Gordon, M. 1975 *Agriculture and Population.* U.S. Bureau of Census, Statistical Training Document No. 1. Washington, DC: U.S. Government Printing Office.

Gore, S. 1978 "The Effect of Social Support in Moderating the Health Consequences of Unemployment." *Journal of Health and Social Behavior,* 19:157–165.

Gottesman, I. I., and J. Shields 1973 "Genetic Theorizing and Schizophrenia." *British Journal of Psychiatry,* 122:15–30.

Gould, Stephen Jay 1980 "Science and Jewish Immigration." *Natural History,* 89:14–19.

Gove, Walter R. 1972 "The Relationship between Sex Roles, Marital Status, and Mental Illness." *Social Forces,* 51:34–44.

Gove, W., and M. Hughes 1979 "Possible Causes of the Apparent Sex Differences in Physical Health: An Empirical Investigation." *American Sociological Review,* 44:126–146.

Granovetter, Mark 1983 "Toward a Sociological-Theory of Income Differences," in Ivar Berg, ed., *Sociological Perspectives on Labor Markets.* New York: Academic Press.

Grant, J. 1982 "The State of the World's Children, 1982–1983." Annual Report of the United Nations Children's Fund.

Grant, L. 1982 *The Cornucopian Fallacies.* Washington, DC: The Environmental Fund.

Gray, C. 1981 *The MX, ICBM and National Security.* New York: Praeger.

Gray, Susan H. 1982 "Exposure to Pornography and Aggression toward Women: The Case of the Angry Male." *Social Problems,* 29:387–398.

Gregory, Dick 1968 Speech given at Rutgers University, New Brunswick, NJ, Oct. 30.z

Green, M. 1981 "Urban Overcrowding Threatens Stability in Less Developed Countries." *Intercom,* Feb. 5.

Green, Richard 1978 "Sexual Identity of 37 Children Raised by Homosexual or Transsexual Parents." *American Journal of Psychiatry,* 135:692–697.

Greenley, James R. 1972 "The Psychiatric Patients' Family and Length of Hospitalization." *Journal of Health and Social Behavior,* 13:25–37. 1979 "Familial Expectations, Posthospital Adjustment, and the Societal Reaction Perspective on Mental Illness." *Journal of Health and Social Behavior,* 20:217–227.

Greenwald, Harold 1958 *The Call Girl.* New York: Ballantine.

Greve, F. 1983 "Warhead Depots: A Weak Line in NATO's Security." *Philadelphia Inquirer,* Mar. 13:2F.

Grimes, D. 1984 "Second-Trimester Abortions in the U.S." *Family Planning Perspectives,* 16:260–266.

Grossman, L. 1983*a* "The Growing Problem of Spouse Abuse." *The William Petschek National Jewish Family Center Newsletter,* 3:1–3. 1983*b* Review of B. Berger and P. Berger's "The War over the Family: Capturing the Middle Ground," in *The William Petschek National Jewish Family Center Newsletter,* 3:5–6. 1985 "Family Policy." *The William Petschek National Jewish Family Center Newsletter,* 5:1–4.

Grusky, Oscar, Kathleen Tierney, Ronald W. Manderscheid, and David B. Grusky 1985 "Social Bonding and Community Adjustment of Chronically Mentally Ill Adults," 26:49–63.

Gusfield, Joseph R. 1963 *Symbolic Crusade: Status Politics and the American Temperance Movement.* Urbana: University of Illinois Press.

Hacker, Andrew, ed. 1983 *U/S: A Statistical Portrait of the American People.* New York: Viking.

Hafner, R. Julian 1986 *Marriage and Mental Illness.* New York: Guilford.

Hagan, John, and Jeffrey Leon 1977 "Rediscovering Delinquency: Social History, Political Ideology and the Sociology of Law." *American Sociological Review,* 42:587–598.

Hahn, Jeffrey 1982 "Is Developed Socialism a Soviet Version of Convergence Theory?" in Maurice Simon and James Seroka, eds., *Developed Socialism in the Soviet Bloc.* Boulder, CO: Westview.

Haines, A. 1982 "The Possible Consequences of a Nuclear Attack in London," in E. Chivian et al., eds., *Last Aid,* 163–172. San Francisco: Freeman.

Haney, D. 1984 "Cancer Causes Suspected in Homes." *Philadelphia Inquirer,* June 7:3.

Hansell, Stephen 1982 "Student, Parent, and School Effects on the Stress of College Application." *Journal of Health and Social Behavior,* 23:38–51.

Harring, Sidney L. 1983 *Policing a Class Society.* New Brunswick, NJ: Rutgers University Press.

Harris, I., and Associates 1975 *Myth and Reality of Aging America.* Washington, DC: National Council on Aging.

Harris, L., and Associates 1978 *Health Maintenance.* Newport Beach, CA: Pacific Mutual Life Insurance Co.

Harris, Marvin 1974 *Cows, Pigs, Wars, and Witches: The Riddles of Culture.* New York: Random House.

Harrison, P. 1983 "Land and People, the Growing Pressure." *Earthwatch,* No. 13.

Hartley, Eugene 1964 *Problems in Prejudice.* New York: King's Crown.

Hastings, William M. 1979 *How to Think about Social Problems.* New York: Oxford University Press.

Haupt, A. 1983 "The Shadow of Female Infanticide." *Intercom,* 11(1 and 2):1.

Heath, R. G., and I. M. Krupp 1967 "Schizophrenia as an Immunologic Disorder." *Archives of General Psychiatry,* 16:1–33.

Heather, Nick, and Ian Robertson 1981 *Controlled Drinking*. New York: Methuen.

Hedblom, J. H. 1972 "The Female Homosexual: Social and Attitudinal Dimensions," in James A. McCaffrey, ed., *The Homosexual*. Englewood Cliffs, NJ: Prentice-Hall.

Helmreich, Robert L., Janet T. Spence, and Robert H. Gibson 1982 "Sex Role Attitudes: 1972–1980." *Personality and Social Psychology Bulletin*, 8(4): 656–663.

Helms, Robert B. 1978 "Contemporary Health Policy: Dealing with the Cost of Care," in William Felkner, ed., *Contemporary Economic Problems*. Washington, DC: American Enterprise Institute.

Helsing, Knud J., Moyses Szklo, and George W. Comstock 1981 "Factors Associated with Mortality after Widowhood." *American Journal of Public Health*, 71:802–809; 71:793–794.

Henshaw, S., N. Binkin, E. Blaine, and J. Smith 1985 "A Portrait of American Women Who Obtain Abortions." *Family Planning Perspectives*, 17:90–95.

Henshaw, S., J. Forrest, E. Sullivan, and C. Tietze 1982 "Abortion Services in the United States, 1979 and 1980." *Family Planning Perspectives*, 14:5–14.

Henshaw, S., and K. O'Reilly 1983 "Characteristics of Abortion Patients in the United States, 1979 and 1980." *Family Planning Perspectives*, 15:5–16.

Henslin, J., and D. Light 1983 *Social Problems*. New York: McGraw-Hill.

Herman, Dianne 1984 "The Rape Culture," in Jo Freeman, ed., *Women: A Feminist Perspective*, 3d ed. Palo Alto, CA: Mayfield.

Herrnstein, R. J. 1973 *I.Q. in the Meritocracy*. Boston: Little, Brown. 1980 "In Defense of Intelligence Tests." *Commentary*, 69:40–51.

Hersh, Seymour M. 1982 "Kissinger and Nixon in the White House." *The Atlantic*, 249(5):35–68.

Herzog, Regula A., Jerald C. Bachman, and Lloyd D. Johnston 1979 "High School Seniors' Preferences for Sharing Work and Family Responsibilities between Husband and Wife." *Monitoring the Future*. Occasional Paper 3, University of Michigan, Ann Arbor, Institute for Social Research.

Heston, L. L. 1966 "Psychiatric Disorders in Foster Home-Reared Children of Schizophrenic Mothers." *British Journal of Psychiatry*, 112:819–825.

Hetherington, E., K. Camara, and D. Featherman 1983 "Achievement and Intellectual Functioning of Children in One-Parent Households," in J. Spence, ed., *Achievement and Achievement Motives*, 205–284. San Francisco: Freeman.

Heyl, Barbara Sherman 1975 "The Training of House Prostitutes." Paper presented at the annual meeting of the American Sociological Association, San Francisco.

Hill, M. 1983 "Trends in the Economic Situation of U.S. Families and Children: 1970–1980," in R. Nelson and F. Skidmore, eds., *American Families and the Economy*, 9–58. Washington, DC: National Academy Press.

Hill, Martha S., and Michael Ponza 1983 "Poverty and Welfare Dependence across Generations." *Economic Outlook U.S.A.*, 10(3):61–64.

Hindelang, Michael J., Michael R. Gottfredson, and Timothy J. Flanagan, eds. 1981 *Sourcebook of Criminal Justice Statistics—1980*. Washington, DC: U.S. Department of Justice.

Hindelang, Michael J., Travis Hirschi, and Joseph G. Weis 1981 *Measuring Delinquency*. Beverly Hills, CA: Sage.

Hirschi, Travis 1969 *Causes of Delinquency*. Berkeley: University of California Press.

Hite, Shere 1976 *The Hite Report: A Nationwide Study on Female Sexuality*. New York: Macmillan.

Hobbs, M. A. 1982 "Congress Confronts a Hidden Problem." *The Philadelphia Inquirer*, May 5:1A.

Hofferth, S. 1983 "Updating Children's Life Course." Center for Population Research. National Institute of Child Health and Human Development. Washington, DC: Unpublished.

Hoffman, S. 1977 "Marital Instability and Economic Status of Women." *Demography*, 14:67–76.

Hole, Judith, and Ellen Levine 1971 *Rebirth of Feminism*. New York: Quadrangle.

Hollingshead, August B., and Frederick C. Redlich 1953 "Social Stratification and Psychiatric Disorder." *American Sociological Review*, 18:167.

Holmes, T., and R. H. Rahe 1967 "The Social Readjustment Scale." *Journal of Psychosomatic Research*, 11:213–218.

Holstrom, Lynda Lytle, and Ann Wolber Burgess 1983 "Rape and Everyday Life." *Society*, 20(5):33.

Hooker, Evelyn 1959 "Symposium on Current Aspects of the Problems of Validity: What Is a

Criterion?" *Journal of Projective Techniques,* 23:278–286. 1966 "The Homosexual Community," in James O. Palmer and Michael J. Goldstein, eds., *Perspectives in Psychopathology: Readings in Abnormal Psychology.* New York: Oxford.

Horowitz, Alan V. 1982 *The Social Control of Mental Illness.* New York: Academic Press.

Horowitz, Irving L. 1968 *Professing Sociology.* Chicago: Aldine.

Horton, P., and G. Leslie 1974 *The Sociology of Social Problems.* Englewood Cliffs, NJ: Prentice-Hall. 1981 *The Sociology of Social Problems.* 2d ed. Englewood Cliffs, NJ : Prentice-Hall.

Hout, Michael 1984 "Occupational Mobility of Black Men: 1962–1973." *American Sociological Review,* 49:308–322.

Hoyle, R. 1984 "A Continent Gone Wrong." *Time,* Jan. 16:26.

Hubert H. Humphrey Institute of Public Affairs 1982 *Public Attitudes toward Youth Crime,* working paper. Minneapolis, MN: Hubert H. Humphrey Institute of Public Affairs.

Humphreys, Laud 1975 *Tearoom Trade.* Chicago: Aldine.

Humphries, Drew 1981 "Serious Crime, News Coverage, and Ideology." *Crime and Delinquency,* April.

Hunt, Leon G., and Carl D. Chambers 1976 *The Heroin Epidemics.* New York: Spectrum.

Hunt, Morton 1974 *Sexual Behavior in the 1970s.* Chicago: Playboy.

Huttman, Elizabeth D. 1981 *Introduction to Social Policy.* New York: McGraw-Hill.

Ilyin, L. 1982 "Evaluation of the Medical Consequences of a Nuclear Attack," in E. Chivian et al., eds., *Last Aid,* 157–162. San Francisco: Freeman.

Inciardi, James A. 1978 *Reflection on Crime.* New York: Holt, Rinehart, & Winston. 1984 "Professional Theft," in Robert F. Meier, ed., *Major Forms of Crime.* Beverly Hills, CA: Sage.

Inhaber, H. 1979 "Risk with Energy from Conventional and Nonconventional Sources." *Science,* 203:718.

Inquirer Washington Bureau 1983 "Lapses among Those Who Guard Doomsday." *Philadelphia Inquirer,* Mar. 13:2F.

Interchange 1983 "The Population of China: One Billion, Eight Million People," 12(2):1–4.

Intercom 1980 "Eugenics Hints in China Press," August:2. 1981 "Feeding the World: The Coming Challenge," February:6. 1983*a* "As *Intercom* Marks Its 10th Anniversary," July:7. 1983*b* "China Steps Up Sterilization as Population Control," May/June:3.

International Institute for Strategic Studies 1984 *Military Balance.* London.

International Monetary Fund 1985 *International Financial Statistics,* 38. Washington, DC: International Monetary Fund.

Jackson, N. 1985 "Hawks, Doves and Owls: Policy Experts Formulate an Agenda for Avoiding Nuclear War." *Harvard Magazine,* May–June: 79–82.

Jackson, Robert M. 1977 "Social Structure and Process in Friendship Choice," in Claude S. Fischer et al., *Networks and Places.* New York: Free Press.

Jacobson, G. 1984 *The Multiple Crises of Marital Separation and Divorce.* New York: Grune and Stratton.

Jeffries, L., and R. Edmonds 1981 "Abortion: The Dreaded Complication." *Philadelphia Inquirer Magazine,* Aug. 2:14–20.

Jencks, Christopher, Marshall Smith, Henry Acland, Mary Jo Bane, David Cohen, Herbert Gintis, Barbara Heyns, and Stephan Michelson 1972 *Inequality: A Reassessment of the Effect of Family and Schooling in America.* New York: Basic Books.

Jencks, Christopher, Susan Bartlett, Mary Corcaran, James Crouse, David Eaglesfield, Gregory Jackson, Kent McClelland, Peter Mueser, Michael Olneck, Joseph Schwartz, Sherry Ward, and Jill Williams 1979 *Who Gets Ahead? The Determinants of Economic Success in America.* New York: Basic Books.

Jenkins, Richard L."Psychiatric Interpretations and Considerations of Treatment," in Lester E. Hewitt and Richard L. Jenkins, eds., *Fundamental Patterns of Maladjustment.* State of Illinois.

Jensen, Arthur R. 1972 *Genetics and Education.* New York: Harper and Row.

Jensen, Gary F., C. S. White, and James M. Galliher 1982 "Ethnic Status and Adolescent Self-Evaluation: An Extension of Research on Minority Self-Esteem." *Social Problems,* 30:226–239.

Johnson, Donald M. 1945 "The Phantom Anesthetist of Mattoon: A Field Study of Mass Hysteria."

Journal of Abnormal and Social Psychology, 40:175–186.

Johnson, J. H., and I. G. Sareson 1978 "Life Stress, Depression and Anxiety: Internal-External Control as a Moderator Variable." *Journal of Psychosomatic Research,* 22:205–208.

Johnson, J. M. 1975 *Doing Field Research.* London: Cassell and Collier Macmillan.

Jones, Brian J. 1982 "Poverty Theory and Welfare Policy: A Network Reformulation." *Policy Perspectives,* 2(3):394–412. 1984 "Toward a Constructive Theory of Anti-poverty Policy." *American Journal of Economics and Sociology,* 43(2):247–256.

Jones, Brian J., Bernard J. Gallagher III, and Joseph A. McFalls, Jr. "Social Network Models of Gender and Health." Under journal review.

Jones, E., J. Forrest, N. Goldman, S. Henshaw, R. Lincoln, J. Rosoff, C. Westoff, and D. Wulf 1985 "Teenage Pregnancy in Developed Countries: Determinants and Policy Implications." *Family Planning Perspectives,* 17:53–63.

Jones, Hardin B., and Helen C. Jones 1977 *Sensual Drugs.* Cambridge: Cambridge University Press.

Jones, Landon 1980 *Great Expectations: America and the Baby Boom Generation.* New York: Ballantine.

Journal of the American Medical Association 1978 "Health Evaluation of Energy-Generating Sources," 240(20):2193.

Kadis, A. L., and C. Winick 1973 "The Cartoon as Therapeutic Catalyst," in H. H. Mosak, ed., *Alfred Adler: His Influence on Psychology Today.* Park Ridge, NJ: Noyes Press.

Kallman, F. J. 1953 *Heredity in Health and Mental Disorder.* New York:Norton.

Kamnuansilpa, P., A. Chamratrithirong, and J. Knodel 1982 "Thailand's Reproductive Revolution: An Update." *International Family Planning Perspectives,* June.

Kandel, Denise Bystryn, Mark Davies, and Victoria H. Raveis 1985 "The Stressfulness of Daily Social Roles: Marital Occupational and Household Roles." *Journal of Health and Social Behavior,* 26:64–78.

Kandel, Denise Bystryn 1966 "Status Homophily, Social Context, and Participation in Psychotherapy." *American Journal of Sociology,* 71:640–650.

Kanin, Eugene J., and Stanley R. Parcell 1977 "Sexual Aggression: A Second Look at the Offended Female." *Archives of Sexual Behavior,* 6:67.

Kaplan, Berton H., John C. Cassell, and Susan Gore 1979 "Social Support and Health," in E. Gartly Jaco, ed., *Patients, Physicians and Illness: A Sourcebook in Behavioral Science and Health,* 3d ed. New York: Free Press.

Kaplan, Howard B., Steven S. Martin, and Cynthia Robbins 1984 "Pathways to Adolescent Drug Use: Self-Derogation, Peer Influence, Weakening of Social Controls, and Early Substance Use." *Journal of Health and Social Behavior,* 25:270–289.

Kaplan, Roy H., and Carlos E. Kruytbosch 1975 Unpublished manuscript.

Karno, Marvin 1966 "The Enigma of Ethnicity in a Psychiatric Clinic." *Archives of General Psychiatry,* 14:516–520.

Kasteler, Josephine, Robert L. Kane, Donna M. Olsen, and Constance Thetford 1976 "Issues Underlying Prevalence of 'Doctor-Shopping' Behavior." *Journal of Health and Social Behavior,* 17:328–339.

Katchadourion, Herant, and Donald Lunde 1975 *Fundamentals of Human Sexuality.* New York: Holt, Rinehart, and Winston.

Kazis, Richard, and Richard L. Grossman 1982 *Fear at Work: Job Blackmail, Labor, and the Environment.* New York: Pilgrim.

Kegley, C., and C. Wittkopf 1985 *The Nuclear Reader.* New York: St. Martin's.

Kelly, J. 1982 "Thinking about the Unthinkable." *Time,* Mar. 29:10–14.

Kempe, C. 1978 "Child Abuse—The Pediatrician's Role in Child Advocacy and Preventive Pediatrics." *American Journal of Disease in Children,* 132:255–260.

Kennedy, F., H. R. H. Hoffman, and W. H. Haines 1947 "A Study of William Heirens." *American Journal of Psychiatry,* 104:113–121.

Kenyon, F. 1968 "Studies in Female Homosexuality." *British Journal of Psychiatry,* 114:1337–1350.

Kerson, Toba S. 1981 "A Nation of Laws: Social Response to Genetic Disease." *Social Science Forum,* III:15–31.

Kessler, Ronald C. 1979a "A Strategy for Studying Differential Vulnerability to the Psychological Consequences of Stress." *Journal of Health and Social Behavior,* 20:100–108. 1979b

"Stress, Social Status, and Psychological Distress." *Journal of Health and Social Behavior,* 20:259–272.

Kessler, Ronald C., Roger L. Brown, and Clifford L. Broman 1981 "Sex Differences in Psychiatric Help-Seeking: Evidence from Four Large-Scale Surveys." *Journal of Health and Social Behavior,* 22:49–64.

Kessler, Ronald C., and Jane D. McLeod 1984 "Sex Differences in Vulnerability to Undesirable Life Events." *American Sociological Review,* 49:520–631.

Kessler, Ronald C., and James A. McRae, Jr. 1981 "Trends in the Relationship between Sex and Psychological Distress: 1957–1976." *American Sociological Review,* 46:443–452. 1982 "The Effects of Wives' Employment on the Mental Health of Married Men and Women." *American Sociological Review,* 47:216–227. 1983 "Trends in the Relationship between Sex and Attempted Suicide." *Journal of Health and Social Behavior,* 24:98–110.

Kety, Seymour S. 1971 "Mental Illness in the Biological and Adoptive Families of Adopted Schizophrenics." *American Journal of Psychiatry,* 128:302–306.

Keyes, R. 1973 *We, the Lonely People.* New York: Harper & Row.

Kidder, Louise H., Claire Sellitz, Lawrence S. Wrightman, and Stuart W. Cook 1981 *Research Methods in Social Relations.* New York: Holt, Rinehart, and Winston.

Kinsey, A., and P. Gebhard 1953 *Sexual Behavior in the Human Female.* Philadelphia: Saunders.

Kinsey, A., and C. E. Martin 1948 *Sexual Behavior in the Human Male.* Philadelphia : Saunders.

Kirkpatrick, Clifford, and Eugene Kanin 1957 "Male Aggression on a University Campus." *American Sociological Review,* 22:53.

Kitagawa, E., and P. Hauser 1973 *Differential Mortality in the United States: A Study in Socioeconomic Epidemiology.* Cambridge: Harvard University Press.

Kitsuse, John I., and Malcom Spector 1973 "Toward a Sociology of Social Problems: Social Conditions, Value-Judgments, and Social Problems." *Social Problems,* 20:407–419.

Klausner, Samuel Z., Edward F. Foulks, and Mark H. Moore 1979 *The Inupiat, Economics and Alcohol on the Alaskan North Slope.* Philadelphia: Center for Research on the Acts of Man.

Kluegel, James R., and Eliot R. Smith 1982 "Whites' Beliefs about Blacks' Opportunity." *American Sociological Review,* 47:518–532.

Kobasa, Suzanne C., Salvatore R. Maddi, and Sheila Courington 1981 "Personality and Constitution as Mediators in the Stress-Illness Relationship." *Journal of Health and Social Behavior,* 22:368–378.

Koffler, R. 1984 "Nuclear Safety Is Questioned." *Philadelphia Inquirer,* Feb. 28:17.

Kohn, Melvin L. 1976 "Looking Back—A 25-Year Review and Appraisal of Social Problems Research." *Social Problems,* 24:94–113.

Kollock, Peter, Philip Blumstein, and Pepper Schwartz 1985 "Sex and Power in Interaction: Conversational Privileges and Duties." *American Sociological Review,* 50:34–46.

Komisar, Lucy 1977 *Down and Out in the U.S.A.* New York: New Viewpoints.

Kotarba, Joseph A. 1983 *Chronic Pain: Its Social Dimensions.* Beverly Hills, CA: Sage.

Kramarae, Cheris 1981 *Women and Men Speaking: Frameworks for Analysis.* Rowley, MA: Newbury House.

Kramer, Ronald C. 1983 "Controlling Corporate Crime through Strategies of Organizational Intervention: A Critical Evaluation." *Policy Perspectives,* 3(2):181–215.

Kraus, R., and P. Buffler 1979 "Sociocultural Stress and the American Native in Alaska." *Culture, Medicine and Psychiatry,* 3(2).

Krause, Neal, and Kyriakos S. Markides 1985 "Employment and Psychological Well-Being in Mexican-American Women." *Journal of Health and Social Behavior,* 26:15–26.

Krauthammer, C. 1984 "How to Prevent Nuclear War," in K. Finsterbusch and G. McKenna, eds., *Taking Sides,* 304–314. Guilford, CT: Dushkin.

Kristol, Irving 1984 *Reflections of a Neoconservative.* New York: Basic Books.

Kronus, Sidney 1978 "Race, Ethnicity and Community," in David Street, ed., *Handbook of Contemporary Urban Life.* San Francisco: Jossey-Bass.

Kruttschnitt, Condare, and Donald E. Green 1984 "The Sex-Sanctioning Issue: Is It History?" *American Sociological Review,* 43:471–483.

Kutchinsky, Berl 1970 *Studies on Pornography and*

Sex Crimes in Denmark. Copenhagen: New Social Science Monographs.

Ladd, Everett C. 1981 "205 and Going Strong." *Public Opinion*, 4:7–12.

LaDuke, W., and F. Brown 1983 "Water, Water Everywhere...and All of It Imperiled," in J. Allen, ed., *Environment 84/85*. Guilford, CT: Dushkin.

Lambert, Wallace E., Eva Libman, and Ernest G. Poser 1960 "The Effect of Increased Salience of a Membership Group on Pain Tolerance." *Journal of Personality*, 28:350–357.

Langor, Elinor 1975 "The Shame of American Medicine," in R. Giallombardo, ed., *Contemporary Social Issues*. Santa Barbara, CA: Hamilton.

Lanza-Kaduce, Lonn 1980 "Deviance Among Professionals: The Case of Unnecessary Surgery," *Deviant Behavior*, 1 (3-4): 333-359.

LaPiere, Richard T. 1934 "Attitudes versus Action." *Social Forces*, 13:220–237.

Larson, Clavin J., and Stan R. Nikkel 1979 *Urban Problems*. Boston: Allyn and Bacon.

Lasagna, Louis, and Gardner Lindzey 1983 "Marijuana Policy and Drug Mythology." *Society*, January–February:67–80.

Lauer, Robert H. 1971 "The Middle Class Looks at Poverty." *Urban and Social Change Review*, 5:8–10. 1976 "Defining Social Problems: Public Opinion and Textbook Practice." *Social Problems*, 24:122–130.

Lee, Rex E. 1980 *A Lawyer Looks at the E.R.A.* Provo, UT: Brigham Young University Press.

Lemere, F., and J. W. Smith 1973 "Alcohol-Induced Sexual Impotence." *American Journal of Psychiatry*, 130:212–213.

Lemert, Edwin M. 1972 *Human Deviance, Social Problems and Social Control*. Englewood Cliffs, NJ: Prentice-Hall.

Lenski, G., and J. Lenski 1982 *Human Societies*. New York: McGraw-Hill.

Leo, J. 1986 "Sex and Schools." *Time*, Nov. 24:54–63.

Leontief, Wassily W., Ann P. Carter, and Peter Petri 1977 *The Future of the World Economy*. New York: Oxford.

Lester, Marilyn 1980 "Generating Newsworthiness: The Interpretive Construction of Public Events." *American Sociological Review*, 45:984–994.

Lever, Janet 1978 "Sex Differences in the Complexity of Children's Games." *American Sociological Review*, 43:471–483.

Levinson, Richard M., and Georgeann Ramsay 1979 "Dangerousness, Stress, and Mental Health Evaluations." *Journal of Health and Social Behavior*, 20:178–187.

Levy, Leo, and Louis Rowitz 1973 *The Ecology of Mental Disorder*. New York: Behavioral Publications.

Lewis, C. 1982 "Reagan Finally Says Something That Makes Sense." *Philadelphia Inquirer*, June 30.

Lewis, Michael 1978 *The Culture of Inequality*. Amherst: University of Massachusetts Press.

Lewis, Oscar 1966 "The Culture of Poverty." *Scientific American*, 215(4):19–25.

Liazos, Alexander 1972 "The Poverty of the Sociology of Deviance: Nuts, Sluts, and Preverts." *Social Problems*, 20:103–120.

Lifton, R. 1982 "Psychological Effects of the Atomic Bombings," in E. Chivian et al., eds., *Last Aid*, 48–68. San Francisco: Freeman.

Lifton, R., and K. Erikson 1982 "Survivors of Nuclear War: Psychological and Communal Breakdown," in E. Chivian et al., eds., *Last Aid*, 287–292. San Francisco: Freeman.

Lin, N., W. M. Ensel, and J. C. Vaughn 1981 "Social Resources and Strength of Ties: Structural Factors in Occupational Status Attainment." *American Sociological Review*, 46:393–405.

Lingeman, Richard R. 1974 *Drugs from A to Z: A Dictionary*. New York: McGraw-Hill.

Link, Bruce 1983 "Reward System of Psychotherapy: Implications for Inequities in Service Delivery." *Journal of Health and Social Behavior*, 24:61–69.

Lloyd, Robin 1976 *For Money or Love: Boy Prostitution in America*. New York: Ballantine.

Lofland, John 1974 "Styles of Reporting Qualitative Field Research." *The American Sociologist*, 9:101–111.

Logan, J. 1984 "Venereal Disease: Chilling Side-Effect of Child Abuse." *Philadelphia Inquirer*, Nov. 20.

Lombroso, Cesare 1911 "Introduction to Gina Lombroso Ferrero." *Criminal Man, According to the Clarification of Cesare Lombroso*. New York: Putnam.

Lopata, H. 1984 "Social Construction of Social Problems over Time." *Social Problems,* 31:249–272.

Lown, B. 1981 "Summary Proceedings of the First Congress of International Physicians for the Prevention of Nuclear War," Airlie, VA, Mar. 20–25, in E. Chivian et al., eds., *Last Aid,* 299–325. San Francisco: Freeman. 1982 "Physicians and Nuclear War," in E. Chivian et al., eds., *Last Aid,* 7–15. San Francisco: Freeman.

Lueck, M., A. Orr, and M. O'Connell 1982 "Trends in Childcare Arrangements of Working Mothers." *Current Population Reports,* (p-23)(117).

Luft, H. S. 1980 "Trends in Medical Care Costs: Do HMOs Lower the Rate of Growth?" *Medical Care,* 18(1):1–16.

Lynch, J. 1977 *The Broken Heart: The Medical Consequences of Loneliness.* New York: Basic Books.

Lynn, Robert 1971 *Personality and National Character.* Oxford: Pergamon.

MacDonald, J. Fred 1983 *Blacks and White TV: Afro-Americans in Television since 1948.* Chicago: Nelson-Hall.

MacDonald, J. M. 1973 *Indecent Exposure.* Springfield, IL: Thomas.

Mack, J. 1982 "Prologue," in E. Chivian et al., eds., *Last Aid,* 1–4. San Francisco: Freeman.

MacKinnon, Catharine A. 1979 *Sexual Harassment of Women: A Case of Sex Discrimination.* New Haven, CT: Yale University Press.

Madigan, F. 1957 "Are Sex Mortality Differentials Ecologically Caused?" *Milbank Memorial Fund Quarterly,* 35:202–223.

Magnuson, E. 1983 "Child Abuse: The Ultimate Betrayal." *Time,* Sept. 5:20–22.

Makofsky, Davis 1977 "Malpractice and Medicine." *Society,* January–February:25–29.

Malamuth, Neil M., and Victoria Billings 1984 "Why Pornography?: Models of Functions and Effects." *Journal of Communications,* Summer: 117–129.

Malamuth, Neil M., and Edward Donnerstein 1984 *Pornography and Sexual Aggression.* New York: Academic Press.

Manautou, J., ed. 1982 *The Demographic Revolution in Mexico, 1970–1980.* Mexico City: Mexican Institute of Social Security.

Manis, J. 1974 "Assessing the Seriousness of Social Problems." *Social Problems,* 22:1–15. 1984 *Serious Social Problems.* Boston: Allyn and Bacon.

Mare, Robert D., and Christopher Winship 1984 "The Paradox of Lessening Racial Inequality and Joblessness among Black Youth: Enrollment, Enlistment, and Employment, 1964–1981." *American Sociological Review,* 49: 39–55.

Margolis, Robert, and Nancy Popkin 1980 "Marijuana: A Review of Medical Research with Implications for Adolescents." *Personnel and Guidance Journal,* September:7–14.

Marshall, James R., and Donna P. Funch 1979 "Mental Illness and the Economy: A Critique and Partial Replication." *Journal of Health and Social Behavior,* 20:282–289.

Marshner, C. 1985 "Why the Family Matters: From a Business Perspective." *Currents in Family Policy.* Washington, DC: The Child and Family Protection Institute.

Martin, Del, and Phyllis Lyon 1972 *Lesbian Woman.* New York: Bantam.

Martinson, Robert 1974 "What Works?—Questions and Answers about Prison Reform." *The Public Interest,* 35.

Martire, Gregory, and Ruth Clark 1982 *Anti-Semitism in the United States.* New York: Praeger.

Marx, John H., and S. Lee Spray 1972 "Psychotherapeutic 'Birds of a Feather': Social Class Status and Religio-Cultural Value Homophily in the Mental Health Field." *Journal of Health and Social Behavior,* 13:413–428.

Massey, Douglass S., and Nancy A. Denton 1985 Spatial Assimilation as a Socioeconomic Outcome." *American Sociological Review,* 50: 94–106.

Masters, R. E. L., and J. Houston 1971 "Toward an Individual Psychedelic Psychotherapy," in B. Aaronson and H. Osmond, eds., *Psychedilis.* New York: Hogarth.

Masters, W., V. Johnson, and R. Kolodny 1985 *Human Sexuality,* 2d ed. Boston: Little, Brown.

Matras, Judah 1980 "Comparative Social Mobility." *Annual Review of Sociology,* 6:401–431.

Maugh, Thomas H. 1982 "Marijuana Justifies Serious Concern." *Science,* 215:1488–1489.

Mauldin, W., and B. Berelson 1978 "Conditions of Fertility Decline in Developing Countries, 1965–1975." *Studies in Family Planning,* 9(5).

Mauss, Armand L. 1975 *Social Problems as Social Movements.* Philadelphia: Lippincott.

Mays, E. 1973 "Cigarette Smoking: Its Relationship to Other Diseases." *Journal of the National Medical Association,* 65:520.

Mazur, Allan 1968 "The Littlest Science." *The American Sociologist,* 195–200.

McAuliffe, William E., Mary Rohman, Paul Fishman, Rob Friedman, Henry Wechsler, Stephen H. Soboroff, and David Toth 1984 "Psychoactive Drug Use by Young and Future Physicians." *Journal of Health and Social Behavior,* 25:34–54.

McCleary, Richard, Barbara C. Nienstedt, and James M. Erven 1982 "Uniform Crime Reports as Organizational Outcomes: Three Time Series Experiments." *Social Problems,* 29(4).

McFalls, J. 1979a "Frustrated Fertility: A Population Paradox." *Population Bulletin,* 34(2). 1979b *Psychopathology and Subfecundity.* New York: Academic Press. 1981 "Where Have All the Children Gone? The Future of Reproduction in the U.S." *USA Today,* 109:30–33.

McFalls, J., and M. McFalls 1984 *Disease and Fertility.* New York: Academic Press.

McGrath, Ellie, and *Time* editorial staff 1981 "Cocaine: Middle Class High." *Time,* July 6:56.

McGuinness, D. 1976 "Away from a Unisex Psychology: Individual Differences in Visual, Sensory and Perceptual Processes." *Perception,* 5:279–294.

McLanahan, Sara S., and Jennifer L. Glass 1985 "A Note on the Trend in Sex Differences in Psychological Distress." *Journal of Health and Social Behavior,* 26:328–336.

McNamara, R. 1979 "Address to the Board of Governors, World Bank." Belgrade, Yugoslavia, Oct. 2:9–10.

Mead, Margaret 1969 *Sex and Temperament in Three Primitive Societies.* New York: Mentor.

Mears, Walter R. 1977 "Ending the Welfare Myths." *New York Post,* May 27: 36.

Mechanic, David 1969 *Mental Health and Social Policy.* Englewood Cliffs, NJ: Prentice-Hall 1978 *Medical Sociology.* New York: Free Press.

Medvedev, Z. 1979 *Nuclear Disaster in the Urals.* New York: Norton.

Merry, S. 1981 *Urban Danger: Life in a Neighborhood of Strangers.* Philadelphia: Temple University Press.

Merton, Robert K. 1938 "Social Structure and Anomie." *American Sociological Review,* 3:672–682. 1949"Discrimination and the American Creed," in R. H. MacIver, ed., *Discrimination and National Welfare.* New York: Harper and Row. 1975"Structure Analysis in Sociology," in Peter M. Blau, ed., *Approaches to the Study of Social Structure.* New York: Free Press.

Merton, Robert K., and Robert Nisbet, eds. 1976 *Contemporary Social Problems.* New York: Harcourt Brace Jovanovich.

Miley, James 1981 "Values," in Arthur W. Frank, senior advisor, *The Encyclopedia of Sociology.* Guilford, CT: DPG Reference.

Milgram, Stanley 1973 *Obedience to Authority: An Experimental View.* New York: Harper and Row.

Miller, G. E. 1979 "Existing Systems of Command and Control," in F. Griffiths and J. Polariye, eds., *The Dangers of Nuclear War.* Toronto: University of Toronto Press.

Miller, G. T. 1975 *Living in the Environment,* 1st ed. Belmont, CA: Wadsworth. 1985 *Living in the Environment,* 4th ed. Belmont, CA: Wadsworth.

Miller, Gale 1981 *It's a Living: Work in Modern Society.* New York: St. Martin's.

Mills, C. Wright 1956a *The Power Elite.* New York: Oxford University Press. 1956b *The Sociological Imagination.* New York: Oxford University Press. 1960 *The Causes of World War Three.* New York: Ballantine.

Milton, P. 1984 "A 'Happy' Baby Jane Doe Turns 1." *Philadelphia Inquirer,* Oct. 11.

Mindiola, Tatcho 1979 "Age and Income Discrimination against Mexican Americans and Blacks in Texas, 1960 and 1970." *Social Problems,* 27:196–208.

Mintz, Beth, and Michael Schwartz 1981 "Interlocking Directorates and Interest Group Formation." *American Sociological Review,* 46:851–869.

Miranne, Alfred C. 1979 "Marihuana Use and Achievement Orientations of College Students." *Journal of Health and Social Behavior,* 20:194–199.

Mirowsky, John 1985 "Depression and Marital Power: An Equity Model." *American Journal of Sociology,* 91:557–592.

Modlin, Herbert C. 1974 "The Medical Profession Addict," in J. G. Cull and R. E. Hardy, eds., *Types of Drug Abusers and Their Abuses*. Springfield, IL: Thomas.

Moffitt, A. D., and C. D. Chambers 1970 "The Hidden Addiction." *Social Work*, 15:54–59.

Mohr, J. W., R. E. Turner, and M. B. Jerry 1964 *Pedophilia and Exhibitionism*. Toronto: University of Toronto Press.

Moloney, Thomas W., and David E. Rogers 1979 "Medical Technology: A Different View of the Contentious Debate over Costs." *New England Journal of Medicine*, 301(26):1413–1419.

Moore, Gwen, and Richard D. Alba 1982 "Class and Prestige in the American Elite," in Peter V. Marsden and Nan Lin, *Social Structure and Network Analysis*. Beverly Hills, CA: Sage.

Moore, Mark H., and Dean R. Gerstein, eds. 1981 *Alcohol and Public Policy: Beyond the Shadow of Prohibition*. Washington, DC: National Academy Press.

Morash, Merry 1984 "Organized Crime," in Robert F. Meier, ed., *Major Forms of Crime*. Beverly Hills, CA: Sage.

Morgan, David L. 1982 "Failing Health and the Desire for Independence: Two Conflicting Aspects of Health Care in Old Age." *Social Problems*, 30:40–51.

Morris, D. 1971 "Developing Global Units for Elementary Schools." *International Education for Spaceship Earth*. New York: Foreign Policy Association.

Morrison, P. 1983 "The Spiral of Peril: A Narrative of the Nuclear Arms Race." *Bulletin of the Atomic Scientists*, January.

Morrow, Carol Klaperman 1982 "Sick Doctors: The Social Construction of Professional Deviance." *Social Problems*, 30:92–109.

Mott, G. 1983 "Mexico City, and Its Problems, Growing Out of Control." *Philadelphia Inquirer*, Sept. 14:2A.

Moynihan, Daniel P. 1970 *Maximum Feasible Misunderstanding*. New York: Free Press. 1977 Speech given at the commencement exercises of the Capitol Page School, June 6.

Mumford, S. 1977 *Population Growth Control: The Next Move Is America's*. New York: Philosophical Library.

Murch, Arvin W. 1971 "Public Concern for Environmental Pollution." *Public Opinion Quarterly*, 35:100–106.

Murphy, E. 1983 *The Environment to Come: A Global Summary*. Washington, DC: Population Reference Bureau.

Murphy, E., and P. Cancellier 1982 *Immigration: Questions and Answers*. Washington, DC: Population Reference Bureau.

Murray, C. 1984 *Losing Ground: American Social Policy 1950–1980*. New York: Basic Books.

Myers, N. 1979 *The Sinking Ark*. New York: Pergamon.

Nadler, R. P. 1968 "Approach to the Psychology of Obscene Telephone Calls." *New York State Journal of Medicine*, 68:521–526.

Nathanson, B. 1979 *Aborting America*. New York: Doubleday.

Nathanson, Constance A. 1977 "Sex, Illness and Medical Care: A Review of Data, Theory, and Method." *Social Science and Medicine*, 11:13–15.

National Academy of Sciences 1969 *Resources and Man*. San Francisco: Freeman.

National Academy of Sciences, Institute of Medicine 1982 *Marijuana and Health*. Washington, DC: National Academy Press.

National Cancer Institute 1982 "Cancer Patient Survival Statistics." National Cancer Institute Office of Cancer Communications, December.

National Center for Health Statistics 1978a *Health—United States: 1978*. Hyattsville, MD: NCHS. 1978b *Vital Statistics of the United States 1975. vol. 1, Natality*. Tables 1–30. Hyattsville, MD: NCHS. 1980 Health—United States: 1980. Hyattsville, MD: NCHS. 1982 "Advanced Report of Final Natality Statistics, 1980." *Monthly Vital Statistics Report*, 31(8), Suppl. 1983; L. Lawrence and T. McLemore: "1981 Summary: National Ambulatory Medical Care Survey." *Advance Data from Vital and Health Statistics*, No. 88. 1985 Health—United States: 1985. Hyattsville, MD: NCHS. Suppl. 2. 1985a "Advance Report of Final Divorce Statistics, 1982." *Monthly Vital Statistics Report*, 33(11), 1986; "Annual Summary of Births, Marriages, Divorces, and Deaths: United States, 1985." *Monthly Vital Statistics Report*, 34(13). Annually-*Vital Statistics of the United States, vol. III*.

Hyattsville, MD: NCHS. 1985b "Advance Report of Final Mortality Statistics, 1983." *Monthly Vital Statistics Report*, 34(6), Suppl. 2. 1985c "Advance Report of Final Natality Statistics, 1983." *Monthly Vital Statistics Report*, 34(6), Suppl. 2. 1985d "Annual Summary of Births, Marriages, Divorces, and Deaths: United States, 1984." *Monthly Vital Statistics Report*, 33(13). 1985e "Births, Marriages, Divorces, and Deaths for September, 1985." *Monthly Vital Statistics Report*, 34(9). 1985f "Births of Hispanic Parentage, 1982." *Monthly Vital Statistics Report*, 34(4).

National Commission on Marihuana and Drug Abuse 1973 *Drug Use in America: Problem in Perspective*. Washington, DC: U.S. Government Printing Office.

National Conference of Catholic Bishops 1985 "Nuclear Strategy and the Challenge of Peace: Ethical Principles and Policy Prescriptions," in C. Kegley and E. Wittkopf, eds., *The Nuclear Reader*, 43–57. New York: St. Martin's.

National Institute of Mental Health 1976 "Deinstitutionalization: An Analytical Review and Sociological Perspective." DHEW Publication No. (ADM) 76-351. 1977 "Patient Care Episodes in Mental Health Facilities, by Type of Treatment Facility." Statistical Note 139, DHEW Publication No. (ADM) 77-158.

National Institute on Alcohol Abuse and Alcoholism 1975 *Facts about Alcohol and Alcoholism*. Washington, DC: U.S. Government Printing Office.

National Institute on Drug Abuse 1981 *Demographic Trends and Drug Abuse, 1980–1995*. Washington, DC: U.S. Government Printing Office.

National Opinion Research Center 1985 *General Social Surveys 1972-1985* [machine-readable data file]. Chicago: National Opinion Research Center.

National Safety Council 1980 *Accident Facts*. Washington, DC: U.S. Government Printing Office.

National Sporting Goods Association 1982 *The Sporting Goods Market in 1982*. Quoted in *Nautilus Magazine*, April-May 1983:82.

Neidert, Lisa J., and Reynolds Farley 1985 "Assimilation in the United States: An Analysis of Ethnic and Generation Differences in Status and Achievement." *American Sociological Review*, 50:840–850.

Nelson, B. 1984 *Making an Issue of Child Abuse*. Chicago: University of Chicago Press.

Nelson, Hart M., and James F. Rooney 1982 "Fire and Brimstone, Lager and Pot: Religious Involvement and Substance Use." *Sociological Analysis*, 43:247–256.

Nelson, Margaret K. 1982 "The Effect of Childbirth Preparation on Women of Different Social Classes." *Journal of Health and Social Behavior*, 23:339–352.

Neubeck, Kenneth J., and Jack L. Roach 1981 "Income Maintenance Experiments, Politics, and the Perpetuation of Poverty." *Social Problems*, 28(3):308.

Newcomb, Michael D., George J. Huba, and Peter M. Bentler 1981 "A Multidimensional Assessment of Stressful Life Events among Adolescents: Derivation and Correlates." *Journal of Health and Social Behavior*, 22:400–415.

Nicholi, Armond M. 1983 "The Nontherapeutic Use of Psychoactive Drugs: A Modern Epidemic." *New England Journal of Medicine*, 308(16):925–933.

Nisbet, Robert A. 1970 *The Social Bond*. New York: Knopf.

Nuckolls, C. G., J. Cassel, and B. H. Kaplan 1972 "Psycho-Social Assets, Life Crises and the Prognosis of Pregnancy." *American Journal of Epidemiology*, 95:431–441.

O'Connell, M., and C. Rodgers 1984 "Out-of-Wedlock Births, Premarital Pregnancies, and Their Effect on Family Formation and Dissolution." *Family Planning Perspectives*, 16:157–162.

Office of Technology Assessment, U.S. Congress 1982 "The Effects of Nuclear War," in E. Chivian et al., eds., *Last Aid*, 111–136. San Francisco: Freeman.

Ogburn, William F. 1950 *Social Change*. New York: Viking.

O'Hare, William P. 1985 "Poverty in America: Trends and New Patterns." *Population Bulletin*, 40(3).

Oliven, John F. 1974 *Clinical Sexuality*. Philadelphia: Lippincott.

Oliver, Melvin L., and Mark A. Glick 1982 "An Analysis of the New Orthodoxy on Black Mobility." *Social Problems*, 29:511–523.

Oppenheimer, J. R. 1963a "International Control of Atomic Energy," in M. Grodzins and E. Rabinovitch, eds., *The Atomic Age*. New York: Basic Books. 1963b "The Failure of International Control," in E. Grodzins and E. Rabinovitch, eds., *The Atomic Age*. New York: Basic Books.

O'Reilly, J. R. 1983 "Wife Beating: The Silent Crime." *Time*, Sept. 5:23–26.

Orshansky, Mollie 1974 "How Poor Is Measured," in Joan Huber and H. Paul Chalfont, eds., *The Sociology of American Policy*. Cambridge: Schenkman.

Osmond, Marie W., and Patricia Y. Martin 1975 "Sex and Sexism: A Comparison of Male and Female Sex-Role Attitudes." *Journal of Marriage and the Family*, 37:744–758.

Packard, V. 1972 *A Nation of Strangers*. New York: Davis McKay.

Parcel, T., and C. W. Mueller 1983 *Ascription and Labor Markets: Race and Sex Differences in Earnings*. New York: Academic Press.

Parker, K. E., and B. J. Stelman 1973 "The Development of the Black Bar." *Annals of the American Academy of Political and Social Sciences*, 407:144–155.

Parsons, Talcott 1951 *The Social System*. Glencoe: Free Press. 1968 *The Structure of Social Action*. New York: Free Press.

Pasamanick, Benjamin 1962 "A Survey of Mental Disease in an Urban Population VII: An Approach to Total Prevalence by Race." *American Journal of Psychiatry*, 119:304–312.

Pearce, Diana M. 1979 "Gatekeepers and Homeseekers: Institutional Patterns in Racial Steering." *Social Problems*, 26:325–342.

Pearlin, Leonard I. 1981 "The Stress Process." *Journal of Health and Social Behavior*, 22:337–356.

Peccei, A. 1977 *The Human Quality*. New York: Pergamon.

Pelman, David J. 1971 "The Male House of Prostitution." *Trans-Action*, 8:21–27.

Peplau, Letitia Anne 1981 "What Homosexuals Want." *Psychology Today*, March:28–38.

Pesch, Marina 1981 "Sex Role Stereotypes on the Airwaves of the Eighties." Paper delivered at the Annual Convention of the Eastern Communication Association, Pittsburgh, Apr. 23–25.

Peters, M. F. 1974 "The Black Family—Perpetuating the Myths: An Analysis of Family Sociology Textbook Treatment of Black Families." *Family Coordinator*, 23:349–357.

Peters, Ruth K., Lee D. Cady, Jr., David P. Bis-

choff, Leslie Bernstein, and Malcolm C. Pike 1983 "Physical Fitness and Subsequent Myocardial Infarction in Healthy Workers." *JAMA*, 249:3052–3056.

Peterson, Ruth D., and John Hagan 1984 "Changing Conceptions of Race: Towards an Account of Anomalous Findings of Sentencing Research." *American Sociological Review*, 49:56–70.

Pettigrew, Thomas F. 1971 *Socially Separate or Together?* New York: McGraw-Hill.

Peyrot, Mark 1984 "Cycles of Social Problem Development: The Case of Drug Abuse." *The Sociological Quarterly*, Winter: 83–96.

Pfohl, S. 1984 "The Discovery of Child Abuse," in D. Kelly, ed., *Deviant Behavior*, 45–65: New York: St. Martin's.

Phillips, David P. 1979 "Suicide, Motor Vehicle Fatalities, and the Mass Media: Evidence toward a Theory of Suggestion." *American Journal of Sociology*, 84:1150–1173.

Phillips, Derek L. 1963 "Rejection: A Possible Consequence of Seeking Help for Mental Disorders." *American Sociological Review*, 29:963–972.

Pickard, J. 1973 *Urbanization and Economic Change in North American Regions*. Mimeograph.

Picou, J. Steven, Richard H. Wells, and Alfred C. Miranne 1980 "Marijuana Use, Occupational Success Values and Materialistic Orientations of University Students: A Research Note." *Adolescence*, 59:529–534.

Pieragostini, K. 1983 "Cooperative Verification." *Arms Control Today*, June.

Pittman, David J., ed. 1967 *Alcoholism*. New York: Harper and Row.

Piven, Frances Fox, and Richard A. Cloward 1971 *Regulating the Poor*. New York: Pantheon.

Platt, Anthony 1969 *The Child Savers*. Chicago: University of Chicago Press. 1974 "The Triumph of Benevolence: The Origins of the Criminal Justice System in the United States," in Richard Quinney, ed., *Criminal Justice in America*. Boston: Little, Brown.

Platt, Richard, Frank Polk, Bridget Murdock, and Bernard Rosner 1982 "Mortality Associated with Nosocomial Urinary-Tract Infection." *New England Journal of Medicine*, 307(1):637–641.

Playbill Magazine 1978 "Who's Who in the Audience: A Study of the New York Theatre-Going Market." New York.

Pleck, Joseph, and Robert Brannon 1978 "Male Roles and the Male School Experience." *Journal of Social Issues,* 34:1–4.

Poinsett, Alex 1980 "Rocky Road for Black Collegians." *Ebony,* September:54–61.

Pomer, Marshall I. 1986 "Labor Market Structure, Intragenerational Mobility, and Discrimination: Black Male Advancement Out of Low-Paying Occupations." *American Sociological Review,* 51:650–659.

Pontell, Henry N., Paul D. Jesilaw, and Gilbert Geis 1982 "Policing Physicians: Practitioner Fraud and Abuse in a Government Medical Program." *Social Problems,* 30(1):117–125.

Popline 1982 "Fertility Survey Winding Down," 4(8):1–2. 1983 "More Than Just Numbers," 5(4):1. 1984 "Family Planning Can Reduce Infant Mortality," 6(3):1.

Population Action Council 1983 *Why Should I Care about the World Overpopulation Problem?* Washington, DC.

Population Institute, The 1984 *Background Statement of the Public Policy Committee,* March. Washington, DC.

Population Reference Bureau 1981 *United States Population Data Sheet.* Washington, DC. 1982 *U.S. Population: Where We Are; Where We're Going. Population Bulletin,* 37:2. Washington, DC: Population Reference Bureau. 1985*a United States Population Data Sheet.* Washington, DC. 1985*b World Population Data Sheet.* Washington, DC: Population Reference Bureau.

Population Reports 1983 "Migration, Population Growth, and Development," (M)(7), September.

Population Today 1984*a* "China by Age and Sex," 12(3):5. 1984*b* "China's Birth Data Show Anomaly in Sex Ratios," 12(9):3. 1984*c* "No Easy Answers to Poverty, Malnutrition," 12(1):3.

Pothier, D. 1983 "Couple Changes Lifestyle to Help Haitian Children." *Philadelphia Inquirer,* Dec. 25:1B.

Pratt, W., W. Mosher, C. Bachrach, and M. Horn 1984 "Understanding U.S. Fertility: Findings from the National Survey of Family Growth, Cycle III." *Population Bulletin,* 39(5).

Preston, S. 1983 "Estimation of Certain Measures in Family Demography Based upon Generalized Stable Population Relations." Paper presented to the IUSSP Conference on Family Demography, New York, Dec. 12–14. 1984 "Children and the Elderly: Divergent Paths for America's Dependents." *Demography,* 21:435–457.

Public Opinion 1983 "Opinion Roundup." April-May:31.

Purdy, Dean A., D. Stanley Eitzen, and Rich Hufnagel 1982 "Are Athletes Also Students? The Educational Attainment of College Athletes." *Social Problems,* 29:439–448.

Quester, G. 1976 "Presidential Authority and Nuclear Weapons," in House Committee on International Relations, First Use of Nuclear Weapons: Preserving Responsible Control, Hearings, March.

Quigg, P. 1983 *A Pole Apart: The Emerging Issue of Antarctica.* New York: McGraw-Hill.

Radelet, Michael L. 1981 "Health Beliefs, Social Networks, and Tranquilizer Use." *Journal of Health and Social Behavior,* 22:165–173.

Rainwater, Lee 1973 "Poverty, Living Standards, and Family Well-Being," in Joint Economic Committee of Congress, *Studies in Public Welfare,* Paper No. 12.

Randell, John 1976 *Sexual Variations.* Westport, CT: Technomic Publishing.

Rankin J. 1983 "The Family Content of Delinquency." *Social Problems,* 30(4):45.

Raspail, Jean 1982 *Camp of Saints.* Institute for Western Values.

Ratner, Ronnie Steinberg 1980 *Equal Employment Policy for Women.* Philadelphia, PA: Temple University Press.

Ray, Oakley 1983 *Drugs, Society and Human Behavior.* St. Louis, MO: Mosby.

Reid, Sue Titus 1976 *Crime and Criminology.* Hinsdale, IL: Dryden.

Rein, Martin, and Sheldon H. White 1977 "Can Policy Research Help Policy?" *Public Interest,* 49:119–136.

Reiss, Albert J., Jr. 1981 "Public Safety: Marshalling Crime Statistics." *The Annals of the Academy of Political and Social Science,* 453:222–236.

Resnick, H. 1972 "Erotized Repetitive Hangings." *American Journal of Psychotherapy,* 26:4–21.

Rettig, Richard A. 1980 "The Federal Government and Medical Technology: Crossing Policy and Management Thresholds." *Policy Sciences,* 11:343–356.

Revelle, R. 1974 "Food and Population." *Scientific American,* 231(3):160.

Rexroat, Cynthia, and Constance Shehan 1984 "Expected versus Actual Work Roles of Women." *American Sociological Review,* 49(3):349.

Rheingold, H. L., and K. Cook 1975 "The Content of Boys' and Girls' Rooms as an Index of Parents' Behavior." *Child Development,* 46:459–463.

Rhoads, Steven E. 1978 "How Much Should We Spend to Save a Life?" *The Public Interest,* 51:74–92.

Richardson, George, and Ingrid Frank 1977 *Junkie: The Deadliest Cover-Up!* New York: Manor Books.

Richardson, Laurel Walum 1981 *The Dynamics of Sex and Gender: A Sociological Perspective.* Boston: Houghton Mifflin.

Ries, Janet K. 1977 "Public Acceptance of the Disease Concept of Alcoholism." *Journal of Health and Social Behavior,* 18:338–344.

Ringler, D. 1983 "Nuclear War Education: Teaching the Most Important Academic Subject." *Academe,* November–December:11–16.

Rist, Ray C., Lee J. Haggerty, and Don C. Gibbons 1973 "Public Perceptions of Sexual 'Deviance': A Study of the Inter-relations of Knowledge and Crimes." Paper presented at the annual Meeting of the Pacific Sociological Association, Scottsdale, AZ.

Robbins, Thomas, Dick Anthony 1982 "Deprogramming, Brainwashing and the Medicalization of Deviant Religious Groups." *Social Problems,* 29: 283-297.

Roberts, Benjamin J. 1981 "Interracial Interaction and Social Marginality." *Phi Delta Kappa,* 62:747.

Roberts, Bertram H., and Jerome K. Myers 1954 "Religion, National Origin, Immigration, and Mental Illness." *American Journal of Psychiatry,* 110:759–764.

Roberts, Robert E. 1980 "Prevalence of Psychological Distress among Mexican Americans." *Journal of Health and Social Behavior,* 21:134–135.

Robertson, I. 1981 *Sociology.* New York: Worth.

Robertson, Leon S., and Paul Zador 1978 "Driver Education and Fatal Crash Involvement of Teenaged Drivers." *American Journal of Public Health,* 68:959–965.

Rock, R. S., M. A. Jacobson, and R. M. Janopaul 1968 *Hospitalization and Discharge of the Mentally Ill.* Chicago: University of Chicago Press.

Roman, P. M., and H. H. Floyd, Jr. 1981 "Social Acceptance of Psychiatric Illness and Psychiatric Treatment." *Social Psychiatry,* 16:21–29.

Roner, Philip, and Carol Leon 1979 "Employment and Unemployment during 1978: An Analysis." *Monthly Labor Review,* 102:10.

Rosenberg, D. 1982 *International Security.* Cambridge, MA: Center for Science and International Affairs, Harvard University.

Rosenberg, Morris 1984 "A Symbolic Interactionist View of Psychosis." *Journal of Health and Social Behavior,* 25:289–302.

Rosenfeld, Rachel A. 1980 "Race and Sex Differences in Career Dynamics." *American Sociological Review,* 45:583–609.

Rosenfeld, Sarah 1980 "Sex Differences in Depression: Do Women Always Have Higher Rates?" *Journal of Health and Social Behavior,* 21:18–24.

Rosenhan, David L. 1973 "On Being Sane in Insane Places." *Science,* 179:250–258.

Rosenthal, D. 1970 *Genetic Theory and Abnormal Behavior.* New York: McGraw-Hill.

Rosenthal, Robert 1966 *Experimenter Effects in Behavioral Research.* New York: Appleton-Century-Crofts. 1984 "In a Lifetime, Valleys and Forests Have Turned to Sand." *Philadelphia Inquirer,* May 14:2A.

Rosenzweig, N. 1961 "A Study of the Reliability of the Mental Status Examination." *American Journal of Psychiatry,* 117:1102–1108.

Ross, Catherine E., and Joan Huber 1985 "Hardship and Depression." *Journal of Health and Social Behavior,* 26:312–327.

Ross, Catherine E., John Mirowsky, and Joan Huber 1983 "Dividing Work, Sharing Work and In-Between: Marriage Patterns and Depression." *American Sociological Review,* 48:809–822.

Rossi, Alice S. 1984 "Gender and Parenthood." *American Sociological Review,* 49:1–19.

Rossi, A., J. Kagan, and T. Hareven, eds. 1978 *The Family.* New York: Norton.

Rossi, Peter H., and Zahava D. Blum 1969 "Class, Status and Poverty," in Daniel P. Moynihan, ed., *On Understanding Poverty.* New York: Basic Books.

Rossi, Peter, and Howard E. Freeman 1985 *Evaluation: A Systematic Approach*. Beverly Hills, CA: Sage.

Rotblat, J. 1982 "Movement of Scientists against the Arms Race," in J. Rotblat, ed., *Scientists, the Arms Race, and Disarmament*. London: Taylor and Frances.

Rothschild, E. 1983 "The Delusion of Deterrence." *New York Review of Books,* Apr. 14.

Rowden, David W. 1970 "Judgements about Candidates for Psychotherapy: The Influence of Social Class and Insight-Verbal Ability." *Journal of Health and Social Behavior,* 11:51–58.

Roy, M., ed. 1982 *The Abusive Partner: An Analysis of Domestic Battering*. New York: Van Nostrand Reinhold.

Rubin, Jeffrey Z., Frank J. Provenzano, and Zella Luria 1974 "The Eye of the Beholder: Parents' Views on Sex of Newborns." *American Journal of Orthopsychiatry,* 44:512–519.

Rubington, Earl, and Martin S. Weinberg 1981 *The Study of Social Problems*. New York: Oxford University Press.

Rubinstein, Carin 1982 "Psychology's Fruit Flies." *Psychology Today,* July:83–84.

Rule, James B. 1978 *Insight and Social Betterment*. New York: Oxford University Press.

Rushmer, Robert E. 1975 *Humanizing Health Care: Alternative Futures for Medicine*. Cambridge, MA: MIT Press.

Russakoff, D. 1984 "Endangered Species Act: An Attempt to Stop a Time Bomb." *Philadelphia Inquirer,* Jan. 3:2A.

Russell, D. 1982 *Rape in Marriage*. New York: Macmillan. 1984 *Sexual Exploitation: Rape, Child Sexual Abuse, and Workplace Harassment*. Beverly Hills, CA: Sage.

Ryan, William 1971 *Blaming the Victim*. New York: Pantheon.

Sack, Saul 1961 "Student Life in the Nineteenth Century." *The Pennsylvania Magazine of History and Biography,* 85:255–288.

Sadker, M., and D. Sadker 1974 "Sexism in Schools: An Issue for the 70s." *Journal of the National Association for Women Deans, Administrators, and Counselors,* 37:69–74.

Sagan, Carl 1980 *Cosmos*. New York: Random House. 1983 "The Nuclear Winter." *Parade Magazine,* Oct. 30:4–6.

Saghir, Marcel T., and Eli Robins 1973 *Male and Female Homosexuality*. Baltimore: Williams and Wilkins.

Saghir, Marcel T. 1970 "Homosexuality." *American Journal of Psychiatry,* 126:1079–1086.

Sahlins, Marshall 1972 *Stone Age Economics*. New York: Aldine-Atherton.

Salkeld, R. 1970 *War and Space*. Englewood Cliffs, NJ: Prentice-Hall.

Salloway, Jeffrey Colman, and Judy A. Baruch 1973 "Illness and Social Control." *Review of Social Theory.*

Sampson, S. F. 1968 "A Novitiate in a Period of Change: An Experimental and Case Study of Social Relationships." Ph.D. dissertation, Department of Sociology, Cornell University (University Microfilms, No. 69-5775). 1969 "Crisis in a Cloister." Ph.D. dissertation, Department of Sociology, Cornell University.

Sanday, Peggy Reeves 1981 "The Socio-Cultural Context of Rape: A Cross-Cultural Study." *Journal of Social Issues,* 37(4):5.

Saxton, Lloyd 1983 *The Individual, Marriage and the Family*. Belmont, CA: Wadsworth.

Scanzoni, Letha D., and John Scanzoni 1981 *Men, Women and Change*. New York: McGraw-Hill.

Schacter, S., and B. Latone 1964 "Crime, Cognition, and the Autonomic Nervous System," in D. Levine, ed., *Nebraska Symposium on Motivation,* 12. Lincoln: University of Nebraska Press.

Schafer, Siegrid 1977 "Sociosexual Behavior in Male and Female Homosexuals: A Study in Sex Differences." *Archives of Sexual Behavior,* September: 362.

Scheff, Thomas 1975 *Labelling Madness*. Englewood Cliffs, NJ: Prentice-Hall.

Schell, Jonathan 1982 *The Fate of the Earth*. New York: Knopf. 1984 *Abolition*. New York: Knopf.

Schelling, Thomas 1960 *The Strategy of Conflict*. Cambridge, MA: Harvard University Press.

Schofield, William 1964 *Psychotherapy: The Purchase of Friendship*. Englewood Cliffs, NJ: Prentice-Hall.

Schohno, N., and T. Akiba 1982 "Fatalities from a One-Megaton Explosion over Tokyo," in E. Chivian et al., eds., *Last Aid,* 173–180. San Francisco: Freeman.

Schultz, L. 1980 *The Sexual Victimology of Youth*. Springfield, IL: Thomas.

Schuman, Howard 1978 In J. Milton Yinger and Stephen J. Cutler, eds., *Major Social Issues*. New York: Free Press.

Schur, Edwin M. 1984 *Labelling Women Deviant: Gender, Stigma, and Social Control*. New York: Random House.

Schurr, S. 1979 *Energy in America's Future: The Choices before Us*. Baltimore: Johns Hopkins University Press.

Schwartz-Nobel, Loretta 1981 *Starving in the Shadow of Plenty*. New York: Putnam.

Segall, Alexander 1976 "The Sick Role Concept: Understanding Illness Behavior." *Journal of Health and Social Behavior*, 17:163–170.

Seidman, Lawrence S. 1977 "A Strategy for National Health Insurance." *Inquiry*, 14:321–329.

Select Committee on Aging 1977 *In Search of Security: A National Perspective on Elderly Crime Victimization*. Committee Publication No. 95-87. Report by the Subcommittee on Housing and Consumer Interests of the Select Committee on Aging, 95th Congress. Washington, DC: U.S. Government Printing Office.

Select Committee on Population 1978 *Legal and Illegal Immigration to the United States*. U.S. House of Representatives. Washington, DC: U.S. Government Printing Office.

Sells, Lucy 1978 "Mathematics—A Critical Filter." *Science Teacher*, February:28–29.

Selye, Hans 1978 "Stress." *The Rotarian*, March.

Sennett, Richard, and Jonathan Cobb 1973 *The Hidden Injuries of Class*. New York: Vintage.

Shannon, James A. 1976 "The American Experience with Biomedical Science," in the U.S. Department of Health, Education, and Welfare, *Health in America: 1776–1976*. Washington, DC: U.S. Government Printing Office.

Sherman, Lawrence W., and Richard A. Berk 1984 "The Specific Deterrent Effects of Arrest for Domestic Assault." *American Sociological Review*, 49:261–272.

Shinn, R. 1982 *Forced Options*. San Francisco: Harper and Row.

Sidel, Victor, and Ruth Sidel 1977 *A Health State*. New York: Pantheon.

Sidey, H. 1982 "Launching Armageddon." *Time*, Mar. 29:26.

Siegel, Larry J., and Joseph J. Senna 1985 *Juvenile Delinquency*. St. Paul, MN: West Publishing.

Silberman, Charles 1964 *Crises in Black and White*. New York: Random House.

Silverstein, Brett, Scott Feld, and Lynn T. Kozlowski 1980 "The Availability of Low-Nicotine Cigarettes as a Cause of Cigarette Smoking among Teenage Females." *Journal of Health and Social Behavior*, 21:383–388.

Simmel, George 1978 *The Philosophy of Money*. Translated by Tom Bottomore and David Frisly. Boston: Routledge and Kegan Paul.

Simmons, Roberta G., Leslie Brown, Diane Mitsch Bush, and Dale A. Blyth 1978 "Self-Esteem and Achievement of Black and White Adolescents." *Social Problems*, 26:86–96.

Simon, David R., and D. Stanley Eitzen 1982 *Elite Deviance*. Boston: Allyn & Bacon.

Simon, J. 1981 *The Ultimate Resource*. Princeton, NJ: Princeton University Press.

Simon, William, and John H. Gagnon 1967 "Homosexuality: The Formulation of a Sociological Perspective." *Journal of Health and Social Behavior*, September:179.

Simpson, D. D., and S. B. Sells 1982 *Evaluation of Drug Abuse Treatment Effectiveness: Summary of the DARP Follow-up Research, NIDA and DHHS Publication*. No. 82–1194.

Skerry, Peter 1971 "Race Relations at Harvard." *Commentary*, 71:62–64.

Slovic, Paul, Baruch Fischoff, and Sarah Lichtenstein 1980 "Facts and Fears: Understanding Perceived Risk," in Richard B. Schwing and Walter A. Albert, Jr., eds., *Societal Risk Assessment: How Safe Is Safe Enough?* New York: Plenum.

Smeeding, Timothy 1977 "The Antipoverty Effectiveness of In-Kind Transfers." *Journal of Human Resources*, 12(3):360–375.

Smith, H. W. 1981 *Strategies of Social Behavior*. Englewood Cliffs, NJ: Prentice-Hall.

Smith-Lovin, Lynn, and Ann R. Tickamyer 1978 "Nonrecursive Models of Labor Force Participation, Fertility Behavior and Sex Role Attitudes." *American Sociological Review*, 43:541–557.

Snow, David A., Susan G. Baker, Leon Anderson, and Michael Martin 1986 "The Myth of Pervasive Mental Illness among the Homeless." *Social Problems*, 33:407–423.

Snow, M. E., C. N. Jacklin, and E. E. Maccoby 1983 "Sex-of-Child Differences in Father-Child Interaction at One Year of Age.'' *Child Development,* 54:227–232.

Song, J., C. Tuan, and J. Yu 1985 *Population Control in China.* New York: Praeger.

Sowell, Thomas 1981 *Ethnic America.* New York: Basic Books.

Spanier, G. 1982 "Married and Unmarried Cohabitation in the United States: 1980." Paper presented at the annual meeting of the Population Association of America, San Diego, May.

Spector, Paul E. 1981 *Research Designs.* Beverly Hills, CA: Sage.

Spilerman, Seymour 1970 "The Causes of Racial Disturbances: A Comparison of Alternative Explanations." *American Sociological Review,* 35:627–649. 1977 "Careers, Labor Market Structure, and Socioeconomic Achievement." *American Journal of Sociology,* 83:551–593.

Spilerman, Seymour, and David Elesh 1971 "Alternative Conceptions of Poverty and Their Implications for Income Maintenance," in L. Orr, R. Hollister, and M. Lefcowittz, eds., *Income Maintenance: Interdisciplinary Approaches to Research.* Chicago: Markham.

Srole, Leo, T. S. Langner, S. T. Michael, P. Kirkpatrick, M. K. Opler, and T. A. C. Rennie 1975 *Mental Health in the Metropolis: The Midtown Manhattan Study.* New York: Harper and Row.

Stack, Carol B. 1974 *All Our Kin.* New York: Harper and Row.

Staines, Graham L., and Joseph H. Pleck 1983 *The Impact of Work Schedules on the Family.* Ann Arbor, Michigan: Institute for Social Research, University of Michigan, Survey Research Center.

Stalker, P. 1982 "Urban Sprawl in the Third World." *Popline,* 4:5.

Steadman, Henry J. 1981 "Critically Reassessing the Accuracy of Public Perceptions of the Dangerousness of the Mentally Ill." *Journal of Health and Social Behavior,* 22:310–316.

Steadman, Henry J., and Stephen A. Ribner 1981 "Life Stress and Violence among Ex-mental Patients." Paper presented at the Annual Meeting of the Society for the Study of Social Problems, New York.

Steinmetz, S. 1977 *The Cycle of Violence: Assertive, Aggressive, and Abusive Family Interaction.* New York: Praeger.

St. John, Nancy 1975 *School Desegregation: Outcomes for Children.* New York: Wiley.

Stoller, R. J., and R. H. Ciertsma 1963 "The Consistency of Psychiatrists' Clinical Judgements." *Journal of Nervous and Mental Disease,* 137:58–66.

Stolte, John F. 1983 "The Legitimation of Structural Inequality: Reformulation and Test of the Self-Evaluation Argument." *American Sociological Review,* 48:331–342.

Stone, L. 1982 "The Historical Origins of the Modern Family." The Fifth Annual O. Meredith Wilson Lecture of History. Salt Lake City: Dept. of History, University of Utah.

Strategy Council on Drug Abuse 1976 *Federal Strategy for Drug Abuse and Drug Traffic Prevention.* Washington, DC: U.S. Government Printing Office.

Straus, M. 1980 "Social Stress and Marital Violence in a National Sample of American Families." *Annals of the New York Academy of Sciences,* 347:229–250.

Straus M., R. Gelles, and S. Steinmetz 1980 *Behind Closed Doors: Violence in the American Family.* New York: Anchor/Doubleday.

Stub, H. 1982 *The Social Consequences of Long Life.* Springfield, IL: Thomas.

Sumner, William Graham 1934 In A. G. Keller and M. R. Davis, eds., *Essays of William Graham Sumner.* New Haven, CT: Yale University Press.

Sundquist, J. 1975 *Dispersing Population.* Washington, DC: Brookings Institution.

Surgeon General, U.S. 1980 *Living Well: An Introduction to Health Promotion and Disease Prevention.* Washington, DC: U.S. Government Printing Office.

Sutherland, Edwin H. 1939 *Principles of Criminology.* Philadelphia: Lippincott. 1956 *The Professional Thief.* Chicago: University of Chicago Press. 1971 *White Collar Crime.* New York: Holt, Rinehart, and Winston.

Sweet, J. 1979 "Estimates of Levels, Trends, and Characteristics of the 'Living Together' Population from the Current Population Survey." *Center for Demography and Ecology Working Paper 79-49.* University of Wisconsin-Madison, December.

Szasz, Thomas S. 1970 *The Manufacture of Madness.* New York: Harper and Row. 1974 *The Myth of Mental Illness.* New York: Harper and Row. 1978 *The Myth of Psychotherapy.* New York: Doubleday.

Szymanski, Albert 1983 *Class Structure: A Critical Perspective.* New York: Praeger.

Talbott, S. 1982*a* "Living and Mega-Death." *Time,* Mar. 29:18–26. 1982*b* "A Grim Manifesto on Nuclear War." *Time,* Apr. 19:20–21.

Tavris, Carol, and Carole Offir 1977 *The Longest War: Sex Differences in Perspective.* New York: Harcourt Brace Jovanovich.

Temerlin, M. K. 1968 "Suggestion Effects in Psychiatric Diagnosis." *Journal of Nervous and Mental Disease,* 147:349–353.

Thoits, Peggy A. 1983 "Conceptual, Methodological and Theoretical Problems in Studying Social Support as a Buffer against Life Stress." *Journal of Health and Social Behavior,* 23:145–159. 1985 "Self-Labelling Processes in Mental Illness: The Role of Emotional Deviance." *American Journal of Sociology,* 91:221–249.

Thoits, Peggy, and Michael Hannan 1979 "Income and Psychological Distress: The Impact of an Income-Maintenance Experiment." *Journal of Health and Social Behavior,* 20:120–138.

Thornton, Arland, Duane F. Alwin, and Donald Camburn 1983 "Courses and Consequences of Sex-Role Attitudes and Attitude Change." *American Sociological Review,* 48:711–727.

Thornton, A., and D. Freedman 1983 "The Changing American Family." *Population Bulletin,* 38(4), October.

Thornton, A., and W. Rodgers 1983 "Changing Patterns of Marriage and Divorce in the United States." Final Report to the National Institute for Child Health and Human Development, Ann Arbor.

Tien, H. 1983 "China: Demographic Billionaire." *Population Bulletin,* 38:2.

Tienda, Marta 1983 "Nationality and Income Attainment among Native and Immigrant Hispanic Men in the United States." *The Sociological Quarterly,* Spring:253–272.

Tietze, C. 1984 "The Public Health Effect of Legal Abortion in the United States." *Family Planning Perspectives,* 16(1):26–28.

Time 1982 "Goal: Every Child an Only Child," Apr. 19:46. 1984*a* "Capitalism in the Making," Apr. 30:31–35. 1984*b* "A Sinking Defense," Sept. 3:57.

Titmuss, R. M. 1950 *Problems of Social Policy.* London: H. M. Stationery Office.

Tittle, Charles R., Wayne J. Villemez, and Douglas A. Smith 1978 "The Myth of Social Class and Criminality." *American Sociological Review,* 43:643–650.

Tocqueville, Alexis de 1955 *The Old Regime and the French Revolution.* Garden City, NY: Doubleday. 1961 *Democracy in America.* New York: Schocken.

Toffler, Alvin 1970 *Future Shock.* New York: Random House.

Tomasson, Richard F., ed. 1978 *Comparative Studies in Sociology,* vol. 1. New York: JAI Press.

Tong, Rosemary 1984 *Women, Sex and the Law.* New Jersey: Rowman and Allanheld.

Treiman, Donald J. 1977 *Occupational Prestige in Comparative Perspective.* New York: Academic Press.

Treiman, Donald J., and Heidi I. Hartman, eds. 1981 *Women, Work, and Wages: Equal Pay for Jobs of Equal Value.* Washington, DC: National Academy Press.

Tsipis, K. 1982 "The Physical Effects of a Nuclear Explosion," in E. Chivian et al., eds., *Last Aid,* 28–39. San Francisco: Freeman.

Tumin, Melvin H. 1953 "Some Principles of Stratification: A Critical Analysis." *American Sociological Review,* Aug. 18:387–393.

Turco, Richard, Owen Toon, Thomas Ackerman, James Pollack, and Carl Sagan 1983 "Nuclear Winter: Global Consequences of Multiple Nuclear Explosions." *Science,* 222:1283–1291.

Turner, R. Jay 1981 "Social Support as a Contingency in Psychological Well-Being." *Journal of Health and Social Behavior,* 22:357–367. 1983 "Labelling Theory and the Attitudes of Mental Patients: A Review." *Journal of Health and Social Behavior,* 24:70–84.

Turner, T. 1979 "The Inhaber Imbroglio." *Not Man Apart,* 9(10):19.

Twaddle, Andrew C., and Richard M. Hessler 1977 *A Sociology of Health.* St. Louis: Mosby.

Twomey, S. 1983 "The Rape of the West." *Inquirer Magazine,* Oct. 9:21.

Tyree, Andrea, Moshe Semyonov, and Robert W. Moore 1979 "Gaps and Glissandos: Inequality, Economic Development, and Social Mobility in

24 Countries." *American Sociological Review,* 44:410–424.

United Nations 1979 "Prospects of Population: Methodology and Assumptions." *Population Studies,* (67), New York. 1980 "Comprehensive Study on Nuclear Weapons." Prepared by a group of experts and submitted to the 35th session of the General Assembly, Sept. 12. 1984 *1982 Demographic Yearbook.* New York: United Nations.

University of Pennsylvania Law Review 1970 Comment, "The Corroboration Rule and Crimes Accompanying a Rape," 118(3).

U.S. Agency for International Development 1972 *Desert Encroachment on Arable Lands: Significance, Causes, and Control,* August. Washington, DC.

U.S. Bureau of Labor Statistics 1982 *Labor Force Statistics Derived from the Current Population Survey: A Databook,* vol. 1. Table C-11:716. Washington, DC: U.S. Government Printing Office.

U.S. Bureau of the Census 1960 "Marital Status and Family Status, March 1960." *Current Population Reports,* (P-20)(5), Table 1:8. 1973 *The Social and Economic Status of the Black Population in the United States, 1973.* Washington, DC: U.S. Government Printing Office. 1975 *Historical Statistics of the United States, Colonial Times to 1970.* Washington, DC: U.S. Government Printing Office. 1980*a Statistical Abstract of the United States.* Washington, DC: U.S. Government Printing Office. 1980*b Social Indicators III: Selected Data on Social Conditions and Trends in the United States.* Washington, DC: U.S. Government Printing Office. 1981*a* "Child Support and Alimony: 1981." *Current Population Reports,* (P-23)(124). 1981*b Statistical Abstract of the United States.* Washington, DC: U.S. Government Printing Office. 1982*a Characteristics of the Population below the Poverty Level: 1980.* Washington, DC: U.S. Government Printing Office. 1982*b Money Income of Households, Families, and Persons in the United States: 1980,* (P-60)(132), July. Washington, DC: U.S. Government Printing Office. 1983*a Current Population Survey,* (P-60)(140), July. Washington, DC: U.S. Government Printing Office. 1983*b Current Population Survey,* (P-60)(142), March. Washington, DC: U.S. Government Printing Office. 1983*c* "Marital Status and Living Arrangements: March 1982." *Current Population Reports,* (P-20)(380), Table 1:8–10. 1983*d Lifetime Earnings Estimate for Men and Women in the United States,* (P-60)(139). Washington, DC: U.S. Government Printing Office. 1984*a Voting and Registration in the Election of November 1982,* (P-20)(383). Washington, DC: U.S. Government Printing Office. 1984*b Statistical Abstract of the United States.* Washington, DC: U.S. Government Printing Office. 1985*a* "Marital Status and Living Arrangements: March 1984." *Current Population Reports,* (P-20)(399). 1985*b* "Household and Family Characteristics: March 1984." *Current Population Reports,* (P-20)(398). 1986 "Money Income and Poverty Status of Families and Persons in the United States 1985." *Current Population Reports,* (P-60)(154), Table 11:17.

U.S. Department of Agriculture 1979 *Is the World Facing Starvation?* Washington, DC: U.S. Government Printing Office.

U.S. Department of Commerce 1980 *Social Indicators III.* Washington, DC: U.S. Government Printing Office.

U.S. Department of Health and Human Services 1980 *Health United States.* Washington, DC: U.S. Government Printing Office. 1983 "Health Care Financing Review." Health Care Financing Administration. Washington, DC: U.S. Government Printing Office. 1986 *Surgeon General's Report on Acquired Immune Deficiency Syndrome.* Washington, DC: U.S. Government Printing Office.

U.S. Department of Health, Education, and Welfare 1976 *Health in America: 1776–1976.* Washington, DC: U.S. Government Printing Office. 1979*a The Nation's Use of Health Resources.* Washington, DC: U.S. Government Printing Office. 1979*b Use Habits among Adults of Cigarettes, Coffee, Aspirin, and Sleeping Pills.* Washington, DC: U.S. Government Printing Office.

U.S. Department of Justice 1984 *Sourcebook of Criminal Justice Statistics.* Washington, DC: U.S. Government Printing Office. 1986 *Attorney General's Commission on Pornography: Final Report.* Washington, DC: U.S. Government Printing Office.

U.S. Department of Labor 1977 *Dictionary of Occupational Titles,* 4th ed. Washington, DC: U.S. Government Printing Office. 1979 *1979 Employ-*

ment and Training Report of the President. Washington, DC: U.S. Government Printing Office.

U.S. Department of State 1978 *Proceedings of the U.S. Strategy Conference on Tropical Deforestation,* October. Washington, DC: U.S. Government Printing Office.

U.S. Department of Transportation 1976 *Societal Costs of Motor Vehicle Accidents*. Washington, DC: U.S. Government Printing Office.

U.S. House of Representatives Select Committee on Aging 1985 *Elder Abuse: An Examination of a Hidden Problem*. Washington, DC: U.S. Government Printing Office.

U.S. House of Representatives 1976 *Cost and Quality of Medical Care: Unnecessary Surgery*. Report of the Subcommittee of Oversight and Investigation of the Committee on Interstate and Foreign Commerce, 94th Congress, 2d session. Washington, DC: U.S. Government Printing Office.

U.S. News and World Report 1982 "A World That Grows More Crowded." Reprint from Aug. 2:1–4.

U.S. Office of Technology Assessment (U.S. Congress) 1982 "The Effects of Nuclear War," in E. Chivian et al., eds., *Last Aid*, 111–136. San Francisco: Freeman.

van der Tak, J. 1981 "Food and Population: The Margin Narrows." *Intercom*, 9(9):1.

van der Tak, J., C. Haub, and E. Murphy 1979 "Our Population Predicament: A New Look." *Population Bulletin*. Washington, DC: Population Reference Bureau. 1983 "A New Look at the Population Problem," in K. Finsterbusch, ed., *Social Problems 83/84*. Guilford, CT: Dushkin.

Vanfossen, Beth Ensminger 1979 *The Structure of Social Inequality*. Boston: Little, Brown.

Verbrugge, L. M. 1983 "Multiple Roles and Physical Health of Men and Women." *Journal of Health and Social Behavior*, 24:16–30.

Veroff, J., E. Douvan, and R. Kukla 1981 *The Inner American: A Self-Portrait from 1957–1976*. New York: Basic Books.

Vrazo, F. 1984 "The Chilling Story of Child Sexual Abuse." *Philadelphia Inquirer*, Sept. 23:1H.

Waite, Linda J. 1981 "U.S. Women at Work." *Population Bulletin*, 36(2), May 1981.

Waitzkin, Howard 1983 *The Second Sickness: Contradictions of Capitalist Health Care*. New York: Free Press.

Wallace, A. 1982 "A Soft-Spoken Activist Brings Horrors to Life." *Philadelphia Inquirer*, June 13:1.

Wallerstein, J., and J. Kelly 1980 "California's Children of Divorce." *Psychology Today*, January:67–76.

Wallerstein, James S., and Clement J. Wyle 1947 "Our Law-Abiding Law-Breakers." *Probation*, 25:107–118.

Walters, Vivienne 1982 "Company Doctors' Perceptions of and Responses to Conflicting Pressures from Labor and Management." *Social Problems*, 30:1–13.

Warner, W. Lloyd 1949 *Social Class in America*. New York: Harper.

Wasserman, H., and N. Solomon 1982 *Killing Our Own*. New York: Delacorte.

Weber, Max 1949 *On the Methodology of the Social Sciences*. New York: Free Press.

Weeks, J. 1981 *Population*. Belmont, CA: Wadsworth.

Weinberg, Martin S., Colin J. Williams, and Charles Moser 1984 "The Social Constituents of Sado-masochism." *Social Problems*, 31:379–389.

Weinberg, Thomas S., and Vern L. Bullough 1986 "Women Married to Transvestite Men: Stresses and Adjustments." Paper presented at the annual meeting of the Society for the Study of Social Problems, New York.

Weiner, Stephen M. 1980 "Health Care Policy and Politics." *American Journal of Law and Medicine*, 5:331–341.

Weinstein, Jay A. *Sociology-Technology: Foundations of Post-Academic Social Science*. New Brunswick, NJ: Transaction Books, 1982.

Weisskopf, V. 1981 "A Soviet Inquiry." *Worldview*, 24:8.

Weitkamp, Lowell R. 1981 "Depressive Disorders and HLA: A Gene on Chromosome 6 That Can Affect Behavior." *New England Journal of Medicine*, 305:1301–1306.

Weitzman, Lenore J. 1984 "Sex-Role Socialization: A Focus on Women," in Jo Freeman, *Women: A Feminist Perspective*, 3d ed. Palo Alto, CA: Mayfield. 1985 *The Divorce Revolution: The Unexpected Social and Economic Consequences for Women and Children in America*. New York: Free Press.

Weitzman, Leonore J., and Diane Rizzo 1974 *Images of Males and Females in Elementary School*

Textbooks. New York: National Organization for Women's Legal Defense and Education Fund.

Weitzman, L. J., D. Eifler, E. Hokada, and C. Ross 1972 "Sex-Role Socialization in Picture Books for Preschool Children." *American Journal of Sociology,* 77:1125–1150.

Weller, R., and L. Bouvier 1981 *Population: Demography and Policy.* New York: St. Martin's.

Wellman, B. 1981 "Applying network analysis to the study of support," in Benjamin H. Gottlieb, ed., *Social Networks and Social Support.* Beverly Hills: Sage.

Wells, John Warren 1970 *Tricks of the Trade.* New York: New American Library.

Wepner, R. S., and M. H. Agar 1971 "Immediate Precursors to Heroin Addiction." *Journal of Health and Social Behavior,* 12:10–17.

Westoff, C. 1978a "Marriage and Fertility in the Developed Countries." *Scientific American,* 239:51–58. 1978b "Some Speculations on the Future of Marriage and Fertility." *Family Planning Perspectives,* 10(2):79–83.

Westwood, Gordon 1960 *A Minority: A Report on the Life of the Male Homosexual in Great Britain.* London: Longmans, Green.

WGBH-TV 1984 *China's Only Child.* Boston. WGBH Educational Foundation. A BBC film.

Whyte, William Foote 1982 "Social Inventions for Solving Human Problems." *American Sociological Review,* 47:1–13.

Wiesman, A. 1967 "Self-Destruction and Sexual Perversion," in E. Shneidman, ed., *Essays in Self-Destruction.* New York: Science.

Will, Jerrie, Patricia Self, and Nancy Datran 1974 Paper presented at the 82d annual meeting of the American Psychological Association, as cited in Carol Tavris and Carole Offir, *The Longest War: Sex Differences in Perspective.* New York: Harcourt Brace Jovanovich, 1977.

Williams, Ann W., John E. Ware, Jr., and Cathy A. Donald 1981 "A Model of Health, Life Events, and Social Supports Applicable to General Populations." *Journal of Health and Social Behavior,* 22:324–336.

Williams, E. 1984 "Abortion Foe Turns to Politics." *Philadelphia Inquirer,* Mar. 2.

Williams, J., E. Giles, J. R. Edwards, D. L Best, and J. T. Daws 1977 "Sex-Trait Stereotypes in England, Ireland, and the United States." *British Journal of Social and Clinical Psychology,* 16:303–309.

Williams, William 1983 *Health Care Cost Containment and Cost Shifting.* Unpublished pamphlet. Provident Mutual Insurance Co.

Williamson, Jeffrey G., and Peter H. Lindert 1980 *American Inequality: A Macroeconomic History.* New York: Academic Press.

Willie, Charles V. 1982 "The Inclining Significance of Race," in Kurt Finsterbusch and George McKenna, eds., *Taking Sides: Clashing Views on Controversial Issues.* Guilford, CT: Dushkin.

Wilsnack, Sharon C. 1973 "Sex Role Identity in Female Alcoholism." *Journal of Abnormal Psychology,* 82:253–261.

Wilson, G. T., and D. M. Lawson 1976 "Effects of Alcohol on Sexual Arousal in Women." *Journal of Abnormal Psychology,* 85:489–497.

Wilson, Thomas C. 1985 "Urbanism and Tolerance: A Test of Some Hypotheses Drawn by Wirth and Stouffer." *American Sociological Review,* 50:117–123.

Wilson, W. Cody 1971 "Facts versus Fears: Why Should We Worry about Pornography?" *Interim Report of Annals of the American Academy of Political and Social Sciences,* 397:105–117.

Wilson, William J. 1980 *The Declining Significance of Race.* Chicago: University of Chicago Press.

Wohlstetter, A. 1985 "Bishops, Statesmen, and other Strategists on the Bombings of Innocents," in C. Kegley and E. Wittkopf, eds., *The Nuclear Reader,* 58–76. New York: St. Martin's.

Wolf, Deborah Goleman 1979 *The Lesbian Community.* Berkeley: University of California Press.

Wolfgang, Marvin 1983 "Delinquency in Two Birth Cohorts." *American Behavioral Scientist,* 27:75–86.

Wolfgang, Marvin, Robert Figlio, and Thorsten Sellin 1972 *Delinquency in a Birth Cohort.* Chicago: University of Chicago Press.

Wood, Michael, and Michael Hughes 1984 "The Moral Basis of Moral Reform: Status Discontent vs. Culture and Socialization as Explanations of Anti-pornography Social Movement Adherence." *American Sociological Review,* 49:86–99.

Wood, Pamela Lakes 1973 "The Victim in a Forcible Rape Case: A Feminist View." *American Criminal Law Review,* 7(2):348.

Woodhouse, R. Y. 1981 "Equality Faces a Dangerous Decade." *Vital Speeches,* 47:242–246.

Woodward, K. 1985 "The Hardest Question: At Issue Are Clashing Views of the Self and the World." *Newsweek,* Jan. 14:29.

World Bank 1983 *World Development Report, 1982.* New York: Oxford.

World Population Conference 1976 *World Population Plan of Action,* August. Washington, DC: U.S. Agency for International Development.

Wright, Eric Olin 1979 *Class Structure and Income Determination.* New York: Academic Press.

Wright, Erik Olin, David Hachen, Cynthia Costello, and Joey Sprague 1982 "The American Class Structure." *American Sociological Review,* 47:709–725.

Wright, Eric Olin, and Luca Perrone 1977 "Marxist Class Categories and Income Inequality." *American Sociological Review,* 42:22–55.

Wright, James B., Peter H. Rossi, and Kathleen Daly 1983 *Under the Gun: Weapons, Crime and Violence in America.* New York: Aldine.

Wrigley, E. 1969 *Population and History.* New York: McGraw-Hill.

Yamaguchi, Kazuo, and Denise B. Kandel 1985 "On the Resolution of Role Incompatibility: A Life Event History Analysis of Family Roles and Marijuana Use." *American Journal of Sociology,* 90:1284–1296.

Yankelovich, Daniel 1981 *New Rules.* New York: Random House. 1982a *Health Vote 82.* Research project conducted by the Public Agenda Foundation, New York. 1982b "Problems of Concern of the American Public." Unpublished poll.

Yankelovich, Skelly, and White, Inc. 1979 *The General Mills American Family Report: Family Health in an Era of Stress.* Minneapolis, MN: General Mills Corporation.

Yergin, D., and M. Hillenbrand 1982 *Global Insecurity: A Strategy for Energy and Economic Renewal.* Boston: Houghton Mifflin.

Yin, Peter 1982 "Fear of Crime as a Problem for the Elderly." *Social Problems,* 30(2).

Young, Michael 1958 *The Rise of the Meritocracy 1870–1933.* Baltimore: Penguin.

Zachariah, K., and M. Vu 1979 *Population Projections 1975 and Long Term (Stationary Population),* July, unpublished tables. Washington, DC: World Bank.

Zborowski, M. 1952 "Cultural Components in Responses to Pain." *Journal of Social Issues,* 8(4):16–30.

Zelnick, M., and J. Kantner 1980 "Sexual Activity, Contraceptive Use, and Pregnancy among Metropolitan Area Teenagers: 1971–1979." *Family Planning Perspectives,* 12(5):230–237.

Zill, N. 1978 "Divorce, Marital Happiness and the Mental Health of Children." Findings from the CCD National Survey of Children. Unpublished report.

Zill, N., and J. Petersen 1982 "Trends in the Behavior and Emotional Well-Being of U.S. Children." Manuscript prepared for the 1982 Annual Meeting of the American Association for the Advancement of Science. Washington, DC: Child Trends.

Zillman, Dolf, and Jennings Bryant 1982 "Pornography, Sexual Callousness, and Trivialization of Rape." *Journal of Communication,* 32:10–21.

Zimbardo, Philip G. 1972 "Pathology of Imprisonment." *Society,* 9:4–8.

Zinberg, Norman 1967 "Facts and Fancies about Drug Addiction." *The Public Interest,* 6:75–90.

NAME INDEX

SUBJECT INDEX

Environmental pollution (*Cont.*)
  progress in solving, 464–465
  strategies for solution, 464–465
  subjective dimension, 464, 466
  in Third World countries, 467
  water pollution, 464
Epidemiology of mental disorder,
    133–139
Equal Rights Amendment, 161
  abortion and, 184
Etiology (*see* Mental disorder, causes
    of)
Eugenics, 246, 426
Excretory perversions, 210
Exercise, health effects of, 109
Exhibitionism, 210, 215
Expectations:
  defined, 26–27
  effect on revolutions, 27
  family problems and, 162
  improvement-expectation-concern
    cycle, 27

False consciousness, 440
Family:
  definition of, 154
  extended, 154
  government policies and, 156
  size of, attitudes toward, 160–162
  skewed, 125
  traditional (*see* Traditional family)
Family problems, 152–185
  conservative views on, 155,
      158–159, 161, 162, 165,
      176–178
  liberal views on, 158, 161, 165, 176
  moderate views on, 158
  sociological views on, 155, 161
  survival of, 160, 162
Family violence, 166–172
  child battering (*see* Child battering)
  child sexual abuse, 168–169
  definition of, 166
  history of, 166
  husband battering, 171
  links to other problems, 167
  marital rape (*see* Marital rape)
  negative consequences of, 167
  parent and elder abuse, 171–172
  prognosis for, 172
  reasons for, 167
  reporting of, 167
  ridding society of, 172
  subjective dimension of, 166–167
  types of, 167–172
  wife battering (*see* Wife battering)

FBI (Federal Bureau of Investigation)
    index crimes, 373
Feminist movement:
  abortion and, 178, 184
  and family problems, 156, 157
  marital rape and, 170
  National Organization for Women,
      156
  wife abuse and, 170
Feminization of poverty, 161
  divorce and, 174–175
Fertility, 157, 227
  average number of children, 157
  definition of, 227
  level of, 229, 253–255
  out-of-wedlock, 164
  reasons for baby bust, 254–255
Fetal alcohol syndrome, 48
Fetishism, 210, 216
Fire fatalities, social factors of, 6
Firestorm, 472
Fishery problems, 444–446
  aquaculture, 445–446
  linkage to other problems, 445
  overfishing, 444–445
Fixation, 128
Food stamps, 290, 292
Friendship choices, social influences
    upon, 5
Frontal lobotomy, 139
Frotteurism, 210
Frustration-aggression theory of
    prejudice, 316
Functional theory (functionalism), 19
  dysfunctions, 19

Gay Activists Alliance, 198
Gay rights movement, 201, 202
Gender:
  definition of, 331
  measured in terms of masculinity and
      femininity, 331–332
Germ theory, 106
Ghetto-gouging practices, 277
Gigantic cities, 417
Glutethimide, 42, 67
Group therapy, 141
Growth of racial and ethnic groups,
    245–249
  black population, 246
  differential fertility and, 245
  differential migration and, 246
  differential mortality and, 246
  eugenics and, 246
  future change, 249

Growth of racial and ethnic groups
    (*Cont.*)
  Hispanic population, 247
  Native Americans, 247
  policy, 249
  problems in other countries, 246
  problems in the United States,
      245–249
  white, non-Hispanic population, 247
Gun control, 383–384

Hallucinogens:
  consequences of, 75
  health effects, 75
  patterns of use, 74–75
  types of, 74
Happiness:
  factors related to, 13, 14
  health effects upon, 86
  relationship of, to income, 287
Hashish, 62
Health Maintenance Organizations
    (HMOs), 115
Hermaphrodite, 217
Heroin, 41, 45, 46, 48
Herpes, 89
Hidden addiction, 47
Hippocratic oath, 98
Hispanics, discrimination against, 322,
    323
Hmong refugees, 324
Homophobia, 191
Homosexuality, 189, 191
  causes of, 196
  cross-cultural views, 194, 195
  differences between gay males and
      lesbians, 200, 201
  gay lifestyles, 197, 198
  laws regarding, 201, 202
  prevalence of, 195
  psychological profiles of, 197
  role-playing, 201
  "tearoom," 15
  types of gays, 198–200
  visibility of, 192, 193
Hospitals, 101–102
House prostitutes, 205
Housing affordability gap, 265, 286
  satisfaction with income-related,
      286
Human extinction, 407–408, 452, 479
Hunger:
  increasing, 285
  objective extent of, in the United
      States, 285

Teenage childbearing, 166
  problems faced by, 166
Temperance movement, 368
Terrorism, 26, 494–495
Therapeutic community, 147
Thyrotoxicosis, 83
Traditional family, 154–158
  definition of, 154
  number of, 154, 159
  problems of, 155–156
  sex roles and, 157
  social movements and, 157
  in transition, 156–158
Tranquilizers, 42
Transexualism, 210, 217, 218
Transference, 140
Transitional deviance, 207
Transvestism, 210, 216, 217
Trephination, 119
Trickle down theory (see Assimilation
    policy)
True prevalence, 118
Twin studies, 126

Unemployment, 29, 34
  among blacks, 304
  (See also Economic development and
    unemployment)
Unmarried pregnancy, 158
  attitudes toward, 165
  prevalence and trends, 163–164
  social policy toward, 166
Unmarried sexual activity, 158
  attitudes toward, 165
  consequences of, 164
  prevalence and trends, 163–164
Urban growth policies, 418–419
  population growth and, 418–419
  problems with, 418
Urbanization:
  family and, 155
  divorce and, 174
  and urban growth, 414–419
    components of urban growth, 414
    conflict and unrest, 417–418
    consequences of, 415–419
    gigantic cities, 417
    Iran, problems in, 418
    Mexico City, 417
    migration and, 414
    natural increase and, 414
    nuclear war, 418
    problems associated with, 415
    rates of, 414

Urbanization, and urban growth
    (Cont.)
    reclassification, 414
    squatter settlements, 416
    subjective dimension of, 415
    urban growth policies, 418–419
United States population policy,
    432–433
  development programs, 433
  family planning programs, 432

Value-free science, 31–32
  (See also Research methods)
Value trade-offs, 32
Values:
  defined, 27–28
  family problems and, 162
  magnify objective harm, 28
  minimize objective harm, 28
Vertebrate chauvinism, 452
Vigilante groups, 394–395
Visibility:
  defined, 25
  of family problems, 162
  intrinsic drama, defined, 26
  media exposure, defined, 26
  "newsworthiness," 26
  population problems and, 229
Voting Rights Act, 321
Voyeurism, 189, 210, 215, 216

War on Poverty, 276
  effects of, 291–292
  perceptions of, 291
Watch queen, 198
Water pollution, 464
Water shortages, 447–449
  history of, 447
  implications for the United States,
    448–449
  linkage to other problems, 448
  objective dimensions, 447–448
  policies on, 448–449
  population growth and, 448
  subjective dimensions, 447–448
  in the United States, 448–449
  water requirements and, 447
Weak ties, 272
Wealth:
  concentration of, 263
  definition of, 263
"Welfare for the rich," 294–295
Welfare fraud, 292

White-collar crime:
  Buffalo Creek disaster, 380
  deaths attributed to, 380–381
  defined, 380
  economic damage, 381
  Great Electrical Conspiracy, 381
  income tax evasion, 381
Whitiko psychosis, 121
Wife battering, 169–170
  attitudes toward, 170
  history of, 169–170
  prevalence and rates, 169
  socioeconomic class and, 169
Winnable nuclear war, 485
Witchcraft hysteria, 366
Women, working, 345–352, 356–362
  college and, 354
  doctoral degrees and, 353
  earning ratio, education and,
    352–354
  expected lifetime earnings and, 352
  homemaker role and, 351–352
  job type and, 348–350
  sexual harassment and, 350–351
Women's movement:
  expectations and, 335, 337
  The Feminine Mystique (Friedan)
    and, 336
  history of, 335–336
  National Organization for Women
    and, 336
Women's work patterns, 158, 159
  abortion and, 179
World Fertility Survey, 429
World hunger, 436–447
  aquaculture and, 445
  bystander apathy and, 439
  carrying capacity, 441
  causes of, 440–441
  children and, 437
  deforestation and, 442–444
  desertification and, 442–443
  false consciousness, 440
  famine, definition of, 436
  FAO and UNFPA study, 441–442
  fisheries, problems with, 444–446
  food surpluses, 446
  future prospects, 441–446
  gender and, 440
  Green Revolution, 441–442
  heroic response to, 439
  implications for the United States,
    446–447
  irrigation and, 444
  maternal depletion syndrome, 440

ACKNOWLEDGMENTS

Material in Chapter 14 from Dick Ringler, "Nuclear War Education: Teaching the Most Important Academic Subject," *Academe,* December, 1983. Reprinted by permission.

Material in Chapter 9 from Gordon Allport, *The Nature of Prejudice,* copyright © 1954, Addison Wesley Publishing Company, Reading, Massachusetts. Reprinted with permission.

Material in Chapter 11 from p. 313 of James B. Wright, Peter H. Ross, and Kathlyn Daly, *Under the Gun.* Hawthorne, New York: Aldine Publishing Company, 1983. Reprinted by permission.

Material in Chapter 14 from Jonathan Schell, *The Abolition.* New York: Alfred A. Knopf, Inc., copyright © 1984. Reprinted by permission.

Material in Chapter 8 from pp. 246–247 and pp. 255–256 in Richard Sennett and Jonathan Cobb, *The Hidden Injuries of Class,* NY: Alfred A. Knopf, 1973. Reprinted by permission.

Material in Chapter 4 from pp. 250–256 of R. L. Rosenhan, "On Being Sane in Insane Places," *Science,* Vol. 179, February, 1973. Reprinted by permission of the American Association for the Advancement of Science.

Box 11-3 contains excerpts of ABC News, "20/20," July 5, 1984, copyright © 1984, American Broadcasting Companies, Inc. Reprinted by permission.

Material in Chapter 5 from Lawrence Grossman "Family Policy," *The William Petschek National Jewish Family Center Newsletter.* New York: The American Jewish Commission, 1985. Reprinted by permission.

Material in Chapter 4 from *American Psychological Association Diagnostic and Statistical Manual of Mental Disorders,* Third Edition. Washington, D.C., copyright © APA 1980. Used with permission.

Material in Chapter 5 from *Here to Stay,* by Mary Jo Bane. Copyright © 1976 by Mary Jo Bane. Basic Books, Inc., Publishers. Reprinted by permission.

Material in Chapter 8 from *Reflections of a Neoconservative,* by Irving Kristol. Copyright © 1984 by Irving Kristol. Basic Books, Inc., publisher. Reprinted by permission.

Material in Chapter 12 from "China's Only Child," Horizon Series, 1984. Quoted by permission of the British Broadcasting Company.

Box 10-3 is by Marilyn Hoffman, copyright © 1983, *The Philadelphia Inquirer.* Reprinted by permission of *The Philadelphia Inquirer* and *The Christian Science Monitor.* Copyright © 1983, The Christian Science Publication Society. All rights reserved.

Table 2-4 from "Drinking Patterns and Drinking Problems of College Students, 1983." Copyright © 1986, *The Chronicle of Higher Education.* Reprinted with permission.

Table 2-2 from p. 46 of Vic Pawlak, *A Conscientious Guide to Drug Abuse.* Copyright © 1984. D. I. N. Publications. Used by permission.

Material in Chapter 1 and Chapter 8 are excerpts from *The Old Regime and the French Revolution* by Alexis de Tocqueville. Copyright © 1955 by Doubleday and Company, Inc. Reprinted by permission of the publisher.

Material in Chapter 12 is from p. 230 of Donald Morris, *International Education for Spaceship Earth.* New York: Foreign Policy Association, 1971. Reprinted by permission.

Table 3-1 "Your Personal Health Inventory" based on adaption by Center for Health Education and Blue Shield of Greater New York, reprinted by permission of Grosset and Dunlap from *How to be Your Own Doctor (Sometimes).* Copyright © 1975, 1981 by Keith W. Sehnert, M. C. and Howard Eisenberg.

Material in Chapter 12 is from p. 522 of Kingsley Davis, *Human Society.* Stanford, CA: Hoover Institution, 1948. Reprinted by permission.

Material in Chapter 12 is from Calvin Goldscheider, "Modernization, Migration, and Urbanization," in P. A. Morrison, ed., *Population Movements.* Liege, Belgium: Ordina, 1983. Reprinted by permission of the International Union for the Scientific Study of Population.

Material in Chapter 8 from Edward Banfield, *The Unheavenly City Revisited,* Boston, MA: Little Brown and Company, Inc. 1974. Reprinted by permission.

Table 8-3 is reprinted with permission of The Free Press, a Division of Macmillan, Inc., from *The American Occupational Structure,* by Peter M. Blau and Otis Dudley Duncan. Copyright © 1967 by Peter M. Blau and Otis Dudley Duncan.

Material in Chapter 3 is from Robert E. Rushmer, *Humanizing Health Care: Alternative Futures for Medicine.* Cambridge, MA: The MIT Press, 1975. Reprinted by permission.

Material in Chapter 2 reproduced by permission from Oakley Ray, *Drugs, Society and Human Behavior.* St. Louis, 1983, The C. V. Mosby Company.

Material in Chapter 1 from Guido Calabresi and Philip Bobbitt, *Tragic Choices.* New York: W. W. Norton and Company, Inc., 1978. Reprinted by permission.

Box 9-2 from *In the Matter of Color. Race and the American Legal Process: The Colonial Period,* by A. Leon Higginbotham, Jr. Copyright © 1978 by Oxford University Press, Inc. Reprinted by permission.

Material in Chapter 8 from p. 7 of Herbert J. Gans, *More Equality.* New York: Pantheon Books, a Division of Random House, Inc., 1973. Reprinted by permission.

Material in Chapter 14 from Carl Sagan, *The Nuclear Winter,* copyright © 1983 by Carl Sagan. First publication in *Parade.* Reprinted by permission of the author and the author's agents, Scott Meredith Literary Agency, Inc., 835 Third Avenue, New York, NY 10022.

Table 4-1 reprinted with premission from *Journal of*